NICHOLAS OF CUSA'S EARLY SERMONS: 1430 - 1441

Translated and introduced

by

JASPER HOPKINS

THE ARTHUR J. BANNING PRESS
LOVELAND, COLORADO

Special acknowledgement is due to Manfred Meiner of Felix Meiner Verlag for permission to translate from the Latin texts contained in *Nicolai de Cusa Opera Omnia*, Volume XVI, Fascicles I-IV (Hamburg, 1970-1984).

Library of Congress Control Number: 2003115881

ISBN 0-938060-52-X

Printed in the United States of America

PREFACE

Now that critical editions of the texts of Nicholas of Cusa's sermons are available through the combined accomplishments of the Institut für Cusanus-Forschung in Trier, the Akademie der Wissenschaften in Heidelberg, and the publishing house of Felix Meiner in Hamburg, the time has become opportune to translate these texts into English. The translation of the present twenty-six sermons represents a beginning; and it is meant to supplement my previous two volumes entitled *Complete Philosophical and Theological Treatises of Nicholas of Cusa*. In undertaking this project, I have striven for accurate as well as for readable English renderings. The former aim required that I avoid paraphrase—that I resist the temptation, at many turns, to restate more elegantly Nicholas's expressed ideas. Since these ideas are often articulated by Nicholas in abbreviated form, I have resorted to the use of brackets in order to show how I have construed his meanings. Although the English renderings would read more smoothly without these interrupting devices, I nonetheless insert them so as to make clear that all translation involves interpretation and that this fact is especially true of works that are hastily written, as were many of Nicholas's sermons.

I here express my appreciation of the scholarly achievement on the part of the members of the Cusanus-Institut, who have so reliably collated, transcribed, edited, documented, and dated. The few *corrigenda* that I add at the end of this present book in no way detract from the masterly accomplishment of the several editors. All scholarly works are continually being perfected; and only those individuals who are not engaged in historical and textual scholarship can regard such asymptotic perfecting as signaling negligence on the part of the scholars who give us the initial products. The misprints, etc., listed in the present appendix were observed *en passant* and are cited in addition to those already recorded by Rudolf Haubst at the end of Volume XVI, Fascicle zero, of *Nicolai de Cusa Opera Omnia*.

Finally, I express gratitude to the University of Minnesota's Alice A. Welch, of the Department of Interlibrary Loans, and Richard J. Kelly, Professor and Librarian. Both have been of invaluable help to me in my gathering of source-materials.

Jasper Hopkins, Ph.D.
Professor of Philosophy
University of Minnesota

TABLE OF CONTENTS

INTRODUCTION TO CUSA'S SERMONS

1. The *importance* of Nicholas of Cusa's sermons, considered as a whole (years 1430-1463), dare not be underestimated. For these 293 sermons are replete with philosophical and theological motifs that both shed light on themes in Nicholas's major works and also introduce metaphors, similitudes, and symbolisms that insightfully convey spiritual truths. To quote from Rudolf Haubst:

> In the long string of Cusa's sermons—above all since the time of his *De Docta Ignorantia*—Cusa displays his intellectual individuality so keenly that these sermons afford a unique perspective on the liveliness and the development of his theological quest for knowledge. For again and again we are able not only to hear in them the echo of what he has already said in his major works but also to trace the germinating and maturing of ideas that he later expressed.[1]

Haubst is right to call attention to the sermons written and preached *after* the completion of *De Docta Ignorantia* (1440). For the early sermons—even some of those as late as 1444—do not have the same weightiness, the same philosophical and theological depth, as do many of the subsequent ones, in which Nicholas's thoughts have also become more creative and captivating. Nonetheless, a sermon such as Sermon IV is certainly weighty, and all of Nicholas's sermons are highly didactic and intended to educate as well as to edify; indeed, they aim to edify by means of educating. This fact means that the sermons are not such as nowadays would be called *inspirational*. And yet, the not-infrequent allusions to the Canticle of Canticles, to the Book of Psalms, and to the writings of Augustine and of Anselm serve to insert poignant passages, such as the following passage from Anselm: 'Jesus' is "a sweet name, a delightful name, a name that consoles the sinner, and a name of blessed hope. Therefore, O Jesus, be Jesus to me."[2]

2. We must also take cognizance of the *general characteristics* of Nicholas's sermons, in addition to their being highly didactic.

a. To begin with, we should note the fact that most of the sermons are sermon-sketches and first-drafts. That is, they are not fully worked out; they are in rough-form literarily, if not always organizationally; they are unrevised; they show signs of having been written down hastily; they are, at times, repetitive with respect to both their topic and the execution of their topic; some of them are even incomplete qua sketches; they not-infrequently give the wrong reference for a Scriptural verse. Edmond Vansteenberghe appraises Nicholas's sermons, rough though some of them may be, as follows:

> Especially of the sermons we can say that if they are the products of a *thinker*, they are not the products of a *writer*. Nonetheless, they remain a treasure-house of lofty ideas and of sentiments that are, by turns, warm and sensitive. Once sewn throughout Germany, Austria, and Italy, they assuredly caused to well up in many souls illumination and zeal. In any event, they reveal, still nowadays, the soul of their author.[3] (my italics)

Josef Koch sees the roughness of style as offering a benefit: "Perhaps the very unliterary sermons now hold for us the greatest appeal, inasmuch as they make possible deep glances into the spirit and the heart of this great German [figure]."[4] Elisabeth Bohnenstädt points out that sometimes a sermon-sketch is really a collection of notes drawn from different times.[5] And, on occasion, a single sermon-sketch contains, in reality, several different sketches, as is the case with Sermons XIII, XIV, and XV—which were conflated.[6] Almost all of the sketches are such as to leave one impressed by Nicholas's extensive familiarity with Scriptural texts and by his rich knowledge of Latin vocabulary.

Thus, we must not hold against Nicholas his roughness of style, given its beneficial consequence and given that Nicholas wrote down his sermons primarily for his own immediate use, not for immediate dissemination to the wider religious community. Many times, the written sermons are intended as notes and memoranda to be used as help-sheets for the sermons as actually preached more or less extemporaneously. And this fact calls to our attention two further points, viz., *b* and *c* below.

b. The sermon-sketches, written in Latin, were usually not the sermons that Nicholas actually preached. For most of the time his preaching was done in a variant of Middle High German or in his moselfränkisch (German) dialect. Koch has marshalled evidence of the fact that this preaching was done extensively in one form of German or another,[7] rather than in Latin. And, as he emphasizes, "one cannot stress enough that [Nicholas's] *Latin drafts give us no picture* of how Nicholas preached to the people."[8] For in preaching, he omitted ideas (found in his Latin text) that he regarded as too difficult for the congregation to grasp; and likewise he improvisingly inserted other points that also were not present in the written notes. This oral refashioning of a given sermon was sometimes quite successful, sometimes less so. Thus, the testimony of his contemporaries is conflicting. There is evidence that his preaching was very engaging. Hermann Schnarr cites this testimony and comments: "Obviously he, [Nicholas], possessed the rare gift of presenting highly speculative contents in a form such that all his listeners not only understood him but were even gripped by the manner of his presentation." [9] And Walter Euler[10] refers to a chronicler (from Nuremberg) who called one of Nicholas's sermons "daz schonst ding, daz ich je gehort habe": "the loveliest thing I've ever heard." On the other hand, any number of Nicholas's sermons were still perceived as too abstruse and too high-flown for the congregation.[11]

 c. But if Nicholas preached so many of his sermons in German or a German dialect, and if his written sermons were intended primarily for his own immediate use, why, then, did he write them out in Latin? Here we must remember that although Nicholas preached to the lay congregations in German, he usually spoke Latin when preaching to clergy. Moreover, those sermons of his that were intended for the clergy—e.g., Sermon III and Sermons CCLXXXIX - CCXCII[12]—are often better worked-out, more polished, even lengthier, than are the sermons meant exclusively for the laity. So it would be a mistake to think of all of his sermons as being mere first-drafts. Be that as it may, all of Nicholas's sermons that we possess[13] were composed in Latin— except, that is, for Sermon XXIV, which Nicholas wrote by his own hand in German. (We must keep in mind that Sermon LXXVI was also written down in German—but by a listener, not by Nicholas. We have no Latin text of it.)

 Thus, the question arises: Why did Nicholas compose the sermons in Latin if the majority of them were preached in German? Koch suggests two reasons:[14] (1) Nicholas's sources were Latin sources. The Scriptures that he used were in Latin, as were the commentaries by Jerome, Gregory the Great, Bernard of Clairvaux, John Chrysostom, and others. It was easier to incorporate these sources into a Latin text than into a German text. (2) By writing in Latin, Nicholas could keep the sermons from being read before they were preached—read by those who had no need of seeing them in advance.[15] However, this latter reason advanced by Koch seems implausible. For even had Nicholas written in German, he could still have kept his written drafts from others' eyes. In fact, it seems that Nicholas composed the sermons in Latin because he intended to revise them at a later time and to disseminate them along with his other works. Indeed, some of the so-called sermons are really minor treatises. Of this sort are *De Aequalitate* and *De Principio*. In order that the sermons be widely read by scholars, they needed to be in Latin—not in moselfränkisch! Koch may well be right when he comments further: "Even when the Cardinal [viz., Cusanus] let his first-drafts be bound together in the two handsome manuscripts V_1 and V_2, he was not thinking of letting them be published. Rather, his concern was that these fruits of his meditation not be lost." [16] Nonetheless, Nicholas would still have expected to revise and polish these preserved sermons so that they might later be made available to a wide circle of priests, students, and scholars, all of whom were required to know Latin. His duties as bishop and cardinal, together with his continued composing of new sermons, left him no time for such re-workings. And this fact signals a third reason for Nicholas's having penned his sermons in Latin: viz., that such was the established practice in his day. Even Meister Eckhart, a century earlier, had drafted his sermons in Latin. [17] His German sermons are *reportationes* from *auditores* or are later translations from the Latin.

Some of the early Cusan sermons, especially, are organized around dramatic dialogues, a fact singled out by Hundersmarck and Izbicki. [18] Of special interest in this regard are Sermons VII and XII, where Mary Magdalene speaks. Sermon XVII hypostatizes and personifies Mercy, Justice, Truth, and Peace and presents them as pleading a legal case before God in Heaven, with Justice and Truth arguing for man's punishment, while Mercy and Peace are cast in the role of his defenders. Yet, amid the dramatization we find highly theological speculations. In Sermon XVII, for example, Nicholas instructs his congregation that Jesus, from the very moment of His conception in the Virgin's womb, was a complete human being. In this same sermon he explicitly rejects the Christological claims of Mani, Arius, Apollinaris, Nestorius, and Eutyches. And in Sermon VII (**2-4**) he alludes to Ambrose's and Augustine's definitions of "sin"; and he vividly illustrates the vileness of sin:

> Sin is like a bodily wound which, when it is fresh, permits itself to be touched and pressed against—but scarcely does so after three days. Likewise, in the case of sinners …, etc. And there are three days—viz., the committal, the habituation, the obstinate persisting—after which the sin does not admit of being touched.

When we recognize that Nicholas's sermons constitute almost one-third of his corpus of writings, [19] it should be no surprise to us that his prodigiously speculative mind infused into his sermons philosophical and theological tenets. Yet, the simultaneous inclusion of many comparisons, metaphors, and symbolisms serves to counter-balance the interjection of speculative doctrines, with the result that most of the sermons appeal also to ordinary people and not exclusively to the learned. In a few of the sermons Nicholas introduces divisions in such a way that one part of the sermon is meant for the more learned and another part for the less learned. Thus, Part One of Sermon XII is for the common people; Part Two is for those who are more capable; Part Three is for those who are more contemplative.

Moreover, the question arises: "Just how long did Nicholas's sermons last when they were being preached?" And the quick answer is that we do not really know, since there is no correlation between the length of a Cusan written sermon and the shortened or the expanded version of it that was actually preached. We may not presume, for example, that the whole of sermon V or VI, as written, was actually delivered orally. On the other hand, it would be tempting to presume that a sermon preached to the clergy would have lasted longer than would have a sermon preached to a lay congregation of the populace. However, we have no evidential basis for entertaining such a presumption—a presumption that is not even fully supported by comparing with one another (insofar as we can identify these two groupings) the respective written-lengths of the sermons meant to be preached to the clergy and of the sermons meant to be preached to the laity. Some scholars have supposed that an inference to the typical length of Nicholas's preaching could be made from considering the common practice in Nicholas's day. Accordingly, Peter Niederkofler judges that all of Cusa's sermons probably lasted for an hour, with some of them lasting for two or three hours.[20] Bohnenstädt observes that in Nicholas's day sermons were sometimes three- to six-hours long among the Brothers of the Common Life.[21] Nonetheless, although Nicholas's sermons conform to the pattern of a priest-scholar's writing them in Latin—he was, after all, a doctor of canon law—we have no firm evidence for concluding that his sermons fit the foregoing pre-established patterns of length. For they also do not correspond to the pattern of his period whereby few bishops undertook at all to preach;[22] for Nicholas, during his residence (1452-1458) in Brixen as bishop, preached 167 sermons (viz., Sermons CXXII - CCLXXXVIII).[23] Indeed, during 1454-1457 he composed no philosophical or theological works but concentrated on his sermons.[24]

3. The *style and organization* of Nicholas's sermons fall into various classes: some of the early sermons, such as Sermon III and Sermon V, proceed in accordance with the then-prevailing standards of

sermonizing: viz., to enunciate a Biblical text that constitutes the theme of the sermon; next, to plead one's own inabilities; then, to invoke God's help, either invoking it directly or by way of the intercession of the Virgin Mary or other of the saints; thereafter, to indicate the parts (usually three in number) into which the theme is divided; finally, to proceed to expounding each of these thematic parts. Oftentimes, Nicholas's sermons in this class do not have all of these five features. For example, Sermon III *does* have them all; and, yet, it does not perfectly expound the three divisions that it articulates. Likewise, Sermon V also has all five features; however, it skirts swiftly and indirectly over the allusion to inability: "Inasmuch as I must speak of him [viz., John the Baptist] who is greater than, and more than, a prophet ..., let us invoke God's grace." By comparison, Sermon I has all the features except for the anticipatory division into parts.

A second, and larger, class of sermons consists of those that are homilies—i.e., those that expound a passage of Scripture in a fuller way than do sermons of the first type. Sermon X expounds the Beatitudes; Sermon XXIV, the Lord's Prayer. Sermon XI expounds John 1:14; Sermon XII, Mark 16:6. A third class of sermons consists of those that are more highly speculative, as is Sermon XXII, which addresses the doctrine of the Trinity. In last analysis, these three classes overlap, with the result that a number of sermons can be viewed as falling into more than one class. And, to be sure, Nicholas himself nowhere explicitly *classifies* his sermons, nowhere assigns them to different *rhetorical types*. Hence, the attempt on a reader's part to impose such classifications must be understood as purely heuristic.

4. In the sermons, Nicholas makes use of all the *methods of interpretation* that were available to him. These include literalism, autonomasia, allegory, anagogy, and hypostatization.[25] We have already noted the example of the hypostatization of Justice, Truth, Mercy, and Peace; and it is obvious what literalism, or literal interpretation, is. Autonomasia (1) has to do with the use of a metaphor to substitute for a personal name or for a proper noun; or (2) it has to do with the use of a personal name to substitute for something non-personal. Thus, the city-name "Bethany" (meaning, according to Nicholas, "House of obedience") is used as a name for the Virgin Mary; and "Martha" is used as a name for the power that motivates the active (vs. the contemplative) life. Autonomasia occurs throughout Sermon VIII but especially in VIII, section **5**. In Sermon IX (**4**) Mary, because of her

virginity, is called *heaven* and, because of her fertile motherhood, is called *earth*. The use of allegory is found in Sermon VI, where the Genesis story of the Garden of Eden is construed in the following ways: The reference to Paradise is a reference to the Virgin Mary. The "Tree of life" signifies Christ. The "Tree of the knowledge of good and evil" stands for the Virgin Mary's rational and intellectual faculties! Or again: in Sermon XII the Apostle Peter is said to symbolize the assembly of the Gentiles; and the Apostle John is said to symbolize the Jewish synagogue.

In Sermon XVIII the Magi are allegorizations for sinners; the Star of Bethlehem is the allegorization that represents a preacher. Other symbolisms also abound in this same sermon: The Old Testament account of the slaying of Adonias is said to befigure a putting an end to the lust of the eyes. The condemning of Abiathar to death represents our condemning the lust of the flesh. And the killing of Joab symbolizes our ridding ourselves of the pride of life.[26] Anagogy, or anagogical interpretation, understands the words and teachings of Scripture in a proleptic way, a way that discloses truths about the redeemed soul's status in Heaven.[27] For example, Jesus's Last Supper discloses the truth about the future Heavenly reunion with Christ, about future spiritual feasting upon Christ, who is the Bread of life. Nicholas also accepts typology: Joseph—son of Isaac, sold into bondage—is a type of Christ, as is also Jonas (Jonah), who spent three days and three nights in the belly of a great fish.[28]

5. Nicholas of Cusa is an eclectic writer whose *sources* are especially numerous. There are, of course, the usual and expected sources: Proclus, Augustine, Pseudo-Dionysius, John Damascene, Anselm, Bonaventure, Peter Lombard, Albertus Magnus, Aquinas, Eckhart, Gerson, Llull, Bernard of Clairvaux, Petrus Comestor, Hugh of Strassburg, Nicholas of Lyra. Yet, there are many others, as well— such lesser figures as Henry of Ghent, Matthew of Cracow, Aldobrandinus of Tuscanella, Jordan of Quedlinburg, and others. The Heidelberg Academy edition of Cusa's sermons is magnificent in its identification and tracing of these sources, which need not all either be mentioned here or repeated in the notes of the present English translations.

6. Some interpreters have thought it desirable and helpful to distinguish Nicholas's sermons into *periods* that correspond to his various ecclesiastical roles and to his various stages of life. Thus, Koch prefers

to group the sermons into four time-periods:[29] (1) the time before the composing of *De Docta Ignorantia* (1439),[30] (2) the decade from 1439 to 1449, (3) the period of Nicholas's mission as papal legate to Germany (March, 1451 - March, 1452), and the time of his bishopric in Brixen (April, 1452-1458). The four additional sermons in 1459 and the last sermon in 1463 do not constitute a further grouping. The foregoing groupings by Koch are indeed helpful in calling our attention to some of the differences that characterize Nicholas's sermons over time. For example, the early sermons (i.e., before 1439) allude—more extensively than do the subsequent ones—to such works as the *Decretum Magistri Gratiani*, the *Glossa Ordinaria*, and the *Corpus Iuris Civilis*. Or again, the sermons of the Brixen period (when Nicholas's bishop's responsibilities left him with less time) are more concentratedly homiletical, expounding at length a given Scriptural pericope. Yet, should an interpreter care to, he might well sub-divide the Brixen period (as does Koch implicitly) into (4a) April, 1452 - November, 1455 and (4b) December, 1455 - September, 1458, thereby distinguishing sermons that were more hastily drafted from sermons less hastily prepared.

Now, of course, other ways of grouping the 293 sermons are both possible and plausible. Rather than grouping them chronologically, one might group them into the shorter written-ones and the longer written-ones or into the more speculative ones and the less speculative ones or into those that deal with Biblical figures other than Jesus (e.g., with Mary Magdalene, the Virgin Mary, John the Baptist, the sisters Mary and Martha, the Apostle John, etc.), those that deal principally with Jesus, those that deal with non-Biblical figures, and those that do not focus on individual figures at all. Or again, if we knew the exact year in which Nicholas was ordained a priest—his ordination occurred some time between 1436 and 1440—we might group the sermons, chronologically, into the period of his being a cleric, the period of his being a priest (but not yet a bishop), the period of his bishopric, further sub-divided into the time before and the time after his elevation to the cardinalate (December, 1448).[31]

7. Even Nicholas's early sermons include, as concerns their *content*, many philosophical and theological considerations. We have already noted that the whole of Sermon XXII expounds the doctrine of the Trinity, introducing at the same time teachings about the Incarnation. However, in that same sermon there are other speculative themes, as well. For therein Nicholas tells us that "the theology of

negation is the truer theology—that God, who is all things, is not any
one of these things but is the altogether simple Beginning, who enfolds
all things by means of His infinity."[32] Moreover, we are told that God
is all perfections, is Perfection itself. Furthermore, Nicholas instructs
us as regards the rationality of belief in God, when he draws the following conclusion: "Whether God is understood to exist or understood
not to exist: since either alternative is affirmed as *true*, God [who is
Truth] is affirmed to exist."[33] Here we must recall the Augustinian
background of Nicholas's line of thought. For in *De Libero Arbitrio*
(*On Free Choice*) Augustine argues: 'If there are immutable truths,
then there is immutable truth. Either Immutable Truth is God or, if
there is anything higher than Truth, then that thing is God. In either
case, God exists, since, clearly, there are immutable truths, such as
arithmetical truths.'[34] In Sermon XXII Nicholas also speaks of God as
beyond all opposition, as so everywhere that He is nowhere, as so
nowhere that He is everywhere, as so One that He is Trine, and as so
Trine that He is One.[35] Similarly, Nicholas introduces the metaphysical claim that in God not-being is in some sense existent.[36] And, theologically, under the influence of Eckhart, he sets forth the doctrine of
the three births of the Son of God: (a) the eternal begottenness of God
the Son from God the Father; (b) the birth of Jesus, the Son of God,
from the Virgin Mary; (c) the birth of Christ in a religious believer at
the time of the believer's conversion, which is also the time that the
believer is born in Christ.[37]

Sermon XXII dates from 1440, and it discloses Nicholas's interest in the very themes that he addressed in *De Docta Ignorantia*.
Nonetheless, even his earlier sermons betray glimpses of his speculative tendencies. In his very first sermon, from 1430, he stresses God's
infinity, God's unknowability by any finite mind, God's ineffability
qua Triune Deity.[38] In Sermon II he makes the theological point—following in the steps of Anselm of Canterbury and others—that Adam
and Eve are among the elect and did not sin irredeemably.[39] He there
also makes the theological points (1) that God alone knows future
events, (2) that the Devil cannot enter the rational soul, cannot alter
either reason or intellect, although he can insinuate thoughts into the
mind.[40] In Sermon IV Nicholas inserts the theme of the disproportionality between the finite and the infinite,[41] the theme of God's nature as

in itself unknowable by creatures' natural reason.[42] Nevertheless, he clings to the claim that God's *existence* can be known by making rational inferences from a consideration of finite creatures.[43] In Sermon IV we see, theologically, that Nicholas employs the term "emanation" when speaking both of the Son's begottenness from the Father and of the Holy Spirit's procession from the Father and the Son;[44] and he there explores at length the notion of faith. Likewise, Sermon VI is sprinkled with theoretical and doctrinal considerations. For in it Nicholas discusses original sin, mentioning Anselm's view.[45] He introduces the themes of self-knowledge[46] and of moral virtue,[47] citing Augustine's definition of "theological virtue." The cardinal virtues are adduced in Sermon VIII, as is also the distinction between political virtue, purifying virtue, and the virtues of a purified mind.[48]

As we see, then, Nicholas's theological thrustings are as penetrating and as bold as are his philosophical propoundings. Speaking of the Virgin Mary, he states radically (in Sermon IX (**19**)): "According to Dionysius this mother was so great and was of such marvelous beauty that anyone who would have no knowledge of her Son would readily believe *her* to be God." And he goes on to maintain that God loves Mary more than all others (except Jesus).[49] Moreover, he asserts that Mary was free not only of original sin but also of all venial and personal sins.[50] In fact, as he declares radically, Mary never sinned and *was never able to sin.*[51] Moreover, after her death she was resurrected and raptured.[52] She was of exceptional beauty and had, in the highest degree, all of the perfections that were ever had, or ever to be had, by any other saint. Using sources that contain unscientific physiological observations and surmises, Nicholas infers that Mary had dark hair and dark eyes, as did also Jesus.[53] As for Jesus Himself, Nicholas refers to Him both as *maximus homo* and as *minimus homo.*[54] He is maximal man in that He is the most perfect of all human beings; He was the smallest human being in that He was fully a human being, and fully wise, at the time of His conception.[55]

8. In *manuscript form* Nicholas's sermons (except for Sermon XXIV, in German) are found, most importantly, in Codices Vaticani Latini 1244 and 1245, which Nicholas commissioned to be copied for himself and which he himself corrected. Although we do not possess all of the originals from which these Vatican manuscripts were copied,

we do possess an autograph (viz., Codex Cusanus 220) of the sermons from 1430 through 1445 (viz., Sermons I - LVI, exclusive of XL and XLI, which are not in Cusanus 220). Other manuscripts are listed and described by Rudolf Haubst in Vol. XVI, Fascicle zero of *Nicolai de Cusa Opera Omnia* (Hamburg: Meiner, 1991).[56]

9. In *last analysis* we may be glad that Nicholas put his sermons into writing—rough drafts though many of them be. For these drafts afford us a keener understanding of the devotional matrix from which there issued forth his metaphysical musings. Thus, they bring us into closer *rapport* both with him himself and with the God of Abraham, Isaac, and Jacob. And they summon us to order our lives in such a way that we not become alienated either from God or from ourselves. And thus it is that Nicholas beckons us unto the spiritual awareness that

> there is no better or healthier art than [the art of] knowing oneself. For when a man sets himself before himself and looks at his own baseness, he recognizes his miseries and the torments of his sin, and, consequently, he grieves. He observes the emptiness of present things, with the result that he despises them. He recognizes the benefits of God, with the result that he is grateful. He recognizes God's mercy, so that he has hope; he recognizes God's justice, so that he fears; he recognizes the uncertainty of his end, so that he worries and shows himself to be always prepared. And, hence, he who at first was alienated from God and from himself and said "My heart has forsaken me," now [says], having returned by way of entering into himself: "Your servant has found his heart."
>
> . . . .
>
> And after a man has thus entered into himself, he finds the child, together with Mary, in the temple (i.e., in the Church), in the desert (i.e., in the place of penance), in the house of a rightly ordered conscience, in the manger (i.e., in humility).[57]

No doubt, Nicholas's sermons, uninspiring though they oftentimes are, will be best appreciated by those for whom the Biblical stories and images are familiar and in whom religious devotion wells up at the recital of the Scriptural verses that these Biblical stories embed. For such individuals are likely, after the fashion of the Prodigal Son and after that of the disciples on the Road to Emmaus, to "come to themselves" and to re-utter the sigh, "Did not our heart burn within us when He ...opened to us the Scriptures?"[58] For it is really Christ and the Holy Spirit who, through Nicholas of Cusa, open the Scriptures to us.

NOTES TO THE INTRODUCTION

1. Rudolf Haubst, *Die Christologie des Nikolaus von Kues* (Freiburg: Herder, 1956), p. 6.

2. Quoted from Cusa's Sermon XX (**14**).

3. Edmond Vansteenberghe, *Le Cardinal Nicolas de Cues (1401-1464): L'action - La Pensée* (Paris, 1920) [reprinted by Minerva Verlag, Frankfurt am Main, Germany, 1963], p. 164.

4. Josef Koch, *Cusanus-Texte. I. Predigten. 7. Untersuchungen über Datierung, Form, Sprache und Quellen. Kritisches Verzeichnis sämtlicher Predigten* [Sitzungsberichte der Heidelberger Akademie der Wissenschaften. Philosophisch-historische Klasse (1941/42, 1. Abhandlung). Heidelberg, 1942], p. 15.

5. [Nicholas of Cusa], *Predigten. 1430-1441*, translated by Elisabeth Bohnenstädt and Josef Sikora; introduced by Bohnenstädt (Heidelberg: Kerle, 1952), p. 14.

6. *Ibid.*, p. 18.

7. Koch, *Untersuchungen über Datierung, op. cit.*, pp. 22-29. See especially p. 27: "Steht es nun einwandfrei fest, daß Cusanus auf der Legationsreise deutsch gepredigt hat, so hat er es auch sonst getan." Cf. Vansteenberghe, *Le Cardinal, op. cit.*, p. 157.

8. *Ibid.*, p. 22. My italics.

9. Hermann Schnarr, "Nikolaus von Kues als Prediger in Trier," pp. 120-132 in Helmut Gestrich, editor, *Zugänge zu Nikolaus von Kues* (Bernkastel-Kues: Cusanus-Gesellschaft, 1986), p. 120[b].

10. Walter A. Euler, "Die Predigten des Nikolaus von Kues," *Trierer Theologische Zeitschrift*, 110 (2001), p. 291.

11. *Nicolai de Cusa Opera Omnia*, Vol. XVI, Fascicle zero, edited by Rudolf Haubst. Haubst calls attention (on p. xxix) to Nicholas's preaching in Latin Sermons CCLXXXIX - CCXCIII.

12. Euler, "Die Predigten," *op. cit.*, pp. 290-291. Wilhelm Egger, "Die Kirche von Brixen zur Heiligen Schrift hinführen. Die Brixner Predigten des Nikolaus Cusanus," *Trierer Theologische Zeitschrift*, 110 (2001), p. 298.

13. Karl Zani attests to his having discovered a document in which Hieronymus Baldung (1485-1533) speaks of Cusa's *several* German sermons ("Neues zu Predigten des Kardinals Cusanus 'ettlich zu teutsch'," *Der Schlern*, 59 (1985), 111-115). See especially p. 112. But even granting that Nicholas wrote various other sermons in German, we possess only one sermon that has come down to us in German from his own hand. A second German sermon, written down by a listener, is found in but a single manuscript and has been published by Josef Koch and Hans Teske, editors, on pp. 96-121 of *Cusanus-Texte. I. Predigten. 6. Die Auslegung des Vaterunsers in vier Predigten* [Sitzungsberichte der Heidelberger Akademie der Wissenschaften. Philosophisch-historische Klasse (Jahrgang 1938/39. 4. Abhandlung). Heidelberg, 1940].

14. Koch, *Untersuchungen über Datierung, op. cit.*, p. 23.

15. Koch, *ibid.*, p. 23: "Die lateinische Sprache hütet den Predigttext vor unberufenen Augen. Was hat eine Predigt für einen Sinn, welche die Zuhörer schon vorher kennen?"

16. Koch, *Untersuchungen über Datierung, op. cit.*, p. 14.
17. Koch, *ibid.*, p. 23.
18. Lawrence Hundersmarck and Thomas M. Izbicki, "Nicholas of Cusa's Early Sermons on the Incarnation: An Early Renaissance Philosopher-Theologian as Preacher," pp. 79-88 in Thomas M. Izbicki and Christopher M. Bellitto, editors, *Nicholas of Cusa and His Age: Intellect and Spirituality* (Boston: Brill, 2002), p. 81. Note also Peter Niederkofler, "Über die Predigtweise des Kardinals Nikolaus von Cues," *Priester-Konferenzblatt*, 75 (1964), p. 123.
19. Klaus Reinhardt, "Raimundus Lullus und Nicolaus Cusanus: ihr Umgang mit der Bibel in der Predigt," pp. 133-145 in Fernando Domínguez y Jaime de Salas, editors, *Constantes y fragmentos del pensamiento luliano* (Tübingen: Niemeyer, 1996), p. 139.
20. Niederkofler, "Über die Predigtweise," *op. cit.* (n. 18 above), p. 120.
21. Bohnenstädt, *op. cit.* (n. 5 above), p. 22.
22. Egger, "Die Kirche von Brixen," *op. cit.* (n. 12 above), p. 296. See also Alois Trenkwalder, "Zur Geschichte der Predigt in der Diözese Brixen," *Konferenzblatt für Theologie und Seelsorge*, 95 (1984), p. 148.
23. Euler, "Die Predigten," *op. cit.* (n. 10 above), p. 284.
24. Walter A. Euler, "Die Christusverkündigung in den Brixener Predigten des Nikolaus von Kues," *MFCG*, 27 (2001), p. 66.
25. Vansteenberghe signals the fact that Nicholas distinguishes four senses of Scripture: the literal, or historical, sense; the tropological, or moral, sense; the allegorical sense; and the anagogical sense. *Le Cardinal, op. cit.* (n. 3 above), p. 158.
26. Sermon XVIII (**15**).
27. Restated verbatim from p. 5 of *Hugh of Balma on Mystical Theology: A Translation and an Overview of His De Theologia Mystica*, translated by Jasper Hopkins (Minneapolis: Banning, 2002).
28. Matthew 12:40.
29. Koch, *Untersuchungen über Datierung, op. cit.* (n. 4 above), pp. 29-37.
30. *De Docta Ignorantia* was completed in February, 1440. It was composed chiefly in 1439.
31. I myself plan to draw together into a future book those of Nicholas's sermons (in English translation) that I deem to be his best ones if only because they are of the most interest to me, a theologically oriented historian of philosophy. And, of course, I have drawn together into this present volume not simply the sermons composed before the composition (1439) of *De Docta Ignorantia* but the sermons up until and including the year 1441.
32. Sermon XXII (**10**).
33. Sermon XXII (**9**).
34. Augustine, *De Libero Arbitrio*, Book II. The excerpt above is not a quotation but is a summarizing paraphrase.
35. Sermon XXII (**15-16**).
36. Sermon XXII (**13**).
37. Sermon XXII (**5 & 42-44**).
38. Sermon I (**3 & 7**).
39. Sermon II (**6**). Anselm, *Cur Deus Homo* II, 16.
40. Sermon II (**16-17**).

41. Sermon IV (**34**).

42. Sermon IV (**32-34**).

43. Similarly, a rational glimpse of God's triunity can be gained from an examination of creatures, although the mind needs the stimulating assistance of revelation: "However, for those who nowadays hold, by faith, that [God is] a Trinity, it would not be difficult to find, subsequent to their faith, rational grounds for [this belief in] a Trinity—as states Richard of St. Victor at the outset of his *On the Trinity*…. However, from merely naturalistic considerations and without their having had faith, they would not have arrived at these reasons." [Sermon XIX (**6**)]

44. Sermon IV (**35**).

45. Sermon VI (**6 & 13**).

46. Sermon VI (**27**). See also Sermon VIII (**16**) and Sermon XXI (**15**).

47. Sermon VI (**16-18 & 34**).

48. Sermon VIII (**38**). See also my article "Die Tugenden in der Sicht des Nikolaus von Kues. Ihre Vielfalt, ihr Verhältnis untereinander und ihr Sein. Erbe und Neuansatz," *MFCG*, 26 (2000), 9-37.

49. Sermon IX (**35**).

50. Sermon VI (**13**).

51. Sermon VIII (**13 & 27**).

52. See n. 86 of Notes to Sermon VIII.

53. Sermon IX (**13**).

54. Cf. Sermon XXII (35) with Sermon XVII (**11**).

55. Like Anselm (*De Conceptu Virginali* 7 & 14), Nicholas did not believe that ordinary human beings have a rational soul from the moment of their conception.

56. On p. xxiii of Vol. XVI, Fascicle zero, Haubst notes that the Vatican Latin mss. 1244 and 1245 contain all but eighteen of Nicholas's 293 sermons.

57. Sermon XXI (**15-16**).

58. Luke 15:17 & 24:32.

Sermon I: In Principio Erat Verbum
("In the beginning was the Word ....")[1]
[December 25, 1430; preached perhaps in Koblenz]

[1] "The Word was made flesh." John 1:[14].

Since, O most reverend Bishop of Trier and others who are beloved in Christ, I, who am the most unsuited of all, was never gifted in explaining concepts even in regard to very trivial instances of clear expression: there is no doubt that in regard to this mystery of the ineffable [Christmas] celebration not only will all the joints of my body tremble but also because of my constricted spirit all the powers of my soul will be numbed with fear-of-failure as concerns the examining of so wonderful and so marvelous a sacred teaching. For who dares to explicate the name of the so infinite, immense, and inconceivable Supreme God—a name that is not known even to angels? And who will declare the generation of the Only-Begotten Word?[2] [Indeed,] the beast which touches so high and imperceptible a mountain will be stoned.[3] If with regard to those features that are nature's most evident features our intellectual eyes are as are the eyes of a bat in regard to light, what [would our eyes be like] if we were to attempt to investigate nature itself and its curious secrets? Clearly, it would profit us little or nothing [to do so]. What if [we were to seek to investigate] the natures of immaterial substance, the order of the heavens, and the order of the stars' power? [Clearly, it would profit us] still less.

But since, as infinite, the Disposer, Orderer, Director, Conservator, and Creator of all the foregoing things exceeds all created things with respect to His simplicity, immateriality, luminosity, and perfection, it is evident that the human intellect through its own vision not only is weak as concerns its perceiving such excellent Light but even remains altogether blind in and of its own nature. Since these are the facts of the matter, let no one wonder why holy and very literate Aurelius Augustine ([in commenting] on the beginning of this most sacred Gospel [of John]), and why other orthodox Catholic men, being also theological luminaries, are so hesitant (as regards an exposition of our present theme) that they add little to the words of [John's] Gospel, after having made a previously appended excuse as best they could. For the loftier the meaning of John's Gospel, the more risky is the discussion [of it], since the feeble intellect cannot assist itself with

1

the exposition. For our pure, priestly John writes the things that you have all heard in the reading of the Gospel. As an eagle flying very high he drew these secrets, by special privilege, from the divine, most sacred breast [of Jesus] at the [Last] Supper. And because contained in John's words are sacred teachings of truth so lofty that neither heaven nor earth nor the entire universe (even if [creatures] numbered in the millions) could comprehend them:[4] all of us wretched sinners must all the more devoutly beseech the Almighty (from whom are all things and without whom there is nothing) to grant us as much illumination from this Gospel as suffices, by His assisting mercy, for our salvation.

Let us, therefore, by means of the consummate joyous salutation at the birth of the Only-Begotten One,[5] pay respect to the bearer of the Word [viz., Mary], so that the most delightful infant Son, with His most gracious mother entreating, may enlighten us as we say with devout mind: "Ave, Maria, …," etc.

PART ONE
The Names of God

[2] "In the beginning was the Word, and the Word was with God, and the Word was God …," etc.

I profess …, etc.

Because God, from whom all things derive, is the independent Origin of all good, all perfection, all virtue, and all truth, He is, necessarily, the Supreme Good. Now, that which is supreme admits nothing into superlativeness with it. Otherwise, it would completely lose the characteristic of supremacy. Accordingly, God is singular and, hence, most simple. It is not the case that anything precedes what is Supreme. Now, the parts precede the whole, and the union of the parts depends on the power of a higher power. Therefore, it is evident that only the Supreme Good—whose being, because supreme, depends on none other—is singular, most perfect, and most simple. And so, it is, properly speaking, the only God. Hence, God is called (among other Hebrew names) *va-heie*, i.e., "He who is," even as elsewhere [in Scripture] He is called "I am I-who-am." [6] Now, because this Divine Being is supreme it must exist through itself and on account of itself. And since it is not the case that anything is the cause of itself (otherwise it would exist before it existed—something that implies a contradiction), it exists eternally and unchangeably and was at the very beginning.

Now, it is evident that nothing is lacking to the singular, most perfect, most simple Divine Being; for it exists most perfectly. And it is evident that there befits it only that which is compatible with the Supreme Good; for whatever falls short of the supremacy of the good does not befit most perfect Being. It is now evident that supreme being, supreme duration (i.e., eternity), supreme power, supreme majesty, supreme glory, supreme justice, supreme truth are one simple God, outside of whom there is nothing supreme and nothing infinite. Therefore, the world is not eternal, nor is anything [other than God] of infinite power or might. [3] Hence, this so immense God remains unnameable, inexpressible, and fully unknowable[7] by any creature. He is assigned names with different human words, in different languages of different nations, although His own name is unique, supreme, infinite, ineffable, and unknown. When the created intellect ascends in order to apprehend the power of such a Supreme Good, (1) it finds Him alone to be the most just Provider: hence, among the Jews the created intellect gave Him the name "El." (2) It finds Him to be the Governor of the universe who foresees all things: [hence,] it called [Him] "Adonai." (3) It finds [Him to be] most powerful: [hence,] it called [Him] "Jah." (4) It finds [Him to be] most kindly: [hence,] it called [Him] "Sabaoth," "Schaddai," etc. And according to the tradition of the Hebrews there are eight such names. However, the one most holy [name], whose meaning the human intellect cannot apprehend, is given by God. It is "Tetragrammaton," i.e., "of four letters." It is ineffable; i.e., it is inconceivable by the intellect. And it is voiced by the Jews only once a year after a preceding fast. This name is "Jehova." And wherever this name occurs in the Hebrew Bible we have [in our Bible the name] "Dominus" ["Lord"]. Etc.

[4] Because this same most holy and most exalted divine name [viz., "Jehova"] signifies God not according to any individual external power, as do other names, but according to omnipotence and to internal properties without regard to things exterior: Rabbi Moses in his *Guide for the Perplexed* states that all the divine names are derived from the divine works, except [the name] "Tetragrammaton," which is assigned to the Most High Creator. That name signifies the Divine Being together with His inner properties, and it is [a name] of maximal mystery. And by means of this [name], as certain say, the Ancients worked all the things that nowadays we call magical operations, which have no apparent cause. And in those books which Adam and his righteous son Abel are said to have written, and in a certain book that is

ascribed to Solomon and is called *Sepher Raziel*, there is found how it is that the Ancients thought there to be contained in this name (and in countless other divine names) all wisdom regarding both higher and lower matters. But today [these] books have been destroyed because they were written in unintelligible language and were rightly despised and condemned. (We must speak of these matters elsewhere, rather [than here].) [5] Likewise, the Greeks have different names for the one God: e.g., "*ischyros*," indicating power; "*kyrios*," indicating dominion; and He is properly called "*theos*." Similarly, too, in Latin "*deus*" is derived from "*theos*"; and, in Tartar, "*birtenger*," i.e., "one God," [is said]; and in German, "*ein got*," i.e., "*eine gut*" ["one Good" is said]. Likewise, in the Slavic language God is called "*boeg*," and in the Turkish and Arabic languages "*olla uhacber*," i.e., "the Great and Just God." And in Chaldean and Hindi He is called "*esgi abhir*," i.e., "Creator of the universe." Hence, although the One God is one in all respects, He is named differently by different peoples in accordance with different attributes.

[6] Now, this God of Supreme might, who has in His being nothing imperfect, small, and minute, necessarily abhors idleness. Otherwise, God would be supremely idle; and, consequently, supreme happiness would consist of laziness and idleness—an impossible consequence. And since it is the case that no idleness can possibly be found in the Supreme Being, it follows that He is of supreme activity. But in every action there are found, necessarily, three perfect correlations. For nothing acts on itself but on an object of the action that is distinct from the agent. And from the agent of the action and the object of the action there arises a third thing: viz., the doing. In the Divine Being these correlations will be the three Persons by reason of which we call God trine. For God whom we call Father deifies, begets, justifies, loves (along with infinite other perfect activities). And God is deifiable, begettable, justifiable, lovable, etc.; and we call Him the Son, who proceeds from the Father. And, thirdly, there is the Deifying on the part of the One who deifies and on the part of the One who is deifiable, i.e., the Deifying on the part of the Father and on the part of the Son (and, similarly, there is the Justifying, the Begetting, and the Loving on the part of the One who loves and on the part of the One who is lovable); and we call this the Holy Spirit, who proceeds from both [the Father and the Son].

[7] By means of the aforementioned concepts the human intellect lays hold of a firm and certain faith in the immense, ineffable,

and inconceivable Divine Trinity, and it assists itself by means of the authoritative claims of those who have spoken with a divine spirit. For the sacred teaching regarding this most simple Trinity is often disclosed in the Old Testament in accordance with Hebrew truth. For example, the beginning of the Sacred Writings says: "In the beginning Elohim created." [8] And at the end of Joshua [we read]: "You will not be able to serve the Lord, for He is a holy God." [9] And in Jeremias 33 [we read]: "You have perverted the words of the living God, of the Lord of hosts, your God." [10] And in Psalms 42 there is said: "The *God of gods*, the *Lord* [11] has spoken" (in Hebrew *El Elohim Jehova*). That is, because the works of the Trinity are undivided, the *three Persons,* the *one God,* [12] created the earth, etc. However, the Jews, wanting to evade [the notion of God as] Trinity, say that one ought to understand, regarding the trinity that is expressed in their [sacred] books, three properties: viz., divine wisdom, divine goodness, and divine power, through which properties they say all things to have been created. But Nicholas of Lyra, in a certain book against the Jews, destroys this [interpretation]; and he shows, on the basis of many authoritative considerations the Trinity in the Old Testament. I, too, when once disputing, discerned that wise Jews can be influenced to believe in the Trinity. But as for the fact that, in God, the Son became incarnated: this is [a teaching] against which they have become hardened and want to hearken neither to arguments nor to the Prophets.

There are other sacred documentations of this undoubted Most Holy Trinity. For the sake of brevity I will now pass over them.

PART TWO
The Eternal Nativity in God and the Creation of Man

[8] Let us now ascend unto an understanding of the sacred Gospel: "In the beginning was the Word." We call this Word, in God, the Son. In Greek, the words are *"in archi henu tu logos."* [13] "Word" is understood not as perceptible word but as intellectual word. For since, in regard to God's Being, there is, necessarily, God who understands Himself or conceives of Himself, who is called God the Father, then His Word, or Concept, is His Son, who is eternally begotten from the Father. Therefore, this most holy Word was in the beginning, in eternity itself, before all time; indeed, He was in the Supreme Beginning, i.e., in God the Father. And He proceeded from the Father, from the Father's substance and nature. For Jehovah who is God the Father, said to Jehovah who is Lord, i.e., said to God the Son: "Sit at my right

hand," etc.[14] "With You is the beginning in the day of Your strength,"
etc.[15] "From the womb," i.e., from my own substance, "I begot You
prior to the morning star, which was created at the beginning of the
world."[16] The Chaldean [Book of] truth contains this [point] more
clearly. It says: "The Lord spoke by means of His Word." "For God's
speaking is His having begotten His Word," according to Gregory in
Moralium Libri XXIII.[17] But God spoke once, because He has no
Word other than the Only-Begotten Word. For God speaks and does
not repeat His Word. But God *speaks* a Word, because no time—
whether past or future—befits God.

[9] Firmianus Lactantius says: "God comprises a vocal Spirit
that proceeds from His mouth. He conceived it—not by means of a
womb but by means of His mind through a certain mental power that
is inconceivable [for us]—into an Image that lives with its own sensing and wisdom."[18] Hence, in Psalms 44 [we read]: "My heart has uttered a good word. I speak of my works to the king,"[19] attesting, that
is, that the works of God are known to no one except to the Son alone,
who is the Word of God and who must reign [as king] forever. "The
Greeks say '*logos*,' whereas we say '*verbum*' or '*sermo*' ['word']; for
'*logos*' signifies word and concept [*sermo et ratio*], because Logos is
God's Word (*vox*) and Wisdom."[20] [10] Who can fittingly state of that
ineffable birth that [the Logos] was born from eternity and is born as
co-eternal and that He who is begotten before the ages is begotten in
such a way that He is not later than His Begetter?[21] For according to
Basilius, the Word was in the beginning and is neither human nor angelic but is God's inner Expression. Together with the Father, this Son
of God is (as is said in the first book of the *Sentences*, Distinction
5)[22] one Wisdom and Substance. The Son is such as the Father.[23] O
marvelous birth, where the One Begetting imparts to the One Begotten His own essence and nature, His own perfection, power, glory, infinity, and omnipotence! For the Son is consubstantial with the Father, because the three Persons are one God. Whatever befits God befits all of the Persons equally. Although the Father is distinct, the Son
is distinct, the Holy Spirit is distinct, nonetheless the Father is not of
another essence, nor is the Father one thing, the Son another thing,
the Holy Spirit still another thing. For of Father, Son, and Holy Spirit there is one essence, co-equal glory, eternal majesty. Therefore, since
the Son is ever in the Father with respect to essence, [the following]
is said in accordance with Origen:[24] " 'And the Word was with God.'
In the beginning in which the Word was, there was not any separa-

tion of the Word and of God who spoke the Word, because 'the Word was God.' Hence, there is nothing less in the Son than there is in the Father, since [the Son is] 'God from God, Light from Light'."[25]

[11] Supreme Truth revealed to some extent this inexplicable begottenness—[revealed it] if not with full light, nevertheless with a small ray [of light] to those situated in the darkness of heathenism. Many examples [hereof] are adduced in writing by Firmianus Lactantius in his *De Falsa Sapientia* [*On False Wisdom*].[26] Indeed, he reports apropos of Hermes Trismegistus: "In the book that is entitled *Logos Gelios*, i.e., *Perfect Word*, [Hermes] used the following words: '*kyros ke ton panton politis on theon kalei*,' etc. That is: 'The Lord and Creator of all, whom we are seen to name *God*, made a second God,' etc."[27] And there follows [the passage]: "Because [the Creator] made Him as First and Uniquely One, the [One that was made] seemed good to the Creator and seemed to comprise completely all goods. The Creator was pleased, and He exceedingly loved, as His own Offspring, [Him whom He had made]."

Likewise, [Lactantius writes]: "Sibyl Erithraea, at the beginning of her song, proclaims the Son of God as Leader and Ruler over all things, when she says: '*panto profton ktistin*,' etc.: i.e., [she proclaims Him] 'Sustainer and Founder of all things, who imparted to all things His sweet Spirit and who made His Spirit the Director-God of all things."[28] And another Sibyl [said]: "He must be known; know to be your God Him who is the Son of God."[29] Hermes speaks of this Son as ineffable. But the reason for this [ineffable] Cause is the will-for-the-good, which has exalted Him whose name cannot be uttered by the mouth of men. And subsequently Hermes says to his own son: "There is, O Son, a secret word of wisdom that comes from the sole Lord of all things, from God who foreknows all things, of whom to speak is beyond man's capability," etc.[30] Zeno calls Him Logos or Word, the Disposer over nature and the Maker of all things. He also calls Him Fate and the Necessity-of-things and the Mind of Jove (by virtue of their custom of referring to God as Jove).[31] But the words are not an obstacle, since the meaning agrees with the truth; for it is the Spirit of God whom he has called the Mind of Jove. For Trismegistus, who somehow has investigated almost all truth, has often described the power and majesty of the Word. Moreover, another Sibyl [says]: "... doing all things by the Word," etc.[32]

[12] Augustine reports in Book VII of his *Confessions* that he found among the Platonists the beginning of our Gospel: "In the be-

ginning was the Word, and the Word was with God, and the Word was God," etc.[33] Then come the words: "And all things were made by Him."[34] For all things depend on one Beginning. The Uncreated Will, which is omnipotent, one, uniform, and of infinite power, did all things as it willed to.[35] But because the Word (*sermo sive verbum*) of the Father, who wills and speaks, is the Son, all things have been made through the Word. For He spoke and they were made; He command-ed and they were created.[36] He said "Let there be light,"[37] and light was made; for by the Word of God the heavens have been formed.[38] Hence, in Psalms 42 [we read]: "The God of gods, the Lord, spoke and called forth the earth."[39] The Psalmist says the following: "Elo-him Jehovah spoke"—[the Psalmist thereby] showing that the works of the Trinity are undivided. He combines "Elohim" with "Jehovah," [thus] showing that by means of God the Son the earth was created.

Supreme and incommensurable Goodness, willing not only to beget within itself *ab aeterno*, even multiplied His goodness by cre-ating in the order of time and outside Himself. But the Most Perfect God could not create all things in accordance with the image of some-thing external, since He is all things; nor could He create all things to an end other than the Highest End, viz., Himself. Therefore, all things were made by Him in accordance with the image of Divinity and unto God [as their End]. [**13**] But how it is that all things flow forth from God with respect to their being would be lengthy and im-possible for me to explain. But in order that we may understand to some small extent, let us take an example from [Robert] of Lincoln's book *De Forma Prima* [*On the First Form*]: just as an artifact flows forth from the mind of an artificer, so we may imagine God, who is the Supreme Artificer, (1) to have had in His Mind, *ab aeterno*, all the things that have existed, that do exist, and that will exist and (2) to have brought them into temporal being, [doing so] through His om-nipotence and in conformity with His will and without intermediary or external assistance. For omnipotence is in need of no one's assistance. And rightly so. By comparison, an artificer who conceives in his mind the form of a house or of a chest wants to bring that object into exis-tence in accordance with his will. But because, in him, his power does not coincide with his will—as is the case with Omnipotent God—he must have many intermediaries (e.g., wood, an ax, and so on) in order to apply the preconceived form. These intermediaries are not neces-sary in the case of God. For every form flows forth from God's Form; every being flows forth from God's Being; all goodness, from God's

Goodness; all truth, from God's Truth. And we call such a flowing forth *creation*.

(**14**] And because the one God is trine, three kinds of creatures flow forth from God: immaterial only; corporeal only; and mixed. Angels and intelligences are immaterial [creatures]; vegetating, sensing, and elemental [creatures] are corporeal; man is a mixed nature, proceeding, as it were, from both [of the other two natures]. And because [the Divine] Trinity exists in Oneness, it follows that in the case of the immaterial nature there is a trinity: viz., three orders; and each order enfolds a trinity, [so that] there are nine choirs. Similarly, in the celestial-corporeal nature and the elemental, sensing, and vegetating natures: the image of the Trinity is present. And the case is similar with the mixed nature. Now, it would be very lovely to contemplate the orderings of things and these domains as regards the fact that the Most Wise made to be exceedingly good whatever He made. And by means of these contemplations St. Dionysius ascended unto [a knowledge of] the hierarchies. But because [the Divine] Trinity exists in Oneness, every created thing bears within itself, in its own being, an image of the Trinity. [It does so] through the fact that it has being, power, and activity; through the fact that it consists of power, of objectification, and of actuality; through the fact that it consists of innate correlations. For just as Divine Goodness consists of the Father, who is the Power to make good, the Son, who is the Power to be made good, and the Holy Spirit, who is the very Act of making good, so goodness that has issued forth [from God] bears within itself this trace of the Trinity. Consequently, no created goodness can be without the power to make good, the power to be made good, and the very act of making good. A similar point holds with regard to love, being, truth, and all the other things that have flowed forth from God.

O, if some contemplator would ascend hereunto! How pleasant he would find his speculations to be! Assuredly, no unbeliever, no one haughty, miserly, unchaste, or cloaked with other sordid sins will be able to apprehend this pleasantness. And no one is so hard-hearted that if he enters upon this pathway of contemplating, his heart will not be softened. [**15**] Let each one here take note: God created all things for His own sake, so that every creature would have its own best End. But God created man last, as being him in whom the fulfillment and perfection of creatures consisted. But man's perfection is in God; and so, every creature is ordered unto God by way of man. Accordingly, the Ineffable God of graciousness created man last and adorned him with

gifts—with free will and with reason—(1) so that through reason he
would understand, and through free will would love, his Origin and
Creator, and (2) so that he would uphold the naturally good principles given to him by God and naturally ordered unto God, and (3) so
that by means of the virtues, by means of obedience, and by means
of love he would increase morally. God situated man in a Paradise of
pleasantness; He placed a most pure soul into a most suitable earthly
body—one manipulable and compliant. He gave to man power over
the entire Paradise, over his entire body, so that he could make use of
all his material and immaterial senses. He commanded that man not
eat of the tree placed in the middle of Paradise, in order that man
would not through free choice misuse his reason and would not
through pride disorderedly direct his principles toward the earth
below—[principles] which were rooted in obedience directed upwards.

[16] Because of the Devil's envy,[40] that First Parent (viz.,
Adam) fell, having been seduced by an empty hope. And in this way
nothing was done without [the assistance of] the Word; i.e., sin was
done, for sin has no being (otherwise sin would bear the image of the
Trinity and of Goodness). Immediately after the sin, after the disorderedness of principles, man became as an exile from Paradise and as
a wanderer, since rebellion arose in the body against the soul. But because of the stain on human nature (a stain contracted from the First
Parents), all the propagated descendants from Adam contracted and
continue to contract this root of sin. O, the Devil's very perfidious
envy, through which death entered into the world! O how great the
sin that would have deprived all the posterity of their [destined] End
had not the Savior mercifully rendered aid!

PART THREE
*The Incarnation's Rationale, Which Is Explained by Means of a
Pious Conflict among the Divine Attributes*

[17] Now, O Venerable Lords, a true priest of God has disclosed—
by means of the singular clause "without Him nothing was done"—
the reason that God was made a [God-]man. Here, very briefly, I will
now discuss the case of a certain pious conflict before [I take up a discussion of] the restorative verdict concerning the Incarnation of the
Word of God. Man was created and ordained for salvation and for the
best end. His sin introduced a disorderedness; and justice condemned
[him] to punishment. The Lord's mercy and His justice's truth met
each other.[41] And so, it happened that between God and man a pious

conflict occurred in the presence of the most holy Trinity, which is called Elohim, i.e., Gods, or Judges. God was the Accuser; man was the defendant. The accusation [had to do with] the crime of *lèse majesté*; God's advocates were Truth and Justice; man's advocates were Peace and Mercy.

[**18**] Truth adduced against man the magnitude of the crime, saying that man, most wicked, had blasphemed the Majesty's honorableness and divinity, because man judged God mendacious and judged the Devil to be veracious. God, who is Truth, had said: "On whatever day you eat of the tree of the knowledge of good and evil, you shall die." The Devil, who is a liar, interjected: "You will not at all die." Man disbelieved the true affirmation, and he believed the false denial. He believed in greater measure the Devil who was falsely promising: "For God knows that on whatever day you shall partake, you will be like Him." [42]

"Do You not, O God, detest those who work iniquity? Therefore, may You cause to perish all who speak a lie![43] And let there remain outside of Your Kingdom dogs, sorcerers, the shameless, murderers, those serving idols, and all who love and do that which is false![44] And because man committed the crime of *lèse majesté*, let this sentence pass down to his posterity, because You are a Jealous God, holding the sin of the fathers against the Sons." [45]

Secondly, Truth adduced once again the sentence of God in saying: "You have stated, O Lord: 'It is not the case that God is as man, so that He lies; nor is He as a son of man, so that He is changed.'[46] You have said, O Lord: 'On whatever day...,' etc.[47] Man the prevaricator did it; let him, therefore, die eternally."

[**19**] In defending man against [the accusation], Mercy spoke and endeavored to minimize the sin by [citing] the magnificence of Goodness: "It is not fitting that Supreme Goodness damn man. O God, You created man for Yourself;[48] and this work of Yours, O God, would be in vain and would be empty and imperfect and would not reach the goal that You purposed for it because of Your Goodness, O God. The charge brought by Truth applies to the angels who with no one urging sinned and fell. However, let man, who was deceived and impelled and deluded by the prompting and cunning of Satan, have a remedy. Will You be angry unto the end, O Lord?[49] Be mindful, I pray, of what human substance is; for You have not formed in vain all the children of men.[50] Truth said, O Lord, that You cannot be a Liar—[a statement] than which nothing is more true. See to it, then, that there

be fulfilled the oath that You swore to Abraham, etc.,[51] viz.: 'In your seed all nations will be blessed.'[52] Therefore, blessed be the Lord God of Israel, who effects the redemption of His people.[53] O Lord, You will keep Your promises, and David will not be disappointed.[54] You will not profane Your testament, and You will not make void [the words] that proceed from Your lips.[55] O Lord, You have said: 'If his children forsake my testament …,'[56] etc., 'I will visit their iniquities with a rod.[57] But I will not take away my mercy from him, nor will I blemish my truth.[58] And so, I will keep my mercy for him forever.' [59] This decree of Yours, O Lord, which is a decree of graciousness, will remain unchangeably. Your purpose, O God, will remain—the purpose by which You predestined [some men] to become conformed to the image of Your Son.[60] The testament that You gave to Your elect will remain in effect: 'I have sworn to David my servant, I will prepare …,' etc., 'and build up your throne forever.'[61] Through Jeremias You have said, O Lord, in Chapter 18: 'I will suddenly speak against a nation and a kingdom in order to uproot and disperse and destroy [it]. If that nation [against which I have spoken] will repent of their evil, then I, too, will repent of the evil that I have thought to do to them.'[62] The human race repents. 'How long will You forget [it]? Unto the end?' [63]

[20] Justice, weighing against man his sin, said that man's sin had done harm to Truth, had rebelled against Mercy, had abused Peace, had despised Justice. For Truth intended for man to be saved; Mercy intended for him to be predestined in order to be conformed to the image of God's Son.[64] Justice offered merit, by way of grace in the present lifetime; Peace offered a reward, by way of glory in the future lifetime. O Adam, you believed a lie! Not only does man die but he lapses downward, as does water.[65] Even Mercy would not be merciful to one who does not repent, O Lord. Now, Adam substituted blasphemy for penitence, haughtiness for confession. For when God walked at the time of the afternoon breeze, He called Adam to repentance, saying: "Who told you that you were naked—except that you have [learned from having] eaten [of the tree]?" etc.[66] Adam answered: "The woman, whom You gave me as a companion, gave to me [the fruit], and I ate [of it]." [67] It was as if he had answered: "The blame ought to be imputed to You, who gave me the wife," etc. Because the Lord is just and has loved justice …, etc., and because You have commanded …, etc.[68]: judge him, O Lord, in accordance with the multitude of his impiety; and cast him out, since he has provoked

You, O Lord."

[21] But Piety, seeing that it could not have, in favor of man, any arguments against Truth and Justice, resorted to pleading—adducing in favor of man's reconciliation the twofold honor of God: with respect to His graciousness and with respect to His integrity. Piety adduced honor with respect to God's graciousness, saying pleadingly: "O God, for Your own sake incline Your ear and hear—open Your eyes and see—the tribulation of [Your] people.[69] O Lord, bring it about that You do not forget to be merciful[70] and it be said 'God is cruel and pitiless.'[71] [For in that case] there will be a detracting from the honor of Your graciousness, O God, You to whom being merciful and ever-sparing are proper." Likewise, Piety mentioned honor's graciousness, saying: "You have sworn that You would give to our fathers the Land of Promise, i.e., [would give them] glory. Therefore, give [it]. Otherwise, demons and Egyptians will be detracting from Your power. And they will speak of that for which Moses prayed in Numbers 13: 'Let not, I ask, the Egyptians hear [of it] and say, "He was not able to lead them into the land of Promise; therefore, He slew them in the desert …"' etc. Therefore, let there be peace in Your strength,[72] O Lord, for the sake of honor with respect to Your graciousness."

[22] Once the accusations of both parties were understood, a silence was made in Heaven for half an hour, as it were.[73] For the course of all time is a single hour; the first half of the hour is the time before the Incarnation; the other half is the time after the Incarnation. Wisdom 16 [says]: "While all things were in the midst of silence and night was in the midst of her course …," etc.[74] In other words, it is as half an hour from the time of man's sin to the time of Christ, in whom silence came about, in whom a pact was awaited between Truth and Mercy, Peace and Justice, man and God. Then there was discussed in the sanctuary of the Divine Council how the legal case between God and man could be put to rest. There was discussion among those who give testimony in Heaven: the Father, the Word, and the [Holy] Spirit.[75] And there was consideration of to which of them would be committed the judgment between Mercy and Truth, Justice and Peace, God and man. The Father was suspect on account of His intimate acquaintance with Truth, because "You are powerful, O Lord, and Truth is round about You."[76] Moreover, Justice is an intimate acquaintance of His, because He is just and has loved Justice.[77] Furthermore, the Holy Spirit is suspect, because He sides with Mercy and with Peace; for it is known that the Spirit of Wisdom is kind and benevolent.[78]

Both parties [to the lawsuit] shouted in agreement: "O God, give Your judgment to the King and Your justice to the King's Son."[79] And it was decided that the Father of mercies would give all judgment to the Son,[80] because the Son could not be suspect; for although the Son is God, nevertheless His eyes look upon him who is poor.[81] He "shall reprove, with equity for the meek of the earth."[82] And He is God's Son, whom John in the Apocalypse saw sitting on a judicial throne and having a rainbow of reconciliation round about [Him].[83] For [as says] Genesis 9: "I will place a [rain]bow in the clouds of heaven, and it will be a sign of the covenant between me and you."[84]

[**23**] After the merits of the case had been discussed, [the Son] rendered a decision: (1) that in accordance with the plea of Piety man would be saved and (2) in order that the condemnatory judgment of the Creator would be inviolable, one [individual] would die for the people, and the whole race would not perish.[85] Hence, a human being (and not anyone else) would die, because it was said: "At whatever time ...," etc.[86] But the death of *which* human being will be able to satisfy this condemnatory judgment? For among those born of women no one suitable is found. Since an angel will not effect redemption but [only] a man will: how, then, [can] man, who is enshrouded in misery and is corrupt with guilt, [do this]? To redeem is to restore lost innocence and lost glory by means of a just and worthy payment. If, then, neither an angel nor a man nor any lower creature can [do this], only God can. And so, it is necessary that it be a God-man [who accomplishes redemption: it is necessary that it be] God, because of the pleadings of Piety; [it is necessary that it be] a man, because of the punitive judgment of the Creator. In this way, "Mercy and Truth have met each other,"[87] when they have come together in one gracious agreement, so that through Mercy man is freed and so that on account of Justice man satisfies the condemnatory judgment of the Creator. However, Justice wills that he who has sinned make satisfaction and that he make satisfaction according as he has sinned. Man sinned; let man make satisfaction. Man willed to be God. Therefore, he sinned as greatly as God is great. Therefore, let a man-God make satisfaction. And because man willed to be wise as is God and because the Son is the Wisdom of the Father, it was fitting that not the Father, not the Holy Spirit but the Father's Son-made-man make satisfaction.[88] And so, let the Son of God be made, on account of Justice, a son of man, on account of Peace.

[**24**] At this point ascend unto contemplating the goodness of

this Divine Judge, who in order to grant you peace rendered a condemnatory judgment such that, on account of it, it was necessary that He empty Himself and take on the form of a servant.[89] O the infinite Graciousness of the Father, because "He spared not His own Son ...," etc.![90] This Son of the Supreme King made to be proclaimed—after the execution of His condemnatory judgment was pleasing to His Wisdom and after night had passed—His advent in the midst of the world at the half-way point in time. And He caused the proclaiming [to be made] to every nation, since the Savior of the world will come, the Giver of life and the Regenerator, and Illuminator, of life. But the darkness apprehended Him not.[91] Those who were seated in darkness and in the shadow of death[92] were awaiting Him and shouting: O Lord, rend the heavens.[93] Come, O Lord, and do not delay. Forgive the transgressions of Your people. Come, O Lord, God of hosts, in order to free us. Remember Your favorable disposition. Visit us with Your salvation.

[25] Many saints and prophets have come, giving witness of His advent. Some [have given witness] of the [birth]place in Bethlehem, etc. Some [have testified] regarding His miraculous conception: "Behold a virgin shall conceive ...," etc.[94] Some [have borne witness] regarding His glorious birth: "Unto us a child is born and a son is given," etc.[95] Some [have borne witness] about the exact time [of His nativity]: "The Lord [foreshortened] yet seventy weeks upon His people ...," etc.[96] Psalms 83: "Truth has sprung out of the earth";[97] i.e., God, who is Truth, has taken on an earthly body in order to disclose the way of salvation to those who are earthly. Let the heavens rejoice![98] Let the clouds put on justice! Let the earth be opened and bud forth a savior![99] And Daniel: Lo, with the clouds of heaven the Son of man comes ..., etc.[100]

NOTES TO *SERMON I*

1. John 1:1.
2. Acts 8:33. Isaias (Isaiah) 53:8.
3. Hebrews 12:20. Exodus 19:12-13.
4. John 21:25.
5. Luke 1:28.
6. Exodus 3:14.
7. Nicholas holds the view that no finite mind knows—or can know—*what* God is or what He is like in and of Himself. All "knowledge" of what God is is symbolical and metaphorical. By contrast, *that* God is is knowable to finite minds.
8. Genesis 1:1. Here the verb accompanying Nicholas's use of "Elohim" is singular: "creavit". In Hebrew "Elohim" is a plural noun.
9. Joshua 24:19. Here the adjective modifying Nicholas's use of "Elohim" is plural: "sancti".
10. Jeremias (Jeremiah) 23:36. Here the adjective modifying Nicholas's use of "Elohim" is plural: "viventium".
11. Psalms 49:1 (50:1).
12. Nicholas here alludes to the point that in Hebrew "Elohim" ("God") is plural but that "Jehova" ("Lord") is singular.
13. That is, ἐν ἀρχῇ ἦν ὁ λόγος. Nicholas's rule for transliterating Greek letters differs from ours.
14. Psalms 109:1 (110:1).
15. Psalms 109:3 (110:3).
16. Psalms 109:3 (110:4).
17. Gregory the Great, *Moralium Libri, XXIII*, Ch. 19, n. 35 (*PL* 76:272B).
18. Lactantius, *Divinae Institutiones*, IV, Ch. 8 (*PL* 6:467 B).
19. Psalms 44:2 (45:1).
20. Lactantius, *ibid.*, IV, Ch. 9 (*PL* 6:469).
21. Gregory the Great, *Moralium Libri, XXIII*, Ch. 19, n. 36 (*PL* 76: 272C).
22. Peter Lombard, *Sententiae I, Distinctio* 5.6 (*PL* 192:536).
23. Basilius, *Homilia* XVI, 136 (*PG* 31:477A).
24. Origin, *In Evangelium Johannis*, cf. Vol. II, n. 1 (*PG* 14:105C).
25. Nicene-Constantinople Creed (381).
26. Lactantius, *Divinae Institutiones*. Book IV: *De Vera Sapientia et Religione*, Chs. 1-30 (*PL* 6:447C, etc.)
27. Lactantius, *Divinae Institutiones*, IV, Ch. 6 (*PL* 6:461D).
28. Lactantius, *Divinae Institutiones*, IV, 6 (*PL* 6:462A).
29. Lactantius, *ibid.*, IV, Ch. 6 (*PL* 6:462C).
30. Lactantius, *ibid.*, IV, Ch. 7 (cf. *PL* 6:463B).
31. Lactantius, *ibid.*, IV, Ch. 9 (*PL* 6:469B).
32. Lactantius, *ibid.*, IV, Ch. 15 (*PL* 6:492D).
33. John 1:1.
34. John 1:3.
35. Psalms 134:6 (135:6).
36. Psalms 32:9 (33:9).

37. Genesis 1:3.
38. Psalms 32:6 (33:6).
39. Psalms 49:1 (50:1).
40. Wisdom 2:24.
41. Psalms 84:11 (85:10).
42. Genesis 3:5.
43. Psalms 5:7 (5:5-6).
44. Apocalypse 22:15 (Revelation 22:15).
45. Exodus 20:5.
46. Numbers 23:19.
47. Genesis 2:17.
48. Augustine, *Confessiones*, opening sentence.
49. Psalms 88:47 (cf. 89:46).
50. Psalms 88:48 (89:47).
51. Luke 1:73.
52. Genesis 22:18.
53. Luke 1:68.
54. Psalms 131:11 (132:11).
55. Psalms 88:35 (89:34).
56. Psalms 88:31 (89:31).
57. Psalms 88:33 (89:32).
58. Psalms 88:34 (89:33).
59. Psalms 88:29 (89:28).
60. Romans 8:29.
61. Psalms 88:4-5 (89:3-4).
62. Jeremias (Jeremiah) 18:7-8.
63. Psalms 12:1 (13:1).
64. Romans 8:29.
65. Psalms 57:8 (58:7).
66. Genesis 3:8-11.
67. Genesis 3:12.
68. Psalms 10:8 (11:7). Psalms 118:138 (119:138).
69. Daniel 9:18.
70. Psalms 76:10 (77:9).
71. Cf. Jeremias (Jeremiah) 6:23.
72. Psalms 121:7 (122:7).
73. Apocalypse 8:1 (Revelation 8:1).
74. Wisdom 18:14.
75. I John 5:7.
76. Psalms 88:9 (89:8).
77. Psalms 10:8 (11:7).
78. Wisdom 1:6.
79. Psalms 71:2 (72:1).
80. John 5: 22.
81. Psalms 10:5 (cf. 11:4).
82. Isaias (Isaiah) 11:4.
83. Apocalypse 4:2-3 (Revelation 4:2-3).

84. Genesis 9:13.
85. John 11:50.
86. Genesis 2:7.
87. Psalms 84:11 (85:10).
88. This reasoning is adapted from Anselm of Canterbury's *Cur Deus Homo*.
89. Philippians 2:7.
90. Romans 8:32.
91. John 1:5.
92. Psalms 106:10 (107:10). Luke 1:79.
93. Isaian 64:1.
94. Isaias (Isaiah) 7:14.
95. Isaias (Isaiah) 9:6.
96. Daniel 9:24.
97. Psalms 84:12 (85:11).
98. Psalms 95:11 (96:11).
99. Isaias (Isaiah) 45:8.
100. Daniel 7:13.

Sermon II: Ibant Magi
("The Magi journeyed ....")
[January 6, 1431; preached somewhere in the Diocese of Trier]

[1] "The Magi journeyed following the guiding star which they had seen. They seek after light by means of light. They acknowledge God with a gift."[1] ([Words contained] in the hymn of the present celebration [of Epiphany]).

Properly speaking, today is the feast of the Church, which was led by the three Magi from heathendom unto Christ. By baptism the Church is united to Christ in matrimony. By means of a miracle it is transformed from its own insipid wateriness into a most succulent partaking of the Bridegroom and into a state of inebriating love for Him. Hence, we sing forth: "Today the Church is joined to the Heavenly Bridegroom ...," etc. [2] First of all,[2] [I note] that the Greeks name their wise men *philosophers*; the Hebrews, *scribes*; the Latins, *sages*; the Persians, *magi* (especially because of the great extent of their knowledge of astronomy). According to Seneca (in the Golden Age), they are called kings, who were governing at that time. Seneca [writes]: "There was supreme happiness at that time, when there was no one superior in power who was not also superior in wisdom."[3] According to Gregory,[4] wise men are those who, first of all, govern themselves; and so, they are rightly kings. Hence, I will say some things, first, for wise men who, in the first place, endeavor to seek God by the light of their knowledge; but, at length, it is necessary that they be led by Divine Light; otherwise, they would never reach their goal. To this discussion I want to append the Gospel-story: that the Magi set out from afar ..., etc.

Secondly,[5] [I will note] that those who set out only as magi or magicians (as, according to Gregory in his homily, some claim that those kings first were), and who follow only the star that they see, and who seek after the light of insightfulness only by means of their own light—these men acknowledge God only with a gift. They are at odds with God, the Father of lights; and they are ever learning but never coming to their goal;[6] and they will fall into heresy, deserting the true light. Hence, together with the Prince of darkness they are forever separated from the light of glory. ([I will speak] of these matters in the second part and [will direct my statements] to the laity.)

19

Thirdly,[7] [I will note] that a pagan, magical soul—for a long
time bedarkened with the darkness of unbelief and by the blight of
sin but now turned toward the Star that has arisen from Jacob[8]—follows, with loving steps, the star on the day of its appearance. The soul
follows it to the place of the crib, offering itself as a whole to God
..., etc. Then it inquires after the Light—[inquires] by means of the
light present on the day of the epiphany that is related to Christ's baptism, when, with faith in the Trinity, the soul purifies itself (by means
of the baptismal fount) as a bride adorned for its Creator ..., etc. Next,
the soul acknowledges God with a gift when it obtains the glory with
which the Lord recompenses those who love Him ..., etc. And this
[third] part will be for contemplatives. And this [third stage] is [sym-
bolized by] the epiphanic festival at the house [in Cana] at which
Christ changed water into wine ..., etc.[9]

PART ONE
How It Is that the Ancients Endeavored To Seek
God by their Own Natural Light

(a) *What the Ancients were able to presage about the Divine*
    Trinity and about the re-creation of man.

[3] As regards the first [issue]: how it is that the Ancients endeav-
    ored to seek the one God through rational considerations.

Since it is not the case that anything is the cause of itself, hence there
is one Beginning, hence only one Originator of all things, from whom
are all things, etc. And since the being of this Beginning derives from
no other, it is eternal and infinite and most simple, without any composition; for otherwise it would not be eternal. And in this way the Platonists posited God as the Creator of the world—God, who created immortal souls according to His image. And, as St. Augustine relates in
his Book of *Confessions*, Plato not only discovered that God is *one* but
also spoke of the *Word of God*. Indeed, Plato spoke of almost the entire Gospel (as writes the same Augustine), to the point [of saying]:
"There was a man sent from God."[10] [4] And by means of rational
considerations certain men investigated the Trinity: the Unbegotten
Father, the Only-begotten Son, and the Holy Spirit, who proceeds from
both [of them]. For it is necessary that in that divine, supreme, most
perfect Being there be supreme intelligence. Accordingly, [in God
there is] He-who-understands, He-who-can-be-understood, and He-
who-is-the-understanding. [Or again, there is] He who loves, He who

is lovable, and He who is the loving. And in this way the Word in God proceeds in the manner of intellect, and the Holy Spirit proceeds in the manner of will. And in this way the Son—like a mental word that flows forth from the intellect—is the Image of the Father. In and through this Word, as in and through His own Understandability, the One who understands, [viz., the Father], understands Himself; and in and through this Word [the Father] understands all things that are outside Himself. For in and through this Word all created things were conceived from eternity; through this Word all things are created, etc.[11]

Eusebius Pamphilus, in his books of *Preparations for the Gospel*, relates many things concerning the foregoing [topic]—i.e., relates that even the philosophers spoke about the Trinity. They all had certain modes (nevertheless not precisely demonstrative modes) of investigating God and His Being, insofar as the Divine Being can be apprehended and understood by creatures. Although one mode draws nearer to Him [than does another], the situation is analogous to a circle's never being measured definitively by means of angular figures. Even though some [of these figures] tend more closely to roundness, nevertheless what is angular is always infinitely distant from what is round, etc. [5] Because the Ancients saw themselves entangled in many errors (even where the deformity of every nature ceased), they saw that each man comes to possess understanding [only] with difficulty, they saw [man's] proneness to evil, [and] they understood the fall-of-human-nature resulting from the offence and the guilt. Still, because of the fact that man was created by God, who is Best, unto an end that is best (this best end is God): they thought that unless created man were re-created, he could not attain his end. They thought that because God is *one* He created one world and because He is *trine* He created a threefold nature: immaterial, corporeal, and mixed. Therefore, in order that every creature might be exalted to the highest degree, God Himself would one day unite Himself to a common creature, viz., to human nature, in order that it might be re-created and in this way man might be led to his end. With great zeal some men (e.g., Messalaha the Arab and others) wrote astrologically about the fact that the Son of God, who was to become incarnated, was to be born of a virgin, so that both the incarnation and the birth would surpass the exercise of the common nature. For Messalaha said: "A young virgin who is weaning a child shall arise ...," etc.[12] Others [write] with respect to other linkages; for example, Ovid tells about a procuress, etc.[13] Moreover, there were female soothsayers; there were various female diviners—nine in number, according to Isidor.[14] What these venerable women foretold of Christ is written about by Lactantius, in his last book on false religion [15] (and by Augustine, etc.).

(b) *The continued transmission from the first parents through their descendants, and the one common faith of all living human beings.*

[6] And there is no doubt that the transmission [of sin] from the First Parent was continued through their descendants. Adam and Eve, as it is commonly held, were not among the condemned but were among the elect. And so, having turned to God after completing much penance (as can be inferred from the beginning of Genesis), they received many consolations from God—especially the promise of a Son who would be born and who would make satisfaction to Divine Justice for themselves and their descendants. Through this disclosure they were lovingly inflamed toward God, pleading for the coming of the Son. Indeed, with this disclosure all wisdom and knowledge flourished in the first human beings [viz., Adam and Eve]. And they made this divine revelation known to their blessed offspring Seth, who was raised up in Cain's place. And Henoch, a just man who was the seventh from Adam, after having lived a long time, viz., three hundred years, while his forefather Adam was alive, learned the very great mysteries that had been revealed to Adam. And, at length, he was caught up [unto Heaven]. But he revealed the mysteries to his son Mathusala, who lived a long time, while Adam and Henoch were alive. Because Mathusala lived until the Flood, he instructed Noe and Noe's sons. For the patriarch Sem, Noe's son, lived during the time of Mathusala and lived one hundred years before the Flood.

Now, Noe, who befigured Christ both in the building of the Ark and in the planting of a vineyard, knew many things about the Mediator. For Noe, according to the calculation whether of the Hebrew Bible or of our Bible, saw Abraham (the Father of faith), for at least ten years. During this long period of time when Sem lived, he revealed what he had heard. For Sem lived more than two hundred years, because after the Flood he lived five hundred years, and there were [only] two hundred twenty-two years from the Flood until Abraham. However, according to the Septuagint there were one thousand seven hundred years [from the Flood until Abraham]. Augustine in Book XV of *The City of God* approves of this [latter calculation], although according to Jerome, who is believed more greatly in matters of history, the first [set of dates] is calculated more correctly. Nevertheless, none of this matters, since nothing as regards human salvation has been lost because of this [disagreement]. More-patent promises about the Son were made in the time of Abraham; after the time of Moses they were made through sacrifices, symbolisms, signs, and prophecies. Later, under David and Solomon, at the time of the construction of the temple, the promises were renewed and the oracles were clarified. Subsequently, there came the prophets, who proclaimed His imminent coming, His actual advent, and all things. O with what great desire the holy fathers were desirous of seeing Him!

[7] But when, at length, He was born in Bethlehem, as you have recently heard,[16] then although He manifested Himself in a public place as a living and true Incarnate Word, He was proclaimed beforehand, by an angel, to simple shepherds. For from among the simple Hebrews He selected shepherds as apostolic ones. So too, it was fitting that He was announced by an angel, through whom the Jews received the Law, as is stated[17] in Acts 7. About this matter, then, you have heard. However, His birth was not supposed to be manifested to all men, (1) so that justification (*iustitia*) would be by faith in Jesus Christ (according to Romans 3),[18] and (2) so that His manifestation would not impede the crucifixion (according to I Corinthians 2: "If they had known, they would never have crucified the Lord of Glory"[19]), and (3) so that the mystery of His humanity would not come into doubt. (As Augustine [wrote] to Volusianus: "Were He to have imitated none of the life-stages from childhood to adolescence …," etc., "would He not have confirmed an heretical view, and would not people fail to believe that He had received a true human nature?"[20] Nevertheless, He was supposed to be manifested marvelously to every kind of man (although not to all men): to Israelite shepherds, to Gentile magi flocking to the one Cornerstone,[21] to just Anna and Simeon,[22] etc.

[8] At length, through His own efforts and those of His apostles, Christ manifested Himself so greatly—by preaching of Himself and sowing seed of Himself in the hearts of men—that His word was apprehended throughout the whole world. For throughout the whole world it is believed that Christ, the Son of God, was born from a virgin. The inhabitants of India believe this; Muslims believe this; Nestorians, Armenians, Jacobites, Greeks, Western Christians (as are we) believe this. The Tartars do not deny this; rather, they commonly believe it, although they do not pay attention to it. And nowadays there

is no nation of the world that does not believe that Christ, the true Messiah whom the Ancients were expecting, has come—[no nation] except for the Jews, who believe only that He is going to come. For there is one common faith of all living men—[faith] in one supreme, omnipotent God and Holy Trinity.[23] If [only the Jews] would understand, [they would believe], as do we! Because they think that we believe there to be three Gods, they reproach our faith. Belief as regards the Incarnation of the Word is widespread, as I indicated. Nevertheless, [these peoples] do not understand the Word of God [viz., Jesus] to be the Son of God, as do Christians.

(c) *The Magi were led to Christ by a star.*

[9] But in order now to approach our proposed topic, let us speak briefly of how it is that the manifestation [that is celebrated] today was made to the Magi. When the Savior was born, a star of marvelous brightness revealed to the Gentiles Jesus, the Splendor of the Father and the ray of his mother. For the Splendor of the Father did not have to be revealed by a more fitting physical sign. That star was created from the elements by the Divine command—[created] only for those Magi, who, alone, saw it. It was small but of great light. It was small because it showed the child who was born but did not cover the entire town, as does every smallest star of the heavens. Perhaps in Arabia Felix, in the region of Saba (from where incense is brought, because of which the kingdoms are called sacred)—perhaps in Arabia Eudaemon [i.e., Arabia Felix], in the area of Mecca—the Magi were desirous of investigating the truth about the upper heavens. And a new star, which was brightly shining, appeared to them, showing them the image of the [new-]born child, having a cross on His head. Inwardly aroused with regard to this new, truly-guiding, wondrous star, they inquired of God, asking: "O God, Creator of the stars, what new thing is this?" … etc. And because they were inflamed with love (perhaps because of a certain earlier divine presage), they desired to see the Incarnate Word, after having received an answer from on high: "Here is a sign of the Creator of the stars, of the Incarnate Word. The Word is Truth and is true Light. Abandon works of darkness." Therefore, seeing the star, and now knowing that it was supposed to be a sign indicative of a great king, and being exceedingly enlightened within, they trusted the outer sign and proceeded toward the star. And because the star was present with them in the region of Saba, [a region] east of Jerusalem, they journeyed a great distance, after having seen the

star in the East—[journeyed] toward the West with gifts, [in order] to adore Him. They heard a voice: "In Judea a child has been born." Hastening onwards with the star miraculously guiding [them] for a brief time, they arrived in Judea.

[**10**] When they came to the royal city, Jerusalem, they asked: "Where is He who is born King of the Jews? We have seen His star in the East and have come to adore Him."[24] When they [thus] asked for human assistance, they dismissed the guidance of the star. Although they knew that Herod was reigning, they did not give heed to the fact that to look for another king was to incur the law of death. They now chose, according to Chrysostom, to die for the sake of Christ.[25] When Herod, who then ruled, heard that the scepter of Judah was raised up (in accordance with the ancient prophecy), he feared (now that Christ was born) that he, being of another lineage, would be ejected from the kingdom. A child in a cradle now frightened a ruler. (Let kings now fear Him who reigns in Heaven at the right hand of the Father!) And Herod called together the elders and the Jewish wisemen, [asking them] where Christ would be born. They answer him according to the prophecy of Micah: " 'In Bethlehem of Judea.'[26] The dead show [signs of] life, just as a hand shows the way with a dry piece of wood ...," etc. Having convoked the Magi secretly once the place [of birth] was known [to him], he learned of the timing of the star; and he said [to the Magi] deceitfully: "Go to Bethlehem; ask attentively about the child; and after you have found [Him], report [it] to me, so that, coming there, I may adore Him too."

O Hypocrite, inasmuch as you devise evil by means of a false and simulated good! Simulated holiness is a twofold iniquity, according to Jerome.[27] Suspecting nothing evil, the Magi departed from Herod and went to Bethlehem. And they again saw the star, which went before them to the place above the head of the [new-]born child—as if it were pointing out [the child] and were saying: "Here is He who is born ...," etc.[28] And the star, after its mission was accomplished, returned into pre-existing matter.

[**11**] And entering into the dwelling, or house, [the Magi] found the child with Mary His mother. And they rejoiced with great joy—rightly, according to Chrysostom—because they had found the Most Beloved, who was being sought. O happy Mary, without whom Christ would neither be born nor be found nor die! Joseph is believed (according to Rabanus)[29] not to have been present at that time, lest any suspicion that God was not born of a virgin be given to the nations,

who immediately sent their first-fruits for the purpose of adoring Him. And so, having entered [the house, the Magi] kneel down humbly before the child Jesus, prostrating themselves in mind and body; and they adore the Incarnate Word. O Magi, how is it that (according to Bernard) you venerate as King and God a child still taking milk from His mother's breasts?[30] Where is His purple? Where is His diadem? Does not the dwelling place of a lowly stable offend you? Does not the cradle, viz., the manger, [offend you]? Consider whether this is a king's mother dressed in a very lowly garment (not for adornment but for covering) such as it befits a travelling carpenter's wife to have! [The Magi] can reply: "We seek the King of eternal glory, not a king of earthly glory ....," etc.

Or, again, [one may ask]: "Why do you *believe*, [since] you have not seen either miracles or signs?" [The Magi] reply: "The supreme humility of Christ draws us toward adoring and professing, as does also the star that we saw, which no mere man could have produced ....," etc. The Magi, having opened their treasures, each offered gold, frankincense, and myrrh. By law, no one appeared empty-handed before a god and a king. Arabic gold and frankincense and myrrh are preferred to all things found there. Nevertheless, [the Magi] offered these [gifts] in very great mystery, because they knew Him to be a man, a king, and God. For they said: "Where is He who is born" (here is the man) "King of the Jews?" (here is the king); "we have come to adore Him" (here is God). Gold is a regal gift; frankincense is a divine gift, because [it is used] by the priest in the sacrifice; myrrh [has to do with] a lordly burial, etc. [The Magi offered] gold (according to Bernard) for sustaining the child and His mother; [they offered] frankincense [for use] against the foul odor of the stable; and [they offered] myrrh for strengthening the child's very tender members, etc. According to this interpretation these three kings were befigured by the three strong men who drew water for David from the cistern of Bethlehem.[31]

[12] At length, when the Magi wanted to return [home]—having completed their mission and after having kissed the feet of the infant and having received a blessing—they received in their sleep a [divine] message that they not return to Herod.[32] And going down to the ship they were transported to Tarsus of Cilicia and returned to their own country by another route. Therefore, Herod, angered, vehemently broke up the Tarsian ships and burned them, etc. And Chrysostom claims that, after having returned, [the Magi] became very devout ser-

vants of Christ and were subsequently baptized by Thomas, with
whom they were associated in preaching the Gospel of God ..., etc.[33]

This [concludes] the first [section of our topic].

PART TWO
The Deceptive Light of Superstition and Its Varieties

(a) *A multitude of things are gathered together.*

[13] Secondly, I mentioned that evil magi [also] follow a star ..., etc.
And the star that they follow is the one of which [we read] in Apocalypse 8: "The third angel sounded his trumpet, and a great star, burning like a torch, fell from heaven. And it fell on the third part of the
rivers and upon the fountains of waters. And the name of the star is
Wormwood. And many men died ...," etc.[34] There are many—even
infinite—superstitious [practices], which by means of deceptive, diabolical light lead every soul away from the true foundation of the
Christian faith. Now, he who falls away from the foundation of faith
is a child of perdition. Hence, such superstitious individuals are to be
cast out and not to be tolerated. [As] Deuteronomy 13 [states]: "If
there rises up in your midst a prophet or one who says that he has
dreamed a dream, and if he foretells a sign and a wonder and it comes
to pass, do not hearken to the words of this prophet or dreamer, because the Lord your God is testing you in order to make known
whether you love Him or not. Follow the Lord your God with your
whole heart, and fear Him, and keep His commandments ...," etc.[35]
But that prophet, that forger of dreams, shall be slain, (1) because he
has spoken in order to turn you away from the Lord your God[36] and
(2) because if you wish to be happy, it is necessary not to regard lying
follies, since God hates all who regard vanities.[37] According to the
laws [false prophets] are punished with death, and their goods are con-
fiscated, as [prescribes] the law *Nemo* (in the chapter on wrongful
deeds) and as [is prescribed] by Hostiensis in his *Summa*.[38] And according to the canons, secret sin is to be expiated by a penance of forty
days. Public sin has [as a penalty] that the sacrament of the eucharist
be denied to the [wrong-doer] (*De Cons.* D. 2, "Pro Dilectione");[39]
and there are other dreadful penalties if [the wrong-doer] does not correct his ways. (See Hostiensis's *Summa*.)[40]

[14] Now, the reason that so many men are deceived by these
vanities is that human nature is corrupted; consequently, men believe
errors rather than the truth. Secondly, there is in a diabolical affair a

power by which it happens that men are blinded, so that the truth does not shine forth to them. Likewise, because there are found *there* some holy words, the men think that [the affair] is not evil, although it is. Similarly, [deception occurs] because [what happens] follows as the result of more than one [cause]. And this fact ought not to influence us, as [warns] Deuteronomy 13 above. For example, in the case of a ring made of three iron nails that have been found, the effect is that when the ring is worn it is protective against certain infirmities. [This effect] happens (according to St. Thomas)[41] in such a way that, at first, men have experienced, through diabolical inducement or by chance, something of the truth; but later when they begin to entangle their mind in these matters, many demonic deceptions occur.[42] For demons do these things in order to tempt and lure [men] into idolatry, according to Augustine[43] in his *On Christian Doctrine* II. And although the Devil has no power of doing anything except by God's permission, nevertheless by God's permission he works, healing the feeble or foretelling future things, with the result that those who hear about and witness [these things] are tested. [15] And because superstition takes its origin and foundation from the Devil's illusion, then first of all one must know that the Devil has the power to deceive and transform man's outer senses. Augustine[44] gives examples in *The City of God* XIIII: Just as men can trick the sense of sight with real colors, so evil spirits can do so with unreal figures. In *The City of God* [we also read] about a landlady who turned men, through their eating cheese, into pack-animals for a certain task; when the task was completed, the men became as they previously were. There, too, [we read] about Apulegius, who admits in a certain book that this [metamorphosizing] was done to him ..., etc.[45] Regarding these deceptions, [we find] in Clement's *Journey* the examples of Simon the Magician.[46] Now, such transformations can occur by an altering either of the senses or of the medium or of the object. Examine [this issue] elsewhere: [viz.,], in Nicholas Gauwer's *Soothsayers*.[47]

[16] Secondly, [the following] must be known: because the Devil cannot enter the rational soul, being present there intimately and inwardly (since only God can do this), he cannot alter reason or intellect. Thus, although a spirit can be in the body at the same time as is the soul, nevertheless a spirit cannot with respect to its essence be in the soul; for the intimate part of the soul and the supreme part of the soul are the same thing. Accordingly, God—who is Supreme and of whom the soul in its supreme part is the image—is the one who

can be present in the [soul's] intimate part. Augustine in his *Ecclesiastical Doctrines* [writes]: "Only He who created the mind can enter it."[48] But although the Devil does not enter into the soul through his essence, he may certainly do so through his effect [on the soul], so that the sinful soul is punished ..., etc. And because the Devil will not enter in, he does not know the secrets of hearts; rather, God alone knows [these]. For no creature knows the secrets of a consciousness except by means of outer signs. Yet, subtle spirits apprehend inner matters from many signs.

[17] However, [both] good and evil spirits can introduce thoughts. Evil spirits [can do so] by illuminating the images already possessed or by furnishing images not already possessed; moreover, good spirits [can do so] by directly impressing [thoughts] ..., etc. Now, this introducing has a certain influence. And so, although a demon cannot motivate the appetites or the affections immediately, nonetheless it can well incite [them] in persuasive fashion ..., etc. In regard to the instigations of the Devil: he first introduces divinations against faith, [doing do] when he wants to make a man to be a foreteller and a diviner. Hence, because it would be very lengthy to speak of this matter—of how the effect depends upon the cause and of how spirits sometimes know from causes future events, as do also men ([who know], for example, of eclipses and about [forthcoming] conditions of rain, etc, and as physicians know about [future states of] health, etc.)—[I will say only what follows]. In all these matters error occurs both with regard to demons and with regard to men. For there is no [pre-]determined truth about the future; and so, foretelling, etc., [the future] is foolish. Moreover, in Isaias 41 it is said: "Make known what things are going to happen in the future, and we will know that you are gods."[49] Therefore, he who arrogates to himself the role of foretelling future things blasphemes God, who alone knows—in and of Himself—future things. Understand this [fact] continually and without hesitation. Otherwise, if in persuasive fashion ..., etc. Telling of future things is "divining," because it befits God alone. Astronomers [who divine] pass beyond their limitations and fall into false interpretation and are led astray by the Devil in their judgments. A wise man is a master of the stars. According to Ptolomy all judgments are in between what is necessary and what is possible. Many things present themselves as mental images, presentiments, etc. (More about this topic elsewhere, etc.) For the Devil, who often induces [one] either to harsh penance in order to destroy [him] or to foretelling certain

things on account of the safety of the people, is recognized as the Devil because of the fact that he is a liar.[50] Oftentimes [what is foretold] does not come to pass; or if it does come to pass, it must not be believed [to have come to pass] for *that* reason. [See] Deuteronomy 13.

Furthermore, one must consider whether from the point of view of the right judgment of reason, this [foretelling, etc.,] could occur. For according to Origen, whatever men do that exceeds right reason will not be done apart from [the power of] demons. Likewise, whatever is contrary to Sacred Scripture is neither to be believed nor accepted. See Bonaventure, *Sentences* III, Distinction 9: "It is not the case that every spirit is straightway to be believed. A certain [man] to whom the Devil appeared in the guise [of Christ] closed his eyes, saying that he did not want to see Christ during this lifetime." Because of these and other temptations the solitary life is dangerous for the inexperienced.

[18] Now, the kinds of divinations that the Devil introduces are multiple: from air, from fire, from water, from earth, etc. (Examine the *Decretals* [of Gratian], etc.) To geomancy pertains inquiry by means of the mirror of Apollo, by means of a handle and cleaned-off stones, by means of a boy's fingernail, etc. [There is] divination by means of the entrails of sacrificed animals and by means of palm branches, etc. Augury is of the kind that deals with (1) the hour of one's birth, (2) the position of the stars, (3) fate. It deals with the chatter of birds, with sneezings, etc., or with an omen that is made when something expressed spontaneously by a man is interpreted as applying to the future. Augury also includes within itself chiromancy, spatulamancy. Furthermore, there are ways for knowing hidden matters—[ways] that take many forms: with weight-scales, with dice, with molten lead, with a rotated wheel, with treasures or stolen goods that are to be found, with trials having to do with a hot iron, with boiling water …, with a duell, a piece of cheese, etc. All of these are forbidden (throughout Deuteronomy 18 [Gratian, *Decretals*, Ch. 26, Question 2]). But as to how it is that this accursed, diabolical sect began at the beginning of the world's creation and through books was handed down by succeeding generations, consult [the works of] Roger Bacon.

[19] Let us likewise touch upon how there are certain works of nature (in the case of herbs and of stones and as regards men's subtle detections—for example, in physiognomy, in chiromancy, and in dreams and in astrology) which appear to be wondrous. And there are works of natural magic and of wondrous origins and wrondrous appearances that occur by nature (as truly occurred on Mount Pincius),

and works of treasure-[finding], and works of deceivers who travel throughout the world. An example is taken from [William of] Paris in your lifetime. He said that he knew the art of finding treasures, etc. [Another] example regards a cross with a magnet, etc. Or again: there is no power on earth that can compare with the power of the Devil (Job 41).[51] For God alone—and angels and men by divine grace—has power over demons. Man has [such power] not of himself but [only] insofar as God gives it to him. Therefore, those peasants who by means of signs and certain words and songs endeavor to cast out a demon by the power of signs, etc., err. And although, on occasion, the Devil withdraws without doing harm, etc. (as we read about in St. Bartholomew's *Legends*), this departing occurs in order to seduce, etc. The enchanters who claim to enclose a spirit in a claw or a jar are foolish, because a spirit is not enclosed in a material object. The astrologers with their imaginings are foolish. Nothing material has an effect on what is immaterial, although the text in Tobias speaks of the heart of a fish.[52] Nevertheless, according to [Nicholas] Lyra the following is understood by [the text's word] "smoke": [viz.,] meritorious expulsive-power.

[20] Moreover, because—according to William of Paris, in his book *On Faith and the Laws*—[our God is a] Jealous God,[53] He wills with righteous jealously that the soul betrothed to Him live a pure life. For he who truly loves his bride does not (1) tolerate another man's coming close or (2) tolerate anything suspicious being done as concerns touch, conversation, nods, signs, or nearness. Nor is it enough for a wife to shun adultery, unless she also shuns the forms of adultery: [viz., in the present case,] seeking help from elsewhere than from God; clinging with steadfast hope to someone other than to God; expecting prosperity from someone other than from God. [Such conduct] displeases God, as someone who is jealous with regard to the [soul] betrothed to Him. And so, for safeguarding His betrothed He gave the command:[54] "Do not suffer wizzards to live" (Exodus 22), because they are idolaters. Because those who captured a mother bird in her nest, with eggs, ascribed this [nesting] to fertility and to evidences of love, God commanded[55] that the mother not be captured (Deuteronomy 22). He commanded that vessels be covered because of the abundant powers and spirits (*holdi*), etc. For [*holdi*] are nothing but demons, to whom sorceresses offer things eatible and drinkable while cleaning house, etc. Nevertheless, [these demons] do not eat; rather, they seduce.

God proscribed men's putting on the garment of a woman, and vice versa, because of idolatry. For women used to put on men's clothes and weapons in honor of Mars. O, Deranged Ones! etc. And, conversely, men [put on women's clothes] in honor of Venus, etc. This festival is held among Christians at the [time just before] Lent, etc. Furthermore, why through blessings and incantations do you foolishly seek from the sun—and why do you through fasting on the first day of the new moon foolishly seek from the new moon—that, as an aid, it safeguard you? The Lord, your Bridegroom, is their Creator; and you are an idolater. What are you looking for in amulets, in characters, in unfamiliar diabolical names? Your God is one. In all of these there is diabolical seduction. At times, [the Devil] appears as a sorceress whisking away a boy; at times, he appears as a boy. And the boy is said to be transformed; and, at length, the boy disappears; he "*verweselt*," (properly speaking, [in German]). At times, the Devil is permitted to slay the boy whom perhaps you exceedingly love—[permitted] in order that you be tempted as regards whether for this reason you wish to depart from God and to render divine honors to the Devil, in the guise of sorceresses, in order that he spare the boy. O accursed sorceresses in whom have remained all the relics of idolatry and who promulgate these [rites] daily! [As] the Apostle [says] in Titus 2: "Instruct women old in spirit that they teach prudence"[56]—as if to say: "… [that they teach prudence], not foolishness."

Another consideration is that man is not permitted to use the Devil's help (IV Kings 1, where [Ochozias] is reproached, etc.).[57] Brigitta, in her *Revelations*, [wrote] about this to Bernard, Archbishop of Naples, etc. Augustine [wrote about it] in his sermon *On Auguries*.[58] William [of Paris wrote about it] in his "Why evil-doers want to have virgins for their practices." [21] Likewise, [consider] how it is that by their own superstitious light they seek God and acknowledge Him with a gift, praying otherwise, and seeking other things, than the Church has instituted. In regard to the worship of God no one is permitted by his own authority to add or subtract from the things instituted by the Church, etc. Moreover, it is superstition when worship owed to God alone is given to someone other than to God; indeed, it is idolatry. Accordingly, a pact with demons, sacrifices made to them, counsel taken from them is idolatry. It is superstition to seek health in marks, amulets, incantations, and in those things that the physicans condemn. When demons are openly invoked, it is called necromancy. If [they are invoked] by means of presentiments, it is *praestigium* [enchantment], because of a blunting [*praestringere*] of men's ears. And when [they are invoked] by means of a dream, it is called divination of dreams. Necromancy is like divination of the dead, because the dead seem to be revived by means of blood applied together with an incantation. If in regard to living men future things are [fore-]told—as occurs by means of those who are demon-possessed—it is called pithonica (from Pytho Apollis, the originator of divination).

[22] As regards herbs and stones, it is clear that when they are made use of for their natural effects, this is done without sinning. However, if [they are made use of] for another reason, then [the use is] not [without sin]; for it is done unto the honoring of the Devil. And the Devil pretends that he flees when one wears on his neck a gem of pionia or of Jasper. [He does so] in order in this way [i.e., through one's wearing the gem] to be honored. If [the herbs and stones] are gathered otherwise than together with [the use of] incantations, nevertheless the Lord's Prayer or the Credo is not used. Here take note of the fact that if consecrated objects are put to a use other than their proper use, this [improper use] is superstition. [Superstition occurs], for example, with holy water that is drunk as a remedy for sickness or that is sprinkled for [acquiring] fertility and is sometimes given to brute animals. [It occurs] also with the light of an Easter candle, with the use of baptismal water. And, likewise, [superstition occurs] with regard to many other things: a withholding of oneself from the source of consecrated light in honor of St. Apollo or [St.] Blasius; a cross made from palm-twigs, etc.; baths on the eve of the [feast of the] Nativity and on the eve of the beginning of Lent as a remedy against fevers and dental pain; not eating meats on the birthday of our Lord, as a remedy against fevers, etc., or as a way of honoring St. Nicholas in order to acquire wealth, etc.; seeking alms for going to St. Valentine [in quest of] a remedy for epilepsy; weighing a boy by means of wheat or wax; carrying a cross all around a field in the springtime as a prevention for storms.

Moreover, [superstition occurs] with regard to certain things offered on the altar: for example, stones [offered] on the day of St. Stephan and arrows [offered] on the day of St. Sebastian, etc. Likewise, various superstitions arise from words mingled with things. [They arise] as regards hate and love and an evil, diabolical procedure with a needle that has touched the garment of a dead man; as regards fork-shaped pieces of wood, pieces of wood joined together as a remedy for fevers, as a remedy for jaundice; as regards an unconsecrated host as a remedy for fevers; as regards urine, etc.; as regards chicks, etc. (See the details in the small book.)[59] [Superstition occurs] with regard to the healing of sheep and of cows by means of a fire to drive away evil spirits; as regards incantation of mares as a remedy against worms or other evils; as regards the lifting of any heavy man who has [but] four fingers; as regards the holidays of the year in their order and together with their superstitious observances, beginning with the feast of our Lord's birth; as regards carvings, writings, etc.

[23] According to Thomas, [*Summa Theologica*] II-II.96.4: "with respect to all incantations two things require caution, whether in the case of words or letters or verses hung [around the neck]. For if there is anything therein that pertains to the divining of demons, obviously it is superstitious and illicit. Likewise, if [the amulet] contains words [whose meanings are] unknown, [it is not to be worn], lest among these meanings something illicit is hidden. Chrysostom [writes in his Commentary] on Matthew: 'by the example of the Pharisees who enlarge their fringes, many men now invent, write, and adduce certain Hebrew names for angels—names that seem awesome to those who do not understand them.' And we must beware lest [these names] contain any falsity." Moreover, we must not believe that there is in those words a certain power that God has not given—as some men believe that if they wear the Gospel of John, they will not be able to be drowned or taken captive. Furthermore, one must beware lest there be mixed with the sacred words things that are vain, for example, marks other than the sign of the Cross. Or one must not rely on the manner of writing, of speaking, or of reading [of words]. If all of these [superstitious aspects] are absent, then—and then only—is [the practice] permitted ....[60] Not only may the Gospels and the Lord's Prayer and relics permissibly be worn if nothing *vain* is mixed [with them]—[i.e.,] nothing which is done in such and such a manner or with regard to such and such a vessel or to such and such [an end], etc.—but in that case it is also required that there be respect for God. And let there not be supposed to be such exactitude that only those words have power and not other things divine. But not the writing or the words [have power] but their signification and meaning do.

[24] As regards fortune and misfortune, things fortuitous, sneezing, dancing flames of fire, footwear, the observance of days of ill-omen, etc.: all of these [practices] are abominable. It is permitted to observe times insofar as they are natural occurrences. But [observance] is not permitted with regard to those things that are not subject to the

influence [of nature]—for example, men's choices of these times or of other times, and similarly regarding other things, regarding the day of the [Holy] Innocents, etc. (Consult teacher Nicholas Gauwer's *Soothsayers*.) A similar point holds regarding things found: e.g., (1) a bird's nest with the mother ([a finding] that signifies fecundity, and abundance, of goods) and (2) a piece of iron or a nail or a half-penny ([a finding] that is good fortune) and the finding of (3) a treasure ([a finding] that is ill-fortune), etc. [25] Rather, the one faith in the Lord Jesus Christ is sufficient for us. For "there is no name under the sun …," etc.[61] "In the name of Jesus every knee shall bow :," etc.[62] "If [you have] faith as [the size of] a mustard seed …," etc.[63] "In whom, through whom are all things."[64] Let us seek Him with our magic light left behind; let us seek Him by the light of His grace and by our light of love; let us adore Him together with the Magi, so that with joy we may return to our native land by another route …, etc.[65]

The following things [I will now say] regarding the second part [of the sermon].

(b) *The order of things-to-be-said is determined.*

[26] The order of things to be said in the second division [of the Second Part]: The star that fell into the inner recesses of absinthian bitterness[66] works adultery and a form of adulterous departing from true Christian faith. Hence, all operations that do not have a reasonable mediate-cause are superstitious. Therefore, as regards evident and experienced natural causes—e.g., in medicines and in the case of certain astrological [phenomena]—and as regards the changes of the moon as they bear upon planting, trimming, and sowing, we must know [the following]: they are allowed, as long as nothing superstitious is mixed in [with them]. There are other things which, although they are secrets of nature, are concealed from us and in which the Devil intermingles himself. These are discussed by Nicholas Horem and Albertus [Magnus] and others (viz., Roger Bacon, John Batem in his *Mirror of Divine Things*, and others writing about the almanac; Alkindus, [writing] about starbeams; Ben Rabas, writing about physical connections; Avicenna; Algazel; etc.). They affirm that works of magic have natural causes, etc. [But] even if such things have [natural] causes, it is not for a Christian to make use of [such things]. For the Devil often intermingles himself amid these secret matters in order to deceive.

Other things occur by means of subtle hand-movements and by means of optics, etc. If such things are not done in order to deceive, they can all be done [permissibly] and without idolatry. But many things, even countless things, that are condemned and evil are accomplished without any explanation or cause—things that our Jealous God does not will to be done (Deuteronomy 13, etc.). [Our attention is] chiefly on these things. And we must be aware of how it is that from the beginning a perverse generation from the church-of-evil-doers always runs together with the elect and with the church-of-the-predestined. Hence, books of divination and of enchantments are found carved on stones before the Flood—[found] by Hermes. These books came into the hands of Cham and his son Chanaan; they came to Zoroaster and to Aristotle and to Zuippus, according to Democritus and Plato, although Zepher Razahel says otherwise. And in these books are handed down manifold ways of using divination, using incantations, etc.—ways that are prohibited for a Christian.

PART THREE
On the Birth That Occurs by the Light of Grace

[27] As regards [this] third part, we must briefly become aware that after the soul (long defiled through faithless infidelity, as was mentioned, and through sins) turns to God, the true Light, then there is present the star of grace, the Eastern light-of-intelligence that guides [one] to understanding all things that fall outside of God. And [the intellect] follows this light of grace in order to apprehend where in that light Christ was born. Then comes the invisible sending of the Father's Splendor, viz., the Word of God in God. This sending is the Begotten Wisdom's entering into the mind of the rational creature for the spiritual and free illumining of it. And although the Word of God—indeed, the Trinity as a whole—is everywhere, with respect to essence, nevertheless the Trinity is not everywhere with respect to its freely-given light. Accordingly, when in your darkened heathen-mind, or your less illuminated mind, a greater light arises and is begotten, then through the light of grace and by faith [in]formed by love you apprehend Christ born in you. Although this [birth] is the work of the Trinity, nevertheless the Son is born in you, because He is the Brightness of eternal light [67] (Augustine, *On the Trinity* I). For it belongs to the Word to illumine and unveil the mind; and it belongs to Wisdom to make the mind wise; and it belongs to the Brightness of light to make the mind bright. And such minds are made to be spiritual sons of God. And when in this way Christ is born in us, then just as the sun accomplishes three things with respect to the earth, so too does Christ, who dwells

in us: in particular, He illumines, warms, and produces fruit. He illumines and brightens the mind qua intellect by means of its contemplation; and He kindles and warms the mind qua affection by means of its love and its fruition, two things that relate to the contemplative power in us. And, thirdly, He causes to be fruitful the practical power—[causes it] by means of the teaching of practical wisdom and by the exercise of the moral virtues, to the end that we may go and bear fruit and that our fruit may remain.[68]

[28] Therefore, in order that, at the outset, Christ may be born in us, let us enter into contemplation, and let us go with the shepherds, at the beckoning of the angels, unto the house of bread, unto Bethlehem;[69] and let us see with the eye of the intellect and of the affections this Word that was made flesh.[70] Moreover, let us go humbly—with those three kings from the East and with the guiding star—toward the West. [Let us proceed] by means of the humbleness of our own mortification, in order that our soul may devoutly find in Bethlehem the humble Christ, the Bread of life.[71] Let us behold! All the things that we see *there* are super-marvelous: the infant sucking on the most sacred breasts—[the infant] whom the heavens could not contain—and the mother, still a virgin. Let us behold the King of kings, wrapped in thick and ordinary swaddling clothes. Let us behold the adornments of the mother! Where are the wreaths? Where are the golden garments? Where, the servants? Where, the courtiers? Where the festive meals, the reclining sofas? Where, the cradle of the newborn King? Lo! All things are very humble! He who thunders amid the clouds lies in a manger. O you who rely on your riches, look at your poor King. O you who live in comfort and in fleshly delight, look at these [lowly] things. If Christ's action is our guiding-instruction, what do you suppose? It will happen [that] …, etc. [29] Reflect on how it is that the mother handles the son, the Ruler of the world. O how often she kisses His holy hands, which a band links together! Reflect on how it is that the royal majesty of paganism devoutly adored Him by prostrating itself on the ground. And, you, what ought you to do for One who reigns in Heaven? Etc.

When the soul reflects in the foregoing way on the foregoing things, it laments with devout and loving remorse; and it asks of the mother permission to approach the child so that, with the Magi, it may kiss His feet. Thereafter, the soul asks more affectionately for permission to kiss the hands; thereafter, to kiss the cheek, etc. Then after it has tasted and seen that the Lord is sweet,[72] it opens its vessels and, with the Magi, offers the child three gifts; myrrh, by mortifying our members; frankincense, through the sweetness of prayer; gold, through purity of contemplation. For when such great beauty appears in the soul, Christ betroths to Himself the soul as an adorned bride. And then, daily, our gold is purified, illumined, and polished in the fire of contemplation and love. And on the part of the soul there arises a maximal desire directed upwards toward God—[a desire] to enjoy and possess its Bridegroom in eternal glory. And so, in this way the soul—united to Christ in this life, espoused to Him in the stable of humility through three gifts—is exalted, after death, unto an intuitive viewing of the essence that is present in the outward manifestation of the Glorious Trinity. And this intuitive viewing is ever-enlivening and happily-restive and solemnly-deifying.[73] Now, with Christ, our Bridegroom, our life will be hidden in God.[74] According to Colossians 3: "when Christ, your Life, appears, you too will appear in glory."[75] And while we journey here below in faith, it suffices us to glory in hope.[76] [As] the Psalm [says]: "I will appear in Your presence in justice; I will be satisfied when Your glory appears."[77] "For then we shall be like [Him], since we shall see Him as He is. And everyone who has this hope sanctifies himself, because He is holy."[78] And because of the form of holiness that [the believer] puts on, God will then be known face to face.[79]

May Jesus Christ, the Enlightener of nations, lead us by a guiding star unto this vision. Amen.

NOTES TO *SERMON II*

1. These words come not from Scripture but from the Breviary of the Roman Catholic Church.

2. See Part One of this sermon.

3. Seneca, *Liber* XIV, *Epistula* 2 (90). See *Epistularum Moralium Libri XX* [Fridericus Haase, ed., *L. Annaei Senecae Opera quae Supersunt* (Leipzig: B. Teubner, 1853), Vol. III, p. 260].

4. Gregory the Great, *Moralium Libri sive Expositio in Librum B. Job*, Book XI, Chap. 13 (*PL* 75:963B).

5. See Part Two of this sermon.

6. Cf. II Timothy 3:7.

7. See Part Three of this sermon.

8. Numbers 24:17.

9. John 2:1-10.

10. John 1:6. Augustine, *Confessiones*, VIII, 9.

11. Colossians 2:16.

12. The allusion is wrongly to Messahalla. See, rather, Albumasar, *Introductorium in Astronomiam* VI, Ch. 2 ("De Naturis Signorum"). Augsburg, 1489. [The relevant passage is on p. 8 of Book VI; pages are without pagination.]

13. Paul Klopsch, editor. *Pseudo-Ovidius de Vetula. Untersuchungen und Text* (Leiden: Brill, 1967).

14. Isidore of Seville, *Etymologiae*, VIII, 8, 3 [See Vol. I of *Isidori Hispalensis Episcopi Etymologiarum sive Originum Libri XX*, edited by W. M. Lindsay (Oxford: Oxford University Press, 1966; reprint of the 1911 edition)].

15. Lactantius, *Divinae Institutiones*, Book IV, Chs. 15-19 (*PL* 6:490-513).

16. An adaptation of this written (Latin) sermon was preached (in German) shortly after Christmas.

17. Cf. Acts 7:53.

18. Cf. Romans 3:22.

19. I Corinthians 2:8.

20. Augustine, *Epistola* 137, 3, 9 (*PL* 33:519).

21. Ephesians 2:20.

22. Luke 2:25-32 and 36-38.

23. This theme Nicholas later develops in his *De Pace Fidei*.

24. Matthew 2:2.

25. Pseudo-Chrysostom, *In Evangelium Matthaei*, Homilia 2 (*PG* 56:637).

26. Micah 5:2. Matthew 2:4-5.

27. Cf. Jerome, *Commentaria in Isaiam Prophetam*, VI, 16, 14 (*PL* 24:248A): "Et in comparatione duorum malorum, levius malum est aperte peccare, quam simulare et fingere sanctitatem."

28. Matthew 2:2.

29. Rabanus Maurus, *Commentaria in Matthaeum*, Book I, Ch. 2 (*PL* 107:759BC).

30. Bernard of Clairvaux, *In Epiphania Domini*, Sermon 2, n. 1 (*PL* 183:147CD).

31. I Paralipomenon (I Chronicles) 11:18.
32. Matthew 2:12.
33. Pseudo-Chrysostom, *In Evangelium Matthaei, Homilia* 2 (*PG* 56:638).
34. Apocalypse 8:10-11 (Revelation 8:10-11).
35. Deuteronomy 13:1-4. Nicholas's punctuation here differs from the Vulgate's.
36. Deuteronomy 13:5.
37. Psalms 39:5 and 30:7 (40:4 and 31:6).
38. Henry of Segusio [Cardinal Hostiensis], *Summa Aurea* (Venice, 1574), Book V, Column 1650.
39. Taken from Henry of Segusio, *loc. cit.*
40. *Loc. cit.*
41. Aquinas, *Summa Theologica*, IIa-IIae, 96, 3, *ad* 2.
42. That is, men begin to wear the ring for reasons of health; later they become superstitious with regard to wearing it—thinking it to have magical powers, etc.
43. Cf. Augustine, *De Doctrina Christiana*, II, 23, 35 (*PL* 34:52).
44. Augustine, *De Civitate Dei*, XVIII, Chs. 15-18.
45. Apulegius: i.e., Apuleius, *Metamorphoses*, III, 24-25.
46. Pseudo-Clemens, *Recognitiones* X, 53 (*PG* I:1445-1446).
47. Nicholas Gauwer, i.e., Nicholas Magni de Jawor, *De Superstitionibus*. (See *Codex Latinus Monacensis* 27417.)
48. Gennaidius Massiliensis (not Augustine), *De Ecclesiasticis Dogmatibus*, 83 (*PL* 58:999).
49. Isaias (Isaiah) 41:23.
50. John 8:44.
51. Job 41:24 (41:33).
52. Tobias 6:5-9.
53. Exodus 20:5.
54. Exodus 22:18.
55. Deuteronomy 22:6-7.
56. Titus 2:3-4.
57. IV Kings 1:2-4 (II Kings 1:2-4).
58. Pseudo-Augustine, *Sermon* 278 (*PL* 39:2268-2269).
59. Nicholas's reference here is unknown.
60. Gratian, *Decretum*, Pars II, Causa XXVI, Quaestio V, C. III (*PL* 187:1346).
61. Acts 4:12.
62. Philippians 2:10.
63. Matthew 17:19.
64. Romans 11:36. Colossians 1:16.
65. Matthew 2:12.
66. Apocalypse 8:10-11 (Revelation 8:10-11).
67. Wisdom 7:26.
68. John 15:16.
69. "Bethlehem," in Hebrew, means *place of food*.
70. John 1:14.
71. John 6:35.

72. Psalms 33:9 (34:8).
73. The theme of deification is one that Nicholas takes up more fully in his treatise *De Filiatione Dei*.
74. Colossians 3:3.
75. Colossians 3:4.
76. Romans 5:2.
77. Psalms 16:15 (17:15).
78. I John 3:2-3.
79. I Corinthians 13:12.

Sermon III: Hoc Facite
("Do this ....")
[March 29, 1431; preached somewhere in the Diocese of Trier]

[1] "Do this in remembrance of me." (Luke 22).[1] [See] *Clementinae*, "Si Dominum in sanctis suis," *De Reliquiis et Veneratione Sanctorum.*[2]

Honorable men, most beloved brothers in Christ! The devotional period is now present in which each one—even one who formerly was very indolent—ought to recall to mind, and to consider in diligent meditation and with a heart inflamed with the fervor of love, his own salvation.

An excusing [of myself]. With all pretense of eloquence spurned, with pleadings set aside, and although I am most unsuited with regard to knowledge and with respect to life, I will endeavor most simply and as best I can to arouse your minds by the grace of the Almighty—[to arouse them] along the lines of healthy meditations, so that by means of my meditation, which I have undertaken to express in words, a spiritual fire of affection may be kindled in each of you and thus your soul may glow vitally with the joy of divine love at this most sacred time of suffering. Accordingly, most Beloved, I make use of the teaching of [Pope] Urban on relics and the veneration of saints, his "*Si Dominum.*"[3] At the outset of his stated aim regarding his commendation of the sacrosanct sacrament of the new law he uses the following beginning: "Do this in remembrance of me."

[2] *Epilogue on three things*. We ecclesiastics ought especially to meditate, with greatest attentiveness, on three things at this season: viz., (1) on the memory of the very bitter passion of our Savior, and (2) on the salvific sacrament of the eucharist (given and bequeathed most graciously to us on this day through a testament), and, (3) thirdly, on the preparing of this same sacrament, along with the preparation's four causes: viz., in terms of effect, of material, of form, and of the reception [of form].[4] All of these things are disclosed in the aforementioned words of Christ our Savior.

The reason for [this] topic. Now, whom He loved He loved unto the end.[5] And according to the doctors [of the Church] it is evident that after the supreme priesthood was conveyed to the Apostles by means of these words—[uttered] with respect to the preparation of this most sacred sacrament during the final hour of love, at the principal

42

evening meal, at the supreme meal of love—He did that supreme act than which He could do, and could give, nothing greater for the salvation of our souls. Therefore, I rightly direct this theme to you priests to whom my sermon is addressed and who are successors of the Apostles with respect to this consecrating power.

Subsidiary prayer. [We have] nothing from ourselves qua from ourselves,[6] since God has made us and not we ourselves[7] and since all our power is by the spirit of His mouth.[8] Nevertheless, as regards this very excellent, divine, supernal, spiritual matter: the less we are *able*, the more we must implore God. With a sincere heart and a devout prayer we must seek the favor of the Incarnate Word's virgin mother, Mary, the intercessor and advocate for our prayers. [I ask] regarding myself that when I open my mouth, it may be filled with the spirit of wisdom; for you [yourselves I ask] that when your ear hears, your heart may obediently be inflamed. Accordingly, let us say with a single and pious mind: "Ave Maria."

PART ONE
Man's Creation and Fall and the Purpose of the Son of God's Incarnation Are Set Forth

[3] *The Trinity.* When—from eternity and in His essence and without inactivity or sluggishness—the Lord, the God of infinite goodness, made to be good what can be made good and loved what can be loved and understood what can be understood, He had *Making-good* and *Loving* and *Understanding* in the oneness of His essence. This altogether simple trinity is an altogether singular oneness. It is easy for someone who is alive to believe this, for if God is good without inactivity: then in His essence there is One-who-makes-good, whom we call Father; and in the same essence there is the correlate of the One-who-makes-good, viz., the God-who-is-makeable-as-good, whom we call Son; and there is each's Act-of-making-good (and loving), whom we call Holy Spirit. It was pleasing to God's goodness, which flowed out from His essence, to make-good and to create. Therefore, God created a threefold nature: a nature that is only immaterial, a nature that is only corporeal, and a mixed nature. The nature that was only immaterial—to pass through [this topic] briefly—remained, in part and through free will—standing upright in humble and loving subjection; but, in part, it fell because of pride, rebellion, and blasphemy.[9]

But God created man as a mixture of body and spirit—[created him] in the image and likeness of His most holy trinity and essence.

He adorned man outwardly with the delightfulness of Paradise; and inwardly He most perfectly filled him with a full knowledge of things. Indeed, as with the angels, He gave man intellect, will, and memory; as with brute animals, He gave man bodily senses. And just as this man [Adam] issued forth from the supremely good Beginning, so the Alpha and Omega,[10] [viz., God,] equipped man for the Highest End. [God equipped him] (1) with reason, by means of which man subjugated the senses; (2) with will, by means of which man, in loving, entered into God; (3) with memory, by means of which man established himself firmly. God gave [man] an appetitive power and a power of desire by means of which powers man would, with delight and affection, remain upright in love. God gave [man] the [power] of anger, by means of which man would indignantly repel, with hope and boldness, things contrary to God, his Beloved. And God saw all the things that He had made, and they were exceedingly good.[11] From Him who is Best [come] only the best of things; for, [made] from nothing, they were, through the goodness of God, good in accordance with a likeness to the forms of them; [and, similarly, they were] great, true, etc., [in accordance with the corresponding forms]. Sadness, pain, etc., were in man only conditionally and potentially. Through sin they were actualized. There was a single oneness, a single harmony among all [three of] these powers. The senses obeyed the will and reason. And by the saints this harmoniousness is called original justice, which God bestowed on Adam.

[5] *The fall of man.* The first created human beings, (1) esteeming the foregoing [facts] lightly and (2) perverting the concreated-ordering that directed [them] toward God, and (3) separating themselves from God through a transgressing of the precept—being transgressors of the imperial, very just commandment through the eating of the fruit, they fell most gravely into the penalty attached to the commandment: viz., "At what time you eat [the forbidden fruit] you shall surely die."[12] Not only [did they fall] but [so also did] the entire human race, which was hidden in them by a certain productive power or seminal cause. And, as Bernard says, "We fell at one and the same time into the mire and onto the pile of stones; hence, we were polluted with original guilt and were battered and broken and were gravely wounded" in all of the perfectly disposed powers and potencies of our soul.[13] For by the just judgment of God, and after original justice was lost through the Fall, the soul's powers and affections—having fallen from their [original] station—became

diminished and disordered. They were not altogether destroyed but functioned in a manner opposite [to the previous manner].

Do we not experience nowadays the fact that sensuality, the power of desire, and the power of anger are contrary to the will? And although the will cannot go beyond reason, frequently it acts against reason. All these powers are prone to evil and inclined toward desiring what is illicit. Reason is made blind and errant; often it uses things false in place of things true; and often it involves itself with idle curiosities and with things useless. The will loves things carnal more often than things spiritual. The power of desiring has lapsed into concupiscence of the flesh, concupiscence of the eyes, and carnal pleasures. The power of anger has lapsed, as disordered, into the pride of life and worldly glory. Hope is not placed in God but in riches and in one's own merits. We are made sad by the loss of riches, by the world's contempt [for us]. We are angry with our brother. See how it is that through the loss of original justice the entire man has fallen from the way of rectitude into discord! As a result of this disproportion among his powers and this turning away [from God] through the evil exercise [of them], man has contracted filthiness and a certain stickiness in the soul's desires and powers. Man was held back, having been pinned down, as it were, by this gluey lewdness; and like the Prodigal Son he went off into a distant land and wasted his entire provision through fornication. And departing very far from God, he made himself a keeper of swine; and he served the Devil, keeping the Devil's precepts. And in this way man came into a land of dissimilitude and [wandered] very far from God and was unable to turn back.

[6] *The reason for the Incarnation.* God sees that man cannot arrive at the goal of salvation, because justice opposes. Moreover, Adam and Eve, together with their descendants, could not of themselves—because they were dead as a result of the [condemnatory] judgment—rise up from eternal death. For nothing gives life to itself; rather, just as every creature exists from God, so too every creature has life from God. Therefore, man, created for life, is not restored unless he is elevated unto a likeness with [those] angels in whom there is no sin. [Man] cannot bring about this [state of likeness] except by means of a preceding complete-satisfaction, which must be [such] that there is given to God something (1) that is not owed and (2) that exceeds all that is not God.[14] To sin is to dishonor God—something which a man ought not to do even if all the things that are not God were to perish [because of man's not dishonoring God]. Assuredly,

reason and immutable truth require that he who sins render to God, in place of the honor stolen, something greater than is that for the sake of which he ought not to dishonor God. Human nature, by itself, did not have this [payment]; yet, without satisfaction human nature was not able to arrive at its goal and at the Kingdom. Hence, God's goodness and love led Him to come down [from Heaven] for the sake of our salvation. His goodness and love are so efficacious that—in the midst of time (and, according to some men, in the midst of the world[15]) when all things kept half-silent[16]—the *One who loves* and *that which is loved* unite with an intermediate creature, viz., man, so that in this way there would be the common union of all creatures. [God descended] in order that through the union of God and man every creature would be exalted and would arrive at its end-goal. This Christ Jesus, the Incarnate Word, took onto Himself the extensive sentence of death in order to exempt us from death by dying our death.

[7] *The reason for [Christ's] sacrifice.* Now, because the infraction was infinite and the besmirching infinite, and because the crime of *lèse majesté* that was committed against God was infinite, it was necessary (according to the precept of Leviticus 9)[17] that this Christ, the High Priest, approach the altar and offer a pure, acceptable, worthy sacrifice in order to make satisfaction for so infinitely great a wrong-doing. And there was found only one pure sacrificial victim, viz., Christ Jesus. Accordingly, He offered Himself for us and died, because He willed to. Augustine aims to say the foregoing things in *On the Trinity* IV, Chapter 12: "The one true Mediator reconciled us to God by means of a sacrifice of peace. In order to remain one with Him to whom He was offered, viz., the Father, He would make to be one in Himself those on behalf of whom He made the offering, [and] He would be the one who made the offering [for them]."[18] [8] And in this [eucharistic] sacrament, Christ left a memorial of this sacrifice, so that just as He Himself bore [our] original sin ..., etc. Such excellent love has left after itself priests, and has instituted this sacrament, so that with this same body of Christ and sacrifice of Christ the priests may make offerings for the actual sins of the people—as will be touched upon here a bit later. In this way He wanted to leave behind for us this sacrifice which He offered for us on the altar of the Cross. And since (1) Christ Himself (our Priest and Sacrifice) and (2) He to whom the sacrifice was made were one: ... He left behind a sacrament in terms of food (because there is no greater union than the union of food and the one fed), so that priests, in making this sacrifice, would

be one with the sacrifice. However, this Immaterial Food changes into itself the one who has partaken of it. Augustine heard [the words]: "I am the Food of grown-ups ..., etc. You will not change Me into yourself, as being the food of your flesh, but I will change you into Myself." [19] And in this way priests are, through this transformation, gods and sons of the Most High. [20] These topics are to be taken up below, in a different section.

PART TWO
The Theme of the Sermon Is Set Forth

(a) *Memory of Christ's suffering.*

[9] Let us here and now elevate our mind unto contemplating the mystery of the suffering and sacrifice [of Christ]. We have heard, Most Beloved, that our first parents became corrupted and abominable in and through their iniquities; and, hence, down to the time of our Lord Jesus Christ there was no one who did what is [perfectly] good. For in Christ the deity exalted, in the highest degree, the humanity—[exalted it] by means of a hypostatic union. And, consequently, every creature is united to God through [Christ's] human nature; and the one created world, because of the one Son of God's becoming incarnate, came to its end-goal through the Word-made-flesh. [Christ's] humanity, as united to the deity, was supposed to pay the greatest honor to God. And, thus, in order to [satisfy] God, Christ freely offered Himself on the altar of the Cross in supreme humility. O Christian soul, soul raised up from grievous death, soul redeemed from wretched slavery by God's blood: engage now in contemplation, arouse your mind, remember your having been raised up, redeemed, and set free; [21] receive instruction, and learn the way of honoring God. Let each one take up his own cross, following this pathway of Christ, [22] in order to be united to Christ. For unless one ascends through this Mediator, he will not come to his own end-goal. For he who humbles himself will be exalted, [23] and he who endeavors to safeguard his life in this world will lose it. [24] One does not come to this pathway except by means of perfect love, in which to live and to die is the one Christ. [25] To cling to Him and to place all one's hope in Him is a good thing. For He is the Life of the living, the Hope of the dying, the Salvation of all those who hope in Him. Do not forever fail to be mindful that Christ Himself died in order that by you an inheritance might be obtained in the Eternal Homeland, viz., [the inheritance of] seeing Christ—who is

God and man—face to face and without a symbolism.

[**10**] O how great that love was which caused God to descend, and caused a human nature to ascend, into a oneness of person! O how great was that love on the part of the God-and-man [viz., Jesus]! [It was so great] that our Priest, the King of kings, the true Shepherd of souls, being without any guilt, removed the sorrows of all earthly tribulation and, at length, offered His own soul and life for His sheep—[doing so] while lifted up from the earth, with hands extended on the Cross, in order by a most shameful kind of death to draw all things unto Himself.[26] O Lord, how sweet are Your words to my palate—sweeter than honey to my mouth![27] You say: "If anyone thirsts after grace and love, if anyone wills to enter through the door, if anyone desires to have whatsoever thing, let him ask and he will receive abundantly.[28] I am the unfailing Fount; I am the Door; I am the Way, the Truth, and the Life."[29] Cause my soul to taste the sweetness of Your most bitter suffering. O Lord, are You not the Light of lights? For in Your light we shall see such great light of glory.[30] How You were darkened on account of me, O Sun of justice[31] and Glowing Gold![32] O Lord, You who are the Life of the living, how Your perfect complexion has been changed, how You have been made a worm, not a man, and made the reproach of men and the outcast of the people.[33] O Lord, are You not the true Samaritan, who heals our wounds? And only he whom You heal is [really] healed. How have You become so despised and infirm that from the sole of Your foot to the tip of Your head there is no soundness?[34] O Sweetness and Piety, since the human intellect cannot grasp You, open to me Your side so that I may enter into You. I know, O Lord, that I am safe nowhere except there from where there flowed blood and water, medicines, remedies, and sacraments for human salvation. O You who are the spotless Lamb led to the slaughter,[35] grant to me, inflamed with desire, to approach the altar of the Cross and to wash my robe in the blood of the Lamb.[36] O Lord, my soul is melted when I recall that beloved-You said on the Cross [that] the mystery of suffering is finished. For I faint with love; in You my soul begins to thirst in very many ways, etc.

[**11**] O Foundation of all humility, I see that life does not consist in reveling and drunkenness but in the Cross and in putting on the Crucified One.[37] For whatever is sought elsewhere is found only there. For so that through an assumed humanity You might furnish aid to all creatures, You did not assume an angelic nature, which lacks a body. Your humanity is a ladder by means of which creatures ascend

unto God. Of the finite to the infinite there is no proportion;[38] nonetheless, there is a symbolic concordance between creatures and Your humanity. Accordingly, by means of our love for You we ascend unto You and are transformed into You;[39] and, thus, by means of You, insofar as Your humanity is united to God, we are united to God. And in You, our Head, we are united [to God] through our ascent of love and Your descent through Your infinite loving-kindness and grace. Hence, Paul says to the Hebrews: All things exist in You and on account of You;[40] and we have nothing of ourselves qua of ourselves,[41] because we are from nothing; rather, all things exist because of You. To You, O God, is given power in Heaven and on earth, because You are God and a man and the Victor over death. Thus, to the extent that we fell through Adam's sin, You were most powerfully able to restore us. Accordingly, by means of Your death, we have been translated unto life, even as the priest transubstantiates bread into Your Body on the altar.

[12] Who could measure the degree of Your suffering? For Your very noble and strong physical body suffered to a very great degree outwardly; and [You] felt pain inwardly and spiritually with human nature generally, with Your mother, with the saints who were going to suffer for Your sake, and with all the human sufferings of all future human beings. Because You knew and loved all men equally You bore all their sufferings in Yourself. And even as You willed to die, so [You died] by a most grievous death—one that had as much suffering as [is contained in] the deaths of all past and future men.

Ascend here [in contemplation] unto the many sufferings which resulted from His knowledge of future happenings, because of the fact that He knew that many men would be damned in spite of His suffering and knew of the many transgressions even of Christians and knew of heresies, sects, etc., wars, tribulations, etc. Who will give my head water and my eyes a fount of tears[42] so that I may suffer, O Christ, with You, who died for me? Etc.

(b) *The instituting of the sacrament of the eucharist.*

[13] "Do this ...," etc. In instituting this sacrament of the eucharist (which is a sacrament of good grace and of love on the part of God and of us) God manifested in it His very great love for us, and He especially inflamed our affection of love for Him. Christ said "Do this ...," etc. God gave to the Incarnate Word, our Source of restoration, most sufficient power and wisdom; and in accordance with this [giv-

ing] He conferred on us the sacraments. And so, in abundantly giving remedies for diseases and gifts of grace, He instituted not only the sacrament that begets us into the presence of grace (viz., baptism) and the sacrament that increases us,[43] once begotten, (viz., [the sacrament of] confirmation) but also the sacrament that nourishes us, once begotten and increased (viz., the sacrament of the eucharist). Hence, these sacraments are given to all those who come to faith. But our nourishment, with respect to its grace-given being, is observed in each believer in terms of his continued devotion toward God, his continued love for his neighbor, and his continued delight within himself. Moreover, devotion toward God is exercised through the offering of a sacrifice; love for one's neighbor is exercised through the mutual partaking of a single sacrament; delight within oneself is exercised through the eating of one's provision for the journey. Therefore, Christ, our Source of restoration, gave [to us] this [eucharistic] sacrament as a sacrificial offering, as a sacrament of communion, and as our restorative provision for the way.

And because the Source of restoration is very wise, He arranged to present the sacrifice, the sacrament, and the viaticum according as befits the time of revealed grace, our capability, and the condition of the pathway. [14] And because the time of revealed grace now requires a pure and full offering, and because there is no such offering except the offering that was offered on the Cross, viz., the body and blood of Christ, it is necessary by means of this sacrament not only to *signify* but necessary also that in the sacrament the body of Christ truly be contained as a due offering for this time. Likewise, in the time of grace the sacrament ought not only to signify communion and love but ought [also] to inflame toward mutual love and ought especially to unite the members to the oneness of the Head, from whom mutual love flows into us by means of the diffusive, unitive, and transforming power of love. Hence, in this sacrament is contained the one Body of Christ, the immaculate flesh—[contained] as that which diffuses itself to us and unites us with one another and transforms us into itself[44] through very fervent love. Through this love [Christ] has offered Himself for us and has given Himself to us, and is present with us until the end of the world.

(c) *The executing of the sacrament of the eucharist*
and the sacrament's four causes.

[15] As the Devout Doctor[45] says, the following [truths] are to be held

regarding this sacrament: [viz.,] that in this sacrament not only are the true body and true blood of Christ signified but also they are truly contained under a twofold form, viz., of bread and of wine—[contained] as under a single sacrament, not a twofold sacrament. But this [transformation] occurs after the priestly consecration, which is done by means of the utterance, over the bread, of the verbal formula instituted by the Lord, viz., "This is my body," and, over the wine, "This is the cup ...," etc. By means of these words, uttered by the priest with the intention of executing [the sacrament], each [of the two] elements is transubstantiated (i.e., [is changed] according to its substance) into the body and blood of Christ Jesus—with the perceptible forms remaining, in each of which form the whole Christ is totally contained, contained not in a circumscribed way but in a sacramental way. In these [elements] Christ is set before us as Food. He who worthily receives it by spiritually partaking of it not only sacramentally but also by faith and love is more greatly incorporated into the mystical body of Christ and is renewed and purified within himself. But he who approaches [the sacrament] unworthily, eats and drinks judgment upon himself, not discerning the body of Christ.[46]

[**16**] But [Christ is present] in the form of bread and of wine because (on account of the cloak of symbolism and on account of the merit of faith) it does not befit the condition of our [pilgrim-]pathway to view Christ unveiledly. Moreover, it is not fitting to chew Christ's flesh with one's teeth, because of our horror at barbarism and because of the immortality of His body after the Resurrection. Therefore, it was necessary that the body of Christ be handed down hidden in most sacred symbols and by means of fitting and expressive likenesses. And there is nothing more suitable for signifying the oneness of the body of Christ than is the wheat-bread [made] from many very clean grains and than is the wine [made] from grapes and berries. And so, [Christ] ought to be presented under these forms more than under others.

[**17**] Hence, according to St. Cyprian in a certain letter, Christ is the grain of wheat that, having been placed in the earth, yielded much fruit.[47] But bread is not prepared from many grains by themselves but from flour and water. Now, water signifies the people, as John says in the Apocalypse: "the many waters are many peoples."[48] Hence, the union of the head of true grain and of water into a oneness of wheaten bread is the material of the sacrament. Then too, water is added to the wine of the cup because Christ, the true Vine, willed that we be united to Him through this sacrament. Hence, the wisdom

of God employed bread and mixed the wine [with water]. [18] Now, this [sacramental] refection is enlivening, because the refection of the spirit is the word of life. Likewise, spiritual refection in the flesh is the Incarnate Word, i.e., is the Word's flesh, which is a universal and health-giving food; although it is one flesh, all are healed through it. Therefore, because it is not possible to give any other universal and health-bringing spiritual food than the true body of Christ, truly it is necessary that His body be present in this sacrament, something which is required by the perfection of the sacrifice, the perfection of the unitive sacrament, and the perfection of the refective viaticum—all of which there ought to have been at the time of the New Testament and of revealed grace and of the truth concerning Christ.

[19] And because the true body of Christ cannot be divided into parts, the body [and] the soul and the deity are there as a single and most simple sacrament. And the entire body is present under the entire form [of bread] as well as under each part of the form, whether the form be whole or divided. And for this reason the body is not circumscribed there, as occupying a space, as having position, as perceptible by any human, bodily sense; rather, it is hidden from every sense, in order that there may be room for faith and merit. And in order that the body not be apprehended, the accidents have the entire operation that they previously had, although they are independent of their subject as long as they have within themselves the body of Christ. The body of Christ is present there as long as the accidents continue in their natural properties and are fit for being eaten.

[20] And so, four things are necessary for this sacrament: (1) that there be a consecrating priest, (2) that there be the required material (viz., bread and wine); (3) thirdly, there is required the [proper] intent of the consecrater and (4) fourthly, the [proper] form of words. Special or general intention is always required; attentiveness is not always required. If inattentiveness results from carelessness or neglect, the consecrator sins; if it results from infirmity, the case is otherwise [i.e., he does not sin]. Moreover, not only the intent of the consecrator but also that of the Institutor [viz., Christ, counts]. Accordingly, the priest would not transubstantiate all the bread in the market-place while pronouncing the words with the intention [to transubstantiate].[49] Although the priest could consecrate as many hosts as would suffice for the entire world, nevertheless it was not the intent of the Institutor that this was to be possible in jest or in folly. In the verbal formula the word " for" ("*enim*") ought not to be omitted, since it is of

proper form, even though it is not necessary.[50]

Likewise, the necessary material is wine and wheaten bread; the required material is non-leavened wheaten-bread and is wine mixed with water, because the one who instituted [this sacrament] used these. Christ, too, was without the leaven of sin; and water, which symbolizes the Church, is joined to the wine, i.e., to Christ, through love. Nevertheless, the water ought to be assimilated by the wine; otherwise, the consecration is impeded. For when we are converted to Christ, we are changed into Him and not vice versa. In the sacrament of the eucharist: the form of bread and the form of wine are the only sacrament; the mystical body of Christ is the only substance (*res*); the true body of Christ, [contracted from the Virgin],[51] is the substance and the sacrament, being the substance of the first thing [viz., of the bread and the wine] and the sacrament of the second thing [viz., of the mystical body].

[21] *Symbols of the sacrament.* [We see such a symbol] in the offering on the part of Melchisedec,[52] with respect to its outer form and its refection, a refection that occurred there antecedently and figuratively, even as it occurs in reality in this [eucharistic] sacrament. Likewise, [we see such a symbol] in the manna, wherein the effect of grace was symbolized. [We see it], furthermore, in the paschal lamb, which symbolized the freeing from bondage in Egypt, even as this [eucharistic] sacrament [symbolizes] the freeing from the Devil. Or again, [symbolizing occurs] in the many sacrifices about which we learn in [the book of] Leviticus. In these sacrifices there was signified the offering [constituted by] Christ's suffering [on the Cross], where He was the host, with respect to reconciliation, and was the victim, with respect to satisfaction for our sins, and was the holocaust, with respect to the maiming of His entire body. It would take a long time to explain everything regarding these topics. But one may consult William of Paris, *On Faith and the Laws.* Wine, [used] for indicating refection, was the symbol of Christ's blood (Canticles: "The king brought me into ...," etc.).[53] Water [symbolized] cleansing ("I saw the water flowing out").[54] Blood [was used] for signifying redemption (according to Hebrews 4: "Without the shedding of blood there is no remission").[55]

[22] From the following factors the worthiness of the sacrament is apparent: viz., that it was instituted by Christ, that it was prefigured both in the Law and prior to the Law, that it was foretold by the Prophets ("Man ate the bread of angels ...," etc.)[56] and observed by

the Apostles ("When you come together into one place, ..." etc.).[57]
The excellence of the sacrament is maximal, since God, who excels
all things, is present there and since the soul that excels all other souls
is present there and since there too is present the body that takes prece-
dence over all other bodies. For in Christ things in the heavens and
on earth are united as something most noble.

A PRAYER
The wonders of the sacrament of the eucharist

[23] Let our mind now be elevated for pondering a bit the wondrous
delights of this most sacred sacrament. Let us say: O Lord, how sweet
the sweetness of Your goodness is! You will that in our partaking of
life we daily proclaim Your death. What more were You able to give
to man, who was dead through [Adam and Eve's] eating than life
through [eucharistic] eating? O Food of life, who was fastened to the
Cross: who can mentally grasp Your most bountiful gift?, [viz.,] that
You who are most high, most gracious, most noble, present Yourself
in food. The following exceeds every degree of generosity and exceeds
every measure of love: [viz.,] where what is given is identical with
the giver. What other nation is similarly great? What other nation has
its own gods who draw near to them, as You, the true God, are present to us in Your own substance but under another form? O Food
that truly nourishes, refects, and most fully fattens not the flesh but the
soul, not the stomach but the mind! O most noble memorial, to be
recommended to intimate hearts, to be bound steadfastly to the mind
and diligently safeguarded in the womb of the heart! In this com-
memoration there are present to us delights, joy, and tears. Let us weep
while rejoicing devoutly. For a heart perfused with great joy sheds
sweet drops by way of the eyes.

   [24] When I elevate myself, O Lord, unto such a lofty reflection, I recognize that the light of my intellect can accomplish nothing; rather, You are He alone who can do all things. [Those who are
merely] curious look for causes and reasons and signs, whereas I approach You through faith. What wonder that in such a terse utterance
of words a transubstantiation occurs? Is not a certain seed, because
of heat, turned suddenly into living animals called silk-worms? Is not
a serpent enchanted by words, and does it not shut its ears in order
not to hear the voice of the enchanters, lest after having heard the
words it comply of necessity? Did You not, O God, make all things
by means of a unique Word? ("He spoke and they were made.")[58]

Was not Lot's wife, as a result of looking, turned into stone or a pillar of salt? Do not certain fountains change pieces of wood into stones and change iron into copper? Who would be surprised at Your power? Does not our stomach change bread and wine into its own nature as flesh and blood? Does not a glassmaker bring forth from ashes of stone a beautiful glass vessel? Does not fire suddenly come forth from the striking of a flint-stone? What is astounding about the fact that You, who are both divine and human, are present in the sacrament as one who is not contracted in terms of the quantitative wholeness wherewith You hung on the Cross? Does not a stork ..., etc.?[59] Does not the eye of a small bird see a very large mountain, etc.? Is there not in a small mustard seed very great power and potentially a large tree, etc.? Did not Eliseus [i.e., Elisha], a great man, place each of his own [bodily] members on top of each of the [bodily] members of a dead boy (Kings 4)?[60] What is astonishing about the fact that [accidental] forms are supernaturally present without their [natural] subject, [i.e., substance]? Does not a diamond ..., etc.? A befiguring of the fact that the concealed sacrament ought to be given to us under [accidental] forms occurred in the figure of Jacob in the guise of Esau, when Isaac was deceived.[61] Thus are all the senses deceived—sight, taste, touch, etc. But Isaac was not deceived in his hearing, because he recognized the voice that came from the interior regions. Similarly, faith is not deceived.

[25] What is astonishing, O my God, about the fact that the body and the blood are sacramentally present in different places as a whole [at the same time]? Is not a single word uttered by me heard and understood wholly and equally and perfectly by many people [at the same time]? For I know that it befits God to be everywhere, [whereas] it befits man to be in only one place [at a time]. Why is it strange if [it befits] Him who is God *and* [a] man [to be present] in an intermediate manner—not in every place [at once] and not in only one place [at a time] but in more than one place [at the same time]? Is not a single definition of "species" equally fitting for more than one individual? Did not the Word, who as a whole is with the Father from eternity and unto eternity, also descend as a whole into the womb of the Virgin? And did He not both come into the flesh as a single whole in order that men might partake of Him and remain wholly with the Father in order that He might feed angels? I am no less amazed that He is present as a whole in each aspect of the host when it is divided. For just as Christ is totally and indivisibly in many places [at

once], so He is present as a single whole in each aspect of the host, [i.e., is present as a whole in both the bread and the wine]. Does not something similar occur in the case of a mirror, which captures a single figure; and if the mirror becomes broken, its fragments likewise capture the entire figure. In things homogeneous: is not each part, for example, of water, also water, just as is the whole? Is it not the case that (1) [one man] who gathered more manna, which rained down in the desert, had no more than did another, and that (2) he who gathered less had no less [than did another]?[62] Is not the soul that is in a small man as "large" as the soul that is in a big man, and is not the soul as a whole in the whole man and in his every part? [26] It is less amazing that although [the body of Christ] is [sacramentally] eaten every day, it is not diminished? For what is glorified and incorruptible is not corrupted after the Resurrection, because it is not turned into the nature of the one who is nourished, but, rather, the one who partakes spiritually of Christ is turned into Him by way of the mind's ecstasy and love.

If many lights are lit from one candle, does not the light of [that] candle nevertheless remain undiminished? One ought rather to be amazed by the fact that the mystical body of Christ (i.e., the Church with the Bridegroom Christ as its head) is diminished by *not* being partaken of. Through partaking worthily a man is made a member of this [mystical] body; and, thus, through having been partaken of, the mystical body is made greater (I Corinthians 6: "Do you not know that your bodies are members of Christ?").[63] Hence, one who partakes unworthily augments the mystical body of the Devil,[64] even as knowledge that becomes more widespread becomes increased (Ephesians 4: "Let us in all respects grow in Him who is our Head, [viz.], Christ."[65]). Does not water flow daily from a fount and nevertheless is not diminished? Why is it strange [that the outflow] from the Fount of our Savior [should be undiminished]? What is strange about the fact that for some [individuals] the sacrament [of the eucharist] is beneficial unto health but for other [individuals] is harmful unto condemnation? From the same flower does not the bee extract honey and the spider venom? (One [and the same thing] is medicine for the one [individual] and death for the other.) Does not the same sun melt ice and harden clay?

[27] I have no doubts, O Lord. Grant that through this sacrament I may obtain the life that You have promised. O Lord, if one loves this life—which consists of a concordance between body and soul,

which life is full of miseries and is near to death, which life is momentary and bears no comparison with the subsequent eternity—how much greater [for us] to be in You, who are Eternal Life! O, [blessed are] those who approach this sacrament worthily, because they draw from the Fount of life! Woe [to those who approach] unworthily, because from the Fount of life they drink death! I see, O Lord, that this wretched life, full of weeping, deceives all men with its gladness, its riches, and its pleasures. When I reflect on losing You, Eternal Life, in order to possess a transitory, perishable life, I groan and tremble as a whole. This present life is ordained unto You. He who improperly makes use of this life does not come unto You. O what a mistake this is—viz., that the greater part of mankind serves You feignedly. Truth has perished and has been suffocated by falsity. O, priest, reflect upon your life; reflect upon your power; reflect upon your words and deeds; reflect upon the nobleness of your office, etc.

NOTES TO *SERMON III*

1. Luke 22:19.

2. See *Clementis Papae V Constitutiones*, Book III, Titulus 16 [Aemilius Friedberg, editor, *Corpus Iuris Canonici* (2nd edition, Leipzig, 1881 (Vol. II)), columns 1174-1177.]

3. *Loc. cit.*

4. This distinction stems from Aristotle, whose four causes are: efficient cause, material cause, formal cause, and final cause.

5. John 13:1.

6. II Corinthians 3:5.

7. Psalms 99:3 (100:3).

8. Psalms 32:6 (33:6).

9. The respective angelic nature of the good angels remained upright; the respective angelic nature of the evil angels fell.

10. Apocalypse 1:8 (Revelation 1:8).

11. Genesis 1:31.

12. Genesis 2:17.

13. Bernard of Clairvaux, *In Coena Domini Sermo*, n. 3 (*PL* 183:272C).

14. This present line of reasoning is adopted from Anselm of Canterbury's *Cur Deus Homo*.

15. Galilee and, in particular, Jerusalem were considered to be the center of the world.

16. Wisdom 18:14-15.

17. Leviticus 9:7.

18. Augustine, *De Trinitate*, IV, 14, 19 (*PL* 42:901). N.B.: Chap. 14, not Chap. 12.

19. Augustine, *Confessiones*, VII, 10, 16 (*PL* 32:742).

20. Psalms 81:6 (82:6).

21. Taken from the opening words of Anselm's *Meditatio Redemptionis Humanae*.

22. Matthew 16:24.

23. Matthew 23:12.

24. John 12:25.

25. Philippians 1:21.

26. John 12:32.

27. Psalms 118:103 (119:103).

28. John 7:37 and 10:9. Matthew 7:8.

29. John 4:13-14 and 10:9 and 14:6.

30. Psalms 35:10 (36:9).

31. Malachias 4:2 (Malachi 4:2).

32. Lamentations 4:1. Canticle of Canticles 5:11 (Song of Solomon 5:11).

33. Psalms 21:7 (22:6).

34. Isaias (Isaiah) 1:6.

35. Isaias (Isaiah) 53:7.

36. Revelation 7:14.

37. Romans 13:13-14.

38. This theme becomes central to Nicholas's conception of learned ignorance. See, for example, Nicholas's *De Docta Ignorantia* I, 3 (9).

39. The theme of the believer's being transformed into God is drawn from the tradition of mystical theology. See pp. 7-9 in the introduction of my translation of Hugh of Balma's *De Theologia Mystica* (Minneapolis: Banning Press, 2002).

40. Hebrews 2:10.

41. I Corinthians 4:7.

42. Jeremias (Jeremiah) 9:1.

43. Cf. I Corinthians 3:7.

44. See n. 39 above.

45. The *doctor devotus* is Bonaventure.

46. I Corinthians 11:29.

47. John 12:24-25.

48. Apocalypse 17:15 (Revelation 17:15).

49. See Hugh of Strassburg, *Compendium Theologicae Veritatis*, VI, 12. [Falsely ascribed to Bonaventure, this work is found in Vol. VIII of *S. Bonaventurae Opera Omnia*, edited by A. C. Peltier (Paris: Vivès, 1866). The cited passage is on p. 209.

50. See Hugh of Strassburg, *op. cit.* The verbal formulae are *"Hoc est enim corpus meum"* and *"Hic ist enim calix."*

51. See Hugh of Strassburg, *Compendium Theologicae Veritatis, op.cit.,* VI, 12.

52. Hebrews 7.

53. Canticle of Canticles 2:4 (Song of Solomon 2:4).

54. Note Ezechiel (Ezekiel) 47:1.

55. Hebrews 9:22 (not Hebrews 4).

56. Psalms 77:25 (78:25).

57. I Corinthians 11:20.

58. Psalms 32:9 (33:9).

59. Does so large a stork originate from so small an egg?

60. IV Kings 4:32-35 (II Kings 4:32-35).

61. Genesis 27.

62. Exodus 16:14-18.

63. I Corinthians 6:15.

64. Interestingly, Nicholas speaks not only of the mystical body of Christ, who is omnipresent, but also of the mystical body of the Devil, who is ubiquitous.

65. Ephesians 4:15.

Sermon IV: Fides autem Catholica
("The Catholic Faith")
[May 27, feast day of the Trinity,1431; preached in Koblenz]

[1] "Now, this is the Catholic faith: that we worship one God in Trinity and Trinity in oneness." (from the Athanasian Creed)

The saints say that man fell from a state of innocence through the sin of his first ancestors and that, [as a result], darkness arose in the intellect and that greediness and coveteousness arose in the will. But since man as recreated and regenerated was supposed to be restored and made righteous, his soul (in accordance with its higher part, which consists of the image of the Trinity) has to be made righteous by means of the three theological virtues.[1] Hence, just as the image of creation consists of a trinity of Persons and a oneness of Essence, so the image of re-creation consists of a trinity of fixed dispositions [*habitus*], together with a oneness of grace. Now, by means of these three fixed dispositions the soul is brought unto the Supreme Trinity in accordance with the three traits ascribed to the three Persons. Faith guides unto the *supremely true* by means of believing and assenting. Hope guides unto the *supremely difficult* by means of relying-upon and expecting. Love guides unto the *supremely good* by means of desiring and loving. Faith assents to God; hope trusts in God; love loves [God]. Faith [is centered] in the intellect or reason; hope [is centered] in the irrascible [nature]; love [is centered] in the desiring [nature]. Faith pursues God in the present; hope accompanies God into Heaven; love embraces God forever.[2]

[2] And because, in accordance with the chosen theme, my sermon is on faith, and because the foundation of our salvation consists in faith, and because faith is a gift of God ...:[3] let us pray ..., etc. [3] "Now the Catholic faith ...," etc. My sermon to you, O Christians, is about a most serious matter, viz., about faith. It is not about just any kind of faith but is about the orthodox Christian faith, which is so great that it overcomes this world ....[4] Since faith is the power by means of which those things that pertain to the foundation of religion are steadfastly believed (*Sentences*, Book III),[5] I must first speak about the nature of faith and about faith's disposition—[doing so] in accordance with the beginning of our theme: "*Fides.*" Secondly, I must deal with the topic of the nature-of-faith as it applies to the Catholic faith,

which is the belief that there is one God who exists in trinity, etc., ...[6] And, thirdly, [I must deal with the topic] of the works of faith insofar as they are in our power; ([as it says] there [in the Athanasian Creed]: "... [that] we worship ..."[7]). For [faith] is the just man's life: "The just man lives by faith" ...;[8] and "he who believes in me has life eternal ...."[9] Therefore, in order that someone live by faith it is required that faith be [in-]formed [by love] and not be dead faith, because "faith without works is dead, even as is the body without the spirit ...."[10] For faith's work is through love ....[11] And by faith hearts are cleansed ....[12] Since the effect of faith is so great, then (as will be evident a bit later) if we reverence it, we must attend to it with diligent care and must keep it in mind, lest we err and declare falsely that we are Christians, although we are not, and lest we lose the very great benefit of faith.

PART ONE
The Nature and Disposition of Faith

[4] As regards the first part, let us say with the Apostle that "faith is the substance of things to be hoped for, the evidence of things that do not appear."[13] For faith is the underlying foundation for the spiritual edifice of grace and glory. Faith is—ontologically, not chronologically—the first *habitus* of the virtues. Through faith's assent the things to be hoped for are in us. Faith persuades the mind, because it inclines the mind toward believing things that do not appear. It manifests by its own light past, present, and future things that do not appear.

[5] First of all, it was said that faith is a virtue. Hence, William of Paris in his [work] *On Faith and the Laws* [states] that to believe the improbable is characteristic of power and strength.[14] For what is pleasant and useful presents itself forcefully to the will; and the uprightness of the one who possesses [these characteristics commends itself] to our love, so that pleasantness and usefulness make the object that has them desirable *per se*. Similarly, evidence and truth bring it about that they themselves are things believable *per se*, because they impose confidence [*fides*] and credibility; hence, it requires no effort to believe them. But when improbable things are believed, the belief is due to the strength of the believer and not to the fact that what-is-believed imposes itself. Just as what is bright is to sight, so what is probable is to the intellect and what is pleasant and useful is to the affections. Just as what is dark is to sight, so what is improbable is to the intellect. It requires no effort to see what is bright, since what is

bright is in no way opposed to sight but, rather, imposes itself. The
case is similar as regards believing that which is probable. The fact
that fire ignites dry wood does not require much power, because [dry
wood] is igniteable; but much power is required if [the wood] is green.
Similarly, our loving what is pleasurable, useful, or pleasant approx-
imates [fire's] igniting what is igniteable. For pleasantness, usefulness,
and splendor are three kinds of immaterial fire; and in human souls
they produce three burnings: the lust of the flesh, the lust of the eyes,
and the pride of life[15]—i.e., licentiousness, greed, and haughtiness.
The ignorant are consumed by these three. As dry wood is consumed
by a material fire, so the ignorant are consumed by means of an immaterial fire—[consumed] from the time of the original corruption, not
from the time of the first creation.

Probability is a diffusion of dim and weak immaterial light; and
so, it does not stabilize—as does the evidentness of truth, [which]
strongly penetrates the intellect's certitude, fixes it, and renders it secure. And just as the will has concerning itself the aforementioned
three immaterial fires, so the intellect has the two aforementioned il-
luminations of probability and evidentness. And so, from this [con-
sideration] it is evident that to believe improbable things is characteristic of the strength and robustness of our intellect, even as to love
things that are hurtful and vexing is characteristic of the strength and
robustness of our affection. [6] Now, the light of strong faith is required; it penetrates the darkness of the many improbable things that
pertain to faith, and it illumines them. And so, it is evident that our
initial faith is a grace and is clothed with glory; and without faith glory
has no place. And if it is needful that the whole man be religious,
given that he wishes to obtain glory, then especially the head, viz.,
the intellect, must be religious through faith. For just as, necessarily,
the will will struggle against itself if it strives to arrive at glory, so
too the intellect will, necessarily, do the same thing. And as regards
its operations, the intellect makes war only on believing. *Believing* and
reflecting and *considering* approach the intellect forcefully, and the intellect receives [them] non-voluntarily, but not as things demonstrated. Likewise, [the intellect receives] things that have been proved, because, necessarily, it assents [to them]. But knowledge involves a de-
liberate investigation from books and from teachers; and so, it can be
partly the result of effort and partly not, etc.

[7] Believing, [which is] the foundation of true religion,[16] has,
as opposed to itself, an array of disputings, dissuasions, contradictions,

as well as of improbability. This improbability is directly contrary to [religious belief] because where reason founders [because of the improbability], faith bridges the gap ....[17] For faith is faith regarding things unseen ....[18] Now, every war must be waged with warlike power, because without power one does not triumph. Therefore, faith is a power. [8] [We can discern that] in faith not all things are manifested, because if they were, there would be no dissension, no heresy. No one contradicts [statements] that are manifestly true, because where there is manifest truth, there is no power [to contradict]. Therefore, there is a power of faith on the part of a believer, because there is no evidentness with regard to the things believed. [9] Each thing is believed through persuasion. But God is believed in and through faith, without persuasion and proof. [Faith] honors God supremely in that it believes Him quite readily. Every [form of] superstition and idolatry, every sect and every faith weeds out with the sword and fire those who blaspheme their God or gods. Therefore, the Catholic faith teaches that God is believed-in without proof and without evidentness.[19] [10] The intellect, because of its weakness, seeks props and means of proof, as if supporting itself by the aid of a cane while ambulating from one conclusion to another. But he who believes by his own power does not need a prop; and he believes the more strongly. [The situation is] comparable to a lover who loves his beloved by his own power more than because of the things that accompany his beloved; otherwise, his love, if it were lured away from [focusing on] the beloved, would be crooked and bent.

[11] An intellect that looks for proofs is like a seller who looks for a guarantee of payment and who, otherwise, does not believe. A heathen demands such a guarantee before he believes; but a Christian, knowing that a guarantee is wrested from God because of a deficiency of belief, does not demand a guarantee in order to believe in God, for a guarantee is deemed to be a sign of unbelief. Because of these props derived from proofs and guarantees, the intellect is judged to be infirm—just as a man, because of his many props, is judged to be weak on his feet. Now, canes do not cure one who is infirm; similarly, guarantees do not heal the intellect; hence, they also do not make the intellect strong. Faith is not to be sought by means of signs (as the Jews [sought it]) nor by means of wisdom or art (as the Greeks [sought it]) but, rather, as a result of virtue. For it is known more certainly by virtue than by art. Art is as a painting that displays the outer form; virtue is as a scent and a flavor that manifests inner [aspects].

[**12**] The closer that light is to the sun, the more noble it is; the more diminished it is and the more distant it is from the sun, the more ignoble it is. A similar [truth holds] regarding the heat of fire. Similarly, through grace faith descends from God as light from Light; probabilities descend through a distant light. Therefore, God's Light is more noble than is light that is reflected from creatures. Hence, "every best gift and every perfect gift is from above, coming down from the Father of lights."[20] Accordingly, those things that are given beyond nature are stronger than are natural things, for they conduce to happiness. Hence, nothing is more certain than is faith. [**13**] Therefore, faith is a general good that is freely given by the grace of generosity and of beneficence. And it is a power holding the intellect upright and securing it, making it to stand by itself and to walk rightly along the pathway of salutary truth and without the maintenance or support of canes. Faith protects the intellect against the darts of disputings and against [the need for] props; and it gives the intellect support against the impulses and concussions of contradictions and opinions and against the severity of its own infirmity and sluggishness. And faith is a light of the intellect that triumphs over the natural lights of the senses—as is evident, in the sacrament of the altar,[21] wherein the senses are triumphed over by faith. In this sacrament we believe in worthy God without any guarantee, and we believe in Him by means of the virtue of obedience. And this [believing] is the foundation of religiousness. And just as the intellect is the nobler part of the soul, so its religiousness—in regard to the works of God and in regard to honoring Him by faith—comes first. And no belief that demands more, viz., [that demands] guarantees, is worthy to be called faith.

[**14**] Now, the generation of Christians, which obediently suppresses its understanding and believes, obeys, and honors [God], is not a perverse generation that seeks a sign[22] but is a people given to worshipping God. With head bowed, i.e., with the intellect bowed, it adores God. And so, faith descends from the Fount of life and enlivens the head of man, i.e., his intellect. Habacuc 2: "The just man lives by faith."[23]

[**15**] *Whence the error against faith*: The error against faith arises first of all from the fact that someone does not believe anything unless he understands, for he thinks that his intellect is capable of understanding all possible things. However, the human intellect is measured and delimited by God, its Creator, who set the bounds of its capability. A second cause [of error] is a turning away [from faith], as

when one who loves something discards it and turns to something else. A third cause [of error] is the grossness of the intellect, just as one who has a thick and turbid eye does not see a hair. And so, he claims that there is no hair there where acute vision [detects it]. As Aristotle says: The inexperienced observe as one who is far distant.[24] It is necessary, then, to believe the learned and experienced. Moreover, there is a further folly: wanting the intellect to grasp things impossible for it [to grasp]—analogous to wanting to see with a human eye as with an eagle's eye. Or again, there is the additional folly of those who want to have proofs [that serve] as stairs for ascending unto the Infinite One. Likewise, another cause [of error] is the sin or the neglect by which divine aid is not sought for [believing] the things that ought to be believed. For light does not enter in where someone sets up a barrier. Isaias says: "Your sins have divided between you and your God."[25] As a result of these errors such great darkness is produced in the intellect that the Sun of justice[26] does not illuminate the darkness unless the night recedes.

[16] Now, faith is God's light and grace; it is not naturally present in [anyone], for nature works according to the manner of one who is a servant without freedom. For example, fire does not act in one way on one thing and in another way on another thing; rather, it acts in equal ways [on both]. Hence, too, even faith would be equally in all [individuals, if it were a natural endowment]. Moreover, because faith is a divine light that descends from God and that [does] not [arise] from things, there will be one true faith that descends from the one God—just as the vision from one eye extends itself unto many objects outside itself, and just as the rays of the one sun illuminate many objects. Moreover, there is one faith common to all believers, just as the articles of faith are common to all Christians. Now, all men are bound to a single divine worship that is owed [to God]. Therefore, there will be a single faith. And whatever is counter to this divine and owed worship and to [this] one faith is an error that is to be extirpted by fire and the sword.[27] All men, as creatures of one Creator, agree in their essential nature; likewise, they agree also in the divine worship [that they owe]. With respect to the basis of their subjection, all subjects are acquainted with their master, although they obtain different duties in the court of this same master. The situation is similar as regards faith.

[17] Now, a sign of belief is that you extend to God obedience and worship—[doing so] out of love that is upright and pure, for [such

love] is freely given and does not result from fear of punishment or
from shame or from hope of reward. For upright and pure love is a
sign that you believe Him to be good and to be worthy of your love
because of His goodness. And in one who thus believes, there is most
pure and most sincere love, as well as actual and most pure worship.
And the love is voluntary because it is freely given; hence, it deserves
a reward. And there is room for a reward in that situation only because
of the preceding gift. But he who loves for another reason ([e.g.,] out
of hope or of fear or because of a reward) is not, properly speaking,
rewarded (for, in that case, his love seeks something outside of God),
but he is given his wages, not a reward.

PART TWO
The Things That Are To Be Believed by the Catholic Faith

[18] Whatever things are to be believed about God are present in Him
either *per se*, without respect and comparison to other things, or they
are not. (1) [Exemplifying] the first [alternative] is our believing that
He is Oneness, Trinity, Equality, etc. (2) [Exemplifying what is pre-
sent] comparatively [is] our believing that He is Powerful, Wise, Kind.
(3) In these [comparative conceptions] other [ideas] are included, as,
for instance, His being called Father, Creator, Light, Leader, etc. From
belief of these three [kinds] arise all the aspects of divine worship. Out
of the loftiness of [His] wisdom arise [our] honoring, venerating, purifying, sacrificing, and adoring. These are nothing other than our
inner and outer subjection and the humbleness with which we believe,
with complete justification, that we are subject to Him as regards our
being saved or lost. Herefrom come (a) bowing, genuflecting, prostrating, etc., and (b) petitions (which we most devoutly and with humble submission deliver into His power) and (c) venerating (by which
we fearfully and only as cleansed and purified approach Him for serving Him and approach holy places, holy men, the relics of the saints)
and (d) the attending to divine matters in silence and with lights and
ornaments, etc.

Wisdom produces fear and shame, blushing, dread, etc. For when
you believe that God knows all of your affairs better than do you, what
are you if you are[28] without shame and fear? But if you were not to
believe that He sees all things, you would be a heretic (even though
this [proposition] is not listed in the articles of faith). For of any two
opposites of which the one is a heresy, the other is, necessarily, an article of faith. Therefore, it is an article of faith that God sees all things

and that nothing is hidden from Him. Something similar holds regarding other [attributes]. From out of God's goodness, or loving-kindness, there arise, in our worship, thanksgiving, blessing (i.e., the summoning of good things), praising (i.e., a magnifying of the Creator), glorifying (which is preaching, proclaiming, disclosing, making-known). Glory is renown that is splendid, sublime, wide-spread. From out of God's loving-kindness, or mercy, there arise, in our worship, hope-of-pardon and thankfulness. The latter includes within itself (a) prayer for mitigating and removing evils, (b) prayer for obtaining good things, (c) affliction (for example, fasting and other forms of mortification), (d) sacrifice (for example, both spiritual and corporeal alms-[giving]).

[19] It is now evident that he loves God most purely who believes (1) that God is the Supreme Good and the Creator of all good and (2) that the entire universe (from top to bottom) has, comparatively, in a certain shading, a very faint trace of that Goodness. Accordingly, God is not loved purely unless He is known or believed to be thus. [20] Now, the articles of faith have been handed down to us in a fixed number for the purpose of our apprehending and believing [them]; and no one is excused from believing them. Moreover, no one, if he is of sound reason, has the excuse to offer (on grounds of his incapability) that he cannot with a general sense of credulity believe to be true all that is contained in the sacred writings and all that men who were instructed by the Spirit of God taught—and [that he cannot believe] to be true of God all that the Prophets believed about Him and that the saints believed had to be imitated. Those who are not of sound reason neither believe nor disbelieve. Thus, it is evident that the community of men is required to believe in a general way the principles of faith without contradiction or inconsistency. However, one departs from faith in two ways: when one does not believe to be true the faith which the Catholic Church preaches (or in some such way) and when one stubbornly disbelieves it or believes something contrary to it or dissents from one article in particular. And so, in regard to what is believed there is no difference between whatsoever simple individuals and those who are well-instructed; for in his own way each of them believes equally but rightly, because the simple man believes generally, whereas the well-instructed man believes particularly.

[22] The basis of faith is the fact that God exists. Moreover, thereafter [comes the principle] that there is one Originator, because every multiplicity has prior to itself oneness. Furthermore, nothing that

is first is compatible with anything else's being first; and two con-
traries are always preceded by another thing. This [assertion] goes
against the Manichees, who posited two principles: one of light and
the other of darkness.

[**23**] *What things faith is like.* Faith is like the ark of the testament, for in Exodus 25 it is said that the propitiatory does not exceed
the arc. Likewise, propitiation is had by faith and never without faith.
Faith is like a star of the firmament and a star of the sea, because the
star shows to sailors the port of safety. And it is like the morning star
that precedes the sun of justice[29] and like the star in the East that led
the three kings to Christ. Faith is the foundational stone on which the
Church is built. (Matthew 16: "On this rock ...," viz., the rock of faith,
because Peter confessed his faith: "You are the Christ, the Son of
God," etc.)[30]

[Faith], which comprehends all kinds of magnificent things, is
like a mirror—because the Divine Majesty is attained through faith,
the mirror without blemish (Wisdom 1)[31]—and is like the right eye.
The left eye is reason, which makes judgments only about natural objects; the right eye is faith, which determines all things, both natural
things and miraculous things. Now, someone who has lost his right eye
is useless for combat. For his left eye is covered by his shield; and if
he has no right eye, he can see nothing. Similarly, without faith no one
engages without danger in the combat of spiritual war.

[Faith], is like a ring adorning a finger. In a similar way, faith
adorns reason that is betrothed to God. (Osee 2: "I will betroth you
to me in faith.")[32] And faith is a silver ring, because it gleams by way
of true knowledge and resonates by means of confession. (Romans 10:
"With the heart one believes unto justice; with the mouth confession
is made unto salvation.")[33] Moreover, faith is like the king's flag,
which during the battle exhibits the king's presence, in order to terri-
fy the enemy. In a similar way, faith frightens the spiritual enemy (I
Peter 5: "... whom resist, you who are strong in faith").[34] And just
as the [king's] flag is placed in the citadel of the city, so faith is situated in the citadel of the mind. (Isaias 11: "The Lord has raised a
standard unto the nations.")[35] Furthermore, faith is a military shield,
placed on the left side, that protects the heart from injury (Ephesians
6: "In all things taking the shield of faith.").[36] Likewise, faith is like
the sun's rays, because without candlelight the sun is seen by means
of its own rays; similarly, God is seen without proof, by faith alone.
Hence, Ambrose [writes]: "In matters of faith we believe the pastors,

not the dialecticians."[37] And because with respect to its own disk the sun is not seen except by an eagle, so God is seen only by a soul that is very devout and that is elevated by wings of contemplation. A blind man does not see the sun, but he believes him who does see it; and he does not see the pathway, but he believes the dog that guides him; furthermore, he does not see the pit [in front of him], but he believes his cane, which touches it. Similarly, the simple ones who do not see ought to believe those who do see, viz., the bishops. O how great the danger is if a blind pastor leads someone who is blind! (Matthew 11: "If the blind lead the blind, ..." etc.)[38]

Or again, faith is like a sacramental pillar, like spiritual dawn, and like first light. It is like the pillar that led the people of Israel out of Egypt and that was a light for them; similarly, faith lights [the way] for believers. Moreover, just as dawn is detestable to thieves, so faith is detestable to demons. And faith is like the first created primordial light, which as first-born ought to be blessed, etc.

PART THREE
The Works of Faith

[24] True confession ought to be [made] in faith—lest it say something other [than in faith] and live otherwise [than in faith]—so that the faith may be living faith and not dead faith. A fictional object is not really a thing, even as a dead man is not considered to be a man. Moreover, a depicted lion and a forged denarius exist fictively, not truly. (Corinthians 1: "They profess that they know God; yet, they deny [Him] with their deeds.")[39] Such [false professors] are like a chimera. True faith is a good denarius, one that is good for purchasing Paradise; and true faith is a real tree that produces leaves of divine love and leaves of beneficial confession, flowers of honorable conduct, and the fruit of good works. Furthermore, faith ought to have magnificent devotion; for when natural reason fails, faith trusts in God alone, even as aged Abraham believed God, who promised that from his aged, barren [wife] there would be born a seed in and through whom all nations would be blessed (Genesis 15). Thomas did not have such faith, because he wanted to touch ..., etc.[40] As regards such faith St. Gregory says: "Faith does not have merit ...," etc.[41]

Likewise, great faith ought not to fail during hardship; rather, it ought to grow stronger. (Matthew 4: "If you have faith as a grain of mustard ...," etc.)[42] The more a grain of mustard is threshed, the more vigorously it thrives. Such was the faith of the martyrs, who through faith conquered kingdoms. (I John 5: "This is the victory that overcomes the world, viz., your faith.")[43] Peter, who when he saw the strong wind was afraid, did not yet have faith. (Matthew 14: "Why did you doubt, O you of little faith?")[44] Likewise, when the righteous who lack faith see the strong wind, they immediately waver and sink into the sea of despondency, which is a dead sea, in which nothing can live. Faith is great through its continuedness and uninterruptedness, just as in the case of the woman who was in Cana of Galilee. (Matthew 15: "O woman, great is your faith.")[45]

[25] Likewise, [there are] three creeds: that of the Apostles for instructing in the faith, the Nicene Creed for explaining the faith, the Creed of Athanasias for defending the faith. Moreover, faith is supposed to have universal perfection; i.e., [there ought to be] twelve articles of faith, even as there were twelve Apostles, each of whom laid down an article. Not only are we to believe God—to believe, i.e., that those things that He speaks are true (as also Peter, etc., is believed) but we are to believe in God (as Augustine claims); i.e., in loving-belief we are to go unto Him and be incorporated into His members. Bad and simulated faith (as states Ambrose in his book *On Faith*) is like mixing gypsum with water—a mixture that deceptively resembles milk.

Jottings on Faith and Reason

[26] Ramon: "Faith is a good *habitus*, [i.e., fixed disposition], that comes through God-given goodness, in order that through faith those objective truths which the intellect cannot attain may be apprehended."[46] Faith is great with respect to magnitude; and so, the more of faith there is, the better faith is. Now, a Christian believes more greatly about God because he believes that God is trine and one, incarnate, etc., and believes in the seven sacraments. However, the Incarnation and the like seem to an unbeliever to be things impossible. The intellect can have a fixed disposition (*habitus*) for faith and a fixed disposition (*habitus*) for knowledge. And it has a fixed disposition for faith in order to acquire a fixed disposition for knowledge. As Isaias says: "Unless you believe, you will not understand."[47] Accordingly, a Catholic can understand more about God than can an unbeliever. Faith is a power accompanied by righteousness (*iustitia*), since it is right (*iustum*) to believe about God those truths which the intellect cannot attain. The Catholic faith asserts more true things about God than [any] other faith; therefore, it is a truer faith. Faith

together with hope and love produce delight.

[27] Faith is a fixed disposition by which a Catholic believes that there is clarity in divine matters, so that it prepares a light for the intellect, in order that the intellect may understand clearly, and not confusedly, acts of divine reasoning and, thereby, may understand the agent and the doable [act]. The Catholic faith says that God can, in and of Himself, act to the extent that He can exist, because "with God all things are possible."[48] The faith of unbelievers says that this [viz., what is claimed by Catholics] is impossible; therefore, [the faith of unbelievers] denies the [doctrine of] the Trinity. The Catholic faith is a better means for the intellect to be illumined for attaining the loftiness of God, even as air is illuminated by the light of the sun, so that our visual power can see color and shape. Faith is tranquility of the intellect as a result of believing; but it is a secondary tranquility, because the primary tranquility comes from [the act of] understanding. Nevertheless, faith is superior to [the act of] understanding, because faith believes more greatly than [understanding] understands. To understand occurs with effort and by stages; however, faith is not [like this]. Faith has the enlightenment of truth, which elevates the soul; and it has the correctiveness of authority, which secures the soul. Both of these [characteristics] come through Christ, who is the Splendor and the Word.

Jottings on Proving the Trinitarian Faith

[28] The initial considerations for proving the truth of the Catholic faith are rather general: [viz.], (1) that [the Catholic faith is] God's instruction, God's words, and (2) that in its precepts there is nothing except what is honorable and fitting, in terms of every law. There is (3) the death and martyrdom of the martyrs, (4) the unwaveringness amid suffering, (5) the wisdom infused generally by the Holy Spirit. There are (6) the miracles, (7) the resuscitation of the dead by the power of this faith. And there is a greater miracle: [viz.,] that at many turns persecution is instituted by emperors and tyrants for the purpose of removing [faith] from the world, but faith has always increased between the hands of raging tyrants.

[29] In the Trinity there are three persons of the divine nature. The first Person is from no one; the second Person exists from the first person through begottenness; the third Person exists from the first two through being breathed out. This trinity does not preclude a oneness of essence or the essence's simplicity, immensity, eternity, unchange-

ableness.

Rationale for the Trinity: He who would believe that God is not able to impart Himself supremely would deny in Him power. He who would believe in this [ability-to-impart] but would say that God was unwilling to do it would deny His mercy. He who would confess God's ability and willingness but would say that He lacked the knowledge would deny His wisdom. Therefore, since He was able, willing, and knew how to, He ..., etc. Dionysius: It is the nature of the good to flow forth. The Father is the Fount of goodness from which the Son flows forth; and through liberality and loving-kindness the Holy Spirit emanates from both [the Father and the Son]. The Trinity is evident in the Scriptures. Isaias [says]: "Holy, Holy, Holy"; and there is added: "Lord God"—in the singular.[49] In Genesis [we read]: "Let us make man according to our image"—["image" being used] singularly.[50] In the Psalms [we read]: "May God, our God, bless us,..." etc.[51]

Jottings on the Principal Names of God

[**30**] There shines forth in creatures a trace of the Trinity: In the magnitude of creatures the power of the Father shines forth; in the arrangement of creatures the wisdom of the Son shines forth; in the equipping of creatures, the goodness of the Holy Spirit shines forth. In every individual thing there is oneness, beauty, and usefulness; and likewise, there is being, power, and operativeness. In the sun there is being, splendor, and heat; in the soul there is memory, intellect, and will. As regards the three hierarchies [of angels]: they are a trinity. And in each hierarchy there are three orders.[52] A trinity is there present in oneness (and it is generally present in all creatures), because "there are three ...," etc., as you know from elsewhere.[53] [**31**] An abstract essential name is not taken as a designation of a Person [in God]. Hence, the following [statement] is false: "An Essence begat an Essence." However, concrete essential names are rightly [taken as designating the Persons in God]: for example, "God from God." There are two principal names of God: viz., "He who is" and "the Good." By means of the first name there is signified God's absolute, infinite being. By means of the second name there is indicated the divine being qua Cause; for God made all things on account of His goodness. By means of the [grammatical] neuter-gender, substantive things are expressed; by means of the masculine gender the person [is signified]; by means of the feminine gender things conceptual are expressed.[54]

Jottings on the Manner of Knowing That
the Incomprehensible God Is One and Three

[32] Those who are willing to say something deeper about our comprehension of God [say] that although faith does not have merit, etc., nevertheless when faith comes first it is elevated by means of understanding—just as if water were mixed with olive-oil, then the olive-oil of faith would be enhanced by the water of understanding. However, as Augustine says, the human mind's acuteness is weak; the mind is not established in such excellent light unless it is cleansed by the justice of faith.[55] Bernard: "God is present in non-rational creatures in such a way that, nevertheless, He is not apprehended by them. He can be apprehended cognitively by all rational creatures. But by good men only is He apprehended through love."[56] We can know about God *what He is not* but not *what He is*, for He is great without quantity, good without quality, etc.[57] In Heaven God is known in terms of His essence—known in proportion to the worthiness of one's merits. Hence, Augustine [says]: "We shall behold the essence of Your majesty—each one [among us beholding it] clearly to the degree that he has lived purely here below."[58] There is an illustrative example in the case of the ocean, which offers itself to sight but, nevertheless, cannot be seen in accordance with its entire scope. And this fact obtains both because of the breadth of the ocean and because of the disproportionality of our sight to so vast a surface. Keep the following in mind: Here on earth we can know God with respect to the fact *that He is*; in Heaven we can know Him *as He is*;[59] but neither here nor there can we ever know *what He is*, because He is incomprehensible.[60]

[33] Now, those who will to arrive at a knowledge of God must first of all cast off the darkness of sins and must put on the armor of light. They must cast aside considerations of natural reason, which are as the light of decaying wood giving light at night but of no use during the daytime. They must set aside mutable goods and cling to the Immutable Good. Thereupon, [a believer] attains a knowledge of God either through infusion or through rational inference or through [a consideration of] creatures, which are a mirroring of the Creator in the present era, just as God is the Mirror of creatures in the future [age]. At times God is known as is wine, which is known by our hearing of it, by our seeing it, and by our tasting it. You know of [God] by hearing of [Him] from a preacher. When theologians read [of Him, they know] by sight. When good men love [Him, they know] by taste.

"Taste and see that the Lord is sweet." [61] According to Dionysius, God is known through eminence, so that when power is found to be in a creature, supreme power is to be ascribed to God—and similarly regarding other [attributes]. Although all things are in God, from God, and through God, He is incomprehensible on the basis of [inferences] from creatures. For He walks upon the wings of the winds, i.e., above the understandings of angels. [62] Furthermore, recall to mind how Augustine, seeking God, asked of the earth whether it was God and asked of the air [whether it was God]. They replied: "He made us," etc. [63]

[**34**] In God power, being, might, wisdom, etc., are the same thing. God is infinite to such an extent that if there were infinite worlds, He would fill them [by His presence], because He has, and can have, no end. Rather, although delimiting all things, He Himself is undelimitable, because He is not absent from any place nor is He localized at any place. Wherever He is present, He fills all things. And before the creation of the world He existed in and of Himself, even as He exists today. Through nature He is everywhere; through grace He is present with those who are good. "He who abides in me and I in him brings forth much fruit." [64] Likewise, through His glory He is present, in what is reasonable, as truth; present, in what is desirable, as goodness; present, in what is emotional, as graciousness. Similarly, through union He was united, in the Virgin's womb, to human nature—[united] in the tomb to His flesh; united in Hell to His soul. He exists in and of Himself as Alpha and Omega; He exists in the world as a king in his kingdom. He reigns and commands everywhere ([says] Bernard). He reigns over angels as Comeliness (insofar as He is Truth) and as Tastiness (insofar as He is Goodness). He reigns over the Church as the head-of-household [governs] the household. He reigns over the elect as Liberator from evils; over those who are good He reigns as Helper; over the reprobate, as Terror and Horror; over the believing soul as King in His kingdom, as Fount in His gardens, as Light in darkness, as a ruby in a ring.

Moreover, God is eternal. No time or measure of time befits Him, who is without beginning and end. Pope Leo [writes]: Nothing can be added to or subtracted from the simple nature of Divinity, for [that Nature] is always that which it is. Living and understanding are proper to it and are co-eternal with it and are the same thing as it. Yet, [that Nature] is manifold in its gifts. The excellence of the Divine Worthiness is so great that the mind that endeavors to conceive of God fails, since He is incomprehensible. The senses do not perceive [Him], since He is invisible. The tongue does not explain Him, for He is ineffable. Place does not confine Him, because He is undelimitable. Scripture does not explain Him, since He is inestimable. Might does not attain Him, for He is inaccessible. And because there is no comparative relation of the finite to the infinite,[65] creatures cannot apprehend Him. He alone is omnipotent; He alone is omniscient; He alone knows Himself; though He is the Worker of miracles, He is quiet in His workings.

[35] Every multiplicity is originated from what is one. Every order has an *earlier* and a *later*. Everything imperfect takes its origin from what is perfect. Every union of different things has as the cause of its persistence some one, ultimate thing that we say to be God. And because this God is most powerful, most wise, and most good, He *is able to*, He *knows how to*, and He *wills supremely to*, impart Himself. But this [imparting] is a giving of the fullness-of-His-majesty to another. Therefore, from eternity God the Father begot a co-equal Son, to whom He imparted the essence of His divinity. Isaias [says]: "Shall I, who bestow on others [the gift] of begetting, be barren?"[66] This is most perfect begetting, where the Begotten One is in every respect like Him who begets. And so, power is ascribed to the Father; wisdom, to the Son. And the Father is said to have made all things in wisdom[67]— i.e., by means of Wisdom, which is the Son. The Son is the Image-of-equality, begotten of the Father; man is a created image that imitates; the world is a created image that represents and that is a mirroring of the Creator. As the Apostle [says]: "Now we see through a mirror."[68] The world was made in the likeness of God because God had no other exemplar than Himself. Properly speaking, the corporeal creature is a vestige of God, a likeness of the immaterial Creator. [According to] Ezechiel: "You [were] a seal of resemblance ...," etc.[69]

Furthermore, emanation in the case of God is twofold: one kind is by means of nature, and it is a begetting; the other kind is by means of an act of will, and it is fittingly called procession but is properly called breathing forth. Now, the Holy Spirit is Love; accordingly, He proceeds by means of a volitional act from both [Father and Son]. From the Father He proceeds mediately and immediately: immediately from the Father and also mediately, because the Son breathes forth the Holy Spirit, and the Son has this [assignment] from the Father. The Holy Spirit is Essential Love insofar as He is one God with the Father and the Son. Because these three [Persons] are one in essence, they love one another with an Essential Love, a name given to the

Holy Spirit. Moreover, the Holy Spirit is Personal Love, because He is the Bond between the Father and the Son. The Father and the Son love each other with a Love that proceeds from them—a Love which is the Holy Spirit. The Holy Spirit is called Love in the sense of exemplar-cause. For not only is the Holy Spirit the Efficient Cause of the freely-given love that is in us but also He is the Exemplar and the End-goal [of such love]. The love that is present in us comes from the Holy Spirit as Efficient Cause, insofar as He is God. Or again, the Holy Spirit is said to be the Love—in the sense of Exemplar-Cause— by which we love God and our neighbor, even as Love (i.e., the Holy Spirit) proceeds from both [Father and Son]. But at times "love" is construed formally in the sense of inherence—as when love of virtue is said to be a fixed disposition in the soul, a disposition by means of which we love God and our neighbor. According to this mode the Holy Spirit is not called love.

NOTES TO *SERMON IV*

1. "... the three theological virtues": viz., faith, hope, and love.
2. Hugo of Strassburg, *Compendium Theologicae Veritatis*, Book V, Chap. 18. [Falsely ascribed to Bonaventure, this work is found in Vol. VIII of *S. Bonaventurae Opera Omnia*, edited by A. C. Peltier (Paris: Vivès, 1866). The cited passage is on p. 178.]
3. Ephesians 2:8. *Decretum Magistri Gratiani*, Part III, De Consecratione, Distinctio 4, Canon 145 ("Gratia"). [See Aemilius Friedberg, editor, *Corpus Iuris Canonici* (2nd edition, Leipzig, 1879 (Vol. I)), column 1408.]
4. I John 5:4. *Decretum Magistri Gratiani*, "Sciscitantibus"; Part II, Causa 15, Questio 8, Canon 5. [See Aemilius Friedberg, editor, *Corpus Iuris Canonici* (2nd edition, Leipzig, 1879 (Vol. I)), column 760.]
5. Peter Lombard, *Sententiae*, Book III, Distinctio 23.2 (*PL* 192:805).
6. *Decretalium D. Gregorii Papae IX Compilatio*, Book I, Titulus I ("De Summa Trinitate et Fide Catholica"), "Firmiter", etc. [See Aemilius Friedberg, editor, *Corpus Iuris Canonici* (2nd edition, Leipzig, 1881 (Vol. II)), columns 5-6.]
7. See this present sermon's opening quotation.
8. Habacuc 2:4 (Habakkuk 2:4). Hebrews 10:38. *Decretum Magistri Gratiani, op. cit.,* Part II, Causa 24, Questio I, Canon 29 ("Ubi sana ....") [Friedberg, *op. cit.,* Vol. I, column 977]. See also Part II, Causa 33, Questio III (Tractatus de Penitencia), Distinctio 4, Canon 11 ("In domo ...") [Friedberg, *op. cit.,* Vol. I, column 1233].
9. John 6:47. *Decretum Magistri Gratiani, op. cit.,* Part II, Causa 33, Questio III (Tractatus de Penitencia), Distinctio 2, Canon 14 ("Karitas ...") [Friedberg, *op. cit.,* Vol. I, column 1194].
10. James 2:26. *Decretum Magistri Gratiani, op. cit.,* Part II, Causa 1, Questio I, Canon 28 ("Fertur ...") [Friedberg, *op. cit.,* Vol. I, column 370]. *Decretum Magistri Gratiani, op. cit.,* Part II, Causa 33, Questio 3 (Tractatus de Penitencia), Distinctio 2, Canon 40 (" 'Si enim, omnis,' inquit ...") [Friedberg, *op. cit.,* Vol. I, column 1203, lines 15-16].
11. Galatians 5:6. *Decretum Magistri Gratiani, op. cit.,* Part II, Causa 28, Questio I, Canon 4 ("Uxor ...") [Friedberg, *op. cit.,* Vol. I, column 1080]. *Decretum Magistri Gratiani, op. cit.,* Part II, Causa 33, Questio III (Tractatus de Penitencia), Distinctio I, Canon 52 ("Potest fieri ...") [Friedberg, *op. cit.,* Vol. I, column 1171].
12. Acts 15:9. *Decretum Magistri Gratiani, op. cit.,* Part III (De Consecratione), Distinctio 4, Canon 150 ("Verus ...") [Friedberg, *op. cit.,* Vol. I, column 1410].
13. Hebrews 11:1.
14. William of Paris (i.e., William of Auvergne), *De Fide et Legibus*, Part I, Chap. 1. [See Vol. I (Paris, 1674) of *Guilielmi Alverni Opera Omnia*, p. 2ᵇ, lines 15-13 from bottom. (Reprinted in Frankfurt a. M., Germany by Minerva Verlag, 1963.)].
15. I John 2:16.
16. This idea is repeated in section 13 below.
17. Nicholas, in his text, refers to Gratian's *Decretals*. The passage corresponds to *Decretum Magistri Gratiani, op. cit.,* Part III (De Consecratione), Distinctio 2, Canon 69 ("Revera ...") [Friedberg, *op. cit.,* Vol. I, columns 1339-1340]. But the words "ubi ratio deficit, fides supplet" are not found there. See, rather, Augus-

tine, *Sermo* 190.2.2 (*PL* 38:1008).

18. *Decretum Magistri Gratiani, op. cit.*, Part II, Causa 33, Questio III (Tractatus de Penitencia), Distinctio 4, Canon 11 ("In domo ...") [Friedberg, *op. cit.*, Vol. I, column 1233]. Also note Hebrews 11:1.

19. Distinguish "without evidentness" from "without evidence." What is to be believed is not self-evident; rather, it is supported by some measure of evidence.

20. James 1:17.

21. "... in the sacrament of the altar": i.e., in the eucharist.

22. Matthew 12:39.

23. Habacuc 2:4 (Habakkuk 2:4).

24. Aristotle, *De Sophisticis Elenchis*, 1 (164^b26-27).

25. Isaias (Isaiah) 59:2.

26. Malachias 4:2 (Malachi 4:2).

27. This idea reached its extreme in the Spanish Inquisition.

28. Ms. Vaticanus Latinus 1244 here has "es" (vs. "est" in the Heidelberg Academy's printed text).

29. See n. 26 above.

30. Matthew 16:18 and 16:16, respectively.

31. Wisdom 7:26 (not Wisdom 1).

32. Osee 2:20 (Hosea 2:20).

33. Romans 10:10.

34. I Peter 5:9.

35. Isaias (Isaiah) 11:12.

36. Ephesians 6:16.

37. Ambrose, *De Fide ad Gratianum Augustum*, presumably I, 13, 84 (*PL* 16:571).

38. Matthew 15:14 (not Matthew 11).

39. Titus 1:16 (not Corinthians 1).

40. John 20:24-25.

41. Gregory the Great, *XL Homiliae in Evangelia*, Book II, Homilia XXVI, 1 (*PL* 76:1197C).

42. Matthew 17:19 (not Matthew 4).

43. I John 5:4.

44. Matthew 14:31.

45. Matthew 15:28.

46. Ramon Lull, *Liber de Praedicatione* (edited by A. S. Flores), 3rd Part of 2nd Part of Distinction I (De Novem Virtutibus, Deductis per Principia), section 5. [See Vol. III in the series *Raimundi Lulli Opera Latina*, edited by F. Stegmüller (Palma of Majorca, 1961), p. 243.]

47. Isaias (Isaiah) 7:9.

48. Matthew 19:26.

49. Isaias (Isaiah) 6:3.

50. Genesis 1:26.

51. Psalms 66:7 (67:7). The word "bless" is used singularly: "benedicat" (in Latin translation).

52. Cf. Cusa's *De Ludo Globi*, II (77-78).

53. I John 5:7-8.

54. Cf. Thomas Aquinas, *Summa Theologica*, I, 31, 2, ad 4.

55. Augustine, *De Trinitate*, I, 2, 4 (*PL* 42:822). In citing Augustine, Nicholas was influenced by Hugo of Strassburg's *Compendium Theologicae Veritatis, op. cit.* [n. 2 above], Book I, Chap. 16.

56. Bernard of Clairvaux, *Sermones de Tempore*, "De Laudibus Virginis," Homilia III.4 (*PL* 183:72D-73A). Nicholas, in citing Bernard, was influenced by Hugo of Strassburg's *Compendium Theologicae Veritatis, op. cit.* [n. 2 above], Book I, Chap. 16.

57. Augustine, *De Trinitate*, V, 1, 2 (*PL* 42:912). See also Hugo of Strassburg, *Compendium Theologicae Veritatis, loc. cit.*

58. Cf. Augustine, *De Civitate Dei*, Book XXII, Chap. 29 (*PL* 41:796-801). See also Hugo of Strassburg, *Compendium Theologicae Veritatis, loc. cit.*

59. I John 3:2.

60. Hugo of Strassburg, *Compendium Theologicae Veritatis, op. cit.* [n. 2 above], Book I, Chap. 16. See also Cusa, *Sermo* XXXII (1:7-16). Cf. his *Sermo* XXIX (11:22-23).

61. Psalms 33:9 (34:8).

62. Psalms 103:3 (104:3).

63. Augustine, *Confessiones*, X, 6, 9 (*PL* 32:783).

64. John 15:5.

65. Hugh of Strassburg, *Compendium Theologicae Veritatis, op. cit.* [n. 2 above], Book I, Chap. 16.

66. Isaias (Isaiah) 66:9.

67. Psalms 103:24 (104:24).

68. I Corinthians 13:12.

69. Ezechiel (Ezekiel) 28:12.

Sermon V: Ne Timeas
("Fear Not")
[June 24, feast-day of John the Baptist; 1431;
preached perhaps in Koblenz]

[1] "Fear not, Zachary, for your prayer is heard."[1] ... "And the child grew and was strengthened in spirit and was in the deserts until the day of his manifestation unto Israel," etc....[2]

Inasmuch as I must speak of him who is greater than, and more than, a prophet—[of him who is] a messenger, a virgin, an eremite, a preacher, and a martyr[3]—let us invoke God's grace. [2] "The child," i.e., John the Baptist, still in tender years, "grew" with respect to an increase of his body and "was strengthened in spirit" with respect to an increase of grace and of virtue. He dwelt "in deserts," being separated from other men, lest he be defiled from association with others and so that he might meditate more freely. And [by the Scriptural passage] it is shown that the contemplative life was to be primary [for him] "until the day of his manifestation," etc., when, in fact, he began to mix an active life with the contemplative life by preaching to the Israelite people (as is indicated in Luke 3 as follows: "In the fifteenth year of the emperor Tiberius," etc.).[4] Today, [the feast-day of John], we must rejoice, because Gabriel foretold that "many will rejoice over his birth."[5] In praise of John the Baptist what can be said more effectively than that which Truth said in Matthew 11: "Among those born of women there has not arisen a greater [than John the Baptist]."[6] And "he was sent by God," etc....[7]

[3] First of all, I must, in accordance with the narrative about the child, speak of how he was born and of the kind of life he led. He "grew" in body. (Here [I will speak] against the gluttonous.) Secondly, [I must speak] of grace, for "his name is John,"[8] and grace increased in him, for "he was strengthened in spirit" daily. (Here [I will speak] of the manifold grace that was in him; here [I will also speak] of the doctrine of having grace, etc.; here, too, let the theme of the spirit of prophecy be touched upon.) Thirdly, [I must speak] of the contemplative life and of the active life, because [John] was in the deserts until his manifestation. (Here [I will speak] of *desert* in a threefold sense.)

80

PART ONE

John the Baptist according to the Narrative;
and on Gluttony

[4] As regards the first [topic]: let the Gospel speak for itself, as to how the one who was born on this day entered the world full of the Holy Spirit, even though, initially, he was conceived in sins, since [from the human race] "he rose forth." [Let it speak] as to how the child of tender years led his life most wisely and most virtuously and how the prayer of his father, Zachary, was heard ("Fear not, Zachary," etc.).

[5] There was in the days of Herod, the King of Judea, a certain priest named Zachary, of the order of Abia. And his wife was of the daughters of Aaron, and her name was Elizabeth. And they were both *just* before God, walking in all the commandments and justifications of the Lord without blame. And they had no child, because Elizabeth was barren. And they both were well advanced in years. And it came to pass, when Zachary executed the priestly function in conformity with the ordering characteristic of a priest in those days, he went out dutifully in order to offer incense after he entered the temple of the Lord. And a whole multitude of people was praying outside, at the hour of incense.

And there appeared to him an angel of the Lord, standing on the right side of the altar of incense. And Zachary, seeing [him], was troubled; and fear fell upon him. But the angel said to him: Fear not, Zachary, for your prayer is heard, and your wife, Elizabeth, shall bear you a son; and his name shall be called John. And he will be to you joy and gladness, and many will rejoice over his birth. For he shall be great before the Lord, and he shall not drink wine or strong drink. And he shall be filled with the Holy Spirit, even in his mother's womb. And he shall convert many of the children of Israel unto the Lord their God. And he shall go before the Lord in the spirit and power of Elias, in order to turn the hearts of fathers unto their children and to turn the unbelieving unto the practical wisdom of those who are just. [Thereby he will] furnish the Lord with a perfect people.

And Zachary said to the angel: Whereby shall I know this? For I am an old man, and my wife is advanced in years. And the angel answered: I am Gabriel.[9]

[6] As regards the second [topic] of the first part, viz., how John grew physically: his [way of] life must be mentioned, because [he ate] locusts, etc.,[10] and drank neither wine nor strong drink nor, in general, any intoxicating drink. Here I must touch upon gluttony and drunkenness. St. John, for many reasons, took care to avoid gluttony, because (as says the gloss on Matthew, Chapter 4) "in Christian combat action is taken, first of all, against gluttony; one would labor in vain against other vices if gluttony were not beforehand reigned-in."[11] And another gloss says: If the Devil is overcome with respect

to gluttony, he does not tempt with regard to lust.[12] Now, gluttony is [one's taking] immoderate pleasure in food and drink. Because of this pleasure the first parents of the human race lost the happiness of Paradise and were cast down into this present miserable life, where every man is born through a sinning, lives by toiling, and dies through affliction. Gluttony rules over a man in three ways: (1) when the man because of gluttony [inordinately] anticipates the established [meal-]time; (2) when he orders [his servants] to prepare for him foods that are more sumptuous than bodily necessity and personal condition require; (3) [when and] if, in eating and drinking, he consumes too much as a result of his intemperate desire.

[7] This vice [of gluttony] is odious for many reasons. First of all, nature opposes it—for which reason man has, relative to the size of his body, the smallest mouth of all animals. Secondly, there is [the consideration drawn from] the tranquility of demons.... A legion of demons said to Christ: "If you cast us out, send us into the herd of swine." [13] Here the gloss [reads]: "When anyone lives as do swine, the Devil receives power over him." [14] Thirdly, there is the injury of corrupting one's neighbor, who readily imitates. Romans 13: "Do not destroy with your meat him for whom Christ died." [15] James 2: "In their feasts they defile not only themselves but also others by their example.[16] Fourthly, the gluttonous one spends needlessly that which he ought to give to the poor. Bernard: "Do not suppose that your spending is without obligation; whether you like it or not, you are a debtor to your neighbor." [17]

Moreover, from winebibbery and drunkenness arise outcries and afflictions. Proverbs 15: "Drunkenness is riotous ...."[18] Likewise, [gluttony] insults God, because [the glutton] makes his own stomach to be god. According to Philippians 3: " ... whose stomach is their god." [19] Augustine in a gloss [writes]: "That is worshiped which is loved above [all] other things.[20] Similarly, [gluttony] makes of the temple of the Holy Spirit the kitchen of the Devil. According to II Corinthians 6: "You are the temple of the Holy Spirit," etc.[21] Furthermore, [gluttony] mars the image of the Trinity in man; for it blackens the face more than does coal. Jerome: "Nothing so blocks the intellect as do reveling and drunkenness." Moreover, [gluttony] distances [us] from God and causes [us] to forget Him. Osee 13: "They were satiated, and they withdrew their heart and have forgotten me." [22] Therefore, the Psalmist expresses the desire: "Bind their jaws, so that they may draw near unto You" [23] —as one who hungers is brought to his master. Likewise, the gluttonous despise God, as did Esau. (Genesis 25: "[Esau] went his way, taking little thought of his having sold his birthright.")[24] Hence, [in the book of] Lamentations [it is said]: "They have exchanged all their valuables for food."[25] Similarly, [gluttony] defiles the mouth, in which uncleanness is most vicious and [which is] a member designed for the worship of God. Furthermore, the first prohibition of gluttony was made in Paradise: "Do not eat of the tree of the knowledge of good and evil...."[26]

[8] Moreover, many evils [recorded] in the Old and the New Testament resulted from gluttony: Eve, who was deceived, deceived [another]; Noah became drunk and naked; Lot committed twofold incest ...;[27] Esau sold his birthright; Absalom during a feast killed Amnon his brother;[28] Pharaoh hung his baker, after a great feast.[29] Likewise, because of this vice [of gluttony] the children of Israel incurred God's wrath. [As the] Psalm [says]: "Their meat was still in their mouth."[30] And Job's children, while drinking wine, were taken captive.[31] (Gregory's rationale: "... because during feasts the mind's good intent will be less active, is less guarded."[32]) Similarly, John was beheaded by Herod at a feast. Furthermore, the spirit is weighed down [by gluttony]: "See to it that your hearts not be weighed down by winebibbery and drunkenness."[33] Gregory: "The more the body is stuffed, the more the soul is diminished."[34] Jerome: "He who revels in pleasure is a living dead-man; he who is given to drunkenness is dead and buried."[35] Drunkenness is the paltry tomb of reason.

Furthermore, talkativeness stems from [inordinate] banqueting. Gregory, in his homily on the wealthy glutton, [says]: "The primary fault of talkativeness attends those who are feasting carousingly."[36] Likewise, lasciviousness arises [out of gluttony]: "[The people] ate and drank and rose up to play...."[37] Licentiousness comes from gluttony: "They were satiated, and they committed adultery...."[38] According to Philippians 9: "Do not be drunk with wine, in which there is licentiousness."[39] Proverbs 20: "Wine is a licentious thing."[40] Similarly, [from gluttony] arises a lack of compassion: The wealthy glutton had no pity on Lazarus.[41] Furthermore, drunkenness removes wisdom. Proverbs 20: "Whoever delights in drunkenness will not be wise."[42] Job 28: "Wisdom is not found in the land of those living in pleasure."[43] Jerome: "A fat belly produces dense senses."[44] Drunkenness causes one to rage: Osee 7: "The princes began to rage [because of wine]."[45]

[9] Moreover, St. John was especially wary of winebibbery, be-

cause although the world's wine is pleasant and delightful at the beginning, it kills in the end. Proverbs 22: "Look not upon the wine when it is yellow in the glass and when its color gleams. For the wine goes in pleasantly, but very shortly it will cause burning like a snake-[bite]."[46] Likewise, drunkenness removes all caring and takes no thought of obligations and errs in all its tasks. Isaias 19: "The Lord mingled in the midst of Egypt a spirit of giddiness and caused Egypt to err, as a drunkard staggers."[47] Accordingly, drunkards become impoverished, because they live without concern and without orderliness. Similarly, drunkenness and winebibbery are on sale in the tavern of the Devil. Hence, the Devil by means of three dice—viz., the lust of the flesh, the lust of the eyes, and the pride of life[48]—robs the world within his tavern. Furthermore, in his tavern, where he plays with the die of lust and supplies the wine of drunkenness, the Devil has promoters—viz., sorceresses and procuresses, etc.—who incite to winebibbery and licentiousness. Regarding these accursed couplers it is said in Joel 3: "They have placed a boy in a brothel and have sold a girl for a price, in order to drink wine"[49] —a boy, viz., pure and innocent affection, and a girl, viz., a spotless soul.[50] These procuresses mix wine in the Devil's tavern, and they deceive. Isaias 1: "Your wine is mixed with water," because no pleasure is pure, as states Boethius.[51] And Seneca [says]: "Those things which you seek as if they caused gladness are a cause of grief."[52] Proverbs 13: "Laughter shall be mingled with sorrow, and mourning takes hold of the end of joy."[53]

[10] [Let us be mindful of] the example of the alcoholic rich man who asked his soul why, when he was sick, it would not stay. And because it did not desire to stay, he told it "Go to the Devil!" etc. You who desire to be good and who wish to discern the true: flee such mordant wine on the ground that it is a partner of death. There is no greater tormentor of men than is the liquid of the vine, [viz., wine]: the ears become deaf; then the tongue stammers. Tell me, tell me, O Drunkard: are you alive or are you oppressed by death? Behold, you are lying there pale; you are resting there utterly mindless. You are aware neither of good things nor of bad things, neither of things hard nor of things soft."[54] [11] Moreover, hunger, sleeplessness, and even infirmity follow upon drunkenness and frequent[55] winebibbery. Ecclesiasticus 37: "In many meats there will be sickness, and many have perished because of winebibbery."[56] Many [have become] stooped, lame, leprous, etc. Likewise, this pleasure [of excessive eating and drinking] is more bitter than is death, because it kills by means [both] of

bodily death [and] of mortal guilt and damnation. Similarly, it infects, suffocates, harshly afflicts, is scarcely cured, requires many expenditures, brings about a servitude of most menial labor when one attempts to fill a single sack [viz., the stomach]. Then too, the "pleasure of the throat has a breadth of scarcely two fingers."[57] Therefore, [gluttony] is equivalent to quinsy of the throat, which chokes a man. And [the throat] is a region that is like a sickness that requires many expenditures. Ecclesiastes 5: "All the labor of man is in regard to his mouth."[58] And [the stomach] is like a sack with a hole in the bottom. Proverbs 12: "The stomach of the wicked is insatiable."[59] Aggeus 1: "He has earned wages and put them into a bag with a hole."[60]

The wanton are like swine whom the Devil feeds here [on earth] so that he may consume their shanks in Hell.

> He is a butler
> Who is fat as ham.
> He presently is dying a
> death that is eternal.
> (Verses made by the Devil, etc.)

Gluttony is the Devil's bridle. For when a man sets out to guide himself by means of gluttony, he proceeds unto all [other] sins, etc.: licentiousness, thievery, etc.

> He wants to consume more than
> his plow can provide, etc.

[12] Holy John [the Baptist] despised the world's wine and its inebriating drink, etc.; and he chose God's wine, viz., the wine-of-remorse (which is also penance and martyrdom) and the wine-of-gladness (i.e., contemplation of the saints). A man cannot at one and the same time drink God's wine and the Devil's wine. God's wine would not taste good to him, because he would have the palate of one who is feverish. God's wine, at first, is acidic and, later, is mild. Hence, [we read] in the Canticles: "Drink my wine together with my milk."[61] "You have shown Your people hard things."[62] This wine is sold in the shop of confession, because [the confessional] is God's pantry. In Genesis 49 [the following] is said as regards Juda, who symbolizes confessing: "He shall wash his robe in wine."[63] The soul is a grape squeezed by the wine-press of the Cross and of penance; the torment of the soul (e.g., the shame of sin, the fear and the pain of Hell) is [like] the [squeezed-out] wine of the grape. And this wine [of penance] cleansed the robe of Juda, i.e., the robe of confessing. This wine intoxicates, because it causes one to put off the old man.[64] "Those were

drunken who rid themselves of their goods and placed [them] at the Apostles' feet." [65] "Behold, we have left behind all things," etc. [66]

Moreover, [God's wine] rids [one] of all shame—as is evident in the case of Mary Magdalene, who felt no shame [in the presence of] the banqueters.... [67] Preachers are heralds of this [divine wine]. And so, at first, they are supposed to drink as does a physician. As Augustine said: The physician drinks beforehand, so that later he will not quiver as does one who is sick; and Christ drank first of the cup of suffering. [68] He who does not with Christ drink of the cup of suffering does not love the Lord. But because our sins are pressuring [us], more men hasten to the Devil's tavern than to God's tavern; the reason is, perhaps, that that which is sold at a higher price is sought-after more eagerly. The Lord makes a good business transaction, because He saves us without payment [on our part]. Isaias 55: "Come, buy wine and milk, without money and without any cost," [69] for "the sufferings [of this present time] are not worthy ...," etc. [70] He who lives in penance has jars full of this [divine] wine. [13] The wine of gladness is God's delightful grace. Concerning this wine it is said in Esther 1 that no one is compelled to drink [of it], because services that are compelled are not pleasing to God. [71] "I will sacrifice to you willingly." [72] "My vows are within me, O God; I shall keep them ...," etc. [73] Nevertheless, one is summoned, as in the Canticles: "Eat, my friends, and be intoxicated!" [74] "They shall be intoxicated from the abundance of Your house ...," etc. [75] And regarding the Apostles, upon whom the Holy Spirit fell, it was said: "They are drunken." [76]

Hail, full of grace: Stephen, full of grace. [77] I will speak a bit later of this grace, for John was a vessel of grace, etc.

PART TWO
The Name "John"; and [Discussion] here of the Different Meanings of "Grace".

(a) *The divisions of grace.*

[14] "He was strengthened in spirit," because [he was] John, i.e., he [was] "he in whom there is grace." In Sacred Scripture "grace" ("*gratia*") is understood in a threefold way. [First of all,] it is understood as the love by which one individual holds another to be pleasing. Hence, in the Scriptures it is often said: "If I have found grace in your eyes ...." Secondly, it is understood as a free gift. Thus, we say: "I do this favor [*gratia*] for you." Thirdly, it is understood

as the recompense for a gift and is called an act of thanks (*gratiarum actio*): "Let us give thanks unto the Lord our God." Now, John was full of *grace*, construed in the second sense; for [grace in this second sense] is the twofold effect of grace in the first sense and is a three-fold stimulus.

God's love is twofold. [There is] a general love by which He loves all things, in accordance with the [verse]: "You, O Lord, have hated none of the things that You have made."[78] The other love is a special love by which God especially loves rational creatures, whom He leads back unto a supernatural friendship and participation. And in accordance with this [distinction], "grace" is construed in a twofold way: First, [it is construed] generally as standing for any gift that proceeds from that general love; and in this sense natural gifts and for-tuitous gifts are rightly said to be graces. In a second sense "grace" is construed as specially standing for a supernatural gift that proceeds to rational creatures from God's special love, so that rational creatures are brought unto God by means of a supernatural friendship; [this is the applicable sense of "grace," no matter] whether such goods were actual mental motions by means of which rational creatures are moved by God unto knowing something, willing something, and doing[79] something, or whether such goods were in the soul as permanent dis-positions that are the sources of the aforesaid acts. Furthermore, in accordance with this [twofold sense] we usually distinguish three kinds of divine goods: viz., natural goods, fortuitous goods, and gra-tuitous goods.

[16] Now, such a leading back of the spirit unto God occurs in a double sense: viz., mediately and immediately. (It occurs in the first way so as to dispose toward true friendship and union with God; it occurs immediately in the sense that through it the spirit is united to God in friendship and in joy. Therefore, we customarily distinguish two senses of "grace": viz., the freely given and the making-pleasing. (1) Freely-given grace corresponds to general grace, because the lat-ter is conferred freely. But it differs [from general grace] in that it is given for the purpose of acquiring the grace that makes one pleasing. Examples [of free gifts of general grace] are the divine impulses, and good operations, by which someone is prodded to convert. And, like-wise, there are the gifts of the Holy Spirit, according as it is said: "There are diversities of graces. To one [person] is given the word of wisdom; to another, the word of knowledge ...," etc.[80] (2) [The grace that] makes-pleasing is freely given, and it makes the spirit pleasing

to God; without this grace no one can please God. If from one who is unpleasing there is to be made one who is pleasing to God, then a change must occur. Change cannot occur in God; therefore, it must occur in the creature. Accordingly, a supernatural gift is infused. This [infused] grace is said to be the grace that makes one pleasing. And rightly so. Just as creatures have forms and powers through which they obtain natural perfections, so too the rational creature foresees, through grace, that through grace he will obtain supernatural [gifts].

[17] It is evident that one who does not have grace cannot worthily merit it; otherwise, if grace were from merit, it would not be grace. Yet, grace is altogether fittingly given, because to Divine Goodness it is fitting and suitable that when someone does his best, then God opens His hand and generously pours forth His gifts. For when a sinner endeavors to please Divine Goodness, he no doubt obtains grace; for [God] stands at the door, etc.[81] And in proportion to [a sinner's] having endeavored to be greater and more perfect, grace is infused to him. One who has grace can worthily merit its increase, as well as meriting the Kingdom of Heaven. [Here] we consider merit not according as it derives from ourselves (for, as such, "the sufferings [of this present time] are not worthy ...," etc.)[82] but as it is acquired by the Holy Spirit's special activity and by our co-operating [with Him], so that in this way our work is made to be something supernatural, and it obtains a supernatural end, viz., glory. Whatever our teachers ascribe to grace [is ascribable] also to love. Just as grace makes one pleasing, so love makes one precious.

[18] Prevenient grace works in us; infused grace makes pleasing: "My God, His mercy goes before me."[83] Subsequent grace co-operates, when free will works with it. Psalms 22: "Your mercy shall follow me."[84] [This grace is], at one and the same time, subsequent and co-operating, because grace and free will work together. St. Thomas posits five effects of grace: "the first effect is the soul's being healed; the second is the soul's willing the good; the third is its doing the good that it wills; the fourth is its persevering; the fifth is its persevering unto glory."[85] The first effect of grace is prevenient; the last effect of grace is subsequent.

[19] Now, John, whose birthday is today, was full of grace. For he was not born a child of wrath,[86] even though he was conceived as such a child; but he was sanctified in the sixth month [of gestation] at the time of the visit of Blessed Mary, when the infant leaped in [Elizabeth's] womb[87]—sanctified not only by common grace as are

others whose sins are forgiven and [who] are strengthened for doing good works. Rather, he was given the ability to avoid all mortal sins and to avoid the frequency of venial sins—[a gift] that was conferred on no other of the saints (say our teachers) except for the Virgin Mary. Nor was this [gift] given to Jeremias, although he was sanctified in the womb.[88] This was the promise of [the angel] Gabriel, by which he promised to Zachary that from the womb John was to be filled with the Holy Spirit.[89] Yet, in no holy man—except for Christ, the Fount of grace—was there ever so much grace that he could not obtain a greater abundance thereof. Accordingly, "the child [John] grew and was strengthened in spirit."[90] Now, "fullness-of-grace" conveys the idea of a perfection of virtues and of graces—a perfection such that it elevates the virtuous and holy mind away from earthly desires, and removes and conquers every inordinate passion, and renders one, in the midst of men, as free of passion as is an angel.

[20] The philosophers, knowing only humanly acquired virtues, posited as perfect the virtues that they said to be characteristic of a purified[91] mind; for [these virtues] were only in a soul that was purged of passions and of inordinate desire. And these same virtues they called heroic, i.e., divine, because men who had them were, in comparison with others, gods.[92] And these men were fully virtuous in regard to all virtues; for no one is said to be virtuous who lacks even a single virtue. Nevertheless, the philosophers did not deny that these men could still increase in virtue.[93] However, the perfection of this mode [of virtue] consists in the fact that by means of these virtues someone is moved to virtuous deeds all the more quickly and perfectly, all the more fervently and delightfully. And so, [John] is of greater distinction because of the freely-given virtues and because of God's grace. [21] Therefore, being filled with both prevenient and subsequent grace, John increased continually in all the virtues—in the theological virtues as well as in the cardinal virtues.[94] For as a little child he left the world behind, etc. Each of those who saw in the child such a wondrous origin, such a marvelous life, such established strength, such virtuous resolve rejoiced, saying: "Who, do you suppose, this child will be?"[95] For he was strengthened to such an extent that he was strengthened above all others who existed (except for the glorious Virgin)—strengthened with respect to prevenient grace, with respect to grace that makes pleasing, with respect to sanctification and conduct and glorification. For although the grace of sanctification was not so extensive that in the womb it altogether extinguished

the susceptibility to sin so that [later] he could not be inordinately influenced as regards creatures, nevertheless it was extensive enough
that it weakened the susceptibility and strengthened the spirit and
bound the spirit to God with a bond of love—doing so to such an extent that John's spirit could never be turned away from God.

Turning away from God is the essence of mortal sin; turning toward creatures is the essence of venial sin. Only the Virgin Mary had
this prerogative.[96] Therefore, John, who was not able to sin mortally,
fled [into the desert], lest even by frivolous conversation he could mar
his life by sinning venially. John was the prophet of the Most High
("You shall be called a prophet of the Most High")[97] and even greater
(because "of those born ...," etc.).[98] And [he was] "more than a
prophet,"[99] because not only did he foretell [the coming of Messi-
ah] but he pointed [Him] out with his finger ("Behold, the Lamb of
God," etc.).[100] He was a messenger (*angelus*): "Behold, I send my
messenger, and he shall prepare the way before you," as the Lord said
through Malachias.[101] This [messenger] was John, who in the desert
prepared the way of the Lord. Behold, the purity of John's life! For
he was a child and a messenger (*angelus*), etc. "He [was] more than
a prophet" with respect to the ordering of his life. [He led] a life strict
and solitary, chaste and poor—[a life characterized by] a garment of
camel's hair (i.e., a hair-shirt), by meals out of locusts and honey and
water (in small portions), by speaking and working, etc.

[22] O What kind of man he was! And how great he was!—him
who, in all his conduct, lacked not a single one of heaven's or earth's
perfections. Because of such great gifts of grace, because of such great
merit, because of such fervent, inflamed love, you, [O John], obtained
eternal, infinite, immense glory. For after the fashion of the glorious
Mother of God, John ascended very highly in glory with respect to
an essential reward, which consists of the beatific vision and of the enjoyment and possession of the Blessed Trinity. In regard to an incidental reward he obtained, as well, that which someone obtains not because of his love but because of various deeds that love commands:
[viz.,] an aureole, i.e., a crown that is small in comparison with the
essential reward. [He obtained it] by reason of his victory (for he conquered), even as at one time victorious combatants were crowned.
Against three things in the world—against the flesh, the world, and the
Devil—the soul's battle is threefold and is in accordance with its threefold power: the appetitive power, the irascible power, and the rational
power. Accordingly, there are three aureoles. The first aureole is the

one belonging to virgins. It is given to those who overcome the flesh through most excellent activity of the appetitive power; for it is difficult to mortify all sexual activity for God's sake. The second aureole is the triumph of martyrs over the world by means of most excellent activity of the irascible power; for it is difficult to choose death for God's sake. The third aureole is that of teachers. It is conferred for one's very worthy triumph over the Devil by means of most excellent activity of the rational power. For it is the responsibility of a teacher to repel—by means of his erudition in faith and morals—the Devil not only from his own heart but also from the heart of his neighbor. Now, the aureole as concerns virginity is enhanced by martyrdom and teaching. John was a most chaste virgin, a most glorious martyr, and a most excellent teacher. Hence, in the hymn [it says]: "Lo, thirty garlands ...," etc.[102] For John is an ark of testimony[103] in the tabernacle—an ark gilded inside and out; he is a crown because of his virginity; he is an altar of the Lord, etc.

PART THREE
On John, Who Was in the Desert; and [Discussion] here of the Contemplative Life and the Active Life

(a) *The steps of contemplation, and a comparison of contemplation with the active life.*

[23] "He was in the deserts until the day of his manifestation."[104] "Desert" is taken to mean *contemplation*. Exodus 3: "And while Moses attended the sheep in the interior of the desert, the Lord appeared unto him."[105] For when a man forsakes all things for God's sake, then God appears to him. And the desert is the Sinai desert, where God rained down manna on the *children of Israel* (i.e., on *those who see God*).

[24] The doctors [of the Church] posit various steps of contemplating God and of ascending unto God. At times, the mind of him who is contemplating is directed towards perceptual and imaginable objects; at times, it is directed towards those things which can be known only by reason; at times, towards those things which can be known only by intellect. And each [such] stage has two steps. The *first step* [of these six steps] is in terms of the imagination and accords with the imagination. Indeed, [it occurs] when we, as dazed, simply gaze on perceptual objects, noting how large they are, how varied, how beautiful, how delightful, etc. And in all these objects we admiringly

venerate, and veneratingly admire, God's power, wisdom, goodness, etc. The *second step* is the imagining—on the basis of philosophic inventiveness or of the teaching of the divine books—of the principles and causes of objects. The *third step* [is taken] when by means of the natures and the properties of perceptible objects the imagination ascends to things spiritual, so that "as cinnamon and aromatic balm...," etc.[106] "My spirit is sweeter than honey."[107] Similarly: "Your name is as ointment poured forth," etc.[108] "The voice that I heard was as the voice of harp-players playing their harps."[109] And so on. The fourth step occurs when we ascend above the imagination by means only of reason—i.e., when by means only of spiritual things we ascend unto God. The fifth step is beyond reason but, nevertheless, is neither out of line with reason nor contrary to reason, as, for example, in the case of the simplicity of God's essence ..., etc. The sixth step is beyond reason but also at times is out of line with reason and at times is contrary to reason—as, for example, with regard to the articles of faith, etc.

[25] This contemplative life is the best life because through the soul's most noble power, viz., the intellect, [this life] is occupied principally with the best object, viz., God, and is occupied, secondarily, with God's works, insofar as the divine goodness shows forth in them. Moreover, [the contemplative life] perfects a man with respect to his most noble part. It very greatly makes a man [God-]like. [This likeness] begins in the present life and is perfected in the next life: "We shall be like Him, for we shall see Him as He is."[110] The *active* life will not be present in our future, Heavenly abode, because merciful works, preaching, resisting temptations will have no place there. However, the *contemplative* life will not be removed but will remain eternally in the saints, because, according to the statement of our Savior, the saints' essential reward and essential happiness consist in their contemplating God: "This is true life: that they know You, the only true God, and Jesus Christ, whom You have sent."[111]

[26] Contemplation, in an unqualified sense, is better than is activity, even though not every contemplative life is better than is any given active life. For example, the activity of preaching and of teaching, which derives from contemplation, is preferable to simple contemplation; however, with regard to other outward works that are works of mercy, activity is not preferable. Nevertheless, in certain respects, activity is to be preferred on account of the needs of the present life—just as in an unqualified sense wine is better than water, al-

though in particular cases water is preferable. Moreover, the contemplative life is, in an unqualified sense, of greater merit than is the active life, because it immediately and directly has to do with our loving God, whereas the active life has to do with our loving our neighbor. Now, goodness is is measured by love. Therefore, [if] one man engages in an active life out of greater love than has another man who engages in a contemplative life, the former man is preferred. In and of itself the conducting of an active life can never be more worthwhile than is contemplation. Accordingly, St. Augustine says: "Love and truth require holy leisure. Love's obligations undertake just tasks. If no one imposes a responsibility, time is to be found for discerning and examining the truth; but if a responsibility is imposed, it must be undertaken on account of love's obligation. But not for this reason is delight in the truth to be altogether left aside, lest that pleasantness be eliminated and the obligation become oppressive."[112] Therefore, that blessed man John, whose help is from You, determined in his heart to take ascending steps, by way of contemplation, in the valley-of-tears of the desert in which he was, etc.[113]

(b) *The means of attaining the final goal; and the threefold ascension unto God.*

[27] O most holy John, you have lived your life very harshly. And it is said in the Gospel that from your day [onwards] the Kingdom of Heaven suffers violence.[114] And you proclaimed as a voice in the desert: "Do penance, for the Kingdom of Heaven is at hand."[115] And you said, further, that the axe is placed at the root of the tree; and every tree that does not bear good fruit will be cut down and put into eternal fire.[116] And you add that "the winnowing-fork is in God's hand, and He will cleanse His floor and will gather His wheat into His barn; but the chaff He will burn with unquenchable fire."[117] Therefore, teach me, and procure for me, the pathway of Your commandments, so that before the tree is cut down I may hasten ..., etc.

[28] Now, in order that you, [O Christians], may obtain some fruit from your life, organize your manner of considering and meditating upon your end—[organize it] in such a way that when the end is given, the means to the end are considered. "Therefore, be still and see!"[118] Glory is your end. Consider the means to glory. If you place before your eyes the greedy desire for many things, it is obvious that this is not the [right] pathway, because it is said: "Do not lay up for yourselves treasures where moth and rust destroy and where thieves

break in and steal; but lay up for yourselves treasures in Heaven ...,"
etc.[119] The wanton are far removed from this [right] pathway, because
"he who sows in the flesh shall reap corruption, [but] he who sows
in the spirit shall of the spirit reap eternal life."[120] [Also] far removed
from this pathway are the idly curious, to whom it is said: "Seek not
things that are seen but, rather, things that are not seen. The things
seen are temporal, but the things unseen are eternal."[121] And this pathway is not in the world, because to all it is said: "Love not the world,
because what is in the world is the lust of the flesh or the lust of the
eyes or lust for worldly success."[122]

To those who desire great things it is said: "What does it profit
a man if he gain the whole world ...?" etc.[123] To the greedily rich it
is said: "Do not trust in iniquity. If riches abound ...," etc.[124] To those
who exceedingly love their wealth it is said: "They have slept their
sleep," etc.[125] Of the exalted it is said: "[Even] if you are exalted as
an eagle and you build your nest among the stars, I will cast you down
therefrom, says the Lord."[126] To the avaricious it is said: "Those who
wish to become rich fall into temptation and into the snare [of the
Devil] and into many useless desires, which drown men in destruc-
tion and perdition. The root of all evils is avarice; certain who are
avaricious have erred from the faith and have entangled themselves
in many sorrows."[127] To those loving this present life it is said: "Light
is pleasant; and it is delightful for the eyes to see the sun. If a man live
many years and have rejoiced in them all, he must remember the dark-
some time and the many days ...," etc.[128] To the lazy it is said: "Go
to the ant, O Sluggard, and consider her ways and learn wisdom. Although the ant has no guide or master or captain, she prepares food
during the summer ...," etc.[129] Consider the perils and the labors of
merchants; consider the toils of students. Yet, knowledge inflates, and
only love edifies.[130] Consider this entire life, whose actual course is
like a ship on a stormy sea. See what kind [of man] you ought to be,
O Sailor, in order to draw near to port.

[**29**] If you wish to arrive at your end-goal, determine to take ascending steps in the valley of tears.[131] You have departed far from
God. You were atop a most high mound of delights, having been created in the image of God [and] in a state of innocence, where all the
powers of the body obeyed the soul. You departed, O Man, into sin;
you, O Man, contracted original sin from your parents. There arose
in you deformity, suffering-and-death, proneness to evil, and avarice,
etc. Enticed by inordinate desires, you departed [from God], and you

clung to the world, and you took pleasure in the world, and you brought upon yourself sliminess as a result of your inordinate affections. Stuck in the mud of the pit because of sinning mortally, you departed very far. If you desire to rise up, determine to take ascending steps in the valley of tears. Reflect on the mortal sins within you— on how greatly they displease God. [You have] as much pride as would expel Lucifer from Heaven, as much gluttony and disobedience as [would expel] Adam from Paradise, as much licentiousness as would overthrow Sodom and Gomorrah.

Consider that God, an upright Judge, will, without doubt, judge you according to your works. Consider your past and present sins. Who will count your sins, which you have committed with heart, mouth, and deed? See how Divine Justice will adjudge you, who have sinned so gravely against most benevolent God. Think of your vain desires, your waste of time, etc. Prostrate yourself in prayer with such remorse that God will give you a correcting of your life. Examine your inner man. Etc. Moreover, reflect with grief every day after compline on your excesses for that day, and so arrange your thoughts that in no respect you adulate yourself, flatter yourself, or excuse yourself.

[30] But after you have thus reflected, begin to dispose yourself for ascending, and arrange your exercises in [accordance with] the way in which you wish to conduct yourself, and keep to that ordering. [Arrangements that are] changing, inconstant, and wandering make no progress in any respect. "Do all things," said God to Moses, "according to the pattern that was shown to you on the mount." [132] Just as one-who-wants-to-build-a-house first conceives [of the house] in his mind ..., etc. Likewise, let your disposition be in one manner as regards the *end* and in another manner as regards the *means* to the end. Let purity of heart be your end-goal, and let love be irremovably impressed on, and implanted in, [your heart]; and, in no event, depart from love and purity. And then steer your ship—the ship of your life— into this port, lest you wander about in uncertainty. First of all, ascend unto [the level of] *heart*; secondly, unto a *pure heart*; thirdly, unto a *pure heart that is inflamed* [with love]. You have filled up the measure of mortal sin by means of a threefold descent: (1) through turning away from God out of pride (in which the formal definition of "sin" consists), (2) through turning to creatures out of delight, (3) through working against the law of God.

Rise upwards by means of a threefold gradation. First of all, turn your heart away from creatures, and have [as your] most firm pur-

pose—even if you were to die a thousand times—[the purpose] of
serving God and of not subjecting yourself to creatures. And grieve
over your having turned away [from God], etc. Indeed, such a gradation is called contrition, when a hard heart is thus softened and is made
contrite and is desolidified. Secondly, because while you were arro-
gantly despising, you despised God: it is necessary that you humbly
submit yourself to the man who is the vicar of God and who has the
keys [to the Kingdom]. And humbly, contritely, and grievingly you
must confess your sins to him as to Christ the Lord, our Judge, etc.
Thereupon, in accordance with the purpose of your remorse and in
accordance with your humble ashamedness: your sins, when confessed, are remitted to you. Thirdly, just as through sinning you have
shown your members to be instruments of the Devil, so make them
to be instruments of righteousness unto sanctification,[133] in order to
cure opposite things by means of opposite things. Do things opposite
to those wrongs which you have committed; [do them] in accordance
with the counsel of a priest. And [hereupon] there is satisfaction [for
sin], and [hereupon] you [will] have returned unto your heart.[134]

[31] In order to ascend unto a pure heart, you must know that
impurity consists in three things. [First of all, it consists] in inordinate affection for the vilest things—e.g., for vainglory, for honor and
praise, for gluttony, licentiousness, etc. Secondly, [it consists in] not
loving things that are to be loved but, instead, [in the having] of affections and appetites so impure and unclean that they know nothing
of spiritual and Heavenly things. Thirdly, [impurity consists it] faint-
ness of heart whereby even a man who is to some extent purified and
restored is, nonetheless, not fit to cling to God through perfect love,
because the vigor of love is lacking [to him]. We mount up against
the first impurity by means of our *fear* of the Lord, who shakes the
heart violently, as it were, and breaks it free from harmful affections.
We prevail over the second [impurity] by means of *hope*, because
through hope the heart is elevated unto the tasting of Heavenly things.
From the level of fear we mount up against the third impurity by
means of *love*.

(c) *The states and conditions of life.*

[32] Consider the state of your life! *If you are a male* (since courage
is characteristic of a male ... and since "male" ["*vir*"] is derived from
"virility" ["*virilitas*"]),[135] then consider [the following]: whether you
have overcome your lusts and have put aside the things that are char-

acteristic of a child.[136] According to I Corinthians 13: "When I became a man, I put away [childish things];..." etc.[137] [Consider] whether you are virtuous in your manner of life, whether just as you are a male by sex, so in regard to your affect you are not of the effeminate. Job 36: "Gird up your loins like a man."[138] Etc. *If you are a female*: [Consider whether you are submissive to your husband (in accordance with I Corinthians 11).[139] [Consider] whether you are silent,[140] not wandering, not idle, not nosy[141] —whether you are vain in terms of appearance,[142] whether you are sober and abstinent from wine, since from wine there results shamelessness, etc. [Consider] the example of Augustine's mother, etc.[143] [Consider] whether you are living modestly and chastely; for in women modesty fosters all honorable acts and is compared to the sun's illumining the world....[144] And as regards women's chasteness, [consider] the many examples [pointed to by] Valerius, Guallensis, Ambrose. Let the adornment of women be honorable, without cosmetics being added. Chrysostom, [commenting] on Matthew, [says]: "It is dangerous to add anything to a royal image: you offend God; you undermine sobriety; you kindle the flames of jealousy ..., " etc.[145] [Take] the example, from William of Paris, about the woman who dyed her hair, etc.[146]

If you are obliged to rear children, take care that you not be a nursemaid who is drunken, talkative, lascivious—lest you instill into a new head seeds..., etc. Rear soberly; instruct in God's law, etc. Pubescent boys, because of their inclination towards lust, are to be kept busy with obligatory tasks, lest, like the unplowed earth, they produce thorns and thistles. They are always to be saddled with some task and to be tamed by honest work. [Consider] the example of the philosopher and the example of the two dogs, one of which was a greyhound [i.e., a hunter of hares] and the other of which was a dog of the kitchen; etc. *If you are an adolescent*, determine whether you have grown in virtue as well as in age. In an adolescent paucity of words, continence, and a sense of shame are praiseworthy. Be subordinate, obedient, obliging. Let men be the more virtuous because of their strength. [Let] an old man [be] the more virtuous the older he is. Seneca: "I am grateful for my old age; I cannot keep from willing to do all that I was supposed to."[147] In old age the intellect ought to work hard and steadily, etc. Let there be steadfastness and patience in these [works]. Let the intellect's desire be [for the following: viz.,] to forswear all past pleasures, to keep track of time, and to settle one's accounts before one is called to judgment.

[**33**] Consider your condition, no matter whether you are a nobleman or not. For since you are but earth and ashes[148] and were born in the same way as were all others, you must not for that reason praise yourself. There is no nobleness of the flesh unless there is nobleness of morals. "With God there is no preferential consideration of persons."[149] It is of no benefit to you what kind of person your father was, etc. *If you are of noble stock* but do not live nobly, you are like a filthy place that is shined upon by the sun. O house belonging to so ill-matched an owner! Etc. He is noble who is made noble by his own virtue. Seneca, *Epistle* 43: Philosophy made Plato noble.[150] Gregory, Book II of his *Dialogues*, Chapter 9: "Nobility of race is, for some men, accustomed to give way to ignobility of mind."[151] And such men make for themselves, in regard to their nobility, a shield or a fortress, as it were, for sinning and for defending themselves amid their sins. [They are like] those who have their liberty as a cloak for malice....[152] *If you are not [by birth] noble*: strive to be noble in your practices. Through the virtues, many have risen from least status to maximal status, as did very wise Socrates, who was from a mother who was a midwife and from a father who was a worker-with-marble. Etc.

[**34**] We are not to glory over our natural gifts; rather, [these gifts] are to be governed by the rules of the virtues infused by grace. The [natural] gifts with respect to the soul are intelligence and memory; the [natural] gifts with respect to the body are health, beauty, strength, nimbleness, etc. Let men not be wise when it comes to doing evil.[153] "The children of this world are wiser than are the children of light."[154] Do not misuse your beauty, O woman, by shamelessly seducing men. Proverbs 11 [speaks of] "a golden ring in her nose; a woman comely and foolish."[155] Although a swine have a golden ring in its nose, it excretes no less dung, etc. Thus, a woman shows her beauty to every fornicator, and she mingles it with all ugliness, although she ought to cover and conceal it ..., etc. [Recall] the example of the very handsome young man (as Ambrose relates in Book III of his *On Virgins*) who caused his mouth to fester, in order to appear displeasing.[156]

[**35**] The rich are to be admonished not to acquire [wealth] unjustly—through usury, deceit, robbery, the mammon of iniquity.[157] "For those who wish to become rich fall into various temptations...."[158] Jerome: "Every rich man is either wicked or the son of a wicked man."[159] "If riches abound, do not set your heart [upon them]."[160] It is as difficult for a rich man to enter into the Kingdom

of Heaven as for a camel to pass through the eye of a needle, etc.[161] Riches are dangerous, for many men have perished because of them, etc. The poor are to be comforted. Seneca: "Welcome-poverty is honorable," etc.[162] A poor man is *not* poor, for he no longer desires [to have] ..., etc.[163] [Consider] patience amid tribulation, etc.

(d) *Three ascending steps, viz., fear of God, elevating-hope, love that unites to God through Christ.*

[36] After you have thus pondered all things, take the first step, viz., fear, and sprinkle with bitterness the pleasures of sin—as women do when they wish to wean children. For example, you are full of worldly desires; with all your heart you aspire to a high status; it is difficult for you to be without pleasure-giving foods. In fear of the Lord sprinkle forth bitterness by considering your end and the punishments of Hell, etc. Consider your past transgressions—[consider] how quickly they were over and that the punishment [for them] is eternal, etc. Make lye for washing [them away]. Your soul is approaching God's judgments, which are inscrutable. [Consider] the fact that man does not know whether he is worthy of love or of hatred.[164] He does not know whether contriteness comes upon him because of his love or because of his fear. He is mindful of life's brevity and of the ordeal of severe judgment [that awaits him]. Thereupon—[i.e., upon having these thoughts]—the world passes from your heart, etc. Keep these [thoughts] ever before your eyes, because as one who is about to set out immediately for an unknown region, you are drawing ever-closer to death. Form in yourself the portrayal of a dying man, as if you were going to die right now. Etc. How greatly you will grieve over the fact that you have sinned and have not done penance! Reflect [on the following: viz.,] how bitter it will be for you to pass from worldly delights into Hell. Imagine that your soul is now departing from you. Look at where it is headed, etc. "O Death, how bitter is the memory of you!"[165]

Suppose the hour of death to be most certain and to be going to be present to you very soon [but] at an uncertain time. Recall the ordering, how it is that you are coming toward death amid infirmities and a dread of nature. In the meantime place before your eyes the image of one who is dying; consider the manner [of dying], the form [of dying], and the [right] order [of dying]. Etc. Reflect on how it is that demons will come, on how the soul will be brought to judgment, etc. Focus your thoughts on this judgment—on the Judge, on the plaintiff, and on the witness, etc. Reflect on the punishment of Hell—on how Hell is a very deep, very dark pit full of fire, etc., a fire that burns without light, etc. Reflect on the kind of gnashing of teeth, the kind of trembling, the kind of wailing that is present there. Alas! To what end we have been born! Reflect on the wretched association with demons, etc. Reflect on the fact that the worm will never die.[166]

Accordingly, the first effect of faith is fear: fear tears the heart away from, draws it away from, unclean affections.

[37] The second step is hope. Because of fear hope elevates the mind that is rent away from sins but that is still weighed down by them. It elevates the mind to higher things, and because of the expectation of Heavenly rewards it despises all the vanities of the world. Hope begins to direct its sighs upwards and to yearn mentally for that sublime joy which it has represented [to itself] inwardly. Accordingly, after you have, out of fear, emptied your heart of evil, fill it with the spiritual affection of hope. For hope makes Heavenly things appealing to you, once the slime of sin has been cast aside out of fear. Just as a man who is attached to lower things is made impure, so a man who is attached to higher things is made pure. Hence, imagine there to be above you a place that is very secure, very pure, very restful; and imagine there to be below you a place very unclean, very dark; and imagine that you are in between. The more you proceed downwards through inordinate desires, the more restless and impure [you become]. The more you proceed upwards—toward Heavenly objects of desire, through continual meditation, through longing, and through hope—the more stable and pure, etc., [you become].

As regards remorse on account of love: [consider] how it is that in gazing from afar and through hope, [you see] the holy, beautiful, etc., city of Jerusalem.... The case is similar as regards the glory, the enjoyment, the delights, of Paradise and as regards the gifts to the soul (viz., fullness of knowledge with respect to the rational power; fullness of justice with respect to the appetitive power; superabundance of gladness with respect to the irascible power). Reflect on the benefits given to you by God—[reflect thereon] so that you may have, as it were, an incentive to love God in return. Reflect on how greatly He loves you; for you have very often departed from Him; but He, being merciful, always takes you back again. He created you from nothing. He gave you above all else intellect, etc. He gave you heaven and earth, the sun and the moon. ("You have subjected all things under man's feet," etc.)[167] Reflect on the fact that [God] has exalted you

[and] on how greatly Christ emptied Himself.[168] God called you through prophets, through signs, through His Son, etc. Reflect on what kind of [person] is He who bestowed on you all those [goods]; and [consider] that He is most good, most kind, most merciful. Hope will be elevated in and through love; and in this way the heart is made pure.

[38] Thirdly, ascend through love unto entering into, and being united with, God. By means of many vigils, labors, and periods of study you will, at length, complete these [three] steps—[steps] of those who are beginning and of those who are finishing. It takes no small effort to renounce one's past life and to lament over one's sins. It takes quite great effort to triumph over a prior, long-standing habit, to leave aside inordinate affections, to extinguish particular sins, and, through hope of forgiveness, to raise up the entire mind unto Heavenly things. After many of the aforesaid ascendings, one ascends still higher, unto love, by transforming one's nature into states of virtue. In a certain manner, then, a man puts on virtue by means of his affections. And he makes a habit of virtue, [doing so] not out of fear of punishment or out of hope of reward but solely out of affection for goodness, since he has taken delight in God. And, accordingly, [when he does all of this], he greatly dreads wickedness and uncleanness. Dreading greatly all things contrary to virtue, he does what is good, being delighted by his affection for the good. And in regard to no thing does he receive impurity, etc. And just as the affective power is habituated regarding the virtues, so it is united to God through fervent love. And once aroused, by means of its study in regard to speculating on God, it is always aglow with zeal. A truly just man dreads sin, etc. Here is the fat mountain;[169] he who ascends unto it will find pastures as he goes in and out.[170] He who goes in by means of the appetitive power will find joy, etc.; he who goes in by means of the irascible power will find courage, steadiness, etc. This love is not given to all; certainly, it is not given to those who are asleep, to those who are disdainful [of it], to those who do not co-operate [with it]. Love is a kind of warfare. Go away, O Slothful ones! Yet, man crawls along incrementally and draws near by means of protracted exercises.

[39] In regard to this attachment [to God], it is necessary to ascend through the Way that is Christ ("I am the Way, the Truth ...")[171] and to ascend by first of all walking along by means of pleasing meditation on Christ's humanity—[meditating on] the manner of His birth, on how, and how much, [He grew] in wisdom and in gracefulness, etc.,

and on how the apostles-who-heard-Him forsook all things. Secondly, it is necessary to ascend by means of suffering and to find God in
and through the man Christ. Thirdly, [it is necessary] to rise up, by
way of Christ's humanity, unto spiritual affection and to behold with
mental eyes now God Himself "through a glass darkly" [172] and hereby to ascend from the humanity unto a knowledge and love of
[Christ's] deity. And at that point a man begins to be, in a certain manner, one spirit with God. [173] Augustine, in Book VII of the *Confessions*,
[says]: "Having now been admonished to return to myself, I entered
into my innermost parts, as best I could, with You guiding me. And
with some kind of eye of my soul I saw—above that same eye of my
soul, above my mind—the unchangeable Light of the Lord, not our ordinary light," etc., "but something else, exceedingly other than these
[lights]," etc. "He who knows the truth knows *that* [Light], and he who
knows the truth knows eternity. And whoever knows love knows that
[Light]. O Eternal Truth and true Love and loving Eternity!" [174] Etc.
Let a beast beware that it not touch this Mount. [175] And [let] the exercise of one who loves [God be] such as [to meditate] on the Sacred
Scriptures, on the Prophets, on Christ's life, incarnation, suffering, etc.

[40] Since the vices have pitched their tent within man, and
since there is only free will, [let a man] arm his will with zeal, seriousness, and kindness. Zeal is strength-of-mind that expels all carelessness and disposes the soul toward doing good deeds attentively,
boldly, and gracefully. Seriousness restrains inordinate desire, rendering it bitter, poor, of no account. Kindness excludes wickedness and
produces benevolence, long-suffering, and inner gladness. [176]

NOTES TO *SERMON V*

1. Luke 1:13.
2. Luke 1:80.
3. Matthew 11:9-11. Luke 7:26-28. Matthew 14:10. Mark 6:25-28.
4. Luke 3:1-18.
5. Luke 1:14.
6. Matthew 11:11.
7. John 1:6.
8. Luke 1:63.
9. Luke 1:5-19.
10. Mark 1:6.
11. Re Matthew 4:2. *Biblia Sacra cum Glossa Interlineari, Ordinaria, et Nicolai Lyrani Postilla, eiusdemque Moralitatibus, Burgensis Additionibus, et Thoringi Replicis*, Vol. 5 (Venice, 1588), ff. 15^{ab}D - 15^{va}E.
12. Re Matthew 4:19. *Biblia Sacra cum Glossa, op. cit.*, f. 16^{ra}B.
13. Matthew 8:31. Cf. Matthew 12:43.
14. Re Matthew 8:31. *Biblia Sacra cum Glossa, op. cit.*, f. 32^{ra}B.
15. Matthew 14:15 (not Matthew 13).
16. Jude 12 (not James).
17. Bernard of Clairvaux, *Sermones de Diversis*. Sermo 33.6 (*PL* 183:629B).
18. Proverbs 20:1 (not Proverbs 15).
19. Philippians 3:19.
20. Augustine, *Enarrationes in Psalmo*. Psalm 77, re verses 34-35 (*PL* 36:996).
21. II Corinthians 6:16.
22. Osee 13:6 (Hosea 13:6).
23. Psalms 31:9 (32:9).
24. Genesis 25:34.
25. Lamentations 1:11.
26. Genesis 2:17.
27. Genesis 19:30-35.
28. II Kings 13:27-29 (II Samuel 13:27-29).
29. Genesis 40:20-22.
30. Psalms 77:30-31 (78:30-31).
31. Job 1:19.
32. Gregory the Great, *Moralium Libri* (= *Expositio in Librum B. Job*), II, Chap. 16, division number 27 (*PL* 75:569A).
33. William Peraldus, *De Vitio Gulae*, Part I (See Codex Cusanus 60; folium 34rb.) I have taken this reference from the critical apparatus of the printed edition of the Latin text of Cusa's sermons. I have not looked at Codex Cusanus 60.
34. Cf. Gregory the Great, *Moralium Libri, op. cit.*, Book XXX, Chap. 18, division number 59 (*PL* 76:556B).
35. St. Jerome, *Epistola* 69.9 ("Ad Oceanum") (*PL* 22:663).
36. Gregory the Great, *XL Homiliarum in Evangelia*, Book II, Homilia 40.5 (*PL* 76:1307A).

37. Exodus 32:6.
38. Jeremias (Jeremiah) 5:7.
39. Ephesians 5:18 (not Philippians 9).
40. Proverbs 20:1.
41. Luke 16:19-21.
42. Proverbs 20:1.
43. Job 28:12-13.
44. St. Jerome, *Epistola* 52.11 (*PL* 22.537).
45. Osee 7:5 (Hosea 7:5).
46. Proverbs 23:31-32 (not Proverbs 22).
47. Isaias (Isaiah) 19:14.
48. I John 2:16.
49. Joel 3:3.
50. The word "soul" (*"anima"*) is feminine in Latin; the word "boy" (*"puer"*) is masculine.
51. Cf. Boethius, *De Consolatione Philosophiae*, Book II, Prosa 4 (*PL* 63:684).
52. Seneca, *Epistolae Morales*, Book VI, Epistola 7, end of margin number 14.
53. Proverbs 14:13 (not Proverbs 13).
54. Eugene of Toledo, Carmen 6 ("Contra Ebrietatem") [pp. 236-237 of Fridericus Vollmer, editor, *Fl. Merobaudis Reliquiae Blossi Aemilii Dracontii Carmina. Eugenii Toletani Episcopi Carmina et Epistulae* = Vol. 14 of *Monumenta Germaniae Historica*].
55. Here (at 11:1 of the Latin text) I am reading "crebras" in place of "crebres".
56. Ecclesiasticus 37:33-34.
57. Bernard of Clairvaux, *Sermo de Conversione ad Clericos*, Chap. 8, number 13 (*PL* 182:842A).
58. Ecclesiastes 6:7 (not Ecclesiastes 5).
59. Proverbs 13.25 (not Proverbs 12).
60. Aggeus 1:6 (Haggai 1:6).
61. Canticle of Canticles 5:1 (Song of Solomon 5:1).
62. Psalms 59:5 (60:3).
63. Genesis 49:11.
64. Ephesians 4:22.
65. Note Acts 2:15 and 4:34-35.
66. Matthew 19:27.
67. Luke 7:37-50 (not Luke 8).
68. Augustine, Sermo 142.6.6 (*PL* 38:781).
69. Isaias (Isaiah) 55:1.
70. Romans 18: "… are not worthy to be compared with the glory that shall be revealed in us."
71. Esther 1:8.
72. Psalms 53:8 (54:6).
73. Cf. Psalms 55:12 (56:12).
74. Canticle of Canticles 5:1 (Song of Solomon 5:1).
75. Psalms 35:9 (36:8).
76. Acts 2:15.

77. Acts 6:8.
78. Wisdom 11:25.
79. Here (at 15:18) I am reading "agendum" in place of "augendum".
80. I Corinthians 12:4 and 8.
81. Apocalypse 3:20 (Revelation 3:20).
82. Romans 8:18. See n. 70 above.
83. Psalms 58:11 (59:10).
84. Psalms 22:6 (23:6).
85. Aquinas, *Summa Theologica*, Ia - IIae, 111, 3, corpus.
86. Ephesians 2:3.
87. Luke 1:41.
88. Jeremias (Jeremiah) 1:5.
89. Luke 1:15.
90. Luke 1:80.
91. Here (at 20:3) I am reading "purgati" in place of "purgativi".
92. Aristotle, *Nicomachean Ethics*, VII, 1 (1145^{a}18-27).
93. See my exposition of this theme in my article "Die Tugenden in der Sicht des Nikolaus von Kues. Ihre Vielfalt, ihr Verhältnis untereinander und ihr Sein. Erbe und Neuansatz," *Mitteilungen und Forschungsbiträge der Cusanus-Gesellschaft*, 26 (2000), 9-39 [Trier: Paulinus Verlag].
94. The three theological virtues are faith, hope and love. The four cardinal virtues are wisdom, courage, temperance, justice.
95. Luke 1:66.
96. That is, the prerogative of begetting sinlessly someone sinless.
97. Luke 1:76.
98. Luke 7:28: "Among those born of women there is not a greater prophet than John the Baptist."
99. Luke 7:26.
100. John 1:29.
101. Malachias 3:1 (Malachi 3:1).
102. Hymn "Ut queant laxis." See *Analecta Hymnica Medii Aevi*, Vol. 50 (edited by Clemens Blume and Guido M. Dreves (Leipzig, 1907), p. 121.
103. Cf. Exodus 25:10-11.
104. Luke 1:80.
105. Exodus 3:1-2.
106. Ecclesiasticus 24:20.
107. Ecclesiasticus 24:27.
108. Canticle of Canticles 1:2 (Song of Solomon 1:2).
109. Apocalypse 14:2 (Revelation 14:2).
110. I John 3:2.
111. John 17:3.
112. Augustine, *De Civitate Dei*, XIX, 19 (*PL* 41:647-648).
113. Psalms 83:6-7 (84:5-6).
114. Matthew 11:12.
115. Matthew 3:2.
116. Matthew 3:10.
117. Matthew 3:12.

118. Psalms 45:11 (46:10).
119. Matthew 6:19-20.
120. Galatians 6:8.
121. II Corinthians 4:18.
122. I John 2:15-16.
123. Matthew 16:26.
124. Psalms 61:11 (62:10).
125. Psalms 75:6 (76:5).
126. Abdias 4 (Obadiah 4).
127. I Timothy 6:9-10).
128. Ecclesiastes 11:7-8.
129. Proverbs 6:6-8.
130. I Corinthians 8:1.
131. Psalms 83:6-7 (cf. 84:5-6).
132. Exodus 25:40.
133. Romans 6:13.
134. Isaias (Isaiah) 46:8.
135. Cicero, *Tusculanae Disputationes*, II, 18, 43.
136. I Corinthians 13:11.
137. I Corinthians 13:11.
138. Job 38:3 (not Job 36).
139. I Corinthians 11:3. Ephesians 5:22-24.
140. I Corinthians 14:34.
141. I Timothy 5:13.
142. I Peter 3:3.
143. Augustine, *Confessiones*, IX, 9, 19 (*PL* 32:772).
144. See Ecclesiasticus 26:21 in the context of the entire Chapter 26.
145. John Chrysostom, *In Mattheum Homiliae*. Homilia 30.6 (*PG* 57:370).
146. William of Auvergne (William of Paris), *De Universo*, Part 3 of Part 2, Chapter 25 [Vol. I of *Guilielmi Alverni Opera Omnia* (Paris, 1674. Reprinted by Minerva Verlag, Frankfurt am Main, Germany, 1963), p. 1072^{b}G.
147. Seneca, *Epistolae Morales*, Book III, Epistola 5, margin number 3.
148. Ecclesiasticus 17:31.
149. Romans 2:11.
150. Seneca, *Epistolae Morales*, Book V, Epistola 3, margin number 3.
151. Gregory the Great, *Dialogi*. Book V, Chapter 23 (not Chapter 9).
152. I Peter 2:16.
153. Jeremias (Jeremiah) 4:22.
154. Luke 16:8.
155. Proverbs 11:22.
156. Ambrose, *Exhortatio Virginitatis*, I.12.83 (*PL* 16:376C).
157. " ... the mammon of iniquity": Luke 16:9.
158. I Timothy 6:9.
159. Jerome, *Commentaria in Abdiam Prophetam*, Book II, re Abdias 3:7 (Obadiah 3:7) [*PL* 25:1316C].
160. Psalms 61:11 (62:10).
161. Matthew 19:24.

162. Seneca, *Epistolae Morales*, Book II, Epistola 2, margin number 5.

163. Gregory the Great, *Homiliae XL in Ezechielem.* Homilia 6.16 (*PL* 76:1007C).

164. Ecclesiastes 9:1.

165. Ecclesiasticus 41:1.

166. Isaias (Isaiah) 66:24. Mark 9:43.

167. Hebrews 2:8. Psalms 8:8 (8:6).

168. Philippians 2:7.

169. Psalms 67:16 (cf. 68:15).

170. John 10:9.

171. John 14:6.

172. I Corinthians 13:12.

173. Nicholas picks up, from the tradition of mystical theology, the theme of a believer's "transformation into God." See pp. 7-9 of my *Hugh of Balma on Mystical Theology: A Translation and an Overview of His De Theologia Mystica* (Minneapolis: Banning, 2002).

174. Augustine, *Confessiones*, VII, 10, 16 (*PL* 32:742).

175. Exodus 19:12.

176. I here omit the repetitive materials entitled "Memoriale" ("Reminder") and *"Adnotationes"* ("Notes"). These are not part of the sermon but are jottings meant to serve as a guide in the preparation or the delivery of the sermon.

Sermon VI: Respexit Humilitatem
("He has regarded the humility ....") [1]
[July 2, 1431; preached perhaps in Koblenz]

[1] "He has regarded the humility of His handmaiden." [2]

The Virgin Mary is most worthy of all praise, being of such great loftiness that none of the languages suffice to express praise for her. For suppose it could happen that all of the following were languages: the sand of the seashore and the waves [of the ocean], the droplets of water, a rose, gem-stones, lilies, flames, the currents of air, the occupants of the heavens, snow, hail, both sexes, the wings of the winds, and every kind of flying-thing and of cattle, etc. These could scarcely express who you are and how great you are, O Virgin Mary, O Queen Mary!

[2] However, because Mary was athirst with deepest desire for the salvation of the human race and because she besought God in deepest humility mercifully to make available to the human race the goal of salvation, she said: "My soul has clung to the pavement. Enliven me in accordance with Your word." [3] In the name of human nature she also said: "I was completely abased. Enliven me in accordance with Your word." [4] For human nature fell into evil; but as completely dead it was destined for life, etc. Mary said: "See my abasement, and deliver me .... Look upon me, and have mercy on me," etc. [5] "See that I have loved Your commandments; enliven me in Your mercy." [6] The Lord heard His handmaiden's most devout prayer and regarded her humility and did great things through her, [causing] Israel to receive a child through her, as was [fore]told to our fathers, etc. [7]

Therefore, I am going to say something about the foregoing matters and about the praises for the Virgin, etc.

[3] [I will speak], first of all, about the cause of the fall of human nature, which was exalted through the Virgin Mary. And [I will speak of] what kind [of person] this Virgin was, who through grace deserved to be the mother of our Savior. And here [I will speak] of this [theme]: "He regarded ...;" for "the eyes of the Lord are upon the just ...," etc. [8] And at this point let the Gospel-story first be set forth very concisely. Secondly, because the Lord did have regard for Mary and her humility, some things must next be mentioned about the virtue of humility and about its contrary, viz., pride. And because after God looked with regard upon Mary and her humility and saw that she was His hand-

maiden, He heard her [prayer] and did great things for her: something will be mentioned about our being God's servant and about our serving Him through prayer. And thereupon I will conclude agreeably [by taking up the topic of] how the soul's union with God, and God's union with the soul, arises out of a pleasing harmony between God's regard, man's humility, and man's subservient devotion.[9]

PART ONE
Man's Original Justice, His Fall, and the Virgin Mary's Grace

[4] God created man for Himself. And so, among other things He gave him original justice, by means of which he was originally just because of freely-given grace. Man lost this grace because of his original sin, and he could not fully rise up again except by means of a Savior. Mary, who was full of the Holy Spirit, knew this fact. Hence, she most humbly besought [God] to send the Savior who was promised to be sent. And God regarded her, and hearkened to her, in her humility.

[5] Now, original sin is the sin which, according to the Catholic Faith, each one of us commonly contracts, by virtue of the fact that he descends from Adam by means of seminal propagation. Romans 5: "Through one man sin entered into this world."[10] Actual sin is a fault that each [of us] contracts through his voluntarily doing something or failing to do something. Original [sin is contracted] from one's parents, apart from one's own willing, etc. Certain men say that original sin is a blamable stain that the soul contracts from its union with flesh that has been lustfully propagated. And, hence, what is *material* with regard to [original] sin would be the habitual concupiscence in the soul—[concupiscence] resulting from the soul's union with shameful flesh; what is *formal* [with regard to original sin] would be the absence of original justice. Similarly, what is *material* with regard to actual [sin] is a turning toward creatures; what is *formal* is a turning away from God.

[6] Original justice was the fixed disposition (*habitus*) that was divinely conferred on our first parents and that kept the sensitive appetite subjected (without any rebellion) to the spirit. It was present in the soul's essential being, and it redounded to all the soul's powers, but primarily to the will. Anselm in *On the Virgin Conception* says that original sin is "the absence of original justice together with the obligation to have original justice."[11] Every sin is the privation of an opposed justice. Thus, original [sin] deprives of original justice. (In adults, what is owed is, and was, remitted through faith, through baptism, and (in the

Old Testament) through circumcision. Now, that deprivation is a fault; and the penalty [of original sin]—viz., concupiscence—remains. And so, original justice is not restored; rather, something else [is given] in its place, viz., grace that makes one pleasing [to God]. And so, although there is present in us, by fixed-disposition or by aptitude, a spark [of concupiscence], and although there is found in our members another law (viz., the removal of original justice), warring against the law of our mind, nevertheless no harm [therefrom] is done to those who are in Christ Jesus, who walk not according to the flesh.[12]

[7] This sin [viz., original sin] is, with respect to blame and penalty, passed on to offspring who are begotten by propagation. For when Adam sinned and lost original justice, which he was supposed to keep and to pass on, all those who were in his loins potentially, and who were going to exist through a seminal cause, lost this very justice. And so, because the whole of human nature was in a certain way present in Adam potentially, it follows ..., etc.—even as the blamable defect of someone's will passes over unto his members. And, thus, those who existed in the power of Adam's loins lost original justice when Adam lost it. Therefore, if individuals would have been born at that time or even later, but not by being propagated from Adam, they would not have lost [original justice]. Moreover, it is said apropos of Adam that if Eve alone had sinned, there would have occurred no transmission [of original sin], because the father is the moving principle of begetting and is the principle that transmits to his posterity.[13] Accordingly, if Adam alone had sinned, we *would have* contracted [original guilt]. Furthermore, original sin is not present in the soul by way of propagation, because it is not propagated; nor is it present in the flesh, for the flesh is not capable of virtue or of vice. Rather, original sin is present in a man potentially with respect to his soul, because of divine punishment. In particular, when the soul is conjoined to the flesh, then at that moment the soul lacks original justice and divine grace. And so, the remission of Adam's original sin was of no benefit to us, because [Adam's sin] was remitted not as a *natural sin* that concerned the whole of human nature but as a *personal sin*. Accordingly, baptized parents still beget a child who has original sin. [Consider] the example of a grain that is planted free of [chaff]: it begets a grain that is on an ear. Furthermore, one who is circumcised begets another who is uncircumcised. The pure soul contracts from the flesh concupiscence and original guilt, even as good wine in a contaminated vessel becomes contaminated and as a handsome man becomes soiled when

he falls into the mud.

[8] Moreover, concupiscence, the penalty of original sin, is not extinguished by means of grace, except in the case of the Blessed Virgin, who alone had this particular [trait], etc. Accordingly, it happens that the nature is corrupted by the person and that [thereupon] the corrupted nature corrupts, daily, the person.[14] One's lustful desire transmits sin to one's offspring; and because of the spirit's disobedience to God, the flesh is made to be disobedient to the spirit. Hence, the lustful desire that remains in the flesh is opposed to the spirit,[15] etc., because we are all born as children of wrath on account of this [residual desire].[16] And so, we incur multiple defects: viz., the defect of the loss of our vision-of-God, the defect of our loss of glory, the defect of death. Consequently, in the case of unbaptized infants, in whom no actual sin has been [incurred] through a turning away [from God], original sin results in the penalty of condemnation, not, however, in the penalty of the senses. For [after death] they do not experience pain. For they do not grieve—because they are rational spirits they do not grieve—over the fact that they do not have glory.[17] For they know that they were never made fit [for glory] by means of the grace that makes one pleasing. (Similarly, someone who is rational does not suffer because of the fact that he cannot fly, given that he has no wings ..., etc.)

There are other penal effects [of original sin]: e.g., ignorance, proneness to sinning, sickness, etc.

[9] This most blessed Virgin knew that unless we are incorporated into Christ our Savior (1) through the grace that makes one pleasing and (2) through the merits of Christ, who is the veritable Truth and the veritable Way,[18] no one would ever arrive at the Heavenly abode. Because Mary was most holy and because, having been exalted, she saw, and recognized, in a beatific vision, man's end: she most humbly prayed to God for human beings' salvation. Wherefore, "He regarded the humility of His handmaiden." [10] And over against this general and universal death the Lord planted a tree of life in the midst of Paradise. ("For the Lord God had planted a paradise of pleasure from the beginning"; in this paradise [He placed] a tree of life in the middle ..., etc.[19]) The Lord God separated the waters from the dry land;[20] i.e., He separated the eternal Heavenly abode from the earth, which was desirable and was ever flowing with the milk and honey of His promise. At that time the earth was unknown and was covered over with the watery coldness of disordering sin. By means of the separating, God

intended to show that regeneration would occur with respect to many generations and many fruits, as Genesis 2 states.[21] Thereafter—before God formed all other things, before He formed even man (i.e., before He recreated him)—God first of all made a very temperate and very agreeable place, very high up in location and reaching all the way up to the lunar globe. It was of such height that even the waters of the Flood—waters which covered all the mountains—did not touch this place. And God adorned this place[22] with herbs, trees, plants, and shrubs, by means of which man, whom He was going to place into this very location, would be delighted and nourished. And in Greek this place is called *paradisus* [i.e., παράδεισος]; but in Latin it is called *hortus*. And it is situated where the sun begins to shine in the East. Now, this story from Sacred Scripture recounts one thing and produces another thing, viz., a mystery—as Blessed Gregory states in Book 15 of his *Moralia*; "By its manner of expression Sacred Scripture transcends all forms of knowledge. For when it recounts a deed, then by means of one and the same word it produces a mystery."[23]

[11] "Paradise" is construed in many different ways. At one time it is construed as signifying the empyrean heaven; at another time, as signifying the church triumphant; at another time, as signifying man; at another time, as signifying Christ. But in the present case it will be taken to stand for Christ's mother. For "my sister, my spouse, is a garden enclosed, a garden enclosed, a fountain sealed up. Your plants are a paradise of pomegranates with the fruits of the orchard, cyprus with spikenard. Spikenard and saffron [are present]; sweet cane and cinnamon, with all the trees of Lebanon, [are present]. As cinnamon and balsam ..., etc. The sweet smell of perfumes [is present]. Arise, O north wind!"[24] This paradise[25] is a very temperate place, i.e., [it is characterized] by very virtuous and very lovely devoutness, by loftiest love. It extends unto the lunar globe. It is beyond all corruptible nature. The waters of the Flood, i.e., sins and temptations, have not reached its lofty level. In Paradise [i.e., in Mary] the vegetative power is adorned with the many flowers of the virtues; [also ornate are] the life of the senses and the tree of the knowledge of good and evil, viz., reason ..., etc. Thus, the Second Adam, i.e., Christ Jesus, having been made into a living soul took delight therein, etc.

[12] And so, O Mary, Your Beloved "descended into His garden, to the bed of aromatical spices, in order to feed in the gardens and to gather lilies."[26] This Paradise [symbolizing Mary] was adorned with marvelous and amazing flowers, and trees, of aromatic scents and of

virtues, so that the man whom God was going to place there—viz., [the one who both is] God and man—would take delight, and would feed, [in it]. The Tree that is in the midst of Paradise—viz., the Tree of life, which extended into the heavens[27] because of its height—this Tree of life signifies Christ Jesus, our Savior, who was carried in the womb of the Virgin. The whole of Paradise [viz., Mary] magnified this Tree by giving provisions to it and by flowing into it, so that it would flourish into something better and something best. For "my soul has magnified the Lord"; and the spirit, attaining this Tree, has rejoiced[28] in God its Savior. For this Tree in the midst of Paradise was rooted in humility and chastity and love, for God regarded [Mary's] humility.[29]

[13] O the wondrous nourishment that this Tree drew from the most pure blood of the Virgin! O the wondrous grace that flowed from the Tree into its root, because the Most High sanctified His tabernacle! Anselm in *On the Virgin Conception* 18 [says]: "It was fitting that the Virgin was resplendent with a purity than which none greater (except for God's) can be conceived. The most pure Son of the eternal God was deservedly so given to her as a son that He was the common Son of God and of the Virgin."[30] O such wondrous grace flowed into the tabernacle of God—grace that makes one pleasing and that sanctifies! For the Sun of Justice[31] situated this Paradise at the point of its rising; and He elevated it above all mortal things that exist under the moon— exalted it through grace. And he brought His tabernacle [viz., Mary] into the sun. ("He placed His tabernacle in the sun ...," etc.[32]) He sanctified His tabernacle with such great grace that she never fell into any sin—not even venial sin (free of which no one [else] has ever lived) and, as is fitting, not even original sin, etc.

[14] Moreover, according to St. Augustine this Paradise [viz., Mary] is of such great pleasantness and beauty that she is the "brightness of eternal life and a spotless mirror of God's majesty ...."[33] Never was anyone greater in grace, purer in virtue, more ardent in love, more steadfast in faith, more strong in hope, more untroubled in peacefulness, more full of joy in the Holy Spirit, more modest in word, more holy in deeds! If we would speak with the tongues of men and of angels,[34] who would be able worthily to praise you? You, [O Mary], are the joyous shout, and desired proclamation, on the part of the prophets. You are the stillness of all the wise and of all the scribes. You are the glorious offspring of the patriarchs and of the kings of Israel. You are greater than all these and than all the angels. You are a woman becloaked with the sun and treading the moon under your feet.[35] You

are indued with light that serves as your garment. You everywhere by the brilliance of Your splendor cause to turn away even the angels' gazes. As regards the Tree of the knowledge of good and evil in Paradise—i.e., as regards the rational faculty and the intellectual faculty of the most blessed Virgin—how [amazingly] this Tree had the very tasty fruits of meditating on the fourteen articles of the divinity and the humanity [of Jesus]! Nevertheless, [these] fruits are not tasted and eaten by means of arguments and human reasoning but by the very deep faith by which Mary believed. For she asked, "How can this occur?" [36] And the angel responded: "The Holy Spirit ...," etc. [37]

[15] Lo, by the grace of faith [the Son of God] descended from Heaven into Mary. And, furthermore, she did not question how [it was done] but said [to the angel]: "Let it happen to me in accordance with your word." [38] Take note of the maximal faith that is symbolized by this Tree located in Paradise. For through faith's contemplation one ascends unto a knowledge of good and evil and unto conformity to God and unto the highest theophany. But present in this Paradise are (a) trees of the Holy Spirit's gifts and (b) trees of the forms of happiness, and (c) exceptional trees that are found nowhere else. "And a river went out from the place of pleasure to water the Paradise." [39] That is, a superabundance of the grace that makes one pleasing immediately flowed forth into Mary's soul from that river of living water that proceeds from the throne of God and of the Lamb, who is an unfailing Fount. To this river and its moisture all the trees of Paradise send forth their roots in order that the trees' leaves may be continually green and that the trees may always bear fruit. And [the river] is divided into four heads [40]—i.e., into the [four] cardinal virtues, by means of which Mary's grace flowed outwardly in a certain manner, so that she was best prepared, and most excellent, in all her moral and virtuous deeds. From these four [cardinal virtues] all the [other] moral virtues flow as streams from which the earth has its being watered with the water of virtue. And so, Paradise is a well of living waters and an enclosed garden. It is a sealed up fount that is never made bitter by foreign waters. In Paradise [i.e., in Mary] there was never any sin or any inordinate motion, etc. [41]

[16] With respect to gifts of nature Mary was most comely. And she was most seemly with respect to the source of her spiritual life. She manifested outwardly what she was inwardly—[manifested], viz., her humility, chastity, etc. Accordingly, no one was ever tempted by the sight of her; rather, each one was motivated toward the virtues. Now,

as concerns the beginning of human nature, Eve was also very beautiful in accordance with her destined-end, as was also Adam. So also was Christ in regard to His destined-end. ("Learn from me, for [I am] meek ...," etc.)[42] "The wisdom of man shines in his countenance ...," etc.[43] "You are all-fair, O my love, and there is not a blemish in you."[44] "Behold, you are lovely, O my love. Behold, you are lovely. Your eyes are [as those] of doves."[45] [All her glory] was inward, with golden borders and clothed round about with varieties."[46]

There are two kinds of virtues: natural and adventitious. A natural [virtue] is one's *natural industriousness* with respect to works of prudence or of skill or with respect to acts that display wisdom or knowledge. (This has to do with cognitive virtue.) In addition, a natural virtue is a *natural inclination* toward moral deeds—[deeds] of justice, of temperance, of courage, and of gentleness, etc. Adventitious virtues are usually not acquired apart from natural virtues. However, by means of adventitious virtues there is a development of the natural virtues, because natural virtues are a tool for investigating what, in particular, is true or false; but this [judgment about the true and the false is what] the adventitious virtues teach. Now, natural [virtue] tends only to one [of a pair] of opposites; [but] moral [virtue tends] now to the one [alternative], now to the other—in accordance with what right reason dictates. Hence, the stronger a natural [virtue] is, the more dangerous it is, unless it is governed by reason. An example: natural gentleness always tends toward not being angry; but moral gentleness sometimes tends toward being angry and sometimes toward not being angry, according as right reason dictates. Something similar holds true of justice and other things.

[**17**] From the spark (contracted from Adam) by means of which our sensuality—in accordance with a fixed-disposition [*habitus*] or an appetite—is inclined toward something outside the domain of reason, we contract two things, according to Augustine in Book 22 of his *City of God*: viz., ignorance and concupiscence.[47] Therefore, since "the flesh lusts against the spirit,"[48] then because of the different proportions of the body's mixture-of-components and because of the different degrees of harmony [between body and soul] and of inflow [of soul into body], one [man] is [naturally] inclined toward one thing, and another [man] is [naturally] inclined toward another thing. One man is more talented with respect to one body of knowledge; and another, with respect to a different art ..., etc. One [man] is obtuse; another is prudent; another is adept ..., etc. This Paradise [viz., Mary] has the fol-

lowing disposition: in all her members the Holy Spirit placed, as a vessel and a sacristy for Himself, a best-ordered and very fecund natural virtue. There was no trace of resistance. [Mary] came the closest to the state of innocence—more closely than all other begotten women, etc.

[**18**] Now, adventitious virtue is twofold: either it is acquired from frequent acts or it is infused from on high. From frequent prudential deliberations a fixed-disposition of prudence is produced in the intellect. And the case is similar as regards other [adventitious virtues]. It is natural to all things that are reserved for the soul's power that a fixed-disposition is inwardly produced as a result of frequent acts; [this *habitus*] inclines one to [additional,] similar acts. Thus, it is exceedingly useful to have, frequently, the intent to act rightly and to avoid sins. Theological virtues and graces that make one pleasing are infused from on high. And according to Augustine a theological virtue is "a good quality of mind by means of which one lives rightly, which no one uses evilly, [and] which God works in us without us."[49] And so, acquired [virtue] directs, in public affairs, toward human things; infused [virtue] directs, theologically, toward supernatural things. Moreover, the naturally acquirable [virtues] are conjoined in prudence; the infused [virtues] are conjoined in love. Love, according to the Apostle, is the bond of perfection.[50] He who has love has all the moral virtues, and he who does not have love has no moral virtue. When love increases, the other virtues increase, each in its own manner. By way of comparison: when the hand grows, the fingers grow; however, the little finger always remains smaller than the other fingers, etc.

Thus, since infused virtue cannot be present without love, it is incompatible with mortal sin; but acquired [virtue is] quite [compatible therewith]. Because of one act of lasciviousness the entire *habitus* of chastity is not suddenly corrupted, with the result that one is no longer inclined [toward chastity]. Accordingly, the one who has reverted [from the wanton act] suffers grievously. Secondly, infused virtue is compatible with a bad *habitus*. God can impart love to one who still has a *habitus*, a very stong inclination, toward vice. The case is otherwise with acquired [virtue]. Thirdly, infused virtue, with respect to its own material, is compatible with inordinate passions and with temptations; but acquired [virtue], which has subordinated the sensitive appetite to reason, is not [thus compatible]. And yet, infused [virtue] is still more excellent [than is acquired virtue], because it directs one unto a higher end. Mary was in every respect very beautiful ..., etc.

PART TWO
The Virtue of Humility and Its Contrary, viz., Pride

[19] Pride is the primary spiritual vice, and it is the root-vice. (There are five vices, as well as two carnal [sins], viz., gluttony and licentiousness). And humility, which is most virtuous, is in opposition to pride. Therefore, "He has regarded her humility." For He looked from Heaven unto earth at the humility of His handmaiden. He does not say "nobility" or "loftiness," because "He looks at things lowly, and He knows from afar things lofty,"[51] [and] He has deposed the mighty ..., etc.[52] The Psalm [says]: "Who is like unto the Lord our God, who dwells on high and looks [favorably] upon things humble in the heavens and on earth?"[53] He regarded her humility, inasmuch as virginity without humility is of no benefit; however, humility without virginity is of great benefit. Augustine: "A humble married woman is better than is a proud virgin."[54] Our very humble Savior [said]: "Learn from me, for I am meek and humble in heart."[55] Therefore, God regarded His humility. For, being humble, Christ made for Himself—[made] from a very humble, a very pure, a proven and purified virgin—a vessel and receptacle conformed to His own humility.

[20] Consequently, God dwells only in a humble heart. Accordingly, He resists the proud.[56] For pride destroys all the virtues. Humility is the eagerly awaiting vessel of the grateful, but pride is not receptive. Hence, a certain man said to haughty Alexander [the Great]: "God is ready to offer wisdom, but you do not have the wherewithal to receive it." "Into a malicious soul ...," etc.[57] Pride defiles and mars all things. Ecclesiasticus 13: "He who acts pollutingly with the proud will put on pride."[58] All vices arise from pride. The angels fell because of pride. According to Augustine every sin results from either a commission or a transgression.[59] A transgression does not occur apart from disobedience; disobedience does not occur apart from pride. Consequently, pride is the most grave vice. The reason that pride affects in this way the one who has it is that it inflates.[60] Wisdom 4: "The Lord destroys the inflated."[61] [Pride] renders a man unhappy, because from the seed of God's grace, [the man] reaps unhappy pride; he turns day into night and light into darkness. But, for the humble, night will be as bright as day.[62] [The proud man] makes a very bad sale of his possessions, because he sells things precious for a small amount of vanity.

A proud man is deceived, is blinded, and is stultified. All dangerous heresies [arise] from pride, according to Augustine.[63] A gloss on Jeremias 49 [says]: "Your arrogance and the pride of your heart have deceived you."[64] Pride is detestable to God and to man, because it does injury to God and to man: to God, because it usurps from Him that which is *His*, viz., to govern; to man, because he aims to subject to himself one whom nature has made his equal. Moreover, a proud man is detested by his likes; [and] he detests another who is proud, although they both are sons of one Devil. God came into the world humbly, in opposition to pride; and the day of the Lord of Hosts will come upon all the exalted and the arrogant ...."[65] Very beautiful Lucifer became the Devil. A man who desired to be knowledgeable became unknowing.[66] Saul, when he was humble, was made king; when he became proud, he lost [the kingdom] ....[67] Jeroboam lost the headship over the ten tribes.[68] Nabuchodonosor became a brute animal.[69] Judith slew [proud] Holofernes.[70] The Publican was preferred to the haughty Pharisee.[71] He who is pleased with himself is foolish; a proud man is pleased with himself; therefore, ... Moreover, so much folly is present that he who is pleased with himself is displeasing to all others. Pride is a most dangerous weakness, because it is easily incurred, it is difficult to remedy, [and] it is quickly fallen into again.

[21] [Pride] is likened to the wind. Augustine [writes]: "So that your lamp not be extinguished, let it not be exposed to the wind of pride."[72] It is likened to smoke, because the more it rises up, the more it vanishes. The Psalm [says]: "As soon as the enemies of the Lord will have been honored and exalted, they shall disappear as does smoke."[73] It is likened to foam, which passes away quickly. [It is likened] to a small crow that is said to have stolen its wings from other birds; and after it itself was plucked, it remained most shameful, etc. Something similar is said of the ass that wrapped the hide of a lion around [itself], etc. [Pride] is likened to an air-filled bubble that, when pricked with a thorn, is reduced to nothing; such, too, is a proud man who has died. [Pride] is like straw, because of its unsteadfastness. Gold occupies the lowest place but is the most noble; the case is similar with humility, etc. [Pride] is like a spider, a bier, a hen.

[22] Pride is distinguished into inner pride that is twofold: of intellect and of feeling. [Pride] of intellect is a pride that has four forms. [Remember] the verse:

> Of itself, in proportion to one's merits,
> [pride], more than[74] all other things, falsely inflates.

Pride of feeling is distinguished into presumption of one's own excellence and craving for one's own excellence. There is a threefold excellence: of governance, of mastery, of simple outstandingness. Outer pride is something external that proceeds from, and manifests, inner pride. It is either pride in body or in attire, in family, in one's horses, buildings, books, singing. Moreover, at times pride arises because of goods of nature, at times because of goods of fortune, at times because of goods of grace. Certain *goods of nature* are goods of the body; others are goods of the soul. Goods of the body are the following: health, strength, mobility, beauty, nobleness, freedom. Goods of the soul are these: soundness and alacrity of intelligence, goodness of memory, ability to exert oneself, a natural disposition toward the virtues (i.e., natural virtue). The *goods of fortune* are external goods that are in the power of men and that can be taken away: e.g., luxuries, riches, praise, glory, human favor. *Goods of grace* are knowledge and the virtues.

[23] Pride does five harms to a man. It dessicates men, so that they are more easily burned; i.e., it causes them to be without the moistness of grace and without compassion. Ecclesiasticus 6: "Do not praise yourself," etc., "so that you not be left as a dry tree in the wilderness" (i.e., in Hell, where the proud will be burned).[75] Secondly, pride consumes a man and destroys his goods. Thirdly, it disgraces and deceives. Jeremias 44: "Arrogance and your heart's pride have deceived you."[76] Fourthly, pride elevates, so that it especially casts down. Luke 14: "He who exalts himself shall be humbled."[77] Fifthly, pride renders a man altogether unhappy: from good seed the man reaps a bad harvest; he harvests bad things from the good seeds sown; from life he reaps death; from medicine he reaps wounds, etc. There are seven daughters of pride: viz., presumption, ambition, disobedience, irreverence, shame, contempt for what is good, the mocking of good men, vainglory, and hypocrisy.[78]

[24] According to Augustine pride is "a desire for illicit exaltation."[79] Pride [i.e., the proud man] looks askance at all others: he looks askance at his superiors because he is not equal to them; he looks askance at his inferiors because they are not equal [to him]; he looks askance at his peers because they *are* equal [to him]. And if [this ill-will] is internal, it is pride; if it is outward, it is vainglory. Vainglory takes [the following] forms: viz., disobedience (because it does not wish to seem inferior), contention, boasting, hypocrisy, opinionatedness, disagreement (always maintaining the opposite), presumption of originality.

There are twelve stages of pride ..., etc. [**25**] Remedies for pride: ascend by means of humility. The first stage of these [remedies] consists in man's truly knowing that he is weak, is lacking in the good, is evil, etc. However, two kinds of pride—viz., carnal pride and spiritual pride—attempt to draw a humble man away from his humble state. *Carnal pride* suggests to a man that he is better than he is—[better] with respect to knowledge, to wealth, to dignity. And it does not permit him to know of his baseness. According to Cassian the signs of pride are: "in conversation, boistrousness; in silence, bitterness; in gladness, loud and profuse laughter; in hardship unreasonable sadness; in reproof, rancor; glib in speech ...," etc.[80] [If] you wish to vanquish pride, engage prolongedly in humble works [and] in lowly tasks with regard to your neighbor: by sweeping the house [as does] a woman, by washing dishes, by appearing in humble garment, etc. Use plain words; select the hintermost seat;[81] be not called "Rabbi."[82] Etc. Do not vaunt yourself; think of death and of the hour of death. Accustom yourself to these [acts], and you will acquire humility.

[**26**] The other [form of] pride is more endangering: [viz.,] *spiritual* pride, which causes the mind to become puffed up and which elevates the mind above itself, for one glories in his virtues and his merits. There is no vice [other than pride] that so removes [humility and] all other virtues and that so despoils a man of all justice and holiness. In resistence to pride, always think the following: "Not I but the grace of God with me";[83] "by the grace of God I am what I am";[84] "it is God who works [in me] to will and to accomplish in accordance with His good will."[85] You ought carefully to consider your own baseness and the fact that (1) the goods of your mind are [of] God's [doing], not yours, and that (2) you are going to render an account for [your use of] them, and that (3) your failings are yours and are numerous and are worthy of Hell's punishments. In addition, (4) the good that you have is not yours and is not pure but is imperfect, full of carelessness, of lukewarmness, of vainglory, etc. Likewise, you ought always to heed your betters and superiors—and especially Christ Jesus, who said: "Learn from me, for I am meek ...," etc.[86] And so, abase yourself in relation to others. Then you will begin to know yourself, and as a result of persistent and loving exercise you will put on the garment of humility. And wish to be esteemed as humble by all others. And, at length, as regards your great and sublime gifts, you will not exalt yourself but will ascribe everything to God, from whom are all things ..., etc.

[**27**] And, thus, note that the ascendancy over pride is, properly

speaking, [constituted by] a knowledge of oneself. "We ourselves who have been tried, know ourselves ...." [87] And so, Augustine at the outset of his *Soliloquies* prays that he may know himself. Bernard in his thirty-sixth homily on the Canticles [says]: "This knowledge [viz., self-knowledge] does not inflate but rather humbles." [88] Isidor, in his *Definitions*, [writes]: "Philosophy is self-knowledge ...," etc. [89] On the front of the temple of Apollo [are inscribed] the words of one asking by what route he can arrive at happiness. The Delphic Oracle answers: "Would that you knew yourself!" ... Augustine in Book 4 of *On the Trinity* [writes]: "Superior in knowledge are those who prefer to know themselves. A mind that knows its own weakness is more praiseworthy than a mind that, with its own weakness unexplored, explores the pathways of the stars ...," etc. [90] Gregory, in Book 31 of his *Moralia* [states]: "Unless a soul humbly draws near to the Light, it cannot know itself, because it is not present to itself as a whole." [91] And in Book 14 of the *Moralia* [Gregory further says]: "He who wishes to make a judgment about the darkness ought to look at the light." [92]

[28] From this knowledge of oneself arises true humbleness. "For humility is the virtue through which each one becomes lowly to himself by means of very true self-knowledge ...." [93] Anselm in his *Similitudes*, Chapter 37, enumerates the seven steps of humility: The first step is self-knowledge. [Then comes] sorrow over wrongs committed, confession of sins, a willing sense of conviction that, indeed, one is a sinner, the admission that one is despicable, patience in sustaining injury, the love by which he loves his being humiliated and despised. [94] Gregory, [writing] about the humility of Constantine, [states] ...: "A certain man heard many things about Constantine's fame. He came and saw [him and] said: 'I previously thought him to be a tall man ...,' etc. Constantine, [hearing this], thanked him and said 'You alone are the one who has opened my eyes.' The man: 'Constantine loved more greatly one who despised him.' " [95] Etc.

[29] Many men have a feigned humility and a semblance of humility. Jerome in his Epistle 87 [writes]: "Many men attain unto a semblance of this virtue; few attain unto its true nature." [96] Let all verbal fictions be removed! Let simulated behaviors cease! Tolerance of injury reveals the humble man. Augustine in Epistle 38 [notes]: "There is no other way for grasping the truth than humility ...," etc. [97] And there follows: "A very noble rhetorician, when asked what ought first of all to be observed with regard to the rules of eloquence, replied 'Pronunciation.' 'What second?' 'Pronunciation.' 'What third?'

'Pronunciation!' " A similar answer ought to be given regarding humility, when someone inquires about the precepts of the Christian religion." [98] In Book I of the *Lives of the Fathers* [there are] examples of
humility. [Consider the example] of him who never spoke during distress. When asked why not, he answered: "I said to my mind: be you
and an ass one [and the same] thing." [99] (Psalm [72]: "I have become
as a beast before you." [100]) In the same place [we read] about another
man, who was thrust out; and, when recalled, he said that he had
thought himself to be like a dog. [101] Cassian in Book 4 of his *Conferences* [speaks] of Abbot Phinuterus, etc. [102] In the book entitled
Paradise [we read] of Marcarius, etc. [103] [Reflect] on the humility of
Jesus Christ, who was made a man, etc. [104] "If you do not wish to imitate a humble man, imitate your humble God" ....[105] Gregory in Book
34 of his *Moralia* [says]: "O how great is the power of humility. In
order truly to teach humility, He who is great without measure became
very small, even to the point of suffering." [106]

PART THREE
Servitude, Prayer, Devotion

[30] " ... of His handmaiden." [107] The soul becomes God's handmaiden by serving Him most devotedly; and this service consists in
devotion and prayer. First of all, humility must precede [the other two],
because devotion does not arise unless a man prostrates himself
humbly, in true confession, before the omnipotence of God. God first
looked unto Abel and then at his offerings ....[108] That which is offered
with affection of heart, is accepted ...." [109] "For to pray truly is not to
recite contrived words ... [but] to utter loving groans in remorse"
while turning the heart away from the lips and turning it toward
God.[110] "Prayer is devotion of mind, i.e., is [the mind's] turning
toward God through pious and humble affection, underpinned by faith,
hope, and love ....[111] A devout man ought to lift himself above himself
... by justly praying for just things.[112] For "prayer is an ascent unto
God and an asking for fitting things." [113] [31] And such an asking is
threefold: a morally pure asking for the forgiveness of sins; a still more
morally pure asking for the Bridegroom's gifts; a very morally pure
asking for the Bridegroom ....[114]

Augustine in Epistle 47 [writes]: "Pray for a happy life, which all
long for and desire." [115] "One thing I have sought from the Lord ...,"
etc.[116] Augustine adds: "This [seeking] is done more with groans than
with words, more with weeping than with speaking. Let lengthy utter-

ance be absent from prayer. However, let not frequent and fervent prayer be absent. Let the intent persist. To pray much is to importune Him to whom we are praying—[to importune Him] with daily and pious arousing of our heart."[117] Job 31: "Who would grant me an aid, so that the Almighty may hear my desire?"[118] Concerning this [verse] Gregory [writes]: "A true request is made with words not of the mouth but of the heart; with Him words [alone] do not avail but rather desires [avail]."[119] Matthew 6 "Enter into your chamber and pray with the door closed ...,"[120] etc. Luke 18: "It is needful always to pray and not to faint."[121] I Thessalonians 5: "Pray without ceasing."[122] Psalms: "Praise of Him [shall be] always in my mouth."[123]

Now, prayer is said to be the entire regulation of holy desire, and, hence, it is considered as a good work. Moreover, we read that until the fifth hour the apostle engaged in manual labor, and from that hour until the tenth hour he preached. Thereafter, he attended to the needs of the poor, the wayfarer, and himself. [And] he spent the night in prayer. And in this way he was constantly praying.[124] I Corinthians 1: "always giving thanks ...."[125] Moreover, prayer is like a beam of light or like a rope-chain hanging from a rock—[a rope-chain] by means of which a man ascends upward unto God. Therefore, we must be vigilant in our prayers, in accordance with the command of our Savior ....[126] John 4: Our Savior spent the night in prayer.[127] And on the mountain Moses [prayed] with raised hands ....[128] The extent to which prayer avails [is shown by] the example (in the *Lives of the Fathers*) of [evil] Julian, who sent a devil [on a mission], and the devil was hindered for ten days by the prayer of a monk. Etc.[129] Raise questions about prayer. As [it says] in the Gloss of Clementine "*Si Dominum*": "[Ask] what prayer is, why it is called prayer, how it is distinguished into divisions, to whom it is offered, through whom [it is offered], to what end [it is], of what kind [it is], where [it is offered up], and what is its effect ..., etc."[130]

[32] According to St. Thomas "devotion is a certain willingness to give oneself readily to the things that pertain to serving God."[131] Devotion is benevolent readiness, or a ready benevolence, by which the mind actually, duly, and rationally is influenced with respect to serving God. It is the act by which the mind devotes itself to God when it gives itself readily to worshipping and serving God. And [devotion] takes its name from devout readiness: "Unto the Lord the multitude of the children of Israel offered, with a devout and very ready mind, their first-fruits ...," etc.[132] [Devotion] is an act inferred immediately from *latria* [i.e., from worship owed to God alone]. And it is the foremost of

all the moral virtues and is the closest to love. For it directs all other virtues unto the End, viz., God, because it ordains all the virtues to the end of worshipping God.

[**33**] Furthermore, [devotion] is of two kinds. A certain kind is rational, or spiritual, without noteworthy influence on the sensual nature, which, indeed, is not yet calmed and is not yet readily subject to the spirit; rather, it rebels, as Paul complained: "I see another law in my members, warring ...," etc.[133] Thus, on account of the [residual] spark [of inordinate desire] it happens [even] to others [than Paul] that the "flesh lusts against the spirit."[134] "The spirit is ready; the flesh is weak."[135] The second form of devotion overflows into a submissive sensual nature, etc. According to Damacene and the philosophers the sensual nature is not like the lower powers, although it is not rational. For it can obey reason, in accordance with its partaking [of reason]. Reason controls various other brute things, etc. Spirit can do nothing outwardly unless the sensual nature in the organs consent and obey, etc. Otherwise, we could not understand how the spirit could be overcome by the sensual nature, etc. With regard to what is outer, the sensual nature needs to consent to the spirit; indeed, a sailor casts his cargo into the sea in order to save himself, etc. But when such consent occurs without resistence or murmuring, the devotion is called devotion of the senses: "My heart and my flesh have rejoiced in God."[136] "My soul has thirsted for You. In how many ways my flesh [thirsts also]!"[137] And, at times, this calming occurs as a result of the intellect's strong intent and the will's fervent inclination. In these cases the stronger movements expel the weaker ones. Secondly, [this calming] occurs because of the perfect fixed-dispositions of the moral virtues— [dispositions] acquired either from practice or from infusion. These [dispositions] restrain the passions of the sensual nature. Hence, those [individuals] who are exercised in the virtues are less troubled by the sensual nature. Thirdly, [this calming of the sensual nature] comes as a result of God's special grace.

[**34**] However, three stages of virtue are posited in accordance with the [following] three stages: (1) of beginners, (2) of continuers, and (3) of finishers—[i.e., the stages] *from which* [beginning], *through which* [middle], and *unto which* [end]. Similarly, devotion is [of three kinds]: (1) eager devotion, (2) delightful devotion, and (3) fierce devotion. The first [kind of devotion] is present in beginners, where the sensual nature obeys the spirit readily [and] in harmony with the worship of God, but [does so] without relish. And God often grants this [kind

of devotion] to those who serve Him. Delightful [devotion] is present when the sensual nature is submissive to the spirit in a higher degree, and more readily, and when this [state] is profuse with a certain spiritual sweetness and consolation. When this devotion is increased to such an extent that the heart is quite delighted, it is called spiritual gladness. And [when] it is increased to such an extent that the heart cannot contain [it], then it is called spiritual intoxication. This inward, tasty pleasure [both] delights and refects both body and soul more than does any carnal pleasure. And such [inner pleasures] detest worldly consolations, and frequently they are brought to diverse inward affections and to bodily actions—now by weeping, now by singing—in accordance, oftentimes, with the saporific motion and the constitution of the body.

Devotion is spiritually fierce, or spiritually feverish, when the sensual nature in a still higher way—above all consolation temporally granted to it, or able to be granted to it—seeks God's honor and glory with such great fervor, and endeavors to serve Him so insistently, that in a certain manner it seems to rage spiritually. And because it seems to itself not to be able to accomplish at will its intent, it begins to languish. And [the devotion] is called spiritual languor. "Prop me up with flowers; compass me about with apples, because I languish with love." [138] [The devotion] is also called the wounding of love. "My sister, you have wounded my heart." [139] And this weakness also arises from intense delight, to which the heart clings excessively and [by which] it is weakened and made ill. Common to all passion is that it is something distinctly able to be felt, etc. With such a degree [of devotion] the saints saw wondrous things, and they worked with a sufficiency of this [fierce devotion].

[35] All true devotion proceeds from divine love, which, according to Thomas, has four effects: melting (i.e., softening) of a hard heart; enjoyment (i.e., delight), languor, and fervor). [140] If these effects are considered with respect to the sensitive appetite: by reason of melting, the devotion is given the name *eager devotion*. (In the case of eager devotion [the devotion] melts the heart from its state of frozenness: "My soul became melted ...," etc. [141]) By reason of fruitfulness—insofar as [the soul] now possesses that which it desires—the devotion is given the name *delightful devotion*. By reason of languor and of fervor—insofar, that is, as the sensual nature endeavors fervently to obtain that which it desires (and becomes languid-like because it cannot, at will, obtain that which it desires)—the devotion

is given the name *fierce devotion*.

[36] The aforementioned effects can be considered with respect to spirit. But [the following] must be known: it is not the case that every sensible [effect] is much better than is a rational [effect]; nor is it the case that every more greatly sensible [effect] is better than is a less greatly sensible [effect], although, perhaps, this [excelling] can occur, all other things being equal. The perfection of devotions depends on the intent to serve God most perfectly. Devotion is not the sensual nature's *savoring* [of God] or *taking delight* [in God] but is the *intent to serve* [God]. This intent is considered, conceptually, by reference to the service in which it occurs. For example, [it is present] more perfectly and more extensively in the case of counsels than of precepts, because it [relates] to more services. [It is present] more extensively with regard to many [services] than with regard to few. Thirdly, [it is present] more intensely[142] according as there is the aim to serve God more intently. Now, many who have stronger devotion and stronger intent come more slowly, than do the less devout, to devotion having to do with the senses. The reason, perhaps, has to do with their rigid constitution. Accordingly, women come to sensory devotion because they are gentler, etc., than men; and men of one country [come to such devotion] more quickly than do men of another country. Nevertheless, [people] are not holier because of this [softness or quickness]; for, oftentimes, one who cries quickly also laughs quickly; and one who is of tougher nature remains standing, whereas the other falls.

Behold, greater devotion is of lesser sensuality! Those living criminally are often moved to weeping solely because of a reprimand or because of what they are told. At times, strong temptation and indisposition of the body keep the sensual nature from devotion. At times, grace of this [devotional] kind is especially removed from one; for God removes from His friends[143] that pleasantness, [doing so] because of what is better for them, in order that the [grace] received may be safeguarded more carefully and sought more desiringly. Therefore, devotion of this sensory kind is not always in our power. We ought not for this reason to be sad; nor ought we to be impatient, saying "our soul is disgusted with …," etc.[144] Rather, we ought to say to ourselves: "For our sake He does not give, lest we be haughty and misuse the gifts and cling to that pleasantness rather than to service to God, thus falling into spiritual lasciviousness while aiming at our own delight, contrary to the precept: 'Delight in the Lord!' "[145]

NOTES TO *SERMON VI*

1. Luke 1:48. The word "regarded" ("*respexit*") has not only the sense of *looking upon* but also the sense of *having regard for* and of *taking favorable notice of.*

2. In the calendar of the Church, this day commemorates the day of the angel's visitation of the Blessed Virgin Mary, as recorded in Luke 1.

3. Psalms 118:25 (119:25).

4. Psalms 118:107 (119:107).

5. Psalms 118:153 (119:153). Psalms 118:132 (119:132).

6. Psalms 118:159 (119:159).

7. Luke 1:49 and 1:55.

8. Psalms 33:16 (34:15).

9. Here I skip over the repetitive section entitled by the editor of the printed Latin text "*Exordii et divisionis perscriptio prima*," since it is not a part of the sermon but is Nicholas's initial sketch of the beginning parts of the sermon.

10. Romans 5:12.

11. *De Conceptu Virginali* 3 and 27.

12. Romans 7:23 and 8:1.

13. The present view is taken over by Nicholas from Anselm of Canterbury's *De Conceptu Virginali.*

14. See n. 13 above.

15. Galatians 5:17.

16. Ephesians 2:3.

17. Here (at 8:17-19) there is a manuscript problem. I am construing the text as "Non enim dolent de hoc—quia sunt sapientes spiritus, ideo non dolent—quod gloriam non habent ...," etc.

18. John 14:6.

19. Genesis 2:8-9.

20. Genesis 1:9-10.

21. Genesis 2:4-6.

22. The pronoun "*eam*" stands for "*paradisum*," which Nicholas treats as a feminine noun.

23. Gregory the Great, *Moralium Libri* (= *Expositio in Librum B. Job*), IV, Chap. 1 (*PL* 75:633). Not meant by Nicholas to be an exact quotation.

24. This passage is a composite of Canticle of Canticles 4:12-14 and 1:3 and 4:16 (Song of Solomon 4:12-14 and 1:4 and 4:16). Ecclesiasticus 24:20.

25. See note 22 above, re the gender of "*paradisus.*"

26. Canticle of Canticles 6:1 (Song of Solomon 6:2).

27. Hebrews 4:14.

28. Luke 1:46-47.

29. Luke 1:48.

30. Anselm, *De Conceptu Virginali* 2. Not meant by Nicholas to be an exact quotation.

31. Malachias 4:2 (Malachi 4:2).

32. Psalms 18:6 (19:4).

33. Wisdom 7:26. Note also Augustine, *De Genesi ad Litteram*, VIII, 1, 1-2

(*PL* 34:371-372).
34. I Corinthians 13:1.
35. Apocalypse (Revelation) 12:1.
36. Luke 1:34.
37. Luke 1:35.
38. Luke 1:38.
39. Genesis 2:10.
40. Genesis 2:10.
41. Note Romans 7:5, which, in the King James' Version, speaks of the "motions of sins."
42. Matthew 11:29.
43. Ecclesiastes 8:1.
44. Canticle of Canticles 4:7 (Song of Solomon 4:7).
45. Canticle of Canticles 1:14 (Song of Solomon 1:15).
46. Psalms 44:14-15 (45:13-14).
47. Augustine, *De Civitate Dei*, XXII, 22, 1 (*PL* 41:784-785).
48. Galatians 5:17.
49. See Peter Lombard, *Sententiae*, Book II, Distinctio 27, numeral 1 (*PL* 192:714).
50. Colossians 3:14.
51. Psalms 137:6 (138:6).
52. Luke 1:52.
53. Psalms 112:5-6 (113:5-6).
54. Augustine, *Enarrationes in Psalmos*, LXXV, 12, 16 (*PL* 36:968).
55. Matthew 11:29.
56. James 4:6.
57. "Into a malicious soul wisdom will not enter ...." Wisdom 1:4.
58. Ecclesiasticus 13:1. Here (at 20:9) Nicholas has "*coinquinaverit*", whereas the Vulgate has "*communicaverit*".
59. Cf. Augustine, *De Consensu Evangelistarum*, II, 4, 13 (*PL* 34:1077).
60. Daniel 5:20.
61. Cf. Proverbs 16:18.
62. Psalms 138:12 (139:12).
63. Augustine, *De Genesi contra Manichaeos*, II, 8, 11 (*PL* 34:202).
64. Jeremias (Jeremiah) 49:16. *Biblia Sacra cum Glossa Interlineari, Ordinaria, et Nicolai Lyrani Postilla, eiusdem Moralitatibus, Burgensis Additionibus, et Thoringi Replicis*. Vol. IV (Venice, 1588), f. 171^r.
65. Isaias (Isaiah) 2:12.
66. The reference is to Adam.
67. I Kings 15:12-23 (I Samuel 15:12-23).
68. III Kings 12:1-18 (I Kings 12:1-18).
69. Daniel 5:20-21.
70. Judith 13:8-10.
71. Luke 18:10-14.
72. Augustine, *In Joannis Evangelium*, XXIII, 3 (*PL* 35:1583-1584).
73. Psalms 36:20 (37:20).
74. Here (at 22:5) I am reading "*plus*" in place of "*post*".

75. Ecclesiasticus 6:2-3.
76. Jeremias (Jeremiah) 49:16 (not Jeremias 44).
77. Luke 14:11.
78. Nicholas here lists nine (not seven) products of pride.
79. Augustine, *De Civitate Dei*, XIV, 13, 1 (*PL* 41:420).
80. John Cassian, *De Coenobiorum Institutis*, XII, 29 (*PL* 49:471A).
81. Matthew 23:6. Luke 14:8-11.
82. Matthew 23:8.
83. I Corinthians 15:10.
84. I Corinthians 15:10.
85. Philippians 2:13.
86. Matthew 11:29.
87. Cf. II Corinthians 13:5.
88. Bernard of Clairvaux, *Sermones in Cantica Canticorum*, XXXVI, 5 (*PL* 183:969C-D).
89. Not Isidor of Seville but Isaac Israeli, *Liber de Definitionibus*. See f. ii^{va}, lines 12-13 of his *Omnia Opera* (Lyon, 1515).
90. Augustine, *De Trinitate*, IV, Prooemium, 1 (*PL* 42:885).
91. Gregory the Great, *Moralium Liber*, XXXI, 12, 18 (*PL* 76:583).
92. Gregory the Great, *Moralium Liber*, II, 20, 36 (*PL* 75:573).
93. Bernard of Clairvaux, *De Gradibus Humilitatis et Superbiae* 1.2 (*PL* 182:942B).
94. *Liber Anselmi Archiepiscopi de Humanis Moribus per Similitudines*, 101-108. [See p. 81 of R. W. Southern and F. S. Schmitt, editors, *Memorials of St. Anselm* (London: Oxford University Press, 1969).]
95. Gregory the Great, *Dialogorum Libri*, I, 5 (*PL* 77:180).
96. These words are not found in Jerome's Epistle 87.
97. Augustine, *Epistolae*, CXVIII, 3, 22 (not Epistola 38) (*PL* 33$_2$:442).
98. *Loc. cit.*
99. *De Vitis Patrum*, V, 15, 30 (*PL* 73:960B).
100. Psalms 72:23 (73:22).
101. *De Vitis Patrum*, V, 15, 64 (*PL* 73:964).
102. John Cassian, *Collationes* [*Conferences*], XX, 1 (*PL* 49:1149B). *De Coenobiorum Institutis*, IV, 30 (*PL* 49:190B-192B).
103. *Paradisus Heraclidis Eremitae* [*Appendix ad Vitas Patrum*], Chap. 6 (*PL* 74:273).
104. John 1:14.
105. Augustine, *In Joannis Evangelium*, XXV, 16 (*PL* 35:1604). Cusa wrongly writes "Homily 15 on John."
106. Gregory the Great, *Moralium Liber*, XXXIV, 22, 54 (*PL* 76:748B).
107. Luke 1:48.
108. Genesis 4:4. (Nicholas writes, mistakenly, "Genesis 3.")
109. Gregory the Great, *Moralium Liber*, XXII, 14, 28 (*PL* 76:230A). (Nicholas writes, mistakenly, "Gregory in [Book] XI of his *Moralia*.")
110. Gregory the Great, *Moralium Liber*, XXXIII, 22, 43 (*PL* 76:701B). Nicholas writes "*amorosos*", but Gregory's text has "*amaros*".
111. Hugh of St. Victor, *De Modo Orandi*, Chap. 1 (*PL* 176:979A).

112. Cf. Lamentations 3:28.

113. John Damascene, *De Fide Orthodoxa*, Chap. 24 (*PG* 94:1089C-D).

114. See, for example, Thomas Gallus (Abbot of Vercelli) *Super Cantica Canticorum Hierarchice Exposita*. In particular, see p. 70 (of the second commentary) in *Commentaires du Cantique des Cantiques*. Text and notes by Jeanne Barbet. Paris: Vrin, 1967. Note also the expression *"castissimis precibus"* in Pseudo-Dionysius's *De Divinis Nominibus* (*Dionysiaca*, Vol. I, p. 123).

115. Augustine, *Epistolae*, CXXX, 4, 9 (*PL* 33_2:497). Nicholas wrongly alludes to Epistola XLVII.

116. Psalms 26:4 (27:4).

117. Augustine, *Epistola* CXXX, 10, 20 (*PL* 33_2:502).

118. Job 31:5. Here the Vulgate has *"auditorem"*, whereas Nicholas (at 31:14) writes *"adiutorem"*.

119. Gregory the Great, *Moralium Liber*, XXII, 17, 43 (*PL* 76:238C). Nicholas does not mean this to be an exact quotation.

120. Matthew 6:6.

121. Luke 18:1.

122. I Thessalonians 5:17.

123. Psalms 33:2 (34:1).

124. Haymo Halberstatensis, *In Epistolam I ad Corinthios*, Chap. 1 (*PL* 117:510B-C).

125. I Corinthians 1:4. Ephesians 5:20.

126. Matthew 26:41 (not Matthew 16, as Nicholas insertts into the text).

127. Luke 6:12 (not John 4).

128. Exodus 17:9-12.

129. *De Vitis Patrum* VI, 2, 12 (*PL* 73:1003A-B).

130. *Glossa in Clementinas*, section "De Reliquiis et Veneratione Sanctorum"; sub-section "Si Dominum" (Venice, 1488).

131. Thomas Aquinas, *ST*, IIa-IIae, 82, 1, corpus.

132. Exodus 35:20-21.

133. Romans 7:23.

134. Galatians 5:17.

135. Mark 14:38. Matthew 26:41.

136. Psalms 83:3 (84:2).

137. Psalms 62:2 (63:1).

138. Canticle of Canticles 2:5 (Song of Solomon 2:5).

139. Canticle of Canticles 4:9 (Song of Solomon 4:9).

140. Thomas Aquinas, *ST*, Ia-IIae, 28, 5, replies.

141. Canticle of Canticles 5:6 (Song of Solomon 5:6).

142. Here (at 36:15) I am reading "*intensive*" in place of "*extensive*".

143. Cf. John 15:15.

144. Numbers 21:5.

145. Psalms 36:4 (37:4).

Sermon VII: Remittuntur Ei Peccata Multa
("Many sins are forgiven her ....")
[July 22, feast day of Mary Magdalene,1431;
preached perhaps in Koblenz]

[1] "Many sins are forgiven her because she has loved greatly." [1]

Of Mary the sinner, enveloped by much uncleanness of sin and darkness of sin, there was made a very pure tabernacle of the Holy Spirit; and in most glorious triumph Mary was conveyed, on today's date, unto the joys of Heaven, because she loved greatly, etc. For love covers a multitude of sins ....[2] [This] public sinner, as Luke calls her on account of the enormity of her sins—[this sinner] who was scorned by the proud Pharisee—is received into the grace of Christ because she loved ..., etc.[3] [This] woman—from whom, according to Mark,[4] Christ cast out *seven demons* (i.e., according to Gregory in a homily,[5] cast out *all kinds of sins*)—was reconciled to God because she loved. Wherefore, Christ, the true [Good] Samaritan, washed wounded Mary with wine and oil and restored her to health.[6] Ezechiel 16: "I saw that you were trodden under foot [and lying] in your own blood. And I said to you while you were [lying] in your blood: 'Be alive.'" And a few lines later: "I spread my garment over you and covered your shame. And I washed you with water and cleansed away the blood on you. And I anointed you with oil, and I clothed you with embroidery ...," etc.[7]

Mary Magdalene, "the sinner." First of all [I will speak] of sin and its effect.

"She loved." Secondly, [I will speak] of love.

"Her sins are forgiven her": here [I will speak] about the grace of forgiveness.

[I will speak] briefly about three things: about sin, about love, and about forgiveness.

PART ONE
On Sin—especially on Licentiousness

(a) *What sin is; and about its effects.*

[2] According to Ambrose sin is a transgression of the divine law and is disobedience to the Heavenly commandments.[8] According to

131

Augustine [to sin] is to cling to a mutable good after having spurned an immutable good.[9] "Sin is the desire to obtain or retain that which justice forbids," according to Augustine.[10] Sin, according to Augustine in Book 22 of his *Against Faustus*, "is that which is done, spoken, or desired contrary to the eternal law."[11] That is, it is the commission or the omission of a deed, of something said, etc. But in and of itself sin is nothing. For with respect to the *act* sins pass away; and they remain [only] with respect to the *effect*.

[3] Now, there are many effects of sins. At present, let some things be said briefly but decidedly about these effects. [Sin] exceedingly displeases God—to such an extent that, because of sin, He drowned almost all of His works (viz., almost all men and [other] creatures) by means of the Flood (Genesis 7). Indeed, [He hates] whatever sin touches. He hates not as do men, who hold onto vessels and pour out the bad wine, etc.; rather, together with the sin He hurls into Hell the vessels of sin (viz., the rational soul, [which is] His own image). Wisdom 9: "The wicked and his wickedness are hateful to God."[12] God hates sin to such an extent that, on account of [sin], He gave His innocent Only-begotten [Son] over to death. God first cast out sin from Heaven; and because it remained in the world, He descended in order to drive it away. Matthew 8: "He will cast all our sins into the bottom of the sea."[13] Sin pleases the Devil. For he loves nothing else—neither gold nor silver—but says: "Give me the souls; let [him] take the other things."[14] To that end Satan always works. Job 1: "I have gone around the earth ...," etc.[15] The Devil has an insatiable appetite for sin. "He goes about as a roaring lion, seeking whom he may devour."[16] ... Job 40: "He will drink up a river and will not wonder; and he trusts that the Jordan may run into his mouth ...," etc.[17]

[4] Sin is a weakness by which the world is destroyed. It is a *tertian fever* caused by threefold lust. I John 1: "All that is in the world ...," etc.[18] Sin is a *quartan* [*fever*], because it is characteristic of the heart, of the mouth, of the deed, and of the habit. "Return, return, O Sulamitess. Return, return."[19] Lo, "return" is said four times. Sin is a *daily fever* because of pride, which is present in every sin. Sin is like the rottenness in an apple, because the rottenness removes the color, the value, the taste, and the fragrance. Similarly, sin removes the adornment of life, the fragrance of a good reputation, the value received from grace, and the taste of glory. Sin is like a bodily wound which, when it is fresh, permits itself to be touched and pressed against—but scarcely does so after three days. Likewise, in the case of

sinners …, etc. And there are three days—viz., the committal, the habituation, the obstinate persisting—after which the sin does not admit of being touched. Proverbs 1: "The sinner, when he comes into the depths of sins, despises." [20] [See] Isaias 30. [21] "Their malice blinded them." [22] Hence, "they have hated him who rebukes at the gate." [23] Sin is like a flaw that is in a garment. Just as the merchant displays only the top side, so the Devil shows only [sin's] titillation, not its end-result. Sin is like a game played with *con*-men, who in the beginning allow one to win but who in the end take everything, etc. Sin is like a net in which a fish entangles itself all the more in proportion to its movements, etc. It is like a bond by which a cow is led to the slaughter, a falcon to the perch, and an ape to the tree-trunk, etc. Proverbs 7: He does not know that he is being drawn as is a fool to bonds, etc. [24]

[5] There are two effects of sin: stain and guilt. The stain [of sin] is the privation of beauty in the soul because of a forbidden act. Just as the body is soiled from contact with what is unclean, so the soul is stained from its affection for what is forbidden. Thereupon it loses the gleam of the divine light and the adornment of grace. Moreover, God is the life and the cleanliness of the soul, which, in sinning, falls very far away from God. And mortal sin is just such a stain; it turns [the soul] away from God, and it deprives of love and of the grace that makes [one] pleasing [to God]. Venial [sin] stains only lightly and does not in the foregoing way altogether transform and mar. Accordingly, it removes the act of love and the fervor of love—but not the *habitus* of love, etc. Guilt indicates deservedness of punishment. Now, these effects [of sin, viz., stain (*macula*) and guilt (*reatus*)] are usually called punishment (*poena*) and blame (*culpa*). According to Thomas [25] he sins in one way (contrary to the equal measure of friendship) who sins against God (in that he does not pay the affection that is owed) and does so either by loving creatures more than God (as happens in the case of mortal sins) or by loving creatures less than God, nevertheless inordinately (as happens in the case of venial sins). And he sins in another way (contrary to the equal measure of justice) in that he either does not pay to God, or he takes away from God, a thing that is owed to God—viz., honor, reverence, and service. By virtue of the first [debt] guilt and stain are contracted from the disorderedness of the will; and love is lost (in the case of mortal sins), or the fervor of love is lost (in the case of venial sins). By virtue of the second [debt] a man is made deserving of eternal punishment (because of mortal sins) or deserving of temporal punishment (because of venial sins) and is made

deserving that there be taken from him, through punishment, that which he unjustly took from God through disobedience.[26]

[6] One's delighting in created things less than one's delighting in God is a venial sin if the delight is greater than it should be. However, due delight is without sin insofar as it is natural—as [is true of] the eye in its seeing what is verdant, the sense of taste in regard to what is sweet. Moreover, sometimes delight in created things is meritorious: [viz.,] when it is referred to God. The Psalmist [says]: "You have delighted me, O Lord, by Your works ...," etc.[27] The preferring of creatures to the Creator is a mortal [sin] because of the turning away [from the Creator] and the contempt [for Him]. And because of the incurring of guilt, death comes to the soul, because [in that case] the soul's works are dead works. Augustine: Just as no medication heals the wound unless the iron is first of all extracted, so benefits are of no avail unless the sin is forsaken. Likewise, neither fasting nor praying is of benefit unless one is recalled from iniquity, etc.

[7] Sin is committed *in the heart* in four ways: by the instigatory thought [of it], by taking pleasure [in it], by consent [to it], and by the brazenness of one's defense [of it]. The first [of these is done] by the Devil; the second, by the flesh; the third, by the spirit; the fourth, by taking-pride-in. In these same ways [sin] is accomplished *in deeds*; first [the sin is committed] in secret; then the guilty one acts openly before the eyes of men; next, there comes the habituation; finally, there comes the obstinate persistence or the false hope. According to Jerome we are born of the Devil as often as we sin mortally.[28] Hugh [states]: The Devil works destabilization in those minds which, inwardly, are without ardor from the heat of God's love but which, outwardly, now rejoice in the delight that has come from carnal pleasures and do not foresee what bitterness will resultantly follow [from them], etc.[29] The Serpent induced; Eve was pleased; Adam consented, etc.[30] Sin as habit has bound one with bonds as many times as the habit has been exercised; and so, the habit is broken only with the greatest of difficulty. Hence, the Lord resurrected the girl at home and Lazarus in the sepulcher.[31] [Symbolically speaking]: A dead man lies at home; i.e., sin, at its first stage, is done secretly. Secondly, the sin is subsequently entombed through habit. And when the tongues of those who eulogize the man condone [the sin], it is removed only with very great difficulty. Take note of this [consequence], because a sin that is supported by the tongues of the depraved is removed only with difficulty. We must take care to safeguard, above all, the eye. From sight arises the illicit

thought and, as a result, the sin. Take note of this [fact]! For the ordering is such as follows: from sight comes the thought; from the thought comes the taking-pleasure-in; from the taking-pleasure-in comes the consent; from the consent comes the perverse deed. Later there comes the bad habit, from which a necessity follows; from this necessity comes stubborn persistence, from this persistence comes hopelessness, from which comes eternal damnation.

(b) *Licentiousness: what it is like; and its varieties.*

[8] Licentiousness is a mortal sin that is contrary to the precept "Do not commit adultery." The lust of licentiousness is distinguished in seven ways. *In the first way*, at the time when the lust consists only in its initial motion, it is a venial [sin]. There follows, *secondly*, the consent to the titillation (although there is no wish to proceed to the act); and so, [the sin] is mortal. *Thirdly*, there is consent to the deed, were it to occur; and this [sin] is also mortal. *The fourth way* occurs when the lust is not only had in the heart but is also fed by sight; [this is a] mortal [sin] because "he who looks upon a woman ...," etc.[32] For at that time he fully consents to the inordinate desire. Because of the fact that if someone were to look upon a woman as a thing of beauty, it would not be a sin, there is added [in the Scriptural verse] "... to lust [after her]." *The fifth way* occurs in the case of foolish chatter[33] —as when someone woos a woman or has intimate conversations with her; [this is a] mortal [sin]. *The sixth* [way has to do with] turpitude—for example, with regard to kisses, embraces, and lascivious touching. It is a mortal [sin], and the sin is greater the more the inordinate desire is kindled by such things—[kindled] on account of one's very nearness to the fire. And so, the non-lustful touching of a woman is not an evil; but the lustful touching is a mortal [sin]. *The seventh way* [occurs] when the deed itself ensues; the deed is a mortal [sin], unless marriage excuses it. The initial motions of sensuality are not classified as sin. However, the retention of the receipts [of this motion]—[the retention] with lingering pleasure but without consent—is a venial [sin]. But the consent [thereto] is mortal, etc.

[9] Licentiousness is like Gehenna. For in licentiousness there is the fire, viz., of lust; there is the worm, viz., remorse of conscience; there is the brimstone, [viz.,] the stench of ignominy. Licentiousness is like a foolish merchant who takes something worthless (Proverbs 6: "The price of a harlot is scarcely one denarius.")[34] in exchange for something precious: he frivolously sells to the Devil the thing that

Christ has purchased at great price. Even the poorest licentious man will be condemned, because he has done harm to everything: to God, to the saints, to his soul, his reputation, his substance, to [God's] glory and grace. Licentiousness is like a crow that hangs around corpses; and it is like a foolish warrior who takes no precautions against women who are the Devil's weapons. Licentiousness is like a large net that ensnares all fish, because licentiousness envelops the entire world. It is the Devil's fish-hook. (Habacuc 2: He lifted them all with his hook.)[35] It is like a Greek fire,[36] like a horse that is not directed without reins and spurs. It is like a ship[37] that is not being steered amid the waves. It is like mud, etc. Licentiousness leads to very dire poverty. It is like the Prodigal Son.[38] It casts one into servitude; it causes a man's baser part to dominate; it makes a man, created in the image of God, to be like the beasts. Licentiousness makes one foolish, as in the case of Solomon (III Kings 6: His heart was condemned because of women[39]). Licentiousness kills by means of death from guilt, death from ignominy, and death in Hell. (Ecclesiastes 7: "I have found a woman who is more bitter than death …," etc.)[40] Anguish is present in this sin [of licentiousness]. Oftentimes a five-[hour][41] sleeplessness precedes a festival of one hour. There is a thing most vile: a damsel who allowed herself to be corrupted, believing the episode to be wondrous, wanted to kill herself when she [later] appeared [to herself] so vile. Shamefacedness is present in this sin [of licentiousness]. (Job 23: "The eye of the adulterer watches for darkness.")[42] Stench [is also present in this sin. Consider] the example of the angel, etc.[43] By means of this sin [of licentiousness] the Devil acquires pairs of human beings, etc.

(c) *The eternal punishments of mortal sin.*

[10] Mortal sin effects the soul's death. Now, we must first note the severity of infernal punishment; secondly, the variety; thirdly, the length; fourthly, the universality of the penalties, etc. (i) The punishments of the damned will be very severe, because, according to Augustine,[44] the world's most grievous punishment is less severe than is the punishment of Purgatory. As a sign of this severity, the Savior says there to be weeping and gnashing of teeth there.[45] Descend here, by means of comparisons, to the [consideration of the] harshness of the punishments. For in Scripture there are nine punishments [mentioned]: *fire*,[46] which burns the flesh; the *worm*,[47] which consumes the mind; *stench* (fire, brimstone, winds, etc.)[48]; *cold*, very intermittently;[49] *hunger* and extreme *destitution* (because there is not even a drop of

water there for drinking ...);[50] *lack of a vision of God* [51] (this is the worst thing). Moreover, there is a huge punishment from the *Tormentor*.[52] Likewise, there is *horror* (because *there* there is "no orderliness but is everlasting horror"[53]). Furthermore, there is *darkness*. (Matthew 22: "with hands bound ...," etc.[54] Gregory: "*That* fire has burning but no light."[55]) Likewise, there is pain there.[56] Gregory in Book IX of his *Moralia* [says]: "The damned will be horrified. *There* there will be pain together with dread,[57] a flame together with darkness, death without dying, an unceasing end, an unfailing defect. For the death is a living death, the end is always beginning, and the defect cannot be remedied," etc.[58] The reason is [the following]: Since the Devil and the sinner agree in guilt, it is *just* that [these] creatures be assembled together in the prison of the damned and join in [experiencing] together the punishment of the damned.

(ii) [In Hell] the pain is caused as a result of four factors: [The damned suffer] because they have lost the temporal goods of this world. Secondly, they have lost time, and they would gladly give the whole world in exchange for a single moment of time for doing penance. Thirdly, [they suffer] because they have lost eternal glory and the eternal vision [of God]. (Chrysostom: They have all been tormented in Hell by the lack of seeing God.) Fourthly, [they suffer] because they have gained the vileness of Hell, which is a place dark and needy. *There* there is continuous smoke and stench and the grotesque sight of demons.

(iii) In addition, thirdly, there is *there* continuedness and everlastingness of punishments; for the punishment is maximal and eternal.

(iv) [And, in addition,] there is *there*, fourthly, universality of punishments, because subsequent to the judgmental verdict the body and the soul and all their members suffer. And these punishments remain ever useless and fruitless, because [even] if one who is damned were to shed as many tears as there is water in the ocean, it would profit nothing.

[11] We need to know that there are four places to which souls go immediately after death: viz., the place of unbaptized children, where there is no sensible pain; another place is Hell; another, Purgatory; another, the Kingdom of Heaven. In these places souls are received according to merit or demerit; and these places are suitable for immaterial substances. Augustine:[59] as often as someone commits, not capital wrongs, but very small wrongs, he will arrive in glory by way of antecedent justice—[arrive] as one who has been purified,[60]

either here or there, either by means of fire or by means of intervening alms-giving and fasting. According to this same [Augustine] venial sins [occur] as often as someone takes more food and drink than is necessary, as often as he is impatient with God's chastisement, as often as he speaks more than is needful, is silent more than is expedient, as often as he entertains evil thoughts without consenting [to them], as often as he is careless with regard to the divine office, as often as he loves earthly things less than he does God [but inordinately]. There is no doubt that these and similar things pertain to very small sins. Although the soul is not damned because of these [sins], nevertheless it is marred as if by pustules and by an ugly scab, so that it is not at all admitted to God's embraces in Heaven, etc.

However, there are gradations both with respect to glory and with respect to punishment. St. Thomas: "No bodies are assigned to souls after death. (The souls would be the forms, and the prescribed movers, of the bodies.) Nevertheless, certain physical places are prescribed for these souls because of a fittingness that accords with their merits. Amid these places souls are, as it were, in a place (in the way in which immaterial things can be in a place) according as they come more near or less near to the First Substance, viz., God, to whom (by considerations of fittingness) a superior place is ascribed. (Scripture declares Heaven to be His abode.)"[61] And so, we say that souls that are enjoying God's presence are there [in Heaven] and that other souls are in the opposite place, etc.

Note an example of gradations in terms of the tree of blood-relationships—[note it] by making the main branch of the tree to be a man who through his demerits moves, by degrees, downwards, [farther away from God], and who through his merits moves, by degrees, upwards, [closer to God].[62] Augustine: As far different as a material fire is from a depicted fire, so different is Hell's fire from a material fire. Hell's flame is so ferocious that all the waters of the world would not diminish its heat in the least. Hugh: This fire, where there is the removal of all hope of salvation, does not need to be fed in order always to burn.[63] Thomas: Wherever the elect are [in the next life], they are amidst gladness and glory; wherever the damned are, they are amidst fire and pain, etc.[64] Either the physical fire burns in a consuming way what is combustible in the soul (because the dross, i.e., what is combustible, can be burned away in Purgatory), or else the defiled soul is as a whole forever being burned unconsumably in Hell.

(d) *Virginity, widowhood, and remedies for licentiousness.*

[12] *Stuprum* is the [extra-marital] deflowering of a virgin.[65] How great a sin it is is recognized from the fact that it is an occasioning of all subsequent fornications, just as he who first breaks down a barrier or breaks a lock is a cause of subsequent losses. ([Here give] examples.) "Virginity transcends the condition of human nature; by means of it human beings are like angels. Angels are alive without flesh; virginity triumphs over the flesh."[66] For a virgin has [the opportunity] to reflect on things that are of the Lord ...[67] in order by means of inner and outer holiness to be without blemish, thinking on divine things, renouncing the things of the world, being sincerely earnest, having the oil of Heavenly grace. And, thus, a virgin becomes wise while resisting betrothal. [Virginity] is not commanded. According to Jerome,[68] [writing] to Eustochium, that which is not coerced but is offered [freely] is of greater value. It was very difficult to exercise coercion, in opposition to nature, and to wrest from men a life of angels. The Son of God, having entered into the world, instituted a new family in order that He who was adored in Heaven by angels would have angels (viz., virgins) on earth.

Let the speech of a virgin be prudent, modest, non-loquacious, full of decency. Let a virgin be calm, honorable in company-kept. (Keeping bad company causes many evils.) [Let her be] intent on useful prayers and useful works. (Leisure provides occasion for vices.) [Let her] abstain from gluttony, etc. Beware, O Virgins, [for] God, who can do all things, does not renew [the virginity of] a deflowered virgin.[69] Safeguard this treasure, which is greater than every treasure of the world. Take care not to talk about it; for if you proclaim your treasure publicly, you wish to be robbed.[70] Ambrose in *On Virgins* [tells] about that holy virgin who was at Antioch and was brought into a brothel. She prayed as a dove among hawks, etc.... [He tells] about the soldier who freed her by means of a changed garment; and when he was condemned to death, he was freed by her, etc.[71] [Consider] the example of St. Brigit, who asked that a deformity be produced in her.[72] [Consider] also [the example], from the Book *Paradise*, of the girl who wanted to be sundered into small pieces rather than to consent. [There is also the example] of another [virgin], who secluded herself for ten years in order not to be seen, etc.[73] [There is the story] of the beautiful damsel who secluded herself so that no one would be seduced by her beauty and in whose abode Athanasius hid.[74]

[13] How great this sin [of licentiousness] is in the case of reli-

gious virgins is evident. For it is fornication, adultery, *stuprum*, and
incest. It is adultery because [the virgin is] the bride of Christ. It is
incest because [the sexual relations are] with the wife of our Father,
etc. Let [religious] virgins beware of idle time, of the immoderate con-
sumption of food and drink, of disputes and strife, of procuresses (who
oftentimes are, in this regard, worse than the Devil, because what he
himself cannot do, the procuress accomplishes by her methods.
[Consider] the example of the woman whom the husband escorted, and
she fell into the mud, etc. The procuress is like a poisonous snake. And
so, [procuresses] are cursed, as are serpents; and they are rightly
avoided, because they transmit the fire of licentiousness, etc. Christ
suffered in order to gain souls. A procuress hands over two souls to the
Devil, etc. By the law of the Saxons it was decreed that a virgin who
permitted herself [extra-maritally] to be deflowered would be [hung
and [buried at her parents' house, and the perpetrator would be strung
up above her burial place.[75] Likewise, the Vestal Virgins were
entombed alive if they allowed themselves to be deflowered.

[14] Jerome greatly commends widows who are content with
one [husband]. He offers examples of many [widows. He mentions]
Cato's daughter, who was mourning [the loss of her] husband. When
asked what the last day of mourning would be, she replied: "the last
day of my life."[76] [Jerome tells] of another [widow] who, when it was
recommended to her that she marry for a second time, said: "If I were
to find a good [man] .... I already had one, whom I will never lose.[77]
But if I [were to find] a bad [man], I would be unhappy. [Jerome tells
also] of Porcia and Marcella, etc., and Valeria. Jerome greatly commends widowhood, enumerating—in his letter on widowhood—the
many troubles of the second marriage. There [he speaks] about this
present [topic]: "Let a widow who does not desire to retain [her wid-
owhood] take a husband rather than taking the Devil."[78] Let a widow
beware of bad company, of actors, of singing, of banquets, etc. Let her
garments and her life-style agree with her [state of] widowhood, etc.

[15] Let married women beware of adultery, for it is against the
sacrament of God, against God, [and] against the law of nature: [viz.,
"Do not do unto others] that which you do not wish to be done to
you."[79] By divine law and by human law adultery is punished by
death. Disinheritance of the offspring results. From adultery there also
results incest. [Consider] the example of a brother and a sister who had
sexual relations with each other and who loved each other very pas-
sionately.[80] A lustful mind pursues quite ardently dishonorable things;

it reckons as quite pleasant that which is quite revulsive to God, etc.

[16] The remedies for licentiousness are, [first of all,] to flee what occasions it, e.g., the sight of a woman. David saw [a woman] washing [herself], and he lusted, etc.[81] The wife of Pharaoh cast her eyes upon Joseph ....[82] From the sole of a woman's foot to her head, there is no place that is not full of snares. [Remember] Solomon.[83] "Many have perished because of the comeliness of a woman."[84] [A woman's comeliness] is a fiery sword sending forth arrows from all sides. The eyes are the soul's very swift ravishers. Hence, in Arabia women are veiled, etc. The eyes are to be bound and put into stocks, as are robbers, etc. The eyes are archers that shoot arrows from afar. The eyes are the gateway of the camp: he who controls the gateways controls the camp. And so, if you, O mother, wish to know by whom your daughter is captivated, determine where her eye is, because where one's eye is, there is one's love, etc.[85]

Secondly, [if one is to remedy licentiousness], one must abstain from conversation with women. Ecclesiasticus 9: "Her conversation burns as does fire."[86] It is like a sword that is doubly sharp. [Thirdly,] touching is especially to be avoided. Gregory in his dialogue about the priest who—situated at the point of death and having a concubine who touched him, while the others standing nearby did not know whether or not he was alive—said: "Depart, O Woman, because the small flame is alive. Take away the straw."[87] [Fourthly,] the hearing of lascivious songs and words must be feared. "Depraved communications corrupt good morals."[88] [Fifthly,] dancing must be avoided, because at dances many souls are weakened and captivated as a result of sight and touch, etc. Now, licentiousness is a fire (which is extinguished [or rendered ineffective] either by the removal of the logs or by the application of cold water or by the removal of the cauldron from the fire). Therefore, when you are tempted in thought and deed, inflict on yourself punishments and vexations, just as does he who has burned his fingers. [Sixthly,] remove from your presence food and drink.

One must fight against this vice [of licentiousness] by fleeing. For fire burns straw that has come close. [Licentiousness] is an unclean vice; and so, at the very least, it pollutes. One is better off not to be near the danger, etc. "He who touches pitch shall be polluted from it ...."[89]

Three things usually deceive: women's holiness, self-confidence, and blood-relationship. Love with your mind, not with frequency of physical presence, the woman whom you see living uprightly. Never, [or rarely, let women's feet step into] your guest-chamber ..., etc.[90]

For you are not holier than David or wiser than Solomon or stronger than Sampson. Lust conquers minds of iron, because in the fire even iron melts. Flee blood-related women! Thamar was defiled by her brother.[91] See to it that a man alone not be with a woman alone.[92] For Pharaoh's wife, being alone with Joseph, was tempted, etc. Prayer is effective, as are both study and virtuous activity. If you love a knowledge of letters, you will not love the vices of the flesh. Alms-giving and reflection on death are effective [against licentiousness].

A NOTE ON SIN

[**17**] Rational creatures were created to understand the Supreme Good [and] by understanding it to love it, by loving it to possess it, by possessing it to enjoy it. But when the will departed from the First Beginning—inasmuch as, by nature, the will was to be guided *by* the Supreme Good, *in accordance with* the Supreme Good, and *for the sake of* the Supreme Good—then because every sin is a disordering of the mind, actual sin [93] is a disordering. (With respect to the ordering of the mind, virtue and vice came to be.) Either such a disordering destroys the orderedness of justice (and is called a mortal [sin] because it separates from God, by whom the just soul is enlivened), or it does not destroy the orderedness of justice, but [only] disturbs it, and is a venial [sin]. Forgiveness of this [latter kind of sin] can be obtained quickly, because grace is not lost because of this sin, nor is God's enmity incurred. Now, the orderedness of justice … [stipulates] that an immutable good be preferred to a mutable good, that what is honorable be preferred to what is useful, that God's will be preferred to our will, and that reason's judgment rule over the sensual nature. And since the law of God prescribes this orderedness and forbids the opposite, one who acts against these [decrees] sins mortally. For according to Ambrose "mortal sin is a transgression of divine law and of Heavenly commandments by disobedience." [94] And a sin against the divine law is either a sin of commission or a sin of omission.

Now, if one loves a [given] mutable good more than is due, yet he does not prefer it to an immutable good (and similarly regarding other goods), this [act of love] is not directly against [God's] law; but it does not accord with His law and, thus, is a venial sin. Sensuality does not prevail over right reason unless reason consents to it. And so, mortal sin is not committed as regards reason's [ungiven] consent; but, nonetheless, sin results from the disordered motion of the sensual nature; yet, the sin is venial, because in some manner it does disturb the order of justice. For because of the opposition between the sensual nature and reason, as a result of original sin: we have the necessity of committing some venial sin on account of the first motions [of the sensual nature]. For venial sins cannot [altogether] be avoided (although all those motions can be partially avoided), for venial sins are sins in such a way that they are also the penalty of sin. And so, for this reason, they are suitable for forgiveness. Reason is not constrained to consent—[constrained] by means of these motions [of the sensual nature]. However, if the consent and the actual deed result, then because the consent reaches "the *man*" (i.e., the highest part of reason), then the sin is a sin in the full sense. But if there is consent only to the delight and not to the deed, then the consent remains in the lower part of reason, and "the *woman*" sins. Accordingly, if reason, amid the sensual delight, obeys the judgment of the senses, then "the woman" obeys the Serpent,[95] and the mortal sin is less grave. Nevertheless, this sin is imputed not only to "the woman" (i.e., to the inferior part of reason) but also to the upper part of reason (i.e., to "the man"), because he ought to have prevented the woman from obeying the Serpent. And so, according to Augustine in Book XI of *On the Trinity* there occurs in every mortal sin an imitation of the first sin, etc.[96]

[18] The disorderedness that is present in a mortal sin has the form of everlastingness; and so, the punishment that corresponds to the sin has the absence of an end-point. Thus, just as man by sinning departed from everlasting life, and just as this sin remains everlastingly with the sinner because of his impenitence, so too everlasting death [remains with him]. And just as man in *his* perpetuity does not put an end to sin, so God in *His* perpetuity does not put an end to the punishment.[97] And just as man sinned against the Infinite, [so too] he is punished infinitely. And because on account of his incapability he cannot be punished infinitely in an *intensive* way, he is punished infinitely in terms of *duration*. And just as the will of him who has committed mortal sin always after death clings to evil without the undertaking of penance, so too God always punishes without change of sentence, since the perpetuity of the disorderedness requires this [punishment] in the case of the damned. In the case of mortal sin there is delight together with contempt [for God]; and so, the place of punishment is opposite to the place of glory: i.e., the [punishment takes place] in Hell, where [the soul] is punished by means of a material fire. Because of a divine infusion man is afraid of the Devil, to whom he is at that time sensually bound. Similarly, he fears the punishment, etc. The Judge

condemns men in different ways in accordance with the quality of the crime—just as by means of one and the same fire straw is burned in one way, wood in another. And because the sin always remains in equal degree, the punishment too remains equal and unchangeable. Because of the turning away from God there is punishment by means of the absence of one's vision [of God]; because of the turning to creatures there is the punishment from the material fire; because of the battle between the will and reason there is the punishment from them both. Etc.

PART TWO
The Grace of Justification [Expounded] by means of a Dialogue

[**19**] "Why, O Mary, after having entered, do you throw yourself to the ground, and weep, at the feet of the Lord?" She answers: "Because I seek grace …," etc. Four things are required for enlivening someone wicked: [viz.,] the infusion of grace; the expelling of guilt; contrition; and the movement of free choice. Guilt is expelled by the gift of God—yet, not without free choice. Through freely-given grace free choice is recalled from evil and is motivated toward the good. If [free choice] consents to the grace, and cooperates with the grace, then the grace that makes one pleasing is infused, etc. Sin was not created by God. And nothing is so contrary to God [as is sin], because (1) it turns us away from God by deforming free choice, (2) it destroys [God's] freely-given gift, and (3) it makes one liable to eternal punishment.

The deforming of the image [of God in man] and the destroying of grace is an annihilation even unto death. And since the offense against God is as great as is God (who is infinite),[98] man does not by his own efforts rise up again unless he is re-created with freely-given life and unless his offense is pardoned. Therefore, only He who is the Creative Source—viz., the Word of the Father—is also the Re-creative Source. Nevertheless, the Word re-forms in such a way that He does not weaken the appointed laws. And so, He does not compel free choice, but, rather, its freedom remains. And so, for the expelling of guilt there is required not only the infusion of grace but also, in the case of adults, consent. [One gives consent] by (1) conforming oneself to the expelling of guilt—[doing so] by means of hatred of all sins. (This hatred we call *contrition*.) And [one gives consent] by (2) conforming oneself to the introduction of grace—[doing so] by means of accepting, and taking delight in, the divine gift. (This [acceptance] we call the *motion of free choice*.) When free choice is motivated by means of freely-given grace, and when it consents and cooperates for the sake of the grace that makes one pleasing, it arrives in Glory. (Grace cooperates with free choice, even as the rider does with his horse.) Hence, Mary said: "I came as one sick unto the Physician without whom I could not be healed. And I succeeded in kissing His feet and in bathing them with tears."

[20] "How, O Mary, did you enter?" She answered: "Intrepidly, because I very much needed a doctor. And with humility I ascended, in three stages, unto my Lord's feet. When I was on earth a fear of being punished for sins imposed itself. I beheld the everlasting reward, and I began to love it. On the one hand, I determined to despise all the goods of the world by means of moderation; and, on the other hand, I determined to have patience amid adversity.

"I ascended to the first stage [of humility] by means of contempt for the world, to the second stage by means of self-renunciation, to the third stage by means of humble love for Christ. And, in this way, I found most assuredly, by the quickest route, that which I was seeking. I wailed and shed volumes of tears so that I might empty myself of water and so that there could enter into me fire—viz., the fire of love—and the firewood of compassion and the victim [to be sacrificed out] of devotion. I brought ointment that was precious, lovely, fragrant—because I was in search of something quite precious in value, quite fragrant in aroma, quite pleasing in loveliness. It was ointment of spikenard, because I humbled myself as a small, fragrant tree of spikenard at the feet of the master, so that my spikenard would yield up its fragrance. I bowed down at the feet of the Lord in order, later, to ascend; I reduced myself to ashes in order to emit my fragrance; I mortified myself in order to rise up again.

"When I mounted up to the first stage, I wept *with tears of remorse* in order to cleanse myself in the sight of so great a King. At the second stage I wept *with tears of compassion* when I stood at the tomb with soothing ointment. I wept at the third stage [*with tears*] *of devotion* when after the Resurrection I found what I had sought; thereupon, my soul was at ease amid the bath of tears. At the first stage I wept because I knew myself to be an unclean sinner, and 'my eyes sent forth springs of water.' [99] I lamented the habitation of the present life: 'Woe is me, because my sojourn is prolonged!' [100] I wept because I was afraid of Hell. 'Weeping, I wept at night' [101] (i.e., amid my sin). At the second stage I wept because I knew that Christ had become incarnate in order to liberate me. And these tears were also my bread day and night. [102] I wept because I had compassion for human wretchedness. I wept out of longing for our Heavenly home. I sat above the rivers of Babylon, treading under foot the transitory things of the world, and I remembered Sion, our Heavenly home." [103]

[21] "Why, O Mary, did you not formerly weep? Why have you waited so long?"

Mary: "[I did not weep formerly] because the haughtiness of pride did not allow me to. The high mountains are quite dry, and only the valleys are moist. I was contaminated by earthly things; I had a hardened heart. I, who would not weep, was frenzied and foolish, being exceedingly occupied with other concerns that had to do with pleasures, being dessicated by their heat. My heart was frozen by a multitude of sins—[frozen] until this present day of the heat of the Sun of justice,[104] my Christ. I thought of Anna, ... who, when she had a bitter soul, prayed to the Lord, while weeping copiously; and her prayer was answered.[105] I thought of Ezechias's [prayers'] having been answered because of his weeping.[106] Isaias 28: 'I saw your tears, and, lo, I have healed you.' [107] Likewise Tobias, likewise Sara, received answered prayers because of their tears. Thus too, Judith;[108] thus too, David: 'You have placed my tears in Your sight ...,' etc.[109] And so, I inferred that God is strongly moved by tears. Hence, I approached and wept."

"O Mary, if this lamenting of yours was penitential, indicate what kind it was and how extensive it was."

Mary: "It was loving and sorrowful, so that [my] sins displeased [me] by virtue of their being abominating and because of their offense against God. [My lamenting occurred] with such a great degree of sincere sadness that I have never had a greater degree and never could have had. And [my lamenting] was greater than one's mourning for a lost only-begotten son, because it was mourning for a lost soul. Nothing in this world has displeased me as much as having offended against God; for I have ascended unto God, whom I purposed to love above all other things. My offense against Him was rightly graver to me than all other offenses."

[22] "O Mary, what did you obtain?"

Mary: "... the forgiveness of sins, happiness, and the receiving of grace. I obtained a new Bridegroom, etc. For by means of my tears the grace of God washed away my soul's stain and my soul's unlikeness [to God]. It removed my guilt and punishment; it made of me a bride pleasing to God."

"O Mary, how great a grace you have found! [It is so great] that there was removed not only the guilt of, but also the punishment of, all your sins. Consequently, having been freed from [consignment] to Hell and to Purgatory, you expected only glory, in an immediate way [i.e., without intermediate sojourn in Purgatory]. O how great was your contrition! You approached boldly unto the feet of the Lord—of the God and the man—and you kissed them. Tell us for what reason."

Mary: "I kissed His feet at the first stage of my ascent. I kissed His hands at the second stage—[i.e.,] at the time He was taken down from the Cross. I kissed His mouth in the wilderness.[110] And now, when apprehending Him as a whole, face to Face, I have joined myself to Him in Glory. I kissed His feet by means of a humble turning. While prostrated, I kissed the right foot of His mercy. And the Lord extended to me, in supreme friendship, the foot that up until then had been dreadfully opposed to me, viz., [the foot] of justice and of truth. And by the course of nature a deep love was kindled in me; and, at the same time, the Loving One infused into me love and grace; and He forgave me my many sins, because I had much love. Because of sins my rust-covered soul was greatly contaminated; and a huge fire of love instantly purified [it], etc. All the things that in me were vain have been turned to the worshipping of God. My eyes have shed a fountain of tears for washing His feet. My hair has wiped [His feet]. With the ointment of devotion and of remorse I have anointed [them]. And I—who was a sinner—have been reconstituted into God's bride; and in me there was planted love, which for as long as I have lived has not ceased to increase very fervently in depth."

The foregoing points [conclude] the second part.

PART THREE
The Dialogue Is Continued as regards Love

[23] Now, [I will say] some things about Mary Magdalene's great love [*dilectio*] and about love that is *caritas*.[111] In the text "because she loved ...," etc., there is indicated the fervent love (*dilectio*) on the part of Blessed Mary Magdalene. All the things that the Gospel-writer proclaims, in today's text, that she did indicate nothing other than that she loved very fervently. Indeed, the forcefulness of the love extinguished in her all inordinate desire. For *caritas* is a divine fire that does not allow another fire to burn upon the altar of the Lord, i.e., within a contrite and humbled heart. And so, it has readily burned away all sin, which is contrary to God.

[24] "O Mary, why did the Lord say that you have loved greatly?"

Mary: "The Highest Good, because it is highest, is to be loved supremely. And it is to be supremely enjoyed as Highest Good, and supremely adhered to through love, and [supremely] rested-in as in one's final goal. Now, then, right and orderly love (*amor*), which is called *caritas*, is directed chiefly unto that Good, which it enjoys and in which it finds rest. And this [enjoyment and repose] are the reason for loving it. Hence, it is that *caritas* chiefly loves that Good as a Good that makes one happy; and, consequently, it loves those things which are suitable to be made happy by that Good; for example, our neighbor and our body can be made happy, together with our spirit. Hence, God, our neighbor, our spirit, and our body are to be loved. But the following order is to be retained: first, God *above us* [is to be loved]; secondly, the spirit *within us*; [then] our next of kin *around us*; and [then] our body *below us* as subjected to us. God is to be loved for His own sake; our spirit is to be loved above all other things that revert unto God; and our neighbor is likewise to be loved; and, lastly, our body, as being the least good, is to be loved.

Now, love is the weight of the mind and is the source of all mental affection—[affection] which is easily directed toward [the mind] itself, is directed toward its neighbor with difficulty, and is elevated unto God with more difficulty. Hence, there is a twofold commandment: one commandment directs [our love] toward God; the other commandment [directs our love] toward our neighbor.[112] For all of the commandments have to do with God or our neighbor; i.e., [they direct us] unto the End or unto that which is a means to the End. And so, [Christ] commands that I love greatly, because *caritas* is the form and the end-goal of the virtues. It unites all the virtues with the Ultimate End, and it binds all things together in an ordinate way, because it has one principal object that is loved. This [object] is the reason for loving all the other things that are destined to be bound, by the bond of love, unto the one Christ, as the Head, and to His body, which contains within itself all of those who are to be saved.[113] For in our eternal Heavenly Homeland God will be all-in-all in assured eternity and in perfect peace. And through love all things will be ordained in a common community and will be indissolubly connected by [that] ordination and will be indissolubly ordered by [that] connection."

[25] "O Mary, tells us: In what way did you enter into love?"

Mary: "*Caritas* for God was poured forth into my heart through God's Holy Spirit,[114] for [this pouring forth] is the role of the Holy Spirit. I prepared a dwelling-place for my God, and He dwelt in me by

His very kindly grace, and He motivated me to love Him. He kindled my heart, He aroused my sleeping soul, and He illumined my darkness. I had the Holy Spirit, through whom I loved and without whom I was unable to love. For the [Holy Spirit] alone elevated my soul's affection unto being *caritas* for God. (Without the Holy Spirit this affection is *cupiditas*.)[115] By means of *caritas* the soul is moved unto the End toward whom it tends. All *cupiditas* was extinguished in me so that *caritas* could increase. My soul was moved, by *caritas*, toward enjoying God for His own sake and toward enjoying all other things on account of Him, my Beloved. At first, my soul was moved by *cupiditas* to enjoy all things—[to enjoy them] apart from God and for their own sakes, not for God's sake. Then by the glue of love I clung to God alone when I spurned all things for His sake. Love of the world expels *caritas* for God, and vice versa. It is necessary that he who endeavors to have *caritas* have God, because God is *Caritas* ...," etc.[116]

[26] "O Mary, I understand that earthly things cannot be commingled with love for God; rather, all these [earthly things] must be forgotten. And because the soul cannot exist without love, it was placed among creatures. The soul loves either in an upward direction in the course of being perfected, or in a downward direction, in the course of dying. Since love for the world is delicious, what kept you[117] from loving it?"

Mary: "After I had seen with the eye of the intellect that all created things are vacuous and that all pleasantness, joyousness, power, and wealth—regardless of how they affected me—did not satisfy, because they are mutable: I found that I was in error. And turning about, I sought God alone and found Him whom I have loved, in whom there is all fullness, in whom the inner man senses, without taste, everything delectable; senses, without color, all beauty; without quality, all delightfulness; without tangibility, His kiss and His embrace."

[27] "O Mary, at the second stage [of humility], when you kissed Christ's hand and wailed at His tomb, what experience of *caritas* did you have?"

Mary: "The strength of the Most High increased in me. I returned to recalling the benefits that God had given me, the works of His hands, the fact that He had given me [the gifts of] existing, living, and understanding, and the fact that for my sake He was made a man and gave Himself over to death. And above all else, I recalled that my Beloved gave me the love [*amor*] by which to love Him, so that He bound me to Himself by a very strong bond. 'And my soul melted.'[118]

I lamented very bitterly the times in my past when I was aflame in my filthy lust and did not know my God. I lamented my having squandered so much time. I lamented my being a very unhappy woman—[unhappy] by virtue of the fact that I did not know the Lord. And *caritas* for my God was strengthened in me (1) when I passed over to a knowledge of His existence, His goodness, power, truth, and glory, and (2) when in deepest humility I despised my entire self and recognized that to me, a most base creature, God had given so many goods. I wept with immense joy when I sensed His supreme delightfulness and graciousness—[sensed], viz., that I, a most despicable creature, was bound to Him, and strengthened, by bonds of love. *Caritas* was strengthened in me, in order, at length, to be perfected. I sensed that God is *Caritas*, because since *caritas* was in me, I loved the decrees, and the precepts, of God alone. No knowledge of the world entered into my heart. Whatever pleased God was pleasing [to me]; and whatever was displeasing to God was displeasing to me. When through *caritas* God dwelt in my soul, I loved Him with my whole soul and with all my strength."

[28] "I know, O Mary, that *caritas* is God's work and not man's, even though man has the command to love God. Although of himself man cannot do this, nonetheless he can love in such a way that he loves nothing as much as he loves God or loves nothing more than he loves God. And he can bring it about that in every way possible he conforms himself to love and makes himself fit for love—in spite of the fact that each one does not always achieve that [required] degree of love with his whole soul, mind, and might. Disclose, then, O Consoler, the pathway to love."

Mary: "Offer a contrite heart and your entire self to God, for God bestows on every living creature a blessing.[119] Let there be in you [both] sorrow for [sins] committed [and] good intent with regard to the future. Listen attentively to God's word, just as I oftentimes sat at the Lord's feet listening to His words. Be ready to do a good work. (Love is not idle …, etc.) These, then, are the signs of the first stage of love.[120]

"But [the following are signs] of a robust degree [of love, i.e., of the second stage of love]: frequent[121] examination of conscience in regard to all mortal and venial [sins]; the reducing of lust; the vital exercise of the spiritual senses (just as the body is shown by the outer senses to be alive, so by the exercise of the inner senses[122] the soul is shown to be alive); the diligent keeping of the commandments; the exhibiting of the divine truths (even as I, Mary, preached publicly the word of the Lord)."

[29] "O Mary, tell me the signs of the third stage of *caritas* and of the third kiss." [123]

Mary: "I was dying daily for Jesus, my God, with incentives of love in my heart. The world held no taste for me. I was desirous of being dissolved and of being with Christ. [124] I sought out desert places because all things became worthless to me. I desired to die daily for God [125] or for my neighbor in honor of God. I loved my enemies, and I did good things for them for God's sake. I underwent all adversities with gladness, and I bore them with patience. I renounced all things by following Christ. With a childlike fear [126] I feared God alone, lest I lose Him as Bridegroom. I emitted deep and intimate mental sighs when the recollection of my Beloved touched the inner recesses of my mind. My love sent forth sighs of love as messengers. My desires were lofty, because I desired only the Most High. My thoughts were languid, because where my treasure was, there was also my heart. [127] Because of the magnitude of my love all things except my Beloved were loathsome to me. I was languishing because I desired Him alone, [128] whom I did not yet have as I desired to. I loved at the first stage of the ladder, i.e., [the stage] in regard to the first kiss, [the kiss] on the feet. I loved fervently at the second stage, viz., with regard to the kissing of the hands; at the third stage I languished. Those who are beginners *love*; those who have advanced *love fervently*; those who have been perfected *languish*.

"I was awaiting in drudgery my dissolution and my being with Christ. [129] Wings of very lofty contemplation were given to me, and manna of Heavenly succulence was given to me for thirty years [while I was] in the desert. I was caught up unto God seven times a day, my body having been elevated from the earth by means of a maximal desire to be with my Beloved. I was expecting, with eagerness, to die for my Beloved and in my Beloved. For when love tends toward the object-loved, nothing else tends more swiftly, more pointedly, more penetratingly, more subtly; for by its nature, love does not rest until, supernaturally, it penetrates the entire depths of the lovable and passes over, as much as it can, unto the whole of the lovable. And so, when the course of this love is impeded or delayed in any way, the whole mind is perturbed and grows weary in waiting. Very frequently I fell into states of ecstatic affection, together with ecstasy of mind; for because of [that] very vehement love I did not belong to myself but

was my Beloved's. I sent forth my spirit so fervently to my Beloved
that I was ecstatic in mind. For he who loves perfectly lives not for
himself but for God, whom he loves; and he is directed, governed, and
instructed, etc., by this Beloved."

[30] "O Woman, you were given two large eagle-wings—[a
wing] of affection and [a wing] of intellect—so that you might fly into
the desert of contemplation and of penitence, where you placed your
nest on the cliffs and tarried among the rocks and the jagged stones.
When [you did this], what did you have with you, O Poor one?"

Mary: "I was not poor—I who, in the company of angels, was
elevated seven times a day unto contemplating Him whom my soul
loved. I had gold that was tested by fire and had iron that was made
malleable by fire; I had spiced-wine that was tasty, pungent, and
strong, because I loved strongly, prudently, and perseveringly. I had
birds of prey, which rarely (except when they prey) touch the ground.
I had a large sea-ship that was propelled by the breath of the Holy
Spirit. I had a mallet-of-death by means of which I mortified the flesh.
I had a fountain, and a well, of living water—water [whose tempera-
ture] was opposite to that of the mundane air: the well was cold in the
summertime and vice versa. And the bucket for the well's water hung
on a tightly-twisted rope, which[130] is strong. I had a fine-specimen of
a hunting dog that did not feel the thorns while hunting. My house was
of well-baked brick; it was not broken apart by storms and rains. I had
fruit-bearing trees—[trees] which had fruit of graciousness, blossoms
of honorableness, leaves of truth. I had a wedding dress of wondrous
texture and fabric; the dress was very shiny and was red in color; the
fire of the Holy Spirit wove it from Christ's blood,[131] etc. I had the
bread of angels and manna from Heaven ...," etc.[132]

[31] "O Mary, did you have things other than the aforementioned ones? You were still very impoverished, because for one-who-
loves there is peacefulness only in the beloved."

Mary: "The Bridegroom of my soul was always with me. The
Lord betrothed me with the remission of sins and with the gifts of the
Holy Spirit. And His left hand was at the base of my head, and His
right hand embraced me. I joined myself to Him, and I pressed myself
very closely against Him by the bond of love. And every day I was
bound more closely to Him by the bonds of love; and by the fire of love
I purified and adorned and illumined my soul's tabernacle, wherein
would dwell the Most High, my Beloved. I burned my past filthy
wrong-doings with fire, in order that the Most Pure One would find a

suitable place in me. I pondered and reflected on the beauty of my Beloved; and I reflected on the fact that He who is so great and who loved me before I loved [Him] wanted to be loved by me. And the fire of superabundant love burned; and, yet, I was languishing, because I was not loving as I wished to love. But out of the languor there grew love; and the more this fire of love increased, the more my Bridegroom apprehended me by means of a kindlier and clearer spiritual vision and embrace. And when He wanted my soul to be consoled by His love, He inflicted a deeper wound [of love]. And when He kissed me with the kiss of His mouth, the honey and milk beneath His tongue—and the dripping honeycomb of His lips[133]—called forth [in me] an inner desire for kissing more frequently and more deeply, etc."

[**32**] "Tell us, O Woman: when seven times a day angels (i.e., desires and affections—flaming ones, very subtle ones, and very deep ones) elevated you upwards from earthly things and toward your Beloved, what were these very fervent affections?"

Mary: "When I turned totally to my Beloved, I asked my love to raise me gently unto a degree of great love." And Love answered: 'Consider the love on the part of your Beloved, and consider your Beloved's nature, which is incomparable to all things because there is no comparative relation of the finite to the infinite.[134] And think of what the union of infinite love with finite love is. No [union is] higher and more wondrous [than the union] of a creature with the Creator.' Lo, when my intellect and my affection lovingly reflected on these things and lovingly reposited them in my memory, then I ascended to the first stage [of love]. Having returned from this ascent without having been satisfied by it, I requested of Love: 'Elevate me once again, even higher, to the second stage.' And Love said: 'Examine now all the things situated under Heaven—[examine them as to] what kind of things they are in comparison to your Beloved.' And in viewing their transience, I fled [from them, and] through love of Heavenly things I was elevated unto the second stage [of love]. And I disdained loving any earthly, created things; and amid all created things I loved Him alone. And once again I asked Love to elevate me again—[this time] unto the third stage."

"And Love said: 'Reflect on the eternity of your Beloved and on the fact that you will possess Him eternally as your Bridegroom. And you will soon possess Him with all the more gladness, in proportion as the love by which you apprehend Him is the more fervent.'

"And I was elevated. Continual perseverance increased in me, with the result that I increased continually in love. And, once again, Love elevated me by means of an inseparable love, for I was not able at any time fully to explore the goodness of my Beloved, etc. And I was ever contemplating [it]. And, once again, I asked that Love elevate me by means of a [still] higher degree [of love]."

"And [Love] replied: 'God, your Bridegroom (who is a very subtle Spirit, who is omnipotent, and who is the Creator of all things) is united to one who loves Him—[united] with an embrace that is the tighter the more spiritual the one-who-loves has become. And the more the loving-one suffers for the Beloved's sake, the more the Beloved reciprocates [that love].'

"And I was elevated unto the desire to be free from this present fleshly body and to be honored with martyrdom for the sake of my Beloved. Then I once again asked Love, a sixth time, to elevate me still more highly unto the delightfulness of love."

"And Love said to me: 'Do you sense that your Beloved is within you?' And I replied: 'I do, but only a little.' And Love said: 'Multiply your affection and your understanding, as regards the demands of your Beloved.' And I did so, and I ascended; but, still, I was not completely filled with love—because the more I ascended, the more insatiable my love grew to be. And since I still was hungering insatiably much, I asked Love to elevate me still higher unto my Beloved. And this seventh time Love elevated me most highly of all. And after out of maximal hunger I had begun most avidly to taste, somewhat, the deliciousness of my Beloved: my desire was most fervently inflamed. For I was now much hungrier than before; and my Beloved wounded my heart, and I was languishing because I did not possess my Beloved as a whole, as I was desirous of doing.

"And all the senses of my body were paralyzed within me, because my soul was occupied with my Beloved, asking Him (to whom my soul was indissolubly bound) not thus to wound [me]. And my soul turned again, intermittently, to its work, so that [once again] it produced motion in [the body's] members, without, nevertheless, having withdrawn from its Beloved. And it wanted to admit of no consolation, because all things were, as far as it was concerned, dead; and only its Beloved, who had wounded it, was, as far as it was concerned, alive. This love is like one who has extreme thirst, whose thirst would not diminish—no matter what portion of wine be given to him for drinking. Rather, he would thirst all the more; and his thirst would never be quenched—unless he were to imbibe the world's entire supply of wine. In such a way I ascended daily; and I drank [of love] more and more; and more and more I thirsted. I went around wounded so that I might die from love; but I was unable to die. The more I sought to die of love, the more love was alive within me. I asked of Love that it would bring me to death rather than afflict me with so many wounds and with so much lack of strength.

[33] "And, lo, after Love had terrified me for thirty years and then, at last, had made me languid, it determined to grant my wish because I served it faithfully. And it led me, in spirit, throughout the whole world, in order that I might see how my Beloved is so little known and so little honored in the world. It led me throughout idolaters, blasphemers, the proud, the envious, etc. It led me—throughout all the places of the world—unto wars, schisms, hypocrites, adulterers, so that I envisioned only the gloom of dishonor and of baseness and of sin-against-my Beloved, so that I would die. I was greatly tormented, and I was languishing; but I still could not die. Love led me unto Hell, in order for me to see how many souls were there—[souls] created in the image of God but [now] eternally dead—and how relatively few souls were saved. And I was afflicted with very great sorrow; but I did not die.

"And my Beloved[135] asked me: 'Do you fully wish to die in love?' And I replied: I desire this only: that I may live in You alone. And He said to Love: 'Lead my beloved to Jerusalem.' And Love led me to Jerusalem, and there I beheld the holy city of Jerusalem and the very many holy lovers of God. I saw the glorious Virgin Mary together with many lovers of God. I saw Christ as having been born and as on the Cross. And after I had seen my Beloved on the Cross, a weakness-unto-death beset me, because I saw my altogether just, kind, pleasing Beloved, and Loving One, most abjectly hanging [on the Cross] and now exercising the will to die; and I thought myself unable to leave. And I asked Love (1) not to let me see my Beloved die, because I would die, but that (2) Love first of all feed me with the Beloved,[136] so that then I would die in my Beloved. And, lo, my Beloved arranged through a certain hermetic priest that Maximinus would transmit to me, in church, the Body of Christ, my Beloved. This Body I most eagerly received, being elevated, in mind and body, from the earth towards Heaven. And after I had received it, I asked Love[137] to transport me *from* that moment *unto* [the time of] Christ's death. Love commanded: 'Enter the tomb.' And I entered.

"After I had entered, Christ's Love led me, in spirit, unto [that] most bitter death of my Beloved. And together with my Beloved, I died continually in love. And, straightway, Love buried me in my Beloved and together with my Beloved. But suddenly my Beloved—with whom my soul was united in love—arose. And He led me unto an eternal Heavenly Homeland, where now I eternally possess my Beloved in the full satisfying of hunger."

May Christ Jesus, true God and true man, lead us unto this [Heavenly] beauty and enjoyment! Amen.[138]

NOTES TO *SERMON VII*

1. Luke 7:47.
2. I Peter 4:8.
3. Luke 7:39 and 48.
4. Mark 16:9.
5. Gregory the Great, *Homiliae in Evangelia*, XXXIII, 1 (*PL* 76:1239).
6. Cf. Luke 10:33-34.
7. Ezechiel (Ezekiel) 16:6-10.
8. Ambrose, *De Paradiso*, VIII, 39 (*PL* 14:309B).
9. Augustine, *De Libero Arbitrio*, I, 16, 35 (*PL* 32:1240).
10. Augustine, *De Duabus Animabus*, XI, 15 (*PL* 42:105).
11. Augustine, *Contra Faustum Manichaeum*, XXII, 27 (*PL* 42:418).
12. Wisdom 14:9 (not Wisdom 9).
13. Micheas 7:19 (Micah 7:19), not Matthew 8.
14. Genesis 14:21.
15. Job 1:7.
16. I Peter 5:8.
17. Job 40:18.
18. I John 2:16 (not I John 1): "All that is in the world is the lust of the flesh, the lust of the eyes, and the pride of life ...."
19. Canticle of Canticles 6:12 (Song of Solomon 6:13).
20. Proverbs 18:3 (not Proverbs 1).
21. Isaias (Isaiah) 30:9-11.
22. Wisdom 2:21.
23. Amos 5:10.
24. Proverbs 7:22.
25. I have recast the syntax of this Latin sentence of Cusa's so as to give it the intended sense and emphasis. See Thomas Aquinas, *In Quatuor Libros Sententiarum*, Book IV, Distinction 14, Question 2, Article 1b, corpus [p. 499, column 3 of Vol. I of *S. Thomae Aquinatis Opera Omnia* (Stuttgart-Bad Cannstatt: F. Frommann, 1980 (Vol. I)].
26. This is Anselm's view in the *Cur Deus Homo*. See Book I, Chapter 14.
27. Psalms 91:5 (92:4).
28. Jerome, *Translatio Homiliarum Origenis*, 6 (*PL* 637A). See also John 8:44.
29. Hugh of Folieto, *De Claustro Animae*, I, 2-3 (*PL* 176:1023A-B).
30. Gregory the Great, *Moralium Liber*, IV, 27, 49 (*PL* 75:661).
31. Matthew 9:23-25. John 11:38-44.
32. Matthew 5:28: "... he who looks upon a woman to lust after her has already committed adultery with her in his heart."
33. Ephesians 5:4.
34. Proverbs 6:26 (not an exact quotation).
35. Habacuc (Habakkuk) 1:15, not Habacuc 2.
36. As defined by the *Oxford English Dictionary*, a Greek fire is "a combustible composition for setting fire to an enemy's ships, works, etc.; so called from being first used by the Greeks of Constantinople."

157

37. Here (at 9:21) I am reading "navi" in place of "nautae".
38. Luke 15:11-16.
39. III Kings 11:4 (I Kings 11:4), not III Kings 6.
40. Ecclesiastes 7:27 (7:26).
41. Here (at 9:33) I am surmising that "quinalis" is the intended meaning and the "quinquennalis", found in the manuscripts and in the printed edition, is a mistake.
42. Job 24:15 (not Job 23).
43. *De Vitis Patrum*, VI, 3, 18 (*PL* 73:1014).
44. Pseudo-Augustine, *Sermo* 104, 5 (*PL* 39:1947).
45. Matthew 8:12.
46. Isaias (Isaiah) 66:24.
47. Isaias (Isaiah) 66:24.
48. Isaias (Isaiah) 3:24. See also Psalms 10:7 (11:6).
49. Job 24:19.
50. Isaias (Isaiah) 65:13. Luke 16:24.
51. Matthew 22:13.
52. Matthew 18:34.
53. Job 10:22.
54. Matthew 22:13.
55. Gregory the Great, *Moralium Liber*, IX, 65, 97 (*PL* 75:912).
56. Gregory the Great, *Moralium Liber*, IX, 66, 100 (*PL* 75:914B - 915A).
57. Here (at 10:26) I am reading "formidine" in place of "fortitudine".
58. Gregory the Great, *Moralium Liber*, IX, 66, 100 (*PL* 75:915A).
59. Pseudo-Augustine, *Sermo* 104, 3 ff. (*PL* 39:1946-1947 and 1949).
60. Here (at 11:12) I am reading "purgatus" in place of "purgatis".
61. See Thomas Aquinas, *In Quatuor Libros Sententiarum*, Book IV, Distinction 45, Question 1, Article 1a, corpus [p. 651, column 2 of Vol. I of *S. Thomae Aquinatis Opera Omnia* (Stuttgart-Bad Cannstatt: F. Frommann, 1980 (Vol. I)].
62. See *Corpus Iuris Canonici*, edited by Aemilius Friedberg [Leipzig, 1879 (2nd edition of Vol. I), columns 1425-1426]. Note the diagram in the Appendix of the present volume of translations.
63. Hugh of St. Victor, *De Sacramentis*, II, 16, 4 (*PL* 176:586B).
64. Thomas Aquinas, *In Sententias*, IV, Distinctio 44, q. 3, a. 3, q^{1a} ad 8^m.
65. "*Stuprum*," sometimes signifying *rape*, here has the meaning that Nicholas explicitly assigns to it. The act of *stuprum* may or may not be accompanied by the consent of the maiden.
66. Re I Corinthians 7:26: see *Biblia Sacra cum Glossa Interlineari, Ordinaria, et Nicolai Lyrani Postilla, eiusdemque Moralitatibus, Burgensis Additionibus, et Thoringi Replicis*, Vol. VI (Venice, 1588), f. 43^{va}F.
67. I Corinthians 7:34.
68. Jerome, *Epistola* 22 (Ad Eustochium), n. 20 (*PL* 22:407).
69. Jerome, *Epistola* 22 (Ad Eustochium), n. 5 (*PL* 22:397).
70. Gregory the Great, *XL Homiliarum in Evangelia*, XI, 1 (*PL* 76:1115A).
71. Ambrose, *De Virginibus*, II, 4, 26-32 (*PL* 16:225C - 228A).
72. Jacobus de Voragine, *Legenda Aurea*, Chap. CCIII (De sancta Brigida). Edited by Johann Graesse (Osnabrück: Zeller, 1969). See p. 902.
73. *Heraclidis Paradisus*, c. 1 (*PL* 74:255A).

74. *Heraclidis, Paradisus,* c. 51 (*PL* 74:334C - 335B).

75. *Lex Saxonum* II, 26. See *Leges Saxonum,* p. 63ᵇ of Vol. V of *Monumenta Germaniae Historica* (Hannover, 1889).

76. Jerome, *Adversus Jovinianum,* I, 46 (*PL* 23:288B).

77. Jerome, *Adversus Jovinianum,* I, 46 (*PL* 23:288C).

78. Jerome, *Epistola* 79 (Ad Salvinam), n. 10 (*PL* 22:732).

79. Tobias 4:16. Cf. Matthew 7:12.

80. II Kings 13:1-14 (II Samuel 13:1-14).

81. II Kings 11:2 (II Samuel 11:2).

82. Genesis 39:7 (not Genesis 29, which Nicholas writes).

83. III Kings 11:4 (I Kings 11:4).

84. Ecclesiasticus 9:9.

85. Cusa, *De Visione Dei* 4 (11:3). Cf. Richard of St. Victor, *Benjamin Minor* 13 (*PL* 196:10). Richard writes "ubi amor, ibi oculus." By contrast, Nicholas writes "ibi amor, ubi oculus" (in *De Visione Dei*) and "ubi oculus, ibi amor" in the present sermon.

86. Ecclesiasticus 9:11.

87. Gregory the Great, *Dialogorum Liber,* IV, 11 (*PL* 77:336B - 337A).

88. I Corinthians 15:33.

89. Ecclesiasticus 13:1.

90. Jerome, *Epistola* 52 (Ad Nepotianum), n. 5 [*PL* 22:531: "Hospitiolum tuum aut raro aut nunquam mulierum pedes terant ...." Etc.]. See also *PL* 22:532.

91. II Kings 13:1-21 (II Samuel 13:1-21).

92. Jerome, *Epistola* 52 (Ad Nepotianum), n. 5 [*PL* 22:532: "Solus cum sola, secreto, et absque arbitro, vel teste, non sedeas."]

93. *Actual sin* is to be contrasted with *original sin.*

94. Ambrose, *De Paradiso,* 8, 39 (*PL* 14:309B).

95. The Serpent symbolizes the Devil. Apocalypse 12:9 (Revelation 12:9).

96. Augustine, *De Trinitate,* XII, 12, 17 (*PL* 42: 1007-1008). Not *De Trinitate* XI, as Nicholas writes.

97. God's perpetuity is eternity; man's perpetuity is sempiternity, i.e., everlastingness.

98. This thought derives from St. Anselm's *Cur Deus Homo* but is different from Anselm's view. See *Cur Deus Homo* II, 15.

99. Psalms 118:136 (119:136).

100. Psalms 119:5 (120:5).

101. Lamentations 1:2.

102. Psalms 41:4 (42:3).

103. Psalms 136:1 (137:1).

104. Malachias (Malachi) 4:2.

105. I Kings 1:10 (I Samuel 1:10).

106. IV Kings 20:3 (II Kings 20:3). Ezechias is Hezekiah.

107. Isaias (Isaiah) 38:5 (not Isaias (Isaiah) 28).

108. Judith 13:6.

109. Psalms 55:9 (cf. 56:9).

110. Cf. Hugh of Balma, *De Theologia Mystica*, the beginning of the section on the *via unitiva*. See p. 61 of J. Hopkins, translator and introducer, *Hugh of Balma on Mystical Theology: A Translation and an Overview of His De Theologia Mystica* (Minneapolis: Banning, 2002).

111. In general, Nicholas uses "*caritas*," "*dilectio*," and "*amor*" interchangeably. In this present section, however, he uses "*caritas*" to signify a higher kind of love (viz., love of God) that is contrasted with *cupiditas*. This distinction is reminiscent of Augustine. See n. 115 below.

112. Matthew 22:36-40.

113. Cf. Colossians 1:18.

114. Romans 5:5.

115. See Anders Nygren's splendid exposition of Augustine's distinction between *caritas* and *cupiditas*: *Agape and Eros*, translated by Phillip S. Watson (Philadelphia: Westminster Press, 1953).

116. I John 4:8.

117. Here (at 26:7) I am reading "retraxit" in place of "setraxit".

118. Canticle of Canticles 5:6 (cf. Song of Solomon 5:6).

119. Psalms 144:16 (cf. 145:16).

120. Here Nicholas uses (the genitive of) "*amor*," even though in speaking of the third stage of love he uses "*caritas*."

121. Here (at 28:19) I am reading "*frequens*" in place of "*fervens*."

122. Whereas Augustine and Anselm speak singularly of one inner sense, Nicholas follows Aquinas in considering there to be more than one inner sense, just as there is more than one outer sense.

123. The third kiss is the kiss on the lips. See n. 110 above.

124. Philippians 1:23.

125. Cf. I Corinthians 15:31.

126. Cf. Psalms 33:12 (34:11).

127. Matthew 6:21.

128. Canticle of Canticles (Song of Solomon) 5:8.

129. Philippians 1:23.

130. Here (at 30:21) I am reading " in fune bene torto qui" in place of " in fune bene torta quae".

131. Here (at 30:30) there is a textual problem. I am reading "quam ex Christi sanguine ignis Sancti Spiritus contexuit" in place of "quam ex Christi glutino ignis Sancti Spiritus contexit". The Paris (1514) edition of the Latin text reconstructs it more intelligibly. In English translation the Paris edition would read: "… the fire of the Holy Spirit had fashioned the garment and had colored it by means of Christ's blood."

132. Psalms 77:24-25 (78:24-25).

133. Canticle of Canticles (Song of Solomon) 4:11.

134. Cusa, *De Docta Ignorantia* I, 3 (9). Nicholas adopts this fromula from Hugo of Strassburg (*Compendium Theologicae Veritatis*, I, 16, beginning). Hugo's *Compendium*, once misacribed to Bonaventure, is found in Vol. VIII of the printed edi-

tion *S. Bonaventurae Opera Omnia* (Paris: Vivès, 1866).

135. The Latin word here (at 33:19) is *"amicus"*. But at 33:42 *"amicus"* (in the accusative case) denotes not Christ, the Beloved, but personifed Love. See n. 137 below.

136. The allusion here is to the eucharist.

137. Here (at 33:42) *"amicum"* denotes love qua personified. See n. 135 above.

138. Here I omit translating the section (in the printed Latin text) entitled by the editors "*Memoriale.*" This short section consists only of a kind of outline that may have been of help to Nicholas when preaching. It adds nothing to the sermon but is, rather, thematically repetitive.

Sermon VIII: Signum Magnum
("A great sign ....")
[August 15, 1431; feast-day of the assumption of Mary;
preached perhaps in Koblenz]

[1] "A great sign appeared in heaven: a woman clothed with the sun, the moon being under her feet, and on her head a crown of twelve stars." ..."[1]

Although from the beginning and origin of the world God made there to be signs and great wonders on earth, nevertheless on this day a great sign appeared in heaven—[on this day] (1) when the Queen of the world, the most blessed Virgin Mary passed from this wretched world into Glory, passed from exile into our Heavenly Home, passed from toil into rest, and (2) when in a marvelous manner, [and adorned] with a surely quite excellent and quite stunning wreath [of twelve stars], she was exalted from humble poverty and was caught up to the Throne of the everlasting kingdom. Indeed, *to the angels* [this] was a reverent sign, because (1) the daughters of supernatural Sion saw her and declared her most blessed and (2) the queens praised her[2] (rather, all the rich among the people adored her).[3] *To the demons* it was a sign of sorrow. For on this day (according to a simile in the Book of Kings) the Philistines (who symbolize those who fall as a result of drink)— i.e., the devils, who once were drunk with pride—fell as lightning from the sky.[4] When they heard that the Ark of the Testament had come into the camp of Israel, they were smitten with terror and they groaned, saying: "Woe to us!"[5] *To men* it was a sign of assurance. For now we can have the assurance of approaching more closely unto the throne of Christ's grace; for Mary is the Mother of mercy, the mediator established by God between Christ and the sinner—just as Christ, her son, is the Mediator between God and men. And because this woman who is blessed among all[6] is exalted above all choirs and is all-lovely,[7] she is so great and so full of all grace and glory that if all created things under Heaven were transformed into tongues, they would not at all be able sufficiently to sing her praises. And so, in order that we may nonetheless apprehend something in accordance with our measure, let us invoke her with a pious mind for the sake of our salvation, etc.

[2] A great sign ..., etc. At this present time we see that the whole world is disposed toward wars. Hence, I will say a word about

162

war. The words of our theme ["A great sign ...," etc.] are customarily expounded in regard to the most blessed Virgin Mary and her glorification and in regard to God's holy Church and its foundation. Hence, I am going to speak of two things, in accordance with a twofold exposition, in the following order: First, [I will speak] about the most blessed Virgin's war against the world and about her military service (the life of man on the earth is military service) and about her victory and her reward. Secondly, [I will speak] about the war of the entire Church militant on behalf of its Bridegroom,[8] whom it will obtain in Heaven after its triumph. (In Heaven it will be perpetually united, as triumphant, to its vanquishing Bridegroom.)

PART ONE
Mary's War against the World and Her Victory and Reward

(a) *The New Jerusalem is likened to Mary.*

[3] To begin with, I will take the Gospel-text "Jesus entered ...," etc.[9] This Gospel-text is written about two sisters, Mary and Martha, through whom two ways of life are signified. However, the Gospel writers say nothing about the glorification of the Virgin Mary; yet, [the Gospel-text] befits the Virgin Mary perfectly in a mystical sense, inasmuch as, more than all other holy men and women, she has chosen the best part. [It befits her] insofar as she is the Shelterer of the Lord and as regards her twofold life, [viz.,] active and contemplative. Hence, on this very high feast-day I have taken[10] this Gospel-passage in a mystical sense (1) in accordance with the excellence and the merit of our pilgrim journey and (2) in accordance with the superabundant grace and the reward of our Heavenly Home, both of which are signified in the Gospel-passage.

[4] Indeed, from the beginning of the world, when errant man was expelled from the state of Paradise into this present exile: Eternal Wisdom, wanting to lead man back unto His Holy City, first considered choosing an abode for Himself on earth—[an abode] in which to dwell. And in order that He might instruct these men in spiritual warfare and might bring—with a strong hand and as their Leader [and] by His own blood—[these] exiles back into His own Holy City, He sought for a long time a dwelling place suitable for His habitation. And He did not find a worthy place of lodging until He saw the Holy City, the New Jerusalem, descending from Heaven as a bride adorned for her Husband[11]—i.e., [until He saw] most blessed Mary, adorned and

bedecked from on high with all virtue. **[5]** Therefore, when the fullness of the time of salvation came, He entered into this particular castle, chosen above all others. [It was a castle] small with humility, maximal in immensity of virtues and of graces—indeed, of such great magnitude that the measuring angel for holy Ezechiel was scarcely able to
measure its size.[12] O if only someone would rightly describe for us the
gates of this city—its moats, its walls, its towers, its fortifications, its
bulwarks, houses, and palaces! Then we could see how lovely and
becoming, how strong and fortified this holy Jerusalem was.

God looked upon the twelve stones of this city's foundation, viz.,
the twelve stages of humility. He looked upon the very deep [protec-
tive] moats, viz., obedience: "Let it happen to me in accordance with
Your word."[13] He looked upon the wall, viz., the unassailable chastity that excluded every inordinate desire. He looked upon the outer
wall, viz., moderation; upon the fortifications, viz., sobriety and modesty; upon the tower, viz., courage, by means of which she was altogether protected from all dreadful opponents and against all hardships.
There were bulwarks: magnanimity, patience, long-suffering, grandeur, perseverance. By the "*streets* through which one proceeds" we
understand justice. Hence, he who walks in the paths of justice ...,
etc.[14] Through justice one rightly approaches God and one's neighbor.
By "*consistory*" we understand practical wisdom. By "*gate*" [we
understand] the faith by which the King of Glory enters. Elizabeth
said: "Blessed are you, [Mary], who have believed ...," etc. [15] By
"*chamber*" we understand hope: "In peace—in that very thing—[I
will sleep] ..., etc., since You singularly [have settled me] in hope."[16]
By "*dining room*" we understand love; there Mary's soul is refected by
the fruits of the Spirit, and there the Lord Himself is refected. By
"*houses*" we understand the soul's powers, etc. The name of the castle
is "Bethany," which means "house of obedience," "house of God's
gift," and "house gratifying to the Lord." These three [labels] befit no
created person as excellently as they befit Mary. Accordingly,
"Bethany" is said qua autonomasia,[17] etc. According to Anselm some
men think [the castle] to have been [named] "Magdalus," which means
"largeness of tower." [18]

[6] Or [think of it] this way: For a long time [Eternal Wisdom]
sought a worthy dwelling-place; but He found one only at the predestined time of salvation. At that time He saw the new city of Jerusalem,
etc. And within this new and adorned city He saw a bride adorned for
her Husband.[19] And from the Father's citadel He was sent to dwell

therein. Now, that new city was wonderful. It was strong by virtue of its very deep moats. It had, on the left, a valley of pathways descending from one side of the world and, on the right, the very lofty mountain of the Celestial City of Paradise. The [new] castle, or city, was situated on a hillside of that mountain, and it had thorn-bushes and rocks on the valley-side and had running water in front of its gate. Now, the valley was large and spacious, uneven, full of asymmetries [and] roarings; and because of strong winds of misfortune it did not offer a foothold. And there was in another part of the valley a downward-sloping pit; and into it slid many people, heedlessly, every day. For the descent to the pit seemed pleasant. And the inhabitants of the valley were attracted, by many pleasures and delights, toward descending in the direction of the bottomless pit. And after they had tasted just a little of the pleasantness, then in the [false] belief that they were on safe footing, they fell and perished forever.

[7] Now, the entire valley was on the pit's roadway. There was no sure way leading upwards from the valley; rather, the journey to the castle, which Solomon had built for himself, was through desert and rocks. And the wall that surrounded the castle was high, unassailable, and very strong. And [the castle] had an outer-wall with many bulwarks. And it had seven gates, the most outer of which was leaden; the next one was made of stagnum; the third, of iron; the fourth, of copper; the fifth, of bronze; the sixth, of silver; the seventh, of gold. And each gate had its own guards. And after the seventh gate there were four steps by means of which one reached the courtyard of the castle. And these four steps were made of precious stones, and the steps were guarded. And at each step those who were permitted access were outfitted and adorned with fitting armor, so that they would be worthy to approach the palace and the courtyard. And the courtyard was paved with a variety of precious jewels and was elevated upon seven pillars, because it belongs to the house of wisdom, which has hewn out seven pillars.[20] And above each pillar a banner was raised in the courtyard, and in the middle of the courtyard there was a very tall banner of the Cross. There were two bridges between this courtyard and the pathway of ascent unto the City of Paradise; and by way of the bridges one arrived at the pathway that led upwards to the City of Eternal Paradise that was situated on the mount; and there was no other pathway. By means of this pathway of love Jesus came down [from the Heavenly City] to the castle, viz., to Bethany, i.e., to the House of obedience and of God's gift, the House made pleasing to God. And this Bethany was

an edifice built on marvelous pavement in the middle of the courtyard beneath the banner of the Cross. This Bethany was adorned with all precious stones and was located, above the pillars and metallic gates, in the midst of the banners. And *this Bethany was the Virgin Mary*, all-lovely and as choice as the sun.[21]

    (b) *By the example of the sisters Mary and Martha it is illustra-*
       ed how contemplation and the active life are constituted.

[8] Indeed, in this Bethany there were created two sisters—i.e., two supernatural powers freely given by God to the soul of Mary—viz., Martha and [Mary] Magdalene,[22] i.e., a practical, or active, power and a contemplative power. The first [sister was] Martha. This [name], in Hebrew, is the same as "calling forth" or "stimulating"; and in syriac it is the same as "giving." For the active power has to summon all the powers (including corporeal powers) that are subject to it—[summon] them to obey it in the case of good deeds. Yea, rather, it often has to stimulate them at a time when these lower powers obey their own inclination and have a certain eomplaining reluctance, and melancholy disinclination, to obey reason. But [the active power] also has to give— in the case of works of mercy—whatever love for God or for neighbor requires. (But [the name] "Mary Magdalene" is understood as "illumined tower." For the lofty illumination of the contemplative life is given by God to the soul.) Martha, through the exercising of good works, has to remove all vices, if she finds any; and she has to aim at acts of moral virtue by means of which one is rightly ordered both to oneself and to one's neighbor.

    The second [sister, viz., Mary], having put aside all cares, is fervent with desire to see the Face of her Creator, according to Blessed Gregory.[23] It is important to her, as Gregory says, to retain with her whole mind love for God and neighbor and to adhere only to a desire for knowledge [of God]. Contemplation of divine truth pertains to [such] knowledge, which is, especially, the end of all human life. Secondarily, a contemplation of divine operations pertains to this same thing, insofar as by means of those operations we are led to contemplate God, in that "the invisible things of God are clearly seen, being understood through those things which have been made."[24]

    [9] Now, the woman Martha received Jesus into her house; i.e., by means of a most devout power [the Virgin] Mary received Jesus, offering to Him an undefiled spirit, so that in it He might be nourished by her sacred affections—yea, rather, so that He might be delighted,

He whose delight is to be with the sons of men.[25] She presented a virginal womb in order that He might be incarnated within it. However, the other sister, [viz., Martha's sister] Mary, sat at the Lord's feet [and] heard His word. That is, through a contemplative power [the Virgin] Mary was most excellently devoted to divine contemplation, retaining all that she had heard outwardly about the Lord Jesus or had derived inwardly, gathering it into her heart.[26] In the foregoing words three things are touched upon that are requisite to contemplation: (1) [First of all is] rest, because Mary sat. But rest ought to be not only outer rest but also inner rest—[freedom] from passions and from the roamings of apparitions. For the mind must be tranquil; hence, there is said: "Be still and see that I am God."[27] "His place was made in peace."[28] For in finding rest the soul is made wise.

(2) Secondly, contemplation ought to be engaged in at the Lord's feet—i.e., by reference to the sacred *humanity* by which He made contact with earthly things. From the feet one must ascend unto contemplating the *divinity*, which, with Paul as witness, is Christ's head. Furthermore, by "right foot" we must understand *divine goodness*; and by "left foot" we understand *divine grandeur*, with regard to His governing and ordering perceptible and corporeal creatures in this lower world. And so, in our contemplation we must begin from earthly things. (3) Thirdly, [contemplation] ought to hear the word of the Lord; i.e., the one contemplating ought to rely not upon his own senses but rather upon divine, revealed faith. For there are many things to which weak and restricted reason cannot attain. They must be believed only by faith as being things revealed from [God's] mouth.

[10] "But Martha was busy about much serving"; i.e., [the Virgin] Mary[29] was quite occupied with often serving the Lord. First, she served up to the Holy Spirit (when she was fourteen years old) the very pure blood of her own substance, from whence would be produced a body altogether worthy of Jesus. She carried [Him] in her womb for nine months; and amid a very chaste womb He rested as does a king on his reclining couch. She nourished [Him] with her virginal blood, and she conducted Him to due growth until the time He proceeded from her as a bridegroom from his bridal chamber.[30] Thereupon the child-bearing Virgin fed with milk one who was crying for the bread of angels; she revived one who was hungering for the bread of Heaven on our behalf and who was thirsting because of His impoverishment. With her own garments she clothed [Him who is] the Jewel of the blessed, who was experiencing cold. With her consola-

tions she made glad [Him who is] the Gladness of all the saints, when He was crying and experiencing distress. She carried in her arms [Him who is] the Strength of God [but who was] made weak for our sakes. Fleeing, she carried into Egypt [Him who is] God, the King of all the earth, who was experiencing the persecution of Herod the Tyrant; [and] when Herod was dead, she returned. Hence, throughout the entire peri-od-of-life in which the Lord Jesus was seen on earth and conversed with men,[31] [this] pious mother did not abandon Him. Rather, weeping when He wept, rejoicing when He rejoiced, suffering when He suf-fered, ministering as much as she could to Him in His need, she fol-lowed Him even to the gallows of the Cross—not leaving Him until the closing of the sepulcher separated her who was alive from Him who was dead. Let someone fittingly recount all that the most blessed Virgin did during her active life, including both before the Conception and after the Resurrection, until the day she was caught up unto Glory!

[11] But [Martha] persisted in this active life, rendering herself helpful and ready to serve. And she said: "O Lord, are You uncon-cerned that my sister leaves me to serve all alone?" [It is] as if she were to say: "O Lord, whom no creature suffices to serve fully, who worked all things for Your own sake so that all things would serve You! O Lord, while ministering by way of an active life, I am often disturbed because my sister, whom I see to be at leisure, does not help me. And my sister is pleasantly delighted in her leisure; so when I see this delight, I am perturbed amid my activity. Therefore, tell her to help me." [It is] as if [Martha] were to say: "My soul's activity is inclined more toward ministering than wishing to be directed toward contem-plating divine secrets. And so, the activity desires that the soul be com-pletely occupied with serving."

But the Lord quickly settles this loving dispute. For He says, "Martha, Martha"—He says it twice because of the twofold works of mercy: spiritual works and corporeal works—"you are concerned and troubled about many things.[32] You do well, but you are troubled. Your work has an added perturbance. But [only] one thing is necessary[33]— that thing, namely, which is the final-goal of all those things regarding which you are troubled. And this one thing your sister Mary has cho-sen to obtain. She has chosen to cling to this one thing by *contemplat-ing* and *enjoying*. Therefore, Mary has chosen the best part, viz., the contemplative life, since she is content with the one necessary, best, very pleasing, very sufficient, most final good. This part will not be removed from her.[34] For the contemplative life begins here below; but it will be perfected in the future, when it will continue forever. But your [present] life of turmoil, which is not focused on the one necessary thing but on many transient things, will be removed."

[12] And here below the contemplative life is said to be the best life, because, principally, it has to do with the Best Object [viz., God]; and, secondarily, it has to do with that Object's works, insofar as in them God's wisdom and goodness shine forth. Therefore, this [contemplative] life is exercised through the nobler power, viz., the intellect; and so, it perfects man in accordance with his noblest part. However, man is perfected in the eternal Heavenly Homeland, because there the God of gods will be seen face to Face in Sion.[35] In this Heavenly Home there is no one who is destitute, wretched, or poor; nor is there disquietude or strife. Hence, there is no exercise of the active life there. And although the contemplative life is unqualifiedly better than is the active life, nevertheless in certain respects the operation of the active life happens to be better; and in particular instances it is to be preferred because of the needs of the present life—as wine is unqualifiedly a better drink than is water, though sometimes water is preferred. Hence, Gregory [says]: "[As for] those who tenderly desire the citadel of contemplation: it is necessary that they prove themselves in the field of action by teaching, preaching, doing works of mercy," etc.[36] For since the act of doing [good] works occurs with greater love than does the act of contemplating, no one doubts that the good works are better, because love is the measure of merit. Nonetheless, with respect to the goodness of the objects, contemplation is always better than action. Moreover, although the activity is sometimes of greater merit, nevertheless the act of contemplation is not for that reason of lesser perfection.

(c) *The active life and the contemplative life: what they are.*

[13] Therefore, "Mary has chosen the best part." And she has placed the moon (i.e., the active life) under her feet; and by means of the contemplative life she has clothed herself with the sun of justice,[37] and now she appears in Heaven as thus clothed [and] as crowned with twelve glowing stars.[38]

At this point we must consider, first, Mary's active life and her contemplative life; secondly, her death; thirdly, the glory of Paradise. On the feast-day of her nativity we must speak of her lineage, of the disposition of her body, and of her divine gifts. Right now [I will speak] a bit about the active life, about devotion, and about contemplation.

The active life is a life that diligently pursues *just* deeds. And, first of all, it keeps itself unstained from this world:[39] it guards, or keeps, the mind, the hand, the tongue, and the other bodily members, away from all pollution of tempting guilt; and it devotes them to ever-lasting divine service. Next, it attends to the needs of its neighbor by doing works of mercy. The blessed Virgin Mary had this [active] life in the highest degree, because she was free of all sin:[40] "The Most High sanctified His tabernacle."[41] Moreover, as is evident, she per-formed works of mercy in the highest degree, more than all other pil-grims. Works of mercy have degrees—because of greater love or because [done] for one who is more needy, or for one who is more wor-thy and more needy, or because of their weightier, more necessary, and less superfluous effect. All of these works were in the glorious Virgin in the highest degree. In her, maximal love ministered to Him who was the neediest of all creatures, for no one among [us] pilgrims is poorer than was Jesus Christ. [Mary] ministered to a most-worthy, impover-ished man; for no one who is in want is worthier than is God. A work of mercy done to an impoverished layman would be great; done to an impoverished clergyman, it would be greater; greater [still] to an impoverished monk; even greater to an impoverished bishop; greatest of all to an impoverished pope. Therefore, the work that was done to very needy God was incomparably great. Mary bestowed the greatest work of mercy because as a reward for us wretched captives she gave [birth to] God the Son; to us who are hungering she gave Him as a pro-vision for the way; to us who are laboring, she gave Him as a recom-pense; to us who are weak she gave Him as medicine. And together with Him she gave the Kingdom of Heaven. She did works of mercy— for her son, who was very poor and a stranger—not superfluously but because of real need. She made [for Him] a tunic woven from her own blood; she housed [Him] in the center of her womb; she gave [Him] food and milk from her own body.

Let these points briefly suffice as regards her active life.

[14] As regards the contemplative life: it is present when some-one—after having been taught through the long exercise of good actions, after having been instructed by the pleasantness of divine prayer, after having become accustomed through frequent and tearful remorse, after having found leisure from all earthly tasks, and after having learned to focus his mind's eye only on love of God—(1) will have begun, in the present, fervently to foretaste in a desiring way the joy of perpetual happiness (joy that he will receive in the future life)

and (2) will also, at times, (insofar as it is permitted to mortals) be sublimely elevated, taking leave of his mind. Not every single individual can have that [contemplative] life; nevertheless, one can, without it, (according to Gregory)[42] [still] come to Glory if one does not neglect the good things that one can do. And, according to Gregory, in Book VI of his *Liber Moralium*,[43] the contemplative life befits quiet minds, whereas the active life befits restless minds. According to St. Bernard: for him who wishes to approach the contemplative life there must be refuge from secular life, there must be affliction of the flesh, contrition of heart, frequent and pure confession, [and] tears. And after all uncleanness has been cast out, let his meditation on our wonderful God elevate him. And [let there be] a viewing of undistorted truth; [let there be] undefiled prayer, joyous hymns of praise, and fervent desire for God. Hugh [of St. Victor, commenting] on Chapter 3 of [Dionysius's] *Angelic Hierarchy* [states]: "It is necessary that the contemplative mind first be purified, then illumined, and then perfected and consummated. And the more closely the contemplative mind approaches the Divinity, the more truly it contemplates."[44] Gregory [writes]: "Between the delights of the heart and of the body there is the following difference: When bodily delights are not had, they kindle a strong desire for themselves; when they are had and partaken of, they satisfy and produce boredom. Spiritual delights are not had with [accompanying] boredom; when they are had they arouse one and cause one to hunger."[45] And because Mary always had these [spiritual] delights, she ever hungered and was more and more [spiritually] aroused, etc. If spiritual delights are not had, they cannot be loved; their taste is not known. For who can love what he does not know?[46] Hence, "taste and see!"[47] He who at first tastes begins a bit later to see, because the taste was pleasing, etc.

(d) *The things that prepare one for contemplating. The stages of contemplation.*

[15] There are six preparations for the contemplative life: (1) exercise in the active [life]; then, (2) solitude; in addition, (3) humbleness of mind [and] (4) purity of heart. ("Blessed are those with a pure heart, for they shall see God ....")[48] According to Augustine the Supreme Good is discerned only by very pure minds.[49] It is necessary that the eye that is fixed on that Brightness be exceedingly clear-sighted and strong. (5) There is, fifthly, fervor of love. (6) Stability of mind is sixth.

[16] There are also other factors that conduce to contemplation:

[There is] our consideration of creatures and our praising the Creator, who created all things in number, weight, and measure.[50] For "creatures are certain rays of the Divinity in a variety of forms ...."[51] And vestiges of the Creator shine forth in creatures, etc. According to Paul "the invisible things of God are clearly seen, having been understood through the things that have been made ...," etc.[52] According to Hugh, God's power is apprehended through the immensity of creatures;[53] their decorousness manifests His wisdom; their usefulness, His loving-kindness. Immensity is arrived at in and through multitude and magnitude; decorousness is arrived at in and through location, motion, appearance, and quality; usefulness is attained in and through what is pleasing, fitting, advantageous, and necessary. For the perceptible world is like a book written by God's finger. And by this means beginners contemplate; but the perfected (as is the Blessed Virgin) persist in contemplation only of the Creator. The Creator is praised by reference to His creatures, even as an artisan is praised by reference to his artifacts. And just as the beauty of creatures turns a man away from God because of love of their beauty, so too by means of creatures a man is returned to the Creator through modes of understanding ....[54]

A second factor conducing to contemplation is a knowledge of oneself. Bernard: "To the extent that I progress in self-knowledge, I draw nearer to God."[55] In accordance with the inner man there are in the mind three things that constitute the image of God, as far as concerns natural properties: viz., memory, intellect, and will.[56] And because of sin this image of the Trinity fell from the power, the wisdom, and the purity of the Supreme Trinity unto a shameful trinity, viz., weakness, blindness, and uncleanness.... Etc.[57] According to Bernard memory was the likeness of the Father; intellect, the likeness of the Son; will is like the Holy Spirit, who is Love.[58] Through memory man remembers; through intellect he beholds; through will he embraces. Do you wish to seek for things invisible by means of visible, created things? There is nowhere better [to do so] than in the image of God, viz., in yourself. But for knowing yourself there is required engagement in activity, in meditation, and in prayer. By what right does he who does not know how to enter into himself endeavor to ascend above himself by contemplating? Let us love inner things and spurn other things. When we will have directed all our thoughts and activities toward the inner, we [will] have built within ourselves a church for God ....[59]

[17] Thereupon you hear the Bridegroom-of-your-soul saying:

"Arise, make haste, my love, my fair one." "Open to me, my sister." [60] And after you have opened your heart to Him, all things except for your Beloved are dead for you; and your entire soul is attached to that Heavenly sweetness which it begins to taste. Then your mind, with its cares set aside, is fervent with the desire to see the Face of its Creator. First, the fire of tribulation and of remorse ascends into the heart so that all impurity may be consumed [and] so that all things are new, etc. Next, an inner brightness begins to gleam within the heart. Immediately, the mind is elevated beyond itself, and as from afar it glimpses a new and a bright-shining mansion, the likes of which it does not recall [ever before] having seen. Seeing [the mansion], it greatly marvels. It reproaches the past times of its ignorance; it is amazed at how it lay prostrate in the mire. And, again, it mounts up more highly, etc. All worldly things are set aside, and thoughts of the world become more fully dead. And through the grace of the Savior the light keeps increasing in these elect ones. It increases in proportion as the outer senses withdraw from things illicit and gather themselves into one. Man, by meditating on his reflow [to God], makes of his outflow from God into sin a kind of ladder of ascent and descent—a ladder that consists of a thousand advantages, etc. Here make a ladder of the way in which man, the final goal of creatures and the image of God, is a union of two natures—a spiritual nature and a corporeal nature. And within yourself ascend unto God by way of the elemental [rung], the perceptive [rung], the rational [rung]—and then by way of the heavens and the angels.

[18] And next, the soul wants to apprehend God and His glory; but in this lifetime the soul can do so only through a glass [darkly],[61] although by grace it has a foretaste thereof. According to Albert, Mary (who is of maximal grace) foretasted in this lifetime the sweetness of Glory not as a simple pilgrim. A pilgrim makes an inference from beautiful things to Infinite Beauty; from pleasant things, to Infinite Pleasantness; from light, to Infinite Light; from what is sweet, to Infinite Sweetness. And, yet, all the things that the pilgrim humanly imagines and sees with his intellect are as distant from that Heavenly glory of the Godhead as faith is from actual seeing [*veritas*], as time is from eternity—according to Bernard.[62] Gregory in his *Moralia* [writes] on the following [text]: "How long will You not permit me to swallow my spittle?..." etc.[63] The mind, which is our stomach, was desirous of swallowing the spittle of contemplation that descends from the Godhead, and it could not do so, because the body weighs down the soul.[64] And so, [the mind] cannot remain long in the light but can

remain only briefly; and it cannot swallow. For saliva [i.e., revelation]
rightly flows from the head [i.e., from God] into the mouth with a certain pleasantness. But in this present life it does not satisfy the mental
stomach [i.e., the mind], etc., but is discerned from afar. [The ultimate
Truth] is neither altogether seen nor altogether not seen. According to
Gregory it is seen by means of images, not in terms of [its own] nature.
Contemplatives who are elevated unto God in the highest possible
degree, in order to see Him, are ones for whom the world is dead and
for whom [only] God is alive.[65] He who is alive to the world does not
see God. But he who is dead to the world sees God in a certain manner
through faith and through fervent desire ....[66] Then, for this mind, all
things are possessed of tedium and are vain; and purity alone is pleasing to it. In humility [contemplatives] safeguard the mind, lest because
of their pride they lose [the power of] contemplation.

[19] A higher contemplation is about the trine and one God,
about His properties and the equality of His attributes, etc., about His
power, about how He created all things, how all things were and are in
Him and through Him, how He is everywhere and nowhere, how He
attends to all things, gives being to all things, and conserves all things,
etc. [Furthermore, it is contemplation] of the supercelestial, the celestial, and the elemental orders and of the principles of love that hold
together the universe by means of harmony, etc. [And it is contempla-
tion] of how the infinite God remains unknowable to us and ineffable
for us—even though here on earth He is known [by us] with reference
to the fact *that He is*, and in Heaven He is known [by us] *as He is*, but
nowhere [i.e., neither here nor there] do we know *what He is*.[67] For
that which God is transcends all creatures' understanding. The
Ineffable is not named when we call Him Being or Goodness. He is
above all these things, according to Dionysius in *The Divine Names*.
Nowadays, man's outer sense is repaired by contemplation of Christ's
humanity; his inner sense is repaired by contemplation of Christ's
deity. And so, God was made a man in order to beatify the whole man,
so that man as a whole, whether he goes in or goes out, would find pastures.[68]

[20] The quality of contemplation is changed in three ways.
First, [it is changed] by the expansion of the mind. When vices are ban-
ished from the chamber of the heart, love for God enters in with adorning virtues. "If anyone loves me ...," etc. I "and my Father ...," etc.[69]
Moreover, the fervent warmth of God's love expands the heart. And,
according to Bernard, God is sensed by the soul to be present, and in

that way is spiritually seen, because the intellect is an eye, etc.

[21] Next, the second stage—[viz.,] the elevating of the mind—follows upon one's desiring to see Him by whom one is so agreeably visited and consoled. And having been thus elevated, the soul begins to fall asleep a bit in the arms of its Beloved. As a result, it clings to Him not only pleasantly but also tightly, so that, as if by a certain force, it is so drawn away from the awareness and memory of all visible things that it has almost forgotten itself, in accordance with the text of the Canticles: "I sleep, and my heart watches." [70] And the soul is like someone who is falling asleep, who, nonetheless, is still somehow aware of things that are done near by him but to which he does not pay attention because of his drowsiness. Accordingly, when love for God is seasoned with understanding, it intoxicates the mind and joins the mind closely to God once the mind is freed from outer things. And the stronger the mind's love, and the clearer its understanding, the more soundly [God] raptures the mind unto Himself—until, at length, the mind abandons all things that are beneath God and remains dwelling in a gleaming light, for "the body weighs down the soul, and the earthly habitation presses down the mind that muses upon many things." [71] For by its own power the mind can only weakly think a few things. But when elevated by means of its glimpse of Heavenly light it sees many things at once—in proportion to its being the more sublimely elevated above itself. But the corruptness of the earthly body and the tasks of the present lifetime press the soul[72] down and recall it to itself, so that, groaning with the Apostle, it cries out: "O wretched man that I am! Who will set me free from the body of this death?" [73] For straightway the contemplating soul returns to lower things and is fed from the memory of those things that it has agreeably seen. Thus, devout men attain, weakly and stealthily, something of the Uncircumscribed Light; and, sighing, they return unto their own darkness …, etc., according to St. Gregory. And at this stage different kinds of devotion manifest themselves, viz., a joyous shout, intoxication of spirit, [spiritual] melting, and spiritual enjoyment.

[22] Hereafter, one comes to alienation of mind, i.e., to the third stage of contemplation—[arriving there] at times because of the magnitude of the devotion, at times because of the magnitude of the wonderment, at times because of the magnitude of the exultation—so that the man's mind does not apprehend itself but, having been elevated above itself, passes to a state of alienation. A flame that has flared up beyond human measure softens the man's mind like wax, so that,

oftentimes, the mind is alienated by the stupefying power of the celestial beauty. It is alienated by the magnitude of the exultation when it tastes the intimate aspects of the Heavenly succulence; and [the man] is led into alienation of mind by an excess of joy. And as long as we do not experience these occurrences in ourselves, we love too little, for these occurrences come as a result of fervent love, etc.

[**23**] And more than all other human beings, as no one doubts, the Blessed Virgin Mary, who surpassed all riches,[74] ascended by means of this third stage of contemplation. Hence, in the Canticles the Beloved says of her who is his love: "Who is she who ascends by way of the desert?"[75] Etc. And "who is she who proceeds as does the rising dawn?"[76] Etc. And "who is she who ascends from the desert, flowing with delights, leaning upon her Beloved?"[77] Etc. Few men ascend to these stages of contemplation, although God is near to all these men; for the mind is filled with cares; and being beclouded with images because of its memory, it does not return unto itself, since it is enticed by its desires. Therefore, it does not return to itself through a desire for inner security. Therefore, man is thus situated and does not return [to God]. Nor was he able to return, because the ladder of return was broken by Adam [and remained broken] until the Restorer, Christ, came. And so, it is necessary to return through Christ, etc.

(e) *The Assumption; and Mary's eternal reward.*

[**24**] A certain pathway of contemplation has now been expounded. The Blessed Mary's contemplation surpassed all of the foregoing modes in a way that is ineffable to me, a sinner. For she has trod under foot all corruptible things, even the moon itself.[78] And she was clothed with the full brightness of the Sun of justice in such a way that she remained dwelling incessantly in the light of contemplation (1) in the loftiest manner, (2) in rapture, and (3) in ecstasy of mind, [and] (4) in accordance with the supreme mode of theophany and of deification. For crowned with twelve stars, she was [exalted] above all other purely human beings and creatures, in accordance with twelve prerogatives. And so, now on today's date, we must proclaim how she was rapt, and assumed, into Heaven and how she is exalted above all the choirs of angels, for she has appeared in Heaven.[79]

[**25**] And, to begin with, [let us] in conformity with the [Biblical] story [speak of] the time when she was assumed and of how she was assumed. And because [she was assumed] unto glory, [let us say] what glory is and to what degree of glory [she was assumed]. According to

the opinion of the doctors [of the Church] she was assumed in the six-teenth year after the ascension of Christ, i.e., [it occurred] in the sixty-third year of the glorious Virgin. And according to Albertus Magnus (in his book *On Praise for the Virgin*) and other doctors, five prerogatives accompanied her death. First, she foreknew her death. For even St. Martin and many other saints had from God this [prerogative]. Therefore, the Virgin Mary [had it more than did someone] lesser than she, etc. Secondly, Christ escorted His own celebrate mother, because [even] David escorted the ark [of God] into its house with drum and dancers ..., etc.[80] Christ ought to have been present at His mother's funeral procession, because it is a work of mercy, etc.

Thirdly, Mary was separated from the pain of death, because (as we read in the Prologue to [the Gospel of] John): "after a prayer was said, [John] was placed with the fathers and was as free from the pain of death as from the corruption of flesh."[81] Therefore, *a fortiori*, such was the case with respect to the Mother of God. Now, she suffered most grievously at the foot of the Cross when a sword pierced her soul.[82] Through equivalence of meaning this sword is ascribed to her in the sense of martyrdom. However, subsequent to martyrdom there is no pain; therefore, she no longer grieved. Moreover, she desired to be dissolved, as did Paul ..., etc.[83] Hence, her most fervent love drew [her] upwards to such an extent that her soul was separated, in love, from her body. And she died without pain, for she died through love. Fourthly, she ascended at once. Fifthly, she was at once assumed with both body and soul (although among the Ancients there were many doubts about this [fact]). But in St. Gregory's collect for today's feast, [we read]: "However, she could not be kept down by the bonds of death ...," etc. [The phrase] "... by the bonds of death" [signifies], according to Albertus, "to become ashes." Accordingly, she arose immediately. For the Ark of the Testament was made of setim wood,[84] which worms never eat."Arise unto rest, O Lord—You and the Ark of Your sanctification,[85] viz., the Virgin Mary ..., etc.

The doctors [of the Church] claim, on the basis of a certain pas-sage from Dionysius's *On the Divine Names*, that James, Peter, Diony-sius, and Dionysius's teacher, Hierotheus, were present at the death of Mary and held a discussion after her death. And Hierotheus was caught up [to Heaven]. By the testimony of this same Dionysius and by appeal to Gregory, Augustine, and Bernard it is proven that Mary was taken up into Glory with both body and soul. But to me it [once] seemed to be the case that except for Christ no human being arises prior to the general resurrection (as elsewhere I have briefly stated the reason).[86] And we may piously doubt whether Mary's soul returned to her body on the same day she died or on the third day [after her death], as we read in the apocryphal books, or on the fourth day (viz., September 23), as [we read] in the Revelations of Blessed Elizabeth, or on the fifteenth day, as St. Brigitte of Suecia says to have been revealed to her— [says there] where she also maintains to have been told her that the Virgin Mary lived twenty-five years after Christ). [Similarly, we may piously doubt] the claim of certain others that Mary was raptured only in contemplation but that her soul did not leave her body and that during the interim the proportion among the qualities [of her soul and body] was disrupted and corrupted, so that she was truly dead. And, thus, [it is claimed that] by means of contemplation here on earth Mary arrived at contemplation in Heaven. [Whether any of these accounts are true], God knows ..., etc. I say: she died and was buried; her sepulcher is found today in the valley of Josaphat.

[26] Most blessed Mary obtained an eternal reward. Bernard in his treatise *On the Wretched Condition of Man* says the following:[87] "Our reward is to see God, to live with God, to be in God (who will be all in all), to have God (who is the Highest Good). In God there is supreme happiness, supreme delight, true liberty, perfect love, eternal security, and secure eternity. *There* there is true gladness, full knowledge, complete happiness and beauty, everlasting life, rest, and pleasant harmony. Thus, he in whose consciousness sin will not have been found will be happy in God's presence. For he shall see God at will; he shall possess God at his pleasure; he shall enjoy God in accordance with his delight. He will flourish amid eternity; he will gleam amid truth; he will rejoice in goodness. Just as he will have an eternity of abiding, so he will have ease[88] of knowing and security of resting. Indeed, he will be a citizen of the Holy City of which angels are citizens. O Heavenly City, secure Mansion, Homeland that contains everything that delights! Its people are without complaint; its inhabitants are at rest; its human occupants have no needs.

" O what glorious things are spoken of you, O City of God. For in You is the dwelling-place of all those who rejoice.[89] All are glad in You, whose Countenance is beautiful and whose Face lovely ..., etc.[90] In God the intellect is brightened—and the affection purified—for knowing and loving the truth. And this is man's entire good: to know and to love the Creator. We will wait and see how pleasant the Lord is and how great the multitude of His pleasantness is ..., etc.

Many other things can be said about this glorious Homeland. Let there be made steps that ascend from the lovable, honorable, and pleasant goods of this world up unto that Homeland. And [these goods], in their comparative relationship [to the Homeland], will be like a comparison between the infinite and the finite. No human tongue can [adequately] express, nor human mind [adequately] conceive, the least delight of the Heavenly Homeland, etc. And although in the Heavenly Homeland there is no difference between all men as regards their essential reward (for the enjoyment of the Divine Being is common to all), nevertheless there are differences of degrees in accordance with the merits in the saints. The glory of the intellect consists in clear knowledge, and the glory of the affections consists in very fervent and very tender love. The light of glory is a certain quality of mind that disposes and elevates the mind beyond the limits of its own nature in order that it can see God face to Face. Perhaps [we can] rightly [say]: just as, if the eye of a night owl were to look at the sun, it would need a disposing that strengthened its nature (but would not need any changed appearance on the part of the sunlight, since the sun is sufficient for presenting its light to the owl): so God, who is of Infinite Light, flows unto all blessed spirits. And the more intensely this light of glory is given by God, the more clearly God is seen. Understand in a similar way the degrees [of glory] in the Heavenly Homeland. Now, this light of glory follows upon grace and merit ..., etc.

[**27**] But because—of all holy men and women—the Mother of the Lord was of greatest and best merit, she will be eternally possessed of the best reward. And so, by means of a wondrous sign in the heavens she was seen in terms of her meritorious works of the active life (because the moon was under her feet), in terms of her contemplative life, which was perfected in Heaven (because she was clothed with the sun), and in terms of her very special prerogatives (because on her head was a crown of twelve stars).[91] She was privileged, foremostly, with a prerogative against evil, because *not only did she never sin but she was not even able to sin.*[92] She was privileged with respect to the good—(1) first *in accordance with predisposing corporeal features.* [She was predisposed] within herself because she was a virgin mother; [predisposed] with respect to God, in such a way that she was the Mother of God; [predisposed] with respect to her neighbors, in such a way that she was the Virgin of virgins. [She was also privileged] (2) *with respect to her soul's fixed intellectual disposition* (she was ignorant of nothing), *with respect to her soul's fixed affective dis-*

position (she had purity in the supreme degree, in the likeness of God), and *with respect to her neighbors* (she was the Mother of all). But in regard to her actions she acquired merit for herself by each of her acts; with respect to her neighbors she is, in an exemplary way, the Star of the sea; with respect to [rendering] aid, she is Heaven's gateway. If [it is a question of] suffering, then she is the sharing of suffering. But if the privilege concerns the reward, her exaltation actually exceeds that of all other creatures; and, in terms of [exalted] name, [she is called] Queen of mercy.

Now, the following are Mary's fourteen prerogatives. The first one is that *she never sinned*. The second one is that *she was not even able to sin*. And these prerogatives amount to the highest purity [possible] beneath God. And so, twelve prerogatives remain. [**28**] Since, then, she was so privileged, she was full of grace. For she had all the general and special graces of all creatures. She is full of graces that other creatures were empty of. Her grace was so great that as purely a creature she was not capable of greater grace. For she contained all uncreated grace in herself. She is like an aqueduct of graces, because she receives [grace] and gives [grace]. (Ecclesiasticus 24: "I came out of God's Paradise like an aqueduct ...," etc.[93]) She was a wondrous vessel, because she contained what is greater than herself. She was the Virgin Mother of God. (He whom the whole world does not [suffice to] contain enclosed Himself in your bowels ..., etc.) She was the wondrous vessel that at one and the same time contained the wine of deity and the water of humanity without a confused mixing of the natures or or of the properties. She was the wondrous vessel that, though closed, receives all things into itself and channels them forth.

The Virgin Mary was a fount full of grace and flowing forth into many waters:[94] viz., [into Him who is] the Price of redemption, the Water of cleansing, the Bread of refection, the Medicine of healing, the Weapons of assault, the Price of recompense. Wherefore, having now merited it, she is exalted above all the choirs of angels .... The throne for the Mother of the King is placed next to the Throne of the King.[95] Augustine [writes]: "As ruler over the angels she is higher than the heavens ...," etc.[96] Jerome [writes]: "This is the splendid day on which she merited to be exalted above the choirs of angels—[exalted to the place] where Christ, as Priest forever, entered in on our behalf.[97] And elevated on the Throne of the Kingdom, she was seated as the one [who is the most] glorious after Christ."[98] For it is believed that our Savior—the Savior of all, in and through Himself (as best it can be understood)—hastened joyously to meet her and with joy gathered her unto Himself on the Throne; for He commanded: "Honor your mother ...," etc.[99] Jerome [stated] these things. And according to Albertus, Mary obtains a place in between God and creatures because she is the Mother of God, the Queen of Heaven, the Bride, the one who is the most God-loved of all creatures. But it would take too long to speak right now of the way in which the very blessed Virgin Mary had the properties of all the angels, orders, and hierarchies. No one doubts that because of her very great achievements of intellect, memory, and will, and because of her threefold triumph (over the world, the flesh, and the Devil), etc., the Virgin Mary obtained all the golden crowns of martyrs, virgins, and preachers.

[29] O Christian, contemplate here the Mother of the Lord—how after the prolonged troubles of this present life, after frequent sighs for her Son (out of love for whom she was languishing and desiring His face-to-Face presence), after she had dispatched many holy souls unto glory and had united them with other supernatural, holy souls: at length, after she had completed the work that her Son had given her, her prayer was answered. ("I adjure you, O daughters of Jerusalem: if you find my Beloved, tell Him that I am languishing out of love."[100]) Thereupon the Son came with all Heavenly majesty and led her unto Heaven, etc. I saw [this] lovely Dove ascending over the brooks of waters,[101] whose fragrance in her garments was inestimable;[102] and rose-blossoms surrounded her as a spring day, etc.[103] For then the Queen stood at Your right hand in gilded clothing.[104] And the Ark—the Ark of the Testament—which up until now was situated under leather wraps: when the Heaven was opened, it was seen in its temple. [This] Ark of the Covenant was golden within and without; in it was a Golden Urn (i.e., Christ) that had in it manna (i.e., the word of God).

[30] O how great is the joy that today has come to all the saints! Who, I ask, can express it? The voice of the Father was heard: "Hear, O Daughter, and see, and incline your ear; and forget your people and the house of your father, and come."[105] And the voice of the Son [was heard]: "Arise, hasten, and come, my Mother, my Love, my Dove, my Beauty."[106] The voice of the Holy Spirit [was heard]: "Come, my Chosen One, my Temple, my Dwelling Place, my Sacristy, and I will establish my throne in you." The entire Curia of Heaven [was heard]: "Come, our Queen; come our Mother; come our Governess; for the

King has desired your beauty." [107] The Virgin answered very humbly:
"I come to do Your will, O God ...," etc. [108] All the Heavenly spirits
shouted with a joyous shout: "Who is this who comes forth ...?" [109]
Others could answer: "This is the Virgin, of the root of Jesse; [she is]
the One expected by the patriarchs, the One proclaimed by the
prophets ..., etc. This Queen of Saba carried into Jerusalem many
spices previously unknown. [110] From her garments there arose vapors
of myrrh, aloes, and cassia. [111] One [Heavenly inhabitant] said to the
other: "Who is this who ascends by way of the desert of this world—
[ascends], as a pillar of smoke, from aromatical spices of myrrh and
frankincense? Others could reply to them: "She is a garden enclosed, a
fountain sealed up ...," etc. [112]

When Mary came to the first hierarchy, [the inhabitants] said: "It
is not fitting that you remain with us, O Virgin; you are much lovelier
than are we. Together with your comeliness and your beauty: set out;
proceed prosperously." [113] The inhabitants of the second hierarchy
said: "O most lovely Form—lovely more than [all other of] the children of men—proceed!" And [the inhabitants] of the third hierarchy
said: "Queen of Heaven, Governess of the world, proceed and reign
over us; for you are more lovely than the sun; compared to the light of
the stars, you are found to be superior to their entire arrangement ...,"
etc. Mary thought, most humbly: "O what kind of greeting is this?"
The individuals replied: "[It comes] because of truth and justice ...,"
etc. [114] "You have loved justice ...," etc. [115] Then Mary arrived in the
presence of the King, who said: "Come, my Beloved, my Mother;
come from Lebanon; come and be crowned." [116]

[31] And then the Queen stood at [Your] right hand; and by
every creature she is adored with the adoration of hyper-dulia—i.e.,
[with the adoration] of the most excellent servitude that creatures can
exhibit. Nevertheless, she did not arrive at equal glory with Christ—
i.e., at infinite glory, which is not conferrable on any creature. Hence,
in accordance with our theme, the "great sign" is this: the Woman of
Glory, clothed with the sun to a very excellent degree, has the moon
under her feet (i.e., [has under her feet] all the citizens who are living
in Glory; for just as the moon is illumined by the sun, so the saints in
Heaven [are illumined] by the light of Glory). And Mary has a crown
of twelve stars, i.e., a crown (more excellent than all other crowns) of
the twelve individual prerogatives—a crown acquired in Heaven. Or
[we may interpret as follows]: just as from the twelve signs of stars, [117]
and by the influence of stars, there are produced gold, gems, and other

things, and just as other saints are said to have crowns of gold and of gems, [so] Mary was crowned with the *cause* of gold and of gems: viz., with the twelve signs. She is that Esther who today is brought to Assuerus (who symbolizes beauty)—[brought] clothed with royal garments and having on her head the diadem of the Kingdom.[118]

And these [remarks have now been made] concerning Part One.

PART TWO
How the Church Militant, with Christ as its Head Is Led into the Heavenly Ark

(a) *The ascension of the Church Militant.*

[32] In another sense, the narrated words [of our text] are said of the Church, which is the woman who is shined upon by Christ, the Sun of Justice.[119] At the same time, the Church is clothed with faith in-formed by love and is adorned with every spiritual gift. She treds the moon (i.e., the mutable world) under her feet (i.e., under her affections). She has on her head (i.e., at her origin) twelve apostles, designated by twelve stars shining upon the bedarkened world. And since this woman lives in the castle and since her name is "Bethany" and she has Mary and Martha as her sisters: we are supposed to recognize how we can cross from the valley of [this] world unto Bethany, so that after the weapons of war have come to be received in Bethany, then Jerusalem (situated on the mountain) may be reached in triumph.

[33] As was said already, Christ, whose going out was from the highest heaven,[120] entered into Bethany (viz., into the Virgin Mary) and from Bethany shouted into the valley: "The Kingdom of Heaven suffers violence.[121] Arise, take up arms and a shield, and come to her aid.[122] Do not love the world or the things that are in the world.[123] Beware of the works of the Devil, who is a Liar[124] and who seducingly leads you into the eternal fire of the great furnace and of the deep pit. Awaken, for you know not when the hour comes.[125] Come hither to me, into the Church's Camp, and your faces will not be confounded.[126] Come unto me, you who desire me, and be filled with riches.[127] Hear the words of life, for I am the Way, the Truth, and the Life.[128] All flesh is as straw ..., etc.[129] Do not fear those who kill ..., etc.[130] Be strong. Come, all you who are heavily laden.[131] If you thirst ...," etc.[132]

[34] Here I must begin [to speak] about the world and about the world's deceptions, about sin and the turning away from God, about eternal and most excruciating punishment in Hell, about the glory and

beauty of the Heavenly Jerusalem and about that infinite sweetness, [viz.,] most pleasant fellowship with God, with the glorious Virgin, and with the saints, and about the means of arriving in Heaven, and about the fact that the arrival must occur by means of triumphing. And the first thing that is necessary is to purify yourself from sins through a turning away from sins and a turning unto God by grieving over the fact that you have offended against so great a Good, [viz.,] against your gracious Creator. And, thereupon, you begin to pass through the desert of penance in the direction of the Church's camp—[to do so] by forming within yourself conceptions of how many goods He against whom you have so greatly offended has bestowed upon you and about how many evils you have done against Him. Secondly, by ascending to confession, with weeping and tears, you will come to the camp's water. Thirdly, by making satisfaction [for you sins] you will be in the [camp's] trenches, in which you will struggle to enter at the gate; and you will remain a while on a trench's ascent and descent as you reflect on your fear of God because of the punishments of Hell and as you examine your past offending sins.

Keep in mind that the judgments of God are most just. And, next, reflect upon the fact that you are going to die without advance notice. And consider yourself to be already in a state of death; and make for yourself an envisioning of death. Consider where you will arrive. Reflect on the Last horrendous Judgment and on the punishments of Hell. Thereupon you climb forth from the camp's moat and begin to glimpse the walls, by means of the hope of forgiveness. And love begins to be induced when you consider (1) how many goods God has given you and how many goods He has prepared for you and (2) that our merciful God has invited you to come. And when you begin to view that Heavenly Jerusalem from afar, you are more aroused in your approach and in your ascent, as you reflect on the glory of Paradise. Next, you consider again the benefits from God: that God has given you contrition for, and sorrow for, your wrong-doings and has given you love, by means of which you can enter into the [Celestial] City, inasmuch as without that currency no one is let in. And to the end that your love may increase and become inflamed and may purify your soul, you see the City that has been prepared for you, and you meditate on Christ's life, on His Cross, and on His death for you, and on the fact that He stands always beckoning you and awaiting you. And then, [standing] in front of the camp's gate, you sustain your ascent by means of reading, meditation, and prayer.

(b) *The gates-of-entry and the stages of ascent.*

[**35**] And when you thus arrive at the first gate—the leaden gate of humility—three men, who will examine you, are standing in front of the gate. And if they find you to be manly, each will give you a single word of counsel about what is indispensable for your being able to ascend. These [indispensable things] are: energeticness, discipline, and kindliness. Energeticness disposes the soul to do good works carefully, confidently, and aptly—in opposition to negligence. Discipline restrains all lust and renders the soul fit for love of hardship, of poverty, and of lowliness. Kindliness disposes toward benevolence, forbearance, and inner gladness; and it excludes wickedness. These [aids] are three primary weapons. For after by means of penance and the preceding acts of contrition you have divested yourself of all sin: then, as if naked, you approach the outer-wall, where you become armed and clothed with these three [aids]. Your head is clothed with the very snug hood of energeticness; your body is clothed with a hairshirt of discipline, and your feet [are shod] with shoes of the affection of kindliness. After you have been thus armed, proceed to the first gate, made of lead. This is the gate of humility. One who approaches the Camp must despise his own worthiness. Now, [the metal] lead is a very lowly but incorruptible metal in which dead bodies are laid to rest, etc. Moreover, this gate has three levels: the first [is reached] when a man despises himself; the second [is reached] when he does not despise others who despise him; the third level is [reached] when he desires to be despised. And these levels are called levels of assurance, for in humility alone is there assurance. Furthermore, at the third level there is given to you leaden defensive armor, all the way to your knees. By means of it you may resist pride.

[**36**] Next, you approach the second gate, the gate made of stannite. This is the gate of patience. Patience is likened to stannite, which melts quite rapidly in fire. It is, most enduringly, ductile; and it makes the metals with which it is mixed sonorous and stronger, so that they may sustain all assaults. Patience has three stages: viz., a double stage of martyrdom—with blood and without blood—and the stage of peace. And it furnishes protective armor above the knees all the way to the buttocks.

Hereafter comes the gate of silence and quietness; and it is rightly compared to iron, which without very intense fire is neither ductile, fusible, nor malleable. And silence also has three stages: the silence of beginners, of on-goers, and of the perfected. Although silence is a virtue with respect to many things, it is ordained especially with respect to purity and chastity. Therefore, it serves to protect the groin. Next comes the fourth gate, which is the gate of obedience. It is likened to red copper. It is rightly likened to copper because copper is very fusible and ductile, and it easily receives into itself other colors. And it is subject—as to things superior to itself—to gold and to silver, as occurs in the case of bronze. Similarly, obedience subjects its will to the judgment of a superior in matters of the permissible and the honorable. And obedience is a copper belt that fastens the genital protections firmly. And it too has three levels: of beginners, of on-goers, and of the perfected.

[**37**] Thereafter, there follows contempt for riches; and this is a bronze gate. Bronze is rightly opposed to greed, because it appears beautiful and noble but is, nevertheless, of only little value. And all of the beauty that is present in bronze is of earth that is called zinc. Moreover, this gate has three levels: of beginners, of on-goers, and of the perfected. Those who are beginners do not desire things belonging to others but are content with their own things. Those who are on-goers keep only things that are necessary. But all those who have been perfected despise riches and choose poverty, as do the religious. And just as greediness for goods and avarice of heart are exercised through the hands and the arms, so too the hands, and also the arms, are covered with bronze protective coverings in order to prevent their becoming inordinately defiled by the filth of riches. It is not fitting that a soldier sift flour; nor is it fitting that he whose hands are armed militarily and mightily be besmirched with mud.

Next comes the sixth gate, which is of silver. It is the gate of sobriety. It is both silver and rightly likened to silver; for silver is a pure metal, a noble metal, and a bright metal. It does not become corrupted, and it is ductile, as is also sobriety, etc. And silver has three grades: viz., that of quality, that of quantity, and that of measure. And so, a silver torque is placed on the neck of one entering by this gate; it compresses the neck and represses gluttony.

Thereafter comes the last gate—the golden one. It is the gate of chastity. And chastity is rightly likened to gold, which is extracted from the earth with very great difficulty. And gold is beautiful, bright, incorruptible, noble, and very pure. Similarly, chastity is extracted from our earth with difficulty because of lust that indwells the flesh. But once it is extracted, it is never soiled but always remains beautiful and noble, etc. And chastity has three levels. The first level is abstinence from carnal intercourse, with the intent of remaining abstemious and with the intent of withdrawing consent from all illicit motions. The second level is the mortification of the flesh in order that it become subjugated to the spirit. The third level is the chastising of the flesh in order that lustful desires not be experienced. And next—as a sign of triumph—[the one who is ascending] is crowned with a small, rounded crown that is golden and polished.

[**38**] And when you are thus outfitted, you approach the four steps of the Palace. These are the four cardinal virtues. The first step is the step of practical wisdom, which examines all present, past, and future goods and evils, choosing the good things and spurning the evil things. And so, it arms one with a bow in order that he may defend himself at a distance. The second step is that of temperance, which in no respect exceeds the law of moderation. And temperance furnishes a shield (commonly called a buckler) for resisting the javelins-of-lust that come from the world, the flesh, and the Devil. The third step is that of courage. It protects the upper arms with steel. Just as that part [of the body] receives undauntingly the blows of the enemy, so courage bravely sustains all assaults, and it fears only things that are shameful. The fourth step is that of justice; and justice girds onto the thigh the sword, [used] for rendering to each his own.[133] And justice rightly girds the sword, because justice is symbolized by a sword. "From the mouth of the one seated on the throne there proceeds a sword" ..., etc.[134] Gird on your sword ..., etc.[135] The sword defends justly and strikes justly. It receives onto itself strong blows; it protects soberly and defends cautiously on all sides. Moreover, all the virtues are present in justice, as is evident. Each step is composed of three kinds of precious stones—marble, jasper, and topaz—because virtue is either (1) political virtue or (2) purifying virtue or (3) virtue of a purified mind. Virtues are called *political* insofar as they regulate human life; they are called *purifying* insofar as they conquer vices; they are said to be *of a purified mind* insofar as the possessor of the virtues is at rest, having vanquished vices.

[**39**] Therefore, when you thus ascend, you come to an ornate palace that is called perseverance. And this palace, or courtyard, is erected on seven pillars, which are the seven gifts of the Divine Spirit, who governs the Church—[gifts] opposed to the seven deadly sins. The pillar of fear-of-the-Lord is opposed to pride; the pillar of graciousness is opposed to envy; the pillar of knowledge is opposed to anger (because anger is a kind of madness); the pillar of courage is

opposed to sloth; that of advisedness is opposed to avarice; that of understanding is opposed to gluttony; that of wisdom, to licentiousness. And in this palace these seven pillars are the seven good spirits[136] who rule over the Church Militant; and other spirits, who are evil, rule over the assembly of evil-doers.[137]

[40] Next, you enter among the seven banners placed higher up on the pillars. These banners are—in accordance with a distinction of degrees—the seven beatitudes. And because, according to essence, there are eight banners: the eighth banner—the banner of the Cross, unto which you come—is in the middle. The first banner is black and is poverty-of-spirit, in opposition to lust; and it is mortification of spirit, etc. The second banner is azure and is the banner of meekness and of gentleness. The third banner is yellow and is mourning. The fourth banner is gray (commonly called [in middle high German] *gra*) and is hunger [for righteousness]. The fifth is green in color and is mercy. The sixth is white and is purity of heart. The seventh is red in color and is [the banner] of peace. The Cross, in the middle, is the color of blood and is the suffering of persecution for justice's sake. By means of all these banners our Heavenly Homeland, situated on the Mount, is attained.

(c) *The entrance into the Heavenly Jerusalem.*

[41] Now, the twelve tribes of Israel have twelve leaders. And, [likewise], this holy congregation has a great high priest in the middle, together with the banner of the Cross; and the congregation has twelve apostles together with trumpets sounding the word of God. And this diocese assembles itself—together with Eucharius, Valerius, Maternus, Paulinus, Maximinus, and the other pastors—under the banner of the Cross. And the whole army begins to move itself toward Mount Sion. And because the army is still not entirely armed, the priest at the first bridge gives a shield to those who are approaching.[138] It is the shield of faith;[139] and faith is likened to a bridge because through faith one approaches hidden and very deep matters, in much the way that by means of a bridge one crosses over dangerous waters. And at the second bridge, when now that Heavenly Homeland begins to show its splendor to the eye, the priest places on each [ascender] a helmet [that protects] against hopelessness, so that [the ascender] may hope that he will be a victor. And when, now, he begins to approach more closely to the Mount and to the pathway of ascent, a plate of armor protects [him and the others] who are approaching. Without this armor they could in

no way be safe. And the breastplate of love, or armor of love, is, on its outer side, made of steel because love endures all things; but on its inner side it is iron, in order to be very firm. True love puts up with all things on account of the beloved, and it cleaves uninterruptedly to the beloved with a very strong bond.

[42] On this pathway of love the Standard-bearer[140] ascends very highly. And His mother, the Mother of mercy, follows Him, as do also all holy spirits. And He presses His way through the stars up to the City; and in the [Heavenly] Camp the guardian angels shout out: "Who is He who comes from Edom, with dyed garments from Bosra?"[141] He answers: "I am the Way, the Truth, and the Life."[142] And I am the Living Host; I offered myself to my Father, and I redeemed those prisoners, my exiled brothers. Open the gates, so that the Minister may be there where His Father is." And immediately the doors of the City of Jerusalem are opened. And the whole Heavenly army will shout out: "O Desirable One, O Light and Salvation, You have arrived! Holy, holy, holy!" And [in the army] one [will say] to another: "O how lovely that congregation is! Lo, here are the 144,000 of the twelve tribes![143] Lo, here are a countless number who are marked with the blood of the Lamb!" And all will enter with might; and the voice of the Father will be heard: "Come, Blessed Ones, receive the mansions prepared for you from the beginning." And each one will ascend, in proportion as he is fervent and light-weighted as a result of the fire of his love. And each will receive, in full satisfaction of his desire, a dwelling-place in Glory, where, in accordance with the thirst and hunger of his inflamed love, he is fed with the vision and the enjoyment of immortal life and will live forever. May our Standard-bearer, our very great High Priest, who is blessed forever, lead us triumphantly to this most blessed Glory.

APPENDIX

[43] In the valley of the world the Prince of [this] world[144] has his temple, wherein are diabolical documents and diabolical images and perverse doctrines. There the Devil's business is conducted—his diabolical mass, with gaming-tables, dice, blasphemies, deceits (commonly called [in middle-high German] *velen*). And, in this manner, there are present there, in every circumstance, deceits, etc. Take in hand the painting of the horse on which the Pope is seated and which the Emperor is guiding and which all the attendants are attending: [viz.,] all officials, all merchants, clergy, executioners, citizens,

women, etc. Now, the temple of the Devil has around it seven gates of
the seven capital sins. The higher and more public gate is the gate-of-
pride, decorated in different ways in accordance with the different
forms of pride and of vainglory. And it has four door-posts, because of
the four kinds of pride, and twelve steps, because of the twelve gradations of pride. The next gate, toward the South, is the large gate-of-
greed, decorated in different ways (because of its many offspring) and
having an idol at the top (because greed is likened to idolatry). The
third and larger gate is the gate of licentiousness. It faces East and is
decorated in different ways. It has seven door-posts, because of its
seven offspring and the seven steps by which one ascends unto licentiousness. In between the gate of pride (which is toward the north) and
the gate of greed is the gate toward the west. It is somewhat large; it is
the gate of envy, and it is smaller than the gate of pride. Nevertheless,
it is made in the likeness of the gate of pride, because envy is pride's
offspring. On the other side of pride, toward the gate of licentiousness,
is the gate of anger. Next is the gate of gluttony; it is situated very close
to the gate of licentiousness. And near to the gate of greed is the gate
of sloth. Through these gates the world enters upon the Devil's service.

NOTES TO *SERMON VIII*

1. Apocalypse (Revelation) 12:1.
2. Canticle of Canticles 6:8 (Song of Solomon 6:9).
3. Psalms 44:13 (45:12).
4. Luke 10:18.
5. I Kings 4:6-8.
6. Luke 1:42.
7. Canticle of Canticles 4:7 (Song of Solomon 4:7).
8. Re Christ as Bridegroom, cf. Matthew 9:14-15.
9. Luke 10:38-42.
10. Here (at 3:14-15) I am reading "assumpsi" in place of "assumpsit".
11. Apocalypse (Revelation) 21:2.
12. Ezechiel (Ezekiel) 40:5-16.
13. Luke 1:38.
14. Isaias (Isaiah) 33:15.
15. Luke 1:45.
16. Psalms 4:9-10.
17. Throughout this and other sermons Nicholas uses autonomasia—the use of a metaphor to substitute for a personal name, or the use of a personal name for something non-personal, etc. Not only is the Virgin Mary called Bethany but the power motivating the active life is called Martha, and the power motivating the contemplative life is called Mary, the sister of Martha (not to be confused with the Virgin Mary or with Mary Magdalene). Jesus is called the Standard-bearer, the Bridegroom, the Sun of justice, etc. See n. 22 and n. 29 below.
18. Pseudo-Anselm, *Homiliae*, IX (*PL* 158:646B).
19. Apocalypse (Revelation) 21:2.
20. Proverbs 9:1.
21. Canticle of Canticles 4:7 and 6:9 (Song of Solomon 4:7 and 6:10).
22. Here Nicholas mistakenly believes Mary the sister of Martha to be Mary Magdalene.
23. Gregory the Great, *Homiliarum in Ezechielem Prophetam Libri Duo*, II, 8 (*PL* 76:953).
24. Romans 1:20.
25. Proverbs 8:31.
26. Luke 2:51.
27. Psalms 45:11 (46:10).
28. Psalms 75:3 (76:2).
29. Nicholas, using autonomasia, here ascribes to the Virgin Mary an interest in, and pursuit of, the active life (vs. the contemplative life). He personalizes this interest on the Virgin Mary's part, referring to it by the name "Martha." Similarly, when Nicholas speaks of the Virgin Mary's contemplative power and contemplative life, he refers to it as "Mary" (the sister of Martha).
30. Psalms 18:6 (19:5).
31. Cf. Baruch 3:38.
32. Luke 10:41.

33. Luke 10:42.
34. Luke 10:42.
35. Psalms 83:8 (84:7). I Corinthians 13:12.
36. Gregory the Great, *Moralium Liber*, VI, 37, 59 (*PL* 75:763C).
37. Malachias (Malachi) 4:2.
38. Apocalypse (Revelation) 12:1.
39. James 1:27.
40. Nicholas accepts not only the doctrine of Mary's immaculate conception but also the doctrine that Mary never sinned and was never able to sin. See, below, the passage marked by n. 92. See also Sermon IX: my note 69 and the text marked by it.
41. Psalms 45:5 (46:4).
42. Gregory the Great, *Homiliarum in Ezechielem Prophetam Libri Duo*, I, 3, 10 (*PL* 76:809).
43. Gregory the Great, *Moralium Liber*, VI, 37, 57 (*PL* 75:761).
44. Not an exact quotation. See Hugh of St. Victor, *Expositio in Hierarchiam Coelestem S. Dionysii Areopagitae*, IV (*PL* 175:998B-C).
45. Gregory the Great, *XL Homiliarum in Evangelia Libri Duo*, XXXVI, 1 (*PL* 76:1266A-B).
46. Gregory the Great, *XL Homiliarum in Evangelia Libri Duo*, XXXVI, 1 (*PL* 76:1266B). Augustine, *In Joannis Evangelium*, 96.4 (*PL* 35:1876 (near top). *De Trinitate*, X, 1, 1 (*PL* 42:972).
47. Psalms 33:9 (34:8).
48. Matthew 5:8 (not Luke 21, which Nicholas writes).
49. Augustine, *De Trinitate*, I, 2, 4 (*PL* 42:822).
50. Wisdom 11:21.
51. Bernard of Clairvaux, *Sermones in Cantica Canticorum*, 31, 3 (*PL* 183:941-942).
52. Romans 1:20.
53. Hugh of St. Victor, *Eruditionis Didascalicae Libri Septem*, VII, 1 (*PL* 176:811D - 813A).
54. Isidor of Seville, *Sententiarum Libri Tres*, I, 4, 2 (*PL* 83:543). Nicholas refers to this passage as a passange in *De Summo Bono*.
55. Pseudo-Bernard of Clairvaux, *Meditationes Piissimae*, 1, 1 (*PL* 184:485A).
56. Augustine, *De Trinitate*, XV, 29, 39 - 23, 43 (*PL* 42:1088-1091).
57. Bernard of Clairvaux, *Sermones de Diversis*, XLV, 1 (*PL* 183:667B).
58. Pseudo-Bernard of Clairvaux, *Meditationes Piissimae*, 1, 3 (*PL* 184:487B). Augustine, *De Trinitate*, XV, 23, 43 (*PL* 42:1090).
59. Richard of St. Victor, *Benjamin Minor*, 78-79 (*PL* 196: 55D-56C).
60. Canticle of Canticles (Song of Solomon) 2:13 and 5:2.
61. I Corinthians 13:12.
62. Not Bernard of Clairvaux but William of St. Theodoric, *Epistola ad Fratres de Monte Dei*, II, 3, 17 (*PL* 184:349C).
63. Job 7:19. Gregory the Great *Moralium Liber*, VIII, 30, 49-50 (*PL* 75:830B and 833B. Pages are misplaced and misbound in some printings.) "Saliva," "head," "stomach," etc. are being used metaphorically. For example, "saliva" symbolizes contemplation; "stomach" symbolizes the mind; "food" symbolizes celestial understanding.
64. Wisdom 9:15.

65. Romans 6:11.

66. Augustine, *De Genesi ad Litteram*, XII, 27 (*PL* 34:477-478).

67. I John 3:2. Cusa, *De Theologicis Complementis* 2. *Sermo* IV (32:26-28). Hugh of Strassburg, *Compendium Theologicae Veritatis*, I, 16 [Vol. VIII, p. 72ᵇ of *S. Bonaventurae Opera Omnia*, edited by A. C. Peltier (Paris: Vivès, 1866). This work was, at times, wrongly ascribed to Bonaventure.].

68. John 10:9.

69. John 14:23: "If anyone loves me, he will keep my word. And my Father will love him ...."

70. Canticle of Canticles (Song of Solomon) 5:2.

71. Wisdom 9:15.

72. Here (at 21:28) I am reading "animam" in place of "animas".

73. Romans 7:24.

74. Proverbs 31:29.

75. Canticle of Canticles (Song of Solomon) 3:6.

76. Canticle of Canticles 6:9 (Song of Solomon 6:10).

77. Canticle of Canticles (Song of Solomon) 8:5.

78. Throughout this section Nicholas alludes to Apocalypse (Revelation) 12:1.

79. Apocalypse (Revelation) 12:1.

80. I Paralipomenon (I Chronicles) 15:1-25.

81. *Biblia Latina cum Glossa Ordinaria*, Vol. IV, p. 223 (Strassburg, 1480/81). Reprinted in Brepols by Turnhout, 1992.

82. Cf. Luke 2:35.

83. Philippians 1:23.

84. Deuteronomy 10:3.

85. Psalms 131:8 (132:8).

86. Cusa, *De Docta Ignorantia* III, 8. The passage above is a later addition. Nicholas came to believe that Mary died and was resurrected and raptured.

87. Pseudo-Bernard of Clairvaux, *Meditationes Piissimae*, 4 (*PL* 184:492B - 493A).

88. Here (at 26:18) I am reading "facilitatem" in place of "facultatem".

89. Psalms 86:3 and 7 (87:3).

90. Canticle of Canticles (Song of Solomon) 2:14.

91. Apocalypse (Revelation) 12:1.

92. See n. 40 above.

93. Ecclesiasticus 24:41.

94. Note Esther 10:6 and 11:10.

95. III Kings (I Kings) 2:19 (not III Kings 3, as Nicholas writes).

96. Pseudo-Augustine, *Sermo* 208.5 (*PL* 39:2131).

97. Hebrews 6:20.

98. Not an exact quotation. Paschasius Radbertus (not Jerome), *Epistola* IX ("Cogitis me") (*PL* 30:130A-B). Nicholas continues by borrowing parts of 130C.

99. Exodus 20:12.

100. Canticle of Canticles (Song of Solomon) 5:8.

101. Canticle of Canticles (Song of Solomon) 5:12.

102. Canticle of Canticles (Song of Solomon) 4:11.

103. Ecclesiasticus 50:8.

104. Psalms 44:10 (45:9).
105. Psalms 44:11 (45:10).
106. Canticle of Canticles (Song of Solomon) 2:10.
107. Psalms 44:12 (45:11).
108. Psalms 39:8-9 (40:7-8).
109. Canticle of Canticles (Song of Solomon) 6:9.
110. III Kings (I Kings) 10:10.
111. Psalms 44:9 (45:8).
112. Canticle of Canticles (Song of Solomon) 4:12.
113. Psalms 44:5 (45:4).
114. Psalms 44:5 (45:4).
115. Psalms 44:8 (45:7).
116. Canticle of Canticles (Song of Solomon) 4:8.
117. Apocalypse (Revelation) 12:1.
118. Esther 5:1.
119. Malachias (Malachi) 4:2.
120. Psalms 18:7 (19:6).
121. Matthew 11:12.
122. Psalms 34:2 (35:2).
123. I John 2:15.
124. John 8:44.
125. Mark 13:35.
126. Psalms 33:6 (34:5).
127. Ecclesiasticus 24:26.
128. John 14:6.
129. Ecclesiasticus 14:18.
130. Matthew 10:28: "Fear not those who kill the body and are not able to kill the soul; but rather fear Him who can destroy both soul and body in Hell."
131. Matthew 11:28.
132. John 7:37: "If any man thirst, let him come to me and drink."
133. The analysis of *justice* as "rendering to each his own" is drawn, ultimately, from Cicero's *De Finibus Bonorum et Malorum*, V, 23, 67. See also Augustine's *De Libero Arbitrio*, I, 13, 27 (*PL* 32:1235).
134. Apocalypse (Revelation) 1:16.
135. Psalms 44:4 (45:3).
136. Apocalypse (Revelation) 4:5.
137. Psalms 25:5 (26:5).
138. In section 38 Nicholas spoke already of the ascender's receiving a shield (*clipeus*). Here he seems to repeat himself. But this time he uses the word "*scutum*," indicating that this shield is not a smaller shield worn on the arm but a larger shield that is carried.
139. Ephesians 6:16.
140. The Standard-bearer is Christ.
141. Isaias (Isaiah) 63:1.
142. John 14:6.
143. Apocalypse (Revelation) 7:4. The number here is 144,000.
144. "... the Prince of [this] world": viz., the Devil (John 14:30).

Sermon IX: Complevitque Deus
("And God ended [His work] ....")
[September 8, 1431; feast-day of Mary's birth;
preached perhaps in Koblenz]

[1] "And on the seventh day God ended the work that He had done, and He rested ...." [1]

Rejoice with all your heart, O Mother, O happy Church! [2] Etc. Let us celebrate most devoutly the rise of the Star from [the lineage of] Jacob [3]—the Star, [viz., Mary], from which the Sun of justice, [i.e.,] Christ our God, issued forth. For this birth of the [God-] Bearer was the beginning of our salvation, etc. For today there was born the Ladder by which the Savior came down to man and by which man ascended unto the Savior. There was born, [viz.,] the Mother of orphans in order to lead unto joy those who were weeping, etc. Who could adequately speak of her marvelous origin? Surely, no one! And so, in order to obtain grace, let us beseech this same one in saying "Hail, Mary!"

[2] The words [of our text] can be expounded along three lines: [first,] as regards the Blessed Virgin Mary, through whom God completed all the works of the six periods and in [whom] He rested on the seventh [day]. Secondly, they can be expounded with respect to [the themes] of rest and of quietude: [viz.,] how it is that on the seventh day God rests in man after having completed the six works. Thirdly, because it is necessary to remove all disquietude (even [disquietude] that is unknown to us by nature) before there is suitable rest: it is necessary to speak about disquietude secondly and, after this, to speak about rest.

PART ONE
*The Six Days of Creation and Some Figures
of the Old Testament Are Expounded with reference to Mary*

(a) *The completion of the work of six days is likened to Mary.*

[3] Regarding the first part: How did God rest after having completed in Mary all the works [of creation]? The answer is the following: "The Lord possessed me from the beginning of His ways, before the earth was made ...," etc. [4] By means of eternal predestination God the Father formed, of old—in His infallible Idea, in a marvelous, ineffable man-

195

ner—this most glorious Vessel, [viz., Mary], of the reparation of the human condition. And Moses, expressing this point for us says: "In the beginning God created heaven and earth."[5] That is, He created in the Virgin Mary both a heavenly, angelic life and a human, earthly life. She was "heaven" in terms of her very lofty worthiness and was "earth" in terms of her very lowly humility—heaven because of her very pure virginity and earth because of her very fertile motherhood.[6] But this earth of the Virgin—most fertile with respect to its ancestors— was at the beginning void and empty; and upon the face of the deep, [i.e.,] in terms of her natural issuing forth from Adam, she was dark and cloudy. And then the Spirit of the Lord moved over the waters— i.e., moved over the face of all the people, who are signified by [the phrase] "the deep." For there was a certain obscuring darkness of orig- inal guilt.[7] And the Spirit of the Lord—i.e., Love and Mercy—moved over the waters, i.e., over all the nations.

[4] And then in His own secret council God said: "Let there be light that expels this darkness and that shines forth." And light was made, viz., the light of the world, a light that was exceedingly good. And by means of this light God separated day from night. For, first of all, by means of the light of His word God expelled the darkness of all bedarkening sin, whose author was separated from the light and turned unto night—i.e., unto everlasting darkness and the lack of the true light of seeing God. And this is the first work. Secondly, by the word of God water was separated from water; i.e., nation was separated from nation by the power of faith, and the people beneath the firmament were sep- arated from the people who were above the firmament; i.e., the people who were earthly pilgrims were separated from the people who were in Heaven. And the firmament was in between; i.e., the glorious Virgin, called *heaven*,[8] was in between pilgrims [on earth] and attainers [in Heaven]. And in this firmament there were twelve stars, or signs, because they were the crown of [this] woman who was clothed with the sun and under whose feet was the moon.[9] The crown had twelve stars—[i.e.,] twelve prerogatives .... And the first work was finished when God willed that His mother, predestined from eternity be born— as, [in truth], she was born today.[10] He gave her to the lost for their sal- vation—for the remedying and washing away of all sin and for the expelling of the diabolical, nocturnal power and for the birth of Christ, the true Light.

The second work occurred when at His death Christ passed into the heavens and when by way of the firmament of the glorious Virgin

He assigned to His pilgrims and peoples places in the heavens. And, thus, the most blessed Virgin Mary was separated from the pilgrims and the attainers, since she was above the pilgrims but below the attainers and since she shared, with those above her, the perfection-of-virtues and, with those beneath her, the state of continued meriting. And just as the firmament, which is moved immediately by God or by an intelligence, moves and influences [whatever is] below itself, so the most blessed Virgin Mary was in the midst of the outpouring and influencing of grace, etc. For [like] the firmament, she has together with those above her rejoicing and security against falling; and together with those beneath her she has emotional suffering and the possibility of merit.

[5] And so, on the third day all the waters were gathered together into one place:[11] [i.e.,] at the time of the natural law there was a single locus of faith. This gathering [of waters] was called a sea. That is, under the firmament there are two things in all people, viz., a body and a soul. The body is dry land, and the gathering of the waters is called a sea, because people ought to be given an appellation from a consideration of their soul rather than from a consideration of their body. For although dry land is of different kinds, and although bodies are of very different kinds insofar as the proportion of their elements is pure, impure, or mixed (whence some men are black, others white; some are small, others large, etc.), nevertheless there is one gathering of the waters of all rational souls, which are dependent on the Creator alone, without the aid of the elements. This gathering had a single place: viz., the place of the natural law under which [man] was living. And just as when there is no water the earth begets or produces nothing, so when there is water, i.e., a vital spirit, it produces green herbs and every kind of thing that has seeds, etc.,[12] i.e., that has natural operations, which are likened to the vegetative power, etc. And by means of Him who governs the firmament, and by means of the influence of the firmament, which waters the earth with spiritual moisture and which distributes the water, there springs forth the fruit of affection and of love. And just as all intellectual spirits beneath the firmament (viz., human spirits) are called a sea, so [the Virgin] Mary alone is called an in-between sea and a vast sea, excelling by far all other [seas].

[6] On the fourth day: Because *acting* and *being acted upon* are not without influence in the domain of things active, so too spiritual action of grace and of love and of virtues must have spiritual influence. Therefore, in the firmament of the glorious Virgin Mary God placed

the Sun of justice, which would illumine and irradiate and causally influence the entire firmament. And, likewise, [He placed] the Moon, illuminated by the Sun; i.e., [He placed in the firmament] the excellent, imparted grace of the Virgin Mary, who dispelled the darkness of night from the hearts of those beneath the firmament in order that they could come to the daylight of eternal glory. And [this] was the work of the fourth day. That is, for all those who are gathered together within the natural law there was no ray of true life except in both the Sun of justice and the Moon that were in the firmament of Mary. This Sun and this Moon were placed in the firmament at this later time in order in this way to shine from afar upon those producing natural fruit on earth through their faith in the future Messiah. Seeing this [Messianic] Ray, the prophets manifested it. The Ray intimately manifested Himself on earth during the period of grace, when He conversed with men.[13]

[7] But when it thus happened as a result of this influence of faith in the future Messiah—[an influence that] descended unto souls (which are primarily symbolized by the gathering of the waters)—then at the beginning stage, there arose in the soil of the elemental power operations and seeds. This soil is the vegetative vital force situated in the elemental power. It is as if the life-giving Ray were exercising its influence from very far away—as occurred at the time of the natural law before the Flood. Hereafter [there arose] by means of this [vegetative power] every [kind of] reptile and [all kinds of] fish in the waters (i.e., in the souls). They arose in the earth-of-the-affections as powers of the senses. But the seeds and the plants arose first. Hereafter, the vegetative power becomes rooted in the knowing intellect, and it grows to become the power of the senses—[a power that is] vital, aquatic, changing, and influenceable. This was at the time of the Law and the Prophets, at the time of Abraham, etc.

[8] At length, on the sixth day the life of the senses is elevated more highly by means of the affections—elevated unto becoming the powers of the imagination. And this is called the elevation of the affections and of cognition, [and it extends] to all the beasts of the earth. This was at the time of Moses and of Daniel, when [God] was seen more closely. And, finally, [the imaginative power] is elevated, by means of the highest level of the affections and of the intellect, unto knowing the rational animal (viz., man) and itself. And by means of this knowledge (whereby man recognizes his own maleness and femaleness) the heavens and the earth and every adornment are completed. And then [man] sees that all things are completed, and he

begins to rest in God, etc.

[9] Therefore, on the seventh day God ended the work that He had done, and He rested. For on the seventh day (i.e., [if we speak] in accordance with the flux of time)—on the seventh day He rested in His very excellent work, viz., in the Virgin Mary. For "He created all things together";[14] and "He spoke, and they were made...," etc.;[15] and "by the word of the Lord the heavens were formed."[16] Nevertheless, all six works were completed in the Virgin, in whom on the seventh day—after six emanating times—God rested, etc. For the first work that was unfolded on the first day contained all the other works within itself. And the other works individualize the days up to the day of rest.

(b) *The annunciation and Mary's birth.*

[10] This most sacred Scripture, at its very beginning, posited this pre-destined, eternal, maximal work of the Word's being incarnated from the Virgin. (Lucifer, because of his arrogant disbelief in this work, fell; and, from the beginning, all were saved by humble faith in this work.) Therefore, all who have been enlightened by the Divine Spirit, and who understand this very deep Scripture with an illumined intellect, prophesy about this very excellent mother [viz., Mary] by means of its words and images. In the first verse of Isaias 11: "A virgin shall come forth from the root of Jesse." The gloss [says]: "The Virgin Mary, the Bearer of God, is the virgin [referred to]; her Son is the flower [referred to]."[17] Likewise, Numbers 24: "A star shall arise from Jacob."[18] Again, Isaias: "the sublime fruit of the earth...."[19] The gloss [says]: "... of the Virgin Mary."[20] Again, Isaias 7: "I went to the prophetess."[21] The gloss: "... the Virgin Mary."[22] She is prefigured in the ark of Noah, in the rainbow, in the tabernacle of Moses, in the Ark of the Testament, in the candlestick, in the propitiatory, in the temple, in the throne of Solomon, in the door, in the house of the forest,[23] and in many other things. She is the bush of Moses (Exodus 3),[24] the sapphire throne above the firmament (Osee 1),[25] the mountain from which the stone is cut out without hands (Daniel 2).[26] She is prefigured in the tree that touched the heavens (Daniel 4),[27] in the closed gate (Ezechiel 44),[28] in Gedeon's fleece (Judges 6),[29] in the small fountain that grew into a very great river (Esther 12),[30] in the beautiful gate of the temple (Acts 4),[31] in the woman clothed with the sun (Apocalypse 10)[32] in Rebecca, Rachel, Judith, Esther, Sarah, Elizabeth, etc.

[11] The most glorious Virgin Mary received a special divine message. Because John, Isaac, and Samson received special divine

messages, *a fortiori* [Mary received one also]. John is the morning star; Mary is the dawn; Christ is the sun. If John received a special divine message, then ..., etc. A watchman calls out when he sees the morning star; he sounds the trumpet when he sees the dawn from afar; the sun manifests itself. According to Damascene: just as Anna, who was barren, gave birth to Samuel because of her vow and promise, so Mary was begotten from Joachim and [a different] Anna because of prayers and promises.[33] And, miraculously, Mary was conceived even without original sin—according to the observance of the Church nowadays, although many rational considerations oppose this [view].[34] Nonetheless, she was conceived in accordance with the usual course of nature. Much more than John or Jeremias, she was sanctified while in the womb. Of these [two], John was sanctified because of the fact that he was to show the way by pointing [to Jesus]; and Jeremias was sanctified because of the fact that he disclosed, in quite clear prophecy, the coming of the One-who-would-sanctify.[35] Therefore, *a fortiori*, the Mother [of Jesus was sanctified] ..., etc. For (according to the observance of the Church, which celebrates her conception) she was of such great purity that she never had either original sin or actual sin.[36] Therefore, she was most holy while in the womb, because this [freedom from original sin] has never happened to a [solely] human created-being.

(c) *The disposition of Mary's body; her genealogy; her name.*

[12] **First of all, [let me speak] about the "earth" of the most glorious Virgin Mary**, i.e., about her body and its disposition, [e.g.,] about whether it was exceedingly beautiful, etc. Our first conclusion is that in the most blessed Virgin Mary there was complete congruence both with respect to nature and with respect to grace—to the end that she become the Mother of God. So, too, all the women that symbolize Mary were exceedingly beautiful in body—e.g., Esther, Judith, Rachel, and Rebecca. As regards Esther: she was especially beautiful by virtue of an unbelievable beauty; and she seemed to the eyes of everyone to be friendly and likeable. Now, regarding Judith we read that she was of exceedingly elegant appearance and that there was amazement in the eyes of those who beheld her countenance, etc.[37] And elsewhere [we read]: "There is no such other woman on earth in appearance, in beauty, and in description by words ...," etc.[38] Similarly, as regards Rebecca we read that she was an exceedingly comely young woman and a virgin unknown to a man.[39] Regarding Rachel [we read] that she was of very lovely appearance and of beautiful countenance.[40] But of what

great beauty [Mary] was, and of what great nobility, let each [person] judge from her soul and from her status and from her being the tabernacle of the Most High; for King Solomon made for himself a litter from the wood of Lebanon ....[41] According to the scale of nature, bodies are beautiful and quite beautiful and very beautiful and very noble. But the superlative degree is present in only one thing [of a given kind]. Therefore, just as by a *supernatural* operation the body-of-Christ, which derived from the Virgin, was most perfect, so too the body of the Virgin Mary was *naturally* most perfect as regards the operation of nature in conformity with our pilgrim-state. And although Scripture says nothing about Mary's beauty, nevertheless in remaining silent it intends to say that it would be wrong to believe that there was not present in Mary whatever goodness and beauty was present in other saints. Now, the Gospels praise Mary with regard to her voluntary deeds and with regard to spiritual matters; and they are so occupied with this [focus] that they leave untouched [the topic of her] other, bodily [traits].

[13] Now, bodily beauty consists in three things: in a becoming body-size and in an elegant arrangement of bodily parts and in loveliness of complexion. The body of the Virgin was elegant in quality. It was neither over-weight nor over-developed nor under-weight; rather it was balanced, having its members proportioned very fittingly. The color of her skin was a blend of white and of red—[a ruddiness] which befits a well-tempered body, according to Galen and Constantine.[42] And a brain that is perfectly suited for the *natural powers* produces red hair in infants and reddish hair in others; for the brain is warm and moist, and in the full-grown the hair is red, etc. But a brain that is perfectly suited for the *animal* [i.e., sensing] *powers* is warm and dry; from the warmth comes quickness of apprehending, and from the dryness comes firmness of retaining; and [this brain] produces dark hair. The eyes are the same color as the hair. And such hair and eyes [viz., black] were had by the Virgin Mary. Dark eyes are correlated with acute and quite subtle spirits in a warm brain. And the more subtle the substance, the more form and activity it has. Therefore, although dark eyes do not have much moist crystal, nevertheless their crystal is quite subtle, etc. But Mary was moderately dark in hair and in eyes, just as we believe her blessed Son to have been.

[14] **Secondly: Of what ancestry was she?** It is said: [She was] of the House of David.[43] And by the account of today's Gospel-reading both good men and bad men are reported to have been in her ancestry. [This fact is] not without mystery, according to the doctors [of the

Church]. She is befigured through the rainbow placed in the clouds as a sign of the covenant between heaven and earth.[44] For God could not establish peace with sinners more effectively than by having accepted a daughter of sins as a wife, a spouse, and a mother for His own Son— so that just as she was the mother and the daughter of God, so she was also the mother and the sister and the daughter of the One sinned against. (I leave aside other considerations.)

Now, she was of the genealogy of kings and was very noble in cause, in substance, and in efficacy: in cause, since she took her beginning from a noble Source; in substance, because she had a noble substance and noble properties as regards perfection of nature and fullness of grace; and in efficacy, because she brought forth [Him who was both] God and a man. She had all the gradations of primary nobility because she was of *regal*, *priestly*, and *prophetic* origin—as is evident in consideration of David, Abraham, and Nathan. She had the gradations of secondary nobility because she was a queen ("The queen stood [at your right hand] ...," etc.).[45] She was a priest; for she offered up Christ for the human race's salvation, which (according to Ambrose)[46] she was looking forward to at the foot of the Cross. For she did not stand there in order to view her Son's pain and death but in order to reflect upon the salvation of the human race. She was a prophetess ("I went to the prophetess ...," etc.).[47] She was most noble with regard to the third level of effectiveness, because she begat a Son who was (1) the King of kings ..., etc.,[48] (2) a Priest according to the order of Melchisedech,[49] (3) a Prophet powerful in deed and in word.[50] The foregoing three honors—of which the first is corporeal; the second, spiritual; the third, heavenly and supernatural—are the world's very great honors and distinctions.

[15] **Thirdly, one speaks of her name, which is "Mary"** ..., etc. And this name is most suitable, for it means "Governess," "Star of the sea," "Enlightened one," "Enlightening one," "Sea of sadness." According to Bernard she is rightly called "Mary" because of the worthiness of her person, the usefulness of her action, [and] the distinctiveness of her conception. Her worthiness-of-person is expressed by the nature of light, because she [is called] "the Star of the sea." (Nothing is more worthwhile and noble than is light; for light is like the divine nature, secondly is like angelic nature, and lastly is like physical nature. Moreover, in the case of physical things nothing is nobler than physical light; and in the case of immaterial things, nothing is nobler than is immaterial light.) She is the morning dawn that

ushers forth the sun ..., etc.[51] Secondly, she is the Star of the sea that leads shipwrecked sailors to port. And, thirdly, as a star is to its light-beam, so is the Virgin to her Son ..., etc. Bernard:[52] "Let us say a few things about that which is called "the star of the sea," for [that star] is most suitably likened to the Virgin Mother. She is very fittingly compared to a star because just as a star emits a light-beam without fail, so without injury the Virgin gave birth to a Son. And the light-beam does not diminish the star's brightness; nor does the Son diminish the Virgin's intactness. She is the Star [arising] from Jacob, whose ray illumines the whole world. She illumines minds rather than bodies; she fosters virtues and burns away vices. I repeat: as a bright and extraordinary star elevated above this large and vast sea, she gleams by her merits and shines forth by her examples.

"O you who in the flux of this world understand yourself to be swaying amid storms and tempests rather than to walk on land: do not turn your eyes away from the splendor of this Star if you wish not to be overwhelmed by the storms. If the winds of temptations assail you, if you run into the reefs of tribulations: look to the Star; call upon Mary. If rage or greed or allurement of the flesh shakes the ship that is your mind: look to Mary. If—upset because of an enormity of wrong-doings, confused because of contamination of conscience, terrified because of fear of judgment—you begin to be alarmed by the chasm or to be encompassed by sadness and by the abyss of hopelessness and begin to be in danger, in difficulty, in doubt: call upon Mary. Let her not recede from your heart nor [her name] from your mouth. And in order to obtain the aid of her prayer [to God], do not be at variance with the example of her behavior. If you follow her, you will not go astray; if you reflect upon her, you will not err. If she holds onto you, you will not fall down. If she protects you, you will not fear; if she leads you, you will not become weary; if she is propitious, you will prosper. And in these ways you will experience within yourself how it is rightly said[53] that 'the name of the Virgin is Mary.' "

(d) *Mary's special graces and blessings.*

[16] On other feast-days we will speak of how great Mary was with regard to inner virtues, of how full of grace she was—full of sacramental graces, of twelve prerogatives, of beatitudes, and of gifts of the Holy Spirit. She had the graces of all creatures and, in addition to these, twelve special graces. [17] As regards the special graces that surround her manner-of-life, which by grace stems from God's special

love [for her], it is said that these graces were present most excellently in the Virgin Mary.

Abraham was loved by God because of his faith ...,[54] Moses because of his meekness ...,[55] David because of his humbleness ("I have found David my servant"[56] and "[he is] a man after my heart ...,"[57] etc.), John the Evangelist because of his virginity, and Martha because of her hospitality. Therefore, *a fortiori*, Mary was loved with regard to all these [characteristics].

[18] **Lastly,** because God rested on the seventh day (and immediately [Scripture] adds that He blessed the seventh day) **we must consider the blessings had by the glorious Virgin more than were had by all other women.** Now, her blessing contains within itself three things: viz., consummation of works, freedom from sins, [and] a prefiguring of eternal rest. In the Virgin Mary there was the consummation of works [that comes] when all created things are united to the Creator in one human being and when the first becomes the last, and the last becomes the first.[58] (For there is perfection of motion and of work only circularly). Likewise, in her there is true absence of sins; in her *will* there was never any sin. In her there was restfulness—a sign and a cause of future, [heavenly], rest. She is the true seventh day, blessed multiply because of the sabbath of creation and of true re-creation. For in all things she sought rest, and only in her did the Creator find rest. Therefore, He rested in her tabernacle ...; she is the true Sion, which the Lord chose as His habitation.[59]

Hence, all blessings were excellently present in the glorious Virgin. In particular, the following blessings[60] were present: "Increase and multiply ...";[61] and "Isaac blessed Jacob ...";[62] and all the blessings of the twelve sons of Jacob. (These sons symbolize the virtues. For example, Juda symbolizes love; Zabulon symbolizes zeal for souls; Issachar, the exclusion of false delight and of vain tumult; Dan, judgment; Gad,[63] discipline of the senses; Naphtali, the contemplation of things invisible; Aser, justification of practices, etc. See Albertus's *Words of Praise for the Glorious Virgin.*)[64] Likewise, the blessings of Balaam[65]... [were present in her as were] also those by which Moses blessed Israel.[66] About these blessings something remains to be said at the Advent; but right now it must be left aside because of other things that need to be said, etc.

(e) *Contemplation of the glory of the Virgin Mary is [here] added.*

[19] Here contemplate the marvelous origin of the Virgin Mary.

Contemplate from an outward viewpoint all created things. Mary is elevated above all the heights of contemplation! Contemplate the firmament and its marvelous constellations, its images and signs, its risings and sittings, the marvelous movements of the planets, the marvelous influences of its innumerable powers and beauties. Contemplate this [royal] litter of King Solomon's[67] [made] from very tall and straight trees of Lebanon, ([i.e., made] of the four columns of the cardinal virtues) and of the cedar of unrottable trees ([i.e.,] of very deep inner-love). Contemplate all created things in and through any given thing: in and through a body or a soul, things natural or products of grace. The Virgin Mary excels them all. Contemplate how she is very full of grace and is blessed among all [human beings].[68] Contemplate the Mother of mercy, the Refuge of the poor, the Star of the sea, the Tabernacle which the Most High sanctified for Himself [as a dwelling-place] in her womb. Contemplate how this exceedingly lovely Rebecca went out as the rising dawn. Contemplate: if [any] creature can have knowledge, virtues, gifts of grace, happiness, etc., then Mary had these things most excellently. O most great Possessor of knowledge, most learned in all fields of knowledge! O most gracious, most merciful Mother, who has begotten a Son who is our very gracious and merciful Savior: venerating your origin we gaze upon you who are all-lovely. We your exiled children cry out unto you with a serene mind, for your birth is our salvation and health. We call upon you. Hearken unto our prayer on this our most health-giving feast-day [commemorating] your entrance into the world.

Contemplate [these things], O Christian, in order that you may arouse yourself (1) to devotion for this Virgin, (2) to [imitating] her way of life, (3) to a life full of virtues, (4) to humility, and (5) to [good] works. According to Dionysius this mother was so great and was of such marvelous beauty that anyone who would have no knowledge of her Son would readily believe *her* to be God.[69] O how great a loveliness-of-virtues was in her—[loveliness] with regard to the natural virtues, the adventitious virtues, the theological virtues, and [loveliness] as concerns the particular prerogatives of the virtues and of grace! O how great her grace—she who was full of grace and who was the dwelling-place of the Holy Spirit and who was a fount issuing forth abundant grace. How marvelous the Ark and Vessel, [viz., Mary], that contained infinitely more than itself—[that contained], viz., Him whom heaven and earth could not contain, etc. And in this way her glory is invisible and unknown to all angels and all creatures, because she is exalted above the choirs of angels, etc. If any saints were to see and to apprehend her glory, then they would have the same glory; hence, no one knows [it] ..., etc.

PART TWO
Restlessness, viz., Greed and Busyness

(a) *Greed and the evils arising from it.*

[**20**] "And on the seventh day God ended [the work] ...," etc. As will be spoken of in the last part [of this sermon], those who on the seventh day put themselves into a quiet mood will find rest at the end of their labors of six days. But since the seventh day—which is called the Sabbath (i.e., Rest)—is blessed by God, restlessness is accursed. Therefore, something must be said about the contrary of rest, viz., about restlessness, i.e., about greed, which is odious. Now, it is evident what restlessness resulting from greed is; for immoderate love of riches makes a man excessively concerned about acquiring or keeping riches. By these concerns and cares a man is drawn away from spiritual things, to which he ought especially attend. Hence, in Matthew 6 it is said: "Lay up for yourselves treasures in Heaven."[70] And [the text] continues: "Where your treasure is, there is your heart."[71] Now, greed is an immoderate love, or immoderate appetite, for getting or keeping external, useful goods that are ordained for the needs of life—such as a field, a house, vineyards, money, etc. If, then, that appetite is centered on others' goods and moves the greedy man to seize them and keep them, the appetite is opposed to justice. Or the greed is an immoderate love for one's own riches, and for this reason one clings very tenaciously to them; and in this way, greed is a special vice that is the opposite of generosity. And greed is always a sin.

At the end [of the Epistle] to the Hebrews [it says]: "Let your manners be without greed, contented with such things as you have."[72] The gloss [reads]: "A greedy man is one who is niggardly in giving and avid in acquiring."[73] And, thus, both rich men and poor men can be greedy. Nevertheless, because a wealthy man possesses worldly things, his mind is enticed toward loving them. Chrysostom [commenting] on Matthew [writes]: "The acquisition of riches kindles a quite large flame, and the desire [for riches] becomes stronger."[74] Immoderate love is spoken of notably in regard to one's own goods, etc. For according to Thomas ... : "If a man loves [something] more than he ought but less than, not more than, [he loves] God, and yet does not because of his riches will to do something contrary to divine love or something against his neighbor: then [the sin] is venial, because every *mortal* [sin] is opposed to love for God and to love for one's neighbor."[75] And although temporal goods (which are obtained and safeguarded with effort and with apprehension and with risk) are the lowest of human goods, nevertheless they are desired for no other reason than [the following]: men strongly love honors, positions of leadership, liberties, pleasures, etc., and men see that all these things can be had by means of riches.

[21] Yet, for many reasons, greediness is especially odious. [It is odious] first of all because it is [a form of] idolatry. Matthew 6: "You cannot serve God and mammon."[76] The gloss [reads]: "To serve riches is to deny God."[77] For a greedy man *sins against God.* He ought to distribute God's goods and to love God all the more for having bestowed them on him. But on his[78] balance-scales a coin of money weighs more than do God, his own soul, and the Eternal Kingdom. At times, he sells God for less than a denarius when he commits perjury, etc. [The greedy man] *sins against himself;* for, having been redeemed by God, he sells himself to the Devil for a pittance. He *sins against his neighbor* by keeping for himself things which he ought to expend on the neighbor. (Ecclesiasticus 34: "The bread of the needy is the life of the poor."[79]) He *sins against his wife and children,* whom he causes to consent to his sins. He *sins against his merchandise,* because he keeps it hoarded up until it rots. Money is a greedy man's god, for because of money he disregards all of God's precepts: he lusts, swears oaths,[80] does not worship God, does not love God or his neighbor, etc. He is obedient to money, his master.

[22] All sins are from greed, because pride is from greed.[81] For pride is the worm of the rich. He is great who does not think that because he is rich he is great. Moreover, gluttony and luxuriating arise out of riches. And one who has riches enters the Kingdom of Heaven [only] with difficulty ... ;[82] but, according to the gloss, it is impossible for one who desires [riches] to enter.[83] In one who is greedy, whose heart clings to temporal goods, love for God is extinguished, because he besmirches himself in the world's muck. Like a small bird stuck in birdlime, his heart cannot soar upward. And Caesarius likens a greedy, wealthy man to a ship, tossed about at sea, that either founders and sinks or that is brought to shore almost empty with very great loss after the jettisoning of goods. The ship is very much like riches. See how the

ship is shaken by the winds, the waves, etc.; in a similar way a rich
man is subject to many dangers, etc. Out of a desire for riches arise
wars, combats, murders, strife, betrayals, treason, robberies, sacri-
leges, etc. And so, Ecclesiastes 5 [says]: Desire for riches "is a grievous evil,"[84] especially long-lasting when it concerns what is material,
because many things in the world are desirable on the part of greed and
greed is on-going. Ecclesiastes 2: "All his days are full of sorrows and
miseries."[85]

Greed greatly afflicts at the time one *acquires*; it seriously afflicts
during the time one *possesses*; it most grievously afflicts at the time
one *loses*. Greed will not spare old age, because when other vices
become senescent ..., etc.[86] According to Seneca "the greed of old age
is like a monster. What is more foolish than to take on more provisions
when the pathway is ending?"[87] O what a wretched thing is greed!
How many vain concerns it has with regard to keeping! How many
deceptions with regard to acquiring! For the world is full of deceptions
and of greed. All men—from the most important to the least important—are given to greed.[88] O insatiableness! Unlimited desire is not
satisfied by finite things. The heart of a greedy man is not satisfied
unless land or gold is given to him—just as thirst is not quenched
unless wine is drunk. You have thirsted for gold ..., etc. Consider your
servitude, you who serve riches; you serve a mistress who does not
grant that you eat or that you ever rest. [One who is greedy] must
always labor either physically or mentally (in preparing snares of
deception); and, therefore, he becomes foolish. Luke 12: "You Fool.
This night ...," etc.[89] "The wisdom of this world is foolishness ...,"
etc.[90]

[23] Greed is like the sea, like death,[91] and like Hell—which are
insatiable. It is like a mole, which is blind and which produces many
mounds of earth and is hidden amidst them all, etc. It is like a dung-
pit, like the wheel of a mill-house, like a pig, a box with holes, the
trunk of a tree, a hen, an abscess near the heart, a bag with holes, a man
with dropsy, and like a thorn in the foot. Look at the *A Healthy Diet*,
etc.[92]

[24] Now, just as in regard to love for God rest comes by means
of six stages and by means of the works of six days, so too in regard to
love of one's neighbor one ascends unto rest by means of six works of
mercy. And immoderate love of one's riches, which begets restlessness
with regard to retaining them, removes rest, while being rigidly
opposed to these stages of mercy. And in regard to other goods the

appetite likewise has six gradations, or six stages, of restlessness. For in the case of obtaining goods greed is considered either with respect to the affections (and so the degree of restlessness is inwardly fervent) or with respect to its effect {and, in that case, when it acquires another's goods it uses sometimes force (which pertains to acts of violence), sometimes deceit (which, if it occurs *verbally*, will be deception with regard to the simple [giving of one's] word; but it will be perjury if the swearing of an oath is added)}. But if deceit is committed in a *deed*, it will be fraud if it has to do with *things*, and it will be betrayal if it has to do with *persons* (as is evident from Judas, who out of greed betrayed Christ). And, seventhly and chiefly, restlessness that stems from greed is moved in different directions unstably. For all the species of greed are reduced to the following forms: viz., robbery, usury, unjust pricing, simony, etc., and also commerce.

(b) *Commerce and trade.*

[25] Moreover, with respect to this vice [of greed] I want to dwell upon details, and I intend to touch a bit, first of all, upon commerce and trade and, secondly, upon obstinacy in holding onto one's riches and, thirdly, upon remedies for this vice [of greed].

In order for the contract having to do with buying and selling to be just, there is required (according to Scotus in Book IV, Distinction 15)[93] free will both in the one selling and in the one buying. There is required, secondly, liberty in the case of both parties, so that neither party is forbidden [to act—forbidden] by law or by his position (e.g., clerics, monks, a minor, servants, etc.). There is required, thirdly, that the exchange occur without fraud. Now, fraud is committed in three ways: in terms of species or substance, by selling one thing as if it were another; secondly, with regard to size or weight; thirdly, with regard to quality (substituting what is defective for what is whole, substituting what is corrupt for what is unblemished, etc.) If one does these things knowingly, he commits fraud and the sale is unjust and he is obliged to make restitution. ([See] Book VI of *On Injuries and on Harm Done* ..., etc.)[94] If he knew of these [injustices], he sins; if he did not know, he does not sin but is [still] obliged to make restitution. Now, understand as applying also to the *buyer* that which has just been said with regard to the *seller*. If someone [mistakenly] sells gold in place of silver or in place of bronze, the buyer who knows this is cheating ..., etc.

Fourthly, there is required equality of value between the things exchanged. For selling-and-buying is introduced for the common good, since you need something of mine, and I need something of yours. And so, [the exchange] ought not to be more to the detriment of the one than of the other. Therefore, the price and the value of the thing-sold ought to correspond. Matthew 7: "Whatsoever you will that men do unto you ...," etc. "That which you wish to be done to you ...," etc.[95] No one willingly desires to pay more than [a thing's] value; therefore, one ought not to charge [more] ..., etc. And even though—in a case where fraud is not committed—a contract is rescinded on the basis of the written code-of-law only if the buyer has been cheated by more than one and one-half times a fair price, nonetheless divine law does not leave unpunished anything that is contrary to virtue. According to divine law [a transaction] is esteemed illicit in case equal justice is not preserved. And so, according to God, one who swindles is obliged to make restitution to him whom he has harmed, if the harm is notable. I say this because sometimes the fair price of items is not exactly determinable but consists, rather, in a certain estimate, so that a slight increase or decrease does not seem to detract from equal justice. Although virtue consists in a mean, nevertheless it does not consist in an indivisible mean, etc. Moreover, a just price is determined not always simply from the value of the item but also (1) from the loss that the seller suffers because of the sale and (2) from the gain that the buyer receives. But although someone is greatly aided from [purchasing] some possession of another's, and although that other is not harmed [by selling it], nevertheless the item is not to be sold for more than it is worth; for the usefulness that accrues to the buyer does not result from the sale but from the circumstance of the buyer. However, the one who is thus aided can generously make an extra, non-required payment; and this [act] pertains to his honorableness.

[26] Moreover, an exchange is twofold: (1) a *personal exchange*, when the one party intends to receive the item in order to use it; (2) a *commercial exchange*, [when someone receives the item] not in order to use it but in order to sell it. And to the end that the commercial exchange may be fair, two things are required: First, [it is required] that the exchange be useful to the state—as occurs in the case of merchants who transfer [goods] from an abundant country to a country that does not have [them] but where their use is more needed. A further [example has to do with] those who keep the purchased items on hand so that marketable items are readily found by those who want to buy them. There are other merchants who merchandise in a blame-worthy way; they neither transfer [goods] nor store [them]; nor by their

industry is the salable thing made better. Rather, [the merchant] buys *now* in order to sell immediately, independently of all the aforementioned conditions. Such a [merchant] must be weeded out as being someone harmful to the community, because these men prevent the immediate exchange of those who want to exchange for their own use. And, thus, they make each saleable or ordinary thing to be more expensive for the buyer than it ought to be and less valuable to the seller, [thereby] doing injury to both parties, etc.

A second thing required for commercial exchange is that such a merchant receive in his transaction a price corresponding to his investment of time and effort and to his incurring of risks. For if he serves the state in an honorable manner by transporting [goods] or storing [them], then he ought to [be able] to live from his labor. Each man can justly sell his effort and his investment-of-time; and he is permitted to set the price in conformity to these and to the risks. But he ought not to seek to become excessively wealthy, lest he incur greediness, etc. And according to St. Thomas he ought not to aim at profit as the goal of his efforts; rather, he ought to aim at another goal ([viz.,] at something necessary or at something honorable): [e.g.,] at supporting his household or at assisting the needy, etc.[96]

[27] From the foregoing, note that trade, which ought to be practiced in a fair manner, ought to have the aforesaid restrictions. And it ought not at all be conducted on a feast-day, because God rested on the sabbath day and blessed the seventh day. Should you wish to set aside God's precept for the sake of your advantage, then you would be sinning mortally. Keep the sabbath days holy! It is scarcely possible for trade and commerce to be engaged in without sin. For either deception or perjury or fraud or concealed usury enter in, because you sell too expensively at the time or there is concealed deception, [etc.]. [For example,] you sell cloth in a dark building; and in the open-air the buyer sees that he was fooled with regard to the color. For there are deceptions on the part of all sellers. Draw [this] conclusion from butchers, fishermen, millers, etc. And if you stick to keeping the sabbath holy, how can you practice commerce lawfully [on the sabbath]— unless necessity, which has no law, intervenes? If tasks of service, etc., are forbidden—[tasks] which [in and of themselves] can be done without sin—then, *a fortiori*, why do not also merchants, barbers, butchers, etc., (who ought likewise to keep the sabbath) take heed? Consider the example, found in Guallensis, of how it is that Abbot Aichardus[97] sent to have his [tonsured head] shaved [on the sabbath]. And the Devil

marked all the [remaining] hairs [of his head] with his imprint. After
the Abbot was brought to repentance, he regained his trimmed hair as
a sign of forgiveness. If God commands that one who gathers wood on
the sabbath be stoned ...,[98] then why do those who govern the state
permit the sabbath to be violated in this way? Those who do not keep
the sabbath are for that reason not enriched, as Gregory in his dialogue
tells regarding the man Deusdedit, of a religious order and a shoemak-
er.[99] He kept the sabbath and was not accustomed to make shoes [on
the sabbath]; and he had, happily, all that he desired. Another always
worked and was always poor, etc.

> (c) *On rightly using one's time.*

[28] [I will speak] briefly about *hardness of heart*. In order that someone do what he ought with goods granted him by God, you should
know (according to Armicanus) that one is obliged to distribute goods
that he does not need, etc. [Those goods] are unneeded which are neither necessary for a person nor suitable to his status or his person. With
regard to man, there are four things to be considered, each of which
requires some amount of financial resources. First, there is the *person*,
who wishes to have food, clothing, shelter, etc., in order to live and to
be able to be active spiritually and physically; and [these needs] are
called personal necessities. But that which is sometimes necessary for
one person is more than enough for another, etc., depending on dis-
ability and health. And this [personal] necessity is also seen in the case
of a family-obligation and a wife.

Secondly, *honorableness* is considered. It is a certain excellence
of person with respect to certain good [traits] that are in the person; by
reason of these good [traits] a person is rendered worthy of honor.
Moreover, honorableness is a virtue that confers honor because of
strength and knowledge. Now, the populace has an eye to outward
nobility, family-size, costly garments, magnificence of food and of
domicile. And it judges honorableness [in terms of these]; and it errs,
because [these] are vanity and vainglory. Where there are virtues ...,
etc. And one who is truly honorable can have somewhat more [means]
for his garments and his servants.

Thirdly, one's job and the requirements of one's position are
taken into account. Depending on one's position, one needs servants,
tools, etc. And for this reason he must have temporal [goods] that correspond to his position and obligations. [Consider] the example of a
general, who in order to preserve the peace needs guardians and sol-

diers. And these latter need servants and cooks, etc. And a citizen needs tools for his mechanical craft and needs weapons for the defense of his country and needs money for paying taxes to his lord, etc. The case is similar as regards a teacher, a deacon, a rector, etc., in accordance with the fact that different obligations befall them.

Fourthly, the honorableness of one's position must be considered, because of which honorableness servants, [appropriate] garments, etc., are required. Hence, one is permitted to have temporal resources, by means of which he can obtain all these [required] things. And honorableness has degrees, in conformity with the persons, etc. [Possessing but] few things is sufficient for honorableness; but no amount of possessions suffices for one who is idly curious, pompous, and vain, because by these men all [the goods] are consumed, and nothing is left for the poor. Yet, whatever a man has over and above the aforementioned [goods] belongs as a whole to the poor and must—on pain of mortal sin—be distributed to the poor or else be used to enhance the worshipping of God or be put to some other pious uses.

[**29**] However, no one ought to give alms from those things that are unqualified necessities—things without which a man cannot live—because he would be taking away life from himself and his dependents. [No one ought to do this] except in a case where he would be doing it for some great prince, for a pope, or an emperor—or doing it for a defender of his country. For in order that [that other individual] might live, he himself would, perchance, have to give himself up even to death for the sake of the common good. But alms are permitted to be given from that which is necessary [in such a way that] without it one cannot *conveniently* live. [Such giving] is not commanded; therefore, it is meritorious. With regard to one's super-abundant possessions, there is no merit [in distributing them to the poor], because [to do so] is obligatory. With regard to things without which one cannot live *conveniently*: in time of necessity alms-giving is required: "Feed one who is dying of hunger ...," etc. The wealthy offer excuses because of their children, for whom they say they are keeping [the wealth]. But oftentimes they are lying, because if a son were to die, the wealthy would nonetheless hold onto the goods; and if the [deceased son] could ask [for his share, the father] would not give it to him, according to Augustine.[100] In this way Coloniensis did not want to give his goods to his sons. In this way the Florentines say that only the last inheritor of a usurer goes to Hell, etc. Instead of distributing their excess [goods], the wealthy endeavor, when dying, to found churches;

and they believe that thereby they will be saved [from divine punishment]. The Lord's commandments ought not to be kept in this way but ought to be kept in the way that the Lord commanded. [Consider] the example of Saul [101]... and of Oza[102]..., [and] of the prophet in Bethel who was sent to Jeroboam,[103] etc. Lo, the following is evident from these examples: those who wish to rely upon their own cleverness and to explain away, to excuse, or to conceal their wrong-doings deceive themselves, etc.

(d) *Remedies for greed.*

[**30**] Now [I will speak of] the remedies for greed. First of all, association with the greedy and cupid must be avoided. And, secondly, "lift not up your eyes unto riches." [104] Thirdly, do not pay attention to the advantages of riches but to the infinite number of disadvantages. Shun worldly glory. In whatever condition you were—whether you were a thief or a bandit or a usurer, etc., or a simonizer or a cheat—reflect on the fact that all of your sins will, in the end, come to light and will ruin your reputation, no matter how subtly you have committed them. [Take] the example of two subtle thieves, one of whom stole a goblet, the other of whom stole fish; but both were hanged. Then, too, there was the thief who wanted to measure a church in Paris with a rope ..., etc. Consider the fact that you are going to die and to leave all things *here*, after the example of the king of the Muslims. After he saw that he was going to die, he had his handkerchief carried throughout the state as a banner and had a proclamation made: "Our leader, the King of twelve kingdoms, says the following: 'Of my glory and my riches this [handkerchief] alone will I take with me.'" Consider the virtues of the ancients—the way in which Diogenes, Socrates, Plato, etc., shunned riches because of their virtues. [And consider] the way in which that philosopher who had a silver goblet threw it away when he saw a boy cupping water with his hand.

Moreover, [there is the case] of the other philosopher who, when his house burned down carried nothing out of it and said: "All of my possessions are with me ...," etc. And [there is the story] of another philosopher who had, beneath his head, a purse with silver coins—[a purse] which a thief wanted to steal away from him at night. When that philosopher sensed that a thief was engaged in this [thievery], he said: "Take it, so that you and I can get some rest." And [consider] the way that an empty-handed traveller sounds in the presence of a bandit. And [think] of the pauper who was usually glad [but] who became sad after he found silver coins, etc. See the examples in Guallensis's *Concerning the Laws*. [Consider] the goods of Lord Lenucius de Valle and his son. [Consider the example] of Scipio Africanus, who conquered all of Africa and took away nothing but his cognomen. [Consider the example] of Marcus Curius, who was eating on a country bench next to a small fire. Legates sought to corrupt him with gold. When they offered it, he laughed and said: "You have brought [the gold] in vain. Tell the Sammites that Marcus Curius prefers to command the wealthy rather than to become wealthy." Likewise, [there is the story] of Fabricius, who called himself rich not by virtue of possessing many things but by virtue of desiring few things. [There is the case] of Quintus Tubero, who, when he was using earthen vessels and when legates brought him silver ones, ordered them to go away: "Greater is the treasure of continence," he said, "than is a treasure of money." Similarly, [there is the case] of Arthagloga, King of Sicily, son of a potterer. He used earthen [vessels] and did not want to change his nature because of his good fortune. Furthermore, there is the other philosopher who, when he was offered much by the king, said that because he spurned more things than the king possessed, he was much richer [than the king]; and he accepted nothing.

[31] But when you turn these matters over in your mind and consider how blessed it is to please God in all respects and consider how transitory this life is, you begin to disdain superfluous riches, and God causes you to ascend by means of love—[ascend] to the point where you disdain even necessities that are suitable to your position. And subsequently you will disdain, in turn, necessities of honorableness. And thereafter you will decrease your personal necessities by means of mortification [of the flesh]—and, after this, by means of getting rid of your property and by following, as naked, the naked and impoverished Crucified One. And after you will have ascended in this way for six days, God will rest in you and will sanctify your seventh day, because he will have completed His works in you.

[Let] the foregoing [suffice] regarding the second [topic].

PART THREE
Ascension by means of Seven Stages of Contemplation

[32] "And on the seventh day God ended [the work] ...," etc.[105] God, who wills to prepare for Himself a mansion in order to rest in the soul by enlivening it eternally, causes man to cling to six stages of life by contemplating for six days. And on the seventh day man rests in God

and God in man. All of our works are divided by seven: in seven hours the *conceptus* is formed into a fetus; in seven days it acquires [human] contours; in seven times seven days it is fit for a rational soul; in seven months it is fit for birth; in seven years it is fit for language; in twice seven, for youth; in four times seven, for young adulthood, etc. Similarly, the world is turned in seven seasons; in seven days there is a week; in seven planets there is a causal influence; man's entire life occurs in seven life-stages. Moreover, there are seven angels in the Apocalypse[106] and seven golden candlesticks[107] and seven gifts of the [Holy] Spirit.[108] And when the seventh angel sounds with the trumpet, the mystery will be over, for on the seventh day there is complete rest.

[**33**] At the first stage of contemplation the ascent is unto true, living rest by means of the general work of the first day: [viz., the creation] of basic life, viz., vegetative life, that is present in all living physical objects. The second stage is the work of the second day: [viz.,] perceptual life. At the third stage one ascends unto the life of the imagination; at the fourth stage, unto the life-of-memory, which is common to the learned and the unlearned. At the fifth stage one is elevated when he ascends unto a pure willing of heavenly things. At the sixth stage one is elevated by means of the pure eye of the intellect—[elevated] unto beholding Him who is supremely desirable and is supremely loved. And thereupon, on the seventh day and at the seventh stage, this beholding apprehends the mansion of true Truth. In this way this ascension corresponds to the creation of [six] days—[a topic that] will be left aside for the sake of brevity. But in another way the first stage is called animation; the second, sense; the third, art; the fourth, virtue; the fifth, tranquility; the sixth, entrance; the seventh, contemplation. But [the stages] can also be spoken of as follows:[109] (1) from the body, (2) by means of the body, (3) with respect to the body, (4) unto [the soul] itself, (5) in [the soul] itself, (6) unto God, (7) with God. And [they can be spoken of] as (1) beautiful from another, (2) beautiful through another, (3) beautiful with respect to another,[110] (4) beautiful unto beautiful, (5) beautiful in the beautiful, (6) beautiful unto beauty, (7) beautiful with beauty. O happy is he who can arrive at seeing these things! O he is truly religious, because true religion is to reunite oneself, in reconciliation, to God, from whom one had torn oneself away by sinning.

[**34**] On the first day, seeing occurs by the senses in conformity with the imagination; and at that time [the soul] uses the world as a mirror.[111] On the second [day seeing occurs] by means of the imagi-

nation in conformity with the imagination; here [the soul] uses not the world but the image of the world as a mirror. On the third [day] seeing occurs by means of the imagination in conformity with reason; the reason for the image is now sought and is now found with amazement. On the fourth [day seeing occurs] by means of reason in conformity with imagination; through the likenesses of visible things [the soul] is now caught up unto invisible things. On the fifth [day seeing occurs] by means of reason in conformity with reason; [the soul] now proceeds, by reasoning, from things known to things unknown. On the sixth day [seeing occurs] above reason by beholding amid the elevation those things which transcend the nature of mind or are counter to reason, as are the articles of faith. And next comes rest, because there follows rapture, or ecstasy, in which "Rachel" (i.e., reason) dies and "Benjamin" (i.e., perfection of contemplation) is born.

[**35**] Now, the ascent unto God varies according to the persons and the medium. There are some who ascend by means of the state of this earthly condition and who see through a glass darkly[112] in five ways: (1) by means of a vestige, (2) by means of an image (by a vestige of creatures, by an image of the soul), (3) by means of unformed faith, (4) by means of faith [in-]formed [by love], and (5) by means of contemplation. Other men see beyond [the limitations of this] present earthly pathway—[see] in a mirror, [not darkly but] in light, in four ways: (1) the first vision is that of the prophets; the second [vision] is that of Moses, [viz.,] face to Face;[113] the third [vision] is that of John, who was sleeping on [Christ's] breast;[114] the fourth [vision] occurs, without a darkening—[occurs] in Adam's state of innocence, when his intellect was pure. Above this earthly pathway there is the vision of sleeping Adam, viz., ecstasy. [And] there is the Virgin Mary's rapture and vision. And her vision excels all other visions in three ways: (1) as concerns the Virgin's purity, (2) as concerns the disproportional medium (viz., the means of grace granted only to her), and (3) as concerns God's love. (He loved her more than all others, and He joined her in fellowship with Himself by means of a disproportional love.) Our vision, in our Heavenly Homeland, is that of those who are glorified in body and in soul; it is that of the angels and of the Virgin Mary. Higher than all these visions is our vision of Christ. First of all, [this vision] on the part of the attainer [of Heaven comes] through the grace by which the attainer apprehends more clearly than do any other creatures. Secondly, [this vision comes] with respect to the grace of the deific union by which the soul knows more perfectly that Christ's divine

nature is united to it itself. And with regard to [our seeing Christ's] deity: this is the very vision that is the seeing of the Trinity as a whole. In comparison with this seeing, all of the aforementioned visions and states of knowing are imperfect.

AN ADDITIONAL TREATMENT [OF THE TOPIC]
The six days of creation are likened to the stages and periods
by which rational, human life was elevated and completed in Christ.

[**36**] "In the beginning God created heaven and earth ...," [115] etc. That is, [He created] all things. [He created] heaven, i.e., the heavenly natures, and earth, i.e., earthly natures (coarse natures and subtle natures, etc.). The earth was void, because it lacked a vital, rational spirit. And it was empty of every vital, worthwhile operation, because darkness was upon the face of the abyss—i.e., because in the depths of its nature there was the darkness-of-ignorance of original guilt. [116] And over these waters of the rational creature the Spirit of the Lord moved, because rational creatures are not brought forth from the potency of matter. The Spirit moved by *creating* in this way and by *re-creating* out of love and mercy. And out of love and mercy the Lord spoke, and there was made true light, which illumined and dispelled the darkness. And when God saw within His own depths that that light was good, He separated it from the darkness, which did not tolerate it. That is, He separated it from rational creatures who did not believe this light to be good. Since heaven and earth were created first, there was at that moment no true light in this created [state]; but now true Light was united hypostatically with what was created. And creatures, not believing this Light, turned away from it and withdrew into darkness—as, for example, did the angels, Lucifer, etc., who for this reason fell, from the very first. And thereafter all the unbelieving [angels fell]. But [the angels] who remained in the light were led unto glory, i.e., into everlasting day, whereas those [angels] who departed [from the light] were led into everlasting darkness.

[**37**] The work of the second day determined the way in which creatures were expressly present in this work in a state of unordered-ness, because rational creatures were beneath the firmament and above the firmament, and the firmament was in the middle. The work of the third day [determined] that the waters (i.e., rational creatures) were at first gathered into the one place of the natural law. And the collection was called a lake. And the land was dry; a lake (i.e., rational spirits) in the depth of the dry land (i.e., of the body) produced—by means of the

natural law and in accordance with its own elements—plants and trees, etc. That is, in the first stage of vegetative life, which is situated in elemental life, the sensing (from very far away) of the supernatural, vital ray produced natural operations innate to itself—[produced them] without regulation and prescribed law. On the fourth day, in the intermediate nature (which is the firmament between the heavenly waters and the earthly waters), God placed great lights (specifically, at the time of Noah and of Abraham): viz., the sun of justice[117] in the firmament and the moon, i.e., the most blessed Virgin, who is situated in the firmament *above* all bodily creatures existing in this pilgrim-state but *below* the attainers [of Heaven]. And in this firmament where this moon is situated, there is the humanified Sun-of-justice. And this Sun, [viz., God the Son], rules over the Kingdom of Heaven and over the daylight, whereas the Moon, [viz., the Virgin Mary], is in charge of all darkness, i.e., of all creatures.[118] On the fifth day, at the time of the prophets (who now perceived this ray of the Sun of justice and of the Moon), the waters (i.e., rational souls) produced a reptile, etc., (i.e., produced works of higher life, viz., of perceptual life).

[**38**] On the sixth day (at the time of Moses and of Daniel) the earth (already stirred by faith in the Sun of justice at the time of the commandments) brought forth [still] higher works of life, viz., [works] of the imaginative life. And, at length, the water and the land, being quite extensively distributed by means of faith—that is, the human race being, at length, now spread out—received a living, life-giving man, [viz.,] Christ the Sun (who was God and a man, someone Supreme but united to what was lowest). Previously [He was received] from afar in the firmament; but now [He was received] on earth. (And, likewise, [the human race received] the Moon—previously from afar but now on earth.) That is, [God] created [a man] after His own image. That is, the Father created for His own Image, viz., for the Son,[119] a human nature, which He united hypostatically to the Son.

And that human being of whom it was previously spoken with regard to the works [of creation] and who already came near [to possessing] a life of reason and who already possessed the imaginative life as a whole—that man [God] now created in His image as truly rational both in terms of masculinity and in terms of femininity, i.e., both in regard to the higher part of the intellect and in regard to the lower part of the will ..., etc.

NOTES TO *SERMON IX*

1. Genesis 2:2.
2. Hymn for the feast of Mary's birth. See *Analecta Hymnica Medii Aevi*, Vol. 51 (*Die Hymnen des Thesaurus Hymnologicus H. A. Daniels und anderer Hymnen-Ausgaben* (Leipzig: Reisland, 1908)), edited by Clemens Blume. On p. 144 Blume cites this hymn as having to do with Mary's assumption (not her birth).
3. Numbers 24:17. The immediately subsequent reference to the Sun of justice is taken from Malachias (Malachi) 4:2.
4. Proverbs 8:22.
5. Genesis 1:1.
6. Throughout this sermon Nicholas is using autonomasia in expounding Genesis 1 and 2. See, above, my note 17 in Sermon VIII.
7. Nicholas is here viewing the human race as fallen. He is not implying that the original creation was other than good.
8. See n. 6 above.
9. Apocalypse (Revelation) 12:1 (not Apocalypse 10, as Nicholas writes at the end of the next sentence).
10. "… was born today": i.e., was born on the day commemorated by this present feast-day.
11. Genesis 1:9.
12. Genesis 1:12.
13. Baruch 3:38.
14. Ecclesiasticus 18:1. Nicholas holds the view that God created all things at once and that the days of creation are ways in which Moses wrote in order to accommodate the limitations of human understanding. See Cusa's *Dialogus de Genesi*, II (159).
15. Psalms 148:5.
16. Psalms 32:6 (33:6).
17. *Biblia Sacra cum Glossa Interlineari, Ordinaria, et Nicolai Lyrani Expositionibus, Burgensis Additionibus et Thoringi Replicis*, Vol. IV (Venice, 1588), f. 28^r, column 1. [Volumes V & VI have the variant title: *Biblia Sacra … Lyrani Postilla eiusdemque Moralitatibus …*].
18. Numbers 24:17.
19. Isaias (Isaiah) 4:2.
20. *Biblia Sacra cum Glossa, op. cit.* (n. 17 above), f. 13^r, column 2 (Postilla Nicolai Lyrani).
21. Isaias (Isaiah) 8:3 (not Isaias (Isaiah) 7, as Nicholas writes).
22. *Biblia Sacra cum Glossa, op. cit.* (n. 17 above), f. 22, column 1.
23. III Kings 7:2 (I Kings 7:2).
24. Exodus 3:2.
25. Not Osee 1 (Hosea 1) but Ezechiel (Ezekiel) 1:26.
26. Daniel 2:34.
27. Daniel 4:10-11.
28. Ezechiel (Ezekiel) 44:2.
29. Judges 6:36-37.

30. Esther 10:6 (not Esther 12). This verse is not in the King James version.
31. Acts 3:2 (not Acts 4).
32. Apocalypse (Revelation) 12:1 (not Apocalypse 10).
33. John Damascene, *De Fide Orthodoxa*, IV, 14, 274-275.
34. See, above, my n. 40 in Sermon VIII. See, below, n. 69.
35. Matthew 3:11. Luke 1:41. Jeremias (Jeremiah) 1:5.
36. See, above, my n. 40 in Sermon VIII.
37. Judith 8:7 and 10:14.
38. Judith 11:19.
39. Genesis 24:16. "... unknown to a man": i.e., without having had sexual relations with a man.
40. Genesis 29:17.
41. Canticle of Canticles (Song of Solomon) 3:9.
42. Claudius Galenus. See *Galeni Ars Medicinalis cum Commentariis Francisci Vallesii* (1567), ff. 38^r - 41^r. Pseudo-Albertus Magnus, *Mariale* (1488 edition), Chap. 44. Constantinus Africanus, *L'Arte Universale della Medicina (Pantegni)*, I, 18. Edited and translated from Latin into Italian by Marco T. Malato and Umberto de Martini (Rome: University of Rome, 1961), pp. 65-66.
43. Luke 1:27. John 7:42. If Christ is of the seed of David, then He is so through Mary, not through Joseph. Thus, Mary is of the house of David (as is also Joseph).
44. Genesis 9:13.
45. Psalms 44:10 (45:9).
46. Ambrose, *Expositio Evangelii secundum Lucam*, X, 132 (*PL* 15:1930C-D).
47. Isaias (Isaiah) 8:3.
48. Apocalypse (Revelation) 19:16.
49. Hebrews 7:17.
50. Luke 24:19.
51. Canticle of Canticles 6:9 (Song of Solomon 6:10).
52. Bernard of Clairvaux, *De Laudibus Virginis Matris Homilia*, 2, 17 (*PL* 183:17B - 71A). Mary is called by Bernard not only the Star of the sea but also the Star arising from Jacob (Numbers 24:17).
53. Luke 1:27.
54. Genesis 15:6 (not Genesis 2, as Nicholas writes). James 2:23.
55. Numbers 12:3.
56. Psalms 88:21 (89:20).
57. I Kings 13:14 (I Samuel 13:14).
58. Matthew 19:30 and 20:16.
59. Ecclesiasticus 24:11-12. Psalms 131:13 (132:13).
60. Here (at 18:24) I am reading "illae" in place of "illa".
61. Genesis 1:28.
62. Not an exact quotation by Nicholas. Genesis 27:28-29.
63. Here (at 18:31) I am reading (with the editors of the Latin text) "Gad" in place of Nicholas's "Dan".
64. Pseudo-Albertus Magnus, *Mariale* (1488 edition), Chaps. 201-230.
65. Numbers 23. Pseudo-Albertus Magnus, *Mariale* (1488 edition), Chaps. 214-217.

66. Deuteronomy 28:3-13.
67. Canticle of Canticles (Song of Solomon) 3:9-10.
68. Luke 1:28.
69. This amazing passage is present in manuscripts *C* and in V_J. However, in V_J the passage has been deleted (by someone other than V_1). See, above, n. 34 and the passage that is marked by it.
70. Matthew 6:20.
71. Matthew 6:21.
72. Hebrews 13:5.
73. *Biblia Sacra cum Glossa, op. cit.* (n. 17 above), Vol. VI (Venice, 1588), f. 161^r, column 1.
74. Not an exact quotation. John Chrysostom, *Homiliae in Matthaeum*, 63, 3 (*PG* 58: 606, bottom).
75. Not an exact quotation. Aquinas, *Summa Theologiae*, II-II, 118, 4 *corpus*. Cusa mistakenly writes "q. 58" (instead of "q. 118").
76. Matthew 6:24.
77. *Biblia Sacra cum Glossa, op. cit.* (n. 17 above), Vol. V (Venice, 1588), f. 26^v, column 1.
78. Here (at 21:8) I am reading "sua" in place of "suus".
79. Ecclesiasticus 34:25.
80. See Matthew 5:34-37.
81. Pride is said by theologians to be the root of all evil. (See, e.g., Augustine, *De Musica* 13, 40 (*PL* 32:1184).) *A fortiori* greed is that root if pride stems from greed.
82. Matthew 19:23.
83. *Biblia Sacra cum Glossa, op. cit.,* (n. 17 above), Vol. V (Venice, 1588), f. 59^v, column 1.
84. Ecclesiastes 5:12 (5:13).
85. Ecclesiastes 2:23.
86. I.e., whereas other vices grow senescent, greed alone does not become old.
87. Seneca, *De Moribus Liber*, n. 18 (p. 462 in Vol. I of *L. Annaei Senecae Opera Quae Supersunt*, edited by F. Haase (Leipzig: Teubner, 1862).
88. Jeremias (Jeremiah) 6:13.
89. Luke 12:20: "This night is your soul required of you."
90. I Corinthians 3:19: "… is foolishness with God."
91. Here (at 23:1) I am reading "morti" in place of "mortuo".
92. See, below, n. 44 of my Notes to Sermon X.
93. Duns Scotus, *Quaestiones in Librum Quartum Sententiarum*, Liber IV, Distinctio 15, Quaestio 2, pp. 277^1 - 284^1 in Vol. 18 of *Joannis Duns Scoti Opera Omnia* (Paris: Vivès, 1894). Here (at 25:8) I am correcting Cusa's "dist. 3" to "dist. 15".
94. Instead of Book VI—a mistake by Nicholas—see the *Decretals of Pope Gregory IX*: Book V, Title 36 (*De Iniuriis et Damno Dato*), Chap. 9 [*Corpus Iuris Canonici*, edited by Aemilius Friedberg, Vol. II (Leipzig, 1880), column 880]).
95. Matthew 7:12.
96. Aquinas, *Summa Theologiae*, II-II, 77, 4, *corpus*.
97. Johannes Guallensis, *Legiloquium*.
98. Numbers 15:32-36.

99. Cf. Gregory the Great, *Dialogi*, Book IV, chap. 37 (*PL* 77:388B-C).

100. Augustine, *Sermon* 9, 12, 20 (*PL* 38:89-90). The son dies and is with God. If he were to ask that his inheritance be given to him (and thus to God, by giving it to the poor), the father would refuse.

101. I Kings (I Samuel) 15:1-34.

102. II Kings (II Samuel) 6:6-8.

103. III Kings (I Kings) 13:1-32.

104. Proverbs 23:5.

105. Genesis 2:2.

106. Apocalypse (Revelation) 8:2.

107. Apocalypse (Revelation) 1:13.

108. Isaias (Isaiah) 11:2-3.

109. Augustine, *De Quantitate Animae*, 35.79 (*PL* 32:1079).

110. Here (at 33:24) I am reading "circa" in place of "contra".

111. Richard of St. Victor, *Benjamin Maior*, I, 6 (*PL* 196:70B - 72C).

112. I Corinthians 13:12.

113. Exodus 33:11.

114. John 13:25.

115. Genesis 1:1. Nicholas's subsequent sentences also relate to Genesis 1.

116. See n. 7 above.

117. Malachias (Malachi) 4:2.

118. See n. 6 above.

119. Hebrews 1:3. Colossians 1:15. The Son is the Image of the Father.

Sermon X: Beati Mundo Corde
("Blessed [are those] with a pure heart ....")[1]
[November 1, 1431; feast-day of all saints;
preached perhaps in Koblenz]

[1] "Blessed [are those] with a pure heart, for they shall see God...."

Today, most Beloved, as we celebrate on this feast-day of all saints, let us endeavor with all our might to sing the praises of all their virtues and to praise their happiness. For this glory is to all His saints ....[2] Let us by means of the saints abundantly praise Him who works wondrous things especially in His saints. But in order that for this reason [these] quite devout [saints] may be praised[3] with great abundance of praise, let us ask for aid, saying "Hail, Mary ...," etc.

"Blessed [are those] with a pure heart ...," etc.

I am going to take up three topics in order: First, [I will speak] of the states of happiness of the saints. Secondly, I will speak, additionally, about the purification of the heart; and in that place I will state, briefly, some things about the purifying of souls (in accordance with the feast that comes tomorrow). Thirdly, I will conclude with [the topic of] the purified heart's beatific vision in Glory [i.e., in Heaven].

PART ONE
The Eight Beatitudes[4]

[3] As regards the first topic the following must be said: although free choice is the most powerful thing below God, nevertheless it can by its own doing fall into sin; but it cannot at all rise up again without the aid of divine grace. (This is said to be the grace that makes one pleasing [to God].) Although grace is infused freely, [the infusion does] not [occur] without adult-consent. Thus, the [will's] fault is remedied by the gift of God, not by free choice; yet, [it is] not [remedied] apart from free choice. Through freely-given grace one is recalled from evil and is motivated toward the good. [I will say more] about this [point] elsewhere.

[4] Now, in another way, grace is likened to fixed-dispositions for the virtues. Grace extends at times to fixed-dispositions for the virtues, at times to fixed-dispositions for [God's] gifts, at times to fixed-dispositions for states of happiness. As concerns fixed-dispositions for the virtues, we must maintain the following: although there is one bestowing grace, there are seven bestowed virtues. These are the

224

three theological virtues (faith, hope, love) [and] the four cardinal virtues (practical wisdom, moderation, courage, justice). [I will] also [say more] about this [point] elsewhere. Secondly, [grace] issues forth in [God's] gifts, which, particularly and fittingly, are seven. Isaias names and enumerates these when he speaks of the flower that has proceeded from the root of Jesse, viz., Christ, and when he says that upon Christ the spirit of the Lord rests (i.e., the spirit of *wisdom*, of *understanding*, of *counsel*, of *courage*, of *knowledge*, and of *godliness*) and that the spirit of the *fear-of-the-Lord* will fill Him.[5] [I will] also [say more] about this [point] elsewhere. The third issuing forth [of grace] is in the fixed-dispositions for states of happiness: The following [beliefs] must be held fast: [viz.], that there are seven beatitudes that our Savior lists in the Sermon on the Mount in today's Gospel-reading and that they are, in particular, *poverty of spirit, meekness, mourning, hungering-for-justice, mercy, purity of heart*, and *peace*. [Believers] obtain these beatitudes, the twelve fruits of the [Holy] Spirit,[6] and the five spiritual senses. These [spiritual senses] indicate not new fixed-dispositions but states of delight and the uses of spiritual speculations by means of which the spirits of just men are filled and conforted.

[5] The reason for the beatitudes is that since the Restoring Beginning is altogether perfect, He restores by a free gift. And so, His gift of grace issues forth into fixed-tendencies for perfection. Since these latter resemble that toward which they tend, they are rightly called beatitudes, whose sufficiency is inferred from the order of perfection. There is required for the wholeness-of-perfection (1) complete departure from evil and (2) perfect advancement in the good and (3) perfect dwelling in the best. Now, evil proceeds from either (i) the tumor of pride or (ii) the rancor of malice or (iii) the lassitude of lust. Opposed to the first [of these] is *poverty of spirit*, which SEPARATES from tumescence; opposed to the second [of these] is *meekness*, which SEPARATES from rancor; opposed to the third is *mourning*, which SEPARATES from the evil of lust and of lustful lassitude.[7] And PERFECT ADVANCEMENT IN THE GOOD is directed toward imitating God. (This pathway is mercy and truth, since "all the ways of the Lord ...," etc.[8]) Hence, perfect advancement is a zeal for, and a *hunger for, justice* and is an *affection for mercy*. But since a DWELLING IN THE BEST occurs either through clear knowledge or tranquil affection, there are two last beatitudes: viz., *purity of heart* (for seeing God) and *peace of mind* (for enjoying Him perfectly).

[6] Likewise, if the ways of perfection are attended to, there

ought to be seven beatitudes, or ways-of-happiness. For there is either
(1) perfection of religion or (2) perfection of authoritativeness or (3)
perfection of inner⁹ sanctitude. There are required for the first [of these
perfections] (a) the renouncing of [merely] private good, (b) the
acceptance of fraternal good, and (c) the desire for eternal good. The
first three beatitudes conduce to this [first] perfection. There are
required for [the second perfection]—[viz.], the perfection of authoritativeness—(d) zeal for justice and (e) affection for mercy. (For
"mercy and truth preserve the king." ¹⁰) There are required for the perfection of inner sanctitude (f) purity of conscience and (g) tranquility
of the entire soul.

The seven gifts of the [Holy] Spirit dispose to beatitude: *fear* [*of
the Lord*] disposes to poverty [of spirit], i.e., to humility, which is the
foundation of all perfection; *godliness* disposes to meekness; *knowledge* disposes to mourning; *courage*, to hungering for justice; *counsel*,
to mercy; *understanding*, to purity of heart; *wisdom*, to peace (because
it joins us to Him who is the supremely True and the supremely Good,
in whom are found the end-goal and tranquil satisfaction of our entire
rational appetite).

Let us turn] to [consider] the Gospel, etc.

[7] *"Blessed are the poor in spirit, for theirs is the Kingdom of
Heaven."* ¹¹ "Poverty of spirit" stands for abstaining from love of the
world, i.e., love of carnal pleasures, of riches, and of personal excellence. Love of the world encompasses these three things. I spoke of
carnal pleasure on the [feast-]day of holy Mary Magdalene. I spoke of
riches-to-be-spurned on the [feast-day of the] birth of the glorious
Virgin [Mary]. Certain men spurn their own wishes and all possession
of goods, in order to have more time for contemplating God. Such
were the Apostles; and religious hermits, religious mendicants, etc.,
were supposed to be such. Secondly, those too are called poor who
possess earthly goods but who put them to use in the worship of God,
in accordance with the regulation recently issued, etc.

[8] Regarding humility, I have often said that one who is humble is like one who is inclined toward the ground (according to Isidor
in Book 10 of his *Etymologies*)—i.e., he is like one who clings to the
lowest things. And if such downcastedness results from an outward
cause, it is a punishment; [but] if it results from inner motivation, then
it is a virtue. And [this virtue] has two forms: one is internal and mental; the other is external, i.e., bodily, and involves one's words, deeds,
gestures, disposition. These latter are not the virtue *per se* and are not

acts of virtue—except when they proceed from inner humbleness. Moreover, in Proverbs 19 it is said: "There is one who humbles himself wickedly, and his interior is full of deceit." [12] (Likewise, one is to think similarly about exaltation.) True humility restrains an inordinate appetite as concerns inner excellence—[restrains it] in such a way that a man does not esteem himself as better than he really is or as otherwise than he really is. Of such is the Kingdom of Heaven, because such men are vanquishers and overcomers of the lusts of the world, etc.

[9] *"Blessed are the meek, for they shall possess the land."* [13] Those men who are meek and mild amid affronts—who are long-suffering amid tribulations, who are possessors of the land-of-their-perceptual-power—are blessed and holy in their Heavenly Home, [where] they will eternally possess this Glorified Land. Mildness maintains peace with its neighbor, because it subdues anger by means of the softness of reason. Proverbs 15: "A mild answer subdues anger." [14] God gladly answers the prayers of the meek. Judith 9: "The prayer of the humble and the mild has always pleased You." [15] And God gladly dwells in the soul of him who is meek. Mildness is a soft mattress on the bed of a beautiful conscience. [16] A meek man is known to God, as was Moses, who spoke face to Face and was the meekest .... [17] And so, [the meek] have their inheritance in the land of the living, because God possesses them here [and] they [possess] Him there. According to Augustine no one will possess God unless God possesses him here. [18] The meek possess their own hearts and govern themselves—something that the irate do not do. And so, ..., etc. Proverbs 16: "Better is he who governs his own soul than is a conqueror of cities." [19] The meek well know how to possess spiritual and temporal goods; and they do not squander them, as do the irate. According to the Philosopher mildness is present in men by nature, and cruelty is present by nature in the lion. [20] Therefore, someone cruel is someone bestial. Human physiognomy indicates mildness of nature by means of an attractive face, soft skin, a small mouth, etc. But anger makes a man a beast, and it enflames him and changes him; and thereupon he is like senseless beasts and is made like them. [21] An upright man ought to have three things: gentleness of heart, truth of mouth, and justice of deed.

[10] Just as meekness is long-suffering, so anger desires vengeance, etc. Anger is like a fire that sets a wooden house aflame; and without grace anger is dry wood, etc. It is like a boiling jar that gives off steam; similarly, an angry man, in boiling, exudes folly. And he is like a wild boar that out of rage dashes against a sword. Gregory

in his *Pastorals* [writes]: "Rage impels the mind to a place where desire does not draw it. And as not knowing, it causes detriment; wherefore, as knowing, it later grieves."[22] Furthermore, rage is like a raving man who in a fit of passion hurls himself into fire or water. Or again, it is a coal that emits a glow [and] which, when it is stirred, emits a flame. Similarly, many men seem to be long-suffering—unless they are stirred up. Anger is like an empty vessel placed on a flame, etc.

[11] The harms of anger: It blinds the eye of reason. James 1: "The anger of man does not work justice ...."[23] According to Seneca two things hinder deliberation: haste and anger.[24] Anger makes one prone to [commit] whatever evil. Proverbs 29: "He who is quick to anger will be more prone to sinning."[25] Etc. Anger removes a man from himself and removes from him mercy and compassion. It begets strife, murders, war, arson, and plunder.

[12] As to just how long-suffering the Ancients were, note in the *Short Discourse* [by John of Wales], Part IV, [the passage] on the long-suffering of Julius and of Augustus.[26] [Read also] about him who said, "O Tyrant!" and received the answer: "If I were a tyrant, you would not be calling [me one]."[27] [See the section] on Vespasian, to whom a certain man said that a wolf can change its hair not its mind [but that] Vespasian [could do] neither. [Vespasian] replied: "We owe to such men derision, to ourselves[28] improvement, and to criminals punishment."[29] Additionally, [see the section] on King Antigonus, who after he had heard some men speaking ill of the King, moved his cloak and said in another voice through the medium of the cloak: "Go away from here, lest the King hear [you]."[30] Aristippus the philosopher said to one who was reviling him: "As you are in charge of your tongue, I am in charge of my ears."[31] Likewise, Antitanes [i.e., Antisthenes] did not [directly] answer one who was reviling [him, but] said: "Two ears ought to be stronger than one tongue."[32] Xenophon [replied] to one who was reviling [him]: "You have learned to revile; with my conscience as witness, I [have learned] not to take seriously your words."[33] After it was told to Diogenes that he was being criticized, he replied: "An evil tongue shows to be better him whom it slanders."[34] Socrates said to Alcibiades that he put up with a loquacious woman at home in order that through her he might learn more easily to bear the affront of others. And when he would be struck with blows, he said only that it was annoying that men did not know when they should leave home with a helmet and when without one.[35] Lentulus spit in the

face of Diogenes, who responded: "I will attest to all men that Lentulus has a mouth …," etc.[36] The Ancients saw to it that the angry not adjudicate, lest perchance they exceed the mean.

[13] *"Blessed are those who mourn, for they shall be comfort-ed."* [37] Because the sadness of the saints is turned into joy, this blessed-ness is called the blessedness of weeping. Now, there is the weeping (1) of remorse, (2) of compassion, and (3) of devotion. As regards the first: "My eyes have sent forth springs of water," [38] and [the weeping] is a cleansing eye-salve. The second form of weeping is an assuaging ointment. And here three things are required: viz., fire, ointment, and the rubbing-of-hands. The fire is, indeed, the fire of love; the ointment is the ointment of compassion; the hands are the hands of assistance in deeds of mercy. Job 30: "I once wept over him who was afflicted, and my soul had compassion on him who was needy." [39] The third form of weeping is like a soothing bath: the soul swims in tears of devotion as a fish swims in water. Proverbs 14: "The heart that knows bitterness-es …," etc.[40]) There are six stimuli to weeping, six hindrances, six benefits. *The stimuli*: (1) recognition of one's guilt, (2) passage through this present life, (3) fear of Hell, (4) recalling our Lord's suffering, (5) compassion for human wretchedness, (6) the longing for the Heavenly Homeland. [Consider] the weeping of Peter and of Mary Magdalene because of their sins—[consider it] not just because they were afraid of losing Glory [i.e., Heaven] but because the offense was against the Infinite God. (Look, above, at the sermon of Ramon [Llull], etc.) The *hindrances to weeping* are: (1) pride ([which is] a dry mountain), (2) greed, or the affection for earthly things (Genesis 4: Cain, i.e., posses-sion, slew Abel, i.e., mourning), (3) hardness of heart, (4) excessive busyness, (5) the blinding that results from ignorance, (6) the magni-tude of sin. (Just as excessive cold freezes water, so the magnitude of sin freezes tears.) According to Gregory love is by nature warm; there-fore, where there is love, *there* there are true tears. There are *six bene-fits from tears*: (1) tears bathe a contrite spirit; (2) they lift-up a devout spirit; (3) they oppose an evil spirit; (4) they enrich the soil of the heart; (5) they quench the thirst; and (6) they avail efficaciously when one prays. The first [of these] is symbolized by a bronze sea in which those entering are bathed.[41] The second [is symbolized] by the Flood's lifting up the Ark [of Noe] on high.[42] The third, by the Red Sea, which inundated Pharaoh. The fourth, by the fountain of Paradise, which watered the land.[43] The fifth, by water's extinguishing fire (as weep-ing extinguishes the [searing] thirst that originates from lust). The sixth

has many examples in Scripture. ([Moreover,] examine [what is said] in *A Healthy Diet*.)[44]

[14] "Blessed are those who hunger and thirst for justice, for they shall be filled."[45] Justice is the virtue of giving to each his own (Augustine, *On Free Choice*).[46] Justice is the right pathway, and every other way is a straying. ([God] leads them, viz., the just, in the right way, so that they would go into a city of habitation.[47] But the ungodly walk in circles.[48]) Justice is like a right rule that is regulated by the Lord. Proverbs 15: "He who follows justice will be directed by the Lord."[49] Justice is a lovely straight line that is extended in an upward direction. Canticles 7: "Your stature is like a palm-tree."[50] Man is raised upwards in a straight direction in order that he may be just. Ecclesiastes 7: "I have found out only this: that God has made man upright."[51]

There is *general justice*, which guides unto every good; in terms of this justice a man is said to be holy. There is *judicial justice*, which reproves and keeps one back from evil. There is *moral justice*, or *cardinal justice*, which renders to each what is good. The saints and the blessed, i.e., those existing in grace, are crowned with a crown of grace wherein there are four [precious] stones: in the front, [there is the stone] of practical wisdom for foreseeing even things future; on the right side, [the stone] of moderation for making one sober-headed amid prosperity; on the left side, that of courage against hardship. In the back [there is the stone] of justice; [it is] like [having] the bishop at the end of a procession, the king at the end of a battle-array, the sailor at the aft of a ship, the just verdict at the end of the trial, the crown of victory at the end of the struggle. And the entire crown takes its name from that stone [of justice]. II Timothy 4: "A crown of justice is laid up for me."[52]

[15] Justice is like the North Star, around which all other stars revolve. And just as the stars are sometimes higher, sometimes lower, but the pole always remains, so justice remains forever; and the just man always stays in the same place without being changed because of either hardships or honors. And even as in His majesty God through justice rules over all things in number, weight, and measure,[53] so in the microcosm justice weighs and numbers all works. Therefore, blessed are those who in this world hunger and thirst, with most fervent love, for everlasting justice, for there [i.e., in the next life] they will be filled by the same justice in accordance with their loving hunger. Thirst for justice must always be in our affections, lest anyone ever think that he

is sufficiently just.

[**16**] *"Blessed are the merciful, for they shall obtain mercy."* [54] For the merciful shall be blessed by God through the infusion of grace. They please their neighbor by their just behavior, and they float on olive oil by means of their inward devotion, as is symbolized in Deuteronomy 33: "Blessed is son Aser; he is made pleasing to his brethren, and he soothes his head in olive-oil." [55] Moreover, mercy transacts prudently; for by the ills of others it is improved, by their uncleanness it is washed, by their poverty it is enriched, by their infirmity it is healed, by their burden it is lightened. Mercy has compassion on all, and it endeavors to bear the burdens of all. And the more burdens it takes on, the more it is enriched and the more swiftly it runs. Mercy lends to the Great King in order that in Glory it can have, with interest, profit (viz., grace) and loss (viz., guilt). [56] The prudent virgins took the oil of compassion and of mercy in their vessels. [57] Christ taught this transaction. Matthew 19: "Go and sell all that you have and give to the poor." [58] O of what sort is this merchandising! It receives, in exchange for a drink of water, torrents of pleasure. [59] Augustine: "Give a house, and obtain Heaven." [60]

Two virtues are especially recompensed: [viz.,] love and mercy, which are very rich in judgment. Love makes others' goods its own. ("I am a partaker with all those who fear [You] ...," etc. [61]) Mercy makes others' ills its own. (II Corinthians 1: "... as you are partakers of the sufferings, so also of the consolations." [62]) Penance is a sacrifice of the body; mercy, of the soul. [Mercy] is a river that issues forth goods and that carries away ills. (Corinthians 11: "Who is weak, and I am not?" etc.) [63] Mercy is a judge that is higher than justice. [64] We appeal to mercy from justice, because "His tender mercies are over all His works." [65] Do you desire that the Judge be merciful to you? Then be you also merciful; for it will not be forgiven [to you] unless you forgive. (Matthew 6: "If you will forgive men their sins, then your Heavenly Father will also forgive your sins." Luke 6: "Forgive, and it will be forgiven [you]." [66]) Mercy is Heaven's gateway. It is symbolized in III Kings 6: at the entrance of the temple-posts Solomon made two small doors from olive trees—[i.e.,] from two things, viz., from mercy as regards material things and mercy as regards spiritual things.

[**17**] If you wish to be motivated toward mercy, consider that there is one and the same Origin of all things. Matthew 23: "You are all brothers." [67] Isaias 58: "When you see one who is naked, cover him, and despise not your own flesh." [68] Consider your own need and

necessitude. Ecclesiasticus 31: "Know by yourself what things are your neighbor's."[69] Thirdly, consider the love that God has for him who is poor. Matthew 25: "That which you will have done for one of the least of mine, you have done for me."[70] And then you, O son of man, are seated amid the seven golden candlesticks[71] of the seven physical works of mercy, which are, viz.: feeding the hungry, giving the thirsty to drink, clothing the naked, sheltering the stranger, visiting the sick, freeing the bound, and burying the dead.[72] And you shall have in your hand the seven stars[73] of the *seven spiritual works of mercy*, which are: (a) forgiving the sinner, (b) reproving the sinner, (c) praying for the sinner, (d) instructing the unknowing, (e) advising and reassuring the doubter, (f) consoling the mourner, and (g) having compassion for all afflictions of the heart. Then you will obtain mercy, etc. How great was the mercy of Serapion, who sold himself to the Saracens in order to win their souls! (See Guallensis's *General Discourse*, Part II, Chapter 5.)[74]

[**18**] "*Blessed [are those] with a pure heart, for they shall see God.*"[75] By these words we understand two things: In one way [we understand] the very great purity that is acquired [by us], in this present Church Militant, through [both] grace and merit. In another way [the pure in heart] are also cleansed in the Dormant Church, viz., in Purgatory. (I will speak about this second topic in the next section, where [I deal] with Purgatory.) But the pure [in heart] of all kinds shall see God in the Church Triumphant. Now, in this present life three things conduce to purity of heart: viz., reading the Scriptures, generously giving alms, and shedding tears. Regarding the first [of these, consider] John 15: "Now you are clean because of the word that I have spoken to you."[76] [Secondly,] the shedding of tears makes the heart clean. Night after night I will wash my bed (i.e., the bed of conscience) by my weeping.[77] If you wish to wash [it] well, then you should have, through devotion, the warm water of tears; through contrition, the bitter water of tears; through recalling death, the ash-colored water of tears. And in this way you have true lye, etc. Thirdly, alms-giving purifies [the heart]. Luke 11: "Give alms, and, lo, all things are clean for you."[78] In order to cleanse the wound of sin, apply the cauterizing iron of justice and the protective covering of alms-giving.

Three things are purifying: the broom of confession, the file of correction, and the furnace of affliction. Take heed to be such that you can be purified by the fire of tribulation. Be not chaff, because it is burned up by the unquenchable fire (Matthew 3).[79] Just as the rubbing of a rough cloth produces, and maintains, the cleanliness of a goblet, so tribulation and mortification-of-the-flesh produce cleanliness of soul, provided that the washing of the baptismal stream, of the flame, or of blood precede [it], etc. I must speak subsequently about purification by Purgatory's fire and must speak, thirdly, about our vision of God. (Augustine in his homily [says]: Just as evil eyes cannot see this [Divine] Light, so an impure heart does not see God, etc.) [80]

[19] *"Blessed are the peace-makers, for they shall be called sons of God."* [81] Blessed are those peace-makers who have inner peace, in whom intellect, memory, will, and imagination have peace and infuse the same peace into the lower perceptual powers in harmony with God, their Beginning; for lower powers are supposed to obey higher powers. Such men are sons of obedience with respect to God's commandments. Blessed, too, are those who make peace with their neighbors by means of an outward peace that arises from their inner peace, etc. Peace comes from Heaven. John 20: "Jesus said: 'Peace be with you.'" [82] Likewise, "Glory to God in the highest, and peace ...," etc., is the angel's salutation (Luke 2). [83] Likewise, the Apostles said "Peace be upon this house"—[said it] because of Christ's instruction: "Into whatever house you shall enter, say 'Peace' ...," etc. (Matthew 10; Luke 10). [84] Peace is the last and best gift of Christ—[a gift] which He left for His disciples when He said: "My peace I leave with you ...," etc. [85] Peace is God's vestige. Proverbs 3: "All her pathways are peaceable." [86] Inner peace is present in the heart. Colossians 3: "Let the peace of Christ rejoice in your hearts ...," etc. [87] [Inner peace] is from Heaven: "If it be possible, as much as is in you, have peace with all men." [88] [Inner peace] is eternal. Isaias 32: "My people shall sit in the beauty of peace." [89] Conformity of will, humility, and tranquillity of mind make for peace. Where there is tranquillity of mind, *there* there is God's dwelling-place. "In peace—in the self-same I will sleep ...," etc. [90] "His abode was made in peace." [91]

[20] There is a bad, polluted peace of hearts that are engaged in evil—as were Herod's heart and Pilate's heart in the case of Christ's death. Psalm [72]: "I was jealous of the wicked when I saw the peacefulness of sinners." [92] Feigned [peace] is bad, as in the case of Judas. Like Judas are those who speak peace with their neighbor but who in their hearts speak ill of their neighbor. Disordered peace is bad, when the greater obeys the lesser, as Adam obeyed his wife, although the wife was, instead, supposed to obey her husband. [93] Nevertheless, [wives] do not always obey, for by nature they always strive for what

is forbidden. ([Consider] the examples (1) of the woman who fell into
the water, (2) of another woman who injured her finger, and (3) of
another one who broke her back—[consider them] in your little book.
And [consider the example] of the cheese—[consider it] in [the writing of] Gandavo, etc.) A fourfold peace allays war: *Penance* allays the
war between the flesh and the spirit, and *justice* allays the war between
man and God; *Christ's Incarnation* [allays the war] between man and
the angel [Satan], and *long-suffering* allays [the war] between a man
and his neighbor. And so, pray for the things that are for peace,[94] since
peace-makers will be called sons of God.[95]

[21] "*Blessed are those who suffer persecution for the sake of
justice, for theirs is the Kingdom of Heaven.*"[96] Blessed is that com-
moner or king or prelate who suffers persecution for the sake of justice. Long-suffering is very prudent, very calm, and very noble with
respect to waging war. It is very prudent for governing. It is present in
three [activities]: in obtaining, in keeping, in increasing. It discharges
the debts for those things that seem to be worth nothing. It discharges
guilt by means of the punishment that it endures. Similarly, it frees
from disgrace and reproaches, and it redeems itself with others, [and]
it obtains from God grace and a kingdom. [Long-suffering] holds on to
things spiritual, even at the expense of losing things material. An impatient man does not act in these ways. [See] the example in the case of
Job. [Long-suffering] causes an increase: it transforms disgrace into
gold; and by means of afflictions it is made fat like a bear; and like a
salamander it is nourished by fire.

[22] One who is long-suffering wages war vigorously. [He does
so] first of all by means of a vigorous mind, because he wants to fight
rather than to cease struggling. It is more glorious to be in battle than
to be in a bath, more glorious to dwell with the king in his camp than
to be in bed with one's wife. Paul in Galatians 6: "I bear the marks of
Christ in my body."[97] Secondly, [one who is long-suffering] has a vigorous way of fighting, for he is evasive without fleeing, he gives
ground without [experiencing] the blow of a spear, he conquers without striking back. He is so vigorous that against his enemy he does not
raise an earthen battering-ram. In the Psalm [it says]: "He has broken
the gates, the bow, the shield, the sword, and the battle."[98] In battle he
has a very well-made triangular shield. At the lower angle is fear of
punishment; at the right angle is love of the reward; at the left angle is
the suffering of Christ. And this shield repels all spears—especially
three spears, viz., the harm of property, troubles of body, and verbal

insults. And, thus, according to Paul, in Hebrews 12: "Let us run with patient endurance toward the goal that is set before us."[99]

[23] Thirdly, long-suffering governs very nobly. For it is a peace-making king that has royal dominion over all things. For all the things that are harmful to others benefit the peace-maker. For example, a year's crop-failure [nonetheless] fills his cupboard; his enemies crown him; fevers serve him as medicine; death opens his prison door, and all things work together for good for him.[100] Moreover, one who is patient is summoned to the royal meal; he is pulled, and his clothing becomes rent. This last [occurrence] is a most effective sign that [his presence] is cordially desired. Thus, the inhabitants of Cologne were not accustomed to entertain ..., etc. Likewise, he is invited to the royal meals of Christ, the Supreme King. These are tribulations, persecutions, hardships, etc. It is a great discourtesy to refuse the goblet of kings, offered after the draughts of the king; and, similarly, it is a great discourtesy to refuse Christ's chalice when offered. Our sufferings become sweet when they pass through the sufferings of Christ—just as wine takes on taste from a vase with cloves, etc. Therefore, "blessed are those who [suffer] persecution ...," etc. "And you will be blessed ...," etc.[101] And if in this way you are tried by eight fires and are found to be pure in your heart, you will see God, For as the goldsmiths know, the best and most pure gold undergoes seven processings. And just as silver and gold are processed, proved, purified, etc., seven times by fire, [so the soul] is purged by the fire of long-suffering.

PART TWO
Purgatory and the Intercessions for the Deceased

[24] "Blessed [are those] with a pure heart ...," etc.[102] According to Augustine there are three kinds of men: very good men, of whom Heaven consists; very bad men, of whom Hell consists; and certain men who are [bad but] not very bad, of whom Purgatory consists. Supreme goodness does not permit someone who is good to go unrewarded; likewise, supreme justice does not permit someone who is bad to go unpunished. And so, there is Purgatory. Moreover, there is Purgatory because only the pure in heart shall see God. Therefore, the spirits of the just are purified by the material fire of Purgatory; and dross and that which is combustible are burned away. And that punishment is greater than any punishment of the world's; but it is lesser than Hell's punishment; for [in Purgatory spirits] know that they are not in Hell, although at times they do not take note of this fact, because

of the extensiveness of the punishment. And after sufficient purifying, they fly away to Heaven.

In sinning we do three things: we offend God; we inflict injury upon the Church; we deform the image of God in ourselves. The offense requires punishment; the injury requires satisfaction; the deformation requires purification. And so, the punitive penalty here and in Purgatory ought to correspond to the sin. And because things opposed are remedied by the things to which they are opposed, and because sin arises from pleasure, sin is blotted out by punishment. For once spirits have been purified, then because there is in them the utmost purity-of-heart (which is not present without love), the spirit's love elevates [the spirit], without hindrance, unto its Beginning; and, in the end, [that spirit] finds rest and will see God.

[25] Just as a sinner, in sinning, commits an offense in three ways (as was previously said), so his penalty ought to be (a) justly punitive, (b) fittingly such as to render satisfaction, and (c) sufficiently purifying. And because departing from God and clinging to the creaturely is to sin: a just ordering demands that [the one who departs] be subject to what is lower, viz., to fire. By a just ordering, fire is so united to him that what-does-the-punishing [is united] to him-who-is-rightly-punishable—even as by the order of nature the soul is united to the body for the purpose of infusing life. However, because of the fact that these spirits are in a state of grace, the punishment ought to be temporary [and] ought to be of greater and lesser duration [and] ought to accord with the demands of what is combustible, etc. Some [spirits ought to be punished] for a longer time, some for a shorter time, some more harshly, others more leniently—in accordance with what the charge against them requires [as punishment] for the offenses. The pain hurts in proportion as the love [of the creaturely] was a clinging love, according to Augustine.[103] One is purified more with difficulty the deeper his love of worldly things has stuck to the core of his heart. From the fact that *there* [i.e., in Purgatory] there is no state of meriting, satisfaction is seen [to be made] not on the part of the will but because of the harshness of the punishments. Yet, the state of grace in which [those spirits] are found to be brings it about that they cannot be [totally] engulfed by sadness or fall into hopelessness; they neither desire to, nor can they, burst out into blaspheming. And in the case of that spiritual purifying: material fire has—by divine dispensation—a spiritual power; and inner grace, by means of outward fire, purifies the spirit and removes [from it] all unlikeness [to God] in order that it may

see [God] without delay. I say "without delay" because delay is a punishment that divine justice does not inflict after the purifying, etc. (Introduce here [the example] of Guido, who had a purgatorium in his house, etc., and [the example] of that thief in Mecheln,[104] etc. [Speak] also about the example in Gregory's Dialogue.)[105]

[**26**] As regards intercessory works the following must be held: [viz.,] that the intercessions which the Church makes on behalf of the dead are of benefit to them—[intercessory works] such as sacrifices, fastings, alms-giving, and other prayers and disciplines that are willingly assumed in order to expiate their sins more quickly. However, [such works] are not of benefit for [those dead men who are] saved, because they have no need [thereof]; on the contrary, *their* merits and prayers assist the Church Militant. Nor do [such works] benefit the damned, because the damned are cut off from the Body of Christ,[106] so that the Enlivening Spirit cannot invigorate those members. But in greater and lesser degrees [intercessions] are of benefit to those in Purgatory: either in proportion to the difference of merits among the dead or in proportion to the love on the part of the living—[a love] which is exercised for some [who are dead] more than for others [who are dead]. And this [exercising of love is directed] either toward mitigation of punishments or toward a quicker deliverance [from Purgatory], in accordance with God's disposing. For just as the severity of justice causes them to be in Purgatory, so the mildness of mercy permits their punishments to be lightened because of intercessory works—especially because they cannot, while situated in misery, aid themselves by their merits.

The mercy of God permits, I repeat, [their punishments] to be lightened through intercessory prayers, provided that there is satisfaction of divine justice and that honor is rendered to God. Divine honor demands that payment be made to it through works that are punitive and that make satisfaction (the three parts of satisfaction are fasting, prayer, almsgiving) and through the sacrifice on the altar (in which due honor is very greatly rendered [to God] on account of the pleasingness of Him who is offered there).[107] As for the fact that the mass avails more than do all other things, see Gregory, in [Book] 4 of his *Dialogues*.[108] (He states that by means of these sacrifices many men are freed very quickly from punishments.) And add [to this] the responses of the spirits of Guido and of the thief, etc. Augustine, in his book on *Caring for the Dead*, says that caring for the [bodies] of the dead does not at all avail as intercessory works for the dead. He states: "The preparation of the

funeral, the condition of the grave, and the pomp of the obsequies are
comforts to the living rather than aids to the dead." [109]

[27] Moreover, in intercessory works, just order and just universal governance ought to be preserved. Hereby it happens that in the
imparting of causal influences orderliness is preserved, as is also the
symbolism.[110] Accordingly, intercessory works do not avail for those
who are in Hell, because being cut off from the mystical Body of
Christ they can receive no spiritual influence. So too, [such works] do
not benefit the blessed, who are already at their goal and are in the
highest seats [i.e., who are in Heaven]. Therefore, [intercessions] are
of benefit to those who are in the Dormant Church.[111] By reason of
their inability to do meritorious works they are lower than the living
but are, by reason of their justice, conjoined to the other members of
the Church—conjoined because they are just and are in a state of grace.
Therefore, on account of the symbolism and the ordering,[112] the intercessory works of the Church Militant are of benefit to the Dormant
Church.

Moreover, justice, which considers the demand of merits, ought
to be preserved. Hence, although intercessions are of avail to all who
are in Purgatory—[of avail] in proportion to their measure—nonetheless, they are of more benefit to those who, when they were in the state
of being pilgrims, merited to be benefited. Therefore, regarding those
[intercessions] that are made specifically for someone: because their
intent is upright and they proceed in conformity with God, and because
the institution of the Church is not violated, they avail more for those
for whom they are specifically made, although they are also beneficial
in some way to others—not, however, in a principal way, because
divine justice requires a greater payment for greater guilt and requires
more numerous payments for more numerous instances of guilt.
(Therefore, the example of light and of the basket of apples, etc., is not
applicable, because intercessory works of this kind are like [particular]
redemptive payments rather than wide-spread influences. But just how
much they avail specifically for any given person must be determined
for sure by him who has the task of noting the weight and the measure
in regard to the accusations and the penalties.

[28] Now, as regards the one who makes intercession, it is necessary that he do so in love. For if not, then either he is the one who
commissions [the intercessions] (in which case his intercessions avail
only incidentally, as alms given to the poor cause the poor to pray for
the deceased) or he is the executor [of the intercession] (in which case,

if he is a public [servant] of God and of the Church—as, for example, a priest—then his lack of love does not nullify the work of the good commissioner (as is evident in the case of a just master who gives alms by the intermediary of an evil servant). If one makes [intercession] as the servant of a private-person-who-was-filled-with-love—whether [the servant] of a deceased [private person] or of another—the work is beneficial, even if it is a dead [work] [113] with respect to the servant. If a deceased [master] leaves a command that something be done, then the work is effective (i.e., the merit is acquired) at the time he commands; and he obtains that which is worked (i.e., the fruit of the work) after it has been worked. Masses for small children are celebrated not because of need (since [baptized children] go immediately [to Heaven]) but for thanksgiving. Moreover, it is a tenet that the pope can extend indulgence even to Purgatory, although many disagree.

[29] Durandus states that (1) Augustine in his book *Caring for the Dead* says that intercession was used in the Church[114] and that (2) according to Damascene in a certain sermon[115] and according to Dionysius in the last chapter of the *Ecclesiastical*[116] *Hierarchy*,[117] it had a use from the time of the Apostles. Furthermore, Durandus says that although public prayers avail by way of a public minister, nevertheless because in the mass there are many prayers that precede and that follow, the mass of a good priest is better, he claims, because of both (1) the one working by means of the work and (2) the work that is worked. As regards the saying of St. Jerome (who says: "As often as a psalm or a mass is sung for one hundred souls, it is of benefit to each one of them, as if [it were sung] for each [of them] individually"), Durandus states: "It is understood with respect to the *effect* of the reception and of the rejoicing or of the consolation that all such souls that are amid love have in and through this good work which is done for God's honor; [it is] not [understood] with respect to the *satisfaction* [that is made]. Accordingly, a mass for many persons is not so greatly beneficial as is a special mass."[118] Indeed, according to Durandus: from the fact that the one who does the work has from the work only the fruit that he transfers to a determinate individual by means of his intent, he aids (claims Durandus) only that individual with respect to [obtaining] satisfaction of the punishment, etc.[119]

PART THREE
The Beatific Vision

[30] Thirdly now: *"Blessed [are those] with a pure heart, for they*

shall see God." [120] Let us ascend with the Queen of Saba, lordess of
peace and of restfulness, unto the Heavenly Jerusalem in order to
behold the immense wisdom of supreme Solomon.[121] And let us see
how the 144,000 who are marked assist the Lamb,[122] who is in the
middle of the throne[123] [and who is He] whom they praise and bless
each day. Let us hasten there in hope and with sighs [and] flaming
desires.

Let us contemplate, to begin with, the [Heavenly] City, con-
structed from living stones that are square and completely perfect.[124]
In that City there is not heard the hammer of a mason or an axe or any
tool of iron.[125] For in that world, where [the living stones] are hewn,
Solomon made them perfect by means of penance, tribulation, etc. And
each [stone] suits its place, with the large stones being placed at the
foundation. And that City does not need either sun or moon, because
the beatific Face of God everywhere illumines it.[126] There the Lamb
shows Himself to the saints as true God and true man, with divine light
dwelling in His humanity as in a lamp. O true vision of peace!—for
there God has wiped away all tears from the eyes of the saints, etc.[127]
There there is the peace of God that surpasses all understanding.[128]
There there is the Lord round about His people,[129] defending His City
forever. This is the City of those saints whose [names] have been written in the book of life.[130] In this City there is no spot or wrinkle, etc.[131]

[31] This City has twelve gates—of the [twelve] Patriarchs.
Through each gate a Patriarch enters with 12,000 marked ones.[132] And
on the twelve towers are the twelve Apostles, with trumpets that proclaim the Gospel; and the Apostles call with the trumpet, so that from
all nations and multitudes an innumerable host of people may come—
whom no one can number, [people] from all nations. All the courtyards
of this City (i.e., all the saints) are of pure gold; and the entire City is
gold as pure as clear glass. The courtyards gleam with love and with
divine wisdom, and they glow perfectly with divine brightness. This is
the City of the Great King,[133] the City wherein dwell most wise
Solomon [and] the exceedingly praiseworthy Great Lord, of whose
wisdom there is no measure.[134] Every spirit praises Him, saying:
"Through Him are all things; He has made us, and we [have] not
[made] ourselves."[135] He is the Lord, in whom are all things. By all
citizens He is seen by means of an intellectual vision; and all citizens
enjoy Him with infinite delight. From this immense and excellent City
have been expelled giants who have perished on account of their
folly.[136] Unto their places have ascended from our earth tribes ...,"

etc.[137] Let us rejoice in these words, for mansions have been prepared for us, provided we have lived rightly. Each of the saints rejoices in his chamber there, in accordance with his merits.[138] And before the Throne of God [the saints] serve Him day and night.[139] Around Him are stationed angels, who fall on their faces, because they are ministering-spirits, who serve their triune Lord [and who are stationed] in a threefold hierarchy having a threefold trine order. They are the King's cupbearers, who convey the higher outpourings of wisdom unto those lower down.

[32] And the Lord God Omnipotent is as a Consuming Fire[140] who transforms all others into Himself. And He is like a living Fiery Fount that flows, as it were, into the middle, while gushing forth and emitting a stream of fire in a circle. This Stream and this Fount flow unfailingly and are an enormous Sea surrounded by the infinite bounds of eternity. And this entire Unfailing Fount—the one God who is trine by virtue of the *Source*, the *Stream*, and the *Sea*—will never cease and will inebriate, with infinite savor, His saints. And all created things have, as it were, flowed forth from the steamy vapors of this Fount; but only the saints are returned unto the Fount. In this Holy City King Solomon offers up as a meaty burnt offering those who have followed in his footsteps—[offers them up] on an altar in the sight of God and with the words: "These are they who have come out of great tribulation …," etc.[141] [God] feeds them with the bread of life and of understanding; and He causes them to drink of the water of health-bringing wisdom.[142] And the Lamb, who is in the middle of the Throne, shall lead them unto the Fount of life.[143] He indues them with a robe of glory.[144] "They are clothed with white garments because they have overcome."[145] And they are wrapped with light as with a garment,[146] having crowns on their heads …, etc. They are clothed individually with different ornaments of glory; and they have on their foreheads the name of God and of the Lamb.[147] These joys are spiritual—not carnal, as the wretched Muslims and certain Jews believe.

[33] And in conclusion: Because happiness is what is best, most delightful, and most sufficient, and because perfect activity accords with virtue,[148] happiness exists objectively in God alone and consists formally of our vision and enjoyment of God—as is the common opinion of the doctors [of the Church]. Herefrom it is evident that God is the nourishment and the clothing of the saints. Indeed, He is their entire perfection of happiness; and He is it so efficaciously that He brings about happiness in the saints even objectively, because He

affects them in this way with respect to the fact that He is, as it were, a Living Object. The vision and enjoyment [of God] is the saints' food, drink, clothing, etc. The saints also have incidental happiness because each [of them] rejoices over the glory of the other as if it were his own glory; for there, [in Heaven], love is perfect. Consequently, their neighbor's good as well as their own good makes them happy. The saints rejoice that they are there and that they have escaped afflictions. They rejoice over their God-given gifts and over their merits. The Virgin Mary [rejoices] because she is the mother of the Lord; the Apostles [rejoice] because they are disciples of the Lord God, etc. Virgins, martyrs, and teachers [rejoice] over their halos, etc. Then, prostrating themselves before His countenance, [the saints] praise and bless Him, praying always even for us, to the end that we might be made sharers of the Kingdom. Therefore, let us today join ourselves, in heart, to these [saints], who desire our salvation, who hear and understand us when we pray. Let us make a request of this [Heavenly] Jerusalem: "Praise the Lord, O Jerusalem!" etc.[149]

[**34**] O Lord, cause us to love You truly, so that we may be eternally joined to You most intimately by means of most fervent love. You, O Lord (who have said "I will deliver him; I will glorify him; I will fill him with length of days, and I will show him my salvation"[150]): show us in this life, O Lord, Your mercy, so that we may be blessed with a pure heart. And in the eternal Heavenly Home grant us Your salvation, in order that we can see You, the true God—You who are forever blessed.

NOTES TO *SERMON X*

1. Matthew 5:8.
2. Psalms 149:9.
3. Here (at 2:10) I am reading "extollantur" in place of "extollentur".
4. In the immediately following paragraphs Nicholas discusses only seven of the eight beatitudes found in Matthew 5. He does not mention the eighth beatitude until the passage marked by margin number 21.
5. Isaias (Isaiah) 11:1-3. These seven gifts are usually referred to as "the seven gifts of the Holy Spirit."
6. We learn of the twelve fruits of the Holy Spirit by combining Galatians 5:22-23 and Ephesians 5:9. These fruits must be distinguished from the gifts of the Holy Spirit (note 5 above).
7. These three beatitudes are correlated with a complete departure from evil. The two subsequent beatitudes are correlated with perfect advancement in the good. And the remaining two beatitudes are correlated with one's dwelling in the best. Thus, there are seven beatitudes under three categories.
8. "All the ways of the Lord are mercy and truth." Psalms 24:10 (25:10).
9. Here (at 6:4) and a few lines later (at 6:12) I am reading "internae" in place of "aeternae".
10. Proverbs 20:28.
11. Matthew 5:3.
12. Ecclesiasticus 19:23 (not Proverbs 29, as Nicholas writes and I have corrected, as do the editors of the Latin text).
13. Matthew 5:4.
14. Proverbs 15:1.
15. Judith 9:16.
16. Cf. Canticle of Canticles 1:15 (Song of Solomon 1:16).
17. Exodus 33:11. Numbers 12:3 (not Numbers 22, as Nicholas writes and I have corrected, as do the editors of the Latin text).
18. Julianus Pomerius, *De Vita Contemplativa*, II, 16, 2 (*PL* 59:460A). Not Augustine, as Nicholas writes.
19. Proverbs 16:32 (not Proverbs 26, as Nicholas writes and I have corrected, as do the editors of the Latin text).
20. Aristotle, *Topics*, V,2 (130^{a}26-27). *Historia Animalium*, VIII, 5 (594^{b}17 ff.).
21. Psalms 48:21 (49:20).
22. Gregory the Great, *Regulae Pastoralis Liber*, III, 9, admonitio 10 (*PL* 77:59C).
23. James 1:20.
24. Seneca, *De Ira*, I, 18, 1.
25. Proverbs 29:22.
26. A *breviloquium* is a short discourse. Re John of Wales (Johannes Guallensis) see Joan de Galles, *Breviloqui*, edited by Norbert d'Ordal (Barcelona: Barcino, 1930). [This is an anonymous translation into Catalan—a translation that appears to the editor to have been made in the fifteenth century.] See also John of Salisbury, *Policraticus*, II, 14, 54-108. [E.g., see Dennis Foulechat, translator, *Le*

Policratique de Jean de Salisbury (1372). Introduction and notes by Charles Brucker (Geneva: Droz, 1994).].

27. John of Wales (Johannes Guallensis), *Breviloquium*. (See p. 128 of the Barcelona edition cited in n. 26 above.) See also John of Salisbury, *Policraticus*, III, 14, 81. "… you would not be calling me one"—because of your fear for your life.

28. Here (at 12:9) I am reading "nobis" in place of "non".

29. John of Salisbury, *Policraticus*, III, 14, 112.

30. Seneca, *De Ira*, III, 22, 2.

31. John of Salisbury, *Policraticus*, III, 14, 21.

32. John of Salisbury, *Policraticus*, III, 14, 24.

33. John of Salisbury, *Policraticus*, III, 14, 28.

34. John of Salisbury, *Policraticus*, III, 14, 29-30.

35. Seneca, *De Ira*, III, 11, 2.

36. Seneca, *De Ira*, III, 38.

37. Matthew 5:5.

38. Psalms 118:136 (119:136).

39. Job 30:25 (not Job 3, as Nicholas writes and I have corrected, as do the editors of the Latin text).

40. "The heart that knows the bitternesses of its own soul …." Proverbs 14:10 (not Proverbs 18, as Nicholas writes and I have corrected, as do the editors of the Latin text).

41. Cf. III Kings (I Kings) 7:23.

42. Genesis 7:17.

43. Genesis 2:6.

44. Guillaume de Lanicia, *De Diaeta Salutis* (Lyon, 1496). This work has often been ascribed, wrongly, to Bonaventure. It can be found in Anton C. Peltier's edition of the volumes *Opera Omnia Bonaventurae*, published in Paris by Vivès, 1864-1871.

45. Matthew 5:6.

46. Augustine, *De Libero Arbitrio*, I, 13, 27 (*PL* 32:1235). See also my n. 133 in Sermon VIII above.

47. Psalms 106:7 (107:7).

48. Psalms 11:9 (12:8).

49. Proverbs 15:9. Not an exact quotation by Nicholas.

50. Canticle of Canticles (Song of Solomon) 7:7. Not an exact quotation and not Canticles 1, as Nicholas writes and I have corrected, as do the editors of the Latin text.

51. Ecclesiastes 7:30 (7:29). Not Ecclesiastes 1, as Nicholas writes and I have corrected, as do the editors of the Latin text.

52. II Timothy 4:8.

53. Wisdom 11:21.

54. Matthew 5:7.

55. Deuteronomy 33:24 (not Genesis 33, as Nicholas writes and I have corrected, as do the editors of the Latin text).

56. Cf. Proverbs 19:17.

57. Cf. Matthew 25:4.

58. Matthew 19:21 (not Matthew 20, as Nicholas writes and I have corrected, as do the editors of the Latin text).

59. Psalms 35:9 (36:8).

60. Augustine, *Ennaratio in Psalmum* 36, verse 26, sermo 3, n. 6 (*PL* 36:387). The idea is to give to God that which is earthly and to receive from Him, in exchange, that which is Heavenly.

61. Psalms 118:63 (119:63).

62. II Corinthians 1:7.

63. II Corinthians 11:29 (not Corinthians 12, as Nicholas writes and I have corrected, as do the editors of the Latin text).

64. James 2:13.

65. Psalms 144:9 (145:9)

66. Matthew 6:14. Luke 6:37.

67. Matthew 23:8 (not Matthew 1, as Nicholas writes and I have corrected, as do the editors of the Latin text).

68. Isaias (Isaiah) 58:7 (not Isaias 18, as Nicholas writes and I have corrected, as do the editors of the Latin text).

69. Ecclesiasticus 31:18 (not an exact quotation and not Proverbs 9, as Nicholas writes and I have corrected, as do the editors of the Latin text).

70. Not an exact quotation. Matthew 25:40.

71. Apocalypse (Revelation) 1:13.

72. Matthew 25:35-36.

73. Apocalypse (Revelation) 1:16.

74. Johannes Gallensis, *Communiloquium*, (Strassburg, 1489), Part II, Distinction 5, Chap. 3.

75. Matthew 5:8.

76. John 15:3.

77. Cf. Psalms 6:7 (6:6).

78. Luke 11:41.

79. Matthew 3:12.

80. Augustine, *De Sermone Domini in Monte*, I, 2, 8 (*PL* 34:1232).

81. Matthew 5:9.

82. John 20:19-21 (not John 2, as Nicholas writes and I have corrected, as do the editors of the Latin text).

83. Luke 2:14.

84. Matthew 10:12.

85. John 14:27.

86. Proverbs 3:17 (not Proverbs 10, as Nicholas writes and I have corrected, as do the editors of the Latin text).

87. Colossians 3:15 (not Colossians 4, as Nicholas writes and I have corrected, as do the editors of the Latin text).

88. Romans 12:18.

89. Isaias (Isaiah) 32:18 (not Isaias 33, as Nicholas writes and I have corrected, as do the editors of the Latin text).

90. Psalms 4:9 (4:8).

91. Psalms 75:3 (76:2).

92. Psalms 72:3 (73:3).

93. Genesis 3:6 and 12. Colossians 3:18.

94. Psalms 121:6 (122:6).

95. Matthew 5:9.
96. Matthew 5:10.
97. Galatians 6:17.
98. Psalms 75:4 (76:3). Not an exact quotation.
99. Hebrews 12:1.
100. Romans 8:28.
101. Luke 6:22.
102. Matthew 5:8.
103. Augustine, *De Civitate Dei*, XXI, 26, 4 (*PL* 41:746).
104. Today Mecheln is called Antwerp (in Belgium).
105. Gregory the Great, *Dialogi*, IV, 55 (*PL* 77:416D-421C).
106. Cf. Galatians 5:12. Romans 11:22.
107. The allusion is to the eucharist and to transsubstantiation.
108. Gregory the Great, *Dialogi*, IV, 55 (*PL* 77:416D-417C).
109. Augustine, *De Cura pro Mortuis Gerenda*, 2, 4 (*PL* 40:594).
110. Here (at 27:4) I am reading "et" in place of "est".
111. "Dormant Church," i.e., those believers who are in Purgatory. Cf. Sermon XXI (**4**).
112. Here (at 27:15) I am reading "ordinem" in place of "originem".
113. James 2:17.
114. Durandus de Sancto Porciano, *In Petri Lombardi Sententias*, IV, 45, 1, 6 (Venice, 1586), f. 405va.
115. Durandus (cited in n. 114 above) makes this point. See also John of Damascene, *De Iis Qui in Fide Dormierunt*, 4 (*PG* 95:249C-D).
116. Here (at 29:6) I am reading "Ecclesiasticae" in place of "Caelestis".
117. Durandus (cited in n. 114 above) makes this point. See also Pseudo-Dionysius, *De Ecclesiastica Hierarchia*, 7 (*Dionysiaca* II, 1420-1476).
118. Not an excact quotation. Durandus de Sancto Porciano, *in Petri Lombardi Sententias*, IV, 45, 3 (Venice, 1586), ff. 406va - 407ra.
119. Durandus, *In Petri Lombardi Sententias*, *op. cit.*, IV, 45, 3, n. 7 (406vb).
120. Matthew 5:8.
121. III Kings (I KIngs) 10:1-4.
122. Apocalypse (Revelation) 7:4.
123. Apocalypse (Revelation) 7:17.
124. Cf. I Peter 2:5.
125. III Kings (I Kings) 6:7.
126. Apocalypse (Revelation) 21:23.
127. Apocalypse (Revelation) 21:4.
128. Philippians 4:7.
129. Psalms 124:2 (125:2).
130. Philippians 4:3.
131. Ephesians 5:27.
132. Apocalypse (Revelation) 7:4.
133. Psalms 47:2 (48:1).
134. Psalms 146:5 (147:5).
135. Psalms 150:5 (150:6). Colossians 1:16. Psalms 99:3 (100:3).
136. The allusion is to the fallen angels.

137. Psalms 121:4 (122:4).
138. Psalms 149:5.
139. Apocalypse (Revelation) 7:15.
140. Exodus 24:17. Hebrews 12:29.
141. Apocalypse (Revelation) 7:14.
142. Ecclesiasticus 15:3.
143. Apocalypse (Revelation) 7:17.
144. Ecclesiasticus 6:32.
145. Apocalypse (Revelation) 3:5. Not an exact quotation.
146. Psalms 103:2 (104:2).
147. Apocalypse (Revelation) 14:1.
148. Aristotle, *Nicomachean Ethics*, I, 13 (1102ᵃ).
149. Psalms 147:12).
150. Psalms 90:15-16 (91:15-16).

Sermon XI: Verbum Caro Factum Est

("The Word was made flesh ....")[1]

[December 25, 1431; preached in Koblenz]

[1] "The Word was made flesh and dwelt among us." John 1.

On this day a very glorious festive solemnity—[festive] for both men and angels—rightly illumines the whole world with the brightness of joy and with the radiant splendor of devout rejoicing. [This is the solemn occasion] on which the King of Heaven, our God—who, having been made a man and having been indued with the instruments of our flesh—was seen on our earth ..., etc. Let the heavens be glad! For just as they were formed by the Word, so today they are to be restored by the Word. Let the earth rejoice! For today it produced fruit, and the Word of the Lord came forth in order to water the earth and cause it to flourish. Let the mountains sing His praise! For today the Lord has comforted his people.[2] How many things [should praise Him]? Let all created things rise up, with greatest joy, in praise of God. For the Creator has united to Himself a creature; and the creature was made the End and the Expectation and the highest Exaltation of all creatures, because he was made God. Furthermore, let us most wretched sinners lift up our devotion [unto God] because our Savior is placed in a manger in the presence of cows and donkeys, in the presence of the able, the clever, the strong, and the simple. He was made visible in order that through our love of visible things we might all be drawn unto Him. Therefore, in order to see this Word with the eye of the intellect, let us by means of our devotion and prayer go over to Bethlehem, the house of the bread of this life,[3] imploring that it show to us the Begotten Word—[show Him] through the Word of this sermon. And with a pious mind let each [of us] say, in saluting the Virgin [Mary] in her sanctuary: "Ave, Maria ...," etc.

[2] "The Word was made flesh ...," etc.

It would be better for me, who am most untalented and less discerning than others, to remain silent about the very lofty, very deep, and incomprehensible begottenness and birth of the Son of God. Nevertheless, I will say a few things—subject to the correcting judgment of all—in order that we may be refected somewhat by the nourishing food of the divine word. My sermon will be about three topics successively:[4] first, about the Word and His eternal begottenness; secondly—because He

248

was made flesh—[I will speak] about this same Word's temporal, super-marvelous birth; and because He dwelt among us, I will speak, thirdly, of the way in which He can be born in us spiritually. This three-fold nativity is signified by means of today's three masses. The first [mass is held] in the midst of darkness—[the darkness] of human capability with respect to the incomprehensible divinity [of Christ]. The second [mass is held] at dawn and has a portion of brightness and a portion of darkness, with respect to the divine nature and the human nature [of Christ]. The third [mass is held] in broad daylight, because only in bright and very pure hearts is Christ born-through-grace in the present and born-through-glory in the future. And those who are thus enlightened show, by means of [their received] grace, light to the world; and in the future they will gleam by means of [their received] glory.

PART ONE
The Word and His Eternal Begottenness

[3] On the first [topic I will speak only] very briefly. Because *"verbum"* [*"word"*] is derived from the verb *"verbas, -are,"* (which means "to produce a word"),[5] the meaning of "Word" in the case of God includes [the idea of] a *begetting production*, in accordance with the [verse] "My heart has uttered a good word."[6] Now, this divine nativity is the proceeding of an intellectual Word from God the Father. For God is the Intellectual Beginning of every creature—[a Beginning] that acts through Intellect and Will. For "He did all things whatsoever He willed [to do]," etc.[7] "He spoke, and they were made," etc.[8] And so, it is necessary that in Him there be a mental, intellectual Word, by means of which He understands Himself and other things. And because "word" is said relatively to another, viz., relatively to one uttering the word (*verberantis*), a word is derived from the one from whom it is produced by speaking. It is distinguished from him really, because nothing proceeds from itself, nothing begets itself, according to Augustine in *De Trinitate* I.[9] As is known, this Word proceeds not from a creature. Therefore, it proceeds from God. But [it does] not [proceed] from the divine essence, because such an essence is not really distinct from the Son, since each Person [of the Trinity] is the [divine] essence. Hence, [the Son, or Word] proceeds from God the Father.[10]

The Word proceeds from God. Here "God" is taken in a personal sense to stand for "person" and not for "essence." However, in God this Divine Word cannot be an accidental feature—as in us and in angels [a word is something accidental].[11] For on account of God's immutability and simplicity, there is no accident in Him. Nor is there any created substance adding [to Him anything] intrinsically as form— nor in any way [adding] extrinsically. This [addition would be] incompatible with the divine perfection and is impossible. Inasmuch as every created thing is finite, it cannot represent the Infinite, as the Word of God represents both God and all created things. And so, [the Word] is an uncreated, infinite thing that is God. Hence, the Word, which is in God (who is the Beginning of all things), *is* God. And because there is [only] one God, [the Word] is not *really and essentially* distinct from God, although [the Word] *is personally and really* distinct from the Father.

[**4**] Every essential distinction is a real distinction, but not vice versa. According to the doctors [of the Church] a *formal*, or *modal*, *distinction* occurs when something is affirmed of *a* but is denied of *b*, although there is not denied of *b* that it is one and the same thing as *a*. In this way, the divine essence is distinct from each Person [of the Trinity], because there is affirmed of a given Person something that is not affirmed of the essence. {For example, "The Father begets" is true, but "The Essence begets" is not true. Etc. ([See] *On the Supreme Trinity*, [the section entitled] "We condemn ...," where [you may read] about this [point].)[12]} However, each Person is no less the divine essence, and vice versa. A *real distinction* occurs when one of the things is denied to be the other. This [real distinction occurs] in two different ways: On the one hand, [the two things] may agree in some respect. For example, in God there is a real *personal distinction*, because although the Father is not the Son, nevertheless the Father is some [essential] thing that the Son is, since each is the one God. The Father and the Son are something one, even though [qua] Father and [qua] Son they are not identical. On the other hand, a real distinction can also be an *essential distinction*. For example, each Person and His essence is distinct from creatures.

The first [distinction, viz., formal distinction,] is a weak distinction. The second [distinction, viz., a real, personal distinction,] is a stronger distinction. The third [distinction, viz., a real, essential distinction,] is the strongest distinction. In God there are only formal and personal distinctions, for in God the several things (viz., the three Persons, who are three things) are one essence. Of these [three] it is not the case that the one depends on the other—as a part depends upon the whole or as a form depends upon its subject or as that which is supported by another depends on that which supports it.

[5] And because this Divine Word is *infinite in its essential perfection* (because it is God) and *infinite in representing* (because it represents altogether universally but nevertheless altogether perfectly— [represents] more so than do all created and creatable things [or] all mental and vocal words): therefore, we must affirm that only one, unique Word is present in God. The Word represents, in a primary way, the divine essence; for the primary object of the divine understanding is God. With regard to this meaning John says, "And the Word was with (*apud*) God,"[13] even as we are accustomed to say "His contemplation is of (*apud*) Himself" (that is, God is the object of His own contemplation, or of His own Concept)—as when we say, "His imagining is of (*apud*) this or that thing," etc. Now, God cannot be conveyed beyond Himself through ecstasy (as happens in the case of a man or an angel); nor by contemplating can He direct His attention to something else more than to Himself. Instead, being in need of no one outside Himself, He directs His attention to Himself[14] through contemplation and enjoyment; and He is happily at rest in infinite delight.

Nonetheless, in a secondary sense this very Word most perfectly represents all creatures. The Ideas and Exemplar-Forms of creatures are present in the Divine Mind, which is the Cause of all things. [They are present] in the way in which there is actually[15] present in the mind of an artisan every form of the artifact that he is going to make. And in this way, whatsoever was made [by God] was, eternally, life in the Word[16]—i.e., [was life] not in a real way but in an intellectual way. Indeed, among the gradations of life, intellectual life holds the highest place.

[6] Hence, this Word is called "the Image of the Invisible God."[17] For this Word is rightly a certain Mental Expression in which, as in an Image or a Natural Likeness, God understands Himself. [The Word] is called, for the same reason, the Splendor of God the Father's glory,[18] the Image of God the Father's substance,[19] the Brightness of the Eternal Light.[20] For like intellectual light and a certain conceptual image and an immaterial brightness, the Word radiates intellectually from the light of God the Father. Moreover, with respect to creatures [the Word] is called the Exemplar-Form, inasmuch as in it all creatures have been shining forth from eternity. [The Word, or Son] is called God's Art, inasmuch as God works through Him. He is called God's Law, inasmuch as God judges in and through Him. He is called the Appearance, or Inner-appearance, of things, inasmuch as in Him all

things are naked and open.[21] He is called the Truth of God, inasmuch as in Him are present all true things, which God truly apprehends. He is the Splendor of holy souls, inasmuch as through Him the light of grace and of glory is infused into holy souls. And so, it is evident that the Word, [or Son], proceeds from God the Father after the fashion of [an act of] understanding and after the fashion of a natural likeness and the fashion of a mental image.

[7] Now, as for every individual substance that is alive with an intellectual life or a perceptual life and that proceeds from an individual substance that is [also] alive with an intellectual or a perceptual life—[proceeds] by means of a natural likeness that is at least a likeness of species or the likeness of a close (or very close) genus and in accordance with a numerical identity of essence, or nature: let it be called the son of that from which it proceeds. In conformity with the most proper manner of speaking, it is evident that the Word of God is called the Son of God. Hence the procession of the Word is said to be like that of a son. This same Word is spoken of by the Prophet: "The Lord said to me: You are my son. Today (i.e., in eternity, where there is never a yesterday or a tomorrow) I have begotten You."[22] For God speaks (*verbat*) and understands always, because He is Pure Actuality;[23] for He exists as always actual. Hence, He is always Word, etc. At the end of Isaias [we read]: "Shall not I, who make others to bring forth children, myself bring forth?"[24] From this Father and this Son there proceeds the Holy Spirit after the fashion of [an act of] willing. [For this procession occurs] in the way in which our mind by means of its word breathes forth its love, or volition—since, in our case, nothing is [intentionally] willed unless it is known.[25]

NOTES TO *SERMON XI*

1. John 1:14.
2. Isaias (Isaiah) 49:13.
3. Luke 2:15. The word "bethlehem" means *place of food, house of bread.*
4. Nicholas's sermon is incomplete. Topics two and three remain undeveloped.
5. Nicholas here writes "verbas, -are". At 7:13 he uses the word "verbat". He seems to regard "verbare" as a verb that means *to utter a word or words.* However, at 3:16 he also uses the genitive form of the verb "verberare"; accordingly, the Paris edition of Cusa's sermons (Vol. II, f. 43ᵛ) transforms "verbare" into "verberare".
6. Psalms 44:2 (45:1).
7. Psalms 113B:3 (115:3). Psalms 134:6 (135:6).
8. Psalms 32:9 (33:9).
9. Augustine, *De Trinitate*, I, 1, 1 (*PL* 42:820).
10. The word "proceed" is here being used in a general sense that indicates begottenness. Its use does not conflict with the traditional statement that the Son *is begotten* from the Father, whereas the Holy Spirit *proceeds* from the Father and the Son.
11. "... is something accidental": i.e., is something incidental, is not of or from our substance, is not something substantial (in the Aristotelian sense).
12. Pope Gregory IX, *De Summa Trinitate et Fide Catholica*, Book I, Title 1, Chap. 2 [Vol. II, column 6 in Aemilius Friedberg, editor, *Corpus Iuris Canonici* (Leipzig, 1881)].
13. John 1:1.
14. See Anselm of Canterbury, *Monologion* 33-36 regarding how God thinks Himself and *thereby* thinks all things.
15. Here (at 5:27) I am construing "actu vel habitu" as a pleonasm.
16. John 1:3-4.
17. Colossians 1:15.
18. Hebrews 1:3.
19. Hebrews 1:3.
20. Wisdom 7:26.
21. Hebrews 4:13.
22. Psalms 2:7. Not an exact quotation. Medieval theologians often considered the Psalmist, David, to be a prophet. And they grouped the Book of Psalms with the Books of the Prophets.
23. This is a Thomistic-Aristotelian point.
24. Isaias (Isaiah) 66:9.
25. Augustine, *De Trinitate*, XV, 27, 50 (*PL* 42:1097).

Sermon XII: Jesum Quaeritis
("You seek Jesus ....")[1]
[April 20, 1432; preached in Koblenz]

[1] "You seek Jesus of Nazareth, who was crucified. He has arisen; He is not here." [This text is found] at the end of Mark and in today's Gospel-reading.

Yesterday and the day before yesterday our pious Mother, the Church, lamented her dead Spouse. "Her harp was turned into mourning and her organ into the voice of those who weep."[2] But on this day those devout women who were still tearfully seeking Him in the place where they [had] laid Him—[seeking Him] in order to anoint His crucified body—heard from the angel (1) that they were seeking Jesus of Nazareth, who was crucified and (2) that He had arisen and was not in that place. And their sorrow was turned into joy, because their beloved Deceased One was once again alive, because He who was lost was [now] found.

[2] O the holy women who, being so troubled, sought Jesus Himself very early on the first day of the week![3] (For it was not permitted on the Sabbath.) [They sought Him] as soon as the opportunity presented itself—[sought] Him with faith formed by love and with affection directed directly toward Christ! They knew by the testimony of the angel that Jesus, the Son of Mary, is the Savior, inasmuch as in His name every knee is bowed—[the knees] of those in Heaven, those on earth, and those beneath the earth.[4] And there is no salvation in and through any other.[5] [They sought] Him, that is, who was [very] recently crucified most contemptibly between thieves. O those blessed women, who merited to be the first to hear that the Savior had arisen! What else was [knowing] this than to know the goal of the Incarnation! For just as the Virgin Mary, having been instructed by the word of the angel first learned that the Incarnate Word was in her womb: so these women merited to be the first to learn, from the angel, of the goal of the entire Incarnation, viz., the Resurrection. For through the Resurrection human nature obtained the glorious beauty that the Incarnate Word principally was intending [for it to have] by His having become human. For [those women] were able to say: "Truly, the Lord has arisen. Hallelujah!"[6] O the enormous joy! For the life of our beloved Crucified One has reflourished. "This is the day that the Lord

254

has made; let us rejoice and be glad therein."[7]

[3] Therefore, in order that together with these women we may be remade—[remade] in spiritual joy—by the triumphant Crucified One, who on this present day is sought but is not found on earth, let us raise the mellifluous voice of our heart in angelic salutation. [Let us do so] in order that from what is to be said we, with mortified flesh, may be raised in resurrection—[raised] through [the aid of our] now-consoled Mother [Mary] (who because of her Son's death was recently afflicted with very grievous empathetic suffering[8]). For now she is the Mother of all consolation. Etc.

[4] I will speak of three things successively. [I will speak], first, of how Christ was sought by these women; and for this purpose, the Gospel will there be cited *for the common people*. In particular, [I will mention the theme] that to seek Jesus is to seek Him as the Crucified One. Secondly, [I will speak] of Christ's resurrection. And there [I will speak]—especially *for the [more] capable*—about the gifts of the glorified body and about the mystical resurrection in the case of those of us who have been crucified with Him.[9] Thirdly, [I will speak of the fact] that Christ was not found alive in the earth, [or grave]—even as life is not present in interred individuals. (As long as Christ's body was dead it remained in the earth, or in the stone [tomb].) Rather, [He was found alive] when He raised up [His body] alive by re-assuming His soul.[10] And this [part of the sermon is] *for those who are [more] contemplative*.

PART ONE
On Seeking Jesus as the Crucified One

(a) *Why the Son of God underwent a most bitter death.*

[5] As concerns the first [topic]: The motive of the first sin was (1) the desire for power in regard to one's excellence (for the Devil had said "You shall be as gods ...") and was (2) the vice of idle curiosity with regard to understanding truth (whence the Devil added "... knowing good and evil"). The transgression-of-the-commandment (viz., the eating from the forbidden tree) followed upon these two [faults]. Because of this sin God became a man in order to save all of us who descend from Adam the transgressor. For this sin had such a very great Redeemer! Hence, although the human race could have been set free by the infinite and eternal God—[set free] solely by the directive of God's eternal and infinite will, which nothing can resist, nevertheless

it pleased His infinite goodness to descend for the sake of us human beings and our salvation.[11] For no other means was so suitable for the Restorer [and] for the one who was restorable [viz., man,] and for the process of restoration. And in order to show that in Him [viz., the Son of God] there was unsurpassable patience, wondrous humility, [and] measureless love, He became, for our sakes, obedient even unto death—the death on the Cross[12]—which was the most despicable and bitter death of all deaths. And so, for our salvation He suffered with a most generalized suffering, not only with respect to His human nature but also in accordance with all the major members of His body. And although He could not experience any suffering with respect to His divine nature, He suffered with respect to every power of His soul— [suffered] with most acute suffering. For not only did He feel pain insofar as He suffered because of His wounds, but also He felt empathetic pain insofar as He suffered empathetically because of our wrongdoings. Moreover, He suffered with a most shameful suffering because of the yoke of the Cross and the company of thieves, with whom He was numbered. He suffered a murderous suffering because of the separation of His soul from His body—although the union of each with the deity was preserved.

[6] The Source of our restoration has restored us, *with freedom of choice preserved.* Hence, by His very effective example He summoned us to come to the highest peak of the virtues, even as is His example of enduring death—yea, a most painful death—for the sake of justice and obedience to God. What, then, could motivate us more than does the very great kindness of the Supreme Son of God, who laid down His own life for us[13] not because of our merits but in spite of our many intervening demerits. And He is shown to be all the greater, the more grave and base are the things that He undergoes for us. By His example, we are summoned to love Him and to imitate Him.

Moreover, *while preserving God's honor,* He restored us by offering satisfaction-making obedience, [thereby] repaying the honor due to God.[14] The honor taken away from God, through pride and disobedience with respect to a matter in which man is under obligation, is restored through humility and obedience with regard to this same matter. [But it is a matter] to which Christ is not at all under obligation, inasmuch as qua God He is equal to the Father and qua man is innocent and not at all bound to die. When He emptied Himself, He became obedient even to the point of death;[15] by offering a pleasing sacrifice for the perfect propitiating of God, He paid to God [the honor] which

He Himself had not taken away.

And, thirdly, with *the orderliness of the universe being preserved*, He made restoration through a most suitable remedy by treating opposites with their opposites. For man sinned through an act of pride, because he willed to be as wise as God. He sinned by delighting in the [forbidden] fruit. He was inclined toward lust [and] was haughty with presumptiveness. He infected the human race and removed [from it] immortality. Hence, first of all, God became a man; secondly, [the God-man] suffered on the wooden Cross by means of a most generalized suffering on account of the general infection [of sin]. By means of very bitter suffering, [He sought to] remedy lust; by means of very shameful suffering [He sought to] remedy presumptiveness.

Moreover, because a generality of corruption had infected every part of our body and every power of our soul, Christ likewise suffered in the higher part of reason (by which He delighted supremely in God); and He suffered very intensely as regards that [part] which, on account of its association [with the body], is more lowly in nature. For Christ was [both] pilgrim and attainer. The pain of the flesh was most intense because of the evenness, and liveliness, of His physical constitution. And, in His mind, the pain was very intense because of His supreme love for God and His supreme graciousness toward His neighbor. And although the soul was separated from the body, nevertheless the deity remained united to them both. However, for three days the man [Jesus] was not alive. And, thus, it is evident how in the case of Christ's death, death was swallowed up by victory.[16] In dying, Christ destroyed our death; and in arising, He restored our life.

Now, I have set forth these [points] prefatorily in order that we may know whom these very devout women sought—viz., Jesus, who was crucified.

(b) *The descent of Jesus's soul to those in Hell,*
  and at what time He resurrected them from the dead.

[7] Now, [I will turn] to the Gospel account. Because Christ earnestly desired the redemption of all those who are incorporated into Him by faith, His soul, when He died, immediately descended unto Hell. (His divinity was united to this soul.) And, thus, Christ descended unto Hell and remained in the tomb, because the divinity remained inseparably united also to His body. And so, He descended unto the Fathers, in order to reform even Hell (for He is the Lord of those who are in Hell) and to lead out those who were captives.[17] O enormous joy! What do

you think the saints who were held in Limbo were shouting? Nothing other than: "You have come, O Desirable One, whom we in darkness were awaiting! O One who put death to death, You who have enlivened us with a glorious beauty![18] Blessed is He who comes in the name of the Lord."[19]

How great was the joyous proclamation on the part of the Prophets, because they saw God's prophesied Salvation! How great was the joy of the Patriarchs, because they discerned that in His seed they are redeemed and all nations are blessed! But although this joy was present in Hell, it did not extend to the lower part of Hell, where there neither was nor will be any redemption. Nor does it extend to the place of those who have departed [from this life] with original sin, because after this life grace is not given to anyone who has not obtained it here.[20] And those who were in Purgatory rejoiced over their salvation; and (as is the opinion of most [theologians]) they were led out [of Purgatory] together with those who were in Limbo [and] who, according to Augustine (in [Book] XII of his *Literal Interpretation of Genesis*) were not tormented.[21] Accordingly, while Christ's soul was present with the Fathers, who at that moment obtained full happiness, His body remained in the tomb.

[8] And on the day of burial Mary Magdalene and the other Mary, viz., the mother of Joseph (according to [Nicholas] Lyra),[22] were sitting facing the tomb.[23] Now, the women, viz., Mary Magdalene [and] Salome, and Mary [the mother] of James, bought aromatic spices (on the day of His death or else after the evening of the Sabbath, when the Sabbath was finished, because it was not permitted [to buy and sell] on the Sabbath), in order, when they came, to anoint Jesus after the Sabbath was over.[24] And they came in the early morning; they flocked together in order to accomplish their purpose; and because the place [of the tomb] was not within the [city] walls, the sun began to rise before they came to the burial place. But (according to the Gospel of John)[25] Mary Magdalene came to the tomb early in the morning, when it was still dark, and found the stone already rolled away. And she ran and told it to Simon and to John. Etc. And we do not there read that she saw an angel on that occasion.

But according to Matthew,[26] Mary Magdalene and the other Mary bought aromatic spices (possibly in the evening after the Sabbath was over) in order to anoint Jesus. And after the evening, but before daybreak, Christ arose early in the morning. And according to St. Jerome[27] [the women] came to the tomb at the time the sun began to rise. And there was an earthquake ...,[28] etc., and the angel of the Lord came down ..., etc. And according to Luke[29] there came on the first day of the week those women who had accompanied Christ from Galilee. [They came] very early, at daybreak, carrying aromatic spices which they had prepared; and they found the stone rolled away; and two men stood there in shining garments ..., etc. According to the Gospel of John,[30] Mary Magdalene remained outside the tomb weeping, after the disciples departed from the tomb to their own homes. And while weeping, she bent forward and looked into the tomb and saw two angels in white [garments] seated there. Etc.

[9] All of the following events are of deepest [symbolism and] mystery: first, Mary Magdalene's coming to the tomb when there was still darkness; secondly, her coming with the other Mary and finding an angel. (Now, the other Mary was perhaps Mary [the wife] of Cleophas,[31] who stood beside her at the Cross. Or [possibly it was] Mary [the mother of] Joseph (according to [Nicholas] Lyra),[32] which Mary was sitting with her facing the tomb. And according to Saint Jerome, as the *Scholastic History* tells,[33] etc., [Mary Magdalene] came at dawn. And in-between there came Peter and John—i.e., (according to a homily of St. Gregory's)[34] the Church of the Gentiles and the Synagogue. And the Synagogue, symbolized by John,[35] ran quite quickly; but the Church-of-the-Gentiles, signified by Peter, entered the tomb first; and thereafter entered John; for, in the end, there will be one shepherd and one sheepfold.[36]

[10] And while Mary Magdalene was thus standing there [looking into the tomb], and while Mary [the wife] of Cleophas (or Mary [the mother] of Joseph/Joses[37]) was outside [the tomb], the angel descended from Heaven and sat at her right hand. For after Mary, amid darkness, first found the tomb empty: she recurred, in her sorrow, to the Old and the New Testaments—[i.e.,] to the Church and the Synagogue. And because she found that Christ ought thus to suffer and to rise, she welcomed her companion who had seen Christ die—viz., Mary [the wife] of Cleophas, [who was] the sister of the glorious Virgin Mother and/or [the mother of] Joseph/Joses—and she stood meditating on the death of her Beloved. And in order fully to experience the bitterness of His death, she [now] had a companion and eyewitness who was able to arouse her both as regards the pains of the crucifixion and as regards the suffering of the [Virgin] Mother and [the Mother's] compassion for her Son. Therefore, while those two very holy women were standing there, there descended into their hearts the

divine light of the Resurrection—[light] sent into their hearts by the angel. And the angel spoke, consoling their hearts regarding that sorrow: "Be not afraid! Him whom you seek, O Followers of Christ, [is not here] ...," etc.

Now, after Mary [the wife] of Cleophas had received consolation by seeing the Lord's angel, who was consoling them, perhaps she immediately ran and reported [the happenings] to Mary Salome (who was her sister)[38] and to Mary [the mother] of James; [for] they too were ready with ointments. And perhaps she went to console the very majestic Mother of Christ, the sister of her own mother.[39] And when these three thus assembled, they courageously entered the Lord's tomb; and they saw an angel, clothed with a white robe, sitting on the right side; and they were astonished. The angel said: "Be not afraid! You seek Jesus of Nazareth, who was crucified. He has arisen; He is not here. Behold the place where they laid Him. But depart and say to His disciples and to Peter that He goes ahead [of you] into Galilee. There you will see Him, as He told you." And the women, departing, fled from the tomb, because fear had seized them. The other women [also] fled.

[11] Now, Mary, who came by herself before daylight, was not fearful. But she stood and wept. While, then, weeping, she bent forward and looked into the tomb.[40] And she saw two angels in white sitting (one at the head, the other at the feet) where the body of Jesus had been laid. Accordingly, they said[41] to her: "Woman, why do you weep?" She replied to them: "They have taken away my Lord, and I do not know where they have laid Him." After she had said this, she turned around and saw Jesus standing there; but she did not know that it was Jesus. And Jesus said to her: "Woman, why do you weep? Whom are you seeking?" She, thinking that it was the gardener, said to Him: "Sir, if you have taken Him, tell me where you have laid Him, and I will take Him away." Jesus said to her: "Mary." She, turning, said to Him: "Rabboni" ..., etc.

(c) *A dialogue is composed concerning our seeking,*
together with Mary Magdalene, Jesus and His resurrection.

[12] Now, in order that we may to some extent grasp the sweetness of this mystery and may arouse ourselves at the dawn of this very high feast, let us address Mary Magdalene, who is full of sorrow and love and compassion. And let us say: "Tell us, Mary. Why did you seat yourself with Mary [the mother of] Joseph facing the tomb?"

Mary: "I did not want to desert in death my heart's Treasure, Him whom unbelievers have taken away from me [and] whom I have always greatly loved. So because I was the most sorrowful and the most sadly distressed of all women,[42] I was sitting there in order at least to see the place where they had buried my Beloved. I was not permitted to approach more closely, and so I was sitting opposite the tomb. Being very sorrowful, I desired to be restored, at least from afar, by the fragrance[43] of my Savior—I who was not able to draw nearer. At that time, I, the most unhappy of all [beings], was not alive. For I had witnessed the heart of my Beloved, in whom my life dwelt, pierced by a spear. How, then, could there survive in me a spirit of any courage? Deprived of strength, I prostrated myself on the ground, in order that the residue of my life's spirit might be taken from me and that I might be buried with my Beloved—I who was prevented from approaching the body, with which I chose to bind myself inseparably.

[13] "But my Beloved—who was now established in peace since the Sabbath had already arrived, who was not dead in my breast but was more alive because He died for me and in my sight—said: 'Arise, make haste, my Love.[44] You see that the place of my burial is surrounded by guards. You are waiting in vain. The garden is closed. [But] do not despair. You shall not lose me.' And I [said]: 'O the nature of this consolation, Lord! And because I see the Fount of Life—You, the Lord—to be signaled by, and sealed up by, this large stone, I shall believe [that] no one will remove You from this [tomb]. Therefore, before I am prohibited because of the [coming of] the Sabbath, I will go in order to prepare ointments and to cleanse Your very sacred body with tears; and I will anoint it, now dead, as [I anointed it], once alive. O Fount of Life, help me to find some vital remedy to apply to Your body. For in a certain way I, my miserable self, was the occasion of Your death—[was the occasion] at the first anointing, when Judas, [later] distraught as a result of his deed, purposed to betray You. O most gracious Jesus, what could have happened more infelicitously for me (who merited to be saved by You) than that moment when for my sake you were delivered up unto death traitorously by Judas! You who alone can do all things, grant [that I] may find an ointment contrary to Judas's, so that [Your body] will become enlivened with the life of the living. With these thoughts, sweet Jesus, I take leave of You. That is, I take leave in body, not in mind, by means of which I rest buried with You. I depart, I say, quite quickly, so that the guards will also leave. If they see no one, then they too will decide to go away. And, thereupon,

I shall return straightway.' "

[**14**] "Tell [us], O Mary: What did you do in the meantime?"

"Assuredly, I gathered a remedy of pure nard-oil, the true fragrance of love, into the clear alabaster vessel of my heart. And I closed it with a tight seal, so that it not lose its fragrance but be more strongly disseminated within itself through a continuous circle of glowing, fragrant vapor throughout the entire holy Sabbath—after the fashion of my Beloved, who is inclosed in the tomb. [I have collected this fragrant oil] to the end that if, perchance, an opportunity of approaching [the tomb] is offered me, I may very quickly spread the very warm remedy over the rent and wounded body and may wrap all of myself, alive and warm, around the dead body. [I would do so] in order that the vital spirit—the immortal soul—of my Beloved might be enticed to return and to re-enliven [that] fragrant, glistening body—a body warmed by the pressing-close of my body and bathed by my tears.

[**15**] "Accordingly, after the Sabbath had ended, I hastened [to the tomb] as quickly as I could. For I was not sleeping, but my heart was ever awake. As a woman alone, I was not afraid of the soldiers who were assigned as guards; nor was I, in the darkness of night, terrified of the place of Calvary, to be dreaded because of the corpses of the dead. Rather, although it was dark, I came with ointment to the tomb. And while I was coming to the tomb, I said to myself: 'O how auspicious a day [it would be] if what I wanted were to happen to me: viz., that my Spouse could awaken in my arms.' What will I say when I arrive? Assuredly, I will speak to Him with [the words of] David and the Prophets.[45] At length, He will hearken—He who comes, as the Ancients have foretold, from Heaven to earth at the insistent plea of the Fathers: 'Send, O Lord, Him whom You are going to send.'[46]

"What, then? If the Word was made flesh for the salvation of His people, and if at the lament, prayer, and insistent plea of the sons of Adam He descended from Heaven, then it will be possible for me, I hope, to beseech Him by means of very acceptable prayers and very devout tears. Because He loves me, [it will be possible to beseech Him] who stayed long enough in Hell to console those [there] and to save them by means of [the gift of] supreme happiness (which they have now obtained)—[beseech Him] that His soul (which is united to His deity) return to His body (which [also] is united to His deity). This [return] will, I hope, be much easier for the infinite deity (which is united to both [His body and His soul]) than was the Incarnation—although for this same deity not only is nothing impossible but also nothing is even difficult.

"And I will remind Him that through the Prophet He spoke the psalm: 'I will extol You, O Lord, because You have upheld me until the end.'[47] (In this psalm [Christ] speaks, assuredly, of His resurrection.) And I will say: 'Rise up, my glory; rise up, psaltery and harp.[48] Take [with you] swiftly the spoils of Hell.[49] And rise up, O Light of my eyes.'[50] And if You died because of me, O Lord, and do not deign to hear my prayer, then look unto Your mother and Your brothers, and rise up on account of their groan and their plight. Who doubts what is written about You?: 'I will arise at daybreak.'[51] Therefore, I have hastened anticipatorily to arouse You, so that (according to the prophecy of Osee)[52] Your going forth may be prepared as the morning light.

[16] "But I, being exceedingly unhappy, was thinking of many things that I wanted to speak into His ears by way of lament in order to evoke His graciousness and power, so that He would come alive again. [He is the one] who gave the eagle the power to renew its youth[53] and gave the lion the power to arouse its cub by its roar and gave the phoenix life from burnt ashes. And [I was thinking] of the potter, who from the clay of a weak vessel made another vessel;[54] and [I was thinking] of Jonas, who emerged unharmed from the belly of a whale; and of the grain of wheat that fell into the soil and bore fruit;[55] and of the stag that received horns again; and of Samson, who carried away the gates;[56] and of Joseph, who was led out of prison, who became established as master of all[57] Egypt.[58] While [thinking of these things], I approached [the tomb] and saw that the stone had been set aside. And at that point what grief could be thought to be similar [to mine], when all my hope was thwarted?[59] For I believed that my Beloved had been taken away by unbelievers. I did not find Him whom my soul was seeking.[60] I said: 'O most wretched of all women, although it is still dark, you have come too late, because those who took away the Lord came even earlier. O irreparable neglectfulness! Why did you go away from the buried treasure, which now someone else has dug up and taken away from you?'[61]

[17] "And while I was saying these things with no small amount of lamenting, I understood that I could not proceed, because my Christ, who had been taken away, could not be found by me at this time, because I was seeking [Him] unworthily. For in me was still the darkness of unbelief in the Resurrection. Nor did the writings of the Old and the New Testament fully satisfy me. However, I ran immediately to Peter—the head of the Apostles and of the Church, who loved Christ

more than did the others[62]—to see whether he could help me look. I also went to John, whom Christ loved with a unique love,[63] to see whether, perhaps, Christ had disclosed to him at the [Last] Supper the meaning of the Old Testament scriptures, so that with his help I could find my Beloved. They ran [toward the tomb] immediately. And John was younger than Peter; but Peter entered [the tomb] first and, thereafter, John. And they saw that I had spoken the truth. And although in both the Old and the New Testament there were many very clear passages to the effect that He had to arise, nevertheless Peter and John had not yet understood [them].

[18] "And I, Mary Magdalene, remained [at the tomb] when [Peter and John] went back to their own matters. And, as it happened, during that interval there arrived Mary [the wife] of Cleophas (who stood beneath the Cross with the Mother of the Lord)—or [perhaps] Mary [the mother] of Joseph/Joses[64]—so that she (in accordance with the etymology of her name) enlightened me as regarded the gathering of the others. And, lo, day began to break and the light of dawn began to be seen, so that after a great shaking of the earth darkness was expelled from my heart. For a dark, enclosed place is not easily enlightened unless the locks are opened and put aside and unless existing impediments to the light are removed by a strong moving-force. For although with respect to Christ's *human nature* I was doubtlessly aglow, having lovingly spent a long time in His very agreeable and very virtuous way of life, nevertheless in my darkened earth I had not yet grasped the mysteries of so great a *divinity*. And so, a strong earthquake occurred in the thickness of the earth-of-my-intellect, so that [its clods] would be parted and broken up for the sake of the enlightenment that my Beloved was preparing for me. And after the earthquake had occurred in me especially as a result of my recalling of Christ's very bitter suffering, which we [women] saw at the very end [of His life and] which we began to consider earnestly while standing together: behold the angel-of-the-Lord (who had come down from Heaven and rolled away the stone, whose face was [as brilliant] as lightening and whose garments were [white] as snow, who terrified the guards, so that they became as dead men) sat on the stone and said to us 'Be not afraid. I know whom you are seeking. For [you are seeking] Jesus, who was crucified for man's salvation [and] whom you now remember. He has arisen ...,' " etc.

(While the angel was thus speaking to the women, other women arrived—viz., Mary Salome and Mary [the mother] of James, etc., as [indicated] previously.)

[19] "When you, Mary, looked inside and saw the place where your Beloved was laid, tell us what you said."

Mary: "I said: 'My God, why have You forsaken me at the end? I never left you. I wanted to die with you, but You did not want it. Cause me to die at Your tomb, O Lord, so that at least I may always be found to be there where you were reposited. I look roundabout, O Lord, and there is no one to console me. I do not look for angels, O Lord, but for You, the Creator of angels. Why do you send me creatures to console [me], for I seek and love only You? It cannot be the case that You do not love those who love You. [But] how is it that You love me, O Lord, if You only afflict me? I do not seek beautiful spirits and ministering spirits but seek the Lord. This [help from creatures] is no consolation, O Lord.' "

[20] There [appeared] now, to Mary Magdalene, two angels. And take note of the following: First of all, when there was only affection—i.e., when by herself Mary hastened [toward the tomb] in darkness—she did not see an angel. Secondly, when with the recalling of [Christ's] suffering and with the affection of love [for Him] she stood [at the foot of the Cross] with Mary [the wife] of Cleophas: [then] she saw an angel. But when she sought [Christ] with the intellect, the affection, the memory, and all her powers, then in the company of the women who had come from Galilee (according to Luke), she found *two* angels. But these [two] angels she also saw when she was by herself at the tomb, when she bent forward so lovingly [and] when she so scrutinizingly sought, with all her visual power, to see at least traces of her Beloved.

And the angels said to her: "We know whom you now have been seeking, because you seek Jesus, the Savior. Do you seek that once beautiful and lovely Nazarene—[lovely] more than the sons of men[65]—whom the Jews so vilely treated on the previous day by covering His shining face and the eyes through which the ray of divine wisdom was gleaming? [The Jews treated Him] as if He were a thief and a robber. They lacerated His holy face with wounding slaps; [and] they crowned the King of glory with thorns; and they mocked Him by kneeling down; they bound His very noble hands with bonds as in the case of a robber. He was treated very vilely and was bound, was defiled in His pleasing face by the spittle and the defilements of the worst of the Jews. There was a livid discoloration of His cheeks as a result of the blows from the slaps and from the shedding of tears. He appeared like a leper. All of His five senses—sight, hearing, taste, touch, smell—were shamefully polluted. He was beaten [and] was reckoned among robbers. He died by a very bitter death on the Cross, with every kind of torment preceding it—[torments] from within and without, because of compassion for His blessed mother and for all those who would undergo future punishments for His sake, etc. No living person will be able to detail His countless punishments, which He underwent in mind and in body. After His burial He remained entombed here for three days. Do you seek Him, Mary?"

Mary: "I have been looking and looking for Him Himself, my Soul and my Life—[Him] who is wounded and dead. But, wretched me, I find Him nowhere. For they have taken away my Lord, and I know not where[66] they have laid Him. And looking roundabout, [I do not find Him]." Etc.

[21] "O Mary, when, from behind, you saw him whom you thought to be the gardener and [to whom] you said (in the common language of the Syrians) 'Sir, if you have taken Him away ...,' etc.: whom did you think Him to be?"[67]

Mary: "Wretched me, I thought that every living being could not fail to see and to know my very great distress and grief ...," etc.

"But when He answered you 'O Woman, why do you weep?' where were your ears that you did not recognize your Lord?" etc.

Mary: "His disposition was other than was once that of my Lord. For He was disposed in a far different way—in accordance with the humanity of a mortal—after having suffered many things. And my enormous longing did not allow me to pay close attention, except when [doing so] was pleasing. And, hence, I said: 'If you have taken [Him] away ...,' " etc.

[22] "And when He said to you 'Mary,' why did you [then] recognize [Him]?"

Mary: "At that point my Beloved infused into me the light of consolation and of grace, so that I who was blind would see and understand and notice that He who called me by name knew me—and so that I would then take a closer look at the one who uttered [my name]. Thereupon, He immediately illumined me with His ray in order that I would see Him whom I, being blind, had been seeking for a time. For in seeking, I was inflamed when I did not find Him. He permitted my desire to become inflamed in order that I would seek Him more diligently and would find Him with greater delight. Then I fell to the earth, understanding that by divine ordination the following had to happen: that the Incarnate Word, my Lord, would die for the salvation of the human race and would descend unto Hell for the human race's restoration and would rise up with a glorified, incorruptible body, according to the Scriptures. [He would do so] in order in Glory [i.e., in Heaven] to bestow blessedness, of body and soul, on the redeemed, whom He raised from the dead. He preceded them as being the High Priest who passed through the heavens," etc.[68]

[23] "O Mary, how great was your joy at that moment?" Etc.

Mary: "[It was] exceedingly great, when I found more abundantly my Immortal Life, [viz., Jesus], over whom death will no longer have dominion,[69] [and] when I saw [this] most victorious Triumpher over death and Hell, Him who is my sole desire—[saw Him] in a body glorified with four [glorious] endowments.[70] Thereupon, I rightly said: 'This is the day that the Lord has made ...,' etc.[71] On this day full restoration of human nature was accomplished, etc. O sweet Apostolic commandment! The Lord commanded me to announce [His resurrection] to the Apostles. O how great a grace He conferred on me (1) that I could be the first to announce to them this excellent glad-tiding, (2) that I could cause [them] to sing, throughout all the quarters of Jerusalem, 'Alleluia' to the Lord God.

"He did not command me to announce [His resurrection] to His most glorious Virgin Mother. Doubtlessly, just as by unique faith she was buried with Christ, so too she arose with Christ.[72] As by steadfast faith and clear understanding she clung to her Son in His death, so too [she was with Him] in His resurrection. And so, she knew [of the Resurrection]. And, as was right, no other messenger than her Son was worthy to make known [to her] this glad-tiding.

"I proclaimed [it]! I ran hither and thither! I made known the things I had seen. I interpreted the Scriptures as to why it was so. Yet, the hard hearts of the disciples doubted, so that greater faith in the Resurrection was given to them later."[73]

[24] (However, lest [Christ's] very certain manifestation be prolonged unduly, He manifested Himself five times on the day of Resurrection: to Mary Magdalene, to the women [at the tomb],[74] to Peter,[75] to those en route to Emmaus,[76] to the disciples behind closed doors.[77] And from the day of Resurrection unto the Ascension He appeared five [more] times, etc.)

PART TWO
The Endowments of Christ's Glorious Body

[25] Secondly, we must speak about the glorified body of Christ and

about its endowments. Christ truly died and truly arose. According to
the view of St. Thomas [Aquinas[78] this resurrection occurred] on the
Lord's Day, in between midnight and dawn (in conformity with a har-
monization—as in the *Ecclesiastical History*[79]—of the Scriptural
passages, which are varied). On the basis of this fact [let us ask]
about the kind of body Christ had when, after the Resurrection, the
glory of His soul began to flow abundantly into His body, so that it
became glorious by virtue of the following four endowments: viz.,
impassibility, subtlety, agility, and splendor. In I Corinthians 15 Paul
[speaks of] these [endowments]. In particular, he speaks of whatsoever holy body of anyone: through death the body is sown in corruption; it shall arise in incorruption; it is sown in dishonor; it shall arise
in glory; it is sown in weakness; it shall arise in power; it is sown a
natural body; it shall arise a spiritual body.[80] By "incorruption"
[Paul] understands in that passage *impassibility*; by "glory" [he
understands] *splendor*; by "power," *agility*; by "spiritual being," *subtlety*. And we are hopeful that the Lord will transform the bodies-of-
our-lowliness, in conformity with the body of His splendor,[81] so that
just as He who is the First-fruits of those who sleep[82] received on this
day a glorious body, so too we will one day receive a glorious body.
Therefore, [because of this hope] it would be delightful to experience
[this reality].

PART THREE
The Resurrection of Christ. How We Must Seek
Life by means of the Spiritual and Sacramental Food
of This Paschal Lamb.

[**26**] Thirdly, because He arose and is not here, we must understand
how it is that the crucified Christ, arising from the dead, was not found
on earth. And [we must understand] that for this reason everyone who
seeks Him who has risen from the dead must, if he seeks to find Him,
first carry his own cross by mortifying himself with Christ. According
to Paul in Colossians 3 [a man does this] (1) by walking along the pathway of patience, humility, and love, (2) by exercising the active life in
works of mercy and, thereafter, by contemplating, (3) by resting in the
tomb with Christ and later arising with Him, and (4) by relishing not
things on earth but things in Heaven, where Christ is.[83] For if we desire
to be members of Christ,[84] who is now immortal, we must be without
sin and live without sin. For on account of sin we die, and we cease
being immortal members [of Christ]. For if oftentimes we have fallen

into death through our sin, we must arise on this present day with Christ, and we must seek life in what is distributed at the spiritual and sacramental meal of the Paschal Lamb.

And just as Christ, who arose from the dead, sits amid the Father's glory, so too let us walk in newness of life. Having put off the mortal human nature of corruptible oldness, let us put on a new human nature.[85] And having dispelled darkness, let us put on weapons of light; [let us do so] especially on this day that the Lord is said special-ly to have made; for it is a victorious day and is triumphant, jubilant, joyous, free of labor, and rewarding. Let us exult and rejoice with spir-itual joy together with the angels whose seats are renewed [and] with the Fathers, who were led from the bonds of Hell—rejoice with beau-tifully sounding citharas, especially if we know how to seek, with fer-vor, Heavenly things. And may the Heavenly things taste sweet to us, with an inner relish. And let us walk in newness of life, having cast aside our former way of life.

[27] Now, [to begin with], Christ arose powerfully. For He was not resuscitated by another living man (as the child was raised by Elias)[86] or by someone dead (e.g., the bones of Eliseus).[87] Rather, just as on the Cross He had the power of giving up His soul, with a shout, so He had the power of taking it up again. And in this way He raised Himself on the third day. Now, it is not the case that in order to accom-plish this [arising] he opened the tomb or the seals impressed upon the stone by the guards. (The stone was placed in order to close off the [entrance] of the tomb.) Rather, as He went out supernaturally from His mother's womb, closed up by the seal of [virginal] modesty,[88] so too He went forth [from the tomb] not weakly but powerfully, bringing His body back into submission, etc.

[28] Secondly, by being seen He showed that He had really aris-en …. "See my hands and my feet."[89] And although the splendor of His glorified body is ten times brighter than the sun, it does not injure the eye, as does the sun, but it perfects the eye. Secondly, through being touched [He showed that He had arisen] …. "Touch and see."[90] Thirdly, through taste [He showed Himself to be risen]. For He ate with His disciples, although the food that was eaten and swallowed was not turned into the nature of His body but was vaporized, even as water is vaporized. Likewise, too, our spiritual resurrection ought to be proved through the following: through seeing, so that with a pure heart we may contemplate God and His benefits [to us. Moreover, it ought to be proved] through touch, in order that we may be intimately united

to Him through the affection of love; through *taste*, in order that by divine sweetness we may be re-created with pleasantness through devotion of mind.

[**29**] Thirdly, Christ arose manifestly. [This fact] is evident from His showing His scars (John 20),[91] which He ought not to have had after His body was glorified [but] which He willed to retain in order to show forever His triumphant victory and in order to placate the Father on our behalf by showing His wounds. (I John 2: "We have an advocate with the Father.")[92] Furthermore, [He arose manifestly] in order to demonstrate to us His generosity and the magnitude of His love. He has pierced hands for displaying His generosity. And He invites [us] to *ask* ("Ask and you shall receive," etc.)[93] He has feet transfixed by a single nail in order to signify the union of friendship, just as friends are joined by one bond of love. He has a side pierced-open, in order that we may draw wisdom from His heart, in which are all the treasures of knowledge and wisdom.[94] Likewise, He retained His scars in order on the Judgment Day to put the condemned to silence by saying: "See the wounds inflicted by you and for you. See my opened side; but you have not entered." Thus, whoever arises with Christ must arise manifestly with stigmatic marks so that he can say with the Apostle in Galatians 6: "I bear in my body the marks of Christ."[95]

[**30**] Moreover, the words of our theme-verse[96] can be applied to those who today are sacramentally seeking the Crucified Christ, the sacrificed Paschal Lamb. For He is to be sought by our arising with Him through remembering His crucifixion [and] by our clinging to Heavenly things. And the Immaculate Lamb is to be partaken of by means of the unleavened bread of sincerity and truth.[97] And our Paschal Lamb is befigured by the Jews' paschal lamb [and] is to be eaten, by the faithful and by those of one heart, in the House of the Lord, i.e., in the Holy Church.

[**31**] [I will now speak] about the instituting of this blessed sacrament in the discourse at the Lord's Supper. For our Restorative Beginning [viz., Christ] left for us medicines and sacraments through which (1) to regenerate us (e.g., [the sacrament of] baptism), (2) to confirm and augment us once regenerated (e.g., [the sacrament of] confirmation), (3) to nourish us once confirmed (e.g., the [sacrament of] the Eucharist). Now, the nourishment—with respect to its being freely given—is observed (1) through the preservation of devotion-to-God (something that is exercised by the *offering of a sacrifice*), (2) through the preservation of love-for-one's-neighbor (something that is

exercised through the *communion of the one sacrament*), (3) by the preserving of inner-delight (something that occurs through *refecting on the provision for the way*).[98] The foregoing things are present in this sacrament in accordance with what befits the period of grace, the pilgrim-state, and our capability. In accordance with the period of [grace], the sacrifice ought to be pure and full; but there is no [such] sacrifice except the sacrifice offered on the Cross. Hence, in the sacrament Christ is present not only symbolically but also really.

Moreover, [the sacrifice] ought [not only] to symbolize love and communion but also to inflame [us] to love one another and to unite, maximally, our members to the one Head, from whom—through the *diffusive, unitive*, and *transformative* force of love—mutual love remains in us. Hence, in this sacrament there is contained the true[99] Body[100] of Christ and His immaculate flesh—[contained] as *diffusing* itself to us, uniting us to one another, and *transforming* us into itself by means of most fervent love. Through this love [Christ] sacrificed Himself for us and made payment for us and is present with us unto the end of the world. Moreover, because of the veil of symbolism and because of the merit of faith, 'seeing in a clear manner' does not befit the pilgrim-state. Nor is it fitting to touch Christ's flesh with one's teeth—because of our dread of raw flesh[101] and because of the immortality of His body after the Resurrection. And so, [the Body] was handed down hidden by very sacred symbolisms and by congruent and expressive likenesses—[handed down to us], in particular, under [the symbolism of] many-grained wheaten bread and of wine from grapes, etc.

[32] Regarding this sacrament the following must be believed ..., etc. (Consider further the symbolism of the Lord's Supper.) Christ as a whole is contained under each form [of the Eucharist], after the consecration—[contained] totally, not in a delimited way but sacramentally. And it is necessary to know that if the priestly office and the intention of the consecrator come together with the prescribed utterance of words over the appropriate material, then true Christ (Body, Soul, and God, because these are indivisible) is present as a whole in each [of the two] element[s]. But He is hidden from all the senses, in order that faith may have merit. And in order that He not be detected, the accidents have their entire operation just as before, etc.

[33] One must not come to [the Eucharist] only for consuming the sacrament, for he who comes [only] for this purpose eats judgment to himself.[102] Rather, one must come for [the partaking of] the reality of the sacrament (viz., the spiritual food) through faith and love. And

one must come to the reality and the sacrament (viz., the mystical Body of Christ). The reality of the sacrament is the real Body-of-Christ, which is apprehended by means of the spiritual food. Now, as long as a man is in the flesh he needs life-sustaining refection that refects the whole man.[103] (This refection occurs only in [spiritual refection on] the Incarnate Word. The Word of life is the refection of the spirit; the Incarnate Word is the refection of man, etc.) Therefore, every day we must eat spiritually, and be nourished lovingly, by this agreeable, vital refection in which [He who is] the Way, the Truth, and the Life[104] is present. One cannot have life otherwise than by living by means of this spiritual food. And this [partaking] occurs not in regard to the leaven of iniquity, etc., but in regard to the unleavened [bread] of sincerity and truth[105] [and] by means of spiritual teeth (viz., the intellect, the memory, and the affection), with which this food is gently chewed and swallowed. Thus, a man is digested into Christ, because He is the food of grown men; He transforms into Himself one who eats worthily of Him.[106] All who are to be incorporated into Christ must be present without mortal [sin], although the partaking of the sacrament removes venial [sins]. One must come to the sacramental [partaking] by way of spiritual [partaking], so that being now incorporated into Christ, one is nourished and one grows.

[34] But how a man is made spiritually Christlike through contemplating Christ's divinity in pure and sincere faith that is formed [by love]—this [topic] I will leave aside for now. Secondly, through the recalling of Christ's suffering one ought to elevate himself upwards after the fashion of Mary Magdalene, etc. And next [I will speak] of the wondrous love that Christ displays for us by means of this sacrament, in which He left Himself in food in a wondrous manner when going to cross over from the world. [This was] the most wondrous of all His wonders. Moreover, a man ought to elevate himself by pure faith, in contrast to all the idly curious, who seek examples and signs, etc. For whatever we cannot understand and eat intellectually, we ought to burn up, in accordance with the precept; i.e., we ought to burn it up by means of the Holy Spirit and to believe it lovingly.

[35] And [we ought] to contemplate how it is that the substance of the bread is converted into the Body of Christ, so that in this way a man is transformed into God by the efficacy of God's love. Secondly, we [ought to contemplate] the fact that [in the transubstantiated Eucharistic elements] the accidents do not exist by the power of their natural subject. From this fact you may infer that your will ought in all

respects to depend on the Divine will, through which alone it exists. Thirdly, [we ought to consider] the fact that just as [in the Eucharist] the accidents indicate bread but, nevertheless, bread is not present (because the substance has been transubstantiated), so through the forcefulness of love let your affection be so transformed that there is only the outward manifestation of the human nature together with the presence of the deity [into which you are transformed].

[**36**] We must contemplate the fact that when this [Eucharistic] meal is approached: then, first of all, the one who approaches it in a worthy manner knows that he will obtain (1) immortal life from Christ's immortal, glorified Body, (2) life-giving grace from Christ's Soul, and (3) life-sustaining glory from the deity that is united to Christ's Body and Soul. And according to Exodus 16 one who comes to the food of this Lamb in order to place into his vessel as much manna as a gomor[107] contains must have a new vessel, completely purged of oldness—[a vessel] in which there is no spot of uncleanness. And thereupon you will find, in this most delectable bread, every delight. [This bread] contains every remedy ..., etc. And according to the commandment[108] one ought to eat the lamb with one's loins gird-ed ([i.e.,] with the intent of curbing evil desires) and with one's feet having shoes on them ([i.e.,] with a heart prepared for eagerly follow-ing the pathway of God's commandments[109]) [and] with our feet pro-tected, so that we not bump them against a stone or on the thorns and the thistles of this world[110]); and [we ought to eat it] while having a prop in our hands ([i.e.,] while having divine aid [and] not relying on ourselves presumptuously), and while considering to eat the salt from the lettuce of the fields ([i.e.,] while considering our Lord's suffering, combined with the bitterness of our penance). [And we are command-ed] to eat hastily ([i.e.,] with great desire and ardor and with sensory devotion, if [such devotion] can be had. Otherwise, the intention not to sin suffices, etc.[111]

NOTES TO *SERMON XII*

1. Mark 16:6. I have left aside the question mark in the title because it appears neither in the Scripture-verse nor in the mss. *C* and *V₁* nor in the Paris edition.
2. Cf. Job 30:31.
3. Mark 16:2 and 16:9.
4. Philippians 2:10.
5. Acts 4:12.
6. Cf. Luke 24:34.
7. Psalms 117:24 (118:24).
8. See, below, the last part of the section marked by margin-number 5.
9. Galatians 2:20.
10. Cf. John 10:18.
11. Cf. Anselm's *Cur Deus Homo* I, 12.
12. Philippians 2:8.
13. I John 3:16.
14. This theme is taken from Anselm's *Cur Deus Homo*.
15. Philippians 2:7-8.
16. I Corinthians 15:54.
17. This view corresponds to the Apostles' Creed. See also Acts 2:31. Matthew 27:50-53. Ephesians 4:8-10.
18. Cf. Osee (Hosea) 13:14.
19. Matthew 21:9.
20. This idea belongs thoroughly to the Christian tradition, which does not assume that those who die in unbelief will ever have a further opportunity for salvation.
21. Augustine, *De Genesi ad Litteram*, XII, 33, 63-64 (*PL* 34:481-482).
22. Nicholas of Lyra, *Postilla*, re Matthew 27:56. [*Biblia Sacra cum Glossa Interlineari, Ordinaria, et Nicolai Lyrani Postilla, eiusdemque Moralitatibus, Burgensis Additionibus, et Thoringi Replicis* (Venice, 1588 (Vol. 5)), p. 86rb. Regarding the Scriptural words (in Matthew 27:56) "... et Maria Jacobi et Joseph mater ..." Lyra comments: "Ista erat soror Mariae, matris Christi." And regarding the words "... et mater filiorum Zebedaei" he writes: "Et mater filiorum Zebedai, scilicet Iacobi et Iohannis."
23. Matthew 27:61.
24. Mark 16:1-2.
25. John 20:1.
26. Matthew 28:1.
27. Jerome, *Epistle* 120, "*Ad Hedibiam*," Chaps. 3-4 (*PL* 22:987).
28. Matthew 28:2.
29. Luke 24:1-4. See also Matthew 27:55.
30. John 20:10-11.
31. John 19:25.
32. See the reference in n. 22 above.
33. See the reference in n. 27 above and the one in n. 79 below.
34. Gregory the Great, *XL Homiliae in Evangelia*, 22, 2-3 (*PL* 76:1175B-D).

35. Here (at 9:14) I am supplying an omission in the Heidelberg edition of the Latin text. After "significata" in line 14 there should be added the words: "citius cucurrit sed ecclesia gentilium per Petrum significata ...."

36. John 10:16.

37. Note Matthew 27:56 and Mark 15:47, both of which mention Mary, the mother of James and of Joseph (i.e., Joses).

38. Here (at 10:24) neither *C* nor *V$_I$* has "Matris", which here I have deleted. (In *C* something is deleted in-line and above-line.) At 10:27 *C* omits "matris", which is supplied, above the line, by C*; *V$_I$* has "matris".

39. This passage (10:24-25) is not consistent with the earlier one (10:9-10) where the Virgin Mary is identified as the sister of Mary Cleophas. It can be made consistent by omitting the present sentence's last words—viz., "the sister of her own mother"—as does ms. *U$_2$*.

40. This passage and the one that immediately follows it are taken from John 20:11-16.

41. Here and elsewhere the Latin text, which is quoted from John 20, uses the historical present-tense, which I am translating by the simple past-tense.

42. One would expect Nicholas to say that of all women the Virgin Mary was the most distressed because of her Son's death. But, instead, Nicholas here represents Mary Magdalene as perceiving herself as suffering even more.

43. Here (at 12:15) I am reading "fragrantia" (as does also the Paris edition) in place of "flagrantia".

44. Canticle of Canticles (Song of Solomon) 2:10.

45. These words come two paragraphs below.

46. Exodus 4:13.

47. Psalms 29:2 (30:1).

48. Psalms 56:9 (57:8).

49. Isaias (Isaiah) 8:1.

50. Psalms 37:11 (38:10).

51. Psalms 56:9 (57:8).

52. Osee (Hosea) 6:3.

53. Psalms 102:5 (103:5).

54. Cf. 9:21.

55. John 12:24-25.

56. Judges 16:3.

57. Here (at 16:12) I am reading, with the Paris edition, "totius" in place of "tonsus".

58. Genesis 41 ff.

59. See n. 42 above.

60. Canticle of Canticles (Song of Solomon) 3:1.

61. Cf. Matthew 13:44.

62. John 21:15-17.

63. John 21:20.

64. The Joseph referred to here is not the husband of the Virgin Mary. The King James Bible calls him *Joses*. Interpreters are not agreed on the identities of the different Marys who are referred to in the Gospels. A note on p. 235 of the Heidelberg Academy's edition of the Latin text of this present sermon points to a tradition in

accordance with which the Virgin Mary and Mary the wife of Cleophas (i.e., Mary the mother of James the Younger and of Joseph/Joses) and Mary Salome (i.e., Mary the mother of James the Elder) are all sisters. Certain other commentators identify with each other Mary Salome and Mary the mother of James and Joses. Still others regard Mary the mother of James and Joses as the sister-in-law of the Virgin Mary.

65. Psalms 44:3 (45:2).

66. Here (at 20:46) I am reading "ubi" in place of "ut". Mss. *C* and *V₁* have "ubi".

67. Mary's response to this question appears to be a non-sequitur, indicating that the manuscript-tradition at this point is corrupt.

68. Hebrews 4:14.

69. Romans 6:9.

70. Regarding the four endowments, see PART TWO below.

71. Psalms 117:24 (118:24).

72. Cf. Romans 6:4.

73. Cf. Mark 16:14.

74. Luke 24:10.

75. Luke 24:12.

76. Luke 24:13-32.

77. John 20:19.

78. Aquinas, *Summa Theologica*, III, 82-85.

79. Peter Comestor, *Historia Scholastica in Evangelia*, Chap. 185 (*PL* 198:1636D - 1638A).

80. I Corinthians 15:42-44.

81. Philippians 3:21.

82. I Corinthians 15:20.

83. Colossians 3:1-2.

84. I Corinthians 6:15.

85. Cf. Ephesians 4:22-24. Colossians 3:9-10.

86. III Kings (I Kings) 17:21-23. Elias is Elijah.

87. IV Kings (II Kings) 13:20-21. Eliseus is Elisha.

88. That is, He was closed in by the intact hymen of the Virgin Mary.

89. Luke 24:39 (not Luke 23, as Nicholas incorrectly writes).

90. Luke 24:39 (not Luke 23, as Nicholas incorrectly writes).

91. John 20:25-28.

92. I John 2:1.

93. Matthew 7:7:8.

94. Colossians 2:3.

95. Galatians 6:17.

96. Mark 16:6.

97. I Corinthians 5:8.

98. Each of these three points alludes to the Eucharist.

99. Here (at 31:24) I am reading "verum" in place of "unum".

100. When the word "body" refers to the real presence of Christ's mystical Body in the Eucharistic sacrament, I capitalize the word.

101. Here (at 31:33) I am reading "cruditatis" in place of "crudelitatis", which the mss. have, as does also the Paris edition.

102. I Corinthians 11:29.

103. Re *totus homo*, note Augustine, *Ennarationes in Psalmos*, 37, verse 8 (*PL* 36:402).

104. John 14:6.

105. I Corinthians 5:8.

106. Cf. Augustine, *Confessiones*, VII, 10,16 (*PL* 32:742).

107. A gomor is an ancient Hebrew quantitative measure. Exodus 16:32-33.

108. Exodus 12:11.

109. Psalms 118:32 (119:32).

110. Here (at 36:19) I am reading, with *C* and V_I, "saeculi" in place of "saeculo".

111. I here omit translating the last section of the text of this sermon. That section is but a sketch of what has already been said; it has no importance—not even as showing the points that Nicholas regards as salient.

Sermon XIII: Et Apertum Est Templum
("And the Temple was opened ....")[1]
[August 15, 1432; feast-day of the assumption of Mary;
preached in Koblenz]

[1] "And the Temple of the Lord was opened in Heaven; and the Ark of His Testament was seen in His Temple. And there were lightnings and voices and an earthquake and great hail. And a great sign appeared in heaven: [viz.,] a woman clothed with the sun and [having] the moon beneath her feet and [having] on her head a crown of twelve stars ...."[2]

These words are set forth, in general, regarding the Mother Church and, in particular, regarding the very foremost member of the Church, viz., the glorious Virgin Mary. [2] With respect to the first, general theme [of the foregoing Scripture-verse], it is stated that the Temple-of-the-Lord—i.e., Christ (in whom is the dwelling-place of divinity)—was opened in Heaven; i.e., He was made manifest within the entire world at the time of His birth. Furthermore, this Temple was also opened on the Altar of the Cross, when the soldier pierced Christ's side with his spear, so that from the side of the sleeping Second Adam[3] there would be formed Eve, the holy Mother Church. For this holy Mother Church was formed by the blood of redemption, and by the water of regeneration, from His side. And then after the Temple was opened, the Ark of His Testament was seen, viz., the holy Mother Church, which is like Noah's Ark, which kept everyone [inside] alive. And the Ark of the Testament preserves within itself the Tables of the Law, manna, and Aaron's rod;[4] i.e., it has the Law, the sacraments, and the keys that are invested with power.[5] The rod symbolizes power; Aaron symbolizes the priesthood. Therefore, in the Church there is priestly power, even as in the Ark [of the Testament] there is [Aaron's] rod. Therefore, he who is not subject to the rod of Aaron is not within the Ark of the Church. And then there were lightnings of good examples by means of the gleam of the honorable way of life of the holy martyrs of the Early Church. And there were voices of divine praise and of lofty proclamation; and there was an earthquake of fear and of compunction; and there was the hail of harsh reproof.

[3] Also, expound on the persecution of the Church—how after the Temple was opened and the great Ark was seen, there followed persecution. [The persecution was] against the Ark that was composed of different kinds of wood, i.e., of [different] believers in Christ. [The

persecution occurred] through all the punitive and injurious modes symbolised by lightnings, thundering voices, tremblings of the earth, and a hail-storm. Notwithstanding, there appeared in heaven a great sign of the universal faith of the Catholic Church. For the Church was like a pious and compassionate woman, bearing great fruit, clothed with the sun of justice,[6] being unhindered by the aforementioned afflictions—[a woman] treading under foot the moon of the earthly impermanence [and] having on her head a crown-of-victory that is decorated roundabout with the twelve brightly-shining, fixed, incorruptible stars of the [twelve] articles of faith. Etc.

[4] Also, by *head* understand the *beginning* of the Early Church. And by *moon*, which is under her feet, understand the *last period* of the Church. [The Church] was first crowned with the twelve stars of the twelve Apostles, and [the crown] was on the head. And through the [statement that] the beginning of the Church had its head crowned, understand [that] the state of the Early Church [is being referred to]. And through [the phrase] "its feet on the moon," understand the present state [of the Church]. If we turn to the anatomy of the head, we will find that all the powers-of-senses and all the nerves originate there. And they convey to the lower members the power of sensing and of moving. [The head] has seven outlets,[7] which are instruments of the senses; it has hard, smooth bones; and it has the full substance of the brain; it has but few strands of flesh and has smooth hairs. [Similarly, the Church] has seven virtues as instruments supported by the seven gifts of the Holy Spirit[8]—[gifts given as] remedies for the vices. [These virtues are] (1) the hard bones of very fixed steadfastness, (2) the ample marrow of meekness and (3) of mercy, (4) the reduced flesh of carnality and of lust, (5) the outer, smooth hairs of an honorable mode of life, (6) the nerves of friendship, and (7) the powers of sensory discrimination. Of such kind ought to be all the leaders and rulers, ([for] they are the heads). For granted that the leader ought manifestly to exhibit hardness, even as the bones of the head are hard, nevertheless he [should] have, within him, the marrow of piety and mercy. For in him there ought to be a sense of insightfulness and of discernment and of prudence, etc. These [traits], too, are symbolized by the Ark, which was gilded over inside and out and which contained the Table of the Law (i.e., justice and prudence!), the rod of reproof, and the manna of pleasantness and of compassion and of piety.

[5] At this time the Church has, as it were, its feet on the moon. The feet are the affections; and just as the feet are always on the

ground, [so] the affections are earthly and on the moon nearest to the earth. Therefore, nowadays the Church is, alas, at the lowest gradation, just as a foot is of little nobility. Although [the foot] has in itself the same life as does the whole body and although it is nourished by the same spirit, nevertheless it is not clothed with the sun of justice,[9] [or] with the sun of prudence, or with the splendor of life. Rather, [it is clothed with] the hide of bestiality [and] of ignorance, miring itself in the clay of covetousness and of lust, clinging to the earth through greed, being unsteady, relying on the moon, etc. As regards the nature of the moon and its unsteadiness and its influence and its approach to the sun and its eclipse, etc.—it is known that our sins are opposed to God, etc.

[6] Accordingly, if we wish to preserve ourselves, and reform ourselves, in the Ark and the Church, then we, who are the feet, must walk in the way of equality and of justice. And we must accept the inflow-of-moving-and-of-sensing from the things that are above us and from those who have preceded us in holiness. And we must direct our lunar spirit toward joining with the sun, so that, by means of the conjoining that occurs, our spirit is moved all the way to the full-moon of eternal glory. And furthermore: because walking must be done carefully,[10] you must pay attention to how you walk. It is not the case that the footprints of others are always to be followed—like an ape that has closed its eyes. Because of the fact that the thief closed his eyes, he lost the money. But good pathways must be visualized, lest one fall when he thinks himself to stand.[11] O Man, see …," etc.[12] Fortune affords various pathways …, etc.[13]

[7] Therefore, one must run by way of the paths of the Commandments[14] and of obedience. And one must not despise the key that is invested with the power of the Church. Moreover, you must not despise unjust things [that are done to you]; for they are meritorious for you [to endure]; but they are punitive for him who commands [them to be done]. If a charge which your superior levels against you is not just, then your merit is greater because of your obedience [to God]. And consider—[seeing that] throughout your lifetime you will find yourself to have transgressed—what you merit. And take your transgressions as an accusation against you. Therefore, consider the good of obedience, and do not despise it.

Take an example of patience and obedience from Christ, who— also being obedient, (even unto death)[15] —always taught obedience. ([The Scribes and the Pharisees sat] on the Chair of Moses …, etc.)[16]

Because of disobedience a curse descended upon the human race. (Genesis 3: "Cursed is the earth with regard to your work."[17] And He blessed Simon, i.e., Obedience: "Blessed are you, Simon Bar Jona" (Matthew 16)).[18] Therefore, be not disobedient, because obedience yields great profits with little expenditure of effort. For obedience is like a merchant's ship[19] that continues ever onwards and leads to profits. Nonetheless, one who obeys is tranquil .... And it is like a horseman who is resting [in his saddle] but is nevertheless advancing. ("To my company of horsemen I have likened you, my Love.")[20] And God remains present with those who are obedient. (And Christ entered Bethany, i.e., the House of obedience, etc.) Where there is obedience, there there is love for God. Love for God makes a man pliable and obedient, as fire makes wax pliable. And note the following: If you wish to know in whom love for God is present, look unto his obedience; for obedience is better than sacrifice.[21]

NOTES TO *SERMON XIII*

1. Apocalypse (Revelation) 11:19.
2. Apocalypse (Revelation) 11:19 - 12:1.
3. I Corinthians 15:45.
4. Hebrews 9:4.
5. Matthew 16:19.
6. Malachias (Malachi) 4:2.
7. The seven outlets are the two eyes, the two ears, the two nostrils, and the mouth.
8. Isaias (Isaiah) 11:2-3. The seven Gifts of the Holy Spirit are wisdom, understanding, counsel, courage, knowledge, piety, and fear-of-God.
9. See n. 6 above.
10. Ephesians 5:12.
11. I Corinthians 10:12.
12. *Carmina Medii Aevi Posterioris Latina* II/5 (entry number 33592), edited by Hans Walter (Göttingen: Vandenhoeck and Ruprecht, 1967:

> "Vir videas, quid tunc facias, cum magnus haberis;
> Prospicias, ne despicias, quem ledere queris,
> Et caveas, ne forte ruas, cum stare videris:
> Dat varias fortuna vias, non ergo mireris."

> ("See, O Man, what to do when you are esteemed great.
> Look circumspectly upon—do not underestimate—him whom
>   you are seeking to injure.
> And beware lest you fall when you seem to be standing.
> Fortune affords various pathways; so do not be
> caught unawares.")

13. See n. 12 above.
14. Psalms 118:32 (119:32).
15. Philippians 2:8.
16. Cf. Matthew 23:2. Note also Matthew 23:3: "All things, therefore, whatsoever [the Scribes and the Pharisees] shall say to you, observe and do; but do not do according to their works. For they say, but they do not do."
17. Genesis 3:17.
18. Matthew 16:17.
19. Proverbs 31:14.
20. Canticle of Canticles 1:8 (Song of Solomon 1:9).
21. I Kings (I Samuel) 15:22.

Sermon XIV: Signum Magnum
("A great sign ....")[1]
[August 15, 1432; feast-day of the assumption of Mary;
preached in Koblenz]

[1] "A great sign ...," etc.

[This verse may be expounded] either as regards the life of the Virgin or as regards Glory or as regards the Church Militant.

As regards the life of the Virgin the following [may be said]: A great sign appeared in heaven (i.e., in the loftiness of the Church Militant): [viz.,] a woman clothed with the sun (i.e., existing in the contemplation of the divine light). She had the feet of her affections treading on the moon. With her active life she was touching earthly things; and on her head she had a special crown of 12 stars, the twelve privileges. Now, for expounding this [theme], I introduce the Gospel-text in a mystical sense. In accordance with this sense life was manifestly present in [the Virgin] Mary in a twofold way: [there was] the active life of Martha and the contemplative life of [Mary] Magdalene.[2] The active life pursues *just* works diligently, etc. [I will speak about] the way in which the active [life] befit [the Virgin] Mary, who was busy ..., etc. To begin with, [I will speak of] the way in which she received [the annunciation, of] the way in which she was with child, etc. And in this regard she supremely worked works of mercy—works ordered gradationally in five ways. The contemplative [life is present] when someone by prolonged [mental] exercise, etc., and (according to Gregory)[3] when cares are trodden under foot, etc., and (according to Bernard)[4] when the flesh is mortified, etc. And (according to Hugh)[5] [this life] has three gradations: it purifies, it enlightens, it perfects, etc.

[2] And, first of all, in accordance with the Gospel-verse, three things are necessary [for the contemplative life]: *leisure* (she was sitting) and *being at His feet* and *listening to His word*.[6] And six additional things [are necessary]: the exercise of the active [life], aloneness, humility, purity of heart, fervor of love, and steadfastness of mind. [Here are some] more things: first, a considering of creatures, by apprehending three things (according to Hugh):[7] Grandeur, Wisdom, and Goodness—by inference from [created things'] magnitude, loveliness, and usefulness. Secondly, [the contemplative life requires] one's knowledge of himself through gradations of descent and ascent, etc.

283

The quality of contemplation is varied in three ways: by enlargement of mind, by exaltation of mind, and by renunciation. That in a supreme way the most blessed Virgin had this life [of contemplation] is recognized from her grace and from the twelve privileges of her crown of twelve stars and from the way in which, through this contemplation, she approached death and from the kind of [earthly end she had].[8]

This [is the end of] the First Part.

[3] The Second Part is (a) about her glorification and (b) about what Glory and the light of Glory are and (c) about the way in which in Glory she obtained halos and a station above all the angels and (d) about our contemplating her assumption.

This [will be dealt with] secondly.

[4] Thirdly comes the third exposition, which deals with the Church [Militant], etc.

NOTES TO *SERMON XIV*

1. Apocalypse (Revelation) 12:1. This Sermon and Sermon XV are variant *sketches* of Sermon XIII, which itself is but a longer sketch. Presumably these three drafts were the basis for homilies delivered in German at three different services on Sunday, August 15, 1432.

2. Luke 10:38-42.

3. Gregory the Great, *Homiliae in Ezechielem*, II, 2, 8 (*PL* 76:953B).

4. Bernard of Clairvaux, *Sermones de Sanctis*, "In Assumptione Beatae Virginis Mariae," *Sermo* 2, n. 3 (*PL* 183:418). Bernard quotes the Apostle Paul: I Corinthians 9:26-27 and Romans 6:12.

5. Hugh of St. Victor, *Expositio in Hierarchiam Coelestem*, IV (*PL* 175:998B). See also Hugh of Balma, Prologue to his *De Theologia Mystica*, translated by J. Hopkins (Minneapolis: Banning, 2002).

6. Luke 10:39.

7. Hugh of St. Victor, *Eruditio Didascalica*, VII, 1 (*PL* 176:811C - 813A).

8. See, above, n. 86 of Sermon VIII.

Sermon XV: Et Apertum Est Templum

("And the Temple was opened ....")
[August 15, 1432; feast-day of the assumption of Mary;
preached in Koblenz]

[1] " And the Temple of the Lord was opened in Heaven; and the Ark of His Testament was seen in His Temple. And there were lightnings ...," etc.[1]

[This text] deals, *first of all*, with the very glorious Virgin Mary and her life and her assumption; [it deals], *secondly*, with the Church Militant and with its station and course; *thirdly*, [it deals] with the union of the [Church] Militant with the [Church] Triumphant. [This union occurs] through the military ascent of the [Church] Militant and through its victorious transformation into the [Church] Triumphant.

[2] Let us begin as follows: The Temple of the Lord (i.e., the humanity of Christ) was opened and made manifest to the heavens (i.e., to the world). And in that Temple-of-the-humanity the Ark of the Testament (i.e., the divinity [of Christ]) was seen by faith and understanding. Thereafter, many wonders occurred in terms of miracles that displayed the Temple [i.e., the humanity] and the Ark [i.e., the divinity]. There occurred lightnings (through the [miraculous] restoring of sight to the blind)[2] and voices (because of the dumb who spoke)[3] and hail ..., etc. Hence, in the heavens there appeared a great sign of faith and of the Church—[a sign] more wondrous than any signs seen hitherto and greater, even, than any signs previously told of. For a woman, viz., the Blessed Virgin, was clothed with the sun of very sublime and very holy contemplation. She had the moon of the active life beneath her feet. She was crowned with twelve stars, etc. (i.e., with twelve prerogatives), that were steadfast and resplendent, etc.

And as an introduction to this [topic] let the Gospel-text be taken in hand, etc.

[3] Secondly, [the second theme] is commented on as above [i.e., as in Sermon XIII].

[4] Thirdly, [as regards the third theme, the following idea] is set forth [by the Scriptural-passage]: The Temple of the Lord was opened on the Cross, and the Ark of the Testament was seen in the Temple; and there were lightnings and voices and an earthquake and a hail-storm, etc. And these occurred in the ambience of the Church Militant. Then,

286

at length, there appeared a great sign. For this Holy Woman, viz., the Church, was elevated (subsequently to all the tribulations) above the moon—yea, rather, even treading on the moon—unto the sun. And her garment was the Sun of justice,[4] [i.e.,] Christ; and she was crowned with a crown of twelve stars, which are the twelve Heavenly joys of Glory.

[5] With the foregoing [events] there agrees that which is written in the Canticles: "Who is she who ascends as the morning rising, who is as beautiful as the sun, as excellent as the moon, as fright-evoking as an army set in array?"[5] On this present solemn feast-day Mary is rightly called *the morning rising*. For nothing [symbolically] announces to the whole world the joy of the forthcoming Sun [i.e., Christ] as much as does the daybreak, which announces the imminent arrival of the sun; [and] no brightness (apart from the brightness of the Sun that is Christ) [announces the coming of its sun] as much as does [the brightness] of daybreak. And daybreak is the very light of the sun, by means of which the sun is known—even as the light-of-Glory, which is attained on this feast-day, is the glorious arising Queen.

[6] But who is this woman who is as beautiful as the sun, as excellent as the moon? Surely, it is the Mother Church, which is nourished by the Divine Solar Spirit. She is the bride-without-blemish[6] who bears in herself the likeness of her Bridegroom [and] who is as excellent as the moon, to which the sun imparts all [the moon's] light. But who is that woman who is as frightening as the army set in array? Surely, she is the frightening army of the holy Church Militant, which, with a certain formidable and astute ordering, sets in array its battle-lines and military-camps so as to conquer its threefold enemy[7][8] so that its victory might be over death and so that it might be transformed into the [Church] Triumphant, etc.

NOTES TO *SERMON XV*

1. Apocalypse (Revelation) 11:19. See n. 1 of Sermon XIV.
2. Matthew 12:22. Luke 7:21. John 9:1-7.
3. Mark 7:37 and 9:16-26.
4. Malachias (Malachi) 4:2.
5. Not an exact quotation. Canticle of Canticles 6:9 (Song of Solomon 6:10).
6. Ephesians 5:27.
7. I John 2:16. Each believer wars against the lust of the flesh, the lust of the eyes, and the pride of life.

Sermon XVI: Gloria in Excelsis Deo
("Glory to God in the highest.")
[December 25, 1432 (?); preached perhaps in Koblenz]

[1] "Glory to God in the highest; and on earth peace to men of good will."[1]

This song, beneficial to us and most pleasing to God, was sung by the mouths of angels to the Newborn at the beginning, after the birth of Christ was announced to the shepherds watching over their flock. It is of such great and deep mystery that neither I nor, indeed, anyone else, past or future, will suffice for explaining its sacred truths. For glory is always [due] to the eternal and unchangeable Most Glorious God. For He is the Beginning, existing before all creatures; [He is the One] through whom, in whom, and unto whom all things are.[2] With Him in the beginning was always the Word; and in the beginning the Word was God Himself.[3] Moreover, [glory is due Him] because all things were made by Him and because whatever was made was Life in Him before it was created. And the Life was the Light of men, because the entire illumination of the being, the life, and the truth [of created things] proceeds from this Living Fount, although darkness does not comprehend [this Light].

[2] Is not glory always [due] to Him (who on different occasions and in many different ways spoke in times past through the Prophets[4] and through witnesses and, lastly, through John) inasmuch as He is the Life of the living [and] is He from whom comes every good? But glory in the highest [is due] to Him now because last of all[5] the Word was made flesh,[6] and [God] spoke to us through His Son. What very sublime and super-wondrous and unprecedented gladness! For on the earth of human nature—where by the envy of the Devil,[7] [and] through the fall of our first parents, death and sin and enmity and war were always found—the angels now sing out: "Peace to men of good will." For the Word made flesh has dwelt among us, and His place was made in peace.[8]

[3] How is it that this was done—except because of the fact that mercy and truth have met each other.[9] (They were at odds with each other because of man's sin and God's law.) Moreover, they have kissed each other in peace and in justice.[10] Who [can] conceive of such enormous things? Who will declare the generation[11] of this King of

289

Peace[12] who on this [feast-]day entered the world? And who will disclose such great, super-wondrous mysteries? [It will] not [be] a man,
because man is a finite creature, is grass and a flower of the field.[13]
Hence, since we need divine assistance in proportion to our weakness,
let us recur, with a very devout mind, to the Mother of our Savior—[the
Mother] of Life and of Truth—so that we may merit to have, for our
contemplation of so great a mystery, some of her salvific sweetness.

PART ONE
The Three Masses of This Feast,
and the Threefold Birth of Christ

[4] "Glory [to God in the highest,"] etc.[14]

    If with a vigilant mind anyone will reflect on all the things that
have (by the ordinance of the holy Mother Church) been ordained for
the offices of this present festival: then, to the extent that a man is permitted to know [it], he will arrive at the very lofty contemplation of
salvation, rest, and happiness—[the objects] of all our knowledge
[and] investigation. Now, the first Gospel-text—for the nocturnal
mass—has to do with the description of a man, viz., Caesar Augustus.
The second [text]—for the mass at sunrise—has to do with the angel's
declaration. And the third [text]—for the mass which is sung once the
sun has arisen above the entire hemisphere—is about the Word, which
was with God in the beginning. Man's intellect is darkened and nocturnal; an angel's intellect is bright like daybreak; the Divine Intellect
is like the sun itself, since it illumines every man coming into this
world.[15] The task of man's [intellect] is to describe the world. The task
of angels is to announce the Savior, whom all super-celestial powers
glorify in Heaven and whom on earth all men of peace glorify. The graciousness of the Savior consists in His manifesting Himself to the
world.

    [5] Now, in the darkness-of-night (which symbolizes the human
intellect) our Savior, who is Divine and human, was born and was
placed in a manger as grass is placed before oxen and asses. Therefore,
let us seek—as best we can, if not as strong oxen then at least like the
simple asses—to taste mentally of this food of angels. Now, the mass
that is celebrated around midnight symbolizes our Savior's eternal
begottenness, which is incomprehensible because of its darkness. The
second mass, at sunrise, symbolizes His temporal birth, which is more
comprehensible, as regards His humanity. And the third [mass sym-

bolizes] the spiritual [birth] that is obtained in the present through grace and in the future through glory. Accordingly, let us who are seated around the crib of our Savior at night contemplate these three [births] as best we can.

Indeed, as fully as we can, let us for the sake of the intellectuals consider the eternal begottenness of the Son of God. Next, for the sake of ordinary [believers let us consider] the temporal [birth of Jesus]. And, lastly, for the sake of contemplatives [let us consider His] spiritual [birth in us].

PART TWO
The Son's Eternal Begottenness.
Here His Temporal Begottenness Is Merely Touched Upon

[6] And although the eternal begottenness is not comprehensible [to us] on this pilgrims' pathway, nevertheless in whatsoever measure we can contemplate it, let us elevate ourselves. For the highest perfection of our intellect consists in this [elevated contemplating]. For we who are on this pilgrims' pathway ought to seek or to hope for nothing other than to arrive at a clear knowledge of this [doctrine] in the Heavenly state. It must be known, therefore, that the birth of the Son of God is nothing other than the intellectual proceeding of the Word from God the Father—or nothing other than the bringing forth of the Divine Word. For Blessed God is the Intellectual Beginning of every creature, [and] He acts through Intellect and Will. (For He did all that He willed to …, etc.[16] He spoke, [and it was done] …, etc.[17] Therefore, it is necessary that there be in Him an Intellectual, or a Mental, Word in and through whom He understand Himself and other things.

Now, it is of [the essence] of a word that it be the word of someone other than itself, for it is spoken of as the word, respectively, of the one who utters it; i.e., [it is the word of the one] by whom it is uttered. That is, it is produced by being spoken. Therefore, the Divine Word proceeds from someone from whom [this Word] is, assuredly, really distinguished, by virtue of the fact that nothing proceeds from itself (according to Augustine, in his *De Trinitate*).[18] But [the Word] does not proceed from a creature; therefore, He proceeds from God. He does not proceed from the Divine Essence, since the Essence is not distinguished really from the Son; for each [Divine] Person *is* the Divine Essence. Hence, when we say "The Word proceeds from God,"[19] "God" ought to be construed personally—[ought to be taken] not for the Essence but rather for the Person, viz., of the Father.

[7] Moreover, because of God's simplicity and immutability, His Word cannot be an accident[20] of the Divine Mind, as occurs with us and with angels. Nor can His Word be, as it were, a created substance added intrinsically to Him as form or added in some way extrinsically. For all these [alternatives] are inconsistent with the Divine Perfection—especially since every created thing is finite and cannot represent, [in a non-symbolical way], the Infinite. Therefore, since God understands both Himself and all things in and through His Word, it follows that the Word is a thing uncreated and infinite; and this can only be God. And because there is only one God, the Word is not distinguished essentially and really from God, although the Word is distinguished personally, in a real way, from the Father.

[8] Every essential distinction is real but not vice versa. And the Divine Essence is each of the Persons, and vice versa. Nevertheless, there agrees with the Persons something that does not agree with the Essence (viz., spiration, begetting, etc.). Therefore, it is conceded that in some way the Essence is formally distinguished from the Persons, etc. And, thus, in God distinctions are formal and personal. And it is true to say that the several things in God—viz., the three Persons—are one Essence. [9] Now, this Word is infinite in essential perfection, because He is God. And He is infinite in representing, because He represents very universally, yet very perfectly and very determinately. He represents better than all other mental and vocal words—created and creatable—can represent. (He represents] in the way that super-optimally befits divine knowing. It follows that there is only one Word, which primarily represents God, i.e., [represents] the Divine Essence. For the primary object of the Divine Intellect is God Himself. John seems to speak in accordance with this sense, [when he says]: "The Word was with God"—[says it] in the way in which one is accustomed to say "His contemplation is of himself" (i.e., "He is the object of his own contemplation, or conceptualization").

[10] The next birth is that by means of which that wonderful Only-Begotten of God, and First-born of Mary, proceeded on this day as Bridegroom from His chamber.[21] (On this day He proceeded] into this world of grief and sorrow—proceeded as King of Pe ace [and] (in accordance with the prophecy of Ezechiel) with the gates of the most holy Tabernacle closed.[22] [He was born] in Bethlehem of Juda,[23] the City of David—[a topic] on which I shall speak in another sermon, where [the theme of] this birth of our Savior will be introduced. And because the aforesaid things are exceedingly lofty (for they are about

the Word who from the beginning was with God and was God and who assumed—by means of a wondrous union and for our salvation—a human nature): there was rightly said [by the angels], "Glory to God in the highest."

PART THREE
Christ's Spiritual Birth in Those of Peace

[11] As regards the third, spiritual birth of Christ in us: it must be said that the Word-made-flesh dwelt among men, to whom (in accordance with the theme of good will) peace was given. Moreover, we must know that such a daily "spiritual birth"—which the invisible mission of the Son of God is accustomed to be called—is nothing other than the procession of the Word, or of Begotten Wisdom, from God the Father unto the minds of rational creatures for the purpose of graciously illumining spiritual creatures. For although the Word of God, i.e., Divine Wisdom, is present everywhere and is present in each rational creature through [that creature's] essence (for the Trinity as a whole and at once stretches from end to end mightily and disposes of all things agreeably), nevertheless the Word is not present everywhere through freely given light. Accordingly, when such divine light arises in a bedarkened mind or when more light arises in a less illuminated mind, the Son of God is fittingly said to be born. Although this work is, in fact, done by the Trinity as a whole (since the works of the Trinity are indivisible), nevertheless it is, without doubt, rightly ascribed to the Son, inasmuch as He is the Image of God, the Word of God, and the Wisdom of God, and the Radiance of eternal light.[24] It is [the nature] of a word to illumine the mind; it is [the nature] of wisdom to make wise; and it is [the nature] of an immaterial image to liken, and to refashion, each one's mind to that of which it is the image; and it is [the nature] of radiance to make the mind bright. Hence, of the Word of God it is written: [Wisdom] conveys itself into holy souls and makes [of them] friends and prophets.[25]

[12] And through such a spiritual birth nothing is acquired by the Son of God; rather, those in whom He is born are made sons of God through grace (in the present) and through glory (in the future). Contained in the Gospel is the [statement] that in the following way [Christ] gave us power to become sons of God: not by being reborn by the will of the flesh or by blood but by being reborn from God by the in-breathing [of the Holy Spirit].[26] And this fact is that of which that wise man says, "Send forth that Wisdom …," etc.[27] For after the fashion of

the sun, that Wisdom causes three things in a man; for it (1) illumines and brightens, (2) it warms, and, at length, (3) it makes fruitful. [13] But in what way are we to obtain this brightness and warmth, and fruit? Let us, for the time being, go over to Bethlehem ..., etc.[28] Now, the pathways of the Lord are peaceable. (Proverbs 3: "All her pathways are peaceable.")[29] Therefore, he who wishes to come to Bethlehem (i.e., to the House of Bread) in order that Jesus may be born in him, must be peaceable and of good will. For the new angelic declaration on earth is the following: "Peace to men of good will," etc.

[14] And so, whenever Christ came to meet the Apostles He said: "Peace be with you." And wherever the Apostles wanted Christ to be born as a result of their preaching, [and] into whatever house they entered, they said: "Peace be to this house."[30] And Paul, after having announced his joy over the nearness of Christ, said: "And the peace of God, which surpasses all understanding ...," etc.[31] Likewise, if you want Christ to be born in you, have peace, which consists of *conformity, humility,* and *tranquility.* For he who *conforms* his own will to the Divine Will is at peace. (Job 9: "Who will resist Him and have peace?"[32] Presumably, the answer would be: "No one.") Next, *humility* conduces to peace in such a way that without humility there is no peace. [Among us] it is commonly said that "two fatheads in one sack do not tolerate each other." (Ephesians 4: "Endeavor to keep the unity of the Spirit in the bond of peace.")[33] Thirdly, *tranquility* of mind aids the good of peace. Just as no one can be at ease in a thorny place, so a restless heart cannot have true peace. ("In peace—in that very thing— I will sleep ...," etc.)[34]

He who wishes to be peaceful must observe these things—namely the things that have been said. [15] And [one who wishes to be peaceful] must keep himself from a *defiled peace,* which is the concordance of many things unto an evil end. ([This is a peace such] as Pilate had with Herod.)[35] And, according to the Psalmist, [a defiled peace] is called a peace among sinners.[36] Moreover, [one must keep himself] from a *feigned peace*—the kind of peace that characterized Judas, the Betrayer. The Psalmist [writes]: "They speak peace with their neighbor ...," etc.[37] Furthermore, [one who wishes to be peaceful must keep himself] from a *disordered peace,* [which occurs] when the superior obeys the inferior. Such a peace is worse than is war. Adam had such a peace with Eve, his wife, since *he* obeyed *her.*

Moreover, [one who wishes to be peaceful must safeguard himself], because in Scripture war is found to be fourfold: (1) war between the flesh and the spirit ([a war] which penance pacifies); (2) war between man and God (which justice pacifies); (3) war between angels and men (which the Son's incarnation has pacified); (4) war between a man and his neighbor (which long-suffering pacifies).

[16] Now, he who thus is peaceful and has a house adorned with peace can approach Bethlehem, and in him our peaceable Savior will immediately be born spiritually. Therefore, let us upwardly direct our loving contemplation toward the birth of Christ, in order that when with a pious and peaceful mind we recall His super-wondrous birth, we may experience illumination, warmth, and fruitfulness.

ADDITIONAL COMMENT

[17] Chancellor Gerson states [in his work] *On Mystical Theology*, Chapter 2: "Faith, it seems to me, is peace in and through believing." [38] Hence, when a man no longer seeks to apprehend by means of rational considerations, and when he has peace with respect to the authority of the one who speaks and when he is obedient, then there is peacefulness by means of his believing. But since every sin has its origin from presumption, Christ comes in order to remove all presumption that is innate to us as a result of our first parent, who willed because of his presumptuousness to be like God and, like God, to know good and evil, and who did not will to obey, in order through obeying to be able to eat of the Tree of Life. Hence, in order to recommend to us obedience, [God the Son] became a man and emptied Himself [39] so as to show us two things: viz., (1) how it is that obedience and humility are so pleasing to God that He sent His Son into the world and (2) that the Son Himself was obedient in this regard. Although the Son was in the form of God ...,[40] etc., He became a man in order to obey the Father; indeed, He became obedient to the Father even unto death—even unto death on the Cross.[41] Nothing baser than this kind [of death] could have occurred—[occurred] in order for man to learn in this way that he must be obedient and in order that he would know how it is that through obedience humanity, having the peacefulness that comes from faith, ascends unto the Divinity. For the humanity of Christ crossed over into the person of the Word, because Christ came into the world in order to do the will of the Father.[42] And so, from the peacefulness that comes from faith we have the learning of truth and the experiencing of obedience's usefulness against presumption.

NOTES TO *SERMON XVI*

1. Luke 2:14.
2. Romans 11:36. Colossians 1:16.
3. This sentence and the subsequent ones are adapted from John 1:1-5.
4. Hebrews 1:1.
5. Hebrews 1:1-2.
6. John 1:14.
7. Wisdom 2:24.
8. Psalms 75:3 (76:2).
9. Psalms 84:11 (85:10).
10. Cf. Psalms 84:11 (85:10).
11. Isaias (Isaiah) 53:8.
12. Cf. Hebrews 7:2.
13. Isaias (Isaiah) 40:6.
14. Luke 2:14.
15. John 1:9.
16. Psalms 113:3B (115:3).
17. Psalms 32:9 (33:9).
18. Augustine, *De Trinitate*, I, 1, 1 (*PL* 42:820).
19. Although the usual Orthodox way of speaking states that the Son is *begotten* of the Father, whereas the Holy Spirit *proceeds* from the Father and the Son, Nicholas is not here veering from Orthodoxy. For like others before him, he regards being begotten as a kind of proceeding. See my article "Verständnis und Bedeutung des Dreieinen Gottes bei Nikolaus von Kues," *Mitteilungen und Forschungsbeiträge der Cusanus-Gesellschaft*, 28 (2003), 135-164.
20. "... cannot be an accident": i.e., cannot be an incidental feature of the Divine Mind.
21. Cf. Psalms 18:6 (19:5).
22. Ezechiel (Ezekiel) 44:2.
23. Matthew 2:1. In Sermon XVII Nicholas speaks of Jesus's temporal birth.
24. Wisdom 7:26.
25. Wisdom 7:27.
26. John 1:12-13.
27. Not an exact quotation. Wisdom 9:10.
28. Luke 2:15.
29. Proverbs 3:17 (not Proverbs 4, as Nicholas writes and as I have corrected, as do also the editors of the Latin text).
30. Luke 10:5.
31. Philippians 4:7.
32. Job 9:4.
33. Ephesians 4:3 (not Ephesians 3, as Nicholas writes and as I have corrected, as do also the editors of the Latin text).
34. Psalms 4:9 (4:8).
35. Luke 23:12.
36. Psalms 72:3 (73:3).

37. Psalms 27:3 (28:3): "... who speak peace with their neighbor; but evils are in their hearts."

38. Jean Gerson, *De Mystica Theologia Practica*, Consideratio I [See Vol. VIII, p. 19 in Palémon Glorieux, editor, *Oeuvres Complètes* (Paris: Desclée and Cie, 1971)].

39. Philippians 2:7.

40. Philippians 2:6.

41. Philippians 2:8.

42. Matthew 26:39. John 6:38.

Sermon XVII: Gloria in Excelsis Deo
("Glory to God in the highest.")[1]
[December 25, 1432 (?); preached perhaps in Koblenz]

[1] "Glory [to God in the highest,"] etc.

Secondly,[2] we must consider, chiefly, the temporal birth of the eternal Word of God. And in this regard two things are to be considered: viz., the reason for the Incarnation and the manner of the Incarnation.

PART ONE
The Reason for the Incarnation

[2] As concerns the reason for [the Incarnation], we must first of all consider the fact that, from the beginning, man was created for the following ends: viz., in order to serve and to obey God; secondly, in order thereby to come to the eternal Kingdom. And man was given the commandment not to eat of the Tree of Knowledge, since otherwise he would utterly die. [But] man sinned. [Man's] cause was argued before the Law-Giver. Charges were adduced against man by Justice and Truth; and Mercy and Peace argued on behalf [of man].[3] First, Justice argued against man that God is a just Judge and that for this reason it was decreed that [man, if he ate of the Tree,] ought utterly to die, etc. Therefore, [he deserves death], etc. On man's behalf Mercy contended that by means of this same Justice the Eternal Source of human beings created man for salvation and that because of man's weakness He often made known the law of mercy and that He ought to be merciful, etc.

Truth adduced a counter-argument; Peace responded, etc. And subsequent to the reply (which is stated elsewhere), Peace adduced the graciousness of the Creator-Lord. [And Peace mentioned] that from the beginning [God] had predestined many men and from the beginning had established His Church as His bride and had adorned her in various ways as a Paradise. And He had placed the Tree of life in the middle [of Paradise], where the Tree of the knowledge of good and evil was. And in Paradise He had consecrated the great [marital] sacrament of the perpetual union-of-Adam-and-Eve, befiguring [the union] of the Church and the Savior. [And Peace mentioned] that, from the beginning, the Church derived from Adam, who befigured Christ, and that

Adam was composed of bone and flesh, i.e., of Christ's predestined Church. And in this greatest sacrament there were symbolized (according to Paul in [his letter] to the Ephesians) the sons of adoption and the joint-heirs with Christ,[4] who is the First-born, the true King, and the eternal Heir. And [Peace mentioned] that at different times and in many ways [God] had spoken about this fact through the Fathers [and] the Prophets[5]—[spoken] in shadows, figures, and signs. And [Peace said] that the whole of Scripture endeavored to express, in various ways, this sole truth about the Savior, the Son, the Heir, the Head, the First-born of every creature.[6] And [Peace spoke] of the concordant and harmonious gradations of all the things that have flowed forth from the Creator through the Son: they will all be returned unto the Creator in a certain super-wondrous way. Moreover, [Peace argued] that (according to Ambrose[7] and others and according to all the holy truths) angelic and human rational creatures would, for their ultimate salvation, be united only to this same [Son] in a oneness of Body.

[3] Therefore, seeing that all men have need of a Healing Physician—especially with regard to rest and love for God (by means of which love God ordained unto Himself all things thus created), then lest there be said in vain and meaninglessly all those written things which Paul (especially in Ephesians) expounds very enthusiastically, the Holy Trinity took under advisement these accusations. And Eternal Truth itself—persuaded by Mercy and Peace—came down in order that, having thought of a mode of satisfying eternal Justice, man, who sinned, might be set free. Now, not an angel but a man sinned against God, who is infinite and eternal—[sinned] in that he believed the Devil and not God. [The man] wanted to be equal to the Supreme Being—[equal] not in terms of believing but in terms of knowing. ([He sinned] by means of this crime of *lèse majesté*; by means of an original condemnation this crime passed to the man's descendants.) Therefore, the remedy of satisfaction for so great an offense could not be found by finite and delimited man.

The verdict was rendered that the Lord of infinite graciousness, of justice, of truth, and of mercy and of peace—the Creator, the Word of God—would assume human flesh, would descend from Heaven, would assume a humanity, would make satisfaction, and, having pacified Justice, would lead man back to his Heavenly Home.

And today is the most holy solemn feast of this super-wonderful [re-]uniting.

PART TWO
How It Is That the Eternal Word Was Born in Time

[4] Let us examine briefly the arrangement by which this birth was accomplished. And we must become aware that the birth is twofold: viz., in the Virgin and from the Virgin. As regards the former, it is said: "The man is born in her, and the Most High Himself has founded her."[8] That is, [this occurred] when, with the power of the Most High over-shadowing her and with the Holy Spirit supervening,[9] the Word was made flesh.[10] Assuredly, it is not the case that [the Word] was transformed into flesh or vice versa. Nor was [the Word brought] into a certain confused mingling with flesh. Nor was [the Word] made fleshly by assuming flesh into a oneness of person. Nor was [the Word] made animal flesh without a rational soul, as individual heretics have individually thought. Rather, the Word was made flesh, i.e., was made a complete human being (including a rational soul) with two natures and one person—not with [only] one nature or with two persons, as certain heretics have claimed. Rather, then, the Word assumed flesh, i.e., a humanity. For "flesh" is understood to mean *man*—as in the following passages: "All flesh is grass"[11] and "All flesh will come unto You."[12]

[5] Hence, all at once [and] not as in the case of others who are in time, the Word was made flesh from the very pure blood of virginal flesh—[was made] a complete human being consisting of a rational soul and a human body. For according to the prophecy of Jeremias[13] a virgin all at once encompassed a complete human being, consisting of a soul and a body. In the case of [all] others, this [ensoulment] does not happen, unless the body is older and larger in size.[14] O such great perfection and manliness at the outset of conception! For with respect to His spirit and the higher part of His soul, [Jesus] was a Discerner: by means of a beatific vision He beheld the divine essence and all things—present, past, and future—shining forth in the Divine Word. Already at that time, that most sacred soul was elevated only unto God. It was thinking thoughts of peace;[15] it was full of fixed-dispositions for all virtues, graces, and fields of knowledge. It had within itself all the treasures of knowledge and of wisdom.[16] But as regards the lower part of the soul, viz., the sensibility, He was made like us[17] and was found, in His fixed-disposition, to be like a human being.[18] Thus, He could experience pain and sorrow and could, with us, drink from the torrent of present afflictions[19] and could learn from the things He was going

to suffer,[20] and could suffer with his brethren in all respects[21] —as is written in Hebrews. The following points are to be reflected upon: how at that time He sanctified this Tabernacle,[22] viz., the Blessed Virgin— [sanctified it] abundantly and filled it with inexplicable grace and gladness. "Exult and praise, O Habitation!"[23] Etc. Reflect on how it is that she was the Mother of [Him who is] God and a human being—contrary to [the teachings of] the heretics. Etc.

[6] For in Christ there are not two hypostases, but there is [only] one.[24] And in Christ the hypostatic union of the human nature and the divine nature is so great that the human hypostasis passes into the divine hypostasis but the two natures remain distinct in the oneness of the divine hypostasis. For although the humanity of Christ is purely a creature, it is not a person—i.e., not a hypostasis—and not (properly speaking) a human being. For "a human being" is the designation for a person. For person, or hypostasis, exists and subsists *per se* in such a way that it does not depend—as a part depends on the whole or as a form depends on an object or something else—on anything that supports it through some power and that supplies its personhood and hypostaticness. In short, [person] does not depend on any thing that supports it by means of some power-of-existence other than the person's own.

Two of these three modes[25] are found in natural objects, and the third mode is found only in Christ. (Moreover, every *person* is an *hypostasis*, but not vice versa. "Rational hypostasis," qua signifying *per se*, signifies person.) For in the third way human nature, although it remains in Christ, is so intimately united to the Word that it does not obtain the form of hypostaticness but transfers all such hypostaticness unto the divinity. And because when the Word assumed His humanity, He did not lose His personhood (but, rather, the assumed human nature lost its personhood), the Word is not properly said to have assumed a man, since the Word did not assume the hypostasis of a man. Rather, [the Word is said to have assumed] a humanity, [i.e., a human nature]. And if at some time we read that the Word assumed a *man* [*homo*], the word "man" (*homo*) ought to be taken to stand for a *human nature*, which was assumed by Christ from the beginning and which never existed in and of itself. Therefore, in Christ there was a unique hypostasis—i.e., [only] one person—and there was, unconfusedly, a divine nature and a human nature, and there was the Word, born before all ages,[26] and born today in time, etc.

[7] It is not the case that Christ is composed of the Word and a man. For, in that case, since no whole is its own part: the Word of God

(who is Christ, as we read in today's Gospel of John) would not be
Deity or God; and, by like reasoning, neither the human nature nor
Christ would exist from eternity but, instead, would be a recent[27] God;
and no such hypostasis ought to be believed to have existed from eternity. Do not let the following statement be an obstacle: "Just as the
rational soul and the flesh ...," etc.[28] For an exact analogy is not [there-
by] being expressed. Rather [that statement] means that just as a human
person subsists in a twofold nature of body and soul, so the person of
Christ subsists in the twin substance of the divinity and the humanity.

[8] But we ought to grant that Christ is composed of a body and
a soul; for He is a man of like species with us,[29] who are composed in
this way. Yet, this labeling befits the divine hypostasis only because of
a communication of idioms, i.e., by reason of the union [of the divine
nature] with the human nature. For this holy union is so wondrous, profound, and intimate that the divine nature which remains in Christ
imparts the hypostasis and, by reason of the hypostasis, or person,
applies to itself every name, or idiom, that befits the assumed human
nature. For example, [there is said of the divine nature that] it is a man,
is the Son of man; [and to the divine nature are ascribed] actions, under-
goings, and change. These terms are intended to apply to the human
nature in particular, according as the human nature[30] is the designated
being. Conversely, names and idioms that befit the divine hypostasis
are, by reason of the same union, said, in truest faith, of the human
being, who is God. Still, the divine and the human idioms do not befit
Christ in the same way. For things divine are said of Him *per se* and
unqualifiedly, whereas things human are said of Him not *per se* but *in
a certain respect*, viz., by reason of His human nature. Hence, it is evident that Christ and His blessed humanity [i.e., His human nature] are
not in the same way said to be composed of a rational soul and a body.
For because of the communication of idioms Christ is said *in a certain
respect* [to be thus composed], whereas the humanity [i.e., His human
nature] is said to be composed *per se* [of a body and a rational soul].

[9] From this fact there originate the following marvelous
expressions which faith asserts: viz., that the Immortal One dies, that
the Invisible One is seen on earth, that God, who is not changed, is
weary from the journey,[31] that the Impassible One is crucified, and that
the One who is begotten from eternity is born today, etc. And similarly [compatible are the statements] that the embodied Man [viz., Christ]
is everywhere, that the temporal Man is eternal, that the weak Man is
omnipotent, etc. Indeed, that [hypostatic] union is so super-wondrous

that we say that Christ, the Son of God, descended unto Hell when He died. But because of the separation of His soul from His body it was not true to say that [at that time] He was a man; [yet, it was true to say this] because the union of the Divine Word with the body and the soul was never dissolved. Indeed, by the same reasoning, Christ both lay in the tomb and descended unto Hell. And, at that time, Christ was reigning everywhere in Heaven and on earth in accordance with His divine nature. This is the super-wondrous union which no one apprehends except by faith [and] which Adam tried to apprehend through knowing and, as a result, fell, etc.

[10] But although these very deep divine mysteries—hidden from the beginning in God [but] now revealed at the end of the ages[32]—are altogether incomprehensible, nevertheless they are not unbelievable.[33] For His testimonies are made exceedingly believable.[34] Previously, He declared these things in the writings of peoples and of princes[35] (i.e., of the just and of the Patriarchs)—[declared them] in figures and symbols and in various proclamations of His holy prophets, who are from the beginning.[36] He reveals all these things to us through evangelists, apostles, and teachers[37] and through shepherds whom He found watching over their flock.[38] And in order that they might behold these wondrous things, He brought them to Bethlehem, etc.

[11] From these things, we know already that Christ was the smallest human being who there ever was.[39] [This statement is true] because from the instant of His conception He was a complete human being and because He was in the womb longer than any other human being and because He received more nourishment from His mother than do others [from theirs], since He was in the womb longer and began to grow from a smaller size. And thus He was joined in a more kindred way to His mother than are all others [to their mothers], because such [a joining] arises from consubstantiality, of which Christ had from Mary more [than do all others from their mothers]. Moreover, very great joy redounded to Mary from the Savior, etc. Christ did not bring His body from Heaven into the Virgin, as the heretic Mani claimed. Nor did the Word assume only flesh, without a rational soul, as Arius claimed. Nor did He assume only a perceptive soul without an intellective soul, as Apollinaris claimed. Let the heretic Nestorius—who claimed that there are two persons in Christ—keep silent. And likewise [let] Eutyches [remain silent], who claimed that just as there is one person [in Christ] so there is [only] one nature.

NOTES TO *SERMON XVII*

1. Luke 2:14.
2. This sermon addresses the second of the three themes proposed—in the previous sermon—for the three masses.
3. See Sermon I for a further exposition of this court-case.
4. Ephesians 1:5 and 3:6. Romans 8:17.
5. Hebrews 1:1.
6. "... the First-born of every creature": Colossians 1:15.
7. Ambrose, *Epistola*, 76: *Ad Irenaeum*, n. 11-13 (*PL* 16:1317-1318).
8. Psalms 86:5 (87:5).
9. Luke 1:35.
10. John 1:14.
11. Isaias (Isaiah) 40:6.
12. Psalms 64:3 (65:2).
13. Jeremias (Jeremiah) 31:22.
14. Normally, that is, the soul is not present with the body until "quickening," which comes at a later stage of pregnancy, rather than at conception.
15. Jeremias (Jeremiah) 29:11.
16. Colossians 2:3.
17. Philippians 2:7.
18. Philippians 2:8.
19. Psalms 109:7 (110:7).
20. Hebrews 5:8.
21. Cf. Hebrews 4:15.
22. Psalms 45:5 (46:4).
23. Isaias (Isaiah) 12:6.
24. The English word "hypostasis" translates the Latin word "suppositum," which itself translates the Greek word "ὑπόστασις". The hypostatic union is the union of Christ's two natures—divine and human—into one person, i.e., one hypostasis.
25. The three modes are not distinguished clearly by Nicholas. Presumably, they are (1) the mode whereby a being has one person and one nature (as is the case with human beings), (2) the mode whereby a being has no person but has one nature (as is the case with non-human animals), and (3) the mode whereby a being has one person and two natures (as is the case only with Christ).
26. "... born before all ages": See the Creed of Constantinople (381).
27. "... a recent God": Note Psalms 80:10 (81:9).
28. See the so-called Athanasian Creed: "Nam sicut anima rationalis et caro unus est homo, ita Deus et homo unus est Christus." ("Just as the rational soul and the body are one man, so God and a human nature (*homo*) are one Christ.")
29. Philippians 2:7.
30. Here (at 8:16) I am reading "natura" in place of "nata"—as does *p*.
31. John 4:6.
32. Colossians 1:26.
33. This passage is important for assessing Nicholas's understanding of the relationship between faith and reason.

34. Psalms 92:5 (93:5).
35. Psalms 86:6 (87:6).
36. Luke 1:70.
37. Ephesians 4:11.
38. Luke 2:8.
39. Cf. Sermon XXII (**35**:7), where Christ is called *maximus homo*, in contrast to His here being called *minimus homo*.

Sermon XVIII: Afferte Domino

("Bring to the Lord [glory and honor] ....")[1]
[January 6, 1433(?); feast-day of the Lord's epiphany;[2]
preached somewhere in the diocese of Trier]

[1] "Bring to the Lord glory and honor; bring to the Lord glory to His name. Adore the Lord in His holy court." Psalms 28.

Recently, on the day of [our Lord's] birth we heard at length—after our Savior's genealogy and His eternal and His temporal births were elucidated a bit—how this Word manifested Himself to the nearby Jewish shepherds. Therefore, today, let us consider how it is that we Gentiles, [coming] from afar with gifts, merit to be led by the divine light unto the Savior. And because He Himself is the Lord, and the Great King, over all the earth, whose name is forever blessed, whom all His intellectual spirits adore: we must bring to Him, as Lord, glory and honor; for He is our Father, who is in Heaven. And let us bring glory to His name, which is hallowed; and let us adore Him in His holy court, so that He may give us His Kingdom. To these ends He has given us the instruction by the Holy Spirit through David: "Bring ...," etc.

[2] "Bring to the Lord ...," etc. The three Magi who came to Christ from the East signify the Church, which from out of paganism is united to Christ. Accordingly, the first part of this epiphany will be, namely, how it is that we, as faithful servants, bring glory and honor to our King, who is now manifest. Secondly, in regard to the theophany of the baptism of Christ (where the Church was united to the Savior through marriage), let us bring glory to that name which was given to Him at circumcision—[given to Him] by divine ordinance and angelic revelation and confirmed on the day of His baptism by the voice of the Father, who said "This is my beloved Son." For Jesus (meaning "Savior")[3] is called the Son of God. His is a glorious name, one blessed forever. Thirdly, [let us bring glory to the Lord] in regard to the epiphany at the changing of water into wine; by means of this epiphany the Church, His bride, is elevated unto the intoxicating taste of love.

Let us adore [Him] now by at least contemplating [Him] in His holy court—[contemplating] how Christ, who was recently[4] born among us and circumcised, is presented with gifts and is baptized, and how water is changed into wine.

306

PART ONE
The Manifestation of the Acme of All Holiness in Christ.
How It Is That We Ought To Serve Him

[3] First of all, let an account be set forth of how it is that the Savior, from the beginning, always manifested Himself through the Prophets ever more and more clearly. And the closer the Prophets lived in relation to [the time of] Christ, the more clearly they prophesied and the holier they were (e.g., John the Baptist, etc.). And, thus, immediately after Christ, the very holy Apostles and disciples preached Christ in all the world. And from the beginning of the world unto [the time of] Christ the Church grew successively in holiness—up to [the life of] Christ, the acme of all holiness. And from [the time of] Christ unto the Day of Judgment holiness diminishes, because the Anti-Christ, who is opposed to Christ, is the fount of all wickedness and sin, etc. And [let us contemplate] how it is that on the basis of a lesser manifestation of Christ our fathers wrote, with regard to morals and to life, about the Anti-Christ—[wrote] that at that time his coming was very near. For they saw many evils and saw times that were worse than the times of their fathers (just as each age has complained as regards its own days). And on the basis of this reasoning we infer that the Anti-Christ will come soon, because all things are disposed toward evils; and, furthermore, according to the calculation of some men, the time [of the Anti-Christ] is approaching because (as many [of these men] say) the world is supposed to reach an age of only seven thousand years, etc.

[4] Now, we have recently heard how when Christ was born in Bethlehem He manifested Himself to Jewish shepherds. And you have often heard tell [how He manifested Himself] to pagan kings, etc. And because the pagan Magi, very far removed from Jerusalem, symbolize sinners, and because the Star [of Bethlehem] symbolizes a preacher, I will take up the role of the Star (although I am amid darkness) in order to enlighten and guide you unto the Savior. And just as that Star—created from elements, and corruptible, and unsensing—shows, nonetheless, the Savior: so too, by the word of preaching, the prelate (even one not alive in spirit) [shows the Savior]. But just as a prelate ought to have the characteristics of that Star—viz., ought to go-before, to illumine, to show the way, and to remain there where Christ *is* (indeed, the having of such a prelate is a great joy to the people), so too the people ought to follow the illumination of his teaching, ought to look for it and, at length, ought to find it.

[5] First, then, you ought to know that because Christ is Lord of lords and King of kings, we His servants ought rightly to bring Him glory and honor. For He is "Lord"—the name of power, of jurisdiction, and of authoritativeness—from whom is all power in Heaven and on earth. And "Lord" is the name not only of power but also of equity. He defends the innocent; He punishes wrong-doers through the intermediary of justice. Such is Christ, since (as the Psalmist says) He lifts up the meek.[5] For he who desires to rule follows Christ, etc., and shows his own power over the beasts, as did Noah.[6] {Genesis 9: Let fear of you be upon all the animals (i.e., according to Gregory, [upon all] beasts), etc.}. He who is a plunderer, a robber, an oppressor, he who violates justice (by word, in price charged, or in what he hates), he who receives tributes and does not protect, he who cancels the rights of fathers, he who desires to be feared rather than to be liked, he who in his exactings reckons false appearances for legitimate grounds—he ought to be called a tyrant, not a lord.

But our Lord is not an acceptor of persons;[7] rather, He is a just Creator and Redeemer, a gracious and merciful Father. Although as a gracious Father He chastises us and places us under supervisors and appears intermittently harsh to us, nevertheless [He does] all these things so that we may make progress and may be nourished in the virtues and, at length, may feast with Him at His table. Therefore, we servants ought rightly, as faithful and just servants, to honor this Lord.

[6] There are three kinds of servants. Some who have been born in servitude are *born-again servants* (even as all unbelievers are *not* born-again). There are *purchased servants* (viz., Christian sinners). And there are *hired servants* (as are good Christians who serve willingly, "rejoicing in hope and serving the Lord ..."[8]). If we wish to be good servants, let us not be voracious, drunken, thieving, negligent, idle, lazy, drowsy, opposed to the Lord, presumptuous. ([See] Luke 12, Matthew 24,[9] John 14, II Kings 19, where [you will read] about these things.) Moreover, such servants are like a rhinoceros. Job 39: the rhinoceros will never serve you (which is to say, as it were: such impudent men are like a rhinoceros, which is never subjected to a yoke and is not yoked, by means of any cunning, for the purpose of domestic service).[10] Let us not seek our own profit more than the Lord's. Let us not carelessly expend entrusted goods. Let us not be demanding in seeking grace from the Lord. Let us believe not that many things are owed to us but that we will have all things because of grace. Let us not be quarrelsome, abusive, contentious, fraudulent, deceitful. (About these [traits see]

Philippians 2, Ecclesiastes 7, Matthew 21, Proverbs 30, IV Kings 21,[11] I Kings 25.)

It is characteristic of persons who are servants to despise their masters. And if they are dealt with kindly, they are accustomed to be haughty toward their masters; but if they are treated harshly, they obey more out of fear; but they do not love more, etc. But let us be good servants who are docile, disposed readily to understand, humble and compliant with regard to obeying, cheerful and consoling, friendly and agreeable when it comes to discussing, manly and courageous for battling the Lord's adversaries, faithful and energetic for distributing the Lord's goods. (About these [topics see] Isaias 52, Luke 12, Isaias 49, I Kings 17, Luke 19.)[12] And so, let us be faithful servants, so that with fear and love we may ever be on guard as concerns the tasks entrusted to us by the Lord, since we are going to give an account ..., etc.[13]

[7] And because it pertains especially to servants to be reverent, we ought to have reverence for our Lord and for all His commandments and for His created image. And, first, our Lord [ought] always to be reverenced and, secondly, our angel, in whose sight (as says Bernard)[14] you should be ashamed to do what you would not do in man's presence. Let us hold in reverence holy places, which are fearsome (Genesis 28).[15] Likewise, [let us hold] men [in reverence]. I Peter 2: Honor all men ...,[16] etc. Be subject to every human creature for God's sake.[17] And, according to Paul, prefer one another in honor.[18] And we ought especially to honor the image of God in man. If honor is commanded to be shown to the image of the Blessed Virgin, then even more so [it ought to be shown] to the image of the Trinity that is in man. And men are to be honored on account of the angels assigned to watch over them (Matthew 18).[19] Moreover, because of the human nature that is united to the divine nature, servants are not to be despised. Cyprian: In the manner in which you desire that God deal with you, so deal you with your servant.[20] Seneca: Deal in such a way with your inferior as you wish your superior to deal with you.[21] Ecclesiasticus 33:[22] If your servant is faithful, let him be to you as your soul; treat [him] as your brother.

Do not shun sinners, because a sinner can be made holy. Deuteronomy 23: Do not abhor the Edomite, because he is your brother.[23] Nevertheless, those who are living a good life are especially to be honored, for they are related to God by means of every kind of kinship. Matthew 12: He who shall do the will of my Father who is in Heaven, he is my brother, [my] sister, and [my] mother.[24] Let God be honored in those who are just, because He dwells within them. Nor are the poor to be despised; for what is done to them is done to God.[25] And although all men are to be honored for God's sake, nevertheless lords and leaders are all the more to be honored.[26] (I Timothy 5).[27] Romans 13: Every soul ..., etc.[28] ([See also] Colossians 3, etc.)[29] Moreover, the youth ought to honor the elderly. Leviticus 19: Rise up before the gray-haired, and honor the person of the aged.[30] I Timothy 5.[31] And Seneca: "An elderly man must be treated quite considerately.[32]

Husbands are to be honored by their wives. I Peter 3: Let wives be subject to their husbands.[33] And in the same passage it is next added: husbands, too, are to honor their wives. Accordingly, the Lord did not form woman from the foot of man but from his rib, lest she be despised. A wife ought to obey her husband as being her head. There ought to be [but] one head in marriage, so that there may be peace. For although there are two hands and two feet in the case of a man, there is only one head. If there were two heads, then there would be discord: one head would want to go to the right, the other to the left, etc.

[8] Parents, both spiritual and fleshly, are to be honored. Exodus 20: Honor your father ..., etc.[34] And such honor ought to be by word and by deed. For never be in such straits that you forget your parents— even as Christ on the Cross commended His mother to John.[35] Even unbelievers have that concern. I Timothy 5: If anyone does not provide for his own and especially for his household, he has denied the faith and is worse than an unbeliever.[36] Cranes nurture their parents after they have lost their feathers. And as you do to your parents, so it will be done unto you. [Consider] the example of a certain man who gave all his goods to his son, etc; look at the *Compendium of Vices*, etc.[37] Ecclesiasticus 3: he who honors his father shall have joy in his children; and in the day of his prayer he shall be heard.[38] And in the same passage [we read]: he who honors his father shall live a long life. The same place [says]: honor your father, in order that a blessing may come upon you, etc.[39] The father's blessing establishes the houses of the children, but the mother's curse uproots the foundation.[40] [Consider] the example of Cham,[41] who scoffed at his father, and of Absalom, who drove out David,[42] and of the children who mocked Eliseus [i.e., Elisha],[43] etc. Therefore, when we keep these commands regarding honor—[keep them] in every circumstance—then we honor the Lord in Himself and in His possessions. And, together with kings, we bring to Him gold, whereby we recognize Him as the immortal, incorruptible, and all-powerful King. Etc.

[Let all of] this [have been said] at the outset. Etc.

PART TWO
Theophany; and the Blasphemy That Is the Greatest Sin

[9] Therefore, bring to this great King above all gods,[44] [this King] who does not cast off His people[45] and in whose hand are all boundaries and who Himself beholds the heights of the mountains[46]—therefore, you kindred people, bring to the Lord glory and honor.[47] For He Himself is the Lord our God, and we are His people and the sheep of His pasture, etc.[48] Because it has now been said that we ought to bring to the Lord our God glory and honor, there is rightly added: "Bring glory to His name." For if we are commanded to magnify the Lord, then likewise we are commanded, for the same reason, to exalt His name.[49] First, let us see who, principally, are the glorifiers and who are not. The glorifiers are those who by formed faith[50] believe on His name. In this way they live with true life, [and] they give glory to Him who lives forever.[51] The non-glorifiers are the evil servants who are cloaked with sins and with the darkness of death. Among these the worst ones, and those who give glory the least, are the very wretched blasphemers. Hence, I will make a few remarks about them.

[10] Now, according to Augustine blasphemy occurs when there is ascribed to God that which does not befit Him or when there is denied to befit Him that which does befit Him or when one usurps that which belongs to God.[52] And [blasphemy] can be considered in a twofold way, because a certain [form of it] is *of the heart*, as in the *Lives of the Fathers*[53] we read about a certain man whom the spirit of blasphemy vexed. [See more] about this in the *Compendium of Vices*.[54] For sometimes blasphemy intrudes on what is being thought of [by us—intrudes] without delight [on our part] and as a result of Satan's inbreathing or, frequently, as a result of our fear of God's displeasure. (For example, to a man who is in a dark, desolate place fear brings to mind frightening things, whether he wishes it or not; and the very great love of a mother for her son brings the son [spontaneously] to her mind after he has died.) And [this unwilled phenomenon likewise occurs] whenever the Devil, knowing that revilings displease God, speaks blasphemies [silently] in a man, who hears them; but the blasphemy is the Devil's, not the man's. Such blasphemy does not contaminate a man. But let the man say: "O, Satan, keep your blasphemy to yourself ...," etc., "for it is not pleasing to man." And so, the remedy is contempt for this kind of blasphemy and our having low-esteem for such

thoughts and our keeping quite busy, etc.

[11] The other [form of blasphemy] is blasphemy *of the mouth*, [occurring] when someone speaks in accordance with the aforementioned three [Augustinian] points, etc. And now I intend to speak especially about blasphemy-of-mouth [that occurs] when someone utters a word that is abusive of God (since he wants to strike back at God) and refers to members that ought not to be mentioned. And this sin is very grave, since the blasphemer has a very evil intent; for [the evil intent] is directed against God, and with his tongue the blasphemer penetratingly abuses God and His mother. Neither the Jews had such a wicked intention, nor do heretics have it; for they believe that they are not in error. But a blasphemer *knows* and *believes* and *does*, etc. And there is no sin which is so pointedly directed against God—not licentiousness or greed, …, etc.

Secondly, [blasphemy is a sin that is] very grave because man is not much inclined toward this sin; and sin is measured in accordance with the smallness of the inclination. Acts 7: They all stopped up their ears …, etc.[55] And Matthew 26, etc.[56] Thirdly, [this sin is very grave] because it encompasses more than does any other sin, because [it is aimed directly at] God; and because God is most perfect, one sins most gravely against God. Likewise, fourthly, [the blasphemer sins very gravely] because he offends against Him who is most noble. For a wrong is weighed in relation to the person against whom the wrong is done. And, thus, Thomas holds that [blasphemy] is a sin greater than [the sin of] killing a man[57] … because the blasphemer sins against a commandment of the First [Mosaic] Tablet; and his doing so is more grave than [is a sin] against a commandment of the Second Tablet.[58] Blasphemy is [aimed] more against the person of God in a spiritual way than in an external way against His body. Fifthly, [the sin of blasphemy] is the greatest malice. Cursing one's father or one's mother is punishable by death; and whoever says to his brother "you fool," is worthy of death in Hell ….[59] If so, then a blasphemer is worthy of both physical and spiritual death.[60] Sixthly, [blasphemy is] of maximal disrespect, because God is despised. ([See] *On Heretics*, [the section] regarding Vergentis.)[61] If to curse a king is a capital crime …,[62] the sentence is all the more applicable to a blasphemer.

[12] Blasphemy against God and blasphemy against the saints are a single wrong-doing that are punished in equal measure because of the union [of the saints] with God. {([See] the *Authentica*, [the section beginning with the words] "That one not be licentious unnatural-

ly...," etc.[63]) For when the soul is apart from the body, it cannot be harmed, on account of its union [with God]. Such [is said] there.} Likewise, [blasphemy is] the worst thanklessness. God ...[64] has given you a tongue for your very great benefit, [but] you would use it to revile Him. Moreover, this sin [of blasphemy] distinguishes the sons of God from the sons of the Devil, because blasphemy is the language of Hell, etc. Therefore, those who hear these diabolical voices ought to plug up their ears, to utter the name "Jesus," to kiss the ground, to sign themselves with the sign of the Cross, to strike their chest, and strongly to contend, in private, against [these voices]. Moreover, by means of his blasphemy a most wicked man is recognized, because he has sung the song of the Devil, his father. And because [blasphemy] is so great a sin, all creatures speak ill of a blasphemer, since every creature, except the blasphemer, knows His Creator and praises Him. Therefore, they rightly speak ill of the blasphemer insofar as he is an enemy of God. And because of this [i.e., because he is an enemy] he is punished physically, spiritually, and eternally. ([See] *On the Foul-Mouthed*, Chapter 2.)[65]

[13] Moreover, this sin [of blasphemy] God punishes visibly, more than other [sins are punished visibly]. For example, [this visible punishment occurred] in the case of the boy of whom Gregory [tells] in his Dialogue.[66] And [it occurred] in the case of the soldier in France who, while blaspheming, fell into an epileptic fit and on the third day was suffocated by the Devil. And a certain man hauling hay while blaspheming was killed by a fire. Furthermore, a man who was blaspheming against the eye of the Virgin Mary lost his own eye; he blasphemed against her foot and lost [his own foot], etc. A certain blasphemer who wanted to shoot arrows at God discharged an arrow. It was in the air for three days and then returned, bloodied, and landed [lethally] on the blasphemer, whose soul the Devil [then] had. In the area of Milan a man was blaspheming in the midst of his comrades. He was seized by the Devil, lifted into the air, stripped of his clothes, and carried off to Hell. And at Rome a blasphemer was hanged in front of his window by devils. At Milan a blasphemer was seen to be carried off publicly by the Devil. Or again, at Florence, at the location of hermits, there was a denarius-coin having the image of the Virgin. A certain blasphemer, servant of Count Hugo, struck it, and blood flowed from [it], etc. Then too, [the following] must be known: he who does not love God tolerates a blasphemer; and he who does not correct [a blasphemer] when he has the ability to do so, will perish with the blasphemer, etc.

PART THREE
On Bethphania—i.e., on the Changing of Water into Wine; and by means of Which Contemplation This [Transformation] Is Effected

[14] In a third way let us see from the work of 'bethphania' (i.e., [the work] of changing water into wine) how it is, indeed, that we who are watery and insipid and cold may be changed into red and strong wine. And let this [understanding] come about by means of our reflecting on myrrh, so that our life may be buried in Christ by our putting off the old man, etc.[67] Recently, through contemplation, we stood at the Lord's crib, and we saw the new-born infant in the crib. And because our soul was then made Christ-like: necessarily, in order to be saved, it grows with Christ throughout the eight days leading up to His circumcision. On the first day it grows by meditating on death. On the second day it grows by meditating on the transitory nature of temporal things. On the third day it grows when it meditates on the loss that results from the fact that it is too inclined toward benefits to its body. On the fourth day it grows when it meditates on the Devil's various machinations, by which a man is ensnared.

On the fifth day [our soul] grows when it reflects on its wretched exile. [The soul] is (1) so oppressed by the bulk of the body and is (2) so distracted by various kinds of things—and (3) by the desire for those things it is so fervently inclined toward the lowest goods—that only with difficulty can it raise itself up to Heavenly things that are to be sought gladly. On the sixth day [the soul] grows when it becomes aware of how greatly God is displeased by arrogance, because of which He cast the angel [Satan] out of Heaven and cast man out of Paradise. On the seventh day [the soul] grows by meditating upon the fact that divine grace is of such efficacy that (1) it makes a man to be conformed to the divine purpose in all his actions and (2) it illumines his activities with a certain God-likeness. And, at that point, [the man] recognizes that of himself he is incapable of doing anything. On the eighth day [the soul] grows when it meditates on the abundance and the richness of divine goodness, which is of such great savor that it draws every mind that tastes of it into a state of having no desire for, and having even a disgust for, every ephemeral delight.

[15] And after Christ has thus increased in us for eight days, the soul begins to be circumcised, so that it may be saved and may remain completely saved. It is circumcised, first, with the knife of providence

through the safeguarding of the outer senses. After making progress, [the soul] is circumcised with the knife of justice through the fervent doing of good works. Thereafter, thirdly, [it is circumcised] with the knife of wisdom through the use and continuance of an internal orderly disposition. And when it has been thus circumcised on [these] three additional days: then, as a result of its fervent love on the twelfth day, it understands that after the eight days were completed, it was saved. Hence, at that point, [the soul] makes itself to be a king from the East (i.e., a new king [from the East]) by departing from Saba (i.e., from darkness), by making its kingdom *clean* and *peaceful* and *Solomonlike* by slaying Adonias ([i.e.,] the lust of the eyes), and by condemning Abiathar to death if he leaves Jerusalem (i.e., by restraining and condemning the lust of the flesh, although it cannot be altogether put to death), and by killing Joab ([i.e.,] the pride of life)—after the fashion of Solomon, who killed both his brother Adonias and Joab the leader and who condemned the priest Abiathar.[68]

And thereupon, with the star of grace as a guide, [the soul] will be led, unfailingly, through the true pathways of the Lord, provided it does not rely on human aid but with steadfast hope clings to divine aid. And [the soul] will come to the Lord Jesus, who is God and a man; and humbly it will find Him—in the Judea of confession, in the House of Bread[69]—to be in Himself of infinite succulence. And it will offer Him (1) faith that is steadfast, incorrupt, golden, without blemish, and incorruptible and (2) the incense-bathed hope of an expected reward of eternal glory and (3) the myrrh of very strong love that will persist unto death and will never fail. By means of this love [the soul] will be happily united—in eternal glory and as a beloved, adopted joint-heir—to Jesus, our very relishable Savior, our Lord, the First-born Heir of all, etc.[70]

And so, the third part of our adoration will be completed (1) when we will have entered, in the foregoing way, into His courts with offerings and (2) when we will—as purified, circumcised, mortified, and bathed in myrrh—adore Him in His holy court. And then—as having been anointed and made Christians—we shall enter (since we have found eternal redemption), into the Holy of holies,[71] so that we shall be saved in eternal glory, to which we are led by Him who lives and reigns [forever], etc.

NOTES TO *SERMON XVIII*

1. Psalms 28:2 (29:2).

2. The feast-day January 6 commemorates Jesus's manifestation to the Magi. The two other epiphanies referred to in this sermon are the manifestation on the occasion of Jesus's being baptized and the manifestation at the Feast of Cana, where Jesus changed water into wine.

3. Mathew 1:20-21.

4. "… recently": i.e., the feast-day January 6 is close to the Feast of the Nativity (December 25).

5. Psalms 146:6 (147:6).

6. Genesis 9:2.

7. Acts 10:34.

8. Romans 12:11-12.

9. Matthew 24:45-51 (not Matthew 20, as Nicholas writes and as I have corrected, as do the editors of the Latin text). Luke 12:41-48. John 14:21. II Kings (II Samuel) 19:26.

10. Job 39:9-12.

11. Philippians 2:3. Ecclesiastes 7:22 (not Ecclesiastes 4, as Nicholas writes and as I have corrected, as do the editors of the Latin text). Matthew 21:33-41. Proverbs 30 (not Proverbs 29, as Nicholas writes and as I have corrected, as do the editors of the Latin text.) IV Kings (II Kings) 21:23 (not IV Kings 29, as Nicholas writes and as I have corrected, as do the editors of the Latin text). I Kings (I Samuel) 25:10.

12. Isaias (Isaiah) 52:13. Luke 12:42-44. Isaias (Isaiah) 49:3-6. I Kings (I Samuel) 17:32. Luke 19:11-26.

13. Luke 16:2.

14. Bernard of Clairvaux, *In Psalmum* XC, "Qui Habitat." Sermon 12.6 (*PL* 183:233C).

15. Genesis 28:17.

16. I Peter 2:17.

17. I Peter 2:13.

18. Romans 12:10.

19. Cf. Matthew 18:10.

20. Cf. Cyprian (not Crispianus, as Nicholas writes and as I have corrected, as do the editors of the Latin text), *Liber ad Demetrianum*, 8 (*PL* 4:568-569).

21. Seneca, *Epistolae Morales*, Ep. 47.

22. Ecclesiasticus 33:31 (not Ecclesiasticus 23, as Nicholas writes and as I have corrected, as do the editors of the Latin text).

23. Deuteronomy 23:7.

24. Matthew 12:50.

25. Matthew 25:40.

26. Cf. I Timothy 5:17 (not I Corinthians 15, as Nicholas writes and as I have corrected, as do the editors of the Latin text).

27. Cf. Lamentations 5:12.

28. Romans 13:1: "Let every soul be subject to higher powers."

29. Colossians 3:22: "Servants, obey in all things your masters according to the

316

flesh."

30. Leviticus 19:32.

31. I Timothy 5:1 (not I Timothy 4, as Nicholas writes and as I have corrected, as do the editors of the Latin text): "Rebuke not an elderly man, but entreat him as a father ...."

32. Seneca, *Epistolae Morales*, Epistola 25.

33. I Peter 3:1 (not I Timothy 3, as Nicholas writes and as I have corrected, as do the editors of the Latin text).

34. Exodus 20:12: "Honor thy father and thy mother."

35. John 19:26-27.

36. I Timothy 5:8.

37. William Perald, *Summa Vitiorum*. Codex Cusanus 60.

38. Ecclesiasticus 3:6-7.

39. Ecclesiasticus 3:9-10.

40. Ecclesiasticus 3:11.

41. Genesis 9:20-25.

42. II Kings (II Samuel) 15:7-23.

43. IV Kings (II Kings) 2:23-24.

44. Psalms 94:3 (95:3).

45. Psalms 93:14 (94:14).

46. Psalms 94:4 (95:4).

47. Psalms 95:7 (96:7).

48. Psalms 94:7 (95:7).

49. Psalms 33:4 (34:3).

50. "... by formed faith": i.e., by faith in-formed by love. Cf. Galatians 5:6.

51. Daniel 6:26.

52. Augustine, *De Trinitate*, I, 1, 1 (*PL* 42:819-820).

53. *Vitae Patrum*, 1V, 41 (*PL* 73:840).

54. William Perald, *Summa Vitiorum*. Codex Cusanus 60.

55. Acts 7:57.

56. Matthew 26:65: "Then the high priest rent his garments, saying: He hath blasphemed: What further need have we of witnesses? Behold, now you have heard the blasphemy."

57. Thomas Aquinas, *Summa Theologica*, IIa-IIae, 13, 3, ad 1.

58. Presumably, Nicholas is alluding to the idea that the first five commandments (on Moses' first tablet of stone) are more grave than are the last five (on Moses' second tablet of stone).

59. Matthew 5:22.

60. Spiritual death is eternal separation from God.

61. *Decretales Gregorii IX*, Liber V, Titulus VII (*De Haereticis*, cap. X). [See *Corpus Iuris Canonici*, edited by Aemilius Friedberg, Vol. II, column 783 (Leipzig, 1880): "... longe gravius est aeternam quam temporalem laedere maiestatem."

62. S. P. Scott, translator, *Corpus Juris Civilis: The Civil Law*, Book IX, Title 7 (p. 4 of Vol. 15). Cincinnati, 1932 [reprinted 1973; Vol. 15 is contained in Vol. 7 of the reprinted edition]. Capital punishment is not here mentioned.

63. *Corpus Iuris Civilis*, Vol. III (*Novellae*), pp. 381-383 (Berlin, 1904), pp. 381-383 (*Novella* 77, entitled "Ut non luxurietur contra naturam ...").

64. At 12:7 I am regarding "qui" as deleted.
65. *Decretales Gregorii IX*, Liber V, Titulus XXVI (*De Maledicis*), cap. II. [See *Corpus Iuris Canonici*, edited by Aemilius Friedberg, Vol. II, columns 826-827 (Leipzig, 1880).
66. Gegory the Great, *Dialogorum Libri*, IV, 18 (*PL* 77:349).
67. Colossians 3:9. Ephesians 4:22.
68. III Kings (I Kings) 1:5-7 and 2:24-31.
69. "Hourse of Bread" is the meaning of the word "Bethlehem."
70. Colossians 1:15-16.
71. Hebrews 9:12.0

Sermon XIX: Verbum Caro Factum Est
("The Word was made flesh ....")
[December 25, 1438; preached in Koblenz]

[1] "The Word was made flesh and dwelt among us."[1]

While being now about to say a word about the Word, there occurs [to me] Fulgentius's set of statements in a sermon on the Nativity, where he says:[2]

> We find no words by which we can adequately say anything about the Word. For this is a Word which, having been brought forth, does not perish but remains born. It is not an ephemeral word but is an eternal Word. It is not a word *made* by God but is a *begotten* Word—yea, an only-begotten Word. But how can a man speak fittingly about God? How can a mortal speak fittingly about the Immortal? The visible, about the Invisible? The mutable, about the Immutable? The work, about the Artificer? The creature, about the Creator? The small, about the Immense? The temporal, about the Eternal? The power by which He created us is indescribable; the omnipotence by which He re-created us and saved us is indescribable. We call it omnipotence by which the Word—who was in the beginning and was with God and was God—made everything that previously was not. But we call it grace by which the Word, having been made flesh, came to seek and to save that which was lost.[3]

[2] Hence, since all language is altogether inadequate to say a word about the Word, but since, nevertheless, we are commanded in the [Book of] Psalms to declare His salvation from day to day:[4] let us—on the basis of the teaching of St. Paul, St. Dionysius, and others—obtain today (when the heavens have been made mellifluous) from the Word made flesh, from the very beloved Child, that He make up our insufficiency. And let us say with St. Augustine (Chapter 3 of his *Soliloquies*): "O Word through whom all things have been made and without whom no thing was made, O Word preceding all things but preceded by no thing, O Word creating all things but without whom all things are nothing, O Word through whom You, [O God], said from the beginning 'Let there be light,' and light was made: command now that there be light (and light will be made) in order that I may see light and may recognize whatever is not light. For without You darkness is reckoned for me as light, and light is reckoned as darkness. And, thus, without Your light: error is present, and vanity is present; there is no truth; there is no discernment; there is confusion; ignorance is present; there is no knowledge; there is blindness; there is no pathway, no life,

319

etc. Let there be light, so that I may see the light and avoid the darkness, which does not comprehend You, etc.[5] Therefore, give light in my heart [and] words in my mouth. Open the secrets of the Holy Scriptures, and open the deep mysteries of Your Kingdom."

[3] And once again, praying with Dionysius at the beginning of his *Angelic Hierarchy*, let us say: O Lord, Holy Father, You[6] are the Father of lights[7] and He from whom all enlightenment is present in heaven and on earth. For You illumine; and, thus, in illumining, You make lights. And You draw into the brightness of Your light the darkness of creatures, and You unite [creatures] with You in the unity of Your light. And unto this end You sent to us, on this day, Jesus, Your principal Light, who illumines every man who comes into this world.[8] Through Your only Son deign to enlighten us ..., etc. And in order that this [enlightening] be accomplished, let us approach the Mother of the Incarnate Word ([the Word] who was made flesh from her flesh at the moment when she said "Let it be done with me in accordance with Your word"[9]...) in order that she may intercede with her Son for us, so that we may deserve to be heard, etc.

ORGANIZATION
*Three Parts of the Sermon Are Indicated. Eleven Conditions
for Entering into [an Understanding of] the Gospel
(John 1:1-14) Are Elicited from the Gospel*

[4] First, [I will speak] about the Eternal Word, next about the Word's having been made flesh, thirdly about His having dwelt among us. In order to enter into [an understanding of] these [topics], let us first of all clearly examine the Gospel-text in which John expresses, first, the co-eternity of the Word with the Father when John says: "In the beginning was the Word." Secondly, [let us consider] the distinct property and personality of the Word—distinct from the Father's—because "the Word was with God." Thirdly, [let us examine] the Word's sameness of substance with the Father, because "the Word was God." Fourthly, [let us consider] the effective causal agency of the Word with respect to all things visible and invisible, because "all things were made by Him and without Him nothing was made."

[And let us examine]:

• ... fifthly, the ideal formedness (in the Word) of all created[10] things. For "what was made was life in Him," since a creature has truer existence in God than in itself. Hence, our knowledge of things in the Word is called morning knowledge, and our knowledge of things in their own genus is called evening knowledge.

- ... sixthly, created things' permanent aliveness in the Word, because "in Him was life."
- ... seventhly, the goodness diffused from the Word unto all things, because "the life was the light of men." Hence, every creature is only a certain participated divine goodness [i.e., a certain participation in Divine Goodness].
- ... eighthly, the brightness breathed into John and the other prophets, because "a man was sent [from God] ...," etc.
- ... ninthly, the humanity assumed by the Word, because "the Word was made flesh."
- ... tenthly, the Word's graciousness that was shown to us, because "He dwelt among us and we saw ...."
- ... eleventhly, the full usefulness obtained by us to this end [viz., of salvation], because "[the Word was] full of grace and of truth."

PART ONE
The Loftiness-of-Soaring by means of which
John the Evangelist
Speaks about the Word. And the Reasons
for There Being a Trinity in God

[5] All the doctors [of the Church] admire the height of the eagle-in-flight ...,[11] which, as Ezechiel saw,[12] was above other faces. Hence, Eriugena,[13] [commenting] on [the text] "In the beginning was the Word," [alludes to] the voice of the high-flying bird that soars (not above the material air or the aether or the circumference of the entire perceptible world, but) beyond all speculation, beyond all existing and non-existing things—[the bird] that transcends [them] by means of wings of innermost knowledge-of-God and by eyes of very bright and very lofty contemplation.[14] Now, I mean by "existing things" "things [whose names] do not altogether lack human or angelic meaning." I mean by "non-existing things" "things [whose names], indeed, elude the power of all understanding." The blessed theologian John soars above not only things which can be spoken of or understood but also above those things which surpass all understanding and meaning. And by an ineffable flight of mind he is exalted beyond all things unto the secrets of the one Beginning of all things. And discerning clearly the incomprehensible, singular super-substantiality of this Beginning and

of His Word (i.e., of the Father and of the Son), John begins his Gospel [by writing]: " In the beginning was the Word."

O blessed John, you are rightly called John since in Latin [your name] means "him to whom a gift has been given."[15] For to which of the theologians was there given what was given to you, viz., to penetrate the secrets of the Highest Good? Etc. Likewise, Dionysius[16] in his letter to John (this is his last letter) calls John *the theologian* and *the sun-of-the-Gospel.* Augustine[17] in Homily 20 *On John* tells of how John transcended the earth, the sea, the air, and all other created things. And in Homily 36 on the same [man, Augustine[18] tells of] how at dinner John imbibed from the Lord's breast those things which later he belched forth above all created understanding. Regarding the agreement of the Gospels, [Augustine[19] mentions] how it is that the three other Evangelists walk, as it were, with the man Christ on earth, whereas the Evangelist John soars in the loftiness of the divinity. Etc.

Moreover, Jerome, [in his letter] to Paul[20]—and it is a preface to the Bible—expresses admiration for the voice of [John], the rustic and the fisherman, [who wrote]: " In the beginning was the Word." Plato and Demosthenes did not know of this voice. Etc. [Furthermore], Jerome, in his *Commentary on Ezechiel*[21] and his *Commentary on Zacharias,*[22] says, about this matter, that John told of mysteries unknown perhaps to the angels. Ambrose [comments] in this regard in Book III of his *On the Sacraments* and in his *Incarnation of the Lord.*[23] Gregory in Homily 4 of his *On Ezechiel* says that [John] is rightly called an eagle because by means of his own eyes he focuses on the divinity.[24] And [Gregory] tells of how John passed beyond himself in order to see the Word in the Beginning.[25] Bede in his Homily 1 on the [Gospel of] John [says] the same thing.[26] Likewise, [see] Chrysostom, Homily 1 of his *On John.*[27] [See] Bernard, Sermon 8 of his *On the Canticles.*[28] [See] Haimo, Book III of his *Commentary on the Apocalypse.*[29] [See] Peter Damian, Sermon 2, regarding the present festival.[30]

[6] Furthermore, [consider] how it is that the Platonists, too, affirmed a great part of this Gospel, as Augustine states in Book 10, Chapter 29 of *The City of God* and in Book 8 of the *Confessions.*[31] Nevertheless, Plato spoke of this Word not as being a Person in God but as being the Ideal Form of things through which God created all things. (This Form corresponds to the Son.) Some philosophers posited below God another substance, which they called Supreme Intelligence or Supreme Intellect, through which, they claimed, God created all things. And, thus, from afar they sensed something [of the

truth]. Nevertheless, they did not arrive at a knowledge of the Person [of God]. However, for those who nowadays hold, by faith, that [God is] a Trinity, it would not be difficult to find, subsequent to their faith, rational grounds for [this belief in] a Trinity—as states Richard of St. Victor at the outset of his *On the Trinity*.[32] Likewise, he there investigates [these reasons], as [elsewhere] did also Anselm, Augustine, Damascene, and others. However, from merely naturalistic considerations and without their having had faith, they would not have arrived at these reasons. As Isaias says: "Unless you believe, how will you understand?"[33]

[7] [The second member of the Trinity] is called *Word* because of His immateriality and intellectuality. He is called *Son* because of His consubstantiality and connaturality [with the Father]. He is called *Splendor* because of His co-eternity [with the Father], just as splendor is ever contemporaneous with the sun. He is called *Image* because of His likeness to, and equality with, [the Father].

PART TWO
Likenesses That Befit the Incarnation of the Word

[8] Peter of Tarantasia,[34] at the beginning of his third [book], says that the example of ingrafting besuits the Incarnation—with the exception that (1) [the thing ingrafted and the thing to be ingrafted] are not of the same nature and species and (2) in place of a site [for the ingrafting], an ordering is understood (so that the human nature is understood to be ingrafted into the divine nature in an ordered relationship). And note here that there are many kinds of union with respect to a common nature: for example, (1) matter and form [are united], or (2) as elements [are united] in a composite, or (3) as an accident [is united] with a substance, etc. Note here that just as grafting is done so that a branch (by way of the root) will bear better fruit, etc., so Christ is the Tree of life in the midst of Paradise. And because human nature by eating the forbidden fruit produced only the fruit of death, human nature was, through grafting, transplanted into the Tree of life. Christ says that He is the Vine and that the Apostles are the branches, etc.[35] (Take note of this.) And [consider] that Christ Himself said that He planted the vineyard and expected it to produce grapes, but it produced wild grapes, etc.[36] And thereafter He transplanted that vineyard and ingrafted it into His divinity, etc.

[9] St. Thomas in his compendium that begins "*Aeterni Patris*," says that a likeness obtains between (1) the union of [Christ's] humanity with His divinity and (2) the union of an accident with its substance.

For the accident is united [to the substance] and exists in it and does not lose its own nature; and the case is similar with the subject's hypostasis, personhood, or suppositum,[37] even though the human nature is not an accident in union [with a person, or suppositum], etc. Moreover, the situation is the same as our saying "person" (or "hypostasis," or "suppositum") in the sense of a complement to being. For example, in the case of a stone, which is without a rational soul, we can speak of the suppositum of a stone. However, because of a supervening rational nature that completes him, a man is not, [as is a stone], called a suppositum on the basis of a composition of elements. Accordingly, in Christ there is a suppositum (or hypostasis, or person) only of the soul, the body, and the divine nature.[38]

The Jews, Arius, Manichaeus, Eutyches, and Nestorius have erred regarding the birth [of Christ]. The Jews deny that in Christ there is a divine nature. (John 10: Since you are a man, why do you make yourself out to be God?)[39] Arius affirmed that the Son is inferior to the Father. Manichaeus denied that Christ had real flesh; rather, he said [that Christ had only] apparent flesh. Eutyches asserted that the humanity was absorbed by the divinity. Nestorius maintained that there were two persons, just as there were two natures.

[11] Pope Clement, in his sermon *On Circumcision*, compares Christ with one who is attired, saying that the humanity is to be understood as a garment. [He said this] because a garment is conformed to the one who wears it and because the garment is supported by the one who wears it and because the one who wears it is manifested in and by the garment. Analogously, in Christ the humanity was excellently formed; it was supported in and by the Person [*suppositum*] of the Word, [and] through the humanity the deity was manifested.

[12] An example can be given (as concerns the aforementioned [ideas]) with respect to the attracting of what is attracted. For example, the attracting power of a magnet causes the iron's nature—at rest in and of itself—to exist in such a way that [the following holds true]: If the iron were to exist by itself, it would act conformably to its weight and would [tend] to move downwards. But now, since its own nature, which is being attracted, does not exist in itself but exists in the nature of the attracting magnet, the iron remains united to the magnet.

PART THREE
The Preconception of All the Things in the Word

[13] All existing things derive their *existence* from the Word: all

things were made by Him.[40] All living things derive their *life* from the Word. But in the Word being and living are not distinguished, because that which was made was, in Him, Life.[41] Whatever things have vital light, or living light, have it from the Word, because the Life was the light of men.[42] For when the Gospel says that the Word enlightens every man ..., etc.,[43] it speaks (as regards this world) of the region of human nature. In this region there is found participation in the living light that we call *intellect*. Therefore, *being, living,* and *understanding* are found [to be present] in this world. And, hence, since they exist not from themselves but from God, they are from God only insofar as they are from the Father—and Primal Fount—of being, living, and understanding. And because all existing things are thus from the Beginning, which is from no other, this Beginning is Eternity itself. Therefore, since the Beginning is Eternity, it is Absolute Necessity itself. Therefore, the things that are originated from the Beginning do not constrain it. Hence, they are originated because it pleases the Beginning. And so, all things exist because of the goodness of the Beginning, which diffuses itself without any change of itself or division of itself, etc.

[14] Consequently, God conceived of that which He created; and that of which He conceived He willed. He who wills, wills something. Therefore, the act of will proceeded from the one who wills and from what was willed. Hence, if God the Father willed, then He preconceived that which He willed. Therefore, God preconceived creatures, and the preconceived [creatures] were pleasing [to Him], and so they came into existence. Therefore, all that a creature has it has from the Paternal Beginning in accordance with the fact that it was preconceived by Him and was pleasing to Him. Accordingly, the Beginning preceded every creature and preconceived it, and the preconception was pleasing to Him.

[15] But since time is the measure of the motion of creatures, there is no time prior to creatures. Therefore, before all time there exists the Beginning of creatures and the Conception of creatures and the Love of what is conceived. Now, before all time there is only Eternity. But Eternity is singular [and] simple, because otherwise—[i.e.], if it had parts and were divisible—it would not be Eternity. For in that case—[i.e., if it had parts]—it would exist subsequent to the Beginning and would not be the Beginning but would be quantity and time. Accordingly, Beginning, Preconception, and Love are one Essence, which is called Eternity. The Beginning is Father; the

Preconception is Word, or Son,[44] who proceeds from the Father; the Love is the Holy Spirit, who proceeds from the Father and the Word. The foregoing comes from Genesis: "God saw that it was good. And He said, 'Let us make man in [our] image ….' "[45] Before [what-was-to-be-created] existed, God saw [it] in His eternal Preconception, and [what was preconceived] was pleasing. The expression of goodness is a manifestation of the will, because the good is desired because of itself.

NOTES TO *SERMON XIX*

1. John 1:14. Cf. Sermon XI.
2. St. Fulgentius (468-533, Bishop of Ruspe (located in what today is Tunesia), Sermon II ("De Duplici Nativitate Christi"), paragraph numbers 1 & 3. Nicholas excerpts and paraphrases. (*PL* 65:726-727).
3. John 1:1. Luke 19:10.
4. Psalms 95:2 (96:2).
5. John 1:5.
6. Here (at 3:3) I am regarding the word "qui" as deleted.
7. James 1:17.
8. John 1:9.
9. Luke 1:38.
10. Here (at 4:16) I am reading "factorum" in place of "sanctorum" (as do the editors of the Latin text).
11. Apocalypse (Revelation) 4:7.
12. Ezechiel (Ezekiel) 1:10.
13. Eriugena (not Origen, as Nicholas writes and as I have corrected, along with the editors of the Latin text). See the beginning of Eriugena's *Homilia in Prologum Sancti Evangelii Joannem* (*PL* 122:283BC).
14. In this sentence (at 5:5-10) I am reading "supervolitantis" in place of "supervolitans" and am reading "obtutibus transcendentis" in place of "obtutus transcendens." See the beginning of Eriugena's *Homilia in Prologum Evangeliae Johannis* (*PL* 122:283B).
15. Eriugena, *ibid.* (*PL* 122:283CD).
16. Pseudo-Dionysius, *Epistola* 10 (*Dionysiaca* II, 1572 and 1576).
17. Augustine, Homily 20 (not Homily 19, as Nicholas writes and as I have corrected, as do also the editors of the Latin text). See *In Joannis Evangelium*, Tractatus 20, paragraph number 13 (*PL* 35:1563).
18. Augustine, Homily 36 (not Homily 24, as Nicholas writes and as I have corrected, as do also the editors of the Latin text). See *In Joannis Evangelium*, Tractatus 36, paragraph number 1 (*PL* 35:1663).
19. *Ibid.* (*PL* 35:1662).
20. Jerome, *Epistola* 53 ("Ad Paulinum"), paragraph number 4 (*PL* 22:543).
21. Cf. Jerome, *Commentarii in Ezechielem Prophetam*, Book I, Chap. 1, verse 7 (*PL* 25:21-22).
22. Jerome, *Comentarii in Zachariam Prophetam*, Book III, Chap. 14, verse 20 (*PL* 25:1539C).
23. Ambrose, *De Sacramentis*, III, 2, paragraph number 11 (*PL* 16:454A). *De Incarnationis Dominicae Sacramento*, Chap. 3, paragraph numbers 15-17 (*PL* 16:857-858).
24. Gregory the Great, *Homiliae in Ezechielem Prophetam*, I, 4, paragraph number 1 (*PL* 76:815AB).
25. *Ibid.,* paragraph number 3 *(*PL 76:816D).
26. Venerable Bede, *In Sancti Joannis Evangelium*, Chap. 1 (*PL* 92:637B-638B).

27. John Chrysostom, *Homiliae in Joannem*, I, paragraph number 2 (*PG* 59:26).

28. Bernard of Clairvaux, *Sermones in Cantica Canticorum*, VIII, 7 (*PL* 183:813CD).

29. Pseudo-Haymo Halberstat, *Expositio in Apocalypsin Beati Joannis*, II, 4 (not Book III, as Nicholas writes and as I have corrected, as do also the editors of the Latin text). (*PL* 117:1010AB).

30. Peter Damian, *Sermones*, II, 64, 351 ("De Sancto Joanne") (*PL* 144:874D-875A).

31. Augustine, *De Civitate Dei*, X, 29 (not X, 7, as Nicholas writes and as I have corrected, as do the editors of the Latin text). (*PL* 41:307). *Confessiones*, VIII, 2, 3 (*PL* 32:750).

32. Richard of St. Victor, *De Trinitate*, I, 4 (*PL* 196:892).

33. Isaias (Isaiah) 7:9 (Old Latin Bible).

34. Peter of Tarantasia was born ca. 1225 in Tarentaise in south-eastern France. He became Pope Innocent V. And he died in Rome in 1276.

35. John 15:5.

36. Isaias (Isaiah) 5:2.

37. When applied to a human being, the Latin word "suppositum" is a theological translation of the Greek word ὑπόστασις, often translated as *person*. (See, above, Sermon XVII (**6**).) When applied to non-human beings (e.g., to a stone), the word "suppositum" is closer in meaning to the Aristotelian notion of οὐσία ("substantia"; "substance").

38. The rational soul and the body constitute, together, human nature. In Christ the human nature and the divine nature are said to be hypostatically united, i.e., united in the Person of God the Son. This Person is the suppositum.

39. John 10:33.

40. John 1:3.

41. John 1:3-4.

42. John 1:4.

43. John 1:9.

44. Cf. Cusa's *De Sapientia*, II (34-35).

45. Genesis 1:25-26.

Sermon XX: Nomen eius Jesus
("His name [was called] Jesus.")
[January 1, 1439 or 1440; feast-day of the circumcision
of Jesus; preached in Koblenz]]

[1] "His name [was called] Jesus." [1]

Let us, to begin with, pray that His name may be sanctified in us
in such a way that we may be able to expound the praises of His holy
name—[doing so] with the intercessory help of the Virgin Mary, His
mother, who is blessed among women [and] who has begotten for us
the Word, whose name is eternal.

[2] There are three things that today make the feast-day important: [today is] the eighth day after His birth ([consider] the Collect and
Leviticus 23);[2] [today is] the circumcision of the [Christ]-child (Luke
2; Genesis 17);[3] and [today is] the assigning of the name (according to
the Gospel). The word "name" ("*nomen*") has to do with the first [of
these topics]. The word "His" ("*eius*")—i.e., of Him who was circumcised—has to do with the second [of these topics]. The word "Jesus"
has to do with the third.

PART ONE
*The Names That Are Assigned to God
through Eminence and Removal* [4]

[3] As regards the first [topic], I will speak about a threefold name in
accordance with a threefold birth, etc. For in the introit of the first mass
there is said (in Hebrew): "Jehovah said …," etc. Secondly, in the second introit there is said: "Light will shine on us today[5] because unto us
the Lord was born; and He is called Wonderful, God, Prince of Peace,
etc. As regards the third [introit]: "A child is born …." [6]

[4] The [part of the] sermon that determines His name insofar as
it is wonderful but, nevertheless, ineffable for us and unknown to us
will be brief. The [part of the] sermon that attempts to express symbolically the infinite name of the Word and Son will be lengthy. The
[part of the] sermon that attempts to explicate the name "Savior,"
which is the name of an activity, is the lengthiest.

The first name-for-God, which is ineffable, is attained only nega-
tively. The second name (e.g., "Creator") is disclosed, variously and
extensively, only in and through creatures and through creatures' like-

329

nesses [to the Creator]. The third name is explicated very extensively by means of the grace of the Incarnation. Consequently, we say (together with Dionysius and with the Apostle Bartholomew, mentioned by Dionysius in *The Mystical Theology*) that the sermon on the name of God is very holy and very brief, the sermon on the Creator is extensive, [and] the sermon on the Re-creator is very extensive and very important.

[5] A name derives from observing, because words are signs of the things that are in the mind, etc. We understand nothing except what takes its origin from perceptible things.[7] Thus, God is not comprehensible. Therefore, according to Dionysius, we ascend unto God in a threefold way. [First, we ascend] by way of *perceptible things* qua things caused. According to Augustine, this fact [holds true] for several reasons: either (a) because nothing has brought itself into existence or (b) because from what is changeable we must come [inferentially] to what is unchangeable, from the imperfect we must come to the perfect, from what is good we must come to what is best, etc. Secondly, [we ascend] *by way of eminence*, so that we understand to be in the cause that which we find in the caused as perfecting the thing caused. Thirdly, [we ascend] *by way of removal*, so that we remove from the excellence of the cause the defect which we find in what is caused.

[6] With respect to the true name which should indicate to us what God is, Dionysius says that God is unnameable [and] ineffable because He is not comprehended. For we have the statement, only by Anselm, that God is Something better than can be thought. But this Something Better is unnameable if it is unthinkable. Therefore, "Best" is not a name for God; instead, "Super-best" is. Hence, in accordance with the fact that we know what God *is not* rather than knowing what He *is*, God is unnameable rather than nameable. Nor is the name "Unnameable" a proper name for God; [i.e., it is not a word that] signifies God together with signifying His proper quality. Rather, ["Unnameable"] signifies that which God is not. Etc.

However, among all names, the Tetragrammaton[8] is [God's] proper name. Etc. Likewise, [God's proper name is] a name that is above every [other] name.[9] Hence, just as God is not good but is supergood, so He is not nameable but is super-nameable. Thus, God's name comprehends all things nameable, even as God's being comprehends all being. Therefore, His name is eternal and infinite. Now, the name "Eternal" or "Infinite" is not His name [that is above all other names]. Rather, [the name above all other names] is "Ha-Shem," [meaning] "the Name," in an absolute sense.[10] We cannot [use] this [name that is above all other names] to name [Him] absolutely as He is. Rather, we name Him insofar as ["Name" has] a contracted [sense] and stands for some property (e.g., *eternal, infinite*) that especially befits Him. Hence, God's name is the name through which every [other] name is a name, and His name is the essence of all names, etc.

[7] Therefore, in the name "Jehovah" there is the secret of this ineffability, because, as say Jerome and Rabbi Moses [Maimonides],[11] [that name] was not able to be applied to anything else. That name signifies God in accordance with His omnipotence. Hence, the Ancients affirmed of this name—the Tetragrammaton (i.e., "[the name] of four letters")—all secrets; and the Jews have a book, the *Cabbala*, on the power of this name. But the Jews do not read aloud this name except on one [annual] occasion when fast-days precede it; and they reverently safeguard the books in which this name is written. And they do not esteem as holy a book in which this name is not found. And Jerome states that in the sacred writings of the Hebrews this name always retained its original [Hebrew] characters, etc.[12] Hence, this ineffable name [that is called the] Tetragrammaton is not a name [i.e., a noun], because it does not signify a substance together with [signifying] its proper or common property. Nor is it a verb signifying [something] together with signifying a time and a manner. Nor is it a pronoun or a participle or a part of a meaningful expression; rather, it is a [meaningful] whole at once. Etc.

PART TWO
The Names That Befit God as Cause in relation to the Caused. Fire as a Metaphorical Name for God

[8] "Light will shine upon us, because unto us the Lord was born, and He will be called [Wonderful ...,]" etc.[13] There are many names that befit God as Cause in relation to what is caused [by Him]. For "Creator," "Illuminator," "Savior," "Enlivener," etc. [are such names]. [There are] names which befit God by a [symbolizing] analogy,[14] because [what they name] is found in the case of undefective creatures—e.g., [the names] "Good," "Mighty," "Comprehending," etc. [And some names] somehow [befit God] with some kind of [metaphorical] resemblance—e.g., "Messenger of great counsel," "Lion," "Lamb," "Rock," "Consuming Fire."[15] [There are] names that befit God by way of removal—e.g., "Immortal," "Invisible," and other [names] in the chapter "*Firmiter credimus*."[16]

[9] All nouns signify either a perfection or an imperfection. If

[they signify] a perfection, then [they signify] either (1) a perfection that is not found in creatures (and these perfections—as, for example, *omnipotent, eternal*—befit God properly) or (2) a perfection that is found in creatures in an indeterminate way (and these perfections—as, for example, *comprehending*—befit God less properly) or (3) a perfection that is found in creatures in a determinate manner (and these perfections—e.g., *lion, lamb*—do not at all befit God properly but only metaphorically). Now, *in accordance with the first mode* we have the divine names "Jah," "Adonai," "El," "Elohim," "Vaheie," "Schaddai," "Sabaoth," and other names—from Solomon's *Books of Exorcisms*, from Greek words, and, likewise, from words from inhabitants of India (e.g., "esgi abhir"). *In accordance with the second mode* we have "theos" (from "theoro," "video," or "curro"). We have "deus," "got" (from "bono," "boeg," "tengri"); and in accordance with the different languages we have other names ("logos," "ratio," "verbum," etc.). And, furthermore, as Ambrose says,[17] God created a variety of things in order that by means of the diversity His power would be expressed. Languages, too, are diverse, in order that the one ineffable name might be expressed in different ways. *In accordance with the third mode* [God] is called Lion, Lamb, Light, Consuming Fire, Light in which there is no darkness.

[10] And for the purpose of our being instructed, let us consider the metaphor of fire, according to [the teaching of] Dionysius,[18] in his *Hierarchy*, 15.

Dionysius, in *The Angelic Hierarchy*,[19] Chapter 15, says that among all material things fire represents the image of God most closely.

(1) Fire is invisible in itself, for it is not seen except in something that is on fire. Likewise, God [is invisible ..., etc.].

(2) Fire is present in all things, although invisibly; nonetheless, it is disseminated throughout all material things. Similarly, God is present invisibly in all things.

(3) Fire moves through all things unmixedly, even as God is not mingled with other things. Moreover, in itself fire is unmixed, as is also God.

(4) Fire is set apart from all elements because of its nobility of nature, its sublimity of place, and the efficacy of its activity.

(5) In and of itself fire—and each of its parts—is through and through light. Similarly, God is Light; and in Him there is no darkness.[20]

(6) Although in and of Himself God is Light, nevertheless He is

unknown to the senses, even as fire in terms of its power in a flint-stone [is undetectible to the senses], etc.

(7) Even as fire is invisible, so it is ungraspable.

(8) Fire triumphs over all things. God is a Consuming Fire.[21]

(9) All things are receptive of fire, and in their own measure they too set on fire, once they themselves have been set afire.

(10) Fire conveys itself to all things heatable, illuminable, and ignitable. Likewise, God [communicates Himself] to material natures, to natures capable of perception, and to intellectual natures.

(11) Fire is renewing of all things. By means of enlivening-heat [22] [things] grow, flourish, etc. [The case is similar] with respect to their being nourished, increased, etc. [It is similar] with respect to circulation, with respect to a deer, etc.

(12) Fire diffuses its rays in circular fashion.

(13) Fire is unencompassable, for it is encompassed by the mind alone. There is no material that could encompass it, because everywhere that it is it is a whole, etc.

(14) Since in and of itself fire is unmingled, it divides and separates all things, even as God distinguishes between all things.

(15) Fire is upwardly directed and is always highest. It cannot be kept under foot, etc.

(16) Fire progresses keenly, i.e., swiftly, unless it is retarded, etc. God's word runs swiftly,[23] reaching from end [to end],[24] etc.

(17) Fire is [characterizable as] a movable sameness—as we see in the case of the heavens, where fire discloses God's inner activity, etc.

(18) Fire moves other things; fire's power is the cause of all movement. Similarly, God causes all things to be moved.

(19) Fire is an unencompassable encompassing, since it turns other things into itself but is itself turned into no other thing. And, by comparison, the personal oneness of the Word assumed a human nature into His own Person; and God beatifies souls.

(20) All movable things, insofar as they are moved need fire, whereas fire has need of no other. In this respect fire bears a resemblance to God, who has no need of our goods.[25]

(21) Fire augments itself (just as, in things numbered, number [increases] and, in things lit, light [increases]). Its power is not bounded. [Likewise,] God is unboundable.

(22) Fire is invisibly present to all things. Not only is it present in another thing as light is present in the eye of a blind man, but also it is present there as light is present in the eye of one who has sight; for

fire aids the eye in its act of seeing, etc. Likewise, God invisibly works all things in all things.[26]

(23) Fire gives itself to all things very generously but remains undiminished, even as knowledge, [in being spread, remains undiminished] ..., etc.

(24) When disregarded, fire seems not to be present; but with rubbing, it suddenly is manifest and again becomes unencompassable, etc. Fire is said to be disregarded when we do not take steps to bring it forth. It is manifest suddenly by the rubbing of iron with a stone. And if we take no pains to capture it in material tinder, it flies forth ungraspably. Similarly, the foolish say in their heart, "There is no God."[27] God draws near to the contrite-in-heart with His goodness. But if they neglect to receive Him with perseverance in the tinder of the virtues and of virtuous actions, etc., He flies forth.

And because reason grasps these [truths] about fire, we see how it is that reason is higher than fire and its essence [*ratio*].

PART THREE
The Names Signifying the Son (in the Assumed Humanity)
as Savior. The Son's Circumcision

[**11**] As regards the third [introit]: "A child is born to us, and a son is given to us. His government is upon his shoulder. And his name shall be called 'messenger of great counsel.' "[28] And for this name "[Messenger] of great counsel" the Gospel substitutes [the name] "Savior," or "Jesus," etc. In Apocalypse, Chapter 19, John says (concerning our topic) with respect to circumcision: "He was clothed with a garment sprinkled with blood, and His name shall be called 'the Word of God.' "[29] Isidore, in Book VII, Chapter 2 of his *Etymologies* says, a propos of the names that befit the Son in His [state of] assumed humanity:[30] He is called Christ—i.e., "one anointed with ointment" or "Messiah"—because above all His fellow-men [He was anointed] ..., etc.[31] He is called *Jesus, Soter, Salvator* (in Hebrew, Greek, and Latin). He is called Emmanuel (i.e., "God with us"); so Matthew says "Emmanuel ...," etc.[32] He is called Only-begotten,[33] First-born;[34] He is called Beginning, Middle, and End,[35] [and called] the Way, the Truth, and the Life.[36]

[**12**] But (if we return [now] to the text of the Gospel): He is called *Jesus*, or *Issus*, according to the Greeks, or *Hessus* according to the Arabs, *Jhesus*, or *Jhešua*, according to the Hebrews ..., etc. Because He saves His people, He is called Savior. Now in the Gospel

we are told that He was circumcised on the eighth day; and the name given to Him was "Jesus," i.e., "Savior." The eighth day is a new day and a day of renewal.[37] For after [our] circumcision with the sharp stone of firmness-of-faith in Christ (who was the true Rock), and after all worldly things have been cast aside [by us] on the eighth day of [our] resurrection from the defilement of the world—[cast aside] in order that we might investigate [Christ's] deity by way of negation (as Dionysius says):[38] then our Savior appeared, who, nonetheless, was not at rest throughout the seven days that measure all time and all circular revolution. For on the first day the name of 'Him who on account of His holy name is propitious toward our sins' pardoned our sins.[39] On the second day He protected from the Devil the one who knows Him. (He will protect him "because He knows my name.")[40] On the third day He delivered from evil. ("Help us, O God, our Savior, and deliver us for the sake of Your name's glory …," etc.)[41] On the fourth day He gives a good spirit.[42] ("The Holy Spirit, whom the Father will send in my name …").[43] On the fifth day He multiplies virtues through the Holy Spirit ("You will guide me for Your name's sake.")[44] On the sixth day He works signs ("In my name they will cast out demons.")[45] And after these seven days of this world's flux, Christ eternally saves—[saves] on the eighth day of resurrection. (Hence, whosoever shall call upon Your name shall be saved.)[46]

[13] It must be known that although this salvation chiefly concerns eternal salvation, nevertheless [Christ] also saves from infirmity (Mark 6: "Whoever touched Him was made whole"),[47] from tempest and storms (Matthew 8: "Save us; we perish"),[48] and from all corruption (Philippians 3: "We look for the Savior").[49] All the Prophets proclaim Him, and Paul says about this name of the Savior: in the name of Jesus every knee shall bow—of things on earth, things in heaven, and things beneath the earth.[50] For He is called Savior because of His power to save; and, likewise, [He is called Savior], *ab aeterno*, because He is God and because of His fixed disposition to save. Likewise, [His name] was imposed by the Angel[51] because of His act of saving. And, similarly, [it was imposed] today by Joseph at the circumcision. For the name was ordained [and] consecrated from eternity; it was uttered by the mouth of God. It was desired [and] prophesied by the Fathers. It was prefigured in Joshua, foretold by the Angel, made known by the Virgin Mary, imposed on the eighth day by Joseph, disclosed by the angels, preached by the Apostles, praised by those professing it, foretasted by the holy virgins as being oil poured forth,[52] venerated by

believers. The name "Christ" is the shared name; the name "Jesus" is the personal name. The name "Christ" has to do with grace; the name "Jesus" has to do with glory.

[14] The [name "Jesus"] is the name that is above every [other] Name.[53] There is no other [name] under Heaven ..., etc. [54] For it is honey in the mouth, a melody in the ear, a shout-of-joy in the heart, according to Bernard.[55] When preached, it lights-up, as does a lamp-of-oil; when reflected on, it nourishes; when invoked, it soothes and anoints. According to Peter of Ravenna, [this name] gave sight to the blind, gave hearing to the deaf, walking to the lame, life to the dead; it put the Devil to flight, etc.[56] Anselm: "Jesus" is "a sweet name, a delightful name, a name that consoles the sinner, and a name of blessed hope. Therefore, O Jesus, be Jesus to me."[57] [The name "Jesus"] has cleansing power with regard to a stain, sanctifying power with regard to guilt, justifying power with regard to wrong-doing—all of which things are forgiven through the name "Jesus." ("You are cleansed, you are sanctified, you are justified ...," etc.)[58] Jesus said: "Whatsoever you ask of the Father in my name, He will give to you."[59] Hence, all the prayers of the Church are ended by this name.

[15] Let us now—in accordance with the Biblical account and so that Christ's every action is our instruction—reflect on what was done [for us] on this day and on what is to be done by us. Christ, on account of His love [and] in order to redeem us, was circumcised on this day and was made a bloody spouse[60] of the Church [and] through His name was shown to us. Now, first of all, we ought to consider the wondrous humility of incarnation and of the observance-of-law in the case of Him who did no sin.[61] [And we ought to consider] the fact that for our sakes the Infant, the Law-giving God,[62] did not shun[63] this pain of circumcision, so that we might learn that we are to be subject to the Law through obedience and so that we not allow ourselves something on the basis of a presumption of innocence, etc.

[16] On this day [Christ] began to shed His blood for us; and so, it is the first day of the year for us Christians. Secondly, [He shed His blood] during prayer;[64] thirdly, when whipped; fourthly, when crowned [with thorns]; fifthly, at the crucifixion; sixthly, at the piercing of His side. On the seventh day He rested; on the eighth day He rose up.[65] Hence, just as on the eighth day after His birth He received a name accompanied by the shedding of blood, so after seven days of painful passage, for our sakes, He obtained on the eighth day another name—[a name] of triumph—accompanied by glorification, etc.

Hence, the custom [of re-naming] took its beginning from the changing of the name from "Abram" into "Abraham" [and] from "Sarai" into
"Sarah."[66] Christ was circumcised because, first of all, He was of the
lineage of Abraham, to whom the promise was made.[67] Secondly, [it
was done] so that He would be like His ancestors. Thirdly, [it was
done] in order that He would approve of the Law as having been good;
fourthly, in order to commend the virtues of obedience and of humility; fifthly, in order to be subject [to the Law] that He had given.
Sixthly, He became subject to the Law in order to redeem those who
were under the Law;[68] seventhly, in order for our sakes to be subject
to the Law from the time of His infancy; eighthly, in order to manifest
the reality of His flesh; ninthly, in order to praise chastity and to put an
end to lust. Tenthly, Christ is the end of the Law unto justice to all who
believe …, etc.[69]

[17] Let him who has recently given birth to Christ within himself strive today to circumcise his own soul (which he has wanted to
lead unto Christ and to transform into Christ)[70] in order that (1) he not
be reproachable in outward demeanor, in action, or in word ([see] St.
Bernard)[71] and in order that (2) his thoughts may be holy, his affections pure, and his intentions upright. We ought to be, in heart,[72] circumcised of all harmful and unclean thoughts, of false and injudicious
judgments, of evil intentions, so that in the presence of God we may
fear to think in our hearts that which we would be ashamed to say
before men. [We ought to be], in tongue, circumcised of words that are
shameful, slanderous, lying, idle, and superfluous. [We ought to be], in
all our senses, [circumcised] of things forbidden, illicit, sensual, and
unnecessary. Moreover, [we ought to be circumcised] of every occasion [on which] …, etc. There is little value in being circumcised in the
one part and not in the other. Pope Pius says: "Fasting is of no benefit
unless mind and tongue refrain from things that are forbidden."[73]
Bede [says] the same thing:[74] "Therefore, he is circumcised with true
circumcision (1) who plugs up his ears so that he does not hear of
[brutal] bloodshed[75] and (2) who closes his eyes so that he does not
see what is evil[76] [and] (3) who guards his pathways so that he does
not transgress with his tongue[77] and (4) who keeps an eye on himself
so that his heart is not heavy with drunkenness and winebibbery[78] and
(5) who washes his hands among the innocent[79] and (6) who keeps his
pathways free of every evil way[80] [and] (7) who chastises, above all
else, his own body and subjects it to servitude[81] and (8) who safe-
guards his own heart with all care, since from his heart proceeds his

life.[82] Moreover, his actions that are hidden are not less in need of chastising, in order that when, together with my fasting, I give alms, I do not seek glory. The Apostle earnestly commends circumcision in heart."[83] (Bede [says] these things.)

[**18**] The highest [purpose] of [spiritual] circumcision is to cut away sins (which in man are not at all necessary) by means of penance. And unless [circumcision] occurs in the soul, the soul is a daughter of perdition. For "the male whose flesh will not have been circumcised of its foreskin will perish."[84] However, eight [things] ought to precede this circumcising: (1) the conversion of the sinner to God, (2) - (8) recognition of sin, contrition for sin, confession of sin, loathing of sin, making of satisfaction [for sin], precaution [against sin]; then comes the justification of him who is wicked.

There are three circumcisings. The one that occurs in the body is a sacrament. The two [others] are offshoots of the sacrament: viz., the circumcising away of sin (which occurs daily in the soul) and the circumcising away of the penalty of sin (which will occur at the resurrection).

ADDENDUM

[**19**] [Thoughts] regarding the new year.

Here [I will speak both of] how the [divisions of] the year were introduced and of the fact that [the name] "January" derives from "Janus," according to Rabanus in his [work] *On Computation*.[85] Janus, at his own home, received Saturn when the latter first came to Italy. And because Janus obtained from Saturn the art of planting, he divided his kingdom with him. This present month, according to Numa Pompilius, was dedicated to Janus.[86] And in the opinion of [some] men Janus was conducted up to the stars, and he is depicted with two heads. And because of this [event] witches were accustomed to scurry about on this day. And because such [men] who depict Janus are of the number of pagans rather than of the number of Christians, the saints forbade the new year to start [with him], as [relate] Maximus in a sermon[87] and Augustine in his sermon on the *Calends of January*.[88]

Because we Germans were pagans, we designate the [new] year from the first day [of the month of January], and we say "iar" [i.e., "Jahr"] from Janus—even as we take the name "sontach" from the sun; "maendach," from the moon; "dingestag" or "eretag" from Mars; "gwudenstag," from Mercury; "tonerstag" from thundering Jove;

"fritag" from Venus; "samstag" from Saturn. The beginning of the year is not today but is on the day of the Annunciation. But according to one measure, today could be called the beginning [of the new year] because today Jesus first began to shed His blood for us. There are different beginnings of the year according to different nations, even as there are [differences] of months and of weeks. God ordained it in this way, so that all things would remain doubtful for us in order that we would avoid presentiments and superstitions, etc. Hence, for the new year I give to you today the circumcised Jesus, the Spouse of the Church. From Him you can have whatever you wish, provided you will be circumcised of your sins, etc.

[20] [Here is] the order of things to be spoken of:

"His name [was called] Jesus." This feast-day is important for three important reasons. Moreover, each of the three is commemorated by us today: [viz.,] (1) the giving of His name, (2) His circumcision, and (3) the beginning of the year.

Concerning the giving of His name three things must be considered relative to the eighth day, for in the three introits of the masses for the Day of the Nativity we find three names. Therefore, we have three names. To begin with, then, what is His name, and how can we understand the difference of names in conformity with the difference of understandings? *First*, [I will speak] about the ineffable name, [which], according to Dionysius, is "Jehovah," "Tetragrammaton" [i.e., "YHWH"], "Hašēm" [or: "Ha-Shem"]. *Secondly*, [I will speak] about the names of the Creator and, to start with, about the names that include negation. ([See] Athanathos, etc.—for example, in the Chapter *"Firmiter credimus."*[89]) [Then I will speak] about the names that include the perfection of a threefold order; and there [I will mention] the name "Infinite Activity," etc. Next, [I will mention] the names in the *Books of Solomon*,[90] etc. [I will speak] about the second names and about the third ones and, at that place, about fire. *Thirdly*, [I will mention] the names of the Re-creator, because "a Child is born ...," "He was clothed ...," etc. I add and set forth the fact that the eighth name is "Jesus."

First, [I will take up the topic of His names]: "Releaser," "Propitiator," "Protector," "Giver," "Spirit," "Nourisher," "Healer" (in a threefold sense), "Savior" (in a threefold sense). And in the conclusion [of this section I will say something] about the sweetness of the name "Jesus" according to Bernard and Anselm [and] Peter of

Ravenna—[a name] revered by them all. Secondly, [I will preach] about circumcision, about the reason [for it], about the six sheddings of blood, about our [spiritual] circumcision, etc. [Finally, I will say something] about the [new] year ..., etc.

NOTES TO *SERMON XX*

1. Luke 2:21.
2. Cf. Leviticus 23:21.
3. Luke 2:21. Genesis 17:12.
4. I have moved this editors' heading here, instead of leaving it placed immediately before margin number 6, as in the edition of the Latin text.
5. Cf. Isaias (Isaiah) 9:2.
6. Isaias (Isaiah) 9:6.
7. Here Nicholas shows the influence of Aquinas.
8. See *De Docta Ignorantia* I, 24 (75). The Tetragrammaton is the name for God that consists of four Hebrew letters—Jod, He, Vau, He (or: Yud, Heh, Vav, Heh)—transliterated either as "YHWH" or as "JHVH" and becoming, in English, "Yahweh" and "Jehovah".
9. Philippians 2:9.
10. See, below, the section marked by margin number 20. The word "ha-Shem" (meaning "the name") came to be used by the Jews as a name for God.
11. Cf. Jerome's *Commentarii in Ezechielem Prophetam*, II, 6 (*PL* 25:57D - 58A). Moses Maimonides, *Guide of the Perplexed*, I, 61.
12. Cf. Jerome's *Praefatio in Libros Samuel et Malachim* (*PL* 28:594B - 595A). (Of interest here, as a reference, is but a single sentence.)
13. Isaias (Isaiah) 9:2.
14. Nicholas already stated that there is no comparative relation between the finite and the infinite. (See Sermons III (**11**:9-10); IV (**34**:39-40); VII (**32**:11); VIII (**26**:38-39)). He is not here changing his mind but is pointing out that some symbolisms are more appropriate than are others when it comes to speaking about, and representing, God figuratively.
15. Hebrews 12:29. Deuteronomy 4:24.
16. *Decretales* (of Pope Gregory IX), I, 1, 1. (See Aemilius Friedberg, editor, *Corpus Iuris Canonici* (Leipzig, 1880 (second edition, Vol. II)), column 5.
17. Ambrose, I have not found a plausible referent-passage in Ambrose's works.
18. Pseudo-Dionysius, *De Caelesti Hierarchia*, 15 (*Dionysiaca* II, 994-1000). Not Chapter 16, as Nicholas writes and as I have corrected, as do also the editors of the Latin text.
19. See n. 18 above.
20. I John 1:5.
21. See n. 15 above.
22. Here (at 10:33) I am reading "vivifica" in place of "unifica".
23. Psalms 147:15.
24. Wisdom 8:1.
25. Psalms 15:2 (16:2). (The meaning in the King James version differs significantly from the meaning in the Douay-Rheims version).
26. I Corinthians 12:6.
27. Psalms 13:1 (14:1).
28. Isaias (Isaiah) 9:6.
29. Apocalypse (Revelation) 19:13.

341

30. Isidore, *Etymologiae*, VII, 2, 1-2 & 6 (*PL* 83:264).
31. Hebrews 1:9.
32. Matthew 1:23.
33. John 1:18.
34. Romans 8:29.
35. Cf. Apocalypse (Revelation) 1:8.
36. John 14:6.
37. The "eighth" day is the first day of the week, following the lapse of the week's seven days. The first day, Sunday, commemorates Christ's resurrection.
38. Pseudo-Dionysius, *De Divinis Nominibus*, 13 (*Dionysiaca* I, 551-555).
39. Psalms 78:9 (79:9).
40. Psalms 90:14 (91:14).
41. Psalms 78:9 (79:9).
42. Luke 11:13.
43. John 14:26.
44. Psalms 30:4 (31:3).
45. Mark 16:17.
46. Acts 2:21.
47. Mark 6:56.
48. Matthew 8:25.
49. Philippians 3:20 (not Philippians 4, as Nicholas writes and as I have corrected, as do the editors of the Latin text).
50. Philippians 2:10.
51. Luke 1: 26-31.
52. Canticle of Canticles (Song of Solomon) 1:2.
53. Philippians 2:9.
54. Acts 4:12: "For there is no other name under heaven given to men, whereby we must be saved."
55. Bernard of Clairvaux, *Sermons in Cantica Canticorum*. *Sermo* 15, 6 (*PL* 183:847).
56. Petrus Chrysologus, *Sermo* 144 (*PL* 52:586BC).
57. Anselm of Canterbury, *Meditatio* I (*Opera Omnia*, edited by F. S. Schmitt, Vol. III, p. 79). All volumes reprinted by Frommann Verlag, Stuttgart-Bad Cannstatt, 1968.
58. I Corinthians 6:11.
59. John 16:23.
60. Cf. Exodus 4:26.
61. I Peter 2:22.
62. Cf. Isaias (Isaiah) 33:22.
63. Here (at 15:10-11) I am reading, with ms. *C*, "refugit" and not "relegit".
64. Luke 22:44.
65. See n. 37 above.
66. Genesis 17:5 and 15. Here (at 16:12-13) I am reading "ex" in place of "et$_1$," and am reading "in" in place of "et$_2$".
67. Genesis 17.
68. Galatians 4:4-5.
69. Romans 10:4.

70. The theme of deification is a common theme among the Medievals. See, for example, my *Hugh of Balma on Mystical Theology: A Translation and an Overview of His De Theologia Mystica* (Minneapolis: Banning, 2002).

71. Bernard of Clairvaux, *In Circumcisione Domini. Sermo* 1, 3 (*PL* 183:134A).

72. Romans 2:29.

73. Pseudo-Pius I (Pope), *Epistola* 1, 2 (*PG* 5:1122). Not an exact quotation.

74. Venerable Bede, *In Lucae Evangelium Expositio*, I, 2 (*PL* 92:340AD).

75. Isaias (Isaiah) 33:15.

76. *Loc cit.*

77. Psalms 38:2 (39:1).

78. Luke 21:34.

79. Psalms 25:6 (26:6).

80. Psalms 118:101 (119:101).

81. I Corinthians 9:27.

82. Proverbs 4:23.

83. Romans 2:29.

84. Genesis 17:14.

85. Rabanus Maurus, *De Computo*, 32 (*PL* 107:684-685).

86. Numa Pompilius is referred to by Rabanus Maurus. Nicholas takes his allusion from Rabanus. See n. 85 above.

87. Maximus Taurinensis, *Sermones de Tempore: Sermo* VI ("De Calendis Januariis"). (*PL* 57:543-544).

88. Augustine, *Sermo* 198 ("De Calendis Januariis"). (*PL* 38:1024-1026).

89. See n. 16 above.

90. See, above, the allusion—in the section marked by margin number 9—to Solomon's *Books of Exorcisms*. See also what is said in Nicholas's Sermon I (at **4**:17-19). These *Books* or this *Book* (says Nicholas there) is also called *Sepher Raziel* (or: *Cephar Raziel; Sepher Rezial; Sefer Raziel*). It is sometimes known simply as the *Liber* (or *Libri*) *Salomonis* The word "sepher" means, in Hebrew, *book*; and Raziel was said to be an angel. The book in question was said to have been given by the angel Raziel to Adam and to have been passed down to King Solomon. It contains secrets, mysteries, instruction in magic, cosmological considerations. It belongs to the Jewish mystical tradition.

Sermon XXI: Intrantes Domum
("[The Magi], entering into the house, ...")[1]
[January 6, 1439 or 1440; feast-day of the Lord's epiphany;
preached in Koblenz]

[1] "Entering into the house, [the Magi] found the child with Mary His mother. And falling down, they adored Him" (Matthew 2).[2]

First of all, [I will speak of] the fact that according to the Biblical account the Magi entered into the house, etc.—[entered] as also elsewhere—with their appurtenances. Now, "house" stands for "Church Militant" (I Timothy: "... [in order that] you may know how you ought to behave in the house of the Lord ...."[3] And Proverbs 9: "Wisdom has built for itself a house ...."[4]). Moreover, ["house" stands] for "Church Triumphant" (John 14: "In my Father's house are many mansions."[5] And in the Psalm: "Blessed are they who dwell in Your house, O Lord."[6] And elsewhere: "I have loved the beauty of Your house."[7]). Furthermore, "house" stands for "church made with hands" ("My house shall be called a house of prayer."[8] And Isaias 2: "Come, let us go up to the mountain of the Lord and to the house of the God of Jacob."[9]). And so, [because "house" stands for "Church"], something must be said—*in the second place*—about the Church in accordance with this [meaning]. For today is the Church's feast-day ..., etc.

Moreover, "house" is also [indicative of] a faithful soul. (In the Psalm: "Holiness befits Your house."[10] And Hebrews 3: "The Son is within His own house; we are this house."[11]) Therefore, *in the third place*, something must be said very briefly (1) about this house and (2) about how it is that we ought to enter into our own house in order to find the child with Mary His mother and (3) about the fact that, falling down, we ought to adore [Him].

PART TWO
The Church as the Union of Rational Spirits with Christ, their Head;
and the Way in Which One Enters into the Church

(a) *In the Church Militant, whose goal is the Church Triumphant,*
one is to make his pilgrimage in a oneness of obedience.

[2] Those who enter into the Church find the child, etc. The Church is

344

entered by faith. For the Church is the congregation of believers. It is true that the Church Militant is the congregation-of-believers in which, through faith, there is a union of Christians with their Head.[12] For *there* [i.e., in that Church] truth is apprehended only in a mirror and in a dark manner.[13] But in the [Church] Triumphant, where Christ is seen face to Face,[14] etc., faith ceases.[15] Therefore, the Church [Triumphant] is the union of rational spirits with their Head, Christ.

[3] And so, we must take note of the fact that every creature is required purely and simply to believe and to obey our God (as being Infallible Wisdom), without any presumptiveness on its part. And through obedience every creature clings harmoniously to its Teacher and obtains its goal. For God created all things for His own sake.[16] And Eternal Wisdom Himself made of rational creatures a house for Himself—[a house] in which He delights to dwell centrally. Therefore, rational creatures can, through clinging to Creative Wisdom, taste of the Refection—of the Bread and the Wine—of that Super-celestial Wisdom.[17] Now, this tasting occurs through the unity of obedience and love, by means of which unity rational spirits are one with Christ; and through Christ they are one with God the Father, even as the Son is one with the Father. And when this union is everlasting and unfailing in Heaven, it is called the Church Triumphant. When the union is still on earth and on its pilgrimage, when it is beset by many storms and by the dangers of separation, it is called the Church Militant. If it is present in an intermediate state, it is called the Church Dormant. Hence, Ambrose in his seventeenth Letter, to Irenaeus, shows elegantly how great is the bond that all spirits have with Christ in Heaven.[18]

[4] But the Church Triumphant, which has already passed beyond the boundaries of this present pilgrimage, is first united with the Eternal Word in the company of the obedient angels after the presumptuous, apostate, and disobedient [angels], who willed to be like the Most High, have been separated off. There is a wondrous order among the obedient angels—[an order] that resembles the order in the Trinity. Thus, there are three orders [of angels] after the fashion of the Trinity; and in each order there are three choirs; and the highest [choir] *enlightens* after the fashion of the Father, etc. Hence, this Godlike, [highest] congregation [of angels] is very intrinsically united to God in accordance with its gradations. And just as other rational spirits—[viz.,] human spirits—have joined these blessed [angelic] spirits in place of the evil angels who were cast out [of Heaven],[19] so too the Church of the wicked exists in an opposite way [from the

Church Triumphant]. [It exists] without order, with a disorderedness of demons, who have Lucifer as their head. Moreover, presumptuous and unbelieving and rebellious human beings have descended unto these demons [and] will remain [with them] forever.

But in between [the Church Triumphant and the Church of the wicked] there are two others: viz., the Church Militant and the Church Dormant, which have not yet arrived at their goal. The Church Dormant is exalted above the Church Militant because of the certainty of its reward. Nonetheless, the Church Dormant, being a Church [still] on this pilgrim's way, is still united with the Church Militant, with the result that it is aided by the Church Militant's intercessory works. However, the Church Dormant is closer to the Church Triumphant [than is the Church Militant] because of the certainty of its victory over eternal death. Now, the Church Militant is gathered from men some of whom, by means of death, come immediately unto the Church Triumphant, others of whom come to the Church of the wicked (who are lost), and still others of whom come to the Church of the dormant (who are going to be purified).

[5] To this Church Militant, which is called the Immaculate Bride, there is promised passage to the Eternal Kingdom, passage to union with the triumphant—if through obedience [this Church] perfects its pilgrim pathway (as Paul attests to the Ephesians).[20] And this Church is our mother, whom, from the beginning, the Word of God and Wisdom of the Father espoused to Himself. In Paradise this [espousal] was symbolized when, through Eve's having been created from Adam's side, marriage was instituted, accompanied by the command to obey.[21] For (as says Jerome)[22] just as Eve [was taken] from the rib of Adam, so the Church (symbolized by Eve) [was derived] from Christ; [and] Christ espoused the Church unto Himself, as [Eve was espoused] to Adam. Etc. But since through presumption man, too, elevated himself contrary to obedience, the Second Adam,[23] viz., Christ, came and by His own blood, etc., washed away the stain contracted by disobedience—[washed it away] in order that man would merit to cross over to Heavenly associations [and] to the Church Triumphant, the Immaculate Bride.[24]

(b) *That the Church Militant is ordered hierarchically, after the fashion of the Church Triumphant.*

[6] Now, Dionysius in his *Ecclesiastical Hierarchy* discusses how it is that this Church Militant is wondrously ordered after the fashion of the

angelic [hierarchy].[25] For the ordering is found to be hierarchical in such a way [as in the body] .... ([See] Leo IX's [letter] against the presumptions of Michael, etc.[26] [And] consult your book *On Ecclesiastical Concordance*.[27]) [Note with Dionysius] that just as with respect to the human body, so also with respect to the [Church Militant], [there is the triad] spirit, soul, and body. [And] just as with respect to the Heavenly [Hierarchy there is the triad] God, angels, and men, [so with respect to the Church Militant] there is [the triad] (1) enlightening and purifying *sacraments*, (2) pastoral *priesthood* that is purified and purifying, (3) faithful *people* who are purified. Likewise, [note] that there is a wondrous hierarchy with respect to the sacraments all the way up to the sacrament of sacraments. For just as in Heaven God communicates Himself Face to face, so here below [He communicates Himself] under the forms [of bread and wine]. And at this point [note] that just as the sacraments symbolize the Church Triumphant, so too each of them bears the image of the Trinity, because (1) there is only the sacrament, (2) there is only the reality, and (3) there is the [unity of] the reality and the sacrament.

[7] The ordering of the priesthood—i.e., its ordering to higher divine things—is symbolized by the sacrament. And in this priesthood there is a hierarchy that is structured in an orderly way from the highest episcopate down to the layman. For some [priests] are of a higher order, some of a lower order, some of an intermediate order; and in each order there are three choirs, even as in the case of angels. And the sacraments are as spirit; the priesthood, as soul; the people, as the body. Gregory Nazianzenus, in his *Apologetics*, in the beginning-section, [writes]: in the body of the Church the priesthood has the role that the soul has in the human body.[28] And so, it befits priests to enlighten, enliven, govern. [It is befitting that they] enlighten, as befits reason, etc.; for [they are] the light of the world and the salt of the earth.[29] (Cyprian [said this latter in his work] *On the Gambler*.)[30] Moreover, in the first choir, of pontifs, there is a hierarchical order; for within the one episcopacy diffused throughout the world there is—because of the oneness—a difference that accompanies the concordance of the many in the one (as Cyprian [writes] to Novatianus[31] [and as] Jerome [writes] against Jovinianus[32]). And note that, necessarily, we come to a first and greatest pontif, who has on earth the power of being supreme hierarch—as the supreme minister, viz., the highest angel, [is the supreme hierarch] in Heaven. But the entire priesthood serves as a legation for Christ.[33] For Christ said: "Just as the Living Father has

sent me, so send I you"³⁴—even as angels are messengers of God, etc.

[8] And, hence, the priesthood is considered in a twofold way: either with respect to the ordering that it has to the governance of the Church (insofar as the governance is a necessary governance) or with respect to union (because the soul³⁵ rules over and unifies the body). As concerns the first way, there are hierarchical orderings all the way up to the pontificate; as concerns the second way, [these orderings] are for the purpose of unity, so that there may be oneness. In the Church there is a regulated administrative power, which is the power of jurisdiction. And this priestly power has a single see, just as it has a single episcopacy, etc. And in that see resides a hierarchical ordering as regards those who preside in and from it. (And here let us note the saying of Optatus Milevitanus³⁶ about the angel who is in charge of the see, etc.) Moreover, the see of Peter holds the promise of truth, as say St. Augustine, Alipius, and Fortunatus (writing to Generosus), etc.³⁷

[9] And at this point we must take note of the fact (1) that there is no power of binding and of loosening³⁸ except for one who is attached to the Apostolic See [and] (2) that one must not be reckoned as being in the Church if he does not accept the authority of the Apostolic See. Likewise, [we must note] (1) that all bishops are like the soul of the people because of the people's common consent; (2) that the parishioners are [representatively] in the priest; and (3) the priests are in the bishop; and (4) the bishops, in the pope; and (5) through the pope, the bishops are in Peter; and (6) through Peter (who is the rock, and the foundation, of the Church),³⁹ they are in Christ, who is the [true] Rock,⁴⁰ etc. Moreover, [let us note] that, subsequently, there is a hierarchy among believers—from the supreme emperor down to the farmers, and from the threefold order of kings [down to] ..., etc., and from the threefold governance (which is monarchical, aristocratic, and political (and also economic) [down to] ..., and from the [three] opposing [forms of government] ..., etc. Likewise, [let us note] the hierarchy within each person—[that of] spirit, soul, and body. Etc. [All of] the foregoing constitutes a diverse disposing within a wondrous unity. [See] Decretal 89 ("Ad hoc ...")⁴¹

(c) *We must enter the Church by faith.*

[10] And [let us note] that from righteous Abel down to the last [man] there is a single Church and that on this [commemorative] day the Church was cleansed in the Jordan and that on this day the nations entered into the Church. [We must also note] (1) that the

Church is Noah's ship, or ark, outside of which there was no salvation, and (2) that [this ship] undergoes tossings-about but undergoes no sinkings, because the faith of Peter will not perish. And this [Church, or ship] is the house of the Lord that has been built steadfastly, that is well established on a Firm Rock, and entrance into which is required for salvation. [11] But one enters into it by faith. For it is necessary that each one [who enters] be cleansed through the sacrament of baptism or through the reality of the sacrament, when necessity removes [the availability of] the sacrament. And so, let [each one] through faith cling to Christ, who was baptized on this day.[42]

It is necessary that one be marked with the sign of that Supreme Captain, in order to be in His army. His army is the Church. One must be faithful and triumphant and not a traitor—in order, in triumphing, to have a seat with the Captain, our God and our Lamb. And in this regard one must be obedient, etc. Furthermore, [we must note] that the betrothal is that of the Head [viz., Christ] to the soul of each [of us]. [The situation is] as if the king of the Germans were to betroth the queen of France on the condition that she would subjugate the entire kingdom of France to herself and then would choose to bring him over and to have him united to her. And, in like manner, the soul is obliged [to undertake] that which is difficult but not impossible. And if the soul does so through subjecting its body to itself and by submitting itself to its own spirit, then it finds the child with Mary, etc.[43]

[12] (Keep in mind to mention,[44] among other things, (1) that God has imparted governing power to rational spirits and (2) that the actions of the righteous, as also those of the wicked, have from the Holy Spirit their efficacy, as concerns the recipient [of the actions]. [Then too, mention something] about the Church's laws and regulations, etc.)

PART THREE
On Entering into Oneself; and on Faith,
Which Is To Be Maintained in Humility

[13] Thirdly, we must examine how it is that someone ought to enter into himself in order to find the child, who is with Mary. Etc. Straightway it must be said that the believing soul is betrothed by the Head of the Church, [viz., Christ], on condition that it remain faithful and subject its body to itself and reduce its body to submission. Otherwise, it cannot enter into the tabernacle of the Lord and cannot worship ..., etc. By the word "faithfulness" [on the part of the soul] we

ought to understand that the soul not be adulterous and not seek out lovers other than its Bridegroom. Now, the soul seeks out other lovers when it directs itself, by choice, to creatures; and the more it clings to creatures, the less it clings to God. But this attachment to creatures can be of two kinds: On the one hand, [the attachment occurs] because [the soul] seeks something divine in the creation, and it embraces as divine *that something* in the creation; and [this embracing] is idolatry. On the other hand, [the soul] seeks in the creation some remedy as coming from the creation. In this latter case either (1) there is an intermediate cause that effects this [result] (as happens with regard to things medicinal and with regard to astrological influences that are certain), and so the soul does not hereby stray away from God, or (2) there is no intermediate cause (as happens with regard to physical amulets), and, in this event, the Christian ought to refrain from these [practices], because there is no intermediate cause and the Devil often insinuates himself into them. Hence, Deuteronomy 13 [speaks] about this matter.[45]

[14] Sometimes someone, out of pure wickedness, does not maintain his faith in God. For example, [such is the case with regard to] a blasphemer, who ascribes to God that which does not besuit God or who denies to besuit God that which does besuit Him or who usurps that which is God's [prerogative]. And sometimes [wickedness] imposes itself on the heart because of the Devil's instigation or, frequently, out of fear of God's displeasure—even as in a dark place fear brings up in the heart frightful things. Sometimes the Devil speaks forth blasphemy through a man, but that blasphemy does not contaminate [the man]. Hence, such thoughts ought to be despised, and such works ought to be case aside. Etc.

Blasphemy of mouth [occurs] when someone who wants to strike back at God utters an abusive word against God and names bodily parts that ought not to be named. And [blasphemy] is a very great sin because of the very evil intent [that is present] when one pierces God with his tongue, etc. Neither Jews nor heretics have such an intent, inasmuch as they believe that they act correctly [in asserting what they do], etc. [Blasphemy] is a very great [sin] because man is little inclined to this sin [and because] it is against Him who is Best, Most Noble, etc. And so, Thomas[46] maintains ... that it is a sin greater than murder since it is contrary to a precept of the First Tablet [of the Mosaic Law].[47] Because there is the penalty of death for cursing one's father and mother (Matthew 15),[48] a blasphemer is worthy of physical and spiritual death.[49] [In blasphemy] God is despised. [See] Vergentis' *On*

Heretics:[50] there is the death-penalty for cursing the king ....[51] Similarly, there is this same punishment for cursing the saints ...,[52] because of their union with God.

[Blasphemy] is a very great ingratitude. It distinguishes the sons of the Devil from the sons of God. It is the language of Hell. Those who hear it should plug up their ears, etc. And the [blasphemer] is thereby known to be a very evil man, whom all creatures curse. He is punished physically, spiritually, and eternally for his blasphemy (*On the Foul-Mouthed,* Chapter 2).[53] [Here are] examples of the punishment: (1) in the case of the child of whom St. Gregory [speaks];[54] (2) the case of the soldier, etc.;[55] (3) the one who blasphemed against the eye of Blessed Mary, etc.;[56] (see elsewhere); (4) the case of the arrow, etc.;[57] (5) in regard to the district in Milan, etc.; (6) as concerns the man hung at Rome; (7) as concerns the denarius-coin of Count Hugo, etc.[58] Accordingly, even though such [blasphemers] may seem to be in the Church, nonetheless because they are unbelievers they are not members of Christ but of the Devil. And so, although all individuals who are in mortal sin do not maintain faith in God, nevertheless these [blasphemers] are especially unbelieving in God and offend against Him more [than do others].

[15] Therefore, one who desires to be in the Church must enter into himself and keep to the faith amid humility. Secondly, he must subject his body to his soul, so that the senses may be subordinate to reason. And he does this [subjecting] if he enters into himself by way of self-knowledge. For when transgressors withdraw [from their transgressions], then they return to the heart.[59] And so, there is no better or healthier art than [the art of] knowing oneself. For when a man sets himself before himself and looks at his own baseness, he recognizes[60] his miseries and the torments of his sin, and, consequently, he grieves. He observes the emptiness of present things, with the result that he despises them. He recognizes the benefits of God, with the result that he is grateful. He recognizes God's mercy, so that he has hope; he recognizes God's justice, so that he fears; he recognizes the uncertainty of his end, so that he worries and shows himself to be always prepared. And, hence, he who at first was alienated from God and from himself and said, "My heart has forsaken me,"[61] now [says], having returned by way of entering into himself: "Your servant has found his heart."[62]

[16] Now, we find that we are despoiled of our acquired possessions, are wounded in regard to our natural possessions, are blinded by reason, are bent downwards by our will, are besmirched by our mem-

ory. And when we are more deeply aware of these [conditions], we shall say: "I have sinned above the number of the sands [of the seashore] ...," etc. And then there will occur that of which Wisdom 8 [speaks]:[63] "Entering into my house, I will repose with that Wisdom," viz., with our Jesus. (For He is Light itself. He dwells in us by means of our faith.) And thereupon we shall hear what he speaks within us, etc. Isaias 30: "In silence and in hope shall be [your] courage."[64] For then, [i.e., in silence], there is no multitude of words, etc. One's becoming humble follows, etc. And after a man has thus entered into himself, he finds the child, together with Mary, in the temple (i.e., in the Church), in the desert (i.e., in the place of penance), in the house of a rightly ordered conscience, in the manger (i.e., in humility).

[17] He who enters within himself truly finds God, as is said [in] *The Spirit and the Soul*, Chapter 14.[65] He draws near to life when through love he is fastened to Him who has been thus found within himself. Hence, he must pass beyond everything perceptible, everything imaginable, everything intelligible, and must return centrally to himself, in order to arrive—by means of desire alone[66]—at the Supremely Desirable One. And when in this way you find the child, you shall draw near to Him [and] you shall worship Him—[you shall do so] as a servant who approaches his lord, as a needy mendicant, as someone weak. [You shall do so] with humble prostration of mind, with bare affection, with a magnitude of desire, and with groaning of heart, in simplicity and sincerity. And with confidence you expose all your possessions to Him, and you offer them and commit them to Him. And you extend yourself unto Him. ("Thy will be done ...," etc.)[67] Thereupon you obtain [Him who is] your Ultimate Desire. However, by means of this foretasting of the future life you understand how pleasant are Mary's and her Son's kisses even of you, etc., as you know from other contexts, etc.

FIRST MEMORANDUM

[18] "Entering, ...," etc. Having expounded Christ's ancestry in the order of eternity and in the order of time, and having mentioned both the appearance of the shepherds on the day of Christ's birth and the manifestation of the reason for Christ's coming (for on the eighth day [He was called] Jesus):[68] I must now consider the manifestation made to the Gentiles, so that we who have been called from out of the nations unto a union [with Him] may now enter in with gifts for the child, and so that we may worship Him. And because the Church sings of its

being joined on this day to its Heavenly Bridegroom, today is a feast-day of the Church, which today took its origin by way of the three Gentiles [viz., the three Magi] who on this day were united to Christ. And on this day the Church was cleansed and joined in matrimony and was transformed from a watery state into [a state of] acceptable wine, etc.[69]

[19] First, [I will speak of] the fact that Christ's appearance among the Gentiles was very hidden. Nevertheless, these Gentiles spoke, on the basis of rational considerations, of a forthcoming Redeemer. In ignorance and with difficulty of apprehending and with impeded desire, etc., they were expecting a Redeemer. In this regard, Messalha, Albumasar, the Sibyls, the Platonists, etc., foretold of many things. Likewise, [I will speak of] the fact that Adam and Eve after their penance, received consolation. Abel, Seth, Henoch, Mathusala, Noah, Shem, Abraham, Moses, David, Solomon, etc.—down to [the Apostle] John—revealed [Him]. Then He came to the shepherds; He manifested Himself more greatly to the world; and, at length, He manifested Himself to all.

[And I will speak] of the ascent unto Christ and of the descent unto the Antichrist and of the words of St. Augustine to Hesychius regarding the Last Judgment, etc.[70] And [I will speak of] the fact that the Church sings the following [words] on this present feast-day: "You have made all nations whatsoever ...," etc. And [I will speak of] the Antichrist's approaching, [as evidenced] from two signs.

Secondly, [I will speak] specifically of Christ's manifestation nowadays.

SECOND MEMORANDUM

[20] On this day the Church celebrates the feast of the appearance of its Head (viz., Christ) and of itself. The appearance of the Head of the Church is, in particular, [the appearance] of our Christ. First, [I will speak of] the fact that the appearance of Christ in the natural light possessed by the Ancients was very obscure; in the light of grace [it was still] quite far [from apprehension]; but [it became] clearer and clearer down to [the time of] John the Baptist. Moreover, [I will preach of] the fact that He was to become manifested to the whole world, so that all nations might worship Him, etc. Furthermore, [I will speak of] the fact that the Church of those believing that He *would be crucified*— and of those believing that He now *has been crucified*—is *one* Church. And [I will mention] the fact that holy men and successively holier

men were present in the Church down to [the day of] Christ; and from [the time of] Christ down to the Antichrist men become progressively worse, according to Augustine.[71] And [I will mention] that (as Augustine says) through the role of the Church and through the prophecies we are taught on this day that the entire world ought to receive the Savior before the Antichrist comes, etc.[72]

[21] Secondly, [I will say something] about the record of [Christ's] appearance nowadays—an appearance that has been more fully made. Thirdly, something must be said about the Church's having been washed in the Jordan [River] and about the fact that he who is to be in the Church must be cleansed. Here [something must be said] about the mysteries of baptism and about the fact that he who wants to remain in the Church must keep faith with the things promised at the time of his baptism and that blasphemers and diviners do not remain in the Church and do not keep to the faithfulness that they pledged. Fourthly, it must be said that he who is to pass from the Church Militant to the [Church] Triumphant must be a pilgrim and must fulfill the condition of subduing his sensuality, so that he may be made a spiritual whole. And this [transformation] is accomplished through obedience and humility, which are acquired through a man's entering into a knowledge of himself.

NOTES TO *SERMON XXI*

1. Matthew 2:11. See n. 2 of Sermon XVIII.
2. *Loc. cit.*
3. I Timothy 3:15.
4. Proverbs 9:1 (not Wisdom 9, as Nicholas writes and as I have corrected, as do also the editors of the Latin text.
5. John 14:2.
6. Psalms 83:5 (84:4).
7. Psalms 25:8 (26:8).
8. Isaias (Isaiah) 56:7. Mark 11:17.
9. Isaias (Isaiah) 2:3.
10. Psalms 92:5 (93:5).
11. Hebrew 3:6.
12. Ephesians 5:23.
13. I Corinthians 13:12.
14. *Loc. cit.*
15. Because the believer now sees "face to Face," he no longer needs faith in the sense of "the evidence of things that appear not" (Hebrews 11:1). However, the believer will still need faith in the sense of trust (*fiducia*); for he must continue to trust in God's love, truthfulness, constancy, goodness, etc.
16. Proverbs 16:4.
17. Proverbs 9:5.
18. Ambrose, *Epistola* 76, ll-12 ("Ad Irenaeum"), (*PL* 16:1317). The Church Dormant is the congregation of believers who are undergoing purification in Purgatory. See Sermon X (**27**).
19. Anselm, *Cur Deus Homo*, I, 16-18.
20. Ephesians 4:17 - 6:20.
21. Ephesians 5:24.
22. Jerome, *Epistola* 123 ("Ad Geruchiam"), section 12 (*PL* 22:1053).
23. I Corinthians 15:45.
24. In this section, marked by margin number 5, Nicholas refers to both the Church Militant and the Church Triumphant as "the Immaculate Bride."
25. Pseudo-Dionysius, *De Ecclesiastica Hierarchia*, I (*Dionysiaca*, II, 1079-1085 *et passim*.
26. Pope Leo IX, *Epistola ad Michaelem Constantinopolitanum Patriarcham*, 37 (*PL* 143:767B - 768A). Not Gregory IX, as Nicholas writes and as I have corrected, as do also the editors of the Latin text.
27. Here Nicholas makes a note to himself with regard to his *De Concordantia Catholica*, II, 17 (145-148). The title is not *De Concordantia Ecclesiastica*, as he writes.
28. Gregory Nazianzenus, *Oratio* 2: *Apologetica*, section III (*PG* 35:409/410).
29. Matthew 5:13-14.
30. Pseudo-Cyprian, *De Aleatoribus*, section II (*PL* 4:903).
31. Cyprian, *Epistola* 10 ("Ad Antonianum"), section XXIV (*PL* 3:815).
32. Jerome, *Adversus Jovinianum*, I, 26 (*PL* 23:258C).

33. I Corinthians 5:20.
34. John 6:58 and 20:21.
35. The priesthood, Nicholas has said, is like the soul.
36. Optatus Milevitanus, *De Schismate Donistarum*, II, 2 (*PL* 11:946).
37. Augustine *et al.*, *Epistola* 53 ("Ad Generosum"), Chap. 1 (*PL* 33:195-196).
38. Matthew 16:19.
39. Matthew 16:18.
40. I Corinthians 10:4.
41. Gratian, *Decretales*, 89:7 ("Ad hoc ..."). See Aemilius Friedberg, editor, *Corpus Iuris Canonici*, Vol. I, col. 313 (Leipzig, 1879). The reference is not to Decretal 83, as Nicholas writes and as I have corrected, as do also the editors of the Latin text).
42. See, above, n. 2 of Sermon XVIII.
43. Matthew 2:11.
44. Nicholas makes this note to himself, not to his reader.
45. Deuteronomy 13:1-5 (not Exocus 13, as Nicholas writes and as I have corrected, as do also the editors of the Latin text).
46. Aquinas, *Summa Theologica*, II-II, 13, 3, *ad* 1.
47. See, above, n. 58 of Sermon XVIII.
48. Exodus 21:17. Matthew 15:4 (not Matthew 5, as Nicholas writes and as I have corrected).
49. Physical death occurs when the soul forsakes the body; spiritual death occurs when God forsakes the soul.
50. Gregory IX, *Decretales*, V, 7 ("De Haereticis"), 10. See Aemilius Friedberg, editor, *Corpus Iuris Canonici*, Vol. II, col. 783 (Leipzig, 1881).
51. Here Nicholas adds: "Codex: Ne quis imperatori maledicat, leg. 1." See *Codex Iustinianus*, Book IX, 7. See also the reference in n. 50 below.
52. Here Nicholas adds: "In Authentica: 'Ne luxurietur contra' ". See Novella 77 in *Corpus Iuris Civilis*, Vol. III (*Novellae*), pp. 381-383 (Berlin, 1904). See also the work referenced in n. 55 below: in particular, see section 392 (first sentence), p. 343.
53. Gregory IX, *Decretales*, V, 26. See Aemilius Friedberg, editor, *Corpus Iuris Canonici*, Vol. II, cols. 826-827 (Leipzig, 1881).
54. Gregory the Great, *Dialogi*, IV, 18 (*PL* 77:349).
55. Stephanus de Barbone, *De Diversis Materiis Praedicabilibus*, Part 4: *De Dono Fortitudinis*, Title 9. (In particular, see sections 387-388, p. 342 ("De peccato blasphemie") in *Anecdotes historiques, légendes et apologues* de Étienne de Bourbon (Paris: Librairie Renouard, 1877).
56. Cf., *ibid.*, section 392, p. 343.
57. *Ibid.*, section 386, p. 341.
58. Nicholas mentions these examples in Sermon XVIII (**13**).
59. Cf. Isaias (Isaiah) 46:8.
60. Here (at 15:11) I am construing "cognoscat" as if it were "cognoscit".
61. Psalms 39:13 (40:12).
62. II Kings (II Samuel) 7:27.
63. Wisdom 8:16.
64. Isaias (Isaiah) 30:15.
65. Augustine, *De Spiritu et Anima*, 14 (*PL* 40:791). Not Chap. 20, as Nicholas

writes and as I have corrected, as do also the editors of the Latin text.

66. "... by desire alone": This phrase speaks to a theme explored by Hugh of Balma (and others) in his *De Theologia Mystica*. See J. Hopkins, *Hugh of Balma on Mystical Theology: A Translation and an Overview of His De Theologia Mystica* (Minneapolis: Banning, 2002).

67. Luke 1:38.

68. Matthew 1:21. The name "Jesus" means *Savior*; and this meaning discloses God's purpose in sending Jesus.

69. John 2:1-11.

70. Augustine, *Epistola* 199 ("De Fine Saeculi"), 8, 22-24 (*PL* 33:1:912-914).

71. *Loc. cit.*

72. Augustine, *Epistola* 53 ("Ad Generosum"), 1, 1 (*PL* 33-2:196).

Sermon XXII: Dies Sanctificatus
(The Sanctified Day)
[December 25, 1440; preached in Augsburg]

[1] The sanctified day has dawned upon us. Come, ye nations: worship the Lord.

The Holy Mother Church, the Bride-without-blemish of the Supreme King, breaks forth—amid the jubilation of the supreme harmony-of-delight of today's festival—in this song of gladness: "*Dies sanctificatus ...*," etc.[1]

[2] The captive daughter of Sion sat for many years in darkness and in the shadow of the deprivation of an intellectual life. But she foresaw many stellar rays in the Prophets, who envisioned a certain day and who foretold by means of the life and the word of their spirit that it would be a great day. [And] she was very frequently consoled—this daughter of Sion, i.e., [this] soul most desirous of a viewing of the most longed-for intellectual life. And many days passed; but certain traces of them were corruptible; yet, these traces became progressively more visible in brighter light.

[3] But today the substantial day, sanctified in and of itself—which [day] is holiness itself, incomparable to all other [days] both past and future—has dawned. It has dawned, I say, without any darkness but while repelling all darkness far away—[has dawned] not as some one of the stars but as the true Sun itself in its excellent primordial brightness. Indeed, [it has dawned] not *in* brightness but as Infinite Light—invisible to every physical eye—in which there is no darkness. It has dawned upon us, in order that the way unto the goal would be more manifest to us—so that every deceit might be put to flight by Truth, so that death might be all the more dead by means of Life, and so that these [results might be accomplished] very simply without multiple causes, because [He who is] the Light is the Way, the Truth, and the Life.[2]

[4] Therefore, because this Bridegroom—who has placed His tabernacle in the sun[3] and who has long been most eagerly awaited by us with all desire—has today shined upon His bride, the daughter of Sion: we must arise and not sleep but must come to meet Him with an approach of supreme affection and with the inner movement of a bride accompanied by sweet-smelling spices, which are the very devout

358

prayers of the saints. Come, then, you who in Christ have been prepared for this course, you who have hitherto assembled together for
this purpose; [come] and let us worship Him, in order that in this way
He may be received in our devotion. And in order that He may descend
unto us as a dewdrop of consolation—[descend] by working in me by
means of eloquence-of-word about Him and through Him: let us with
confidence approach the parturient Mother of this Light, so that by her
prayer she may render her Son well-disposed toward us—[let us
approach] with a pious mind and say: "Hail, Mary ...," etc.

[5] The sanctified day ..., etc. There are three births of the Son
of God. Today we celebrate the feast-day of these [three]: (1) There is
the eternal birth, which is hidden in the depth of the understanding
[and] which the midnight mass commemorates. This [birth] is touched
upon by the words: "the sanctified day." (2) There is the birth by which
the Word was made flesh. The mass at dawn befigures this birth. It is
touched upon by the words "has dawned upon us." (3) There is the
third birth, by which in the fullness of His light we are born in Him as
sons of God by means of our devout approach unto Him. The high
mass shows this birth to be for our salvation. This birth is touched upon
by means of the thematic words "Come, let us worship [Him]."

[6] The foregoing are the sections that I have decided to touch
upon briefly. The first section will be about the Son's eternal begottenness [and will be] for those who are more learned, so that the
Gospel of John will be explained a bit in this section.[4] The second section will be for commoners [and will be] about the temporal birth, so
that the part of [John's] Gospel that speaks of this will be noted.[5] The
third section will be for contemplatives, so that this part of [John's]
Gospel will be noted as last: [viz.,] "He gave [them] power ...," etc.[6]

PART ONE
The Eternal Birth of the Son of God

(a) *God as Absolute Oneness enfolds even opposites and transcends all our names.*

[7] As concerns the first section, it must be known that God is not
apprehended by reason or by imagination or by the senses; for He surpasses all the senses and all power of reason. Rather, He is apprehended by faith. For unless you believe, you will not understand, says
Isaias.[7] Therefore, we believe that God is one and three, although neither His oneness nor His trinity is understandable. [8] All nations

admit that the God of them all is the Best, from whom all things derive; and even the heathen have not denied this. For since it is not the case that anything can bring itself into existence (because it would exist before it existed—something that reason does not admit), we must come [in our inferences] to a single first, eternal [Beginning]. [9] Now, this First Beginning we call God, who cannot be understood not to exist.[8] For God is Truth, which cannot be understood not to be; for truth is the object of the intellect. For whether God is understood to exist or understood not to exist:[9] since either alternative is affirmed as *true*, God [who is Truth] is affirmed to exist. Consequently, God—who by means of either of the contradictory alternatives is seen, necessarily, to exist—is beyond all opposition and contradictoriness.

[10] Therefore, when you wish to ascend unto investigating God's quiddity, you see that, of necessity, you will fail. For in order to investigate that Infinity—which as most simple Eternity and maximal Cause surpasses and precedes all opposition—you are not able to assist yourself by means either of names or of concepts [*rationes*]. For God is not anything that has an opposite; instead, He is infinitely above all opposites—as is [expressed by] the teaching of the true theologians. Therefore, when you consider that God is the Supreme Good, then by investigating by way of reason you assert that He is Truth, Justice, Graciousness; and you remove from Him the opposites of these. And when you reflect in this way, there occurs to you a certain multiplicity and otherness, because Justice in its own essence [*ratio*] is not Truth, and Truth is not Graciousness, etc. Hence, you see that these names ("Truth," "Justice," "Light" ..., [etc.]) do not befit God, since they indicate otherness, multiplicity, oppositeness, and [finite essence, or] form—none of which can befit the First, altogether Simple, Infinite [Reality]. Rather, you speak more truly [when you say it] to be the case that these names do not *positively* befit God, who cannot be *this* thing and not *another* thing, since He is all in all.[10] Hence, you discern that the theology of negation is the truer theology—that God, who is all things, is not any one of these things but is the altogether simple Beginning, who enfolds all things by means of His Infinity. For He is Justice in such a way that He is also Truth and Peace and all the things —in Heaven and on earth—[whose names] signify a perfection. For He is Perfection itself, of which all perfect things partake.

[11] Now, all things exist insofar as they are one.[11] Therefore, if all things partake of oneness, which is also called being itself[12]—of which (by degrees) intellect partakes in one way, reason in another, and

perceptible things in still another way—and if it is not the case that all things partake of intellect or of reason: then it is evident that [the name of] Oneness (which is Absolute Being, or Absolute Form-of-being, through which all things are that which they are) befits God more than does any other name whatsoever. Therefore, [the name of] Oneness—Infinite Oneness, to which plurality is not opposed—befits God. Infinite Oneness enfolds all things. It is also Goodness, in that it is understood to be the formal imparting of being, without any intermixing. And in this way we explain the Scripture-texts "I am I-Who-Am,"[13] "God is One,"[14] etc. [12] But when we consider God with respect to contracted being, we see clearly that it is more fitting that He be named in accordance with the contractedness[15] of being that is of more excellence and more enfolding-power rather than of lesser [excellence and enfolding-power]. Hence the names "spirit," "intellect," "reason," "justice," "truth" (and the names of those things that in their simplicity escape all sensory detection) befit God more than do [the names] "fire," "water," "air," etc. [13] So, consider abstract oneness, which is also being itself.[16] [Consider] that it enfolds all things; for it is not the case that anything can exist outside it. (How could [some thing that were] apart from being be understood to *be*?) Moreover, it is not the case that not-being, or nothing, exists apart from oneness. For in Infinite Oneness not-being is most simple Being itself. For outside of Infinity neither being nor not-being can be understood to be. But in most simple Being itself there is nothing of otherness or of multiplicity, because [most simple Being itself is] Infinite Oneness. Therefore, in Infinity all things that can be spoken of and all things that cannot be spoken of, all things that can be understood and all things that cannot be understood, are Infinity itself, which enfolds and encompasses both those things which are and those things which are not.

[14] You now see—if you elevate yourself by means of a very subtle understanding—(1) how it is that God is not understood, inasmuch as He infinitely surpasses all oppositeness [and] (2) how it is that Being itself (which is the Infinite Form of being) is the Beginning, the Middle, and the End of all existing things.[17] And because it is the Beginning, it is eternal [and] prior to everything else; because it is the Middle, it is that in which all else is present; and because it is the End, it is that at which all else aims. [15] You see how it is that God is neither everywhere nor nowhere, since *everywhere* and *nowhere* are opposed [to each other; and, being opposites,] they do not befit God.

Rather, God is above [them]; for in Him everywhere and nowhere are enfolded and are not opposed. Hence, He is so everywhere that He is nowhere; and He is so nowhere that He is everywhere—even as by means of its likeness the substantial form of a thing is in a material everywhere and nowhere. For the form precedes every accident; and it is simple and, hence, is present as a whole in the whole and in each part [of the material thing]. An example [occurs] with regard to the form of a man, i.e., with respect to his body, etc. And, in this way, see how it is that God is present everywhere by means of His Essence [*essentia*]—[present] precisely because His Essence is Being, is Power, is Truth, etc. But the Essence is not received equally by all things, even as the members of the body do not receive the soul in equal measure; and for this reason the soul does not accomplish the same thing in all the members, etc.

> (b) *The way of ascent is shown* from *creatures* unto *God, considered as Absolute Oneness, Absolute Equality, and Absolute Union. And by means of these mathematical names a trinity is asserted to be present in God.*

[**16**] As regards the [doctrine of] the Trinity, it is necessary that you advance [in understanding] by means of the following pathway, because no trinity that is opposed to simplicity and to oneness befits God. But you must understand [the notion of] trinity very abstractly and elevatedly above any rational [conception of] trinity. [You must understand it in such a way] that the trinity is not constituted by one thing and another thing, or by *one* multiplied several times, but [is constituted in such a way] that it is compatible with the oneness—indeed, *is* the oneness.[18] Consequently, it is not a *trinity* but is a *triunity*, just as the oneness is a *unitrinity*. And do not look at the meaning of the name; for in the meaning of the name you will find nothing of Infinite Truth. For names are imposed by the faculty of reason, through comparisons; and they cannot befit [Him who is] Infinite, Disproportional [to all else], very Simple, and altogether One. And for us human beings it is not possible to apprehend the Trinity by means of some sign or image or verbal expression. For the fact that God is One is altogether true; and the fact that God is Trine is altogether true. But these are not two truths, because there is not one truth regarding the Oneness and another truth regarding the Trinity. Rather, [God] is so One that He is Trine; and vice versa.

[**17**] And because we ascribe all names to God in comparative

relation to creatures, we must assist ourselves from creatures in order to ascend unto the Trinity. [For] it is not the case that we have something that we have not received.[19] We recognize in the case of each thing that it is a thing that is *one, distinct,* and *unified*; these [properties] are found in the essence of every being. Moreover, oneness indicates *undividedness, distinctness,* and *union.* Therefore, if we find these [properties] in every being that partakes of being, then we see that the contracted oneness that is partaken of by things does not exist unless it is trine. In a similar way, we say certain things of God transferredly and abstractly. For example,[20] Infinite Oneness is trine in such a way that it is Oneness that is, in and of itself, *Indivisibility*; it is also *Infinite Distinctness* that is *Equality*-of-being-all-things; and it is *Infinite Union.* For by virtue of the fact that God is *Infinite Oneness*: each thing that derives from Him is one and is undivided (considered in and of itself). By virtue of the fact that God is *Infinite Equality*, He enfolds the distinctness of all things. For the fact that a thing is composed of such and such features and not of other features is due to Infinite Form [*ratio*] or Infinite Distinctness, which is Infinite Equality, through which a thing obtains its being distinct. Below this [limit the thing] would not exist; and[21] above this [limit] it does not exist. Therefore, from Infinite Distinctness there is—in accordance with our relational viewpoint—difference in things, and there is no precise equality between any things. Rather, Infinite Equality, which is Infinite Form (*ratio*),[22] enfolds within its simplicity all distinct differences. Next, by virtue of the fact that God is *Infinite Union*: all things have a certain connectedness with one another. Hence, from Oneness, which is present in all things, and from Distinguishing-equality there arises and proceeds a proportional union of all things; and this union is the constituting-bond of the universe.

[18] By such means [as the foregoing] we come *from* a knowledge of contracted oneness, which is not present actually without a trinity, *to* Oneness that, in its own way, is Absolute. Nonetheless, by means of the things that are visible or apprehensible we cannot ascend unto a knowledge of Infinity. For in Absolute Infinity—when we consider it not as Beginning and Cause but in and of itself—we would be able to find nothing other than Absolute Infinity. Many things could here be said about how it is that all created things lead us to a knowledge of the Trinity. According to Dionysius [we could be led] through [a consideration of] being, potentiality, and actuality;[23] and according to Augustine [we could be led] through [a consideration of] mode,

species, and order.[24] And this assertion of Augustine's will be able to be understood in the aforesaid way. Likewise, *measure, number*, and *weight* can be introduced for this purpose; so too can *oneness, truth*, and *goodness*. And these are three fingers by means of which God attaches size to the earth, etc.[25]

[19] Now, we must examine elsewhere how it is that the intellect, when elevated, understands something of this [topic]. But, for now, it suffices for us to know that if we want to behold the Beginning of all things, then we [must] recognize that every rational understanding is encompassed by multitude and magnitude; for reason apprehends nothing apart from multitude and magnitude. But [reason] sees that, necessarily, the First Beginning ought to be altogether simple; otherwise, it would not be the First. And because multitude has oneness as its beginning, necessarily multitude is one thing. Now, magnitude does not exist apart from a trinity. (We observe this fact in the case of magnitude that is contracted to a material size; for there is no physical object apart from length, width, and depth; and the beginning of polygonal figures is a triangle, prior [to which] a [polygonal] figure is not possible, etc.) Hence, reason finds, of necessity, that the First Beginning of all things must be one and trine uncomposedly and altogether simply, so that it is the Beginning, and the Measure (*metrum et mensura*), of all things. We must explore elsewhere the topics of how it is that—with regard to every created thing—(1) in magnitude there is multitude, and vice versa, (2) in compositeness there is simplicity, and vice versa, (3) in trinity there is oneness, and vice versa. These [considerations] show us—in a vestige which we ought to detect above all oppositeness—how it is that Infinite Oneness exists in a Trinity, and vice versa.

[20] But in order to be able to go on now to [the topic of] eternal begottenness,[26] we should know that St. Augustine speaks of the eternal Trinity by means of mathematical names. For example, oneness precedes all otherness, which does not exist apart from duality; therefore, oneness is eternal. Likewise, inequality is subsequent to equality, of which it falls short. For every inequality [can be] reduced to an equality, and there can be no inequality without otherness. Therefore, equality precedes otherness and, hence, is eternal. Union is prior to division, because union derives from oneness, [whereas] division derives from otherness. Therefore, ..., etc.

[21] Our [most holy teachers] wanted Oneness to be called Father, Equality to be called Son, [and] Union to be called Holy

Spirit.[27] [They desired this] because of a certain resemblance, so that we might better arrive at apprehending [the doctrines of] begottenness and procession. Nonetheless, the names "This," "Same," "Identity" are more appropriate, etc.[28] [22] Let us now consider the eternal begottenness of the Son. For begetting is the multiplication of one nature, or is the repeating of oneness (e.g., in the case of a father and his son), which occurs with regard to things transitory. [But] in God begetting is one repeating of Oneness, i.e., is Oneness once. If you were to repeat [oneness] twice or three times, something else—viz., the number two or the number three—would be produced. Therefore, oneness repeated once[29] begets only an equality of oneness; and by this [statement] nothing can be understood other than that oneness begets oneness—a begetting that is eternal. And so, procession is 'oneness of oneness and of the repetition of oneness'—or 'oneness of oneness and of its equality'. For, necessarily, union proceeds from oneness and equality: and it cannot proceed from anything else. Etc.

(c) *Other analogies (brightness, word, art; reason, concept, form) that in like manner elevate us unto a knowledge of eternal generation.*

[23] The doctors [of the Church] have [used] many examples in order to elevate us unto a knowledge of eternal generation. [There is the example] of brightness, which is generated from fire, and [the example] of heat, which is [produced] from both [fire and brightness]. [There is the example] of light; for instance, Hilary says[30] that light is kindled from light and that brightness results from both. [There is the example] of mind: [viz.,] that the mind begets a word resembling itself ([begets], namely, a concept [*conceptus*] of itself); and from these [viz., mind and its word] there proceeds will, or love. Hence, many [of these teachers] turned to [the example of] the word, in order that the gospel might be made known to us. For a word is a likeness of the intellect—[a likeness] in which the intellect enfolds that which is understandable. Hence, the Apostle is seen to mean that, in God, the Son is the Father's mental Word, i.e., is the [Father's] Divine Wisdom, Divine Art, or Divine Concept (*ratio*).[31] For as regards the fact that all things were made by God the Father in His Conceptual Word and Wisdom: just as there is no doubt about this, so too there is no doubt that His eternal Concept, Word, or Wisdom is the Infinite Art. Therefore, in the beginning was the Word, and the Word was with God, and the Word was God.[32] Therefore, if the Concept, or intellectual

Word, or Wisdom) was in the beginning, clearly it was present from eternity, because it was in the beginning. "To have been present in the beginning" indicates eternity. Moreover, if there was a Concept, it was the Concept of something. But it can be the Concept only of the Eternal Beginning, in which it was always present. Hence, in the beginning was the Concept, and it was with God, because it was in the eternity of the Beginning, which is God the Father. And it was God, because it was the Eternal Art and Infinite Concept. Now, the Word cannot be less than God, since there is [but] one Eternity and Infinity. Therefore, all things were created by means of this Infinite Concept.

[**24**] Here contemplate the fact that all things in the Infinite Art are Equality and that the altogether simple Infinite Concept is the Concept of all things. For all differences are enfolded in the oneness of the Infinite Concept. And just as nothing [finite] is found to be so equal to a given thing that it cannot be more and more equal *ad infinitum*, and just as there is only one Infinite Equality of all things, so a reason (*ratio*) cannot be given by anyone for [any of] all created things. As Solomon says:[33] there is no reason [that man can discover] for any of the works of God. There is one Infinite Concept (*ratio*) …, etc.

[**25**] Here consider the fact that the Word is every Art, Form, and Concept. Recur to the likeness with our art, which is within us. [Consider] the fact that in our mind's word, which is its art, are enfolded the mind's artifacts. And [consider] (1) that our art in its simplicity enfolds above time and division artifacts and (2) that these artifacts unfold the enfolded art. See how it is (1) that a church-building is present in the art of the architect—present undividedly and incompositely—and (2) that the church-building that is unfolded from the art becomes subject to multiplicity, division, and temporality. And in one way or another the art is contracted by one kind of material or another.

[**26**] Likewise, consider in this way, as regards the Divine Art, that just as our art introduces into matter (which it presupposes) accidental forms that are likenesses of natural [forms], so the Divine Art, because it is infinite, produces in accordance with a singular and altogether simple Art all existing things. Therefore, the form-of-being of all things flows from the Infinite Form of the Eternal Art as an artifact [flows] from its art. Furthermore, you ought to consider that the higher and more perfect an art is, the more it enfolds within itself the lower arts, even as the art of a goldsmith enfolds the art of a painter, of a sculptor, of a foundry-man, etc.; therefore, [the art of the goldsmith is] nobler, because its simplicity is stronger and more unified. But, neces-

sarily, the Infinite Art is the strongest and most powerful. Consider, too, that an artisan produces various things from a single art; and the more things he produces, the greater and more powerful is his art. By comparison, the Divine Art is undepletable.

[27] Moreover, consider how it is that an artisan produces an artifact—that first of all he forms a conception [*conceptus*] within his art, that next he embraces the conception in such a way that the embracing proceeds from the conceiver and what has been conceived (i.e., the *will* proceeds from the *intellect* and the art, or the *conception*). So too, procession occurs in its own way in God, because God the Father conceives; and the *Embracing* proceeds [from the *Conceiver* and the *Conception*]. And this is the Trinity. We read in Genesis that [God] *created*; then He *saw*; then from these [two] proceeded *Goodness*, for [all the things] were exceedingly good. An artisan acts in a similar fashion. And just as an artifact is to a finite art, so a creature is to the Creator. For in and through an artifact one sees what capabilities the artisan has; similarly, in and through creatures one sees what [attributes] the Creator has. For in the artifact we see a trinity in oneness, even as [we also do] in regard to a creature. For example, a chest has being from an artisan, even as the whole world has being from God. The chest is *one*, is *distinct*, and is *unified*.

[28] And here consider carefully the fact that if the universe is envisioned as present in pure Oneness, then it is God—because it is the archetypal world and is the Word, inasmuch as then it is nothing outside the Word, etc.[34] God is the Oneness of all things; and in each thing Oneness is found by way of the unified whole. For example, [this is true of] each part of a chest. If we consider, for instance, its bottom, then the bottom has a oneness, it has a distinctness qua bottom, and it has a union that proceeds from its being and its distinctness; for [the bottom] unites to itself the chest, to which it bears a comparative relation. And something similar is the case as regards each stone of a tower, as regards a man's hand or foot in relation to the man [as a whole]—even as also regards each part of the universe in relation to the universe [as a whole].

[29] Now, consider that an art agrees with every [feature] of the artifact. For example, the diverse hewings of a stone, in relation to the oneness of the tower's unity, depend upon one and the same art. Similarly, all the differences depend on one and the same art. And [consider] the fact that the form of the artifact is a likeness of the art, of the artisan, and of the artisan's conception. This form, because of the

material in which it is received, is to a greater or a lesser degree like the conception [of it]; but it is never exactly equal to the conception [i.e., never actually corresponds precisely to the conception]. By comparison, the forms of things are images of the Divine Art, etc.

[**30**] And, at this point, the first section, which deals with the begetting of the Word, has been completed. And [I have now explained] how it is that, according to the Gospel, all things were made by Him, and without Him not anything was made." [35] Moreover, [I have discussed] the fact that in Him all things are the [Divine] Art, which is Life, whose image all living natures bear. And [I have spoken of] the fact that the Life is the Light of men, [36] because the Life is the Concept (*ratio*)-and-Wisdom from which derive every concept and all wisdom. And [I have spoken of] the fact that He is the Light of men and shines in the darkness of ignorance but the darkness has not comprehended Him. [37]

PART TWO
On Christ, Born in Time insofar as He Is a Man

[**31**] II Corinthians 5: "God was in Christ reconciling the world unto Himself." John 6: "He is the Bread, who ... gives life to the world." [38]

I promised, in the second place, to add something about Christ's incarnation. In order to introduce this section, I propose to take up the theme that "the day has dawned upon us," for God created man [in His image] ..., etc. [39] [**32**] Here we must take note of the fact that Christ's incarnation was necessary for our salvation. God created all things for His own sake. [40] And [He created] them maximally and most perfectly only for Himself. However, they could not be united to Him, since there is no comparative relation of the finite to the infinite. [41] Therefore, through Christ all things are in God, their End. For unless God had assumed a human nature, then (since that human nature, as being something intermediate, enfolds in itself [all] other [human natures]) the entire universe would neither be perfect nor, indeed, would exist. [42] (Here note that among created natures human nature (*homo*), by reason of its universality, enfolds all [other natures], both immaterial and material.) And hence, too, human nature was created as the goal of all beings, so that all things are present in human nature as in their goal. [43] [**33**] But it was not possible that the whole of created nature could be conveyed unto the Divinity except in and through man, who in glory and honor is a little lower than the angels and who is established above all other animals and all other works of God's hands.[44] And for this reason the spirit of man, which enfolds within itself the natures of all other things, is not at rest in any created thing; rather, it strives [for something] above itself and finds, as something with which it can be satisfied, only immortality, which is eternal life and eternal wisdom. And that man—who was to be the Final-Goal, or Rest, or Sabbath, of all things—was able to be the Supreme Creature (which enfolds within itself all [creatures] in its perfection) only if He was personally God, in whom alone there is rest; moreover, He is all that which is sought. Hence, it was necessary that God become a [God]-man, in order for all things to arrive at their Final-Goal.

[34] Consequently, we must know the following: by means of our eyes and of perceptual considerations we can discern differences only by means of temporal distances, so that in this way Christ, with respect to the fact that He is a man, is seen to have been born, in time, after Abraham and others. Nonetheless, with respect to the fact that He is God, who is beyond all time, He is the Beginning and Head of every creature. As He said: "Before Abraham was made, I am."[45] And Paul writes [of this fact] to the Ephesians and the Colossians. Hence, [Christ is] the Beginning of living things, of dead things, and of the entire Church, both of the Church Triumphant and of the Church Militant. This Christ was seen to dwell among us temporally on earth, even as He was born temporally of the Virgin on today's date.

[35] Here, then, we must take notice of the fact that Christ the Lord—in that He is united (above every creature) to Absolute Maximality, since there cannot be anyone greater than He in whom infinite power is perfect and complete in itself—is God and the Infinite Art, or Infinite Form, of all existing things. But insofar as He is maximal man,[46] He is an altogether perfect man, than whom there can be no more perfect man. And since the human nature in Him is so very lofty that there cannot be a loftier human nature that could be united as closer to Divine Infinity, then by the very fact that He is most perfect and most lofty as concerns the nature of His humanity, He is most closely united to the Divinity. But the nature of His humanity, since it is a creature, cannot pass over, by way of ascent, into becoming His divinity; nor can the divine [nature], by way of descent, [pass over] into becoming His humanity. And so, there is here a oneness, with the distinction of the natures remaining. Now, if what is caused or created passes over to becoming maximal through a union than which a greater union is not possible, then necessarily it cannot exist personally in itself. Therefore,

the human nature [of Christ] subsists in the divine nature, even as (according to Athanasius)[47] the body exists (in its own way) in the soul (although this is not a completely accurate illustration).

[Let all of] the foregoing [be said], to begin with.

[**36**] Secondly, we must now consider the fact that in Christ Jesus the human nature, qua exalted unto the Divinity, is the perfection of the universe[48] and, especially, is the perfection of our human nature. For in that [Christ's human nature] reaches the highest gradation of human nature, than which there is no higher gradation, it enfolds every other [human] nature.[49] And it unifies all the things that are subject to the nature, transforming them into Christ.

[**37**] We recognize how it is that a single art enfolds other arts. What if every art were in one man, and he would be all Perfection and all Wisdom and every Form? Wouldn't the Perfection of that [man] enfold all men? If the man still retained his human nature, wouldn't that humanity, which is one, be present in all [men]? The humanity of Christ is not *other*[50] than [the humanity] of each man—past, present, or future.[51] Rather, it is humanity but is not *other*. And so, we see how it is that our nature, which is not *other* than Christ, is, in Christ, most perfect. (And here take note of the fact that Christ coincides with the nature of humanity, through which all men are men. And, accordingly, He is the equal [i.e., exact] Measure (*metrum et mensura*) of all men; and in Him all men are present as in the Head of, and Ruler over, all things. In the Oneness of Christ—where there is neither Jew nor Gentile nor male nor female but where Christ is all in all[52]—they are present without difference. Accordingly, Christ is the nearest [kin] of each [of us]—indeed, much closer [to us] than a fleshly father or brother. For He is the substantial intimacy of each [of us]. And, hence, all our defects are made-up-for in Him, who is our Fullness and our Perfection. In Him we are justified; in Him we are saved; in Him we live and are moved.[53]

[**38**] And keep in mind that here you can see (1) the wonderful promise that we obtain in Christ and (2) the super-wonderful salvation of the Cross. For Christ's humanity—as elevated unto the maximal degree, insofar as it is united to the divine nature—is the truest and most perfect humanity of all men. Therefore, a man who clings to Christ clings to his own humanity, so that he is one with Christ, even as Christ [is one] with God.[54] Accordingly, each one who adheres to Christ and is united to Christ—not in and through something other than in and through his own humanity, which is also Christ's humanity—

has satisfied the debt [of sin], is justified, is enlivened. For his humanity, which is one in him and in Christ,[55] is united to God the Word. O deepest mystery! Here you see that in Christ human nature has put on immortality through union with the Word. Here you see the inference: 'If Christ has arisen, then we too [shall arise].' Here you see the error of all those who look for salvation apart from Christ. Here you see how much they err and contradict themselves—those (such as pagans and Jews) who believe in resurrection but deny Christ. Here you see that Christ is all in all[56] and that the very profound letter of Paul to the Ephesians is understood as regards the Church Triumphant and is completely true. Here you see [Him who is] your Consoler with regard to all your dire needs. And [you see] endless things of these [kinds].

[39] Now, He is the Light that has shined upon us. But how has [that Light] shined forth? For although God is hidden, He has revealed Himself—as when [someone's] mental word is hidden to you, then in order for it to be revealed to you it takes on vocalization; and beneath the vocalization, which is its sign, lies the hidden mental state. Similarly, the hidden Eternal Word has put on flesh in order to become visible; He did works that someone other than God could not have done. And, in this way, He came for dwelling with men. Therefore, men saw one thing and believed another thing because God was hidden beneath the flesh—even as a voice is heard and the meaning [beneath it] is understood. Christ preached and enlightened. It is the task of a teacher to enlighten by means of his voice; and he imparts light to his student without any diminution of his own light. Similarly, Christ has shined upon us in order to make us partakers[57] of His Wisdom. Note how deep are the mysteries [contained] in the words of Christ, which are vocal sounds in which Eternal Wisdom itself is hidden. But in order to hear the vocal sounds, we must draw near—draw close through faith and devotion. And thereupon we are enlightened and will appropriate His fullness, etc.[58]

[40] (Here [I will mention] a few points about the Blessed Virgin.)

[41] And now you see that he who through faith turns with all his heart to Christ and ceases to be who-he-is and becomes born again in Christ, so that only Christ is in him: he is, in and through Christ, a son of God; he is deified;[59] he obtains the final perfection. And understand the Gospel as teaching that he who wishes to be a son of God must be reborn in Christ, who is God. For before the foundation of the world[60] we were called unto an eternal inheritance in Christ. It follows

that we must believe the following: that the Word was made flesh and dwelt among us.[61] If, in God, the Son assumed a humanity, then it is evident that you, who are a man, can be made to be a son of God by means of Christ's dwelling in you.[62]

PART THREE
Spiritual Birth in Christ

[**42**] If, then, (as concerns this third section) you wish to be reborn in Christ as a son of God, you—who are a Gentile—must come and draw near to this Sun by means of the subtleness of human reasonings. You must come most devoutly by a choice by means of which you choose only Christ—[choose Him] with simplicity, and purity, of your mind. You must dismiss all spiritual presumptiveness. You must put on kindness toward all others and must become tender-hearted. And you must draw near with fervent love; and with concord and peace and very devout prayer you must make your request—together with Peter, to whom God first of all revealed His mystery. Etc.

[**43**] And here consider the fact that just as God is the Head of Christ, so Christ is the Head of the Church.[63] As God is to Christ (for the deity is as the soul; the humanity, as the body), so Christ is to the Church (Christ is as the soul; the Church, as the body). Therefore, it is necessary that you exist in a oneness of body [i.e., of Church], so that through the body [i.e., the Church] you may exist in the oneness of the spirit of Jesus. *Nota bene*!

[**44**] Remember that your soul is not present in any member of your body unless it is united to the body. And the soul is present in the member in such a way that the member is present in it. If you desire that Christ dwell in you nobly, then grow into a noble member [of His mystical body], and see to it that you enter into Christ boldly. And this [admonition] is to be noted the more especially.

A FURTHER NOTE

[**45**] Take note of the following secret: [viz.,] that the sanctified day is that day of which Genesis 2 [states]: "God blessed the seventh day and sanctified it."[64] For we read that God made the other days and, in making them, worked. But we do not read that God worked on the seventh day or that He made the seventh day. Rather, He blessed that day and sanctified it, because on that day He ceased from all work and rested. Therefore, consider carefully and subtly that [the sanctified] day is [to

be understood here as] Eternal Light, or Eternal Wisdom. And things exist gradationally through six stages that partake of that Light, so that by partaking of it they are called days. Moreover, a day was not anything other than it was created to be. But the sanctified day is the day that does not partake of the Light of wisdom with the hopeful expectation of [reaching] a higher stage; instead, it is that highest gradation-of-wisdom, in which God's every work ceases. Take note very particularly of this fact, because today is the sanctified day.[65]

NOTES TO *SERMON XXII*

1. See Genesis 2:3. See also Nicholas's Further Note at the end of this present sermon. Also see Sermon XXIII (**12**:1-4). The phrase "dies sanctificatus," says Nicholas, signifies the Sabbath, the day sanctified by God for the purpose of affording both rest from labor and time for worshipping God. It also signifies the Son of God's being united to a human nature—signifies, that is, the day of Jesus's conception.

2. John 14:6.

3. Psalms 18:6 (19:4).

4. John 1:1-4.

5. John 1:14.

6. John 1:12: "But to as many as received Him He gave power to be made sons of God ...."

7. Isaias (Isaiah) 7:9 (Old Latin Version).

8. Nicholas here uses the phrase "*qui non potest intelligi non esse.*" Anselm rejected this expression when arguing against Gaunilo. He insisted on the necessity of *not* replacing the verb "*cogitari*" by the verb "*intelligi*".

9. Regarding the expression "understood not to exist": see n. 8 above.

10. I Corinthians 15:28. Cf. Colossians 3:11.

11. See Cusa's *De Venatione Sapientiae* 21 (59).

12. Nicholas, in the spirit of the Platonic tradition, identifies being and oneness. See his *De Docta Ignorantia* I, 8. This present sermon repeats a number of the themes contained in *De Docta Ignorantia*, completed on February 12, 1440.

13. Exodus 3:14.

14. Deuteronomy 6:4.

15. Here (at 12:3) I am reading "contractionem" in place of "contractiorem", as do also the editors of the Latin text.

16. See n. 12 above.

17. Cusa, *De Docta Ignorantia* III, 1 (185).

18. Nicholas makes clear, elsewhere, that in God the trinity is not a *numerical* trinity. See *De Docta Ignorantia* I, 19 (57). See also my article "Verständnis und Bedeutung des dreieinen Gottes bei Nikolaus von Kues," *Mitteilungen und Forschungsbeiträge der Cusanus-Gesellschaft*, 28 (2003), 135-164.

19. I Corinthians 4:7.

20. In the examples that follow, Nicholas does not believe that there is any infinite oneness, infinite equality, etc., that is not God, who is Infinite Oneness, etc. But in his writings he sometimes speaks as if there were such an infinite oneness, etc. Similarly, in *De Docta Ignorantia* he speaks of an infinite triangle, an infinite circle, etc., even though he believes there not actually to exist any such figures.

21. Here (at 17:24) I am reading "et" in place of "nec"—as do also the editors of the Latin text.

22. The Latin word "*ratio*" has an especially large range of meanings. In Sermon XXX (**12**:10) Nicholas uses it interchangeably with "*forma*", as I construe it here. But in section 23 (margin number) below, I take it as interchangeable with "*conceptus*".

23. Pseudo-Dionysius, *De Caelesti Hierarchia*, 11 (*Dionysiaca*, II, 930).

24. Augustine, *De Civitate Dei*, V, 11 (*PL* 41:153).

25. Isaias (Isaiah) 40:12 (Douay-Rheims Version).

26. Cf. this entire section with what Nicholas writes in *De Docta Ignorantia* I, 709. See the third sentence of n. 12 above.

27. See *De Docta Ignorantia* I, 9 (26:1).

28. In *De Docta Ignorantia* I, 9 (25) Nicholas uses the triad "hoc, id, idem", as well as the triad "unitas, iditas, identitas". In the present sermon he writes "id, idem, identitas".

29. That is, 1 x 1 = 1, whereas 1 x 2 or 1 x 3 would equal 2 or 3, respectively.

30. Hilary of Poitiers, *De Trinitate*, VII, 29 (*PL* 10:224-225).

31. See n. 22 above.

32. John 1:1.

33. Ecclesiastes 8:17.

34. In God all things are God. In God-the-Word the archetypal world is the Word. See Nicholas's *Sermo* XXX (12:29-32) and *De Docta Ignorantia* I, 5 (119).

35. John 1:3.

36. John 1:4.

37. John 1:5.

38. II Corinthians 5:19 and John 6:33 respectively.

39. Genesis 1:27.

40. Proverbs 16:4.

41. See, above, n. 14 of Sermon XX.

42. *De Docta Ignorantia* III, 3 (197).

43. See *De Docta Ignorantia* III, 3 (198).

44. Psalms 8:6-7. Hebrews 2:7.

45. John 8:58.

46. In Sermon XVII (**11**:1-2) Nicholas refers to Christ as *homo minimus*: minimal man. Christ is *homo maximus* because He is *homo perfectissimus*. He is *homo minimus* because from the moment of His conception He was fully a human being (something that is not the case with other human beings, thinks Nicholas) and because He was in the womb longer than are any other human beings. See Sermon XXIII (**8**:10-12).

47. See the Athanasian Creed (also called the *Quicumque*): "sicut anima *rationalis* et caro unus est homo, ita Deus et homo unus est Christus."

48. *De Docta Ignorantia* III, 3 (198-199).

49. Although Nicholas holds that Christ's human nature, qua microcosm, enfolds every other nature (see divisions 32-33 above), his point here relates to the enfolding of all other *human* natures. Cf. *De Docta Ignorantia* III, 3 (198-199).

50. See Nicholas's late work *De Li Non Aliud* for an expansion of this theme.

51. That is, Christ's humanity is not different *in kind* from the essence of any human being's humanity. It is, however, *numerically distinct*. It is important for us to read the present and the subsequent passages in the light of Sermon XXXV (**5**), Sermon XXXVI (**2**:30-31), *De Docta Ignorantia* III, 12 (255). For example, Sermon XXXV (**5**:1-9) has: "And take note: If you conceive of the fact that Christ has the humanity of all men and that He is man not in the breadth of the human species nor outside [the human species] but as the most perfect final goal of the species, then you see clearly that human nature—present in Him much more intimately than in a broth-

er, a son, or a father, but present in the most precious identity that is positable *with a numerical difference being preserved*—obtains all fullness."

52. Colossians 3:11.

53. Acts 17:28.

54. *De Docta Ignorantia* III, 11 (252-253).

55. See n. 51 above.

56. See n. 52 above.

57. Here (at 39:17) I am reading "participes" in place of "participem"—as do also the editors of the Latin text.

58. John 1:16.

59. See Nicholas's *De Filiatione Dei*, where the theme of deification is explored further. See also, above, n. 66 of Sermon XXI.

60. Ephesians 1:4.

61. John 1:14.

62. Cf. I John 3:1-2.

63. I Corinthians 11:3. Ephesians 5:23.

64. Genesis 2:3.

65. December 25, 1440 was a Sunday.

Sermon XXIII: Domine, in Lumine Vultus Tui
("O Lord, in the light of Your countenance ....")[1]
[January 1, 1441; the feast-day of Christ's circumcision;
preached in Augsburg]

[1] "O Lord, in the light of Your countenance they shall walk, and in Your name they shall rejoice ...,[2] and in Your justice they shall be exalted."[3] ....[4]

The Holy Mother Church finds that the Holy Spirit, through the Royal Prophet,[5] has foretold of Christ's coming as a result of God's very great mercy. And [the Church] receives this psalm, to be read at this time in order that we may see (1) that Christ was announced to our fathers and (2) what our fathers believed and hoped for regarding Him—so that we may walk in light and rejoice in His name and be exalted in His justice. Therefore, let us pray ..., etc.

[2] In the theme-text three points are touched upon: (1) walking in [His] light, (2) rejoicing in [His] name, (3) exaltation in [His] justice. And in accordance with this [text] I will address these three points.[6]

I will expound the first point (related to walking) in three subpoints: (a) how it is that we walk toward the light-of-surmise by means of its transiently-sensed light; (b) secondly, how it is that we advance toward rational light by means of light sensed durably; thirdly, how it is that we enter into very lofty intellectual light by means of the perceptually-received light of the teaching of Christ, who is Truth.[7] Accordingly, the first [form of] walking is from the sensible to the imaginable; the second [form] is from the sensible to the rational; the third [form] is the most perfect for us, viz., from the sensible to the intellectual. And each of these [forms of] walking is from the extrinsic to the intrinsic, from the extrinsic appearance or knowledge to intrinsic [knowledge] ..., etc.

[3] With respect to the second point, where the text says "and in Your name they shall rejoice," I will take up the subject (a) of God's name, which is ineffable, (b) of other names (viz., the name of four letters, and still others), and, thirdly, (c) of the name "Jesus".

[4] [With respect to] the third point, [the text reads]: "... and in Your justice they shall be exalted." In Christ, God reconciled the world to Himself,[8] as says Paul in II Corinthians 5. And because without Christ we are nothing and because in Him we live,[9] He who is Justice

was made justice for us[10] through the shedding-of-blood, which was begun today through Christ.[11] Therefore, there is no justice apart from Christ. And we can be exalted only through Him, who was made justice for us and who, when exalted on the altar of the Cross, drew all things unto Himself.[12] Therefore, we are exalted

- if we are washed in His blood;[13]
- if through withdrawal from the world we are united to Him, because He is on high;
- if, with plurality and inequality and division set aside, we seek those things that are above:[14] [viz.,] oneness, equality, and peace (or union);
- if we follow Christ and His footsteps;
- if we walk as He walked and if in the light of His life and teaching we seek out the Light itself;
- if through devout prayer that is full of love we ascend [unto Him];
- if we bless His name;
- if by means of good works we become conformed to Him.

For when by means of such a loving likeness we are united to Him who is above—so that in us is no one other than He—we shall be exalted in His justice. Etc.

PART ONE
Walking in Christ's Light

(1) *We walk toward the light-of-surmise in the light-of-Christ, sensed transiently.*

(a) *All things are to be seen by us in Christ's light.*

[5] "In His light we shall see light."[15] For just as without light no thing can be seen perceptually even by good eyes, so too without wisdom no thing can be seen immaterially. Now, a given light is visible in and through itself, without the aid of another light; the case is similar with eternal light. There are many [metaphorical] similarities between perceptual light and immaterial light, although [the two] differ incomparably. Now, we measure all things through Christ. If [we see] long-suffering, wisdom, justice, holiness, etc., we see them all—in whomever they are present—only in the Light that Christ is. Apart from this Light there is neither virtue nor holiness. The holiness of Peter is visible only in Christ's holiness; for unless [his holiness] were

present in Christ's holiness, it could neither exist nor be seen. Christ's holiness enfolds all other holiness, even as light enfolds all colors; and although light does not have a contracted color, nevertheless it manifests all colors within itself. But Christ's holiness is intelligible in and of itself, because Christ is Holiness itself, even as He is Light itself; for we know nothing apart from that Light. By means of that Light we know that which we *will*—[know it] the more profoundly and more differingly that we will have received its rays. All things are present in that Light. If we *will* for wisdom to be present in us, and if to this end we walk in [that] Light, then we will find wisdom. Etc.

And this [concludes what was to be said] first.

(b) *The stages of development of human nature and the enfold-edness of these stages in Christ.*

[6] The Apostle Paul—writing to the Galatians and instructing them in the truth of the Gospel as to the fact that in Christ we are free and have been delivered from servitude—says in the text for this present Sunday: "As long as the heir is a child he does not at all differ from a servant ...," etc.[16] "So we also, when we were children, were serving under the elements of the world. But when the fullness of time arrived, God sent His Son ...," etc.[17] It is necessary that one-who-understands turn his attention in all respects to [the phenomena of] both enfolding and unfolding, in order not to err. [7] Lo, the world is one world, and its oneness exists in a plurality. Moreover, human nature is one human nature present in many men; furthermore, there is [but] one man in his many members. And conversely: just as one man, from the beginning of his life until death, passes through many stages of development, so too human nature, which is one, has its stages of development. The situation is similar with respect to the [one] world.

If, then, you consider the human nature of all men from the beginning of men until their end—[consider it] after the fashion of a single man—then you will discover many hidden things that Paul attempts to indicate to us very briefly in his aforementioned letter. For example, at the beginning human nature was like an infant, when God made garments for Adam and Eve, who, shortly beforehand, did not know that they were naked. Subsequently, human nature was childlike and began to use reason with respect to God. [This occurred] at the time of Abraham, in whom the seed of reasoning began—[this seed being] befigured by circumcision of the physical foreskin. Next, human nature progressed to a stronger stage of development, so that it became teachable; and this was at the time of Moses, when human nature was placed under a teacher and under the regulations of the Law—as being under a pedagogue.[18] Thereafter, human nature arrived at the fullness of time and of perfection, i.e., at the unconstrained understanding of wisdom. And, thereupon, wisdom was united to the human nature in Christ our Lord; and human nature, having arrived at an altogether completed stage of development, was no longer able to develop.

[8] We find these [features] in each man. For intellect, which is incorruptible and immortal and is the substance of our soul, is not detected at the time of a child's birth; rather, it lies hidden in the power of the perceptual nature. Thereafter, [the soul] progresses to the stage of reason and then to the stage of learning and then to the stage of intellectual understanding. And because [the soul] is united to God by means of the intellect, it thereupon obtains rest in Him. These [considerations] are to be noted.

Now, although Christ, who fills all things, was altogether perfect and wise at the beginning of His conception, as if in Him, as in its Head, human nature were enfolded:[19] He was an infant; then He was circumcised; then He was a Hearer of the Law and an obedient Observer [of it]; next He was a Teacher, as one having power.[20] [9] Moreover, in accordance with the aforesaid things, there is found no stage of man's development which is not similar thereto. For example, the stage of development of [a man's] perceptual nature did not previously lack reason, learning, and intellect; but by comparison with the subsequent development, [that stage] was perceptual. Similarly, Christ's state [of human being] is [always] an intellectual state in which, however, He shows the other states to be also in Him, as is set forth [in the Gospels]. Therefore, let the whole intellectual state-of-being that is Christ's— [Christ] who is the Truth of, and the Wisdom of, the Father—be unfolded in its stages. And we see that at the beginning Christ began [to appear] among men in simplicity and in an infant-like state (in comparison with His intellectual perfection). [This was a time] when simple fishermen and ordinary people received Him apart from His lofty knowledge and His lofty words. However, after eight days transpired, this infant-like state arrived at the shedding of blood, as concerns the foreskin.

Next came the age of the foreskin and of sacrifice—[an age] in which there were martyrs for Christ. And thereafter came the time that men were under the pedagogue of the Christian law[21] and observed that law. The time approaches in which Christ, as one having power, will elevate [us] most clearly unto spiritual understanding, as if He were about to cross over from this world unto the Father through mortification of the flesh by way of most bitter sensory suffering, because the senses are at odds with the spirit.[22]

(c) *A surmise is made regarding the end of the world.*

[**10**] So let us see from the life of Christ what we ought to believe about our era. And, thereupon, we will find that Christ was born, was circumcised, was led into Egypt, was found in the Temple, etc. Next, from His twelfth year unto about His thirtieth year He is found only to have slept, as it were; for nothing is learned about Him except that He was in the world. Subsequently, He made His appearance; and after a short while He was crucified, and He ascended into Heaven. Let us now consider (a) when the shedding of blood ceased in the foreskin, (b) when Christ ceased to be a child in the temples, (c) when He began to be held in disdain, as it were. And let us compare the times [of historical events] to the era of Christ;[23] and we shall know that the times of Christ's preaching and suffering are near. On the eighth day the circumcision began, when Stephen was martyred; and the circumcision lasted many years. Next, Christ was found, in His twelfth year, to be in the Temple and to be engaged in those things that were of His Father.[24]

[**11**] Moreover, I think that *year one* of [Christ's] adult age symbolizes a duration of fifty years.[25] (And so, [Christ] was found in the Temple, [so to speak], from the six hundredth year A. D. down to the time of St. Gregory.) Thereafter, He was not seen to do anything for seventeen years. (And so too, [there was inactivity in the Church] for eight hundred fifty years. But on the basis of this [inference] He will now very soon begin to appear as One who has power; and His appearance will last one hundred fifty years. Then there will follow the final persecution of crucifixion; then [will come] resurrection and the ascension of the mystical body unto the Church Triumphant. Etc. Moreover, [this inference] agrees precisely with Daniel,[26] who held that there would be—from the going forth of the word [to build up Jerusalem again]—2,300 days[27] (where "days" stands for "years"). And that [going forth] was five hundred fifty-nine years before Christ. Consider carefully, with regard to this issue, that —as Philo says[28]—Moses had a final revelation, after which[29] he died suddenly: [according to the vision,] time is divided into four parts; and two [of them] had already elapsed, but two remained. This [statement] agrees with that [of mine].

Likewise, that which Lactantius[30] says about the seven thousand years also agrees [with what I have said]. Consider, furthermore, Ezechiel's vision about four wheels that went but that did not turn;[31] and these [four wheels] are [four] *times*. And consider that there are four animals, etc.[32] All of these [texts] agree [with one another and with my surmise].

[12] I say, then, that just as the sanctified day is the Sabbath day, which is the day of rest and of our deliverance from bondage, so too it is the day when the Word was united to a human nature.[33] Sanctified years are multiplied from out of that day; for as is said in Leviticus, Chapter 25: the year of Jubilee, i.e., the fiftieth year, is based on the sanctified number seven, which is also a year set aside for rest and liberation.[34] Now, Christ is our Rest and our every Sabbath. Therefore, the years of [the life of] Christ are years of rest, or jubilee, as seems to be evidenced by Luke 4, where [we read]: "... the year of the Lord and the day of reward."[35] [13] Therefore, I declare unto you that we have now been in Christ for twenty-eight years, and the last fifth of the twenty-ninth year is beginning. And [we are] near to the time in which Christ manifested Himself and was bathed [i.e., baptized] in the Jordan and when the Spirit of the Lord descended upon Him and remained upon Him and when He appeared to the world as Messiah, pointed to by the finger of John [the Baptist]. And this is the new year, which I desire to have come to you in Christ on this day. But John [the Baptist] will precede this coming of Christ unto the Church. The time of John's preaching will come forthwith, in order that we may do penance. (Here consider that there are, perhaps, still forty years for Christ to be manifest to all nations successively; and He will experience suffering. After He has thus appeared for one hundred fifty years and a few more,[36] the final tribulation will come—[a tribulation] than which there was never a greater one, viz., that of the crucifixion. But there will follow immediately the resurrection and, after some years, the ascension. And [this] will be the end of the world.

These are the likely [sequences]; but they are not certain to us. Etc.

(2) *From the light perceived durably we advance toward rational light.*

[14] But since there was announced as at hand the time (1) of His appearance, (2) of the washing of the Church in the Jordan, and (3) of the descending of the Holy Spirit upon the Church, and (4) of the Church's being enlightened in every respect with eternal wisdom: we

must have, prior [to these events], the means of ascending unto wisdom. And wisdom is not given prior to [our having] a knowledge of His name. If, then, we ought first to ascend unto a knowledge of His name, and if we wish to turn our attention to gradations, then it does not seem necessary to look at books, since there are countless books. Therefore, if we become involved with a countless multiplicity, we will fall into inescapable vanity. For the first wise men, viz., Pythagoras, Socrates, and even Christ, wrote nothing, as Augustine says in his *Harmony of the Gospels*.[37] For they did not dream of bestowing on wisdom the writing about it; for this [action] would serve rather to diminish and to bedarken wisdom's majesty. Moreover, there is only one Book of life[38] in which is contained all wisdom, which is our goal. The many other books do not have a goal. But the Book of life is spiritual and intellectual. All other books—assimilated by learning, reasoning, or sensing—bear the image of this Book. [15] Therefore, we ought not to concern ourselves with a host of books that have been produced by men. Rather, if we need to ascend from the perceptual to the intelligible, from the outer to the inner, from the visible to the immaterial, then let us turn to the one Book written by the Finger of God.[39]

Therefore, let each individual imagine himself to be Adam and to imagine that he alone has entered the world by birth and that he beholds this world. Seeing all things—the heavens, the stars, the earth, the waters—he conceives first of all of a *multiplicity* of beings. Secondly, when he sees the different sizes of those beings, he conceives of *inequality*. Thirdly, when he sees the stars above and the earth below, and sees East and West and South and North, and sees whatsoever two things in different places: he conceives of discreteness [*divisio*]. And so, he has [the concept of] multiplicity, from which comes [the concept of] inequality. For from one thing and another thing there originates inequality; one thing and another thing constitute a multiplicity. Therefore, inequality presupposes multiplicity, from which inequality is begotten. But from multiplicity and inequality there arises discreteness. For several unequal things are, necessarily, discrete. And no one is so simple-minded that he does not see these matters clearly. Now, multiplicity does not exist from itself but exists from oneness; for multiplicity falls short of oneness. (For it is multiplicity by virtue of the fact that it is not oneness once, or in one respect only, but is oneness made plural.) Hence, you see well enough that multiplicity falls short of *one* and that it does not have existence outside of oneness. For if oneness is removed, there no longer remains anything as regards multiplicity. Therefore, all that which multiplicity *is* it is from oneness, which is present as a whole in all multiplicity and in each part of multiplicity; and multiplicity is present [enfoldedly] in oneness.

[**16**] Next, [the foregoing individual] considers the fact that inequality falls short of equality. For he who says "unequal," first says "equal," of which the unequal falls short. And so, all inequality has, antecedently, an equality unto which it is reduced. Therefore, inequality has no being except from equality, of which it falls short [and] to which it is related as multiplicity [is related] to oneness.

[**17**] Next, discreteness presupposes union,[40] just as multiplicity presupposes oneness and as inequality presupposes equality. Therefore, you see that the world is something originated. And just as that which is originated is multiple, unequal, and discrete, so its beginning is one, equal, and united. And so, you see that the First Beginning is Oneness, Equality, and Union—without which there could be no beginning of that which is originated as multiple, unequal, and discrete. And since multiplicity falls short of oneness, Oneness is as the Father of many nations. And Equality can rightly be called the Son of Oneness, for Equality arises only from Oneness. And Union is called the Holy Spirit.

(3) *By means of Christ's light, received perceptually, we enter into very lofty intellectual light. [This fact] is illustrated by the depth-of-Christ's-teaching in the case of [the prayer] "Pater Noster."*

[**18**] And now, your understanding has been opened, so that you see how great a profundity is present in Christ's word, which bears the image of Eternal Wisdom. The expression of this Wisdom by Christ was [accomplished] in the Holy Spirit. Now, in order for you to see this [point], I do not want to lead you beyond that which you know. Just as I have used only the visible world as the unfolded word of God, so I want to take some word of Christ's—[some word] humanly set forth by Him and known to you. Let [that set of words] be: "Our Father ....," etc.[41] I claim, then, that all of God's wisdom shines forth in that series of words.

[**19**] First of all it is said: "Our Father, who art in Heaven." You see clearly that that which I stated about the oneness of multiplicity and about the Father of all things is here very clearly expressed. For

Christ says "Father," not "fathers". He adds "our" in order that you may see that oneness is the cause of plurality by way of creation or by whatever mode of originating. He adds: "You who art ...." Therefore, if the Father is *one* (because [the text] says "*tu*"[42]) and He *who is*, then it is evident that the entire plurality of the things that exist is from the one and only Father. And in order that you may continue to see very clearly the very fecund, incomprehensible nature of that one and only Father, *who is*, [the Prayer] adds that He is in Heaven (*in caelis*).[43] Therefore, just as Oneness exists absolutely in and of itself but is, as present in plurality, all that which plurality is,[44] so [the Prayer] here says that the one Father is present in many heavens (*in multis caelis*). It says, notably, "heavens" rather than "elements". [It says this] in order that we may know [the following]: that the supreme and very perfect nature that is referred to by the name "heaven," [and] that is present in the many heavens, has being only from the one Being—viz., the Father—which is present in it. And all that is perceptible by us, as regards the Father, is contained in [the meaning of] that word.[45]

[20] Next, there follows [the clause] "Hallowed by Thy name." In this very short sentence is contained all that we can understand about the Son, or Word. For a name, if it is a very true name, is, necessarily, equal to what is named. And because, [in the Prayer], "Thy name" is said: it is evident of what kind the name "Father" is; for it is the image, the splendor, the infinite equality of the Father. Therefore, Christ, through a knowledge of the Father, teaches us to know the Father's name, so that through the name we might have knowledge of the Father. Christ has given instruction that this name, which is "Eternal Truth" and "Eternal Wisdom," be hallowed. But this [hallowing] occurs when [the knowledge of the Name] is infused intellectually into us by the Father. For when we receive the infusion by means of turning our intellect toward Wisdom itself, [and] when we begin to behold Wisdom intellectually, then [its name] is hallowed. For the intellect can magnify, praise, and hallow nothing more than it does Infinite Wisdom. For the pure intellect can prefer nothing else to the Wisdom and Word of God—just as the eye can prefer nothing to beauty, etc.

[21] There follows: "Thy Kingdom come." The Father's Kingdom is only Eternal Union. For elsewhere[46] Christ says that every kingdom divided against itself shall be brought to desolation. Therefore, division (*divisio*) is opposed to the Kingdom. Accordingly, union, or love, is of the essence of the Kingdom, because in union there is rest. Therefore, there is expressed to us [by the foregoing passage]

nothing other than (a) all the knowledge, about the Holy Spirit, that is possible for us and (b) what we are supposed to seek. Hence, we ought to strive for this Kingdom of eternal union, eternal love, and eternal rest—in which Kingdom our every desire is satisfied—to come to us. And just as our intellect is not satisfiable except through the Father's eternal Word and Wisdom, so too our will cannot be brought to rest except in the Holy Spirit, in and through whom it obtains the Kingdom of Peace—[a peace] of which there is no end.[47]

[22] Hereafter, once the trinity of the Oneness of our Beginning has been explained (as concerns those things that instruct us as to what is to be believed and sought and hoped for), there follows what we ought to think about the whole creation in its orderedness to the Beginning; and [Christ's Prayer] adds [the words]: "Thy will be done in Heaven (*in caelo*) and on earth." (Without the hope-of-obtaining we would seek in vain; and, hence, [Christ's Prayer] instructs us, in regard to our petition, as to what we are confidently to hope for.) This [verse] means to affirm that all things whatsoever be done according to His will. In this [verse] the entire outflowing of creatures is expressed; i.e., [there is expressed] the fact that all things in heaven and on earth are from God the Father, are in the Word ([who is indicated], viz., [by the verb] "be done"), and are in the Holy Spirit ([who is indicated], viz., [by the word] "will"). Moreover, the conciseness of the Prayer is to be appreciated—[a conciseness] that no books (whether written already or to be written)—can express as regards the outflowing of creatures [from God].

[23] Once an enlightening about creation has been made [within the Prayer], [Christ] adds something about the Incarnation: "… our bread …," etc. Christ says [elsewhere]: "I am the Living Bread, which came down from Heaven …," etc.[48] He did not intend for us to be obliged to seek anything other than that that super-substantial bread (which is necessary for us daily) be given to us today, i.e., on this day of the present corruptible time. Hence, this bread which is asked for here [in the Prayer] is bread that is necessary for life. Hence, since some bread refects temporally and some eternally (as even the Gospel-writers speak of both kinds), so, necessarily, each kind of bread is sought, viz., super-substantial bread, which is from Heaven, and bread which is from earth. And because immediately beforehand [i.e., before the mentioning of bread, the Prayer] mentioned [the words] "heaven" and "earth" (i.e., the temporally incorruptible heaven and the corruptible earth): here [the Prayer] instructs us about the bread of Heaven

(viz., incorruptible bread) and the bread of earth (viz., corruptible bread). [It instructs us about these] so that from the aforesaid we may believe that such [incorruptible] bread can be given to us by God and so that we may hope that it will be given to us when we ask for it. Every [prayerful] request, however, presupposes love as its form.

And look unto the Greatest Artisan by virtue of the fact that at the outset [of the Prayer]—viz., "Our Father, who art in Heaven"—there is an evincing of all things. And in all that follows [within the Prayer] there is instruction in faith, in hope, and in love. For example, the words "hallowed be Thy name" instruct us (a) as to what we are to believe about the Name, or Son, (b) as to what we are to hope for, and (c) as to what we are to love. For love *seeks*, [inasmuch as] that-which-we-love we desire and seek. [The Prayer instructs us] in a similar way in all [its other passages]. Moreover, as for the petition "Give us our daily (or our super-substantial)[49] bread": in that it says "us," it instructs us that there is one bread for many people; and this multitude is a multitude united for receiving the one bread. And in this way there is expressed (a) the super-wondrous nature of this bread and (b) its relationship to the Church and (c) the fact that the effectiveness of this bread is within the Church.

[24] Next, there comes: "And forgive us our debts." In this [verse] there is shown the fruitful result of the bread, by means of which bread we can ask that our debts be forgiven. [The verse] includes all [aspects] of the fruit of Christ's suffering and of His making satisfaction on behalf of the Church. And it includes the fact that His forgiveness can be asked for only within the oneness of the Church—[as is seen] from the fact that [the verse] says "us". And [there are] an infinite number of things that are contained here [in this verse].

[25] Next, [Christ's Prayer] adds [something about] the law of the Church (which is the Body of Christ) when it says "... as we forgive [our debtors] ...," etc. For to love one another unqualifiedly, with no exception being allowed, is the whole law of oneness, i.e., of the Church. Therefore, no one, if he wants to be loved by God, ought to hate his brother-in-Christ. And there is no law that is not here present in its own fullness. For what is the whole law other than so to do unto others as one would want done unto himself? And this [is what it means] to forgive one another, as Christ says to us [and] as Paul, John, and the other Apostles preach it to us.

[26] Next, [Christ's Prayer] adds: "And lead us not [into temptation]." [This passage] shows that not all of those to whom forgiveness

is extended are confirmed in grace but that they can still be tempted and can fall and that they continually need God's grace. Now, it says: "And lead us not ...," etc., as if to say: 'Since we cannot be in this world without being tempted, and since no one can keep us from falling except You, O God: do not permit us to be led into temptation.' Furthermore, [the text] says "do not lead into"—as if the leading into temptation (whether by the Devil or by the world or by the flesh)[50] could not occur (up to the point of [temptation's] victory and our inducement) except by God's permission. Because God permits [the tempting], He is said to do [the tempting] in His own manner. Thus, a man does not believe that he can be overcome by the strength and power of the Tempter if God does not withdraw His hand of protection. Thus, we attribute all things to God, and we summon Him alone as our Protector. [We do] not [call upon] any creature, since there is no creature that can, of itself, exercise any power over man.

[27] Lastly, [the Prayer] adds: "but deliver us from evil." By this [passage] faith is instructed that only God can free us from evil. And through its being said "but deliver ...," it is shown that this delivering from evil most appropriately befits God. And [there is shown] not [to befit God] that which is stated beforehand, viz., the leading into temptation. For [the leading is done only] permissively, since God is not a Tempter but is a Rewarder. Therefore, Christ instructs us that God can free us from all evil and that we can assuredly hope for this and that we ought to ask for [it] with fervent love. And in this way it is evident that ultimate happiness and the final goal of our desires is God, who can deliver us from all evil only by granting us the highest good. For only the highest good is free from all corruption and from every aspect of evil. Nor is there an intermediate between good and evil. Therefore, in seeking the removal of evil from ourselves, we seek nothing other than the highest good, in which alone we find rest.

By means of such teachings and deeper ones we are enlightened as we walk in the light of Christ's teaching. And the foregoing suffices as regards the first part [of the sermon].

PART TWO
Exulting in the Name of God and of Jesus

(1) *The ineffable name of God.*

[28] So now that the Beginning has been arrived at by means of the foregoing simple method, let us speak of the Beginning's name. And

since a name ought to be the perfect basis for getting to know that which is named—[ought to be the basis] that leads to a knowledge of the thing named—it is immediately evident that no name that befits a multiplicity can befit the origin of multiplicity. Now, every name that is nameable in Heaven and on earth presupposes multiplicity, since it is imposed, by the movement of reason, with respect to distinctness. Distinctness presupposes one thing and another thing. Hence, God's name is above every name that is nameable either in Heaven or on earth, either in this present age or in the future age.

[29] And for the following reason Trismegistus says that God is ineffable: either He would have to be named by the names of all things, or all things would have to be named by His name, since He is Oneness amid the multiplicity; [and] the multiplicity is present in the Oneness. And this is what Solomon says in Proverbs 30: [viz.,] that when the man with whom God is present considers—by way of ascent to the heavens and of descent—all the things in the world, he is led unto an admiration of the name of God and the Name of His Son.[51] And there Solomon remains in admiration (as did also David in the Psalm "O Lord, our Lord,"[52] unto the end). For no one knows God's name except God Himself (Apocalypse 19).[53] [30] Nevertheless, from the immediately aforesaid things we know that the *Name* of the Father is none other than His *Son*. For there can be found no other Name that can lead us to a knowledge of the Father—[no other Name] than that Word, or that Infinite Name, which is the Infinite Equality of the Father. But just as this Name of the Father (viz., the Son in God) is the Infinite Form of all forms, so too it is the Name of all the names that are imposed by reason. And so, this Name enfolds all names, even as infinite equality enfolds all unequal things.

[31] And just as this Name is nothing other than Infinite Form, so every name coincides with form. Therefore, each thing's name comes by way of the arrival of form—as in the case of wax seals we say that they are the king's seals because [they bear] the figure of the king. And on the basis of human nature's in-forming a material we speak of an individual human being. And so on. Therefore, since every form in matter is an image of the Infinite and Absolute Form: then, also, every name is a name insofar as it is an image of the Infinite [and] Absolute Name. Therefore, we now see it to follow that no name of anything whatsoever—no name that is imposed on that thing from a rational inference that takes its basis from something perceptual—is a precise name for the thing. But in the multitude of the names that

unfold the powers of that which is named, there shines forth, in a particular [but imprecise] way the precise name for the thing, just as oneness [shines forth] in multiplicity. For example, the name "*homo*" (i.e.,
"man") derives from "*humus*" (i.e., "soil"); in Greek, man is called
"anthropos" because of his upwardly-turned, i.e., erect, state.[54] And so
on, as regards [words of] other languages. Hence, those names do not
express man's precise quiddity, which is unnameable, just as it is
unknowable.[55] Rather, they express some aspect of man. Similarly, as
concerns the soul: it is called *reason* from the fact of its reasoning;
[and] it is called *mind, intellect, spirit*, etc.

[**32**] Therefore, you see plainly that not only is the Name of God
unnameable but that there is not even a precise name for anything.
Moreover, in all names the Name of God shines forth as in an image.
And just as "Word (*Verbum*) of God" is an Infinite Name, so too it is
an Infinite Expression (*Sermo*). And all languages and expressions are
unfoldings of it. Hence, the plurality of languages derives from that
[Divine] Expression, just as plurality [derives from] Oneness.

[**34**] And so, consider, next, that the naming of God's [true]
Name is not possible for a creature. For just as what is infinite can have
as equal to itself only an infinite name, so too it cannot be named
except infinitely. Accordingly, the Holy Spirit is the Infinite Union of
the Infinite Name and of the Infinite Named. Therefore, in every utterance or locution there shines forth the Infinite Name or Infinite
Locution, even as union is present in division and as oneness is present in plurality. Therefore, there is not found for any thing a locution
that is so precise that there could not be one that is still more precise.
And in every locution there shines forth only the Infinite Locution (i.e.,
the Holy Spirit) insofar as the particular locution tends toward truth.
And, hence, [the Holy Spirit] is properly said to speak in and through
wise men and prophets and all those who declare the truth. For Christ
says in regard to speakers of the truth: "It is not you who speak, but
rather it is the Spirit of your Father who speaks in and through you."[56]
And Paul says: "No one can profess [that] Jesus [is Lord] except by the
Holy Spirit."[57] And in this way the Scriptures are opened.

(2) *The names of God that are found in Sacred Scripture.*

[**35**] Next, something must be said about the names of God that are
found in the Scriptures. First of all, we must note that among all the
names for God there is one supreme and sacred name, viz., the name
of four letters.[58] For that name is said to be the name for God's

Substance and Omnipotence and to be a wonderful name. (Genesis 32: "Why do you ask my name, [which is] wonderful?")[59] And it is not translated but is called, in Greek, *Tetragrammaton*, i.e., "of four letters," viz., Joth, He, Vau, He. Other names signify God, in a restricted way (*contracte*), either with respect to justice or strength or pre-eminence, etc., as these divine names are expounded by Rabbi Solomon[60] and St. Jerome. Now, an infinite number of secrets are hidden in these names, as the wise maintain. (I cannot here explain all of these [hidden matters].)

(3) *Exultation in Jesus's name.*

[36] Thirdly, I must add something about this most sacred name "Jesus," imposed on this day, when the child was circumcised.[61] Now, "Jesus" is a Hebrew name and has the same meaning as "Savior," (as the angel states)[62] because He saves His people. For the Word of God is called by this Name-for-Christ-the-Lord [i.e., the Name "Jesus"] on this day when He began to have a garment red with blood, as John says[63] in Apocalypse 19. For [God] sent His Word and healed them.[64] Therefore, healing is the work of the Word of God. And, hence, the Apostle Peter, being full of the Holy Spirit (Acts 4), says that under the sun there is no name in which there is salvation other than in the name "Jesus".[65] And, for this reason, the Apostle says that at the name of Jesus every knee is bent—[the knees] of those in Heaven, those on earth, and those beneath the earth.[66] For the Name of the Son of God is exalted above every name that is in Heaven or on earth (Philippians 2). For all these things [named] are subject to Him.[67]

[37] O how great are the very deep mysteries of the very sweet name "Jesus," of whom St. Bernard sings very pleasingly![68] Therefore, when whoever is a Christian hears this name, he ought to exult in his innermost heart and ought to incline toward reverencing Christ, whose name this [name "Jesus"] is. See how it is that when those who entreat the Pope and the princes [of the Church] name their lord, they do so only with fitting reverence. Therefore, by himself each person knows well what reverence ought to be shown to the name that is above all principality[69]—[shown to it] when it is heard in the mass or elsewhere. Who does not gladly revere the memory of his friend's, his brother's, or his benefactor's name? How much more [ought he to revere the Name] of his Redeemer, His Regenerator! Note that if reverence and observance are had for the name of him from whom we expect certain suitable things, then how much more reverence and

observance we are obligated to give to this Name!

If we believe that Christ is God and a man and Savior and that this Name of His, [viz., "Jesus"], was first given by an angel, then it is evident that the Apostles worked all their cures and healings in this Name, as we read [in the Scriptures]. We ought, then, also to believe most assuredly that through this Name we can obtain salvation and the anodyne for all hardships, if we call upon Christ with complete faith, steadfast hope, and fervent love. For if, as previously mentioned, we meaningfully utter His blessed Name with our heart turned toward Him, sincerely calling upon Him for our salvation, then there is no doubt that we will be heard. For He is near to all who call upon Him.[70] For the Lord has so magnified His own Holy One that He will hear me when I call out to Him,[71] because He says "Ask and you shall receive."[72] Romans 10: "Whosoever shall call upon His Name shall be saved."[73] And Joel 2 [makes] the same point.[74] And Christ says the following: that the signs that believers will obtain in Christ are that in His name they [will] cast out demons ..., etc. (Mark, last chapter).[75]

[38] Therefore, do not seek salvation in another name, and do not follow magicians or diviners; but whatever you desire seek in this incarnate [*abbreviatum*] Word which God made on earth,[76] and seek it in this Living Fount, and you shall find it (1) by using this Name "Jesus" as a most sacred remembrance of, and sign of, and Name of, Christ, our Savior, and (2) by calling upon Christ by means of the Name. But if He will not always hearken [to your prayer], it will be because He wants from you greater faith, hope, and love and because He wills that these be increased in you as a result of your repeated asking.[77] Hence, He says: "Knock, and it shall be opened."[78] He wills, for the sake of your salvation, that there be knocking. If, perhaps, after you have knocked, He does not grant your request, it is because you do not know what you are asking for. For you suppose that you are seeking from the Savior your well-being, but you are [really] asking for something harmful or lethal, which our Savior and our Life cannot grant. So if you are a true Christian, and if you believe the Gospel, then you are required to believe the foregoing [statements]. And you can be consoled only by our Consoler, whether or not He grants the things that you have asked for. Accordingly, He, who is Best, cannot but do what is beneficial for you. The Lord's Name is forever to be blessed. O blasphemers, O diviners, recognize your error!

[39] Therefore, contemplate now this very pleasing name "Jesus" as being a treasure-house of all desires, and embrace Him as

your only Consoling Refuge. If you are sad because of hardships, flee to Jesus for refuge, and contemplate His hardships, which He suffered for you, and you will find rest in Him. And amid your hardships you will be content to have patience, in imitation of Christ, if He does not remove [the hardships]. And because you will be able to suffer nothing that Christ has not suffered, you have in regard to all matters refuge in Him; and, amid refuge, you have consolation, etc.

[**40**] Therefore, teach your children to depart from every evil and foul name; and make them accustomed to the very pleasant name "Jesus". With attentiveness of heart, pray continually to Christ that by the power of His Name and memory He protect and defend you; and you will obtain [His help], etc.

[**41**] Consider that the reward for honoring the Lord's Name is one hundredfold. Matthew 19: "Everyone who leaves behind his house or his brothers or sisters or father or mother or sons or fields for my Name's sake shall receive one hundredfold and shall possess eternal life." [79] Take note of this reward and of this indulgence.

[**42**] Conclude[80] with the fact that if we praise the Name of the Lord continually, we shall rejoice in Him here below as well as in Heaven amid those who are praising [Him repeatedly] ..., etc. For, as says Augustine at the end of his *City of God*: in Heaven we shall see, we shall love, and we shall praise.[81] Etc.

NOTES TO *SERMON XXIII*

1. Psalms 88:16 (89:15).
2. Here Nicholas omits the words "tota die," as found in the Vulgate.
3. Psalms 88:16-17 (89:15-16).
4. Here Nicholas adds the words: "In Psalmo: 'Misericordias Domini'."
5. Viz., King David, author of the Psalms.
6. The sermon does not arrive at developing the third point.
7. As is often the case in Medieval Latin, Nicholas (in this present passage) forms an indirect question with the use of the indicative mood rather than the subjunctive mood. (Cf. the sentence at 1:9-11.)
8. II Corinthians 5:19.
9. Acts 17:28.
10. I Corinthians 1:30. The Latin word "*iustitia*," translated throughout as *justice* (following the Douay-Rheims translation of the Vulgate), has the sense of *righteousness*.
11. See, above, Sermon XX (**15** and **16**).
12. John 12:32.
13. Apocalypse (Revelation) 1:5. I John 1:7.
14. Colossians 3:1.
15. Psalms 35:10 (36:9).
16. Galatians 4:1.
17. Galatians 4:3-4.
18. Cf. Galatians 3:25.
19. As human nature was enfolded in Adam, the first man, so (according to Nicholas) there is a sense in which the perfection of human nature is enfolded in Jesus, the second Adam.
20. Mark 1:22.
21. See, below, the section marked by margin number 25. See also Matthew 22:37-38 and 7:12.
22. Galatians 5:17.
23. Nicholas correlates the periods of Christ's life with the periods of history generally. Thus, he can compare the time of Christ's being circumcised with the time of Stephen's being martyred (Acts 7:54-60). Etc.
24. Luke 2:49.
25. Christ was 12 (the age of adulthood's onset) at the time He entered the temple. These 12 years of His early life correlate, says Nicholas, with 600 years in the historical calendar; the 17 years correspond to 850 years; and the 3 years correspond to 150 years. Each year of Christ's life symbolizes 50 years of history.
26. Daniel 9:25-26.
27. Daniel 8:14.
28. Pseudo-Philo Judaeus, *Liber Antiquitatum Biblicarum*, XIX, 14-16. [See *Pseudo-Philo's Liber Antiquitatum Biblicarum*, edited by Guido Kisch (Notre Dame, IN: University of Notre Dame Press, 1949), pp. 165-166.]
29. Here (at 11:19) I am reading "post quam" in place of the printed Latin text's "postquam".

30. Lactantius, *Liber Divinarum Institutionum,* VII, 14 (*PL* 6:783A).

31. Ezechiel (Ezekiel) 1:15-17.

32. Ezechiel (Ezekiel) 1:5.

33. This uniting occurred at the moment of Christ's conception, according to Nicholas.

34. That is, the seventh year is also a year of Jubilee.

35. Luke 4:19.

36. Nicholas is still correlating each year of Christ's life with 50 years of history. Reasoning in the reverse direction, we see that 150 years correspond to one and one-half years of Christ's life. Traditionally, Christ is said to have died at age 33.

37. Augustine, *De Consensu Evangelistarum,* VII, 11-12 (*PL* 34:1047-1048).

38. E.g., Apocalypse (Revelation) 3:5.

39. Cf. Deuteronomy 9:10. In the passage above, Nicholas is alluding to the Book that is the Bible.

40. Here (at 17:1-2) I use the one word "union" to translate the Latin phrase "unionem ac conexionem".

41. Matthew 6:9-13.

42. The Latin word "tu" ("You") is singular. In the English translation of the Lord's Prayer the word "You" is implicit and *understood.*

43. The Lord's Prayer, as translated into English, renders "in caelis" by the singular word "heaven," referring to God's abode. Nicholas considers the meaning of "in caelis" to indicate that God, who is omnipresent, is present in the heavens of this world.

44. "... [is] is all that which plurality is": i.e., is the ground-of-being of plurality.

45. Psalms 18:2 (19:1).

46. Luke 11:17.

47. Isaias (Isaiah) 9:7.

48. John 6:51.

49. In Matthew 6:11 the word "supersubstantialem" is used, whereas Luke 11:3 has the word "quotidianum".

50. Cf. I John 2:16.

51. Proverbs 30:4.

52. Psalms 8.

53. Apocalypse (Revelation) 19:12.

54. This English sentence is a paraphrase of the Latin text at 32:8-9.

55. This is a tenet of Nicholas's doctrine of learned ignorance.

56. Matthew 10:20.

57. I Corinthians 12:3.

58. See, above, n. 8 of Sermon XX.

59. Genesis 32:29. Judges 13:18.

60. Nicholas here means Moses Maimonides, whom he misnames.

61. Luke 2:21.

62. Matthew 1:21.

63. Apocalypse (Revelation) 19:13. Nicholas is alluding to the day of Christ's circumcision.

64. Psalms 106:20 (107:20).

65. Acts 4:12.
66. Philippians 2:9-10.
67. I Corinthians 15:27.
68. Bernard of Clairvaux, *Hymnus Jesu Dulcis Memoria.* See F. J. Raby, *A History of Christian-Latin Poetry: From the Beginnings to the Close of the Middle Ages.* Oxford: Clarendon, 1966 (2nd edition), p. 330
69. Ephesians 1:21.
70. Psalms 144:18 (145:18).
71. Psalms 4:4 (4:3).
72. John 16:24.
73. Romans 10:13.
74. Joel 2:32.
75. Mark 16:17.
76. Romans 9:28.
77. Here (at 38:11) I delete the editorial addition "salus" and regard the singular verb "augeatur" as encompassing "fidem ..., spem, et caritatem" collectively.
78. Luke 11:9.
79. Matthew 19:29.
80. Nicholas writes this paragraph as a not to himself.
81. Augustine, *De Civitate Dei*, XXII, 30, 5 (*PL* 41:804).

Sermon XXIV: Jesus in seiner allerdemütigsten Menschheit
("In His very lowly human state Jesus ....")[1]
[January, 1441 (?); preached in Augsburg]

[1] In His very lowly human state Jesus was true God; and His words and His teaching were very lowly; and, hence, the Lord's Prayer, in the simplicity of its words, contains the highest instruction and wisdom. For just as the divinity lay hidden in Christ's humanity, so all graspable wisdom is hidden in the simple words of Christ's teaching, which no one on this earth can completely phantom. [It is hidden there] in order that each person in this visible world may, like the Christian, have an imperishable meal, consisting of the hidden wisdom-of-God that lies beneath the words and the perceivable signs. The Christian has an eye out for an eternal meal having to do with the highest dimension of his mind—a meal that presents itself apart from all detection on the part of the weak powers of the senses. Hence, it happens that, in accordance with the grace of God, one individual can have a superior and more acute understanding of the words of the Lord's Prayer than can another—even as one man has keener eyes for seeing the sun than does another. And although each man in his simplicity can find something especially comforting in this Prayer, God has given one man an [intellectual] advantage over another—[an advantage] that is profitable to each. Thus, one man teaches another; and each desires to learn from the other.

[2] What follows is my understanding of the Lord's Prayer at this time. I trust that from day to day such an understanding will increase in me and will become clearer, even as I desire from God to know that a prayer [for understanding] follows after your longing [for understanding] and that a longing will follow after your hoping. But hope follows believing and understanding. No one hopes for something that he does not believe or know. And, hence, the highest prayer must be accompanied by the highest longing, hoping, and believing. And this [accompaniment] is what you should aim to seek in the Lord's Prayer.[2]

[3] Now, our understanding is disposed to know the truth; and, hence, that which you should believe, you find in the truth: [viz.,] in God and in creatures. And after you have found belief in truth—through which belief you are enlightened as to what perfection a

human being can come—then you also *hope* to come to it. And when
you find that such perfection is good, then you desire it and ask for it,
even as you understand it and hope that you may arrive at it. And, thus,
it happens that our faculty of understanding, which is disposed toward
truth, finds in the Lord's Prayer[3] enlightenment for knowing, with
steadfast faith, what the truth is.

First, [I will speak] of the Beginning and Origin of all things.
Then [I will speak] of the emanation[4] of all things from God, of the
means of the return of all things [to God], and [then] of the ultimate
goal.

[4] The Origin (i.e., the Divine Nature) is referred to by the
words "Our Father, who art in Heaven, hallowed be Thy name. Thy
Kingdom come." The emanation [is referred to] by the words "Thy
will be done on earth as it is in Heaven." The mighty means [are
referred to] by the words "Give us this day our daily bread, and forgive
us our trespasses as we forgive those who trespass against us. [And]
lead us not into temptation." The ultimate goal [is alluded to] by the
words "But deliver us from evil. Amen."

[5] The Origin is disclosed to us, in faith, by the words "Our
Father"; it is disclosed to us, in the hope of understanding, by the
words "hallowed be Thy name"; it is disclosed to us, in the desire for
the good, by the words "Thy Kingdom come." The emanation of creatures is revealed to us in its orderedness by the words "Thy will be
done on earth as it is in Heaven." The means for our pilgrimage must
consist of (a) a nourishing meal, (b) the removal of impediments, (c) a
guide, and (d) a shelter. Without these four requirements no one can
journey well. The first requirement is expressed in the words "Give us
this day our daily bread." The second requirement is expressed in the
words "Forgive us our trespasses; the third, in the words "as we forgive those who trespass against us"; the fourth, in the words "Lead us
not into temptation." The goal of the entire journey toward the Good is
contained in the words "but deliver us from evil. Amen."

[6] Nature, grace, and glory, and all that a human being desires
to know (insofar as in this earthly domain this knowledge, in the order
that the teachers of theology can grasp it, is possible for us)—all this
can be found in this very holy Prayer, in which there is nothing superfluous, nothing deficient, nothing too weighty, nothing too light, noth-
ing too long, nothing too short, nothing without reason and without
right ordering—in which ordering the first is, necessarily, the first and
the last, the last. For the clause "Our Father who art in Heaven" can

tolerate no other sentence ahead of it; and the clause "Hallowed be Thy Name" issues forth from the first clause; and the third clause issues forth from the preceding two. The clause "Thy will be done" issues forth from those that precede it. And all the way to the end [of the Prayer] each clause [or phrase is found] in its right order.

This very holy Prayer I will now very briefly expound.

[7] *"Our Father ...."*

One Father is a naturally first and highest Beginning and is by Himself a Beginning of us all. The word "our" attests to this fact. For "one" is not like "our"; rather, "our" indicates *many*. However, a multitude has a beginning, as number shows us. The number ten or the number twenty is more than *one* and is multiple. But the fact that the number ten is the number ten or that the number twenty is the number twenty it owes to *one*.[5] Ten is none other than *one* ten times; and, thus, were there no *one*, there could be no ten. And so, ten derives from *one* and is nothing in and of itself; rather, [all]-that-it-is comes from *one*; and in ten there is only *one*. Therefore, we are all from One, no matter how many we are. And in and of ourselves we are nothing. And that which we are we are in the Father, without whom we could not exist. And, accordingly, from the words "Our Father" we see how it is that all creatures are from one Father and are present in one Father.

Next comes:

[8] *"[You] who art ...."*[6]

From these words we are made aware that because the Father exists, He is the [Ultimate] Being of all things, since all things are from Him and in Him. And so, God is all that there is in each thing that there is.

Next comes:

[9] *"... in Heaven ...."*[7]

By the word "Heaven" I understand the highest creatures; and, thus, these simple words teach me how it is that God the Father is present in all things, for He is in the heavens. The highest creatures are the intellectual natures. They have in their power the lowest natures, even as the moving, living nature of trees contains within itself the lowest elements, and as the perceptual life of animals contains within itself the motional life [of plants]. (And, thus, an animal grows and increases, as does a tree.) The rational nature encompasses the perceptual nature, i.e., [does so] in the case of human beings. And the intellectual, celestial nature encompasses the rational nature, as in the case of angels. And, accordingly, one God the Father, in whom all things are, is present in the heavens. Likewise, He is present in all things and is one God the Father, who is present in the many heavens. And there are many celestial natures, in which a single God the Father is present as undivided and unintermingled.

[10] From the aforesaid you recognize how it is that this sensory-bound earth is far from having a knowledge of God, inasmuch as God is in the heaven of the highest intellect. And there He is found by the eyes of intellectual natures—[eyes] which we too have, in our souls.[8] [He is found there] because He is the Supreme, Immaterial Nature, which our sensory and physical eyes cannot see. Take note, then, of the fact that God the Father is the Being of all things. And He is present in each and every thing but in no thing more than in another. He is apprehensible and knowable in the heaven of the intellectual natures.

[11] *"Hallowed be Thy Name."*
A name is an identifying sign. By means of names we have [knowledge of] different characteristics. And the more precise and more true a name is, the better it signifies that which is named. And, hence, a true name is an accurate likeness of what it names; it is analogous to an understandable word that flows from the power of the intellect and is a likeness of the intellect. Therefore, the name of God the Father is a supreme word that is equal to the intellectual nature of the Father. And since this Name is most truly equal to the Father and is the Supreme Name, which cannot be truer, more precise, or more resembling, it cannot be less than the Father. Otherwise, i.e., were it less, it could be more [precise] than it would be. And, thus, it would not be the supreme, most true Name. But since it *is* equal to the Father, it is God, as is the Father. Now, God the Father is the sole Origin of all things (as is written above). Therefore, the Name that is equal to the Father must be one and the same God as is the Father, although the Name is not the Father but is the Father's Name. Because the Name is the Supreme Image of the Father, we may call it "Son." [We may do so] in analogy with the physical birth by which a son is from his father. But no son in this earthly domain is so like his father that he could not be still more like him. Similarly, no [earthly] thing can ever be so like another thing that it could not be still more like it. For only the supreme and truest Image is the Father's Son, or Name. Accordingly, all equality in our earthly domain is intermingled with inequality. And in this earthly domain God the Father's Name is not to be found in any equality that

is free of great inequality.

[12] Now, since God cannot be known except in and through His Name, we hope that we can arrive at knowing Him beyond our intellectual power, in that God the Father illumines us in and through His Name in order that we may hallow His name. For when we hallow His Name, this hallowing results from the light given us by the Father—light wherein we see His Name above all other names.[9] If we see His Name there, then we hallow it above all else that *there* is holy, true, and right. For we know how it is that that Name is the true Name and the right Name and the most precise Image and the Mirror of Wisdom, alone wherein God the Father can be seen and known. [And we know] that everything which is named in Heaven and on earth has no true name that is without defect and inequality—unless [it is known in] this Name. And [we know] that, therefore, no thing can be known in truth, unless [it is known] in this Name.

[13] Christ, then, teaches us to pray that this Name be hallowed by us. In this Name is included the phantomless teaching about coming to a knowledge of God. Of ourselves we cannot come to this knowledge; but [we can come] by God's grace, which sanctifies us so that we may be able to sanctify the Name of [Him who is] the Knowledge-of-God, which transcends all other knowledge. When our intellect hallows only God's Name and finds or seeks its pleasure or rest in no other thing, then an individual has that which he entreats of God with the words "Hallowed be Thy Name."

[14] *"Thy Kingdom come."*
A kingdom is a union; a royal kingdom is union with a king; a divine kingdom is union with God. The Kingdom of God is the divine and supreme union, which cannot be a closer union. The union of the Father and the Son (the Son being altogether equal to the Father) is the supreme union. From *one* and its *equal* there arises *union*, just as from the unequal there arises discreteness. And so, from the One and His altogether Equal there arises the Supreme Union. This Supreme Union, which cannot be a closer Union, must be God. For whatever is what it can be is God; and whatever is not God can, through God's working, be other than it is. But God alone is all that which can be.[10] Accordingly, the Supreme Union is God whom we call the Holy Spirit, who comes from the One and His Equal—i.e., from the Father and the Son. Therefore, you see that the Father's Kingdom is the Supreme Union—is the Holy Spirit.

[15] And consequently: If a man is elevated unto the knowledge of God in and through God's Name, and if, therefore, he has seen that God alone is the highest and all-desirable Good, then he finds the following: [viz.,] (1) that God is the Kingdom of all delight, is the Love of all lovingness, and only in this Kingdom is there holy and eternal peace and union and (2) that outside of this Kingdom all love is transient, is intermingled with suffering, and all peace is impermanent, intermingled with lack of peace, and all friendship and union are afflicted with defects. Therefore, we ought to pray with great longing that there come to us this Kingdom in which nothing can be lacking to us but in which, rather, we will be eternally happy.

[16] We pray that Thy Kingdom may come. Thereby we understand that we are to believe [the following]: although we are creatures and live in this earthly domain with many infirmities, and although we must remain creatures,[11] nevertheless there can come to us the peaceful, imperishable Kingdom. And so, we are taught by Christ that we are capable of becoming God's children and that God's Kingdom can come to us as an eternal inheritance and that we have within us an immortality to which God's Kingdom can come. We are also taught that it should be our highest hope to possess this Kingdom of eternal joys. And while we pray for the [coming of the] Kingdom, we are taught that out of grace God can give us the Kingdom but that we have no right to demand it. For of ourselves we are children of wrath[12] and of discord and of sin (i.e., children of dividedness). For sin results from separating, i.e., from dividing.[13] Therefore, not of our own doing but only from grace are we born into this Kingdom of peace and of union. But from the fact that Christ teaches us to pray to God for the Kingdom, we understand that God wills to be entreated to this end and that then His grace will refuse us nothing of the Kingdom. From the fact that you are instructed to pray "Thy Kingdom come," you see that God's Kingdom will first come after the conclusion of this ephemeral [dimension of] time and that the kingdom of this world—the kingdom that now is and in which we now are—is not ready to receive the Kingdom of God and that in this world you ought to have patience and to await with great desire God's Kingdom after the conclusion of this world. And in the domain in which you now find yourself, make an effort to become so dear to God, and so to unite yourself to God, that God's Kingdom may come to you.

[17] From the fact that we pray that His Kingdom come to us, you see that you come to God's Kingdom only by God's Kingdom's coming to you—just as our body comes unto life only by the soul's life coming to it.

Herewith you have, very briefly, the first part of the holy Lord's Prayer; and from that which I have said, you understand well that Christ's teaching is phantomless.

[18] Note now, in addition, from the three portions [of the Prayer] that I have here expounded for you, how it is that you should turn away from this world and turn toward God. First, you find in this earthly domain many things: stars, animals, trees, etc. Secondly, you see that they are very different: a star is different from an animal, and an animal is different from a tree. And you see that no thing is exactly like another. Thirdly, you see that all things are separate and distinct: the stars are above, the earth is here below, the fish are in the water, the birds are in the air. And the one thing is always separate from the others. Each man readily takes note of these three features of this earthly domain: [that things are] *many, different,* and *separate.* From the *many* comes the *different*; and from these two comes *separate.* If you wish now to come [inferentially] to God, note the beginning of *many*: [viz.,] the *one.* Now, since *many* is united to *one* as to its beginning, turn [your attention] from *many* to the One. In this way, you can say "Our Father, who art in Heaven."

Next, note the place where the unequal, or different, is equal, or the same: viz., in God's Son. Hence, turn away from the unequal and the unjust to the equal and the just. In this way you turn to God's Son, and you can rightly pray "Hallowed be Thy Name." Next, note the place where all division and separateness are united: viz., in [the place of] true peace, i.e., in the Holy Spirit. Therefore, turn away from all the separating-power of sin (sin causes separation between you and God[14] and your neighbor, whether with regard to anger or hostility), and turn to the union of love and of peace. Accordingly, you can rightly pray: "Thy Kingdom come." And these pathways are necessary for you; and they are also sufficient, if you follow [Christ's] teaching.

[19] *"Thy will be done on earth as it is in Heaven."*
By these words we are taught that all things emanate from God in accordance with the will of God and that all things have no other cause of their existence than God's will. [Furthermore, we are taught] that the heavens are the heavens and that the earth is the earth and that a human being is a human being. This fact is due to no other reason than that God wills it to be such. Therefore, by the words "be done," together

with [the word] "will," all things [are signified to] issue forth from the Father into their own being. This fact is nothing other than the fact that from the triune God all things are that which they are—[i.e., what they are they are] from the Father, in and through His Word (i.e., the Son), together with His Will (i.e., the Holy Spirit). Note, then, that by means of the three words "Thy will be-done" [15] all things, in their emanation, are designated. By the word "Thy" [they are designated as] from God the Father; by the word "be-done" [they are designated as] from God the Son; by the word "will" [they are designated as] from the Holy Spirit. And just as these three words denote the Trinity and as by means of these words the Holy Trinity is referred to, so too each existing thing has within it an image of God and of the Holy Trinity. By virtue of this image the thing exists; for a thing is something only insofar as it is an image of God. Take note, O Man, of the brief words "Thy will be-done." They make it possible for you to understand, by means of the Holy Trinity, the emanation of all things [from God]. For if you want to know how it is that human beings became human beings, then here you are taught to know that there is no other cause than that the will of God the Father has been done. This point holds [not only for human beings but also] for all things.

Next comes: [20] "... on earth as it is in Heaven." Herefrom you note the orderedness of all things. For all the things that God has created are here named in the Prayer's arrangement. In the Prayer, *Heaven* is named, *earth* is named, and in between is the word *"and"*.[16] Thereby take note of a highest, celestial nature, which is immaterial; a lowest, earthly nature, which is corporeal; and a middle nature, which is united from these two and is both celestial and earthly. This [middle nature] is human nature, which has above it the celestial, angelic nature and which has beneath it the earthly nature, i.e., all the natures of the elements. Herefrom you recognize (1) how it is that all the natures beneath human beings have no common bond with the celestial, immaterial nature and (2) that, therefore, God, who is in Heaven, is not known clearly by means of them. For they are from the earth, which is their common mother. And out of the earth the other elements are raised up. And from these elements are raised up stones and mobile, [i.e., vegetative], and perceptual, [i.e., animal], natures.[17] And because their nature from their mother is earthly, it is subordinate to the celestial nature.

[21] But the celestial nature is immaterial and is more like God and, hence, is more noble. For in the intellectual nature we find imma-

terial being, intellect, and will. The being tends toward eternity and immortality; the intellect tends toward truth; the will tends toward the good. In this way you find that the celestial, immaterial nature is a reflection of God and of the Holy Trinity. [It is] a reflection of God the Father, who is eternal in His immortality. [It is] a reflection of God the Son in terms of its intellect, i.e., in terms of the truth that shines forth in the intellect. (Through truth the intellect possesses the radiance of wisdom, which relates to truth.) [The celestial nature is] a reflection of the Holy Spirit in terms of its will, which desires from the light of the Holy Spirit nothing other than that which is good. Thus, the will desires nothing except the good. For the good flows forth from the Holy Spirit, and [the will] has its striving after the good because of the will's emanation from the Holy Spirit—just as the intellect, because of its emanation from God the Son, has an inclination only for truth.

[22] Now, it happens that human nature, which is a union of the celestial and the earthly natures, finds in the spirit that belongs to its soul[18] the celestial inclination toward immortality, toward truth, and toward the good, and, beyond itself, toward God. And in the earthly, perceptual nature there is a downward inclination toward the perishable, the false, the apparent-good, with the result that the [two] dispositions are dissimilar and opposed to each other.[19]

[23] Therefore, Christ teaches us to pray that God's will be done on earth as it is in Heaven—[to pray this] in order that our sensory, fleshly nature may turn to our intellectual nature and may remain united to it in obedience. For then a man peacefully journeys—in the heaven of his intellect, where God dwells—completely beyond himself. And because of our praying such a prayer we recognize that of ourselves we are of weak nature and that without God's grace we cannot resist the flesh and sensuality. And our earthly nature cannot receive the celestial laws (through which it partakes of the divine eternity) without divine grace, which God indeed wills gladly to give us if we earnestly pray "Thy will be done on earth as it is in Heaven." This [teaching] and many other important teachings are revealed to us in the words of Christ Jesus.

[24] *"Give us this day our daily bread."*
We have just prayed that our earthly [i.e., bodily] nature may be obedient to our immaterial, heavenly nature. But because of the infirmities of our [earthly] nature such [obedience] cannot occur unless we have nourishment which nourishes us daily and continually. Therefore,

Christ instructs us to pray to God for life-giving nourishment through which we are nourished in order to have the strength to face death and infirmity. Because, then, two natures—one celestial and one earthly—are united in us, we pray for bread that is necessary for both natures. That is, [we pray] for Heavenly bread, wherein is present Heavenly, immortal life—present beyond all substantiality of all creatures, as Matthew writes.[20] And [we pray] for bread for all the needs that may ever come upon us today in this perceptual life.

[**25**] Now, hitherto we have seen that the intellectual, spiritual nature is nourished, in an immortal way, with the Word of God (i.e., with the Eternal Son of God, who is Wisdom). Hence, we pray that the Word may become Nourishment for our human nature. Now, food must be united with the one that is fed; otherwise, it is not food. This is the reason we pray that Truth, or God's Word, may be given to us as united to our nature. For this is the Bread by means of which we can have eternal life;[21] and it is our Bread, is Bread for our nature. Therefore, we pray that God give us our Bread (viz., Jesus Christ) in the core of our life as the Nourishment of our life. And this our Bread is given to us—for our life's nourishment—when with complete faith we receive Jesus into our heart as Nourishment of our life. For thereupon our life, in our own human nature, is united to Christ, in whom our nature is immortally united with the divine life. And in this way we are then fed with our Bread, which God has given us for this purpose.

[**26**] Consider now the fact that these words—"our daily bread"—reveal to you, first of all, that our Bread is such [as has been said] and, secondly, that this Bread is necessary for our life and that we are to entertain the hope of being nourished with it and that this [being nourished] cannot happen apart from God's grace and that God wills to be asked for this Bread with devout love and that then He wills to bestow it. All of these things the words of the Prayer show us. Therefrom take note of what goes hand in hand with a being able to have this life. For it is necessary that [such a] man have Christ, who is the Heavenly Bread. However, Christ is appropriated by someone only through the belief that He is the Bread of life and only through hope and love and only by means of a gracious gift of God. Note also that since Christ is Nourishment of our life, He heals in us all infirmities, even as [material] food stills hunger. And, hence, Christ is the Food of all foods—a Food that can completely remove all infirmities. Therefore, whatever we lack—whether with respect to being, justice, wisdom, or truth, whether with respect to peace, love, or goods—we

find it all in this Bread.

Let us next direct our desire toward this Bread; and our faith and our hope and love will be increased. This [increase] is the way in which God gives us, each day, this Bread. And this sacrament is the loftiest, most holy sacrament that we—with great love and devotion— desire, and shall receive, (as the loftiest and highest gift-of-God) by means of this Prayer.

[27] You now well understand that man can come to the eternal, immortal possession, or apprehension, of the highest good only in and through Christ Jesus, through whom all our infirmities are removed. In Him we are all made perfect; and in Him we arise from the dead and are united with life. For He is the Living Bread,[22] which is elevated above all the substance, or substantial existence, of all creatures. And in Him all creatures are present in their highest perfection; and He is the First and the Head of all of God's creations;[23] and all the works of God reside in Him. And He is the Beginning of the flowing forth of all creatures and is the Means of their return-flow and is the End-Goal of all their perfection. Since human nature unites all other natures—celestial and earthly—within itself, and since human nature is united to Christ, the Son of God, Christ is the End-Goal of all perfection.[24] For He alone is the Highest—above all celestial natures and all earthly natures.

[28] From the foregoing you recognize that Christ is not food that is transformed into our nature as is a material meal, for He alone is Highest; rather, He is life-giving Nourishment that unites us to Himself and that renders us alive in His Life, as your soul is nourishment for your body and all your members—[nourishment] that gives natural life. It is not the case that the soul is transformed into the body and that the soul assumes the corporeal nature; rather, it is the case that the soul unites to itself your body and all your members. In this union the body lives in this way in the life of the soul. Herefrom note that all creatures who here come to eternal life are like members of the one Body of Christ—[members] in which Christ's life is such that in them only Christ lives. And this fact is nothing other than the fact that [these] rational creatures are unified in a Body that is unified in Christ's Life.

[29] Now consider [the following] carefully: If you want Christ to live in you, then you must be united to Him—just as if your finger wanted your soul to live in it, it would have to be united to your body and to be united, through your body, to your soul. For if you separate your finger from your soul by cutting it off from your body, then you are separating it from life. And so, you see that you must be united to

Christ if you are to live. But the union with Christ cannot occur unless you are united to Christ's Body, which is the holy community of the Christian Church.[25] And, hence, you pray: "Give us this day our daily bread." In saying "our," you recognize that you are united to this community. In saying "bread," you take note of the living Nourishment of the many who are unified in Christ. In saying "Give us today," you recognize that Nourishment will be given not to one who is separated but to one who is unified with many. Therefore, understand, from Christ's teaching, that faith and the sacraments and all virtue cannot help you to come to eternal life unless you are a member in union with the body of believers-in-Christ.

[30] You should also take note of your being taught to pray every day without ceasing.[26] For just as the influence of your soul is always necessary for the members of your body if the members are to live, so this Heavenly Bread is always necessary for your soul. And you rightly recognize this fact from the word "daily" and the word "today". For if this Bread is needful daily and if we pray that the Bread of which we have daily need be given to us today, then we also are aware (because the Bread is necessary for us every day) that we are every day to pray for it. Because during the period of this perceptible life we as path-breaking wanderers toward the Heavenly life need the Food without which we, as such wanderers, cannot live during this period, Christ teaches us that we ought to pray for that Bread.

[31] Take account now of the fact that Christ is our Bread insofar as we are journeying unto Him. And to the extent that during this time of journeying it is possible for us to receive Him, He is given to us in His Being, His Wisdom, and His Goodness. For at present these physical eyes of ours in this perceptible world cannot see Christ, who is immortal and who, after the Resurrection, is invisible for mortal eyes because of His [resplendent,] penetrating, and ungraspable spiritual glorification. Yet, because of these features Christ is a spiritual Meal for our soul. Thus, it happens that on this pilgrimage [of ours] Christ is given to us under the form of bread since we cannot see Him with our sensory eyes but [only] with the eyes of faith. And so, under the form of bread, Christ is truly present in the sacrament. And none of the things which by means of that form the senses see, taste, smell, or touch are the true Body of Christ; rather, they are characteristic-signs, or sacraments, of that Body, which is present there and which is seen only by means of the intellect's faith. This [seeing by faith] is God's greatest gift, given to us pilgrims for our [spiritual] nourishment—

[given] until such time as we come from this perceptible world unto the intellectual Heaven, where we shall see Christ not as hidden beneath the sacraments and not by means of [the eyes of] faith but in truth [and] as He is.[27]

[32] We pray for this Bread, and we are supposed to receive it with complete *faith*, with greatest *hope*, and with earnest *love*. We should truly receive Christ beneath the sacraments—[receive Him] in the *belief* that in all [instances of the eucharistic] sacrament He is truly and fully present beneath the entire form of the bread. By comparison, our soul is invisible but is truly and fully present in our each and every member, and a single face is present in the many eyes that see it, and a single word is present in the many ears that hear it, and a single skill is present in the many masters who exercise it, and a single truth is present in the many rational beings who know it. And just as our soul does not grow when we are small and then become large, but only our body does, so too Christ is not greater [or lesser] beneath the form of a large or a small piece of bread or beneath many or few [instances of the eucharistic] sacrament. We should also *hope* that we will come from faith to truth; and we should likewise receive Christ with great *love*, in order that through love we may be united to Him as our Good and our Salvation. Together with His wisdom Christ is given to us in His teaching. For in the teaching of the master artisan lies the art-of-mastery; therefore, we find Christ present in His teaching. And this fact is shown to us by the teaching of the holy Lord's Prayer, in which teaching Christ is present. For Christ's teaching is full of all wisdom, full of all virtue and—as in the case of the Master Himself—is as perfect as can be.

[33] Note now [the following] with respect to the words "Give us this day our daily bread": Since we are pilgrims, Jesus teaches us that we are to be without anxiety, inasmuch as God wills to give us that which is necessary for this life—[wills to give it] from day to day until we depart from this life. Accordingly, we should not expend great effort in greedily accumulating many possessions, as if we were not pilgrims but were permanent inhabitants of this earthly domain—or as if God did not know of what we have need and could not grant it in due time. Moreover, we are taught that we ought not to ask God for anything except the daily bread that is necessary. For otherwise He will not hearken to us. And if more comes to us than we have need of, [we are taught] that this [abundance] comes to us from God not as something for our sake but because of the need for it to be given by you to the

poor and the infirm, in order to meet their needs. [This abundance occurs] so that you may know (when you ask God for "our daily bread") that such bread as God gives is not only yours but is also ours—i.e., is for those who have need of it besides you. And if you do not share with the needy the extra bread that remains after your needs are satisfied, then this fact is a sign that you have gathered such bread wrongly and greedily and that you wrongfully possess it and that you are unworthy of God, who has purposed to give to you, and to everyone, that which is necessary. By so acting you are withholding from poor children of God their [rightful] portion—[withholding it] contrary to God's will and as an unfaithful servant.[28]

[34] In this teaching, and in other teachings, of Christ in this holy Lord's Prayer and in the holy Gospels, God gives us Christ, who is the Way, the Truth, and the Life.[29] Moreover, God gives us for our pilgrimage a partaking of the Life of Christ, by means of which partaking we are nourished on our pilgrim's way. For we find in this Nourishment that which we need for this pilgrimage. If because of haughtiness our journey is without resources, then in the humble journey of Christ we find nourishment. If we want to ask for this nourishment and to appropriate it, then our need is met, and our lack of resources (because of haughtiness) is no longer the case. If we mirror our life in the life of Christ, then we see what we are lacking and what we ought to do. If we want to journey to Christ unto eternal life, then we should take pains to walk in this earthly domain as Christ walked.[30] And, for the sake of our salvation, we ought not to scorn the way which Christ (who is God and man) walked (for our salvation) in accordance with His humanity, in which He is like us.

[35] And if you cannot completely keep to the pathway, then you must follow the pathway with such care that you are able to arrive at the goal, where Christ is. But if you leave the pathway and turn your back on it, then you have gone away from the pathway of life unto the pathway of death, and you will not come to Christ. Herefrom note how it is that on your pilgrimage you are nourished from the works of Christ's [earthly] journeying. And if you neither ask for nor receive this Nourishment, then you are lacking Living Bread.

The foregoing is what you can gather from the above-written words.

[36] "*And forgive us our trespasses ....*"
Christ teaches us that we ought to ask God for the forgiveness of our

trespasses. Herefrom we recognize that all of us by nature are bur-
dened by trespasses. Now, since according to the teaching of Christ
everyone should pray in this manner, everyone admits that he has trespassed. And the trespasses are *ours*, for they are ascribable to our
nature. Hence, they are each man's own, and God is not a reason for,
or a cause of, our trespasses. For they are ours; and, therefore, we ask
for forgiveness. Herefrom take note of the fact that God alone forgives
the trespasses that we have committed against Him—[forgives them]
if we earnestly ask Him to. Here learn that you ought to believe that
God can justify the sinner and can forgive his trespasses; and no trespass, whether great or small, is excepted [from this forgiveness].
Herefrom recognize that God's might is His mercy and that through
His very gracious mercy He makes of one who is unjust one who is
just—even as through His omnipotence He makes, in accordance with
His will, something out of nothing, makes one who is alive out of one
who is dead, makes one nature out of another nature, makes wine out
of water. For His will is His might. And that which He wills, He can
do; and [what he wills] must come to pass. Know, too, that no man
should despair of God's mercy but should have, with undiminished
steadfastness, the hope that God will forgive him. For Christ teaches
you to ask for the forgiveness of your trespasses. Were it the case that
you could not be forgiven, then Christ would not have instructed you
that you should hope for forgiveness and should ask for it.

[37] You should also notice that this request begins with the word
"And"; for we read, "And forgive us ...." This word "And" joins this
request to the previous one: "Give us this day our daily bread. *And* forgive us our trespasses ...." For forgiveness of our trespasses cannot be
ours apart from that Bread. Rather, we can ask for forgiveness of our
trespasses [only] if we are united to the Heavenly Bread by faith. For
of ourselves we have a trespass-prone and sin-prone nature, which is
purified only in Christ. And so, the grace of purification from sins can
reach our nature in no other way than through Christ, who also
removes all our infirmities and makes payment for all our trespasses if
we are united with Him in His Body, so that the confirmation of our
redemption can then become ours. If Christ with His merit is united
with us—by means of which merit we have all done in our nature what
amounts to a sufficiency—then we are rightfully listened to by God.
But otherwise we are not heard, because of the unreceptiveness of our
nature.

[38] Note, too, that you are praying "forgive us *our* trespasses."

For he who is separated from the others and who aims to pray only for himself and not for the others cannot say "forgive *us* …"; and, therefore, he accomplishes nothing. For at this point [in the Prayer] we learn that there is forgiveness of sins only in the harmony of the holy community of the Christian Church. Outside the Church the belief in Christ can help no one to be able to be redeemed from his transgressions.

[39] "… *as we forgive those who trespass against us.*"
In the holy Lord's Prayer, in which everything that is necessary for us is brought together in one set of teachings, we find that which we are to do—[find it] only in this clause, viz., "… as we forgive those who trespass against us." Hence, all of Christ's commandments, which we are supposed to keep, are here gathered into one word, viz., the word "forgive". Christ teaches us that God forgives us in no other way than as we forgive [others]. Herefrom note that it is Christ's law that you do unto others as you want them to do unto you.[31] This fact is shown by the words "forgive us our trespasses as we forgive those who trespass against us."Now, if you ask God to forgive you but you do not forgive, then you deprive yourself of being forgiven. He who has trespassed against you is God's creature, even as are you. God wills that that transgressor have his transgressions forgiven by you, even as you deem it good for you that God do for you such a thing as you choose not to do for the transgressor against you. How, then, are you worthy to receive from God the good of forgiveness if you yourself are not good enough to grant forgiveness?

[40] See what a reasonable and clear precept that is—[a precept] which everyone understands and cannot fail to approve of. He who prays that God forgive him and who himself does not forgive and who believes that his prayer is heard: he believes that God is not God and that wrong is right and that evil is good. By contrast, he who believes (as Christ taught us to believe) that God forgives [us] insofar as we forgive [others]: he has the rightful belief in God—[to wit], that He is the just and best God. And from a man's own works of forgiveness he can gage his degree of hoping that he will be forgiven by God; and in love he can pray for forgiveness. Herefrom recognize, O Man, that in this way there is opened to you the only way whereby you can know whether you are heard by God and whether you are a child of God. This way is that, from and by your works, you recognize whether you do unto others as you would wish to have done unto you: viz., whether you sincerely forgive those who trespass against you and whether you

have toward them only love. Thereupon, without doubt, it is the case that you are entitled to have complete confidence (1) that you have obtained from God forgiveness of all your sins and (2) that you are a child of eternal life. For then you do not fail to fulfill any precept. For in the love-of-your-neighbor, which is demonstrated in the forgiveness of trespasses—[as evidenced] by your works—there lies the complete fulfillment of all precepts.[32]

[41] *"Lead us not into temptation."*
Here we are taught [the following]: Even if we have once fulfilled the law and have obtained the forgiveness of our sins, we are nevertheless not sure that we will remain standing and will not fall into transgression through being led into temptation. This means that temptation begins when we are free of sins. Now, we should believe that we can be shielded by God in order to remain standing and not to fall. And we should hope that we arrive at not falling, and we should ask it of God earnestly, i.e., with the words "Lead us not into temptation," as if we meant to say: "O Lord, no deceit (under some aspect or other of the good) has by its temptation the power to seduce me unless You do it—i.e., unless You permit it (since all things happen by Your permission or Your will). And so, I entreat You: Do not withdraw Your protective hand in cases of temptation to evil; in this way I cannot fall. Otherwise, through the withdrawing of Your shield, You are leading me into temptation—even as the sun, through setting, produces for us night, in which we do not see.

[42] Know also how it is that we fall back into sins if we are temptingly seduced through an apparent-good (1) that is deceptively presented to our senses from this visible world or (2) that is presented to our reason by an evil spirit who tries to distract our understanding away from truth. And if we do not implore God to protect and shield us, then we become seduced, to the point that we come into temptation and deem the [object of] temptation as good. In this way we will have fallen away from God, who is the Highest Good—[fallen] unto the deceptive apparent-good. From that situation, we have no way back except, amid all our temptation, to ask God, in accordance with Christ's teaching, that we not be led into temptation—[to ask] in accordance with the [following] words of that holy [Lord's] Prayer:

[43] *"... but deliver us from evil."*
Here, in these last words, we infer, from Christ's teaching, that in this world we cannot be without temptation to evil. For we are situated here

below, where there is evil. Here we pray for deliverance. Thereby, [i.e., by thus praying], we profess (1) that there is another Kingdom, where there is no evil but where there is only the supreme, truthful, and pure Good and (2) that our deliverance from evil is deliverance from this sensory, malicious, deceptive world. And we long for the glory of the Eternal Good; only therein can we be delivered from all evil. For outside of the Highest Glory there is no abode of pure, imperishable, permanent good. We pray for this deliverance. Although we are presently situated amid the life of this sensory world and can come out of this world only through death, we believe and profess, together with [praying for deliverance], that after this bodily death we can have existence in a permanent, eternal Good; and we hope to come to it. And with great love we pray, and long, to come there, though this arrival cannot occur apart from our bodily death. And for this reason in [our praying] this Prayer, our sensory nature is caught up into the immateriality of our understanding, and the will of God is done on this earth of our senses as it is in the heaven of our understanding. For the whole man has wholly turned beyond himself to God and asks to be separated and delivered from this temporal, vain life in order to be in eternity with God, who is the Good (and who, hence, has the name "God" from the word "good").

[**44**] Here note [the following]: He who would not gladly will to die this bodily death in order to come to God, and who does not pray for deliverance from evil, obtains nothing; for he prays contrary to his heart. And he who prefers this vain world to God remains separated from God and the Good and is eternally present amid evil, from which he can never again be freed. And hence, this [part of the Lord's Prayer] is a prayer on the part of a man who harbors a rightful, unstained, and pure love for God. For this man prefers God to his temporal life and to all that is created and that is not God. He prays for deliverance from this insubstantial, transient life, in order to be present with his most beloved Good, without which Good he desires not to live. For he understands that he lives only in and through union with God. To this union his love conducts him, and in this union he exists only through love, although he is still trapped in this sensory world [and] in his fleshly temple. He prays with devotion for deliverance. This life is so sorrowful to him (because of the love that he harbors for God) that he seems to himself to be trapped in a shabby, dismal, unclean prison. And [it seems to him] that if he were out of this prison, he would come to a permanent, good, and supreme joy—would come to his most Beloved,

for whom only he longs.

[**45**] He, then, is in God's love and has come to this love in accordance with the teachings of this holy Lord's Prayer. And in order to belong especially to God, he finds beyond all artifices deliverance from evil, i.e., the gift of eternal life. For eternal life is nothing other than the highest thing that we can desire (and we can desire nothing other than the good). This Highest thing is God Himself. This man speaks: "O Lord, since through the Heavenly Bread [viz., Christ] You have forgiven me my trespasses, lead me not into temptation. Do not let me stay long in this deceptive world, where I cannot be untempted and cannot remain unseduced without Your protection. Rather, deliver me, O Lord, from all evil. For this is Your bequest, far from all evil. To this bequest You have called me through Your Son, Jesus."

[**46**] At this juncture be aware of [the following]: If you want to know what the eternal joy is that no man can comprehend because of its magnitude, then you will find out that eternal joy cannot be understood by us better or more concisely or more clearly than as Christ teaches us here [i.e., in the Prayer]. For joy is deliverance from evil. Do you want to know what Hell is? Christ teaches you that Hell is eternal imprisonment in evil. Deliverance from evil is the highest joy; not being freed from evil or being enmeshed in evil is the deepest sorrow and torment. The highest [and] Heavenly joy is to be in the Good, which is God, [and] to be eternally separated from evil. The most hellish, or most infernal, torment is to be separated from the Good, which is God. The Kingdom in which there is nothing but Good, or God, is called the Kingdom of Heaven. It is the Highest Kingdom. The kingdom in which there is nothing but wickedness and evil is called Hell. For "Hell" means *under* or *beneath*. And since Hell exists in separation, discord, strife, ignorance, and darkness, the princes of Hell are called Princes of darkness [33] or are called devils. But the Kingdom of Heaven is harmony, peace, love, wisdom, clarity, and everything that is good. Thus, its Prince is called the Deliverer from all evil; Him we beseech to deliver us from Hell and from all evil. Amen.

NOTES TO *SERMON XXIV*

1. In this prayer I follow the high German translation (from the Moselfränkisch dialect) made by Wolfgang Jungandreas and revised by Kurt Gärtner and Andrea Rapp: *Die Vaterunser-Erklärung in der Volkssprache* (Trier: Paulinus, 1999). Jungandreas's Moselfränkisch text is published in *Nicolai de Cusa Opera Omnia*, Vol. XVI (*Sermones I (1430-1441)*), edited by Rudolf Haubst and Martin Bodewig (Hamburg: Meiner, 1984). This Moselfränkisch edition uses the title "Jhesus in eyner allerdemutlichster Menscheit," spelled accordingly.

2. The ordering, then, is (1) believing and understanding, (2) hoping, (3) longing, and (4) asking.

3. Matthew 6:9-13. Luke 11:2-4.

4. Nicholas and other Medieval Christians often use the language of emanation, without contrasting emanation (in a Plotinian sense) with creation *ex nihilo*. Cf. *De Docta Ignorantia* II, 4 (116:3); III, 3 (199:16-17). In the passage above, the German word used is "Ausfluß".

5. For Medieval thinkers, as also for Classical Greek thinkers, *one* is not regarded as a number but as the source of all numbers. A number of things is always more than one. The unit "1" is, however, used in numerical calculations.

6. Here Nicholas's German reads "Du bist".

7. Here both the King James version and the Douay-Rheims version of the Lord's Prayer read "in heaven"—in the singular. And by "heaven" they understand *God's abode*. The German translation uses the plural "in den Himmeln"; and the Vulgate has the plural "in caelis". Since God is omnipresent, He is present in the heavens. Nicholas here understands "heavens" to refer symbolically to the angelic natures.

8. The finite intellectual natures are the angels. The highest aspect of human nature is the intellectual power, which Nicholas distinguishes from the rational power, which is lower.

9. Philippians 2:9.

10. This idea becomes central years later in Nicholas's trialogue *De Possest*.

11. That which is *contracted* remains ever so, without ever becoming *absolute*. God alone is absolute, and the divine nature never becomes contracted—not even in the Incarnation.

12. Ephesians 2:3.

13. Isaias (Isaiah) 59:2.

14. Isaias (Isaiah) 59:2.

15. In the Latin Vulgate there are but three words ("Fiat voluntas tua"), as is also true in German ("Dein Wille geschehe").

16. In Latin ("sicut in caelo et in terra") and in German ("wie im Himmel und auf Erden") the word "and" ("et" / "und") occurs—something not true of the King James English translation.

17. See, above, the section marked by margin number 9.

18. Here Nicholas distinguishes the human spirit from th human soul. Note Hebrews 4:12 and I Thessalonians 5:23.

19. Cf. Romans 7:22-23.

20. Matthew 6:11.

21. John 6:33 and 48-52.

22. John 6:41 and 51.

23. Colossians 1:15.

24. I. e., Christ is the Ultimate Perfection of all things.

25. Nicholas is here speaking of the Church as the invisible communion of saints. He is not endorsing the view that there is no salvation outside of the visible Church.

26. I Thessalonians 5:17.

27. I John 3:2.

28. Cf. Matthew 25:14-30.

29. John 14:6.

30. I John 2:6.

31. Matthew 7:12.

32. Matthew 22:39-40.

33. Ephesians 6:12.

Sermon XXV: Quo Modo Deus Creavit Hominem
("God created man ....")[1]
[1441-1444; unknown where preached[2]]

[1] [Let us consider] the fact that God created man on the sixth day and that in that work He placed the goal of creation. He situated man in Paradise, which was planted from the beginning, wherein were all delights. Now, God had commanded man not to eat of the Tree of the knowledge of good and evil; but He did not forbid him [from eating of] the Tree of life. However, man—wanting to seek life in and through his own knowledge in order, through knowing, to become like the Most High—sinned and incurred the death of ignorance. And while being unable to live in and through his own knowledge, he was cast out by God from the Paradise planted from the beginning; and he returned unto the earth of his own sensuality in order to till the earth.[3]

[2] And a Cherubim guarded the Paradise with a flaming sword. For when man did not want to have life in God's Garden but sought, in and through his own knowledge, life and a likeness to the Most High: then, having entered into his own earth, he found thistles and thorns. For our earth does not yield anything else unless in it other things are planted by God. Hence, man, who by his own knowledge raised himself unto the likeness of God, was prevented from extending his power to the point of life and of immortality. For human knowledge does not attain unto the infinite, the eternal, the immense, and the immortal, because the Cherubim with the flaming sword prevents this [attainment]. For the Cherubim is [symbolic of] the seat of God—who sits above the Cherubims.[4] For the intellect, which is supposed to attain unto God and immortality, must come to the simplicity of the Cherubim—unto which simplicity it is not possible that our work on this earth-of-our-human-knowledge arrive. For the very subtle intellect of the Cherubim is higher than our human knowledge to the extent that a firey, flaming sword and the acuteness of fire are superior to the dust of the earth.

[3] Therefore, man, being outside the Paradise of God's Garden attempted to make gardens on his own earth in order to see whether he could obtain nourishment; and he fell into [fashioning] a grove and [worshipping] a multiplicity of gods. But God had mercy upon man and revealed to him that immortal life is to be sought not in a grove and a multiplicity of different philosophical views but in that Simple Oneness from which our entire being derives as from a Father. And

418

God led this people of His from the wisdom of the Egyptians to the desert so that in the desert they might seek salvation in Oneness. And He promised to them, in the desert, a land flowing with milk and honey. And by means of many prophecies and sacrifices He revealed to them that in the renouncing of knowledge they would discover, even in the desert of simple faith, that human nature was to be elevated unto immortality.

[4] Therefore, God gave to His people, in the desert, the Law of servitude,[5] through which they would be kept from fornication, as concerns both idolatry and their own knowledge, and through which they would stand in faith, as concerns one God the Father. God promised that He would lead them from this indeed solitary desert and from the captivity stemming from the laws unto the land of promise and of freedom, where they would be able to taste more fully of the pleasantness and truth of the immortality to be obtained. Therefore, when the fullness of time came, etc.,[6] God gave us through Christ precious and very great promises in order that through them we might be made partakers of the divine nature ....[7]

[5] The Eternal Word is Life, and in the Word all things are life, as says the Gospel.[8] And note this point well: that in order that in Paradise we may live amid all pleasure, there is a prohibition against coming to the Tree of knowledge. Therefore, the Tree of life was planted from the beginning. In it all things are life, because from it sprouts the fruit of life. To us there was made the promise that we can return to this Tree.

[6] Take note of the Gospel of John: "He gave them the power to become sons of God ...," etc.[9] At the end of the same [Gospel we read]: "... so that believing, you may have life in His name."[10] Likewise, He says: "I am the Way, the Truth, and the Life."[11] [7] Note the text in Chapter 1 [of the Letter] to the Ephesians: "I make mention of you in my prayers, [praying] that the God of our Lord Jesus Christ, the Father of glory, may give unto you the spirit of wisdom and of revelation with regard to the knowledge of Him: the eyes of your heart being enlightened, so that you may know what the hope is of His calling and what are the riches of the glory of His inheritance in the saints and what is the exceeding greatness of His power towards us, who have believed in accordance with the operation of that power of His which He wrought in Christ, raising Him up from the dead and setting Him on His right hand in the heavenly places, above all principality ...," etc.[12] He "is filled all in all."[13] Etc.

NOTES TO *SERMON XXV*

1. Genesis 1:27.
2. Sermons XXV and XXVI are obviously sermon-sketches.
3. Genesis 3:23.
4. Psalms 79:2 (80:1). In the sermon-passage above I am reading "sedet" in place of "sedes".
5. Romans 7. Galatians 3:10-11.
6. Galatians 4:4.
7. II Peter 1:4.
8. John 1:3-4.
9. John 1:12.
10. John 20:31.
11. John 14:6.
12. Ephesians 1:16-21.
13. Ephesians 1:23.

Sermon XXVI: Carissimi, Omnes Unanimes

("Dearly Beloved, all of one mind ....")[1]
[1441-1444; unknown where preached]

[1] "Dearly Beloved, be ye all of one mind in prayer ...."[2]

Augustine teaches that prayer is necessary. For no one is saved unless he asks for God's grace, without which grace no one is saved. For prayer reconciles, provided that [praying] is done in spirit with highest faith and trust. For [our] most gracious and most powerful God is a Spirit and, thus, is to be worshipped in spirit.[3] Prayer strengthens the spirit, just as Christ was strengthened, as an example to us, when He prayed more earnestly.[4] Prayer overcomes our Adversary:[5] "Watch and pray, so that you not enter into temptation."[6]

[2] Prayer requires that one be humble. Faith accomplishes this [humbling]; hope makes prayer long-suffering; love brings about prayer's oneness-of-mind. Ecclesiasticus 35: "The prayer of one who humbles himself penetrates the clouds."[7] "The Lord is high and looks upon things lowly."[8] "He has shown regard for the prayer of the humble,"[9] as in the case of the Pharisee [and the Publican], etc.[10] Moreover, [consider] Luke 18: "It is necessary to pray always"; and Jesus spent the night in prayer.[11] Furthermore, [it is necessary that those who pray] be of one mind: Acts 1: With one mind they persevered in prayer.[12] And this [is meant] in the sense that we be of one mind in fellowship, that we live with similar values, and that we make progress ....[13] [3] Likewise, [consider] that prayer is of such great efficacy that it is efficacious for all things. In the case of Daniel and of Moses and of the saints we have countless examples [of prayer's efficacy]. Indeed, prayer moved Christ to come down [from Heaven], as the doctors [of the Church] state.

[4] However, prayer ought to be—according to Exodus 30—like fragrant incense of stacte, onycha, galbanum, and frankincense,[14] so that one's sacrifice may be acceptable. *Stacte* is [symbolic of] a kind of myrrh that keeps the flesh from putrefying, since the lust of the flesh militates against prayer. Isaias 1: When you multiply your prayers ..., etc.[15] Job 16: Prayers are to be pure.[16] By *"onycha"* is understood (1) spice that is like a perfume, (2) humility of mind, and (3) an abundance of spiritual anticipatory relishing. Judith 9: From the beginning the proud have not pleased You; but the entreaties of the

421

humble and the meek have always pleased You.[17] By "*galbanum*,"
which rids of carbuncles, is signified the kindness of benevolence—or
the increase of heart-felt affection—that is extended to all others.
Furthermore, [such kindness] moves one's enemies to kindness.
Moreover, it is said that Stephen by means of prayer brought about the
conversion of Paul. *Frankincense* that is burning indicates [fervent]
prayer ..., etc.

NOTES TO *SERMON XXVI*

1. Adapted from I Peter 3:8.
2. I Peter 3:8.
3. John 4:24.
4. Luke 22:43 (22:43-44).
5. I Peter 5:8.
6. Mark 14:38.
7. Ecclesiasticus 35:21.
8. Psalms 137:6 (138:6).
9. Psalms 101:18 (102:17)
10. Luke 18:9-14.
11. Luke 18:1 and 6:12.
12. Acts 1:14.
13. Cf. Philippians 2:2.
14. Exodus 30:34-35.
15. Isaias (Isaiah) 1:15: "When you multiply prayer, I will not hear you."
16. Job 16:18.
17. Judith 9:16.

ABBREVIATIONS

MFCG   *Mitteilungen und Forschungsbeiträge der Cusanus-Gesellschaft*

PG   *Patrologia Graeca* (edited by J.-P. Migne)

PL   *Patrologia Latina* (edited by J.-P. Migne)

PRAENOTANDA

1. References to Scriptural passages are given in accordance with the Douay-Rheims Version and, in parentheses, in accordance with the King James Version.

2. A reference such as "Sermon III (**4**)" indicates Sermon III, bold-faced division-number **4**.

3. The italicized sub-headings within a sermon are translations of the sub-headings *added by the editors of the Latin text.*

4. Many of the source-references in the notes to the sermons are taken from the printed edition of the Latin texts: viz., from Vol. XVI, Fascicles 1-4 of *Nicolai de Cusa Opera Omnia.* (Not all of these editorial references to sources are repeated in the present English notes; thus, some readers will want to consult the Latin editions directly.)

5. All translations (Latin, German, French) are mine.

6. The following editors are herewith acknowledged:

   Fascicle Zero (1991): Rudolf Haubst

   Fascicle One (1970): Rudolf Haubst with assistance of
       Martin Bodewig and Werner Krämer

   Fascicle Two (1973): Haubst with assistance of Bodewig and Krämer

   Fascicle Three (1977): Haubst and Bodewig

   Fascicle Four (1984): Haubst and Bodewig

CORRIGENDA FOR THE LATIN EDITIONS

Nota bene: An entry such as "Vol. XVI, Fascicle One: II, **5**:4-6" indicates Sermon II, section with bold-faced numeral '**5**', lines 4-6. Such references are to the Latin texts and their numeration.

A. Vol. XVI, Fascicle 1

1. III, **9**:17-21: Add as note: 'Anselm, *Meditatio Redemptionis Humanae*'.
2. III, **10**:15: Change note to read: '*Joh. 14,6*'.
3. IV, **1**:22-26: Add as note: 'Hugo von Strassburg, *Compendium Theologicae Veritatis*, Liber V, Caput 18'. [Contained in Vol. 8 of *S. Bonaventurae Opera Omnia*, edited by A. C. Peltier (Paris: Vivès, 1866)].
4. IV, **13**:2: Add as note: 'commune: ratione *p*'.
5. IV, **13**:5-6: Add as note: 'suppodiatione baculorum protegens: suffultione baculorum protegente *p*'.
6. IV, **13**:10: Add as note: 'vigorositatem: vigorem *p*'.
7. IV, **18**:26: Change 'est' to 'es'.
8. IV, **23**:42-44: Correct note to read '*PL 16, 571*'.

B. Vol. XVI, Fascicle 2

9. V, **5**:1-33: Change note to read '*Luc. 1, 5-19*'.
10. V, **7**:48-49: Change note to read '*Gen. 2, 17*'.
11. V, **8**:10-11: Change note to read '*Job 1, 13-19*'.
12. V, **8**:23-26: Change note to read '*PL 76, 1307A*'.
13. V, **11**:2-4: Change note to read '*Eccli. 37, 33-34*'.
14. V, **13**:5: Change note to read '*Ps. 55, 12*'.
15. V, **13**:8-9: Change note to read '*Ps. 35, 9*'.
16. V, **24**:20-21: Change note to read '*Eccli. 24, 20*'.
17. V, **24**:21: Change note to read '*Eccli 24, 27*'.
18. V, **35**:7-9: Change note to read '*Marc. 10, 25*'.
19. V, **35**:12-13: Change note to read '*PL 76, 1007C*'.
20. VI, **15**:6-7: Change note from '6-7) *Gen. 2, 10*' to '12-13) *Gen. 2, 10*'.
21. VI, **29**:30-33: Change note to read '*c. 22*'.
22. VI, **31**:40: Change note to read '*Exod. 17, 9-12*'.
23. VI, **33**:8-9: Change note to read '8) *Gal. 5, 17*'.
24. VI, **33**:8-9: Add as note: '*Matth. 26, 41. Marc. 14, 38*'.
25. VI, **36**:47: Change note to read '*Ps 36, 4*'.
26. VII, line 6 from top of p. 119: Change to read '*V$_1$* 39vb'.
27. VII, **1**:15-17: Change note to read '*PL 76*'.

28. VII, **7**:19-26: Add to note: '*Cf. Matth. 9, 23-25*'.
29. VII, **31**:24-25: Change note for **31**:25 into a note for **31**:24-25: 'Et ... infligebat: Et dum vellet suo amore consolari animam meam fortius vulnus infligebat amoris *p*'.
30. VII, **32**:23: Add as note: 'caducitatem illorum: illorum caducitatem *p*'.
31. VII, **32**:23: Add as note: 'fugi: et *add. p*'.
32. VIII, **21**:29-30: Change note to read '*Rom. 7, 24*'.
33. VIII, **27**:5-6: Change note to read '*Apoc. 12, 1*'.
34. VIII, **28**:28-32: The reference '*PL 30, 128C*' is incorrect.
35. VIII, **30**:40-41: Change note to read '*Luc. 1, 40-41*'.
36. IX, **18**:11-12: Add as note: '*Matth. 19, 30. Matth. 20, 16*'.
37. IX, **20**:37-39: Change note to read '*PG 58, 606*'.
38. X, **1**:1: Change note to read 'omnium sanctorum *inter capita not. V₁*'.
39. X, **5**:20-21: Change note to read, '*Ps. 24, 10*'.
40. X, **8**:11-12: Change note to read '*Eccli 19, 23*'.
41. X, **11**:3-4: Change note to read 'Seneca *De ira. Cf. I c. 18 n.1*'.
42. X, **14**:3-4: Add as note: 'Cicero, *De Finibus bonorum et malorum*, V, 23, 67'.
43. X, **16**:23-24: Add as note: '*Cf. Ps. 35, 9*'.
44. X, **32**:1-2: Add to note: '*Heb. 12, 29*'.

C. Vol. XVI, Fascicle 3

45. XII, title: Change 'Jesum quaeritis?' to 'Jesum quaeritis'.
46. XII, **1**:1: Delete question mark.
47. XII, **4**:8: Add as note: '*Gal. 2, 19 (2, 20)*'.
48. XII, **9**:14: Add to text after 'significata': 'citius cucurrit sed ecclesia gentilium per Petrum significata'.
49. XII, **10**:24: Revise note to read: 'Matris *om. V₁ om. C (scribit C* supra lin.)*'.
50. XII, **16**:21-23: Add as note: '*Cf. Matth. 13, 44*'.
51. XII, **20**:46: Change 'ut' to 'ubi'.
52. XII, **29**:2: Change note to read '*Joh. 20, 25-28*'.
53. XII, **29**:10-11: Change note to read '*Matth. 7, 7-8*'.
54. XII, **31**:32: Add as note: 'carnem Christi: Christi carnem *C*'.
55. XII, **31**:33: Add as note: 'crudelitatis': crudetatis *C V₁*'.
56. XII, **36**:19: Change 'saeculo' to 'saeculi'.
57. XVI, **11**:23: Change note to read '*Sap. 7, 26*'.
58. XVI, **11**:28-30: Change note to read '*Sap. 7, 27*'.
59. XVI, **14**:13: Change double quotes to single quotes.
60. XVI, **15**:6: Delete from note: '*Ps. 72, 3*'.
61. XVI, **15**:7: Add as note: '*Ps. 27, 3*'.

62. XVII, **10**:9-10: Change note to read '*Luc. 1, 70*'.
63. XVIII, **7**:30-31: Change note to read '*Deut. 23, 7*'.
64. XVIII, **7**:34-36: Change note to read '*Matth. 12, 50*'.
65. XVIII, **7**:42: Change note to read '*Col. 3, 22*'.
66. XVIII, **8**:13: Add missing note.
67. XVIII, **11**:18-19: Change note to read '*Act. 7, 56*'.
68. XVIII, **12**:7: Change 'Deus qui dedit' to 'Deus [qui] dedit'.
69. XX, **8**:9: Change note to read '*cf. Is. 9, 6*'.
70. p. 310, line 8 from bottom: Change to read '*Ps. 13, 1; 52, 1*'.
71. XX, **12**:26-27: Change note to read '*Joh. 14, 26*'.
72. XX, **15**:10-11: Change 'relegit' to 'refugit'.
73. p. 325: move '**11**' down one line.
74. XXI, **14**:24-25: Change note to read '*Matth. 15:4*'
75. In the *Corrigenda* for fascicle III (on p. 547 of fascicle zero) change 'p. 232' to 'p. 323'.

Vol. XVI, Fascicle 4

76. p. 338, line 23 from bottom: Change to '*cf. ib. 15, 28*'.
77. XXII, **23**:9: Change "Verbum' to 'verbum'.
78. XXII, **38**:17-18: Change double quotes to single quotes.
79. XXII, **39**:3-4: Change 'Verbum' to 'verbum'.
80. XXIII, **8**:15-16: Change note to read '*Marc. 1, 22*'.
81. XXIII, **11**:19: Change 'postquam' to 'post quam'.
82. XXIII, **14**:21: Change note to read '*Exod. 32, 32-33*'.
83. p. 386, line 16: Change to read 'E. Bohnenstädt p. 414-441'.
84. XXV, **1**:1-2: Change note to read '*Gen. 1, 27. 31*'.

BIBLIOGRAPHY

Aris, Marc-Aeilko. "Nikolaus von Kues (1401-1464) predigt den Mainzern," *Archiv für mittelrheinische Kirchengeschichte*, 50 (1998), 191-217.

Baum, Wilhelm. *Nikolaus Cusanus in Tirol. Das Wirken des Philosophen und Reformators als Fürstbischof von Brixen.* Bozen: Athesia, 1983.

Billinger, Martin. *Das Philosophische in den Excitationen des Nicolaus von Cues* (Beiträge zur Philosophie, 32). Heidelberg: Carl Winter, 1938 [reprinted in 1979 in Liechtenstein by Kraus-Thomson publishers].

Bodewig, Martin. "Die Predigten des Nikolaus von Kues in Kodex 205 (CCI) der Benediktiner-Abtei Subiaco," *MFCG*, 10 (1973), 112-124.

——————. "Die kritische Edition der Predigten des Nikolaus von Kues. Das Autograph und die Probleme der Quellenanalyse," pp. 133-143 in Helmut Gestrich, editor, *Zugänge zu Nikolaus von Kues.* Bernkastel-Kues: Cusanus-Gesellschaft, 1986.

Dahm, Albert. *Die Soteriologie des Nikolaus von Kues. Ihre Entwicklung von seinen frühen Predigten bis zum Jahr 1445.* (Beiträge zur Geschichte der Philosophie und Theologie des Mittelalters. Neue Folge, Vol. 48). Münster: Aschendorff, 1997.

——————. "Christus—'Tugend der Tugenden'," *MFCG*, 26 (2000), 187-207.

Egger, Wilhelm. "Die Kirche von Brixen zur Heiligen Schrift hinführen. Die Brixner Predigten des Nikolaus Cusanus," *Trierer Theologische Zeitschrift*, 110 (2001), 294-307.

Euler, Walter A. "Does Nicholas Cusanus Have a Theology of the Cross?" *Journal of Religion*, 80 (2000), 405-420.

——————. "Die Christusverkündigung in den Brixener Predigten des Nikolaus von Kues," *MFCG*, 27 (2001), 65-80.

——————. "Die Predigten des Nikolaus von Kues," *Trierer Theologische Zeitschrift*, 110 (2001), 280-293.

——————. "Proclamation of Christ in Selected Sermons from Cusanus' Brixen Period," pp. 89-103 in Thomas M. Izbicki and Christopher M. Bellitto, editors, *Nicholas of Cusa and His Age: Intellect and Spirituality.* Boston: Brill, 2002.

Frost, Stefanie. "Die Meister Eckhart-Rezeption des Nikolaus von Kues. Einige Beobachtungen zu den *Sermones* CXL und CXLI des Nikolaus von Kues," pp. 149-162 in Harald Schwaetzer, editor, *Nicolaus Cusanus: Perspektiven seiner Geistphilosophie.* Regensburg: Roderer Verlag, 2003.

Hallauer, Hermann J. and Rudolf Haubst. "Auf den Spuren eines Autographs von Predigten und Werken des Nikolaus von Kues aus der Brixener Zeit?" *MFCG*, 17 (1986), 89-95.

Hallauer, Hermann J. "Auf den Spuren eines Autographs von Predigten und Werken des Nikolaus von Kues aus der Brixener Zeit. Ein Nachtrag zu MFCG 17, S. 89-93." *MFCG*, 19 (1991), 185-195.

——————. "Auf den Spuren eines Autographs von Predigten und Werken des Nikolaus von Kues aus der Brixener Zeit. Eine Ergänzung zu MFCG 17, S. 89-93 und MFCG 19, S. 185-195," *MFCG*, 24 (1998), 209-232.

——————. *Nikolaus von Kues. Bischof von Brixen 1450-1464.* [Hallauer's collected essays, edited by Erich Meuthen, Josef Gelmi, with the assistance of Alfred

Kaiser.] Bozen: Athesia, 2002.

Haubst, Rudolf. *Die Christologie des Nikolaus von Kues* (Freiburg: Herder, 1956). See pp. 5-21.

_____. "Das Wort als Brot," pp. 21-39 in Otto Semmelroth, editor, *Martyria, Leiturgia, Diakonia*. Mainz: Matthias-Grünewald, 1968.

_____. "Ein Predigtzyklus des jungen Cusanus über tätiges und beschauliches Leben," *MFCG* 7 (1969), 15-46.

_____. "Zu den für die kritische Edition der Cusanus-Predigten noch offenen Datierungsproblemen," *MFCG*, 17 (1986), 57-88.

_____. "Praefatio generalis qua totum Nicolai de Cusa Sermonum corpus eiusque editionis criticae methodus delineantur," pp. IX-LXI in *Nicolai de Cusa Opera Omnia*. Sermones I (1430-1441). Fasciculus 0. Hamburg: Meiner, 1991.

_____. *Streifzüge in die cusanische Theologie* (Münster: Aschendorff, 1991). See pp. 328-334, 402-408, 430-459, 552-572.

_____. "Zur Edition der Predigten und anderer Cusanus-Werke," *MFCG*, 19 (1991), 136-162.

Hoffmann, Ernst and Raymond Klibansky, editors, *Cusanus-Texte. I. Predigten. 1. "Dies Sanctificatus" vom Jahre 1439* (Sitzungsberichte der Heidelberger Akademie der Wissenschaften. Philosophische-historische Klasse. Jahrgang 1928/29. 3. Abhandlung. Heidelberg, 1929).

Hoffmann, Fritz. "Die Predigten des Nikolaus von Kues. Ihre Edition in der Heidelberger Gesamtausgabe," *Theologische Revue* [Münster], 82 (1986), 103-106.

Hundersmarck, Lawrence and Thomas M. Izbicki, "Nicholas of Cusa's Early Sermons on the Incarnation: An Early Renaissance Philosopher-Theologian as Preacher," pp. 79-88 in Thomas M. Izbicki and Christopher M. Bellitto, editors, *Nicholas of Cusa and His Age: Intellect and Spirituality*. Boston: Brill, 2002.

Izbicki, Thomas M. "An Ambivalent Papalism: Peter in the Sermons of Nicholas of Cusa," pp. 49-65 in Joseph Marino and Melinda W. Schlitt, editors, *Perspectives on Early Modern and Modern Intellectual History*. Rochester, NY: University of Rochester Press, 2001.

Jungandreas, Wolfgang. "Zur Überlieferung und Sprache der deutschen Vaterunserauslegung des Nikolaus von Kues," *MFCG*, 7 (1969), 67-88.

Kandler, Karl-Hermann. " 'Unsere Rechtfertigung besteht nicht aus uns, sondern aus Christus.' Die Rechtfertigung des Sünders bei Nikolaus von Kues," *Lutherische Theologie und Kirche*, 23 (April, 1999), 49-61.

Koch, Josef, editor and translator. *Vier Predigten im Geiste Eckharts* (Sitzungsberichte der Heidelberger Akademie der Wissenschaften. Philosophisch-historische Klasse. Jahrgang 1936/37. 2. Abhandlung). Heidelberg, 1937.

_____ and Hans Teske, editors and translators into High German. *Cusanus-Texte. I. Predigten. 6. Die Auslegung des Vaterunsers in vier Predigten* (Sitzungsberichte der Heidelberger Akademie der Wissenschaften. Philosophisch-historische Klasse. Jahrgang 1938/39. 4. Abhandlung). Heidelberg, 1940. See especially pp. 24-95.

_____. *Cusanus-Texte. I. Predigten. 7. Untersuchungen über Datierung, Form, Sprache und Quellen. Kritisches Verzeichnis sämtlicher Predigten* (Sitzungsberichte der Heidelberger Akademie der Wissenschaften. Philosophisch-historische Klasse. Jahrgang 1941/42. 1. Abhandlung). Heidelberg, 1942.

Krämer, Werner. "Die Textform der Cusanus-Predigten in Kodex D," *MFCG*, 10 (1973), 106-111.

Lentzen-Deis, Wolfgang. *Den Glauben Christi teilen. Theologie und Verkündigung bei Nikolaus von Kues*. Stuttgart: W. Kohlhammer, 1991.

Miller, Clyde L. "Meister Eckhart in Nicholas of Cusa's 1456 Sermon: *Ubi est qui natus est rex Iudeorum?*" pp. 105-125 in Thomas M. Izbicki and Christopher M. Bellitto, editors, *Nicholas of Cusa and His Age: Intellect and Spirituality*. Boston: Brill, 2002.

[Nicholas of Cusa]. *"Dies Sanctificatus" vom Jahre 1439*. Edited and translated into German by Ernst Hoffmann and Raymond Klibansky. *Sitzungsberichte der Heidelberger Akademie der Wissenschaften. Philosophisch-historische Klasse*, 1929.

——————. *Die Auslegung des Vaterunsers in vier Predigten*. Edited and translated into German by Josef Koch and Hans Teske, *Sitzungsberichte der Heidelberger Akademie der Wissenschaften. Philosophisch-historische Klasse*, 1940.

——————. *Predigten 1430-1441*. Translated into German by Josef Sikora and Elisabeth Bohnenstädt. Introduced by Bohnenstädt. Heidelberg: Kerle, 1952.

——————. *Tota pulchra es, amica mea* (*Sermo de pulchritudine* = Sermon CCXLIII), edited and translated into Italian by Giovanni Santinello, pp. 21-58 in Atti e Memorie della Accademia Patavina di Scienze Lettere ed Arti, classe di scienze morali, lettere e arti, 71 (1958-59).

——————. *Vom rechten Hören und Verkündigung des Wortes Gottes. Sermo XLI (Prothema) und Sermo CCLXXX*. Translated from Latin into German by Wolfgang Lentzen-Deis. Trier: Paulinus, 1993.

——————. *Sermons eckhartiens et dionysiens*. Translated into French and introduced by Francis Bertin. Paris: Cerf, 1998. [A translation and study of five Cusan sermons: XXII, CXL, CXLI, CCXVI, CCXLIII—from the years 1440 (not 1439!) - 1456.]

——————. *De Aequalitate*. Translated into English by Jasper Hopkins, pp. 74-125 in his *Nicholas of Cusa: Metaphysical Speculations* [Vol. One]. Minneapolis: Banning, 1998. [Includes the Latin text.]

——————. *Predigten im Jahreslauf*. Introduced and translated into German by Harald Schwaetzer, in conjunction with Klaus Reinhardt. Münster: Aschendorff, 2001.

Niederkofler, Peter. "Über die Predigtweise des Kardinals Nikolaus von Cues," *Priester-Konferenzblatt*, 75 (1964), 119-125.

Pauli, Heinrich. "Die Aldobrandinuszitate in den Predigten des Nikolaus von Kues und die Brixener Aldobrandinushandschrift," *MFCG*, 19 (1991), 163-182.

——————. "Die geistige Welt der Brixener Predigten des Nikolaus von Kues," *MFCG*, 22 (1995), 163-186.

Pfeiffer, Helmut. "Der Rückgriff auf das Neue Testament im Denken des Nikolaus von Kues," *Trierer Theologische Zeitschrift*, 94 (1985), 197-211.

——————. "Maria, die Dienerin und Magd des Herrn. Die Schriftauslegung des Nikolaus von Kues am Beispiel seines Dialogs 'De visitatione'," pp. 144-151 in Helmut Gestrich, editor, *Zugänge zu Nikolaus von Kues*. Bernkastel-Kues: Cusanus-Gesellschaft, 1986.

Reinhardt, Klaus. "Wo sollen wir Brot kaufen ..." (Joh 6, 5) – Nikolaus von Kues über die Verkündigung des Wortes Gottes," *Trierer Theologische Zeitschrift*, 102 (April - June, 1993), 101-109.

_____ . "Raimundus Lullus und Nicolaus Cusanus: ihr Umgang mit der Bibel in der Predigt," pp. 133-145 in Fernando Domínguez y Jaime de Salas, editors, *Constantes y fragmentos del pensamiento luliano*. Tübingen: Niemeyer, 1996.

_____ . "Nikolaus von Kues in der Geschichte der mittelalterlichen Bibelexegese," *MFCG*, 27 (2001), 31-63.

_____ . "Herrlichkeit als Grundwort cusanischer Theologie. Eine Analyse des *Sermo* CCIV," *Trierer Theologische Zeitschrift*, 110 (2001), 308-318.

_____ . "Concordancia entre exégesis bíblica y especulación filosófica en Nicolás de Cusa," pp. 135-148 in Mariano Álvarez Gómez and Joâo Maria André, editors, *Coincidencia de opuestos y concordia. Los caminos del pensamiento en Nicolás de Cusa*. Salamanca: Sociedad Castellano-Leonesa de Filosofía, 2002.

Scharpff, Franz A. *Cardinal und Bischof Nicolaus von Cusa als Reformator im Kirche, Reich und Philosophie des fünfzehnten Jahrhunderts*. Tübingen, 1871. [Reprinted in Frankfurt am Main by Minerva Verlag, 1966.] See pp. 262-294.

_____ . *Des Cardinals und Bischofs Nicolaus von Cusa wichtigste Schriften in deutscher Uebersetzung*. Freiburg i. B., 1862. [Reprinted in Frankfurt am Main by Minerva Verlag, 1966.] See pp. 411-624.

Schnarr, Hermann. "Zur Filiation der Handschriften mit Cusanus-Predigten an Hand der Martinspredigt v. J. 1444 zu Mainz," *MFCG*, 12 (1977), 137-154.

_____ . "Nikolaus von Kues als Prediger in Trier," pp. 120-132 in Helmut Gestrich, editor, *Zugänge zu Nikolaus von Kues*. Bernkastel-Kues: Cusanus-Gesellschaft, 1986.

_____ . "Beobachtungen zu einem unveröffentlichten Predigt-Text des Nikolaus von Kues. Überlegungen zur Edition der Sermones des Nikolaus von Kues," pp. 211-238 in Ludwig Hagemann and Reinhold Glei, editors, EN ΚΑΙ ΠΑΗΘΟΣ. Einheit und Vielheit. Würzburg: Echter Verlag, 1993.

Schwaetzer, Harald. *Aequalitas. Erkenntnistheoretische und soziale Implikationen eines christologischen Begriffs bei Nikolaus von Kues. Eine Studie zu seiner Schrift* De Aequalitate. Hildesheim: Olms, 2000.

_____ . " 'Sei du das, was du willst!' Die christozentrische Anthropologie der Freiheit in *Sermo* CCXXXIX des Nikolaus von Kues," *Trierer Theologische Zeitschrift*, 110 (2001), 319-332.

Trenkwalder, Alois. "Zur Geschichte der Predigt in der Diözese Brixen vom Hochmittelalter bis zum Konzil von Trient. – 1. Teil," *Konferenzblatt für Theologie und Seelsorge*, 95 (1984), 147-165.

Vansteenberghe, Edmond. *Le Cardinal Nicolas de Cues (1401-1464). L'action – La pensée*. Paris, 1920. [Reprinted in 1963 by Minerva Verlag, Frankfurt am Main]. See pp. 156-165.

Vogels, Heinz-Jürgen. "Christus und die Toten vor dem absoluten Tod. Die 'visio mortis' nach Nikolaus von Kues," *MFCG*, 13 (1978), 208-213.

Yamamoto, Kuhgai. " 'Dies sanctificatus' und der Ursprung der Religionsphilosophie," *MFCG*, 19 (1991), 221-230.

Zani, Karl F. "Neues zu Predigten des Kardinals Cusanus 'ettlich zu teutsch'," *Der Schlern*, 59 (1985), 111-115.

APPENDIX

(See Sermon VII, endnote 62.)

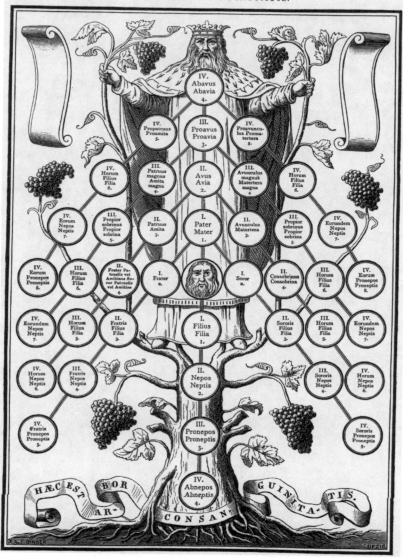